Peter Norton's®

Introduction to Computers

Third Edition

Glencoe
McGraw-Hill

New York, New York   Columbus, Ohio   Woodland Hills, California   Peoria, Illinois

Library of Congress Cataloging-in-Publication Data

Norton, Peter, 1943—
  [Introduction to Computers]
  Peter Norton's introduction to computers.—3rd ed.
   p. cm.
  Includes index.
  ISBN 002-804386-3
  1. Computers. 2. Computer software. I. Title.
QA76.5.N6818   1996b
004—dc20   96-32939
                  CIP

Glencoe/McGraw-Hill

*A Division of The **McGraw·Hill** Companies*

This book was set in 10/13 New Aster by Proof Positive/Farrowlyne Associates, Inc.

Send all inquiries to:

Glencoe/McGraw-Hill
936 Eastwind Drive
Westerville, OH 43081

ISBN: 0-02-804386-3
ISBN: 0-02-804388-X Annotated Instructor's Edition

 3 4 5 6 7 8 9 073 02 01 00 99

BRIEF CONTENTS

Peter Norton's® Introduction to Computers, Third Edition, brings you a completely revised and updated textbook and supplements. The result is an innovative instructional system designed to help instructors teach and students learn about computer technology.

World-renowned computer expert, software developer, and author Peter Norton has once again joined Glencoe in developing an integrated learning system that emphasizes life-long productivity with computers. Peter's straightforward, easy-to-follow writing style is an established winner! His best-selling books—including *Inside the IBM PC* and *Peter Norton's® DOS Guide*—have set the standard in user-friendly computer instruction. Now students can benefit from his unique ability to teach computer concepts in a way that demystifies computing—an approach that truly comes to life in this edition!

This enhanced, updated package integrates text, photos, screen shots, and three-dimensional graphics to take students *inside* the computer. By using this complete from-the-ground-up introduction, students not only learn the basics of computing, but master valuable tools for a lifetime of productivity. Along the way, students will find a treasure trove of valuable insight—not just into the technology itself, but into the human side of computing.

THE THIRD EDITION

Peter Norton's® Introduction to Computers, Third Edition, retains all the high-quality features that have made previous editions so successful, while adding many new features that make this learning system even more indispensable!

As always, this teaching system's primary goal is to introduce students to the technologies (hardware and software alike) that they will most likely encounter in school

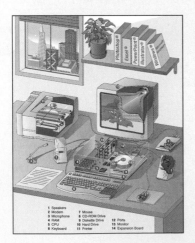

1 Speakers   7 Mouse
2 Modem   8 CD-ROM Drive
3 Microphone   9 Diskette Drive   12 Ports
4 RAM   10 Hard Drive   13 Monitor
5 CPU   11 Printer   14 Expansion Board
6 Keyboard

or the workplace. Therefore, examples focus primarily on the use of IBM-compatible personal computers (PCs) and the Windows 95/98 operating system. Other platforms (such as the Macintosh, OS/2, and UNIX) and sizes of computers (such as mainframes) are also discussed, in the context of their most common applications.

The Third Edition presents technologies in a way that demonstrates how they can be used in school, work, or the home. To keep pace with computer technology, we have thoroughly revised every chapter in this book to reflect new developments. Students will find expanded coverage of the Internet, networking, and multimedia, as well as refined coverage of productivity applications and operating systems, including Windows 98. For students who have never experienced the World Wide Web, a new appendix introduces the process of launching a Web browser and going online for the first time.

Changes and additions to this new edition include:

■ **Reorganized material.** Several chapters have been reorganized and condensed for easier mastery of basic concepts, and to allow students to better understand the relationships among various technologies. In particular, the chapters covering operating systems, productivity software, and networking have been realigned so students can see how these technologies rely on one another. Coverage of applications and information systems has been refined and condensed for easier understanding. All chapters are configured to complement hands-on practice sessions in the classroom.

- **Hands-on introduction to the World Wide Web.** Appendix B, **Getting Started on the World Wide Web**, is entirely new. This brief appendix is designed to introduce students to the Web, and is especially helpful for students who have never "surfed the Web."

- **Completely revised text.** Every chapter has been completely updated to reflect the latest developments in technology.

- **3-D illustrations, new photographs, and software screen shots.** Colorful 3-D illustrations help students visualize computer components and many basic concepts. New photographs show the latest hardware technology, from the smallest chips to complete new computer systems. Screen shots give students the look and feel of many software applications, including Windows 98, the current versions of Microsoft Internet Explorer and Netscape Navigator, and many others.

- **Internet margin notes.** Throughout this edition, students will find dozens of **Norton Online** notes in the margins of the text. These notes direct students to the Norton Online Web site, which provides links to other sites on the World Wide Web. (The Norton Online Web site is discussed later in this preface.) By following these links, students can find more detailed discussions of many topics. Many of the links lead to manufacturers' Web sites, where students can learn about specific products, and even download sample software. Others provide product reviews, up-to-the-minute explanations of technologies and trends, industry analysis, and much more.

To see Norton Online visit this book's Web site at **www.glencoe.com/norton/online**

- **48 completely updated feature boxes.** In each chapter, you will find four different types of feature articles, each focusing on an aspect of technology. These single-page articles are designed to help students relate the concepts they are learning to real-world applications of technology. The **Norton Notebook** feature emphasizes practical uses of technology in the real world, and shows how cutting-edge hardware and software are being used in a variety of professions. The **Techview** feature provides insights into new technology. **Productivity Tips** offer practical advice on using technology to be more productive at school, at work, and at home.

Each chapter features a new section, called **Computers in Your Career**. These single-page articles list and describe careers that rely on the technologies covered in the chapter, and explain how specific technologies are being applied in the workplace. These sidebars are designed to help students understand how computers and computer technology can play a significant role in their professional lives.

Norton Notebook   **Techview**   **Productivity Tips**   **Computers in Your Career**

- **Internet Workshops.** At the end of every chapter, students will find a new section, called **Internet Workshop**. This section provides exercises that take students online, with the goal of finding more information on the Internet that relates to the discussions in the chapter. Many of these exercises give students freedom to surf the Web independently, while others direct students to one or more specific Web sites. (Links to these Web sites are provided in the Norton Online Web page, which is described in the following section.)

NORTON ONLINE

Because the Internet is such a rich source of information, Glencoe now provides students with Norton Online—a Web-based set of resources that complement the Third Edition of *Peter Norton's® Introduction to Computers*. Norton Online, **www.glencoe.com/norton/online**, is a Web site that offers links to various sites and provides additional information related to topics discussed in the text.

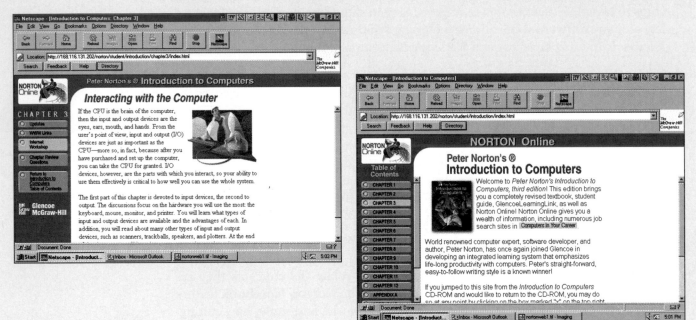

- Frequent **Updates** provide current information about technology news. The **Updates** are archived for continued reference.

- **WWW Links** are provided for students to quickly access Web sites mentioned in the text.

- **Internet Workshops** are exercises that challenge students to find technology information on the Web.

- **Chapter Review Questions** test students comprehension of the material discussed in each chapter.

- **Exercises** provide hands-on activities and projects relating to topics discussed in chapters 6, 9, and 10.

- **Getting Started on the World Wide Web** is an appendix that students should visit before exploring Norton Online.

- **Computers in Your Career** offers links to job search sites that focus on various computer-related fields.

- **Upgrading & Buying a PC** helps students determine which option best suits their computing needs

- Students of Peter Norton's® tutorials, can download template files from the **Norton Tutorials Download Site**.

THE INTERACTIVE BROWSER EDITION™ CD-ROM AND STUDENT GUIDES

To accommodate self-paced study and enhance retention of concepts, this new edition is available on CD-ROM, as *Peter Norton's® Introduction to Computers*, Interactive Browser Edition. This unique, fully HTML-based interactive courseware guide includes all the contents of this book, enhanced with animations, video, audio, hypermedia links, and many other features.

Because the Interactive Browser Edition is HTML-based, students can view it entirely within a Web browser, such as Microsoft Internet Explorer or Netscape Navigator. Using familiar browsing tools, students can easily and intuitively navigate the Interactive Browser Edition by moving from chapter to chapter, jumping to related Web sites, and drilling for information.

In addition to all the content from the printed Third Edition, the Interactive Browser Edition also includes the following features:

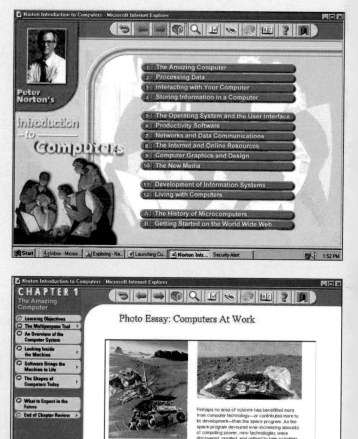

- **Completely illustrated text.** The Interactive Browser Edition is fully illustrated, using all the figures from the printed book, as well as special animations—many of which are clickable or accompanied by special audio captions. Video is also included, whereever appropriate, to enhance the learning experience.

- **Interactive objectives and glossary.** Lesson objectives are clearly defined in the opening screen of each chapter, and can be clicked to take students directly to the related coverage. Key terms are highlighted throughout the text, so students can view the definition of any term simply by clicking it.

- **Navigation hints.** Throughout the Interactive Browser Edition, students will find special buttons and highlighted text that lead to further explanations, examples, audio or video resources, Web sites, and more.

- **Self-Quizzes.** Many sections in the Interactive Browser Edition feature a **Self Quiz**, which enables students to quickly check their understanding of the topics covered in that section.

- **End of lesson review.** At the end of each lesson, the Interactive Browser Edition provides a series of review sections to help students recap the lesson's major points. These sections include an illustrated Visual Summary, a list of Key Terms, and a variety of online quizzes.

- **Links to the Web.** At many points in the Interactive Browser Edition, students can jump to the Norton Online Web site for more information and links to other Web sites. Because students are already working in a browser, moving to the Web is as easy as turning a page in a book.

The Interactive Browser Edition is accompanied by a printed *Student Guide*, which helps studentsget the most from the interactive learning experience. The *Student Guide* provides an up-front overview of the important concepts and terms in each chapter, which students can review prior to using the CD-ROM (or after, as a refresher).

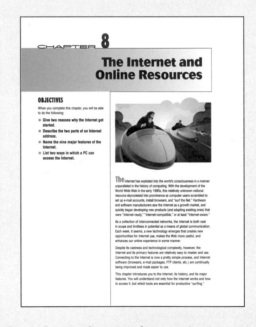

Once students are online, the *Student Guide* provides a series of targeted questions, which direct them through the interactive material. By answering these questions while browsing the interactive material, students are assured of maintaining a deliberate pace while being continually tested for understanding of the concepts and terms as they are being presented.

GLENCOE_ONLINE_LEARNING™

Platform Independent! Glencoe_Online_Learning will run on Windows, Macintosh, Linux, and Solaris servers. Students access Glencoe_Online_Learning via the Internet using a standard Web Browser.

- Full-Content Internet Courseware

- Virtual Classroom Environment

- Interactive and Collaborative Learning on the Web

- Distance Learning Using the Full Potential of Internet Technology

Glencoe_Online_Learning is a full-feature online course environment designed to let students take courses over the Internet. Using TopClass™ course management technology, Glencoe_Online_Learning allows instructors to:

1. Deploy a full-content online course from the school's Web server or hosted from Glencoe's Web server.

2. Manage individual sections of a course from a secure course management system.

3. Modify existing content or add original material to the online course using open HTML standards.

4. Track individual student's progress through the course material.

5. Assess student performance using automated testing.

6. Personalize coursework for all students based on their performance and skill level.

Additional features include:

- Secure collaboration tools such as bulletin boards which support threading, multi-leveled discussion boards, previewing, moderation, and file attachments.

- Built-in electronic mail to allow students to communicate with instructors and other students.

- An integrated environment that provides easy access to all built-in functions for users at all times.

EDITORIAL CONSULTANT

L. Joyce Arntson
Irvine Valley Community College

PROGRAM REVIEWERS

Dr. Mary Astone
Sorrell College of Business,
Troy State University

Dr. Mary Auvil
Foothill College (ret.)

Bill Barakat
Chubb Institute

Dick Barton
El Camino College

Gigi Beaton
Tyler Junior Community College

Anita Black
Laney College

Jeanine Black
Southern Oaklahoma Tech.

Patsy Blankenship
North Lake College

Beverly Bohner
Reading Area Community College

Ron Brock
Yakima Valley Community College

Charles Brown
Atlanta Technical Institute

Jeff Brown
Montana State University

Robert Caruso
Sonoma State University

Wendy Ceccucci
Quinnipiac College

Michael Crompton
Humber College of Applied Arts
and Technology, Ontario

Chuck Decker
College of the Desert

John Ford
National Institute of Technology

Louis Fuxan
Delgado Community College

Lanny Hertzberg
Cosumnes River College

Harry Hoffman
Miami-Dade Community College

Thaddeus Howze
Laney College

Brian Kilpatrick
Sanford-Brown College

Joyce Letourneau
The Sawyer School

Brad Mankoff
Career Point Business School

David Manning
Northern Kentucky University

Michael P. Martel
University of Southern Maine

Jeanne Massingill
Highland Community College

Dr. Samia Massoud
Texas A&M University

Linda McFarland
Indiana Business College

Ray Mollere
North Harris College

Todd Moser
Parks College

Luegina Mounfield
Midlands Technical Institute

Dr. Ravi Nadella
Wilberforce University

Teresa Peterman
Grand Valley State University

Mike Rabuat
Hillsboro Community College

Carole Rogers
Laney College

Patty Santoianni
Sinclair Community College

Helen Shambray-Johnson
H. Councill Trenholm State
Technical College

Bert Spivy
Lake Tahoe Community College

Brenda Stout
Kiamichi Technology Center

Becky Stragand
Western Piedmont Community
College

Al Watkins
Central Alabama Community
College

Rebecca Weier
Bob Jones University

Jim West
Fisher College

Dr. Robert Wurm
Nassau Community College

ACKNOWLEDGMENTS

The following individuals contributed to the content and development of this project: L. Joyce Arntson, Robert Goldhamer, Jeanne Massingill, Pat Fenton, Rob Tidrow, Cheri Manning, Cathy Manning, Chris Ewald, Geneil Breeze, Bill McManus, Elliot Linzer, Jose Lozano, Cynthia Karrasch, Mary Sheskey, and Kurt Hampe.

Special thanks goes to following at Glencoe whose dedication and hard work made this project possible: Corinne Gindroz, Janet Coulon, Bruce Albrecht, Hal Sturrock, Janet Grau, Sarah O'Donnell, Julia Holsclaw, Rachel Laskowski, Kim Harvey, and Denise Phillips. A personal thanks to Gary Schwartz, Satbir S. Bedi, Chris Shira, Colleen Morrissey, and Dave Kunkler.

Last, but by no means the least, it was a privilege to work with Charles T. Huddleston without whose hard work, patience, and professionalism this project would not have become a reality.

October 1998

Additional review provided by:
Maureen Sprankle
College of the Redwoods

CONTENTS

CONTENTS

Chapter 3:

Interacting with Your Computer   72

CONTENTS

Chapter 4:
Storing Information in a Computer 114
Contents 114

Objectives 114

CONTENTS

USING MICROCOMPUTER SOFTWARE

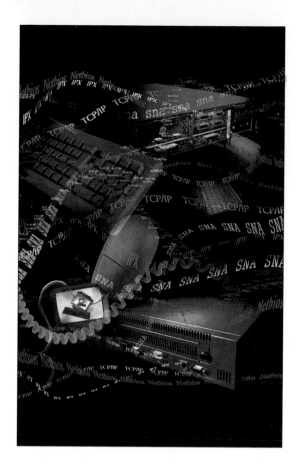

Chapter 6:
Productivity Software   196

CONTENTS

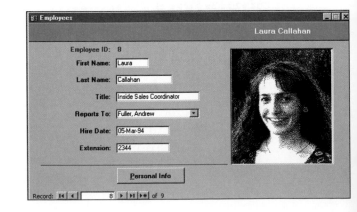

Chapter 7:
Networks and Data Communications   246

CONTENTS

Chapter 8:
The Internet and Online Resources 290

CONTENTS

CONTENTS

OUR TECHNOLOGICAL SOCIETY

PART 3

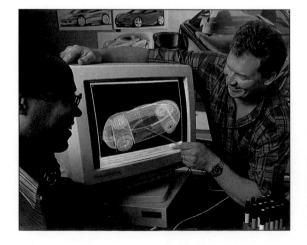

CONTENTS

APPENDICES

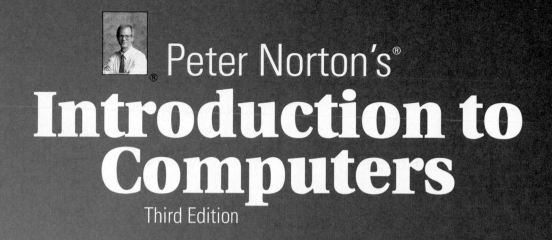

Peter Norton's®
Introduction to Computers
Third Edition

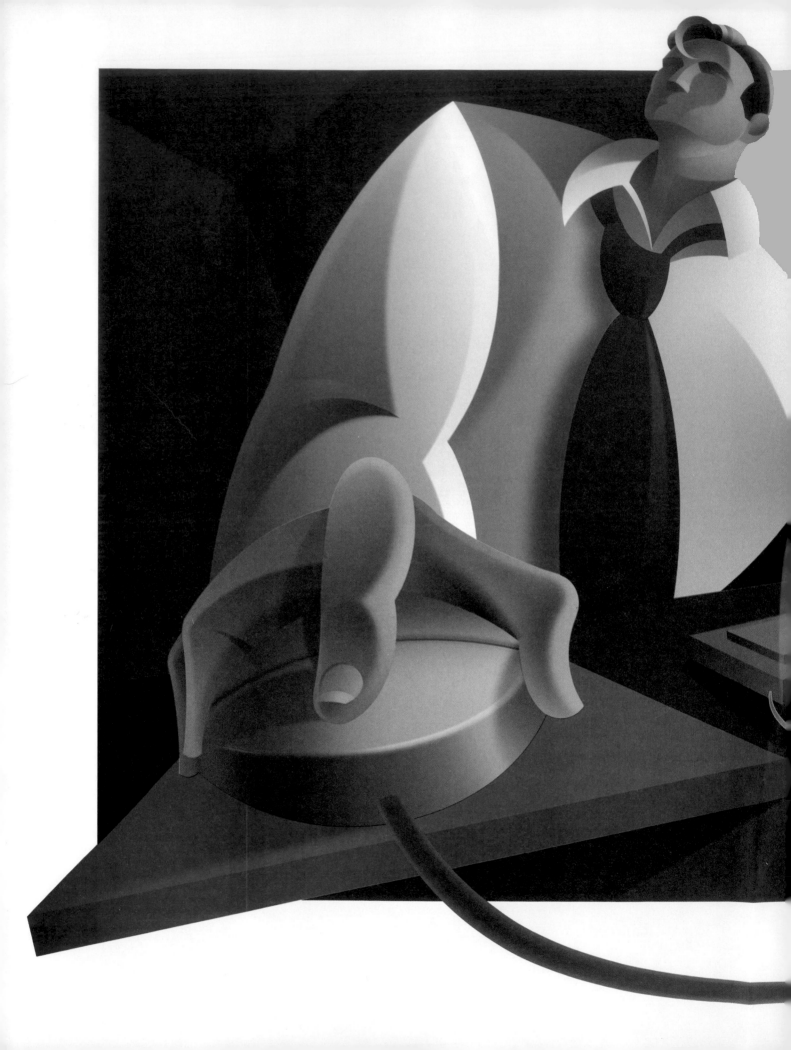

HOW COMPUTERS WORK

CHAPTER 1

The Amazing Computer

CONTENTS

OBJECTIVES

When you complete this chapter, you will be able to do the following:

- List at least five professions in which computers are routinely used and describe at least one of the ways computers have affected the work of people in those professions.

- List the four parts of a computer system.

- Identify four kinds of computer hardware.

- List the two major categories of software and explain the purpose of each.

- List the four most common types of computers available today and describe what kind of job each does best.

would be affected by computers, as well. It was envisioned that consumers would pay bills and do most of their shopping on the computer. In fact, some nervous pundits warned that jobs would be lost as stores and banks closed their doors—their services would be made obsolete by the computer!

The computer is a truly amazing machine. Few tools can help you perform so many different tasks in so many areas of your life. Whether you want to track an investment, publish a newsletter, design a building, or practice landing an F14 on the deck of the aircraft carrier, you can use a computer to do it.

In the early 1980s, when personal computers began gaining popularity, many futurists and analysts made bold predictions about the computer's importance to society. Some people even predicted that, by the year 2000, *no* home would be without a PC! The computer, it was forecast, would become the nerve center of every home, controlling the thermostat, switching on lights, operating the VCR, and more.

People would not only do most of their work on or with a computer, but nearly every aspect of their homes and personal lives

Of course, many of those predictions were over stated. But though we still don't depend completely on computers, our use of them has grown wildly in the past decade. These powerful tools built of silicon, metal, and plastic are so pervasive that virtually no business or organization can function effectively without them. Although not every home has a computer (not even half do), computers are becoming increasingly indispensable personal tools.

In this chapter, you will see some of the many ways computers help shape daily life. You will learn how computers have changed the way some businesses—even entire industries—function. You will also take a peek under the hood of these magnificent machines to see what makes them tick. Finally, you will learn about the various types of computers and which tasks each does best.

THE MULTIPURPOSE TOOL

In general terms, a **computer** is an electronic device used to process data. Today's computers, which are continually becoming smaller, faster, and more powerful, and which are being used in an ever-growing number of applications, are a far cry from the machines of 50 years ago, when the first computers were created.

In the 1940s and 1950s, computers were massive, special-purpose machines that only huge institutions such as governments, the military, and universities could afford. The earliest computers—such as the giant ENIAC (Electronic Numeric Integrator and Calculator) and Universal Automatic Computer (UNIVAC)—were big enough to fill a large room. Even with their enormous electronic "brains," based on the same type of vacuum tubes used in early radios and televisions, these wondrous machines had little more real computing power than a modern-day digital wristwatch or handheld calculator.

In the 1960s, modern computers began to revolutionize the business world. IBM introduced its System/360 mainframe computer in April 1964 and ultimately sold more than 33,000 of these machines. As a result of the commercial success of its System/360, IBM became the standard against which other computer manufacturers and their systems would be measured for years to come.

In the 1970s, Digital Equipment Corporation (DEC) took two more giant steps toward bringing computers into mainstream use with the introduction of its PDP-11 and VAX computers. These models came in many sizes to meet different needs and budgets. Since then, computers continue to shrink in size while providing more power for less money. Today, the most common type of computer is called a **personal computer**, or **PC**, because it is designed to be used by just one person at a time. Despite its small size, the modern personal computer is more powerful than any of the room-sized machines of the 1950s or 1960s.

Computers have become so fundamental to modern society that without them, our economy would grind to a halt. They are such flexible tools that most people in the business community use them every day. Office workers use them to write letters, keep employee rosters, create budgets, communicate with

Today, the personal computer is the most prevalent type of computer in the home and the workplace.

NORTON Online

For information on the **history of the personal computer**, visit this book's Web site at **www.glencoe.com/norton/online**

Salespeople often carry portable computers to give presentations to potential customers.

coworkers, find information, manage projects, and so on. Step into any office building, and you will see a computer on almost every desk. Many businesspeople use computers even when they are away from the office. For example, salespeople use computers to manage accounts and make presentations. Most salespeople who are on the road now carry portable computers—known as **laptop computers** or **notebook computers**—which can be every bit as powerful as models that sit on a desk. With a portable computer, a salesperson can enter orders, write letters, track travel expenses, update customer files, and create colorful presentations to help sell a product. Using a modem and communication software, a traveling worker or a **telecommuter** (that is, an employee who works at home rather than at the organization's office at least part of the time) can communicate and share data with fellow workers by using a standard phone line, from any location.

Modern checkout lines feature computerized scanners that calculate and total the prices of the items you purchase and enable you to pay using cash, check, credit card, or debit card. The computerized card readers usually use a telephone line to connect to the card's issuer for approval.

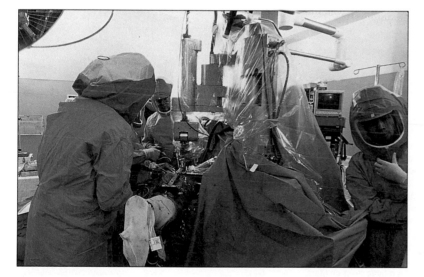

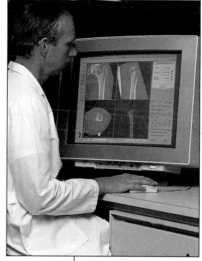

In medicine today, computers are used for everything from diagnosing illnesses to controlling the movement of robotic surgical assistants. These doctors are using a computer system called Robodoc, which helps them with the drilling necessary for an operation on the patient's hip.

Computers are also vital in accounting departments. For organizing and manipulating large sets of numbers, which accounting departments do daily, computers are now considered essential. Computers are used to juggle budgets, create purchase orders, set up employee files, track expenses and income, and pay taxes. Even small businesses—which can comprise just a single person—can afford to set up sophisticated accounting systems using a personal computer and affordable accounting and financial software packages.

Even if you do not work in a business, computers affect you every day. Any time you go to the bank, renew a subscription, call information for a phone number, or buy something out of a catalog, you are benefiting from the power and speed of computers. Even when you buy groceries and gasoline, you are interacting with computers.

Visual Essay: Computers at Work

In classrooms, computers have become as essential to the learning process as books, paper, and pens. Students use computers to develop science projects, prepare reports, and gather information from electronic sources around the world. Increasingly, college students are taking personal computers to school with them, and connecting to school networks.

Computers are used at the Smithsonian in Washington, D.C. to guide museum goers and tell them about the exhibits.

NORTON Online

For information on the **Mars Pathfinder mission**, visit this book's Web site at **www.glencoe.com/norton/online**

Perhaps no area of science has benefited more from computer technology—or contributed more to its development—than the space program. As the space program devoured ever-increasing amounts of computing power, new technologies were discovered, created, and refined to help scientists continue their progress. This progress reached a new peak in the summer of 1997, with the landing of a robotic rover on Mars.

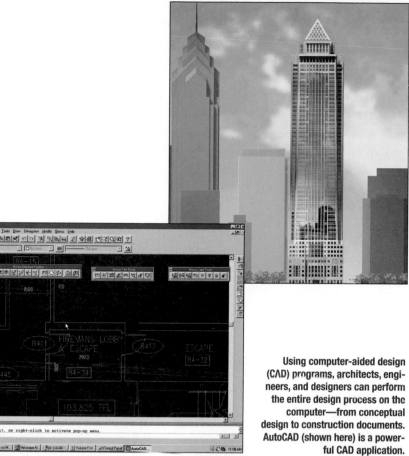

Using 3D CAD tools, designers can create photorealistic three-dimensional renderings of a finished building's interior and exterior. These capabilities enable the designer and client to visualize the completed project before the first shovel of dirt has been turned.

Using computer-aided design (CAD) programs, architects, engineers, and designers can perform the entire design process on the computer—from conceptual design to construction documents. AutoCAD (shown here) is a powerful CAD application.

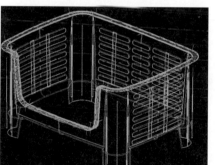

Designers use CAD programs to create products of all kinds. To design a new storage bin, a designer can use a CAD program that creates a three-dimensional wireframe outline of the product. The designer then can add a "skin" to it, which depicts the container's finished appearance.

Factories use computerized robotic arms to do physical work that is hazardous or highly repetitive. Manufacturing with computers and robotics is called computer-aided manufacturing (CAM).

Find Your Way Anywhere with GPS

Imagine you are in Benton Harbor, Michigan, on the eastern shore of Lake Michigan. You want to travel to Chicago, Illinois, which is on the lake's western shore. And you want to make this trip by boat. To do this, you have two options.

First, you can follow the shoreline of Lake Michigan, traveling south along the Michigan shore, west along the Indiana shore, and then north along the Illinois shore. By keeping the shore in sight, you reduce the risk of getting lost, and you'll know when you reach Chicago; it's too big to miss! The trip is about 100 miles.

Or, you could head directly southwest from Benton Harbor, taking a straight line across the lake to Chicago. This trip is about 60 miles.

But unless you're an expert navigator, how can you find your way across such a big lake?

Earthbound GPS receivers determine their location by triangulating with a sytem of NAVSTAR satellites.

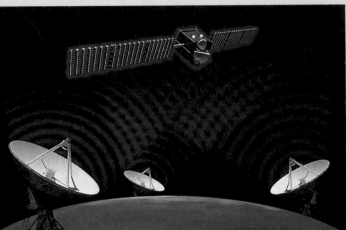

Commercially available GPS receivers can be used on foot and in cars, boats, and planes. GPS units take three forms: handheld devices, dashboard units, and laptop units.

A Global Positioning System (GPS) could help you find your way. GPS is a computerized navigation system that can tell you where you are at any time. GPS also can give you directions to practically any destination, whether you're traveling on foot, by car, by boat, or by plane. This technology makes it virtually impossible to get lost, whether you're hiking through dense woods, driving in a foreign country, or cruising across open waters.

Like the Internet, GPS is a global technology, making use of worldwide resources. It is based on a group of NAVSTAR satellites, each of which orbits the Earth about once every 12 hours. A series of ground stations constantly track and monitor the satellites, updating their positions and checking for errors. GPS users interact with the system through small, highly portable GPS receivers.

The user's GPS receiver determines its position by triangulating with the orbiting satellites. The GPS unit receives radio waves from the satellites and measures the amount of time it takes for the waves to travel the distance

from the satellites. (To do this, the receiver needs to know each satellite's precise location in the sky at any moment.)

The result: the receiver can determine your current location and tell you how to get where you're going.

Current GPS systems are accurate to within a few meters. Emerging systems—such as Differential GPS—are accurate to within a few centimeters.

The US government originally developed GPS for military use, but the system is also available for many civilian applications. For example:

■ Emergency vehicle drivers (as well as taxi and limousine drivers) use GPS in major cities to help reach their destinations in less time.

■ In some national parks, rangers use handheld GPS receivers to help locate and rescue lost hikers.

■ Geologists rely on GPS to measure changes in the height of mountains and the movements of glaciers.

■ Private pilots and boaters use GPS to chart accurate courses and reach their destinations safely across unfamiliar routes.

Basic handheld GPS receivers can be purchased for as little as $100 in department stores and sporting-goods stores. Dashboard-mounted units, for use in cars and trucks, range in price from around $200 to over $1,000. Specialized receivers are also available for use in boats and planes of all sizes.

Most GPS receivers provide a small screen, which displays the user's location and directions to a destination. More sophisticated units also provide a voice-response system, which can give the user audio directions, such as "turn right" or "go west." Some receivers work in tandem with a CD-ROM drive and download map coordinates and other information from databases on compact disk.

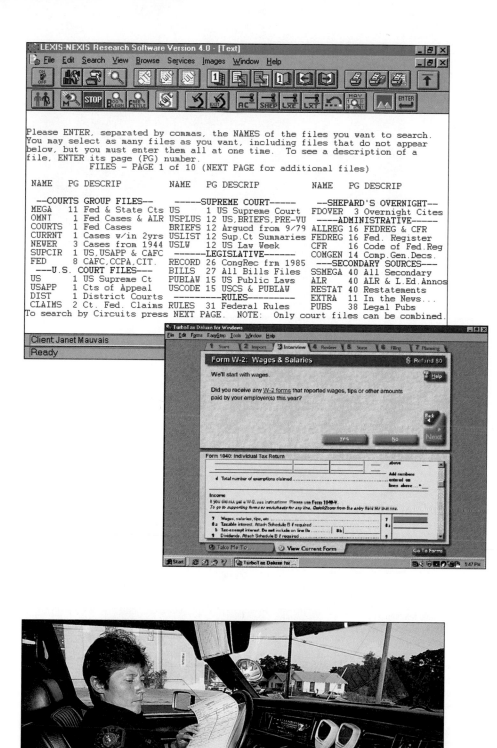

Attorneys use the LEXIS data-base to search for information about federal and state case law. The service has dozens of specialized libraries covering the major fields of practice, including tax, securities, banking, environmental, and international law.

Today, many people use computers to prepare their tax forms and send them electronically to the IRS. TurboTax, a program from Intuit, provides electronic tax forms. The program performs all the arithmetic, and you can send the completed forms to the IRS electronically using a telephone line and modem.

This police officer is using a mobile data terminal (MDT), which provides quickaccess to information, such as license plate numbers of stolen cars. Computers have also enabled local, state, and federal agencies to share data about crimes, criminals, crime scenes, and police activity around the nation.

NORTON Online

For information on **government agency Web sites**, visit this book's Web site at **www.glencoe.com/norton/online**

The military is often at the forefront of technology. This man is using an Airborne Warning and Aircraft Control (AWAC) system to track the in-flight progress of missiles and jets. The military also uses computers to keep track of the largest payroll and human-resource management systems in the world.

The Internal Revenue Service uses its computers to record income tax returns for millions of individuals and businesses every year. Its computers also check and cross-check tax returns with information received from many sources throughout the year. The IRS and other government agencies also host sites on the World Wide Web.

Computers have become a cre-ative tool for musicians. The Musical Instrument Digital Interface (MIDI) allows different electronic instruments to be con-nected to one another, as well as to computers. A musician can touch one synthesizer key to pro-duce the sound of a violin and another to create a cymbal crash, or use one instrument to control another one. This musician is writing an original piece of music with the help of a computer and a MIDI keyboard.

Many movies and television productions now use motion-capture technology to enable computer-generated characters to move realistically. Special sensors are attached to an actor, who moves in a tightly choreographed way. Movements are recorded by a computer. The data can then be assigned to the corresponding parts of a digital character's body, so that its movements exactly mimic the actor's movements.

AN OVERVIEW OF THE COMPUTER SYSTEM

The computer systems you read about in the last few pages come in all shapes and sizes, from the common personal computer, to embedded computers that work inside appliances, to the huge machines used in manufacturing. Despite the differences in size and use, all these computers have several characteristics in common. First, any computer must be part of a system. As shown in Figure 1.1, a **computer system** consists of four parts:

- Hardware, also known simply as the computer
- Software, also known as programs
- Data, which the system converts into information
- People, also known as users

The term **hardware** refers to any part of the computer you can touch. Hardware consists of interconnected electronic devices that you can use to control the computer's operation, input, and output. When people talk about a computer, they usually mean hardware.

The term **software** refers to sets of electronic instructions that tell the hardware what to do. These sets of instructions are also known as **programs**, and each one has a specific purpose. For example, you will probably use a word processing program to enter, edit, and format text documents, such as letters, memos, and reports.

Techview

Man Versus Machine: Round Two

In May, 1997, a new chapter was added to the epic saga of man versus machine, as World Chess Champion Garry Kasparov returned for a rematch with his most highly trained and inscrutable opponent ever: IBM's computerized chessmaster, a souped-up RS/6000 SP system named "Deep Blue."

In their first match in February, 1996, Kasparov bested the machine four games to two. Kasparov won that match through a clever strategy: The computer, he reasoned, would be programmed to defend against most standard moves. Despite its speed and processing power, however, the machine might not be able to adapt quickly to tricky, nonstandard moves and combinations.

Instead of playing in a standard style that would defeat most human opponents, Kasparov adapted his style in hopes of confusing Deep Blue. The plan worked. The world champion zigged when Deep Blue anticipated zags, and the computer's primary weakness was revealed: Although it could analyze and calculate with incredible speed, Deep Blue could not shift its strategy as quickly as its human opponent. It could not develop a longer-term strategy, especially if its opponent's tactics changed.

In the following year, Kasparov prepared for the rematch with Deep Blue by reviewing play logs from the initial match and refining his winning strategy.

World chess champion Garry Kasparov lost his rematch with IBM's Deep Blue computer in May, 1997.

Deep Blue's preparation for the rematch, however, was a different story. At IBM, the Deep Blue development team "bulked up" the computer by increasing it to a 32-node system. Each node contained eight dedicated chess processors-modules designed to analyze chess positions. These 256 dedicated processors could analyze 200 to 300 billion positions in three minutes (the amount of time allowed for a match player to make a move). Deep Blue's processing speed was essentially doubled, and IBM recruited an international chess grandmaster to help improve the computer's "mastery" of the game.

In the end, Deep Blue won its rematch with Kasparov. The final score was Deep Blue, 3.5 games; Kasparov, 2.5 games.

Despite his disappointment at the loss, Kasparov applauded Deep Blue and its developers, suggesting that the team may someday deserve a Nobel Prize for its efforts, which resulted in a machine that could foresee the long-term consequences of its own actions.

The human qualities that Kasparov admired in Deep Blue, however, were disturbing to other observers. The most important aspect of the rematch was not the play itself, perhaps, but the

implications that arose from it. Were computers becoming smarter than humans? Would the computer's future outshine that of its own creator? Was Kasparov a John Henry for the 21st century?

The answer from Silicon Valley was oddly reassuring: Computers, though capable of playing a mean game of chess (especially if you pay enough to build them), are not likely to replace people soon.

"Believe me," wrote Bill Gates, chairman of Microsoft Corporation, "there is no artificial intellect at work inside Deep Blue. It's just a computer running clever software."

In an article written for IBM's World Wide Web site, Dr. Mark Bremen, General Manager of IBM's RS/6000 Division, wrote that the computer's real purpose wasn't to outwit humans. Rather, the research and development that went into Deep Blue benefit business and society in other, subtler ways.

After his loss to Deep Blue, Kasparov immediately issued a challenge for a rematch. After several months of deliberation, IBM declined, saying that Deep Blue and the Deep Blue team were ready to take on other challenges. But Deep Blue's legacy did not end there. IBM also unveiled a new system, named "Deep Blue, Jr.," which will continue playing grandmaster-level chess, and further the research into making computers think and function in more human ways.

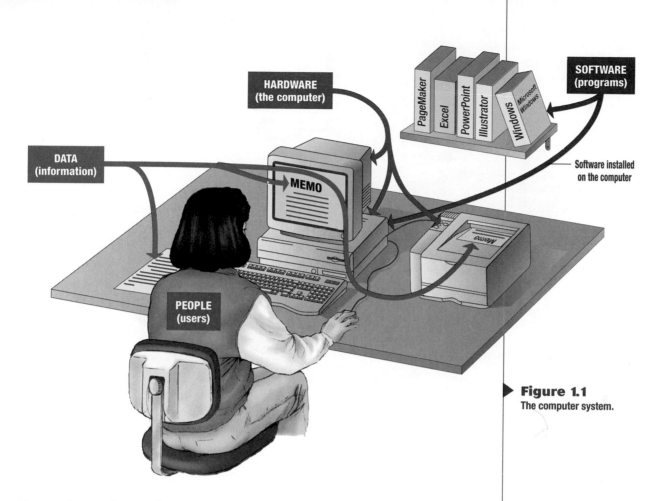

Figure 1.1
The computer system.

Data refers to the raw facts the computer can manipulate. Data can consist of letters, numbers, sounds, or images. However, no matter what kind of data is entered into a computer, the computer converts it to numbers. Consequently, computerized data is **digital**, meaning that it has been reduced to digits, or numbers. Within the computer, data is organized into files.

A computer **file** is simply a set of data or program instructions that has been given a name. A file containing data that the user can open and use is often called a **document**. Although many people think of documents simply as text, a computer document can include many kinds of data. For example, a computer document can be a text file (such as a letter), a group of numbers (such as a budget), or a video clip (which includes images and sounds). Programs are organized into files as well, but because programs are not considered data, they are not document files.

The last part of the computer system is the person who uses the computer. In discussions about computers, people are usually referred to as **users**.

LOOKING INSIDE THE MACHINE

The computer itself—the hardware—has many parts, but each piece falls into one of four categories:

1_ Processor

2_ Memory

3_ Input and output devices

4_ Storage devices

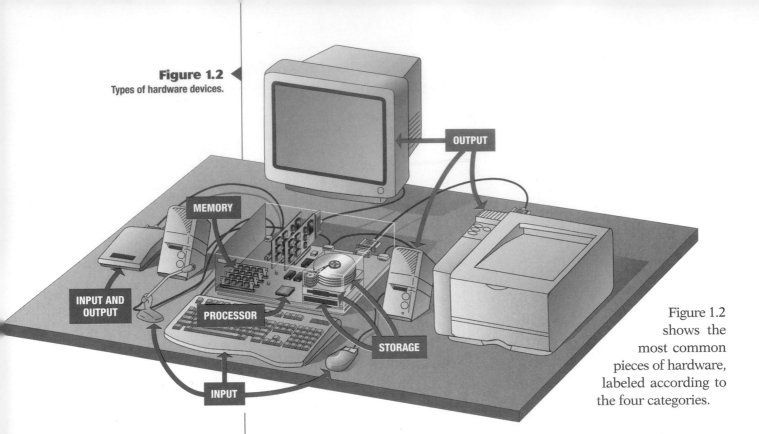

Figure 1.2 ◄
Types of hardware devices.

Figure 1.2 shows the most common pieces of hardware, labeled according to the four categories.

The Processor

NORTON
Online

For information on **computer processors**, visit this book's Web site at **www.glencoe.com/norton/online**

The procedure that transforms raw data into useful information is called **processing**. To perform this transformation, the computer uses two components: the processor and memory.

The **processor** is like the brain of the computer, the part that organizes and carries out instructions that come from either the user or the software. In a personal computer, the processor usually consists of one or more **microprocessors**, which are slivers of silicon or other material etched with many tiny electronic circuits. As shown in Figure 1.3, the microprocessor is plugged into a **circuit board**—a rigid rectangular card containing the circuitry that connects the processor to the other hardware. The circuit board to which the microprocessor is connected is called the **motherboard**.

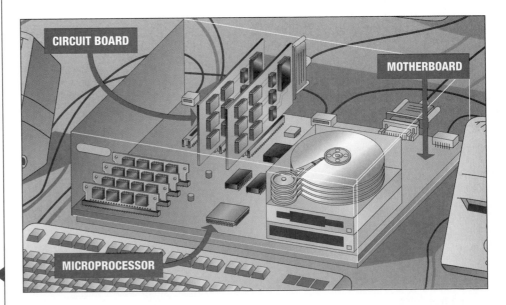

Figure 1.3 ◄
Processing devices.

In some powerful computers, the processor consists of many chips and the circuit boards on which they are mounted. The term **central processing unit (CPU)** refers to a computer's processing hardware, whether it consists of a single chip or several circuit boards. This "vital organ" occupies an amazingly small space in a PC.

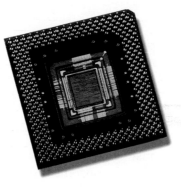

▶ The CPU of a modern computer is a tiny device, not much larger than a thumbnail.

THE COMPUTER AT A GLANCE

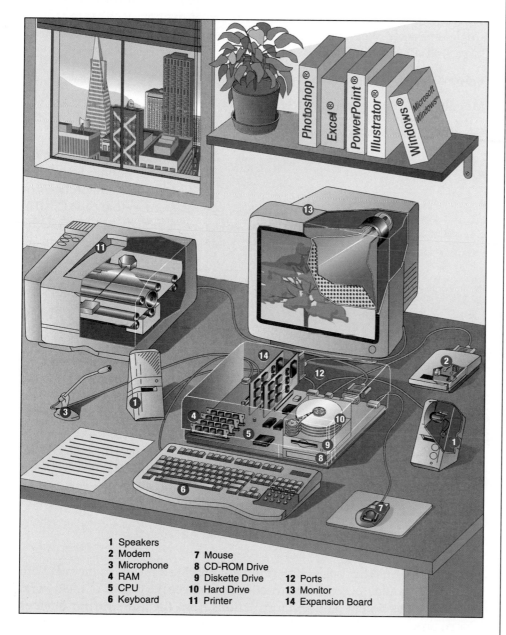

1	Speakers		
2	Modem	7	Mouse
3	Microphone	8	CD-ROM Drive
4	RAM	9	Diskette Drive	12	Ports
5	CPU	10	Hard Drive	13	Monitor
6	Keyboard	11	Printer	14	Expansion Board

Memory

Memory is the computer's electronic scratch pad. Programs are loaded into and run from memory. Data used by the program is also loaded into memory for fast access. Similarly, as you enter new data into the computer, it is stored in memory—but only temporarily. The most common type of memory is called **random access memory**, or **RAM** (see Figure 1.4). As a result, the term "memory" is commonly used to mean RAM.

Perhaps the most important thing to remember about RAM is that it is volatile, so it needs a constant supply of power. When you turn off a computer, everything in RAM disappears. As you will soon learn, this is why you frequently have to save to a storage device everything you are working on.

One of the most important factors affecting the speed and power of a computer is the amount of RAM it has. Generally, the more RAM a computer has, the more it can do. The most common measurement unit for describing a computer's memory is the **byte**—the amount of memory it takes to store a single character. When people talk about memory, the numbers are often so large that it is useful to use a shorthand term to describe the values:

Kilobyte (KB)—approximately 1,000 bytes

Megabyte (MB)—approximately 1,000,000 bytes

Gigabyte (GB)—approximately 1,000,000,000 bytes

RAM

Figure 1.4
Random Access Memory (RAM).

Today's personal computers commonly have from 16 to 128 million bytes of memory (or 16 to 128 MB), although newer systems seldom have less than 32 MB. Increasingly, newer generations of PCs feature more RAM than previous generations because newer generations of operating systems and software require ever-increasing amounts of RAM to operate efficiently. As a rule of thumb, therefore, the more RAM a computer has, the better. Note, too, that it is usually possible to add more RAM to a standard computer; some newer systems can be upgraded to nearly 1 GB of RAM.

Input and Output Devices

Computers would be useless if they did not provide a means to interact with users. They could not receive instructions or deliver the results of their work. **Input devices** accept data and instructions from the user; **output devices** return processed data back to the user. The generic term **device** refers to any piece of hardware.

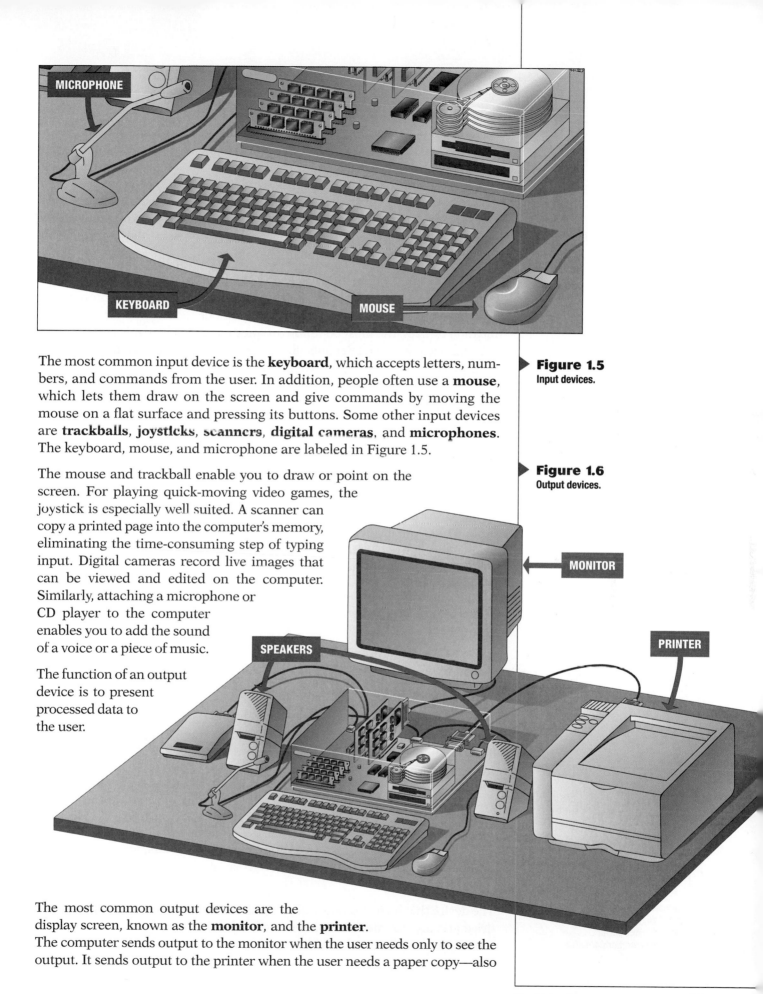

MICROPHONE

KEYBOARD

MOUSE

MONITOR

SPEAKERS

PRINTER

The most common input device is the **keyboard**, which accepts letters, numbers, and commands from the user. In addition, people often use a **mouse**, which lets them draw on the screen and give commands by moving the mouse on a flat surface and pressing its buttons. Some other input devices are **trackballs**, **joysticks**, **scanners**, **digital cameras**, and **microphones**. The keyboard, mouse, and microphone are labeled in Figure 1.5.

The mouse and trackball enable you to draw or point on the screen. For playing quick-moving video games, the joystick is especially well suited. A scanner can copy a printed page into the computer's memory, eliminating the time-consuming step of typing input. Digital cameras record live images that can be viewed and edited on the computer. Similarly, attaching a microphone or CD player to the computer enables you to add the sound of a voice or a piece of music.

The function of an output device is to present processed data to the user.

▶ **Figure 1.5**
Input devices.

▶ **Figure 1.6**
Output devices.

The most common output devices are the display screen, known as the **monitor**, and the **printer**. The computer sends output to the monitor when the user needs only to see the output. It sends output to the printer when the user needs a paper copy—also called a "hard copy." In addition, just as computers can accept sound as input, they can include stereo speakers as output devices to produce sound. The monitor, printer, and speakers are labeled in Figure 1.6.

Some types of hardware can act as both input and output devices. One example is the **touch screen**, a type of monitor that displays text or icons you can touch. Touch screens are popular in libraries, book stores, and music stores because they enable users to quickly locate an item without wandering the aisles or searching through card catalogs. When you touch the screen, special sensors detect the touch, then the computer calculates the point on the screen where you placed your finger. Depending on the location of the touch, the computer responds by displaying new data.

The most common types of devices that can perform both input and output, however, are **communication devices**, which connect one computer to another—a process known as **networking**. Among the many kinds of communication devices, the most common are **modems**, which enable computers to communicate through telephone lines, and **network interface cards (NICs)**, which let users connect a group of computers to share data and devices.

Storage

It is possible for a computer to function with just processing, memory, input, and output devices. To be really useful, however, it also needs a place to keep program files and related data when it is not using them. The purpose of **storage** is to hold data.

Think of storage as an electronic file cabinet and RAM as an electronic worktable. When you need to work with a program or a set of data, the computer locates it in the file cabinet and puts a copy on the table. After you have finished working with the program or data, you put the new version into the file cabinet. There are three major distinctions between storage and memory:

1_ There is more room in storage than in memory, just as there is more room in a file cabinet than there is on a tabletop.

2_ Contents are retained in storage when the computer is turned off, whereas the programs or the data you put into memory disappear when you shut down the computer.

3_ Storage is much cheaper than memory.

Remember the distinction between storage and memory. Their functions are similar, but they work in different ways. Novice computer users often use the term *memory* when they actually mean *storage* or *disk*. This mistake can cause confusion.

Common Storage Devices

The most common storage medium is the **magnetic disk**. A disk is a round, flat object that spins around its center. **Read/write heads**, which are similar to the heads of a tape recorder or VCR, float above and below the disk near its surface.

The device that holds a disk is called a **disk drive**. Some disks are built into the drive and are not meant to be removed; other kinds of drives enable you to remove and replace disks. Most personal computers have a nonremovable

hard disk. In addition, there are usually one or two diskette drives, which allow you to use removable **diskettes**. Typically, a hard disk can store far more data than a diskette can, so the hard disk serves as the computer's primary filing cabinet. Diskettes are used to load new programs or data onto the hard disk, trade data with other users, and make backup copies of the data on the hard disk.

Because you can remove diskettes from a computer, they are encased in a plastic or vinyl cover to protect them from fingerprints and dust. The first diskettes, commonly used in the late 1970s, were 8-inch diskettes (they were 8 inches in diameter). Because the vinyl cover was very thin, the diskette was flimsy, or floppy. As a result, they came to be called **floppy disks**. Next came the 5.25-inch diskettes common in the early PCs. Finally, the 3.5-inch diskette with its hard plastic shell appeared.

▶ Over the years, diskettes have shrunk while their capacity has greatly increased. The 3.5-inch diskette can hold more data than can either of the larger two diskettes.

8-inch diskette

5.25-inch diskette

3.5-inch diskette

Other Storage Devices

Other types of storage devices include **CD-ROM drives**, **tape drives**, **optical drives**, **removable hard drives**, and many others. The CD-ROM drive is the most common type after the hard and diskette drives. **Compact disks (CDs)** are a type of optical storage device, identical to audio CDs, that can store about 650 MB, or about 450 times as much information as a diskette. The type used in computers is called **Compact Disk Read-Only Memory (CD-ROM)**. The name implies that you cannot change the information on the disk, just as you cannot record over an audio CD. The hard disk, diskette drive, and CD-ROM drive are shown in Figure 1.7.

▶ The DVD standard promises to revolutionize home entertainment and is quickly being adopted by the PC industry.

Figure 1.7
Storage devices.

An emerging data storage technology is the **digital versatile disk (DVD)**, which promises to revolutionize home entertainment. Using new compression technologies, a single DVD (which is the same size as a standard compact disk) can store an entire full-length movie. DVD disks require a special player; the new players, however, generally can play audio, data, and DVD disks, freeing the user from purchasing different players for each type of disk.

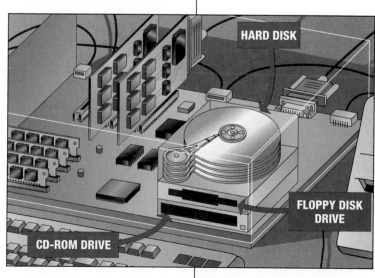

HARD DISK

FLOPPY DISK DRIVE

CD-ROM DRIVE

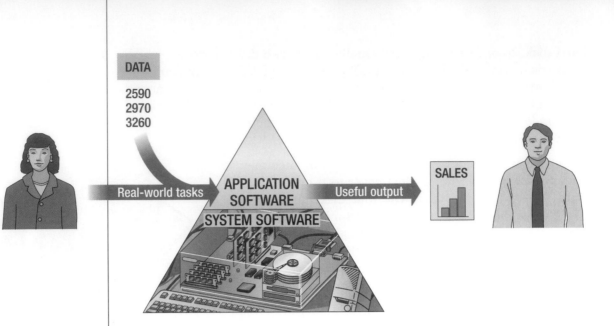

Figure 1.8
Application software and system software.

SOFTWARE BRINGS THE MACHINE TO LIFE

Computers are general-purpose machines. You can use them just as effectively to calculate numbers as you can to create documents or drawings or to control other machines. The ingredient that allows a computer to perform a certain task is the software, which consists of electronic instructions. A specific set of the instructions that drive a computer to perform a specific task is called a program. When a computer is using a particular program, it is said to be **running** or **executing** that program. Because programs tell the machine's physical components what to do, without them, a computer could not do anything. It would be just a box of metal and plastic.

Although the array of programs available is vast and varied, most software falls into two major categories: **system software** and **application software**. One major type of system software, called **operating system** software, tells the computer how to use its own components. Application software tells the computer how to accomplish specific tasks for the user, such as word processing or drawing. Figure 1.8 shows the relationship between the two types of software and the hardware, user, and data.

Operating Systems

NORTON Online
For information on any **operating system**, visit this book's Web site at
www.glencoe.com/norton/online

When you turn on a computer, it goes through several steps to prepare itself for use. The first step is a self-test. The computer identifies the devices attached to it, identifies the amount of memory available, and does a quick check to see whether the memory is functioning properly. This routine is initiated by a part of the system software located in **read-only memory (ROM)**, a chip that contains brief, permanent instructions for getting the computer started.

Next, the computer looks in the diskette drive and then on the hard drive for an operating system. The operating system tells the computer how to interact with the user and how to use devices such as the disk drives, keyboard,

Table 1.1	The Startup Process	
STEP	**SOURCE OF INSTRUCTION**	**TYPE OF INSTRUCTION**
1	ROM	System self-check
2	Hard disk	System software loaded into memory
3	User	Control hardware by issuing operating system commands *OR* Load an application from a disk

and monitor. When it finds the operating system, the computer loads it into memory. Because the operating system is needed to control the computer's most basic functions, it continues to run until the computer is turned off.

After the computer finds and runs the operating system, it is ready to accept commands from an input device—usually the keyboard or a mouse. At this point, the user can issue commands to the computer. A command might, for example, list the programs stored on the computer's disk or make the computer run one of those programs. Table 1.1 shows the process the computer goes through at startup.

Application Software

The operating system exists mostly for the benefit of the computer. Other programs are required to make the computer useful for people. Programs that help people accomplish specific tasks are referred to as application software. Application software has been written to do almost every task imaginable, from word processing to selecting a college to attend.

Thousands of applications are available; however, some major categories you are likely to encounter are:

■ Word processing software

■ Spreadsheets

■ Database management software

■ Graphics, multimedia, and presentation applications

■ Entertainment and education software

■ Utilities

■ Communication software

You will learn about these different types of application software in later chapters.

NORTON Online

For information on all kinds of **application software**, visit this book's Web site at **www.glencoe.com/norton/online**

Visual Essay: Software Makes the System Useful

Word processing software is designed for creating documents that consist primarily of text.

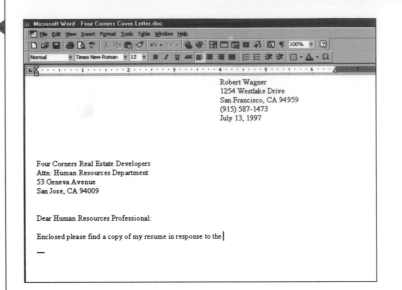

Microsoft Word - Four Corners Cover Letter.doc

Robert Wagner
1254 Westlake Drive
San Francisco, CA 94959
(915) 587-1473
July 13, 1997

Four Corners Real Estate Developers
Attn: Human Resources Department
53 Geneva Avenue
San Jose, CA 94009

Dear Human Resources Professional:

Enclosed please find a copy of my resume in response to the

Spreadsheet programs are perfect for setting up budgets. Your document can contain text, numbers, or formulas for calculating numbers. Spreadsheet programs also enable users to create colorful graphs from their data.

Microsoft Excel - Morton's 1998 Budget.xls

B9   =SUM(B6:B8)

Category	Actual	Budget	Difference
Morton Family Budget			
June, 1998			
INCOME			
Mort's Salary	$ 2,675	$ 2,675	$ -
June's Salary	$ 2,892	$ 2,892	$ -
Other Income	$ 213	$ 197	$ 16
Total Income	$ 5,780	$ 5,764	$ 16
EXPENSES			
Mortgage	$ 889.00	$ 889.00	$ -
Vehicle leases	$ 520.00	$ 520.00	$ -
Child care	$ 329.00	$ 300.00	$ 29.00
Telephone	$ 128.00	$ 75.00	$ 53.00
Water	$ 13.00	$ 15.00	$ (2.00)
Electricity	$ 38.00	$ 45.00	$ (7.00)
Credit cards	$ 268.00	$ 250.00	$ 38.00
Cleaning	$ 120.00	$ 120.00	$ -
Cable	$ 27.00	$ 27.00	$ -
Insurance	$ 69.00	$ 69.00	$ -
Food	$ 229.00	$ 200.00	$ 29.00
Entertainment	$ 78.00	$ 50.00	$ 28.00
Medical	$ 28.00	$ -	$ 28.00

June '98 / July '98 / Aug. '98
Ready

This screen shows a database of names and addresses. Database management software makes it easy to reorganize data. For example, you could easily arrange this list by city or ZIP code.

Microsoft Access - [Employees : Table]

Employee ID	Last Name	First Name	MI	Title	Title Of Courtesy	Birth Date	Hire Date	Ad
1	Davolio	Nancy	A	Sales Representative	Ms.	08-Dec-48	01-May-92	507 - 20th
2	Fuller	Andrew	S	Vice President, Sales	Dr.	19-Feb-52	14-Aug-92	908 W. Ca
3	Leverling	Janet	L	Sales Representative	Ms.	30-Aug-63	01-Apr-92	722 Moss
4	Peacock	Margaret	J	Sales Representative	Mrs.	19-Sep-37	03-May-93	4110 Old F
5	Buchanan	Steven	L	Sales Manager	Mr.	04-Mar-55	17-Oct-93	14 Garrett
6	Suyama	Michael	B	Sales Representative	Mr.	02-Jul-63	17-Oct-93	Coventry H
7	King	Robert	R	Sales Representative	Mr.	29-May-60	02-Jan-94	Edgeham I
8	Callahan	Laura	R	Inside Sales Coordinator	Ms.	09-Jan-58	05-Mar-94	4726 - 11th
9	Dodsworth	Anne	M	Sales Representative	Ms.	27-Jan-66	15-Nov-94	7 Houndst
10	Smith	Adam	B	District Manager	Mr.	13-Jul-59	06-Jan-93	6136 N. Ev
11	Smith	Toni	S	Sales Representative	Ms.	01-Jan-61	01-Jan-94	87 Stickvie
12	Smith	Toni	K	Receptionist/Dispatcher	Mrs.	07-Jun-64	12-Mar-95	1818 Mars
13	Buchanan	Arnold	Z	Driver	Mr.	09-May-49	12-Feb-93	4650-B Pl
14	Fuller	Nikki	L	Trainer	Ms.	05-May-60	12-Aug-94	1616 Weid
15	O'Hara	Shamus	I	Sales Representative	Mr.	08-Aug-58	14-May-94	7654 Take
16	Jones	Nancy	L	Sales Representative	Mrs.	19-Sep-59	16-Feb-93	451 Amos
17	Jones	Steven	P	Sales Manager	Mr.	30-Apr-57	02-Feb-93	1610 Builtr
18	Jones	Harold	M	District Manager	Mr.	11-Nov-62	02-Feb-93	1876 Cann
19	Jones	Steven	L	Driver	Mr.	30-Dec-58	12-Feb-93	5150 Belle
20	Gesner	Rustin	B	Designer	Mr.	10-Aug-56	04-Mar-95	128 Bee Li
21	Tidrow	Robert	A	Tech Writer	Mr.	10-Mar-62	09-May-95	12 Whoop
22	Tidrow	Tammy	L	Illustrator	Mrs.	03-Jan-63	12-Mar-94	12 Whoop
23	Gregg	Tara	L	Sales Representative	Ms.	22-Jul-65	01-Jun-94	8528 Head
24	Gregg	Tracy	L	Trainer	Ms.	17-Aug-67	05-Apr-95	14 May Rc
25	Foster	Steven	A	Developer	Mr.	12-Aug-58	18-Aug-94	444 Latin F
26	Kuhns	Peter	H	Tech Writer	Mr.	03-Mar-65	18-Apr-93	321 Liftoff

Record: 25 of 26

Street or post-office box.

Multimedia authoring applications let you organize text, audio, video, and other graphic elements into a sequenced interactive program.

Presentation software is most often used for creating sales presentations, although it can be effective for any type of electronic slide show.

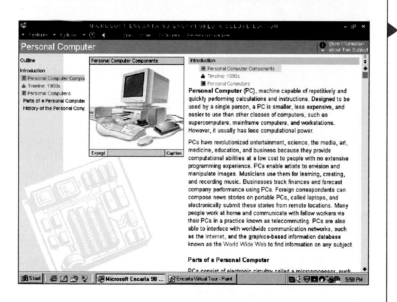

Microsoft's Encarta is a multimedia "edutainment" program that adds video and sound to encyclopedia-like entries. Users can explore the various elements on-screen by clicking them.

THE SHAPES OF COMPUTERS TODAY

Computers come in many sizes and with varying capabilities. The terms that describe the different types of computers have been around for some time, although the capabilities of each type have changed quickly. These are the terms:

- Supercomputer
- Mainframe
- Minicomputer
- Microcomputer

All these types of computers can be connected to form networks of computers, but each individual computer, whether it is on a network or not, falls into one of these four categories.

Supercomputers

Supercomputers are the most powerful computers made. They are built to process huge amounts of data. For example, scientists build models of complex processes and simulate the processes on a supercomputer. One such process is nuclear fission. As a fissionable material approaches a critical mass, the researchers want to know exactly what will happen during every nanosecond of the nuclear chain reaction. A supercomputer can model the actions and reactions of literally millions of atoms as they interact.

NORTON
Online

For information on
supercomputers, visit
this book's Web site at
www.glencoe.com/norton/online

Another complex study for which scientists used a supercomputer involved air pollution in Los Angeles. A model that comprised more than 500,000 variables, including geographic elevations, temperatures, and airborne chemicals, was required to create an accurate simulation of the Los Angeles Basin and to predict the effects of various strategies for pollution control. This simulation would have taken many hours using a less powerful computer, but the supercomputer did it in half an hour.

Because computer technology changes so quickly, the advanced capabilities of a supercomputer today may become the standard features of a PC a few years from now, and next year's supercomputer will be vastly more powerful than today's. Contemporary supercomputers generally cost upwards of $20 million, and they consume enough electricity to power 100 homes.

Cray supercomputers are among the most powerful computers made. This model is the Cray T3E.

Mainframe Computers

The largest type of computer in common use is the mainframe. **Mainframe computers** are used where many people in a large organization need frequent access to the same information, which is usually organized into one or more huge databases. For example, consider the Texas Department of Public

The two employees in the fore-ground of this photo are working on mainframe terminals. Each terminal consists of a monitor and a keyboard. Processing for the terminals is carried out by the mainframe's CPU, which is visible in the background.

Safety, where people get their drivers' licenses. This state agency maintains offices in every major city in Texas, each of which has many employees who work at computer terminals. A **terminal** is a keyboard and screen wired to the mainframe. It does not have its own CPU or storage; it is just an **input/output (I/O)** device that functions as a window into a computer located somewhere else. The terminals at the Public Safety offices are all connected to a common database on a mainframe in the state capital. The database is controlled by a mainframe computer that handles the input and output needs of all the terminals connected to it. Each user has continuous access to the driving records and administrative information for every licensed driver and vehicle in the state—literally millions of records. On smaller systems, handling this volume of user access to a central database would be difficult and more time consuming.

Mainframe computers can cost anywhere from $35,000 to many millions of dollars. It used to be common for mainframe computers to occupy entire rooms or even an entire floor of a high-rise building. Typically, they were placed inside glass offices with special air conditioning to keep them cool and on raised floors to accommodate all the wiring needed to tie the system together. This setup is not used much anymore. Today, a typical mainframe computer looks like an unimposing file cabinet—or a row of file cabinets—although it may still require a somewhat controlled environment.

Minicomputers

When Digital Equipment Corporation (DEC) began shipping its PDP series computers in the early 1960s, the press dubbed these machines "mini-computers" because of their small size compared to other computers of the day. Much to DEC's chagrin, the name stuck. (Later, when even smaller computers built around microprocessors came out, they were first called **microcomputers**, but, eventually, they were named *personal computers*.)

The capabilities of a **minicomputer** lie somewhere between those of mainframes and those of personal computers. (For this reason, minicomputers are often referred to as "mid-range" computers.) Like mainframes, minicomputers can handle much more input and output than personal computers can. Although some minis are designed for a single user, many can handle dozens or even hundreds of terminals.

Minicomputers cost anywhere from $18,000 to $500,000 and are ideal for many organizations and companies that cannot afford or do not need a mainframe system. Minicomputers are relatively inexpensive but have some of the desired features of a mainframe. The major minicomputer manufacturers include DEC, Data General, IBM, and Hewlett-Packard.

This box, which is about the size of a large file cabinet, contains the CPU of an IBM AS400 minicomputer.

NORTON
Online

For information on **minicomputers**, visit this book's Web site at **www.glencoe.com/norton/online**

The first IBM-PC was released in 1981.

Microcomputers

The terms *microcomputer* and *personal computer* are interchangeable, but *PC*—which stands for personal computer—sometimes has a more specific meaning. In 1981, IBM called its first microcomputer the IBM-PC. Within a few years, many companies were copying the IBM design, creating "clones" or "compatibles" that aimed at functioning just like the original. For this reason, the term *PC* has come to mean the family of computers that includes IBMs and IBM-compatibles. The vast majority of the microcomputers sold today are part of this family. The Apple Macintosh computer, however, is neither an IBM nor a compatible. It is another family of microcomputers, made by Apple Computer. So, it is accurate to say that a Macintosh is a personal computer, but some people consider it misleading to refer to the "Mac" as a PC. In this book, however, we will use the term *PC* as a simple abbreviation for *personal computer*, referring to both IBM-compatible models and Apple's Macintosh line.

One source of the PC's popularity is the rate at which improvements are made in the technology. Microprocessors, memory chips, and storage devices keep making gains in speed and capacity, while physical size and price remain stable—or in some cases are reduced. For example, compared to the typical PC of ten years ago, a machine of the same price today will have at least eight times as much RAM, about 50 times more storage capacity,

Productivity Tip

Choosing the Right Tool for the Job

Buying a computer is a lot like buying a car. There are so many models and options from which to choose! But the choice is not just a matter of taste. Some models can meet your needs better than others.

Before deciding which computer is best for you, identify the type of work for which you want to use the computer. Do you want a system for professional use, school work, or home use? Do you need power or portability? Do you want a system that can expand, or will a certain set of features be enough?

Laptop computers enable you to work almost anywhere.

Depending on your job, you may not need to use a computer much. For example, if you want to:

Manage your schedule on a daily or hourly basis. PDAs are popular for their calendar and schedule-management capabilities, which enable you to set appointments, track projects, and record special events.

Manage a list of contacts. If you need to stay in touch with many people and travel frequently, PDAs provide rich contact-management features.

Make notes on the fly. Some PDAs feature small keyboards, which are handy for tapping out quick notes. Other PDAs feature electronic pens, which enable the user to "write" directly on the display screen. Many PDAs have fax and e-mail capabilities, and a port that lets them exchange data with a PC. PDA prices range from around $300 to more than $1,000.

If your job requires you to travel, but you still need a full-featured computer, then consider a laptop or notebook computer. This is the best choice if you want to:

Carry your data with you. If you need to take presentations on the road or keep up with daily work while traveling, portable PCs are ideal. Laptop systems offer nearly as much RAM and storage capacity as desktop models. Many portables have built-in CD-ROM drives; others accept plug-in CD-ROM and hard drives, which can greatly increase their capacity.

Be able to work anywhere. Portable PCs run on either rechargeable batteries or standard alternating current.

Communicate and share data from anywhere. Most portable computers have built-in modems or slots for PC-card modems.

Portables can match many desktop models, feature for feature. Portable systems range greatly in price, from around $1,500 for the most basic units to more than $5,000 for powerful multimedia systems.

If you work in one place and need to perform a variety of tasks, a desktop computer is the best choice. Choose a desktop computer if you want to:

Work with graphics-intensive or desktop publishing applications. Complex graphics and page-layout programs require a great deal of system resources, and a desktop system's large monitor reduces eye fatigue. Desktop models also can accept many different types of pointing devices that can make graphic work easier.

Design or use multimedia products. Even though many portable computers have multimedia features, you can get the most bang for the buck with a desktop system. Large screens make multimedia programs easier to see, and stereo-style speakers optimize sound quality.

Set up complex hardware configurations. A desktop computer can support multiple peripherals—including printers, sound and video sources, and various external devices—at the same time. Desktop systems can easily be connected to a network, and it's possible to interface desktop systems with mainframe and minicomputers, as well.

and a microprocessor at least 75 times as fast. What's more, many analysts believe that this pace of change will continue for another 10 or 20 years.

One result of increasing PC power is that the differences between mainframes, minis, and microcomputers are not as great as they once were. In fact, the processing power of PCs often rivals that of current mainframes. (Mainframes are still popular because they can handle the input and output needs of many users at once, so they are still the right choice for the massive databases that many people need to use at the same time.)

Desktop Models

The style of personal computer introduced first was the **desktop** model. Most desktop computers are actually small enough to fit on a desk but too big to carry around. In the tower model, the main case, which is called the system unit, sits vertically and has more space for devices. Because of its design, this model is often placed on the floor to preserve desk space, allowing more room to place external components, such as removable disk drives or scanners, on the desktop.

Two common designs for PCs are shown here. On the left is the more traditional desktop model, with the monitor sitting on top of the system unit. On the right is a tower model, with the system unit sitting vertically. To save space, system units for tower models are often placed under a desk.

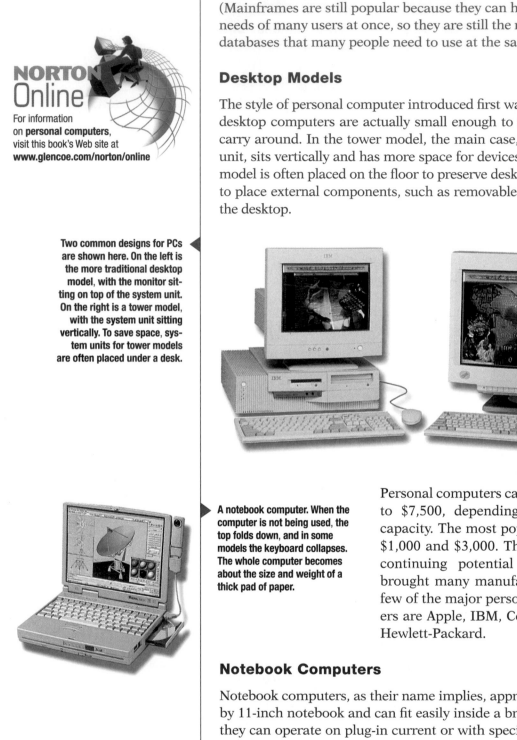

A notebook computer. When the computer is not being used, the top folds down, and in some models the keyboard collapses. The whole computer becomes about the size and weight of a thick pad of paper.

Personal computers can cost anywhere from $600 to $7,500, depending on the capabilities and capacity. The most popular models cost between $1,000 and $3,000. The tremendous growth and continuing potential of the PC market has brought many manufacturers into this arena. A few of the major personal computer manufacturers are Apple, IBM, Compaq, Dell, Gateway, and Hewlett-Packard.

Notebook Computers

Notebook computers, as their name implies, approximate the shape of an 8.5 by 11-inch notebook and can fit easily inside a briefcase. Also called laptops, they can operate on plug-in current or with special batteries. Notebooks are fully functional microcomputers; the people who use them need the power of a full computer wherever they go. Some models can plug into a dock that includes a large monitor, a full-size keyboard, and sometimes an additional hard drive.

Personal Digital Assistants (PDAs)

Personal digital assistants (PDAs) are the smallest of portable computers. Often, they are no larger than a checkbook. PDAs, also sometimes called **palmtops**, are much less powerful than notebook or desktop models. They are normally used for special applications, such as creating small spreadsheets, displaying important telephone numbers and addresses, and keeping track of dates or agendas. Many PDAs can be connected to larger computers to exchange data.

This area of computing is evolving quickly. Some PDAs come with an **electronic pen** that lets users write on a touch-sensitive screen. The latest generation of PDAs can use infrared light to communicate with nearby computers. They may also have built-in cellular telephone, fax, and electronic mail capabilities.

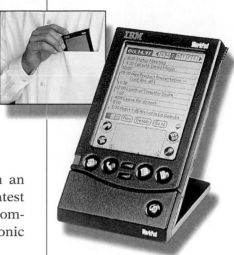

The people who use PDAs generally want to avoid carrying a lot of weight and do not need a full array of applications while away from home or the office. Most use inexpensive standard batteries, the kind sold everywhere. Because of their limited power, however, PDAs usually have no disk drives. Instead, most use devices called PC cards, each about the size of a credit card, to store programs and data. These cards have proved so handy that the makers of notebook and desktop computers have adopted them, as well.

▶ Many PDAs are pen-based computers. You interact with the computer by "writing" on the screen.

A **handheld computer** is like a PDA, but usually features a tiny built-in keyboard. Most users find they must use a pencil or pen to type on the handheld computer keyboard, but the keyboard is more reliable than handwriting-recognition input systems.

Workstations

At the other end of the spectrum, in terms of PC power, are the machines sometimes called **workstations**. Usually scientists, engineers, graphic artists, animators, and programmers use these powerful machines—that is, users who

▶ This personal computer is actually a powerful Ultra 1 workstation from Sun Microsystems.

Computers
In Your Career

Very few jobs do not rely on computers in some way. Remember that computers do not necessarily take the form of a PC, and your career path will likely bring you in contact with one type of computer or another. Whether it is a supercomputer or an automobile, an automated machining tool or a telephone switchboard, many of the tools in today's workplace incorporate computer technology.

This is why it is so important to have a basic understanding of computer technology, which is what this book is all about. Regardless of your career choice, you can benefit from an understanding of computer hardware and software. Even if your job does not require you to work directly with a computer, this knowledge may help you envision ways to use computers as never before in your work, resulting in a more productive work environment. Such knowledge can also lead to advancement opportunities in many jobs.

If you think this case is being overstated, and that computers are not being used that much, think again. Computers are popping up in places and professions that may seem unlikely. For example:

Restaurant and Grocery Store Managers Restaurants, grocery stores, and retail outlet managers use computer systems of all kinds—from handheld units to mainframes—to monitor inventories, track transactions, and manage product pricing. Store managers can frequently be seen using portable devices to check stock levels and change prices. These devices can be networked with a single store's computer system or a chain's wide area network.

Courier Dispatchers Courier services of all types use computerized terminals to help dispatchers schedule deliveries, locate pick-up and drop-off points, generate invoices, and track the location of packages. Such systems are used by cross-town delivery services and by national carriers such as Federal Express.

Construction Managers Construction managers and estimators use specialized PC software to analyze construction documents and calculate the amount of materials and time required to complete a job. These computerized tools—which often read information directly from disk files provided by the architect—help contractors manage costs and make competitive bids. On the job site, construction workers use computerized measuring devices and laser beams to make precise measurements quickly. Field managers and laborers alike routinely use portable computers to check plans and other construction documents, or to manage inventories of materials.

Automotive Mechanics Automotive mechanics and technicians use sophisticated computer systems to measure vehicle performance, diagnose mechanical problems, and determine maintenance or repair strategies. These computer systems are sometimes networked to regional or national databases of automotive information.

Each of the following chapters concludes with a discussion of computers in the professional world. Each discussion focuses on the type of technology introduced in that chapter and is designed to help you understand how that particular technology is being used in one or more professions.

need a great deal of number-crunching power. In days past, workstations implied certain differences in terms of chip design and operating system. However, just as the distinctions between mainframes, minis, and microcomputers have become less clear, so have the differences between workstations and other PCs. This is the result of the incessant increase in the power and popularity of the PC. Some of the major manufacturers of workstations are IBM, Sun Microsystems, Silicon Graphics Incorporated, Hewlett-Packard, and Compaq.

WHAT TO EXPECT IN THE FUTURE

These days, people just assume that in the future, computers will give them more power for less money and that computer manufacturers will pack more power into smaller packages. This is a fairly safe assumption. It is also a good bet that, given the multitude of software packages available for specialized tasks, your job will somehow involve a computer.

Perhaps the most important change likely to take place in our society as a result of the computer industry is a continued explosion in connectivity. In other words, the computers you use, whether at home, school, or work, are going to be connected to other computers. This growth in connectivity will mean that you will be able to send e-mail—electronic messages transmitted on a network—to virtually anybody. You will be able to shop from home, bank from home, and conduct library research without going to the library.

These capabilities assume that everyone will be using the worldwide network known as the Internet. The fact that other types of electronic networks are going to be popping up all over the place is equally important in terms of social impact. Remember, the telephone system, the cable system, and the electrical utility system are all networks. The companies that own these systems are watching the growth of the Internet and trying to figure out how to use their own infrastructures to offer more services to homes and businesses. As they do, you are going to experience a technical revolution that will affect

- How and where you work
- How and where you and your children go to school
- How you communicate with other people
- How and where you shop and how you pay for goods
- How you obtain and share information

VISUAL SUMMARY

The Multipurpose Tool

- The first modern computers were used for complex numerical tasks. They were initially designed for use by the government and military but quickly were adopted by large companies for business uses.

- Modern medicine uses computers in many ways. For example, computers are used to assist in surgical procedures and to diagnose illnesses.

- Educators are interested in computers as tools for interactive learning. Advances in computer and communication technology have made two-way distance learning possible in the classroom.

- The scientific community uses computers to do research and exchange information with colleagues around the world.

- Engineers and architects use computers to design objects and structures with the help of CAD tools and techniques.

- Attorneys use computers to access and create databases that contain records of old cases and data related to current ones.

- The government is a major user of computers; many governmental agencies now even host their own World Wide Web sites.

- Musicians can use MIDI to combine or create sounds electronically, either in the recording studio or during live performances.

- Filmmakers use computers to create special effects.

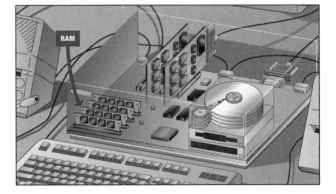

An Overview of the Computer System

- Computer systems include hardware, software, data, and people.

- Hardware consists of electronic devices, the parts you can see.

- Software, also known as programs, consists of organized sets of instructions for controlling the computer.

- Data consists of text, numbers, sounds, and images that the computer can manipulate.

Looking Inside the Machine

- The hardware, or physical components, of a computer consists of a processor, memory, input and output (I/O) devices, and storage.

- The processing function is divided between the processor and memory.

- The processor, or CPU, is the brain of the machine.

- Memory holds data as the CPU works with it.

- The most common units of measure for memory are the byte, kilobyte, megabyte, and gigabyte.

- The role of input is to provide data from the user or some other source.

- The function of output is to present processed data to the user.

- Communication devices perform both input and output, allowing computers to share information.

- Storage devices hold data not currently being used by the CPU.

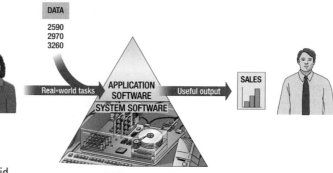

Software Brings the Machine to Life

- Programs are electronic instructions that tell the computer how to accomplish certain tasks.

- When a computer is using a particular program, it is said to be running or executing the program.

- The operating system tells the computer how to interact with the user and how to use the hardware devices attached to the computer.

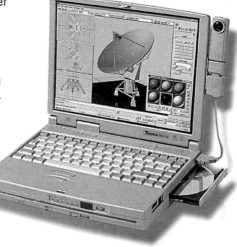

- Application software tells the computer how to accomplish tasks the user requires.

- Seven important kinds of application software are word processing programs, databases, spreadsheets, graphics, education and entertainment applications, utilities, and communication.

The Shapes of Computers Today

- There are four types of computers: supercomputers, mainframes, minicomputers, and microcomputers.

- Supercomputers are the most powerful computers in terms of processing. They are useful for problems requiring complex calculations.

- Mainframe computers, which generally have many terminals connected to them, handle massive amounts of input, output, and storage.

- Minicomputers are smaller than mainframes but larger than microcomputers. They usually have multiple terminals.

- Microcomputers are more commonly known as personal computers. The term PC often denotes microcomputers that are either IBM-PCs or compatibles. The term can also refer to personal computers made by other manufacturers.

- Desktop computers, including the newer tower models, are the most common type of personal computer.

- Laptops (notebooks) and PDAs are used by people who need portable computing power outside the office.

- The most powerful PCs, which are used by engineers, scientists, and graphic artists, are known as workstations.

Visual Summary & Exercises

KEY TERMS

After completing this chapter, you should be able to define the following terms:

application software, 22
byte, 18
CD-ROM drive, 21
central processing unit (CPU), 17
circuit board, 16
communication device, 20
compact disk (CD), 21
compact disk read-only memory
   (CD-ROM), 21
computer, 6
computer system, 13
data, 15
desktop, 30
device, 18
digital, 15
digital camera, 19
digital versatile disk (DVD), 21
disk drive, 20
diskette, 21
document, 15
electronic pen, 31
executing, 22
file, 15
floppy disk, 21
gigabyte (GB), 18
handheld computer, 31

hard disk, 21
hardware, 13
input device, 18
input/output (I/O), 27
joystick, 19
keyboard, 19
kilobyte (KB), 18
laptop computer, 7
magnetic disk, 20
mainframe computer, 26
megabyte (MB), 18
memory, 18
microcomputer, 27
microphone, 19
microprocessor, 16
minicomputer, 28
modem, 20
monitor, 19
motherboard, 16
mouse, 19
networking, 20
network interface card
   (NIC), 20
notebook computer, 7
operating system, 22
optical drive, 21

output device, 18
palmtop, 31
personal computer (PC), 6
personal digital assistant (PDA), 31
printer, 19
processing, 16
processor, 16
program, 13
random access memory (RAM), 18
read-only memory (ROM), 22
read/write head, 20
removable hard drive, 21
running, 22
scanner, 19
software, 13
storage, 20
supercomputer, 26
system software, 22
tape drive, 21
telecommuter, 7
terminal, 27
touch screen, 20
trackball, 19
user, 15
workstation, 31

KEY TERM QUIZ

Fill in the missing word with one of the terms listed in Key Terms:

1. A(n) _____ enables a computer to communicate through a telephone line.

2. Electronic instructions that tell the hardware what to do are known as _____.

3. A(n) _____ is a powerful type of PC, usually used by scientists, engineers, graphic artists, animators, or programmers.

4. Portable computers that can fit easily inside a briefcase are called _____.

5. _____ is the process of connecting one computer to another.

6. A(n) _____ is a device that holds a disk.

7. The _____ refers to the combination of hardware, software, data, and people.

8. A keyboard and screen that are wired to a mainframe are known as a(n) _____.

9. A(n) _____ is a set of data or software that has been given a name.

10. The capabilities of a(n) _____ lie somewhere between those of mainframes and those of personal computers.

Visual Summary & Exercises

REVIEW QUESTIONS

1. List the four key components of a computer system.

2. For each of the following devices, describe the type of component it is and briefly describe its function within a computer system:
- Laser printer
- Mouse
- Modem
- Hard disk

3. Describe at least two ways in which storage complements memory.

4. What are the four size categories for computers?

5. Which type of computer provides a user with mobility as well as essentially the same processing capabilities as a desktop personal computer?

6. What does application software do?

7. Describe the startup process that a computer follows when it is turned on.

8. Name the two major categories of software.

9. What is the difference between a "file" and a "document" in a computer?

10. What are the four values used to describe a computer's memory or storage capacity, and approximately how much data does each value represent?

DISCUSSION QUESTIONS

1. Do you envision computers in the home being used more extensively over the next five to ten years for such everyday tasks as shopping, banking, and communicating with others? If so, list two or three reasons that support this direction; if not, explain why you think this is not likely to occur.

2. Will the "explosion" of connectivity that is now occurring have an impact on your own career goals? In what ways do you think using the Internet might contribute to your productivity in the career you imagine pursuing?

3. Consider some of the improvements that computers have brought to our lives, as addressed in this chapter. What key factors or characteristics do you believe make computers an essential part of our lives in today's world?

inteNET Workshop

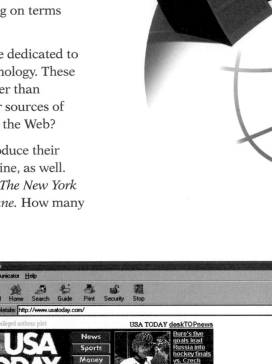

The following exercises assume that you have access to the Internet and a browser. If you need help with any of the exercises, visit this book's Web site at **www.glencoe.com/norton/online**. This book's Web site also lists the URLs you need to complete many of these exercises.

1. Using an Internet search engine such as Yahoo! or WebCrawler, see how much information you can find on the Internet about the earliest computers. Try searching on terms such as "UNIVAC" and "mainframe computers."

2. Many sites exist on the World Wide Web that are dedicated to providing the latest information on computer technology. These sites can inform you of new innovations much faster than printed publications can, and can lead you to other sources of information. How many such sites can you find on the Web?

3. Newspapers are not only using computers to produce their daily editions, but are putting their newspapers online, as well. Check out the World Wide Web sites of *USA Today, The New York Times, The Los Angeles Times,* and the *Chicago Tribune.* How many other online newspapers can you find on the Web?

4. The National Aeronautics and Space Administration (NASA) and the Jet Propulsion Laboratories (JPL) maintain a huge Web site, filled with information about space exploration and technology. There are also several Web sites devoted specifically to the Mars Pathfinder mission and upcoming Mars missions. Starting the with JPL Web site, how many other sites can you find that are devoted to space exploration?

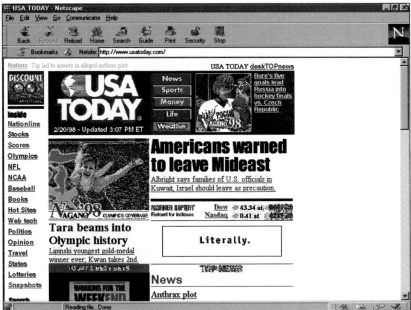

5. Global Positioning Systems are being used by the military, in aviation, in boating, and in many other applications. Starting with the Global Positioning Systems Overview Web page, see how much information you can find about the newest GPS products and their uses. Which GPS products would be most helpful to you, given your interests or travel habits?

6. There are many types of input devices for computers. Generally, most people use a mouse, but many other options exist. Search for and visit the Web sites of input device makers to learn more about different types of input devices for use with computers.

7. Digital Versatile Disk (DVD) is expected to take both the entertainment and computer industries by storm. Before you face a purchasing decision, it's a good idea to study up on this emerging technology. A good place to start is the DVD Industry Web page. Follow the links to find up-to-date information on technologies, terms, products, and companies providing DVD services to professionals and consumers alike.

8. You may decide that a notebook (or laptop) computer is the best PC choice for you. The Web offers several good resources for last-minute information on new notebook systems, product reviews, buyers guides, price comparisons, and so on. How many such sites can you find on the Web? How would you rate these sites?

CHAPTER 2

Processing Data

CONTENTS

OBJECTIVES

When you complete this chapter, you will be able to do the following:

- Identify the main difference between data and information.
- List two reasons why computers use the binary number system.
- List the two main parts of the CPU and explain how they work together to process data.
- Name three differences between RAM and ROM.
- List three hardware features that affect processing speed.
- Name the two best-known families of CPUs and list their differences.

Even people who have been using computers for years still marvel at what they can do: how at lightning speed and with amazing accuracy they can sort a mailing list, balance a ledger, typeset a book, or create lifelike models of objects that have never existed.

Just how a computer does all this may seem magical, but in fact it is a process based on simple concepts. All the words, numbers, and images you put into and get out of the computer are manipulated in relatively simple ways by the computer's processing components.

In fact, it is because this process is so simple that the computer can operate so fast. No matter what you put into a computer—text, numbers, graphics, sound—the computer treats it all the same way, translating the information into simple codes. Because these codes are so small, and because the

computer has so much processing power, the computer can utilize millions of the codes every second.

Not surprisingly, computers are getting faster all the time. Because computers use a process that has changed very little, designers have been able to focus on refining the way computers handle that process—making them faster and more powerful. As a result, today's computers can not only perform a single task very rapidly, but they can also perform many tasks simultaneously.

In this chapter, you'll find out what data is, how it differs from information, and what form it takes in the computer. Then you'll explore the two processing components: the central processing unit (CPU) and memory. You'll also learn about the most important factors affecting a computer's speed. Finally, you'll look at the microprocessors made by the biggest chip manufacturers, with an emphasis on the families of chips from Intel and Motorola.

NORTON Online

For more
information on
transistors, visit
this book's Web site at
www.glencoe.com/norton/online

TRANSFORMING DATA INTO INFORMATION

It often seems as though computers must understand us because we understand the information that they produce. However, computers cannot *understand* anything. All they can do is recognize two distinct physical states produced by electricity, magnetic polarity, or reflected light. Essentially, all they can understand is whether a switch is on or off. In fact, the "brain" of the computer, the CPU, consists primarily of several million tiny electronic switches, called **transistors**.

A computer only appears to understand information because it contains so many transistors and operates at such phenomenal speeds, assembling its individual on/off switches into patterns that are meaningful to us.

The term used to describe the information represented by groups of on/off switches is data. Although the words *data* and *information* are often used interchangeably, there is an important distinction between them. In the strictest sense, data consists of the raw numbers that computers organize to produce information.

You can think of data as facts out of context, like the individual letters on this page. Taken individually, they do not tell you a thing. Grouped together, however, they convey specific meanings. Just as a theater's marquee can combine thousands of lights to spell the name of the current show, a computer turns meaningless data into useful information, such as spreadsheets, graphs, and reports.

It is often necessary to distinguish between data and information.

DATA

FACTS OUT OF CONTEXT

576-21-0102

#37

Felicia

Tone =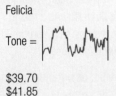

$39.70
$41.85
$16.19

INFORMATION

MEANINGFUL COLLECTIONS OF DATA

Population estimates
Sockeye Salmon
Inverness Creek

Year	Est.
1991	16,500
1992	16,000
1993	17,000
1994	16,500
1995	19,200
1996	19,500
1997	19,000
1998	21,000
1999	20,400
2000	20,900

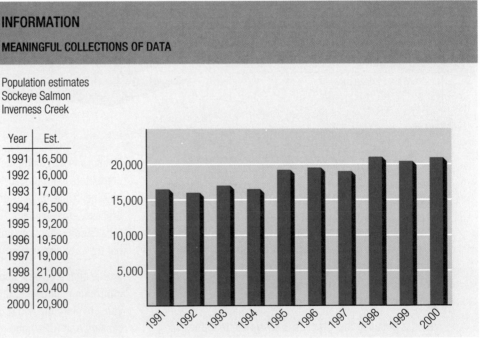

How Computers Represent Data

To a computer, everything is a number. Numbers are numbers, letters and punctuation marks are numbers, sounds and pictures are numbers; even the computer's own instructions are numbers. This might seem strange because you have probably seen computer screens with words and sentences on them, but it is true. When you see letters of the alphabet on a computer screen, what you are seeing is just one of the computer's ways of representing numbers. For example, consider this sentence:

Here are some words.

It may look like a string of alphabetic characters to you, but to a computer it looks like the string of ones and zeros shown in Figure 2.1.

Computer data looks especially strange because people normally use base 10 to represent numbers. The system is called *base 10*, or the **decimal system** (*deci* means 10 in Latin) because ten symbols are available: 1, 2, 3, 4, 5, 6, 7, 8, 9, and 0. When you need to represent a number greater than 9, you use two symbols together, as in 9 + 1 = 10. Each symbol in a number is called a digit, so 10 is a two-digit number.

In a computer, however, all data must be reduced to electrical switches. A switch has only two possible states—"on" and "off"—so it has only two numeric symbols. 0 stands for "off," and 1 stands for "on." Because there are only two symbols, computers are said to function in *base 2*, which is also known as the **binary system** (*bi* means two in Latin).

When a computer needs to represent a quantity greater than 1, it does the same thing you do when you need to represent a quantity greater than 9: it uses two (or more) digits. To familiarize yourself with the binary system, take a look at Table 2.1, which shows how to count in base 10 and base 2.

Bits and Bytes

When referring to computerized data, each switch—whether on or off—is called a **bit**. The term *bit* is a contraction of *bi*nary digi*t*. A bit is the smallest possible unit of data. To represent anything meaningful—that is, to convey information—the computer needs groups of bits.

After the bit, the next larger unit of data is the byte, which is a group of 8 bits. With one byte, the computer can represent up to 256 different values because it is possible to count from 0 to 255 with 8 binary digits.

H	0100 1000
e	0110 0101
r	0111 0010
e	0110 0101
	0010 0000
a	0110 0001
r	0111 0010
e	0110 0101
	0010 0000
s	0111 0011
o	0110 1111
m	0110 1101
e	0110 0101
	0010 0000
w	0111 0111
o	0110 1111
r	0111 0010
d	0110 0100
s	0111 0011
.	0010 0001

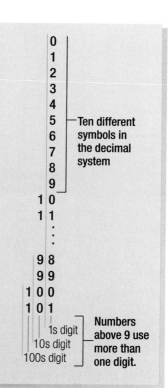

Figure 2.1
1s and 0s representing a sentence. The decimal system uses ten symbols and multiple digits for numbers above 9.

Table 2.1	Counting in Base 10 and Base 2
BASE 10	**BASE 2**
0	0
1	1
2	10
3	11
4	100
5	101
6	110
7	111
8	1000
9	1001
10	1010

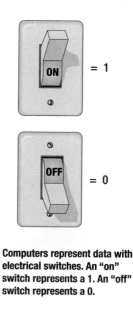

Computers represent data with electrical switches. An "on" switch represents a 1. An "off" switch represents a 0.

1 bit

8 bits = 1 byte

One byte is composed of eight bits.

The byte is an extremely important unit because there are enough different eight-bit combinations to represent all the characters on the keyboard, including all the letters (uppercase and lowercase), numbers, punctuation marks, and other symbols. If you refer to Figure 2.1, you'll notice that each of the characters (or letters) in the sentence "Here are some words." is represented by one byte of data.

Text Codes

Early in the history of computing, programmers realized they needed a standard code—a system they could all agree on—in which numbers stood for the letters of the alphabet, punctuation marks, and other symbols. EBCDIC, ASCII, and Unicode are three of the most popular systems that were invented.

EBCDIC

The BCD (Binary Coded Decimal) system, defined by IBM for one of its early computers, was one of the first complete systems to represent symbols with bits. BCD codes consisted of six-bit codes, which allowed a maximum of 64 possible symbols. BCD computers could work only with uppercase letters and with very few other symbols. For those reasons this system was short-lived.

The need to represent more characters led to IBM's development of the EBCDIC system. **EBCDIC**, pronounced "EB-si-dic," stands for Extended Binary Coded Decimal Interchange Code. An example of some of the symbols in the EBCDIC character set are shown in Table 2.2.

EBCDIC is an eight-bit code that defines 256 symbols. EBCDIC is still used in IBM mainframe and mid-range systems but is rarely encountered in personal computers. By the time small computers were being developed, the American National Standards Institute (ANSI) had swung into action to define standards for computers.

ASCII

The ANSI organization's solution to representing symbols with bits of data was the ASCII character set. **ASCII** stands for the American Standard Code for Information Interchange. Today, the ASCII character set is by far the most common. Table 2.3 shows the ASCII codes.

Table 2.2	Sampling of EBCDIC Character Set	
BINARY VALUE	**DECIMAL VALUE**	**EBCDIC SYMBOL**
1001011	75	.
1001100	76	<
1001101	77	(
1001110	78	+
1001111	79	I
1010000	80	&
1011010	90	!
1011011	91	$
10000001	129	a
10000010	130	b
10000011	131	c

NORTON Online

For more information on **EBCDIC** and **ASCII**, visit this book's Web site at **www.glencoe.com/norton/online**

Table 2.3   The ASCII Table

ASCII CODE	DECIMAL EQUIVALENT	CHARACTER	ASCII CODE	DECIMAL EQUIVALENT	CHARACTER	ASCII CODE	DECIMAL EQUIVALENT	CHARACTER
0000 0000	0	Null	0010 1011	43	+	01010110	86	V
0000 0001	1	Start of heading	0010 1100	44	,	0101 0111	87	W
0000 0010	2	Start of text	0010 1101	45	-	0101 1000	88	X
0000 0011	3	End of text	0010 1110	46	.	0101 1001	89	Y
0000 0100	4	End of transmit	0010 1111	47	/	0101 1010	90	Z
0000 0101	5	Enquiry	0011 0000	48	0	0101 1011	91	[
0000 0110	6	Acknowledge	0011 0001	49	1	0101 1100	92	\
0000 0111	7	Audible bell	0011 0010	50	2	0101 1101	93	]
0000 1000	8	Backspace	0011 0011	51	3	0101 1110	94	^
0000 1001	9	Horizontal tab	0011 0100	52	4	0101 1111	95	_
0000 1010	10	Line feed	0011 0101	53	5	0110 0000	96	`
0000 1011	11	Vertical tab	0011 0110	54	6	0110 0001	97	a
0000 1100	12	Form feed	0011 0111	55	7	0110 0010	98	b
0000 1101	13	Carriage return	0011 1000	56	8	0110 0011	99	c
0000 1110	14	Shift out	0011 1001	57	9	0110 0100	100	d
0000 1111	15	Shift in	0011 1010	58	:	0110 0101	101	e
0001 0000	16	Data line escape	0011 1011	59	;	0110 0110	102	f
0001 0001	17	Device control 1	0011 1100	60	<	0110 0111	103	g
0001 0010	18	Device control 2	0011 1101	61	=	0110 1000	104	h
0001 0011	19	Device control 3	0011 1110	62	>	0110 1001	105	i
0001 0100	20	Device control 4	0011 1111	63	?	0110 1010	106	j
0001 0101	21	Neg. acknowledge	0100 0000	64	@	0110 1011	107	k
0001 0110	22	Synchronous idle	0100 0001	65	A	0110 1100	108	l
0001 0111	23	End trans. block	0100 0010	66	B	0110 1101	109	m
0001 1000	24	Cancel	0100 0011	67	C	0110 1110	110	n
0001 1001	25	End of medium	0100 0100	68	D	0110 1111	111	o
0001 1010	26	Substitution	0100 0101	69	E	0111 0000	112	p
0001 1011	27	Escape	0100 0110	70	F	0111 0001	113	q
0001 1100	28	Figures shift	0100 0111	71	G	0111 0010	114	r
0001 1101	29	Group separator	0100 1000	72	H	0111 0011	115	s
0001 1110	30	Record separator	0100 1001	73	I	0111 0100	116	t
0001 1111	31	Unit separator	0100 1010	74	J	0111 0101	117	u
0010 0000	32	Blank space	0100 1011	75	K	0111 0110	118	v
0010 0001	33	!	0100 1100	76	L	0111 0111	119	w
0010 0010	34	"	0100 1101	77	M	0111 1000	120	x
0010 0011	35	#	0100 1110	78	N	0111 1001	121	y
0010 0100	36	$	0100 1111	79	O	0111 1010	122	z
0010 0101	37	%	0101 0000	80	P	0111 1011	123	{
0010 0110	38	&	0101 0001	81	Q	0111 1100	124		
0010 0111	39	'	0101 0010	82	R	0111 1101	125	}
0010 1000	40	(	0101 0011	83	S	0111 1110	126	~
0010 1001	41	)	0101 0100	84	T	0111 1111	127	
0010 1010	42	*	0101 0101	85	U			

The characters from 0 to 31 are control characters; from 32 to 64, special characters and numbers; from 65 to 96, uppercase letters and a few symbols; from 97 to 127, lowercase letters, plus a handful of common symbols. Because ASCII, a seven-bit code, specifies characters up to only 127, there are many variations that specify different character sets for codes 128 through 255. The ISO (International Standards Organization) standard expanded on the ASCII character set, to offer different sets of characters for different language groups. ISO 8859-1, for example, covers Western European languages. There are many other character sets, however, for other languages that use a different alphabet.

Unicode

An evolving standard for data representation, called **Unicode Worldwide Character Standard**, provides two bytes—16 bits—to represent each symbol. With two bytes, a Unicode character could be any one of more than 65,536 different characters or symbols—enough for every character and symbol in the world, including the vast Chinese, Korean, and Japanese character sets and those found in known classical and historical texts. If a single character set were available to cover all the languages in the entire world, computer programs and data would be interchangeable. Because this is certainly a worthwhile goal, there may someday be a widespread effort to replace ASCII with Unicode. Many software publishers, including Microsoft, Netscape, and Accent, encourage their developers to use Unicode in their programs.

Figure 2.2
Processing devices.

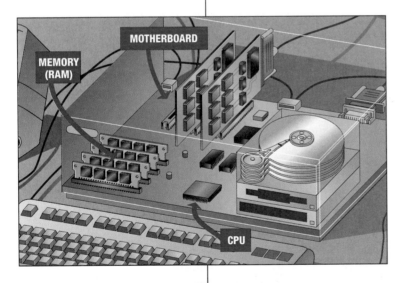

HOW A COMPUTER PROCESSES DATA

Two components handle processing in a computer: the central processing unit, or CPU, and the memory. Both are located on the computer's main **system board**, or motherboard (shown in Figure 2.2), the circuit board that connects the CPU to all the other hardware devices.

The CPU

The CPU is the brain of the computer, the place where data is manipulated. In a microcomputer, the entire CPU is contained on a tiny chip called a microprocessor. The chip is mounted on a piece of plastic with metal wires attached to it. Every CPU has at least two basic parts: the control unit and the arithmetic logic unit.

The Control Unit

All the computer's resources are managed from the **control unit**. You can think of the control unit as a traffic cop directing the flow of data. It is the logical hub of the computer.

This circuit board is the
motherboard for a PC.

NORTON Notebook

Breathing Easier with Dive Computers

When you're 100 feet under water, the last thing you want to worry about is running out of air. When you get back to the surface, the last thing you want to worry about is getting "the bends."

Thanks to recent innovations in diving technology, divers can worry less about these risks and breathe a little easier—both in and out of the water.

Dive computers enable divers to dive more safely than ever and to keep more accurate records of their dives. By using these submersible miniature computers, divers can schedule dives more intelligently, calculating the proper balance of bottom time (the amount of time between reaching maximum depth and resurfacing) and surface intervals (the amount of time at the surface between dives).

For divers, this means more efficient diving and a decreased risk of decompression sickness (DCS), commonly known as "the bends." DCS is caused by the build-up of nitrogen in the body under pressure. When a diver submerges, water pressure causes the body to retain nitrogen instead of releasing it. When the diver leaves the water, the body needs time to expel the excess nitrogen through normal breathing.

Divers, therefore, must carefully monitor bottom time to prevent too much nitrogen build-up. They also must spend adequate time on the surface between dives, to allow the nitrogen to escape. If a diver miscalculates a dive or surface interval, the result can be disastrous; in extreme cases, nitrogen can "bubble up" inside the body with great force, like bubbles in a bottle of soda that has been shaken up. DCS can be extremely painful, even fatal.

Before the advent of dive computers, divers had to master complicated dive tables—arrays of depth measurements, bottom times, and surface intervals—to calculate the effects of diving on the body.

Dive computers, however, are changing all that by monitoring dive conditions and simplifying dive planning. Despite their tiny size (the smallest units are about the size of a wristwatch), the latest dive computers are packed with features. Depending on the model, dive computers can perform some or all of the following tasks:

- Monitor air usage from the diver's tank

- Monitor the current depth and water temperature

- Log the amount of time spent at different depths

- Monitor descent and ascent speed, and warn the diver when to slow down

- Calculate actual bottom time and amount of time remaining before ascent is required

- Assist in calculating adequate surface intervals between dives

- Remind the diver to make required decompression stops when resurfacing from a deep dive (more than 60 feet)

- Store information about a number of "logged" dives, which can be recalled

- Adjust calculations for high-altitude dives (when diving in a mountain lake, for example)

Significant advances are being made in the way computers display information to the diver. Some computers attach to the end of a hose from the diver's tank, like traditional air pressure gauges. Other units connect directly to the hose port at the top of the tank and do not dangle at the end of a hose. These models use radio waves to transmit data about air usage to the diver's wristwatch-style console. The latest dive computers feature "heads-up" display; that is, they project data inside the diver's face mask, freeing the hands from using gauges.

Many dive computers also can be connected to a personal computer. This feature enables the diver to "dump" information from the dive computer into a PC to keep long-term records of logged dives. This information is valuable in helping serious divers plan diving routines and optimize bottom times and surface intervals. The result is more enjoyable, safer diving.

Even though divers are still required to know how to use dive tables, dive computers can perform the required calculations of depth, bottom time, and surface intervals, to help the diver stay within safe limits.

The CPU's instructions for carrying out commands are built into the control unit. The instructions, or **instruction set**, list all the operations that the CPU can perform. Each instruction in the instruction set is expressed in **microcode**—a series of basic directions that tell the CPU how to execute more complex operations. Before a program can be executed, every command in it must be broken down into instructions that correspond to the ones in the CPU's instruction set. When the program is executed, the CPU carries out the instructions in order by converting them into microcode. Although the process is complex, the computer can accomplish it at an incredible speed, translating millions of instructions every second.

Different CPUs have different instruction sets. Manufacturers, however, tend to group their CPUs into "families" that have similar instruction sets. Intel's $x86$ family of processors, for instance, includes the most common type of CPU found in the majority of PCs. Usually, when a new CPU is developed, the instruction set has all the same commands as its predecessor, plus some new ones. This allows software written for a particular CPU to work on computers with newer processors of the same family—a design strategy known as **upward compatibility**. Upward compatibility saves consumers from having to buy a whole new system every time a part of their existing system is upgraded.

The reverse is also true. When a new hardware device or piece of software can interact with all the same equipment and software that its predecessor could, it is said to have **downward**, or **backward**, **compatibility**.

The Arithmetic Logic Unit

Because all computer data is stored as numbers, much of the processing that takes place involves comparing numbers or carrying out mathematical operations. In addition to establishing ordered sequences and changing those sequences, the computer can perform only two types of operations: **arithmetic operations** and **logical operations**. Arithmetic operations include addition, subtraction, multiplication, and division. Logical operations include comparisons, such as determining whether one number is equal to, greater than, or less than another number. Also, every logical operation has an opposite. For example, in addition to "equal to" there is "not equal to." Table 2.4 shows the symbols for all the arithmetic and logical operations.

Remember that some of the logical operations can be carried out on text data. For example, when you want to search for a word in a document, the CPU carries out a rapid succession of "equals" operations to find a match for the sequence of ASCII codes that make up the word for which you are searching.

Many instructions carried out by the control unit involve simply moving data from one place to another—from memory to storage, from memory to the printer, and

CPU

Arithmetic Logic Unit

INPUT DEVICES

Control Unit

OUTPUT DEVICES

MEMORY

STORAGE

All the data that flows through the computer is directed by the control unit in the CPU.

Table 2.4	Operations Performed by the Arithmetic Logic Unit	
ARITHMETIC OPERATIONS	**LOGICAL OPERATIONS**	
+	add	=, ≠	equal to, not equal to
−	subtract	>, ⊁	greater than, not greater than
×	multiply	<, ≮	less than, not less than
÷	divide	≧, ≱	Greater than or equal to, not greater than or equal to
∧	raise by a power	≦, ≰	less than or equal to, not less than or equal to

▶ Examples of arithmetic and logical operations.

so forth. However, when the control unit encounters an instruction that involves arithmetic or logic, it passes that instruction to the second component of the CPU, the **arithmetic logic unit**, or **ALU**. The ALU includes a group of **registers**—high-speed memory locations built directly into the CPU that are used to hold the data currently being processed. For example, the control unit might load two numbers from memory into the registers in the ALU. Then it might tell the ALU to divide the two numbers (an arithmetic operation), or to see whether the numbers are equal (a logical operation).

Memory

The CPU contains the basic instructions needed to operate the computer, but it does not have the capability to store entire programs or large sets of data permanently. The CPU does contain registers, but these are small areas that can hold only a few bytes at a time. In addition to the registers, the CPU needs to have millions of bytes of space where it can hold programs and the data being manipulated while they are being used. This area is called *memory*.

Physically, memory consists of chips either on the motherboard or on a small circuit board attached to the motherboard. This electronic memory allows the CPU to store and retrieve data very quickly.

There are two types of built-in memory: permanent and non-permanent. Some memory chips always retain the data they hold—even when the computer is turned off. This type of memory is called **nonvolatile**. Other chips—in fact, most of the memory in a microcomputer—do lose their contents when the computer's power is shut off. These chips have **volatile** memory.

ROM

Nonvolatile chips always hold the same data; the data in them cannot be changed. In fact, putting data permanently into this kind of memory is called "burning in the data," and it is usually done at the factory. The data in these

NORTON Online

For more information on **computer memory**, visit this book's Web site at **www.glencoe.com/norton/online**

ROM (nonvolatile)

RAM (volatile)

CPU

Motherboard

▶ The CPU is attached to two kinds of memory: RAM, which is volatile, and ROM, which is nonvolatile.

chips can only be read and used—it cannot be changed—so the memory is called read-only memory (ROM).

One important reason a computer needs ROM is so that it knows what to do when the power is first turned on. Among other things, ROM contains a set of start-up instructions, which ensure that the rest of memory is functioning properly, check for hardware devices, and check for an operating system on the computer's disk drives.

RAM

Memory that can be changed is called *random-access memory* (RAM). When people talk about computer memory in connection with microcomputers, they usually mean the volatile RAM. The purpose of RAM is to hold programs and data while they are in use. Physically, RAM consists of some chips on a small circuit board.

ROM chip

ROM usually consists of a small chip, located near the CPU on the motherboard.

RAM chips

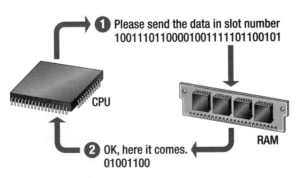

In personal computers, RAM chips are normally mounted on a small circuit board, which is plugged into the motherboard.

A computer does not have to search its entire memory each time it needs to find data because the CPU stores and retrieves each piece of data using a **memory address**. This is a number that indicates a location on the memory chips, much as a post office box number indicates a slot into which mail is placed. Memory addresses start at zero and go up to one less than the number of bytes of memory in the computer.

This type of memory is referred to as random-access memory because of its capability to access each byte of data directly. Actually, though, read-only memory (ROM) is "random access" as well, so the names for the two types of memory can be misleading. It is best simply to remember that the contents of ROM do not change; the contents of RAM do.

❶ Please send the data in slot number 100111011000010011111101100101

CPU

❷ OK, here it comes. 01001100

RAM

To request a byte of data, the CPU sends a memory address to RAM.

RAM Technologies

Many advancements in RAM technology have been made over the years. The following are the major types of RAM used in PC computers:

- **Fast Page Mode (FPM)RAM.** FPM RAM is the oldest and least sophisticated type of RAM. It's still used in many PCs available today.

- **Extended Data Output (EDO) RAM.** EDO RAM is faster than FPM RAM and is commonly found in the fastest computers.

- **Burst Extended Data Output (BEDO) RAM.** BEDO RAM is very fast RAM and is supported by a limited number of CPUs, namely CPUs manufactured by VIA.

■ *Synchronous Dynamic RAM (SDRAM).* SDRAM delivers bursts of data at very high speeds (up to 100 MHz), which provides more data to the CPU at a given time than older RAM technologies. SDRAM is supported by the latest CPUs and is probably the most popular type of RAM on the market today.

Flash Memory

Standard RAM is dynamic; when power to the PC is lost, all data currently stored in RAM is lost. This is why it is important to save your work when working with an application. One type of memory, called **flash memory**, stores data even when the power is turned off. ROM is a form of flash memory used in PCs. Other machines that use flash memory are digital cameras. When you take pictures with a digital camera, the pictures are stored in a flash memory chip rather than photographic film. Because you don't want to lose the pictures you've taken, the memory must store the pictures until you can transfer them to your PC, even when the camera is turned off.

Digital cameras use flash memory to store photographs.

FACTORS AFFECTING PROCESSING SPEED

Although all microcomputers have a CPU and memory, all microcomputers are by no means the same. Over the past 15 years, the power of microcomputers has increased dramatically. Computing power usually refers to the speed with which the computer processes data. Therefore, more computing power really means faster processing. One common axiom is that CPU computing power doubles every 18 months. This is known as **Moore's Law**, named after Intel founder and chairman emeritus Gordon Moore. So far, Moore's Law has held true, as more transistors are being placed on smaller chips, resulting in performance gains and increases in speed. One reason the speed increases is because the distance between transistors is reduced. In the future, CPU construction will be so small that it will be at the atomic level.

The circuitry design of a CPU determines its basic speed, but several additional factors can make chips already designed for speed work even faster. You have already been introduced to some of these, such as the CPU's registers and the memory. In this section, you will see how these two components, as well as a few others—such as the cache memory, clock speed, data bus, and math coprocessor—affect a computer's speed. Figure 2.3 shows how these components might be arranged on the computer's motherboard.

NORTON Online

For more information on **Moore's Law**, visit this book's Web site at **www.glencoe.com/norton/online**

How Registers Affect Speed

The registers in the first PCs could hold two bytes-16 bits-each. Most CPUs sold today, for both PCs and Macintosh computers, have 32-bit registers. Some powerful computers, such as the minicomputers and some high-end workstations, have 64-bit registers, and this trend is working its way down to mainstream PCs.

The size of the registers, which is sometimes called the **word size**, indicates the amount of data with

MOTHERBOARD

RAM

DATA BUS

CPU WITH MATH COPROCESSOR

CLOCK

ROM

Figure 2.3
Devices affecting processing speed.

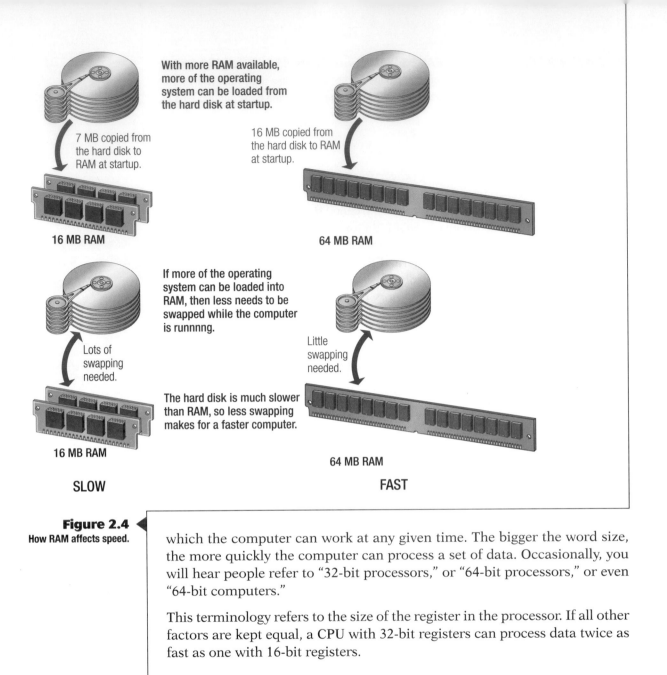

With more RAM available, more of the operating system can be loaded from the hard disk at startup.

7 MB copied from the hard disk to RAM at startup.

16 MB RAM

16 MB copied from the hard disk to RAM at startup.

64 MB RAM

If more of the operating system can be loaded into RAM, then less needs to be swapped while the computer is runnnng.

Lots of swapping needed.

The hard disk is much slower than RAM, so less swapping makes for a faster computer.

16 MB RAM

SLOW

Little swapping needed.

64 MB RAM

FAST

Figure 2.4 ◄
How RAM affects speed.

which the computer can work at any given time. The bigger the word size, the more quickly the computer can process a set of data. Occasionally, you will hear people refer to "32-bit processors," or "64-bit processors," or even "64-bit computers."

This terminology refers to the size of the register in the processor. If all other factors are kept equal, a CPU with 32-bit registers can process data twice as fast as one with 16-bit registers.

Memory and Computing Power

The amount of RAM in a computer can have a profound effect on the computer's power. For one thing, more RAM means the computer can use bigger, more powerful programs, and those programs can access bigger data files.

More RAM also can make the computer run faster. The computer does not necessarily have to load an entire program into memory to run it, but the more of the program it can fit into memory, the faster the program will run. For example, a PC with 12 MB of RAM is capable of running Microsoft Windows 98, even though the program actually occupies about 50 MB of disk storage space. When you run Windows, the program does not need to load all its files into memory to run properly. It loads only the most essential parts into memory. When the computer needs access to other parts of the program on the disk, it can unload, or **swap out**, nonessential parts from RAM back to the hard disk. Then the computer can load, or **swap in**, the program code or data it needs. As shown in Figure 2.4, however, if your PC has 16 MB of RAM or more, you will notice a dramatic difference in how fast Microsoft Windows 98 runs because the CPU will need to swap program instructions between RAM and the hard disk much less often.

Fortunately, if you decide that you need more RAM than you have, you can buy more, open up your computer, and plug it in. In today's computers, chips are usually grouped together on small circuit boards called **Single In-Line Memory Modules (SIMMs)** or **Dual In-Line Memory Modules (DIMMs)**. Each SIMM or DIMM can hold between 1 MB and 64 MB of RAM and connects to the motherboard with 30-pin or 72-pin connections. The cost of upgrading the memory of a computer is between $10 and $25 per megabyte, so this is often the most cost-effective way to get more speed from your computer.

On the top is a SIMM; on the bottom is an example of a DIMM.

The Computer's Internal Clock

Every microcomputer has a **system clock**, but the clock's primary purpose is not to keep the time of day. Like most modern wristwatches, the clock is driven by a quartz crystal. When electricity is applied, the molecules in the crystal vibrate millions of times per second, a rate that never changes. The speed of the vibration is determined by the thickness of the crystal. The computer uses the vibrations of the quartz in the system clock to time its processing operations.

Over the years, clock speeds have increased steadily. For example, the first PC operated at 4.77 megahertz. **Hertz** is a measure of cycles per second. One clock cycle means the time it takes to turn a transistor off and back on again. **Megahertz (MHz)** means "millions of cycles per second." Clock speeds of 400 MHz and higher are common. Processor speeds are increasing rapidly. By the time you read this, clock speeds probably will have exceeded 500 MHz. Experts predict that clock speeds of 1 GHz (gigahertz) will be achieved shortly after the turn of the century. All other factors being equal (although they never are), a CPU operating at 300 MHz can process data more than twice as fast as the same one operating at 133 MHz.

The Bus

In microcomputers, the term **bus** refers to the paths between the components of a computer. There are two main buses in a computer: the data bus and the address bus. The one that you hear the most about is the data bus, so when people just say "the bus," they usually mean the data bus.

The Data Bus

The **data bus** is an electrical path that connects the CPU, memory, and the other hardware devices on the motherboard. Actually, the bus is a group of parallel wires. The number of wires in the bus affects the speed at which data can travel between hardware components, just as the number of lanes on a highway affects how long it takes people to get to their destinations. Because each wire can

NORTON Online

For more information on **processor speeds**, visit this book's Web site at **www.glencoe.com/norton/online**

The motherboard includes an address bus and a data bus. The address bus leads from the CPU to memory (RAM and ROM). The data bus connects the CPU to memory, as well as all the storage, input/output, and communication devices.

RAM

Data bus

ROM

Address bus

Motherboard

CPU

Disk drives

16-bit bus
2 bytes at a time

32-bit bus
4 bytes at a time

With a wider bus, the computer can move more data in the same amount of time (or the same amount of data in less time).

NORTON Online

For more information on the **PCI bus technology**, visit this book's Web site at
www.glencoe.com/norton/online

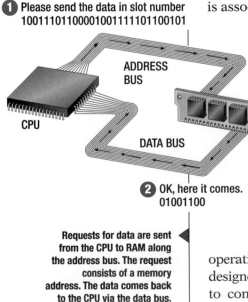

1 Please send the data in slot number 100111011000010011111011001101

ADDRESS BUS

CPU

DATA BUS

RAM

2 OK, here it comes. 01001100

Requests for data are sent from the CPU to RAM along the address bus. The request consists of a memory address. The data comes back to the CPU via the data bus.

transfer one bit at a time, an eight-wire bus can move eight bits at a time, which is a full byte. A 16-bit bus can transfer two bytes, and a 32-bit bus can transfer four bytes at a time.

PC buses are designed to match the capabilities of the devices attached to them. When CPUs could send and receive only one byte of data at a time, there was no point in connecting them to a bus that could move more data. As microprocessor technology improved, however, chips were built that could send and receive more data at once, and improved bus designs created wider paths through which the data could flow.

When IBM introduced the PC-AT in 1984, the most dramatic improvement was an enhanced data bus that was matched with the capabilities of a microprocessor introduced in 1982, the Intel 80286. The data bus of the AT was 16 bits wide and became the de facto standard in the industry. It is still used for PC devices that do not require more than a 16-bit bus. The AT bus is commonly known as the **Industry Standard Architecture (ISA) bus**.

Two years later, however, when the first 80386 chips (commonly abbreviated as the 386) began shipping, a new standard was needed for the 386's 32-bit bus. The first contender was **Micro Channel Architecture (MCA) bus**, from IBM. Then came the **Extended Industry Standard Architecture (EISA) bus** from a consortium of hardware developers who opposed IBM's new standard because it was not backward compatible. The winner of the bus wars was neither MCA nor EISA. It was the **Peripheral Component Interconnect (PCI) bus**. Intel designed the PCI bus specifically to make it easier to integrate new data types, such as audio, video, and graphics.

The Address Bus

The second bus found in every microcomputer is the **address bus**. The address bus is a set of wires similar to the data bus that connects the CPU and RAM and carries the memory addresses. (Remember, each byte in RAM is associated with a number, which is the memory address.)

The address bus is important because the number of wires in it determines the maximum number of memory addresses. For example, recall that one byte of data is enough to represent 256 different values. If the address bus could carry only eight bits at a time, the CPU could address only 256 bytes of RAM.

Actually, most of the early PCs had 20-bit address buses, so the CPU could address 2^{20} bytes, or 1 MB, of data. Today, most CPUs have 32-bit address buses that can address 4 GB (more than 4 billion bytes) of RAM. Some of the latest models can address even more.

One of the biggest hurdles in the evolution of PCs was that DOS, the operating system used in the vast majority of PCs for more than a decade, was designed for machines that could address only 1 MB of RAM. When PCs began to contain more RAM, special software had to be devised to address it.

Programmers came up with two devices called expanded memory and extended memory. Windows 95 largely did away with these, although extended memory still exists in the operating system for purposes of backward compatibility.

Most cache memory is visible on the motherboard as a group of chips next to the CPU.

Cache Memory

Moving data between RAM and the CPU's registers is one of the most time-consuming operations a CPU must perform, simply because RAM is much slower than the CPU.

A partial solution to this problem is to include a cache memory in the CPU. **Cache** (pronounced "cash") **memory** is similar to RAM, except that it is extremely fast compared to normal memory, and it is used in a different way.

Figure 2.5 shows how cache memory works with the CPU and RAM. When a program is running and the CPU needs to read data or instructions from RAM, the CPU first checks to see whether the data is in cache memory. If the data that it needs is not there, it reads the data from RAM into its registers, but it also loads a copy of the data into cache memory. The next time the CPU needs that same data, it finds it in the cache memory and saves the time needed to load the data from RAM. Knowing the size of most programs and many data files, you might think that the odds of the CPU finding the data it needs in the cache memory are small, but it actually does find the data it needs there often enough to improve the performance of a PC.

Program instructions are often found in cache memory. Frequently, programs ask computers to do the same operation repeatedly until a particular condition is met. In computer language, such a repetitive procedure is called a *loop*. For example, when a word processing program searches for a specific word, it must check each word in the document until it finds a match. If the instructions that tell the arithmetic logic unit how to find a match are in cache memory, the control unit does not have to load them from RAM each time. As a result, the search is completed more quickly.

Since the late 1980s, cache memory has been built into most PC CPUs. The first CPU caches came with 0.5 KB, then 8 KB, then 16 KB, then 32 KB. Today, some chips have as much as 64 KB built in. In addition to the cache memory built into the CPU, now cache is also added to the motherboard. Many PCs sold today have 512 KB or 1024 KB of motherboard cache memory. Cache memory clearly provides performance benefits, so you can expect to see the new chips and new motherboards continue to leapfrog the old with more cache memory.

Figure 2.5
The cache speeds up processing by storing frequently used data or instructions in its high-speed memory.

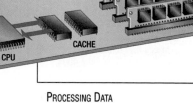

Passing Math Operations to the Math Coprocessor

Some computers speed up certain kinds of processing by adding a **math coprocessor** to the CPU. A math coprocessor is a chip specially designed to handle complicated mathematical operations. Newer CPUs have math coprocessors built in. Earlier CPUs did not have them, so many users chose to upgrade their machines by adding them.

The ALU (arithmetic logic unit), which handles most processing operations, can manipulate binary code representing numbers, text, images, sound—any form of data that the computer can store. In terms of processing, the ALU is a generalist.

The ALU, however, has difficulty performing certain mathematical operations. For example, say that the processor needs to compute $(314.15927)^4$. The ALU is designed to manipulate whole numbers that are not too large or small. If it is forced to work with decimals, it can really get bogged down. The math coprocessor, on the other hand, is a processing specialist designed to work with exactly these kinds of numbers. It can execute arithmetic routines much more quickly than the ALU because it uses **floating-point arithmetic**, a computer technique that translates numbers into scientific notation. (In some computers, the math coprocessor is called the **floating-point unit**, or **FPU**.) In floating-point arithmetic, the computer represents

$$0.0000586 \quad \text{as} \quad 5.86 \times 10^{-5} \quad \text{or} \quad 128,610,000,000 \quad \text{as} \quad 1.2861 \times 10^{11}$$

This technique simplifies complex arithmetic because the computer is not forced to store large numbers of decimal places.

When the computer must do much floating-point arithmetic, the presence of a math coprocessor's floating-point unit can speed up processing considerably. Applications that benefit from math coprocessors include spreadsheets and drawing programs. Software for computer-aided design (CAD) and 3-D rendering generally will not even run without a math coprocessor because each point in a complex design must be plotted numerically.

CPUS USED IN PERSONAL COMPUTERS

The two biggest players in the PC CPU market are **Intel** and **Motorola**. Intel has enjoyed tremendous success with its processors since the early 1980s. Most PCs are controlled by Intel processors. The primary exception to this rule is the Macintosh. All Macs use chips made by Motorola. In addition, several firms, such as AMD (Advanced Micro Devices) and Cyrix, make processors that mimic the functionality of Intel's chips. Several other companies manufacture chips for workstation PCs.

The Intel Processors

The Intel Corporation is the largest manufacturer of microchips in the world, in addition to being the leading provider of chips for PCs. In fact, Intel invented the microprocessor, the so-called "computer on a chip," in 1971 with the 4004 model. This invention led to the first microcomputers that began appearing in 1975. However, Intel's success in this market was not guaranteed until 1981, when IBM released the first IBM PC, which was based on the Intel

Ted Hoff, inventor of the microprocessor.

Intel's first microprocessor, the 4004.

8088. Since then, all IBM machines and the compatibles based on IBM's design have been created around Intel's chips. A list of those chips, along with their basic specifications, is shown in Table 2.5. Although the 8088 was the first chip to be used in an IBM PC, IBM actually used an earlier chip, the 8086, in a subsequent model, called the IBM PC XT. The chips that came later—the 286, 386, 486, the Pentium, and Pentium II line—correspond to certain design standards established by the 8086. This line of chips is often referred to as the 80x86 line.

Table 2.5	Intel Chips and Their Specifications			
MODEL	YEAR INTRODUCED	DATA BUS CAPACITY	REGISTER SIZE	ADDRESSABLE MEMORY
8086	1978	16 bit	16 bit	1 MB
8088	1979	8 bit	16 bit	1 MB
80286	1982	16 bit	16 bit	16 MB
80386	1985	32 bit	32 bit	4 GB
80486	1989	32 bit	32 bit	4 GB
Pentium	1993	64 bit	32 bit	4 GB
Pentium Pro	1995	64 bit	32 bit	64 GB
Pentium II	1997	64 bit	32 bit	64 GB

The steady rise in bus size, register size, and addressable memory illustrated in Table 2.5 has also been accompanied by increases in clock speed. For example, the clock attached to the first PCs ran at 4.77 MHz, whereas clock speeds for Pentium chips started at 60 MHz in 1993 and quickly rose to 100, 120, 133, 150, and 166 MHz. Pentium II chips are rated at speeds of 233, 266, 300, 350, 400 MHz and higher.

These statistics, however, do not convey all the improvements that have been made. The basic design of each chip, known as the architecture, has grown steadily in sophistication and complexity. For example, the architecture of the 386 contained 320,000 transistors, and the 486 contained 1.2 million. With the Pentium, that number grew to more than 3.1 million, and the Pentium Pro's architecture brought the total number of transistors on the chip to 5.5 million. Pentium II's architecture includes an amazing 7.5 million transistors.

The growing complexity of the architecture allowed Intel to incorporate some sophisticated techniques for processing. One major improvement that came with the 386 is called virtual 8086 mode. In this mode, a single 386 chip could achieve the processing power of 16 separate 8086 chips each running a separate copy of the operating system. The capability for virtual 8086 mode enabled a single 386 chip to run different programs at the same time, a technique known as multitasking. All the chips that succeeded the 386 have had the capacity for multitasking.

The 486

Introduced in 1989, the 80486 did not feature any radically new processor technology. Instead, it combined a 386 processor, a math coprocessor, and a cache memory controller on a single chip. Because these chips were no longer separate, they no longer had to communicate through the bus. This innovation increased the speed of the system dramatically.

The Pentium

The next member of the Intel family of microprocessors was the **Pentium**, introduced in 1993. With the Pentium, Intel broke its tradition of numeric model names—partly to prevent other chip manufacturers from using similar numeric

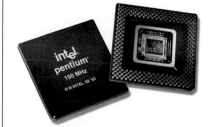

The Intel Pentium

names, which implied that their products were functionally identical to Intel's chips. The Pentium, however, is still considered part of the 80x86 series.

The Pentium chip itself represented another leap forward for microprocessors. The speed and power of the Pentium dwarfed all its predecessors in the Intel line. In practical terms, this means that the Pentium runs application programs approximately five times faster than a 486 at the same clock speed. Part of the Pentium's speed comes from a **superscalar** architecture, which allows the chip to process more than one instruction in a single clock cycle.

The Pentium Pro

Introduced in 1995, the **Pentium Pro** reflected still more design breakthroughs. The Pentium Pro can process three instructions in a single clock cycle—one more than the Pentium. In addition, the Pentium Pro can achieve faster clock speeds.

The Intel Pentium Pro.

Intel coined the phrase "dynamic execution" to describe the chip's capability to execute program instructions in the most efficient manner, not necessarily in the order in which they were written. This out-of-order execution means that instructions that cannot be executed immediately are put aside while the Pentium Pro begins processing other instructions.

Pentium with MMX Technology

The Pentium also supports a technology called **MMX**. MMX includes three primary architectural design enhancements: new instructions, SIMD process, and additional cache. MMX includes a set of 57 instructions that increase the multimedia capabilities of a computer chip. These instructions process audio, video, and graphical data more efficiently than non-MMX processors. The **MMX Single Instruction Multiple Data (SIMD) process** enables one instruction to perform the same function on multiple pieces of data, reducing the number of loops required to handle video, audio, animation, and graphical data.

Intel's MMX Bunny People showcase the "fun" built into Pentium processors with MMX technology.

The Pentium II

The newest Pentium series of processors from Intel is the **Pentium II**. Released in the summer of 1997, the Pentium II has 7.5 million transistors, and execution ratings of 233MHz, 266MHz, 300MHz, 333MHz, 350MHz, 400MHz, and higher. Like the Pentium Pro, the Pentium II supports MMX

Productivity Tip

To Buy or To Upgrade?

At some point, you probably will face the problem that plagues nearly every computer user. That is, you will need a computer that is faster, has more features, or runs newer software than your current system.

This problem leads to another question: Should you buy a new computer or upgrade an existing system? Both approaches have advantages, and you should consider them carefully before deciding. It's a choice that can bring satisfaction or regret.

Evaluate Your Needs Before deciding whether to buy or upgrade, look at your computing needs, especially if you are buying your first computer. The more complex your tasks, the more computing power you need.

If you need only to use basic applications, or usually use one or two programs at a time, an older PC may provide adequate performance. If you need to multitask, run powerful applications, or use the latest multimedia software, then you need the most powerful system you can afford.

Buying a Computer If you are a "power user" or use sophisticated software for graphics, databases, multimedia, or programming, then purchase the most powerful system you can afford. Affordability is the key, so here is a good rule of thumb: *Invest the most in the features that will give you the most benefit.* Purchase add-ons only if you can afford to, and only after your primary needs have been adequately addressed.

Will you work with large or multiple applications? Then RAM and processing power are important considerations; look for a system with at least 32 MB of RAM (64 MB or more is better) and the fastest Pentium II processor you can afford.

Will you use large files, such as book-size documents or graphics? If so, storage is a primary concern. While most new computers feature hard drive capacities of 4 GB or more, you should consider an even larger drive or multiple hard disks.

Is cutting-edge multimedia a requirement? Then your system needs a large monitor, a high-speed graphics card with enhanced 3-D capabilities, and a 32-bit sound card with high-quality speakers. These enhancements are costly, but they can increase overall performance when using multimedia-intensive products.

On the other hand, if your needs are limited, consider buying one of the new breed of "budget" systems, many of which sell for less than $1,000. These systems can easily be found in computer stores, department stores, and mail-order outlets. Budget systems offer plenty of horsepower for desktop applications (usually an AMD K5 or Intel Celeron processor are included). Because they are designed primarily for home users, however, these systems usually provide minimal RAM, smaller hard disks, and smaller monitors.

For the true beginner or the user with very simple needs (strictly word processing, for example), a used computer may be the perfect solution. Early Pentium-class systems can easily be found for a few hundred dollars. These older systems are perfectly adequate for basic applications, and can easily be upgraded in the future. In fact, if you want to try your hand at upgrading, an inexpensive used PC can be an excellent way to start.

Upgrading a Computer Everything in a computer can be upgraded. The CPU, RAM, disk drives, motherboard, pointing devices, video and audio systems can all be replaced to improve your computer's performance. Consider upgrading your current computer, however, only if you can get the performance boost you need while spending less than you would for a new system.

A new processor is the quickest way to a faster computer. Current upgrade packages can increase a Pentium computer to a Pentium Pro CPU with MMX technology for under $200. A processor upgrade can be as simple as removing the current processor chip and inserting the new one in the same socket. (If you want to upgrade to a Pentium II processor, you need to install a new motherboard that will accommodate a "Slot One" socket. This type of upgrade can cost nearly as much as a new computer!)

Many devices are available to boost your current PC.

A RAM upgrade can enable your PC to process data faster, by keeping more information on hand for the processor. Currently, 32 MB is the practical minimum, with 64 MB yielding faster performance; the more RAM, the better. A RAM upgrade can be as easy as plugging one or two additional SIMM (Single Inline Memory Module) chips into the motherboard.

For greater storage capacity, add or replace a hard disk. Newer disks also tend to be faster than older ones, and are reasonably inexpensive. A hard disk upgrade is more challenging than a RAM upgrade, but most kits provide everything you need.

Changing the sound or video display card is another easy upgrade; just replace the current card with a newer one. Older computers may have less than 1 MB of video memory (VRAM). The minimum VRAM for most systems now is 2 MB, with 4 MB the norm for systems you routinely use for graphics work and navigating on the World Wide Web.

For more information on buying or upgrading a computer, visit this book's Web site at **www.glencoe.com/norton/online**.

technology and dynamic execution. The Pentium II differs from other Pentium models in that it is encased in a plastic and metal cartridge instead of the wafer format used for other chips. This is due to the Pentium II's new **Single Edge Connector** connection scheme. Rather than plugging into the regular chip slot on your motherboard, the Pentium II plugs into a special slot called Slot One (called the Single Edge Connector), which requires a new motherboard design. Enclosed within the Pentium II cartridge is the core processor and the L2 cache chip, enabling high-performance operations.

In 1998, Intel expanded the Pentium II family by announcing two new processors—Celeron and Xeon—which adapted Pentium II technology for new markets. The **Celeron** processor features many of the capabilities of the Pentium II, but operates at slightly slower speeds and is designed for entry-level personal computers priced in the $1,000 range. The **Xeon** Pentium II incorporates a larger level 2 cache on the processor, and features enhanced multiprocessing capabilities. The Xeon is designed for use in network server computers and workstations.

Intel's Competitors

Advanced Micro Devices (AMD) and **Cyrix** are the two main competitors to Intel's dominance. You usually find AMD and Cyrix processors in low-end, low-priced home and small business computers that sell for less than $1,000.

AMD has three lines of processors. The **5x86** processor line has a clock speed of 133MHz and is roughly equivalent to the 75MHz Pentium chip. AMD's **K5** chip is a Pentium-class processor and comes in 100MHz and 116.7MHz versions. These chips are equivalent to the 133MHz and 166MHz Pentium processors, respectively. One of the fastest AMD processor is the **K6** chip. This chip supports the Intel MMX technology (AMD's other two lines do not) and comes in speeds of 166MHz, 200MHz, 233MHz, 266 MHz, 300MHz, and higher. The K6 line of chips is comparable to the Pentium Pro line of processors of the same clock speed.

Cyrix originally began as a math coprocessor manufacturer in 1988. It now works with IBM Microelectronics and SGS-Thomson to manufacture chips in two main lines. The **MediaGX** processor, introduced in February 1997, integrates audio and graphics functions and comes in speeds up to 233MHz. **The Virtual System Architecture (VSA)** combines the technology of a memory controller, video card, and sound card in the MediaGX processor. One example of a PC that uses the MediaGX processor is the Compaq Presario 2100 PC. The Cyrix 6x86MX processor is MMX-compatible and comes in 133MHz, 150MHz, 188MHz, and 208MHz versions. The Cyrix MII offers Pentium II-class performance.

The Motorola Processors

Motorola Corporation is the other major manufacturer of microprocessors for small computers. As mentioned earlier, Apple's Macintosh computers use Motorola processors. Other computer manufacturers, including workstation manufacturers, such as Sun Microsystems, have also relied heavily on Motorola chips. They were an early favorite among companies that built larger, UNIX-based computers, such as the NCR Tower series and the AT&T 3B series.

The Intel Pentium II is one of the most popular chips ever made.

NORTON Online

For more information on **Advanced Micro Devices'** line of microprocessors, visit this book's Web site at www.glencoe.com/norton/online

The AMD K6.

The Cyrix MediaGX.

Techview

Parallel Processing: On the Fast Track

In the race to make computers faster and more powerful, the CPU is the star athlete, and it's already going just about at top speed. So what's next?

The answer: teams of CPUs. This is called *parallel processing,* where multiple processors work together in a single system.

The processor is the crucial determinant of a computer's speed because it is involved in every computer task from scientific or engineering calculations to the placement of colors and character fonts on screen. There are several ways to make a faster processor. One is to increase the number of bits of information a chip can handle at once.

Another is to increase the pace at which the chip handles these bits. This "clock rate" of the computer is measured in megahertz (MHz), which stands for millions of clock ticks per second. With each tick, a processor takes another step in calculating. Where computers once operated at 1 MHz or less, many now operate at 300 MHz, some reach 400 MHz or more, and 1GHz (GigaHertz or 1000 MHz) processors are currently on design boards.

One way developers have increased the speed of computers is to increase the number of CPUs in a system. This is parallel processing, also called *multiprocessing* (MP) or *symmetric multiprocessing* (SMP) In fact, most of today's computer processors have some measure of parallel processing built in. This is called *pipelining*—overlapping some of the steps of processing within a single processor.

SMP systems are already common among high-end servers and workstations. Some of the fastest computers use thousands of individual processors. Parallel processing has not moved to the desktop, however, because of cost and complexity.

Microprocessors are one of the most expensive components in a PC. Putting in more than one raises prices substantially. Adding another Pentium II chip to a PC, for example, can raise the overall price more than $1,000, a cost most users and businesses do not want to incur.

Also, operating systems and software traditionally are designed to be used by one processor. Windows 98, for instance, does not support multiple processors. This means that adding processors to most users' PCs would not improve performance.

Many users and businesses, however, are adapting Microsoft's advanced operating system, Windows NT, to gain parallel processing capabilities on the desktop and server. With Windows NT's SMP capability, users' desktop computers and companies' network servers will be able to process much more data in shorter amounts of time, making real-time video, high-speed animations, and mathematical-intensive calculations a reality.

Desktop computers that support multiple processors are becoming more popular.

Someday you may be looking for a PC that includes not only a high-speed CPU (over 1 GHz perhaps) but also multiple processors to help you tackle your everyday job.

Table 2.6	Motorola Processors for Personal Computers			
MODEL	YEAR INTRODUCED	REGISTER SIZE	DATA BUS CAPACITY	ADDRESSABLE MEMORY
68000	1979	32 bit	16 bit	16 MB
68010	1983	32 bit	16 bit	16 MB
68020	1984	32 bit	32 bit	4 GB
68030	1987	32 bit	32 bit	4 GB
68040	1989	32 bit	32 bit	4 GB
68060	1993	32 bit	32 bit	4 GB
MPC 601	1992	64 bit	32 bit	4 GB
MPC 603	1993	64 bit	32 bit	4 GB
MPC 604	1994	64 bit	32 bit	4 GB
MPC 620	1995	128 bit	64 bit	1 TB*
MPC 740	1997	128 bit	32 & 64 bit	1 TB
MPC 860T	1997	128 bit	64 bit	1 TB

*terabyte, equal to 1000 GB

NORTON Online

For more information on Motorola's line of products, visit this book's Web site at www.glencoe.com/norton/online

Table 2.6 shows the specifications for the most popular Motorola processors.

As you can see, Motorola offers two families of processor chips. The first is known as the "680x0 family," similar to the way that Intel's group of PC processors is known as the "80x86 family." The second, designated MPC, has a different architecture and is known as the PowerPC family.

The 680x0 Series

Although the 68000 chip is best known as the foundation of the original Macintosh, it actually predates the Mac by several years. In fact, IBM considered using the 68000 in the first IBM PC. (IBM's decision to use the Intel 8088 chip in its first PC was apparently driven by cost considerations.) Although Motorola's 68000 chip was more powerful than Intel's 8088, subsequent improvements to the Motorola chip were made in smaller increments than Intel's giant performance leaps. By the time Motorola introduced the 68060 chip, Intel was promoting the Pentium. In an attempt to regain market share, Motorola initiated the development of the new PowerPC chip.

The PowerPC Series

The **PowerPC** chip had an unusual beginning. Two industry rivals, IBM and Apple, joined forces with Motorola in 1991, ostensibly to dethrone Intel from its preeminence in the PC chip market. The hardware portion of their efforts focused on the PowerPC chip, the first of which was the 601. Following closely on its heels was the 603, a low-power processor suitable for notebook computers. Its successor, the 604 and 604e, is a high-power chip designed for high-end desktop systems. With the introduction of the 620 late in 1995, PowerPC chips established a new performance record for microprocessors. A handful of small 620-based machines working together offers about the same computing power as an IBM 370 mainframe. The PowerPC 750 chip (266 MHz) was released for desktop and mobile computers that need significant computing power in a low-voltage processor. The PowerPC 750 was designed for multimedia, small business, and mobile applications. The new G3 chip provides even more power for such applications. As you will see in the next section, PowerPC and G3 chips are different from the earlier 68000 series from the ground up.

RISC Processors

Both the Motorola 680x0 and Intel 80x86 families are **complex instruction set computing (CISC)** processors. The instruction sets for these CPUs are large, typically containing 200 to 300 instructions.

A newer theory in microprocessor design holds that if the instruction set for the CPU is kept small and simple, each instruction will execute much faster, allowing the processor to complete more instructions during a given period. CPUs designed according to this theory are called **reduced instruction set computing (RISC)** processors. The RISC design, which is used in the PowerPC but was first implemented in the mid-1980s, results in a faster and less expensive processor. Because of the way the Pentium Pro and its spin-offs process instructions, they are called RISC-like, but their architecture is still based on complex instruction set computing.

RISC technology has been the engine of mid-size computers such as the IBM RS/6000 and high-end UNIX workstations such as those built by Sun Microsystems, Hewlett-Packard, and NCR. RISC CPUs are also found in printers and other devices that have their own internal CPUs. The PowerPC and G3 processors reflected a major move on the part of industry giants toward using RISC technology in desktop and notebook computers.

Motorola is not alone in producing both RISC and CISC processors. In 1989, Intel introduced the i860, which was a 64-bit RISC chip that earned the distinction of being the first chip to contain more than one million transistors. Other RISC processors include the Intel i960, the Motorola 88100, NEC Electronics' VR4000 series, and the DEC Alpha. Sun Microsystems also produces a RISC processor, known as SPARC, which it uses in its UNIX workstations. Members of the NEC VR4000 family are meant to be used by the same range of computers as the PowerPC chips, namely, for machines from notebooks through high-end systems. NEC's VR4111 processor, on the other hand, is intended for battery-powered devices such as handheld and wallet PCs.

Whether CISC or RISC technology will be the basis of most future microprocessors has yet to be determined, but early bets are on models of RISC chips with reduced power consumption.

Parallel Processing

Another school of thought on producing faster computers is to build them with more than one processor. This is not a new idea in the mainframe and supercomputer arena. In fact, the IBM 3090 has two to four processors, and the Cray X MP 4 has four processors. Some companies are developing computers with 256, 512, and even thousands of microprocessors, known as **massively parallel processors (MPP)**. For example, Intel, in conjunction with the U.S. Department of Energy's Sandia National Laboratory, constructed what is touted as "the world's fastest supercomputer." It included more than 7,200 Pentium Pro processors and achieved speeds of 1.06 teraflops—or trillions of floating point operations per second. (The previous record was 386.2 gigaflops, or billion-operations-per-second.)

At the other end of the spectrum, dual-processor and quad-processor versions of PCs are available today. Unfortunately, the DOS operating system

▶ Motorola's PowerPC 750 chip.

◀ Motorola's PowerPC 604e chip.

▶ A RISC chip from NEC, the VR4111 processor.

▶ This Ultra 1 workstation from Sun Microsystems is based on a RISC microprocessor called the UltraSPARC. The Ultra 1 is designed for exceptionally high performance for networking and graphics programs.

Computers
In Your Career

Processing Data

If your career involves the use of a computer, it's a good idea to become familiar with how a computer processes data. Even if your activities are limited to using a computer and not supporting or building one, it is helpful to have an idea of which components are key in processing data and which components affect the speed of your computer.

This knowledge will enable you to make sound decisions on upgrading and replacing your hardware.

Depending on your career track, it may be necessary to learn all you can about how a computer processes data. The following list describes some of the fields in which you need to know the details of how computers process data.

■ **Information Systems Managers and Technicians** If you're interested in a career in information systems, an understanding of how a PC processes data is a must. In many organizations, IS managers have the responsibility of choosing the types of computers that a company uses. Further, the IS department usually must set up and administer a company's PC installation. All three of these tasks require that the IS manager and staff have an in-depth knowledge of how PCs process data, use RAM, and are affected by CPU type and speed. IS personnel also must understand the different types of data bus architecture and on which type (ISA, EISA, PCI) their company has standardized.

■ **Software Engineers and Programmers** Although software is usually described as separate from hardware, software engineers and programmers must understand how a PC processes data in order to write computer programs. Software engineers and programmers must know how to optimize their program to take advantage of the CPU (speed and type), bus architecture, and RAM that a computer uses. Also, programmers working with certain types of software must become proficient in the different text codes used by the PCs they work on, in particular the ASCII and Unicode tables.

■ **Hardware Configuration Personnel** If you're interested in a hardware support career, knowing how a computer represents data in binary code is a must. This will enable you to troubleshoot many problems that users encounter between the hardware and operating system. Likewise, knowing in-depth how a computer uses the CPU to process data, as well as keeping up to date on the types of CPUs available is essential to success in a hardware support position. Finally, to round out your knowledge to support as many hardware problems as possible, you should become familiar with the different types of memory a PC uses and the types of data buses available.

cannot make use of an additional processor. Some UNIX programmers, however, have developed software that takes advantage of an additional processor. One of Microsoft's operating systems, Windows NT, can also make use of parallel processor computers. These computers are often based on the Pentium Pro, and they look much like ordinary desktop PCs.

WHAT TO EXPECT IN THE FUTURE

For 20 years, advances in CPU technology have driven the rapid increases in computer power and speed. CPUs have doubled in performance roughly every 18 months (in keeping with Moore's Law), so today's fastest chips are about 1,000 times faster then those of 20 years ago. Although some industry analysts claim that this trend has to taper off soon, others predict that it will continue for another 20 years. How can technology keep up this pace?

There will probably be a continuation of existing trends—more cache built into the motherboard, faster clock speeds, and more instructions executed in each clock cycle. There may also be continued growth in register and bus size. Chip manufacturers may continue to reduce the size of the electrical pathways on the chip. A new chip design, called CMOS 7S, announced in September 1997 by IBM, uses copper rather than aluminum to create the circuitry on chips. These advances enable manufacturers to squeeze more transistors onto the microprocessor chip and reduce chip size.

Many analysts predict that RISC technology will be a major factor in CPU improvements. RISC architecture is only half the age of CISC architecture, and the makers of RISC chips say there is room for improvement.

The greatest boost in CPU speed may come from multiprocessing, a design innovation that builds more than one chip into the CPU. In microcomputers, multiprocessing systems appeared first as network servers, the machines that form the hub of some computer networks. You are soon likely to see multiprocessing systems on the desktop.

The next leap in multiprocessor technology is expected to be the Merced chip, now under design by Intel and Hewlett-Packard. The Merced (which gets its name from a Western river), will incorporate a Pentium processor along with a RISC processor and several separate parallel processors, all on the same chip. The chip may hold as many as ten million processors on board, possibly more, and will be able to run DOS, Windows, and UNIX operating systems and software simultaneously. When the chip is released (probably in 2000), it may give minicomputer power to PCs and enable businesses to consolidate software and applications from different programs into a single system. Look for the Merced to appear in server-class systems and workstations.

Visual Summary & Exercises

VISUAL SUMMARY

Transforming Data into Information

- Computer data is reduced to binary numbers because computer processing is performed by transistors that have only two possible states, on and off.

- The binary numbering system works the same way as the decimal system, except that it has only two available symbols rather than ten.

- A single unit of data is called a bit; eight bits make up one byte.

- In the most common character-code set, ASCII, each character consists of one byte of data.

How a Computer Processes Data

- A microcomputer's processing takes place in the central processing unit (CPU), the two main parts of which are the control unit and the arithmetic logic unit (ALU).

- Within the CPU, program instructions are retrieved and translated with the help of an internal instruction set and the accompanying microcode.

- CPUs in the same family are made with backward compatibility in terms of instruction sets, so that a new CPU can work with all the same programs that the old CPUs used.

- The actual manipulation of data takes place in the ALU, which is connected to registers that hold data.

- Read-only memory (ROM) is nonvolatile (or permanent); it is used to hold instructions that run the computer when the power is first turned on.

- Random-access memory (RAM), is volatile (or temporary); programs and data can be written to and erased from RAM as needed.

- The CPU accesses each location in memory by using a unique number, called the memory address.

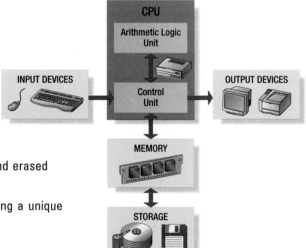

Factors Affecting Processing Speed

- The size of the registers, also called word size, determines the amount of data with which the computer can work at a given time.

- The amount of RAM can also affect speed because the CPU can keep more of the active program and data in memory rather than in storage.

- The computer's system clock sets the pace for the CPU by using a vibrating quartz crystal.

- There are two kinds of buses—the data bus and the address bus—both of which are located on the motherboard.

- The width of the data bus determines how many bits at a time can be transmitted between the CPU and other devices.

- Bus architecture in the PC has evolved from the ISA bus to the PCI bus.

- The size (or width) of the address bus determines the number of bytes of RAM the CPU can access.

- The cache is a type of high-speed memory that contains the most recent data and instructions that have been loaded by the CPU.

- A CPU relies on either a math coprocessor or an integrated floating-point unit to perform floating-point arithmetic.

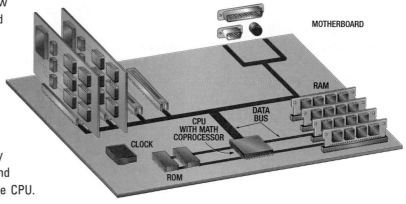

CPUs Used in Personal Computers

- Since 1978, Intel's processors have evolved from the 8086 and the 8088 to the 286, the 386, the 486, the Pentium, the Pentium Pro, and the Pontium II.

- Moore's Law states that computing power doubles every 18 months.

- Intel competitors, AMD and Cyrix, are commonly found in low-end, low-priced (under $1,000) consumer and home PCs.

- Motorola makes the CPUs used in Macintosh and PowerPC computers: the 68000, 68020, 68030, and 68040 were for Macintosh; the PowerPC series is now used in the Power Macintoshes. The G3 is now available as well.

- Instruction sets for RISC chips are kept smaller than CISC chips so that each instruction executes more quickly.

- Some high-end micros and mid-size computers, as well as a growing number of PCs, use RISC chips.

- One trend in computer architecture is to incorporate parallel processing.

Visual Summary & Exercises

KEY TERMS

After completing this chapter, you should be able to define the following terms:

5x86, 60
address bus, 54
Advanced Micro Devices (AMD), 60
arithmetic logic unit (ALU), 49
arithmetic operation, 48
ASCII, 44
binary system, 43
bit, 43
Burst Extended Data Output (BEDO) RAM, 50
bus, 53
cache memory, 55
Celeron, 60
complex instruction set computing (CISC) processor, 62
control unit, 46
Cyrix, 60
data bus, 53
decimal system, 43
downward (backward) compatibility, 48
Dual In-Line Memory Module (DIMM), 53
EBCDIC (Extended Binary Coded Decimal Interchange Code), 44
EISA (Extended Industry Standard Architecture) bus, 54
Extended Data Output (EDO) RAM, 50
Fast Page Mode (FPM) RAM, 50

flash memory, 51
floating-point arithmetic, 56
floating-point unit (FPU), 56
G3, 60
Hertz, 53
Industry Standard Architecture (ISA) bus, 54
instruction set, 48
Intel, 56
K5, 60
K6, 60
logical operation, 48
massively parallel processors (MPP), 63
math coprocessor, 56
MediaGX, 60
Megahertz (MHz), 53
memory address, 50
microcode, 48
Micro Channel Architecture (MCA) bus, 54
MMX, 58
MMX Single Instruction Multiple Data (SIMD) process, 58
Moore's Law, 51
Motorola, 56
nonvolatile, 49
Pentium, 57

Pentium II, 58
Pentium Pro, 58
Peripheral Component Interconnect (PCI) bus, 54
PowerPC, 62
reduced instruction set computing (RISC) processor, 63
registers, 49
Single Edge Connector, 60
Single In-Line Memory Module (SIMM), 53
Single Instruction Multiple Data (SIMD) process, 58
superscalar, 58
swap in, 52
swap out, 52
Synchronous Dynamic RAM (SDRAM), 51
system board, 46
system clock, 53
transistor, 42
Unicode Worldwide Character Standard, 46
upward compatibility, 48
Virtual System Architecture (VSA), 60
volatile, 49
word size, 51
Xeon, 60

KEY TERMS QUIZ

Fill in the missing word with one of the terms listed in the Key Terms:

1. The base 2 number system used by computers is known as the _____.

2. A(n) _____ is the common path between the components of a computer.

3. The smallest possible unit of data is called a(n) _____.

4. In a CPU's instruction set, each instruction is expressed in _____.

5. _____ is the most common character-code set.

6. A location in the memory chip is indicated by the _____.

7. A(n) _____ is a chip designed to handle complicated mathematical operations.

8. Tiny electronic switches in the CPU that register on or off are known as _____.

9. _____ is the capability of a new hardware device or piece of software to interact with the same equipment and software as its predecessor.

10. High-speed memory locations built directly into the CPU that hold data currently processed are called _____.

Visual Summary & Exercises

REVIEW QUESTIONS

1. What is a CPU composed of primarily?

2. Which bus technology has emerged as the winner of the bus wars?

3. What characterizes a binary system? Explain briefly why it is used to represent data in a computer.

4. Which is the most common character set in use today?

5. Name the device that connects the CPU to a computer system's other hardware devices. What two processing components reside on it?

6. Explain briefly the roles of the CPU's control unit and arithmetic logic unit.

7. Explain briefly what the phrase "upward compatibility" means.

8. Under what conditions does the CPU's arithmetic logic unit (ALU) receive an instruction from the control unit?

9. How does cache memory speed up the computer?

10. What is a register, and what aspect of processing does it most affect?

DISCUSSION QUESTIONS

1. Do you think the international interchange of data provided by the Unicode character set is a worthwhile goal for computing technology? Do you see any other benefits to Unicode's widespread implementation?

2. Why do you think the CPU is commonly referred to as a computer's brain? Can the CPU really "think" like a human's brain?

3. What significant factor led to advancements in bus technology, such as the EISA and PCI architectures?

4. Consider the evolving power of CPUs and the parallel increase in the number and arrangement of transistors they contain. Do you think there is a physical limit to the number of transistors in a CPU's design? What significant factor common to today's PCs occurred in evolution of CPUs, beginning with the 80386 processor? What change in the Pentium II processor is likely to change chip design in the future?

The following exercises assume that you have access to the Internet and a browser. If you need help with any of the exercises, visit this book's Web site at **www.glencoe.com/norton/online**. This book's Web site also lists the URLs you need to complete many of these exercises.

1. Visit at least three sites on the World Wide Web that describe new innovations in CPU design. How do competitors of Intel describe their products? Can you find charts that show performance of Pentium chips against other chips?

2. The Web provides excellent tutorials on learning standard code systems. Can you find a site that lists the Unicode Worldwide Character Standard? Compare this standard to the ASCII table located in Table 2.3.

3. Many computer users use the Web to order hardware devices to upgrade their PCs. PC manufacturers and hardware resellers often post bargain prices for different devices. Find a site or group of sites that offer to sell you the following devices:

- CPU upgrades
- Motherboards
- Cache memory
- Memory (RAM)

4. PC processing speeds are constantly increasing, bringing more power to the home user as well as the business user. Search the product listings at the Web sites of popular computer manufacturers. What are the fastest systems currently available from each manufacturer? Check this information for both desktop and portable PCs.

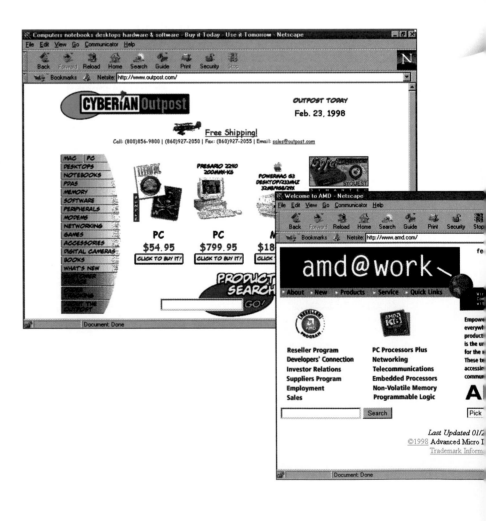

5. Remember that Intel is not the only maker of CPUs for computers. Check the Web sites of some of Intel's primary competitors. What are the fastest chips these companies are offering? Using information from these Web sites and Intel's Web site, what comparisons can you make about these different processors?

6. RISC-based workstations are an essential tool in many professions, including engineering, high-end graphic design, animation, and others. Visit the Web sites of workstation manufacturers. Aside from raw processing speed, what other features do workstations possess that make them so powerful?

7. The supercomputer represents the ultimate in computing power. Search and visit the Web site of a supercomputer manufacturer to learn more about these amazing systems. Can you find out how supercomputers are being used, and by whom? How many applications can you find for supercomputers?

CHAPTER **3**

Interacting with Your Computer

CONTENTS

OBJECTIVES

When you complete this chapter, you will be able to do the following:

■ List at least three common input and output devices.

■ Name the components of a mouse and list the common techniques used to maintain a mouse.

■ Describe the processes a video monitor uses to display images.

■ Name three types of printers and list the advantages and disadvantages of each.

■ Explain how input and output devices communicate with the other parts of the computer.

devices enable the computer to give you information about the tasks being performed, or the results of a completed task. Common output devices are the monitor and printer, but other kinds of output devices also are available for special purposes.

Some computer devices provide both input and output functions. An obvious example is the modem. Although it is generally considered to be a communications device, it receives input from and sends output to other sources. When you send and receive e-mail, for example, the modem functions as an input and output device, enabling you to share information with someone using another computer.

The first part of this chapter is devoted to input devices, the second to output. The discussions focus on the hardware you will use the most: the keyboard, mouse, monitor, and printer. You will learn what types of input and output devices are available and the advantages of each. In addition, you will read about many other types of input and output devices, such as scanners, trackballs, speakers, and plotters. At the end of the chapter, you will learn how ports, expansion cards, and expansion slots are used to connect I/O devices to the rest of the computer.

IF the CPU is the brain of the computer, then the input and output devices are the eyes, ears, mouth, and hands. From the user's point of view, input and output (I/O) devices are just as important as the CPU—more so, in fact, because after you have purchased and set up the computer, you can take the CPU for granted. I/O devices, however, are the parts with which you interact, so your ability to use them effectively is critical to how well you can use the whole system.

Input and output devices do exactly what their names suggest. Input devices enable you to input information and commands into the computer. Common input devices include the keyboard and mouse, but many other types of input devices exist. Output

THE KEYBOARD

The keyboard is the primary input device for entering text and numbers. It is a relatively simple device, consisting of about 100 keys, each of which sends a different character code to the CPU. It was one of the first peripherals to be used with PCs, and it is still the most common; you will find a keyboard either built into or attached to every PC.

If you have not used a computer keyboard or a typewriter, you will learn one important fact very quickly: you can use a computer much more effectively if you know how to type. The skill of typing, or **keyboarding**, as it is often called today, implies the ability to enter text by using all ten fingers—and *without* having to look at the keys. Certainly, you can use a computer without being able to type, and many people do. Some people claim that when computers can understand handwriting and speech, typing will become unnecessary. For now, however, keyboarding is the fastest way to enter text and other data into a computer.

The Standard Keyboard Layout

Keyboards for personal computers come in many styles. The various models differ in size, shape, and feel, but except for a few special-purpose keys, most keyboards are laid out almost identically. The most common keyboard layout used today is the IBM Enhanced Keyboard. It has 101 keys arranged in five groups, as shown in Figure 3.1.

The **alphanumeric keys**—the parts of the keyboard that look like a typewriter—are arranged the same way on virtually every keyboard and typewriter. Sometimes this common arrangement is called the **QWERTY** layout because the first six keys on the top row of letters are *Q, W, E, R, T,* and *Y.* In addition to letters and punctuation marks, the alphanumeric keys include the **modifier keys**, so named because they are used in conjunction with the other keys. You

Figure 3.1 ◀
The standard keyboard layout.

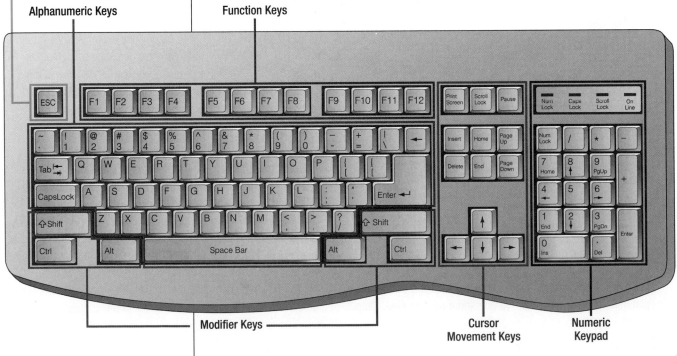

Escape Key
Alphanumeric Keys
Function Keys
Modifier Keys
Cursor Movement Keys
Numeric Keypad

press a letter or number while holding down one of the modifier keys. On a PC, the modifier keys are Shift, Ctrl (an abbreviation of "Control"), and Alt (an abbreviation of "Alternate"). The modifier keys on a Macintosh are Shift, Ctrl, Option, and Command.

The **numeric keypad**, usually located on the right side of the keyboard, looks like an adding machine, with its ten digits and mathematical operators (+, –, *, and /).

The fourth part of the keyboard consists of the **function keys**. The function keys (F1, F2, and so on) are usually arranged in a row along the top of the keyboard. They allow you to give the computer commands without keyboarding long strings of characters. Each function key's purpose depends on the program you are using. For example, in most programs, F1 is the help key. When you press it, a screen displays information about the program you are using.

The fifth part of the keyboard is the set of **cursor-movement keys**, which let you change the position of the cursor on the screen. In a word processing program, there is a mark on the screen where the characters you type will be entered. This mark, called the **cursor** or **insertion point**, can appear on the screen as a box, a line, or a symbol that looks like a capital I, known as the **I-beam cursor**. Figure 3.2 shows a typical cursor.

Keyboards also feature four special-purpose keys, each of which performs a specialized function:

- **Esc.** This key's function depends on the program or operating environment you are using. Typically, the Esc key is used to "back up" one level in a multilevel environment. For example, if you open several dialog boxes, one from the other, you can press Esc to close them in reverse order.

- **Print Screen.** This key sends an "image" of the screen's contents directly to the printer. The Print Screen key, however, works only when a text-mode display is on the screen; it does not work with graphics programs or graphical environments.

- **Scroll Lock.** Despite its name, the Scroll Lock key does not necessarily make the screen's contents scroll. Although it does stop a scrolling screen in a DOS program (or a DOS command window), it may serve another purpose, depending on the program you are using. Usually, this key controls the functions of the cursor-movement keys. With some programs, Scroll Lock causes the cursor to remain stationary on the screen, and the document's contents move around it. When Scroll Lock is turned off, the cursor moves normally. This key does not function at all in some programs.

- **Pause.** In some programs, the Pause key can be used to stop a command in progress.

Many variations have been made on the standard keyboard, primarily for the sake of comfort and to reduce repetitive stress injuries. People who type a great

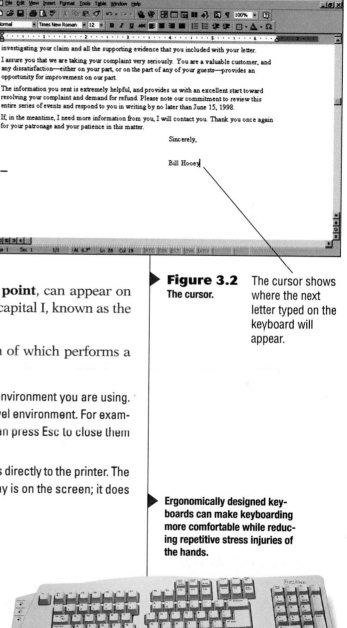

▶ **Figure 3.2**
The cursor.

The cursor shows where the next letter typed on the keyboard will appear.

▶ Ergonomically designed keyboards can make keyboarding more comfortable while reducing repetitive stress injuries of the hands.

deal are susceptible to arm and hand fatigue and strain; new ergonomically correct keyboards can help reduce those problems.

How the Computer Accepts Input from the Keyboard

When you press a key on a keyboard, you might think the keyboard simply sends that letter to the computer—after all, that is what appears to happen. Actually, it is more complex than that, as shown in Figure 3.3.

A tiny computer chip, called the **keyboard controller**, notes that a key has been pressed. The keyboard controller places a code into a part of its memory, called the **keyboard buffer**, indicating which key was pressed. This code is called the key's **scan code**. The keyboard controller then signals the computer's system software that something has happened at the keyboard. It does not specify what has occurred, just that something has. The signal the keyboard sends to the computer is a special kind of message called an **interrupt request**. The keyboard controller sends an interrupt request to the system software when it receives a complete keystroke. For example, if you type the letter *r*, the controller immediately issues an interrupt request. (If you hold down the Shift key before typing *R*, the controller waits until the whole key combination has been entered.)

When the system software receives an interrupt request, it evaluates the request to determine the appropriate response. When a keypress has occurred, the system reads the memory location in the keyboard buffer that contains the scan code of the key that was pressed. It then passes the key's scan code to the CPU.

Actually, the keyboard buffer can store many keystrokes at one time. This is necessary because some time elapses between the pressing of a key and the computer's reading of that key from the keyboard buffer. Also, programmers must put instructions into their programs to read keystrokes (reading does not happen automatically) because the program might be doing something else at the moment a key is pressed. With the keystrokes stored in a buffer, the program can react to them when convenient.

Figure 3.3
How input is received from the keyboard.

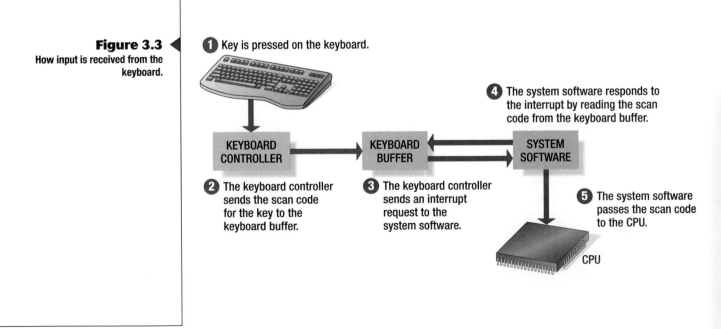

① Key is pressed on the keyboard.

④ The system software responds to the interrupt by reading the scan code from the keyboard buffer.

KEYBOARD CONTROLLER

KEYBOARD BUFFER

SYSTEM SOFTWARE

② The keyboard controller sends the scan code for the key to the keyboard buffer.

③ The keyboard controller sends an interrupt request to the system software.

⑤ The system software passes the scan code to the CPU.

CPU

THE MOUSE

If you had bought a personal computer in the early 1980s, a keyboard would probably have been the only input device that came with it. Today, all new PCs come with some kind of **pointing device** as standard equipment. If the computer is a desktop or tower model, the pointing device is usually a mouse. A mouse is an input device that rolls around on a flat surface (usually on a desk) and controls the pointer. The **pointer** is an on-screen object, usually an arrow, that is used to select text, access menus, move files, or interact with programs, files, or data that appear on the screen.

NORTON Online

For information on **mice** and other **pointing devices**, visit this book's Web site at www.glencoe.com/norton/online

The mouse first gained widespread recognition when it was packaged with the Apple Macintosh computer in 1984. Initially, some users scoffed at this simple tool, but it quickly became apparent that the mouse is very convenient for certain types of input. For example, a mouse lets you position the cursor anywhere on the screen quickly and easily without having to use the cursor-movement keys. You simply move the pointer to the on-screen position you want, press the mouse button, and the cursor appears there.

The mouse's strengths are so numerous that its use changed the entire personal computing industry. Although the Macintosh operating system was the first widely available system to take advantage of the mouse, the tool's popularity grew rapidly. By the late 1980s, DOS programs were incorporating the mouse, and Windows would soon emerge as the new standard in mouse-aware computer interfaces.

Instead of forcing you to type or issue commands from the keyboard, the mouse and mouse-based operating systems let you choose commands from easy-to-use menus and dialog boxes. The result is a much more intuitive way to use computers. Instead of remembering obscure command names, users can figure out (sometimes pretty easily) where commands and options are located.

Mouse

Most modern personal computers come equipped with a mouse.

A mouse also allows you to create graphic elements on the screen, such as lines, curves, and freehand shapes. With this new capability, the mouse helped establish the computer as a versatile tool for graphic designers, starting what has since become a revolution in that field.

Using the Mouse

You use a mouse to point to a location on the screen. Push the mouse forward across your desk, and the pointer moves up; push the mouse to the left, and the pointer moves to the left. To point to an object or location on the screen, you simply use the mouse to place the pointer on top of the object or location.

Everything you do with a mouse you accomplish by combining pointing with four other techniques: clicking, double-clicking, dragging, and right-clicking. Clicking, double-clicking, and dragging are illustrated in Figure 3.4.

Pointer

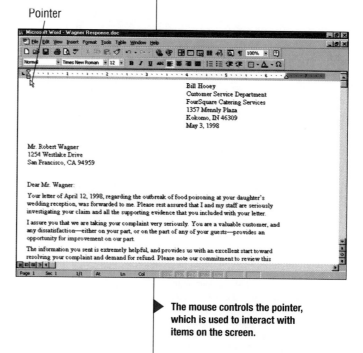

The mouse controls the pointer, which is used to interact with items on the screen.

To **click** something with the mouse means to move the pointer to the item on the screen and to press and release the mouse button once. To **double-click** an item means to point to it with the mouse pointer and then press and release the mouse button twice in rapid succession. To **drag** an item, you position the mouse pointer over the item, press the mouse button, and hold it down as you move the mouse. As you move the pointer, the item is "dragged" along with it. You then can drop the item in a new position on the screen. This technique is called **drag-and-drop** editing.

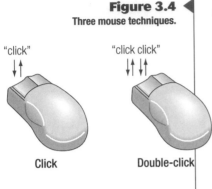

Figure 3.4
Three mouse techniques.

"click"
Click

"click click"
Double-click

Drag

Although most mice have two buttons, clicking, double-clicking, and dragging are usually carried out with the left mouse button. Many mice have only one button, whereas other types of mice can have three or more buttons. The buttons' uses are determined by the computer's operating system, application software, and mouse-control software.

The mouse usually sits to the right of the keyboard (for right-handed people), and the user maneuvers the mouse with the right hand, pressing the left button with the right forefinger, as shown in Figure 3.5. For this reason, the left mouse button is sometimes called the primary mouse button.

If you are left-handed, you can configure the right mouse button as the primary button (this is done by an operating system command). This configuration lets you place the mouse to the left of the keyboard, control the mouse with your left hand, and use your left forefinger for most mouse actions.

Although the primary mouse button is used for most mouse actions, an increasing number of programs also use the right mouse button. Windows 98, for example, uses the right mouse button extensively to open shortcut menus (as does its predecessor, Windows 95). Using the right mouse button is known as **right-clicking**.

The Inner Workings of a Mouse

A mouse is really a simple device. The most common type has a ball inside it that extends just below the housing. When you slide the mouse around on a flat surface, such as a desktop or a mouse pad, the ball rolls. Figure 3.6 shows an exploded view of a mouse.

Inside the mouse, on two sides of the ball, at a 90-degree angle to each other, are two small rollers that touch the ball and spin when the ball rolls. Figure 3.7 shows how moving a mouse diagonally causes the rollers to rotate.

Figure 3.5
Right-handed users generally keep the mouse to the right of the keyboard, so that they can manipulate the mouse with their right hand. Left-handed persons can easily place the mouse on the left side of the keyboard and switch the mouse buttons' functions.

A sensor detects how much each roller spins and sends this information to the computer. The computer translates the information and changes the position of the on-screen pointer to correspond to the position indicated by the mouse.

Using simple operating system commands, you can change the mouse's "sensitivity." That is, you can configure the mouse so that it responds more sensitively to your hand's movements, and so that the pointer moves faster or slower on the screen. You can even set mice pointers to leave "trails" behind them, to make their movements easier to follow.

Like the keyboard, a mouse does not actually send a message directly to the program that the computer is running. Rather, it sends an interrupt request to the CPU. The program that is running checks regularly to see whether the mouse has been used; if it has, the program reads a memory location to see what happened and then reacts appropriately.

Figure 3.6
Coverplate and mouse ball removed to show rollers.

Although most mouse units are connected directly to computers with a cord, some are not. A cordless mouse communicates with a special controller in or near the computer by transmitting a low-intensity radio or infrared signal. Cordless mice are more expensive than their tailed cousins, but many people like the freedom of movement they allow without the restriction of a cord.

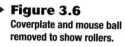

NORTON Online

For more information on **optical mice**, visit this book's Web site at www.glencoe.com/norton/online

Another difference between mice is the way in which they sense movement. Most track the rotation of rollers, but a few track movement optically by sensing the movement of dots or a grid on the mouse pad. These optical models are generally more expensive. They are also less versatile because they can be used only on their own special pads. Their chief advantage is that they are highly sensitive and therefore more accurate than standard mice.

Figure 3.7
How the mouse controls the pointer.

Taking Care of a Mouse

A mouse rolls around on the surface of a mouse pad or a desk, so it tends to pick up tiny objects that are scattered there, such as dust and hair. After a while, the mouse will not work well because it is dirty. The pointer will seem to get stuck on the screen, and the mouse will bump along as though it had a flat tire. When this happens, it is time to clean your mouse.

1 When the mouse moves...

2 ...the rolling mouse ball spins the rollers.

3 The information from the spinning rollers is sent to the system software, which controls the pointer.

To clean the mouse, disconnect it from your computer. Then turn it over and find the coverplate (see Figure 3.8). Rotate the coverplate in the direction of the arrows about a quarter turn; then turn the mouse over in your hand. The coverplate and the mouse ball should fall out. Wipe the mouse ball with a dry, clean cloth; then set it aside.

The problem with the mouse is almost certain to be with the rollers. Use a pair of tweezers to remove any debris stuck to or wrapped around the rollers. If the rollers appear grimy, you can gently wipe them with a cotton swab soaked in alcohol and then let them dry completely before reassembling the mouse. When the rollers are clean, replace the ball and coverplate. That should get you rolling smoothly again.

1 Take the coverplate off and remove the mouse ball.

2 Remove the debris and fuzz that is stuck to the rollers.

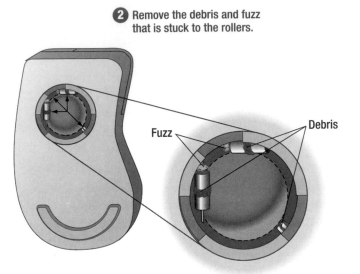

Fuzz

Debris

Figure 3.8
Cleaning the mouse's rollers.

The Trackball

A trackball is a pointing device that works like an upside-down mouse. You rest your thumb on the exposed ball and your fingers on the buttons. To move the pointer around the screen, you roll the ball with your thumb. Because you do not move the whole device, a trackball requires less space than a mouse; so when space is limited, a trackball can be a boon. Trackballs gained popularity with the advent of laptop computers, which typically are used on laps or on small work surfaces without room for a mouse.

Like mice, trackballs come in different models. Some trackballs are large and heavy, with a ball about the same size as a cue ball. Others are much smaller. On portable computers, trackballs may be built directly into the keyboard, slide out of the system unit in a small drawer, or clamp to the side of the keyboard. Most trackballs feature two buttons, although three-button models are

NORTON Online

For information on many different **alternatives to the standard keyboard**, visit this book's Web site at www.glencoe.com/norton/online

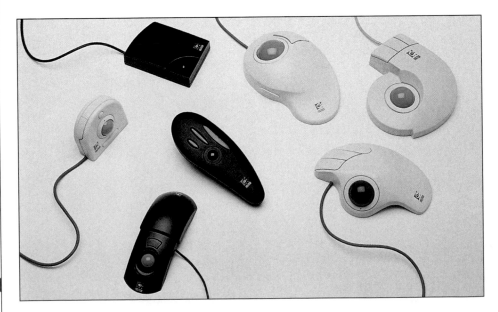

Trackballs come in many different shapes and sizes.

also available. Trackball units also are available in right- and left-handed models.

Some trackballs, such as the Trackman Live from Logitech, are not even attached to the computer and act like a remote control for the pointer. They are especially useful when giving presentations because the presenter often walks around the room instead of sitting at a computer. Another wireless innovation—the Surfman cordless Internet controller—is a handheld trackball designed specially for navigating the Internet. It includes special software that adapts the user's Internet browser for use with the controller.

The Trackpad

The **trackpad** is a stationary pointing device that many people find less tiring to use than a mouse or trackball. The movement of a finger across a small touch surface is translated into pointer movement on the computer screen. The touch-sensitive surface may be just between 1.5 and 2 inches square, so the finger never has to move far. The trackpad's size also makes it well suited for a notebook computer. Some notebook models feature a built-in trackpad rather than a mouse or trackball.

The Trackman Live, from Logitech, is a remote control trackball. It is especially handy for giving stand-up presentations.

Like mice, trackpads usually are separate from the keyboard in desktop computers and attach to the computer through a cord. Some special keyboards, however, feature built-in trackpads. This keeps the pad handy and frees a port that would otherwise be used by the trackpad.

Pointers in the Keyboard

Several companies now offer another space-saving pointing device, consisting of a small joystick positioned near the middle of the keyboard, typically between the *g* and *h* keys. The joystick is controlled with either forefinger. Two buttons that perform the same function as mouse buttons are just beneath the spacebar and are pressed with the thumb. Because it occupies so little space, the device is built into several laptop models. Another advantage is that users do not have to take their hands off the keyboard, so the device saves time and effort.

IBM's ThinkPad comes with the TrackPoint pointing device, as do several models of desktop keyboards. The pointer is controlled by pushing the red TrackPoint device forward, back, left, or right. Commands are executed by clicking the TrackPoint buttons, just below the spacebar.

No generic term has emerged for this device yet, although several manufacturers are referring to it as an **integrated pointing device**. On the IBM laptop called the ThinkPad, the pointing device is called the **TrackPoint**. The TrackPoint is also available on some models of desktop computer keyboards.

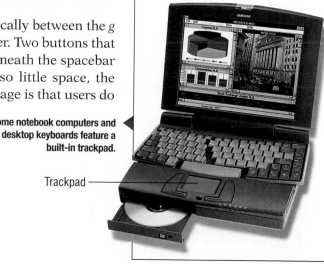

Some notebook computers and desktop keyboards feature a built-in trackpad.

Trackpad

Productivity Tip

Perfect Navigation

In the 1980s, as programmers began packing more features into PC software, they also developed ways for users to issue an ever-increasing number of commands. Software packages came with long lists of commands, all of which had to be entered at the keyboard. As a result, the computer keyboard rapidly became valuable, but crowded, real estate.

To make things easier, programmers began devising *keyboard shortcuts*, which enable users to issue commands quickly by typing a short combination of keystrokes. Keyboard shortcuts involve using a special-purpose key (such as Ctrl on the PC or Command on the Macintosh) along with one or more alphanumeric keys. To print a document in many applications, for example, the user can press Ctrl+P on a PC or ⌘+P on a Macintosh.

Function keys (the "F keys" on a PC's keyboard) became important, as well. The F1 key, for example, became the universal way to access online help. Personal computer keyboards originally had 10 function keys; eventually that number was expanded to 12 keys.

Still, a keyboard can hold only so many keys, and the lists of keyboard shortcuts started to become unmanageable. A single program could have dozens of *hotkeys,* as the shortcuts came to be called. If you used several programs, you had to learn a different set of shortcuts for each one.

The Common User Access (CUA) standard led to standardization of many commonly used hotkeys across different programs and environments. CUA dictated that different programs use many of the same hotkeys, to make them easier to remember, for example:

Windows	Mac	Function
Ctrl+N	⌘+N	Open the New file dialog box
Ctrl+O	⌘+O	Open the Open file dialog box
Ctrl+Z	⌘+Z	Undo an earlier command
Ctrl+F	⌘+F	Open the Find dialog box

These are some of the shortcut keys available in Microsoft Word.

Microsoft Word

Help Topics | Back | Options

Keys for editing and moving text and graphics

Delete text and graphics

To	Press
Delete one character to the left	BACKSPACE
Delete one word to the left	CTRL+BACKSPACE
Delete one character to the right	DELETE
Delete one word to the right	CTRL+DELETE
Cut selected text to the Clipboard	CTRL+X
Undo the last action	CTRL+Z
Cut to the Spike	CTRL+F3

Copy and move text and graphics

To	Press
Copy text or graphics	CTRL+C
Move text or graphics	F2 (then move the insertion point and press ENTER)
Create AutoText	ALT+F3
Paste the Clipboard contents	CTRL+V
Paste the Spike contents	CTRL+SHIFT+F3

Despite such standards, pointing devices (such as the mouse) came along none too soon for hotkey-weary computer users. Microsoft Windows and the Macintosh operating system gained popularity because of their easy-to-use, mouse-oriented graphical interfaces, and even DOS-based programs began using toolbars, pull-down menus, and dialog boxes. This made commands easier to issue because users could select them visually from menus and dialog boxes, using the mouse. Emphasis rapidly began shifting away from the keyboard and to the screen; today, many users of popular programs probably can't tell you what their function keys do!

Because pointing is a manual process, however, it can slow you down. As menus and dialog boxes become increasingly crowded, commands can be hard to find, and their locations can be as difficult to remember as keyboard shortcuts.

Many computer users are overcoming these problems by using a combination of keyboard shortcuts and a pointing device. You use one hand to issue many basic shortcuts (such as Ctrl+P, Ctrl+S, and others), or to launch macros. A **macro** is a series of commands that a program memorizes for you; macros enable you to issue an entire set of commands in just a few keystrokes. These techniques minimize keystrokes and leave a hand free to use a pointing device.

Digitizing tablets and other sophisticated pointing devices can replace keyboards entirely. Tablets can be configured to work with command templates; the user issues a command or macro simply by pointing to a specific spot on the tablet template.

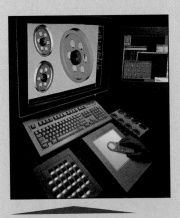

Sophisticated pointing devices, such as tablets, can actually replace the keyboard in pointing-intensive applications, such as CAD programs.

OTHER INPUT DEVICES

Although the keyboard and mouse are the input devices with which people work most often on the desktop, there are a number of other ways to get data into a computer. Sometimes the tool is simply a matter of choice. In many cases, however, the usual tools may not be appropriate. For example, in a dusty factory or warehouse, a keyboard or mouse can become clogged with dirt pretty quickly. Also, alternative input devices are important parts of some special-purpose computers.

NORTON Online

For information on **alternative input devices**, such as specialized mice and other pointing devices, visit this book's Web site at www.glencoe.com/norton/online

Pens

Pen-based systems use an electronic pen as their primary input device. You hold the pen in your hand and write on a special pad or directly on the screen. You can also use the pen as a pointing device, like a mouse, to select commands. It is important to realize that the screen is the input device, not the pen. The screen detects pressure, light, or an electrostatic charge that comes from the pen and then stores the position of that signal.

Although pen-based systems would seem like a handy way to get text into the computer for word processing, perfecting the technology to decipher people's handwriting with 100 percent reliability is so complex that pens are not generally used to enter large amounts of text. They are more commonly used for data collection, where the touch of a pen might select a "yes" or "no" box, or to mark a box next to a part that must be ordered or a service that has been requested. Another common use is inputting signatures or messages that are stored and transmitted as a graphic image, such as a fax. The computer may not be able to decipher your scrawled note, but if it appears on your coworkers' screens and they can read it, that is all that is required. When delivery-service drivers make deliveries, they often have recipients sign their names on such a computer-based pad. As handwriting-recognition technology becomes more reliable, pen-based systems will undoubtedly become more common.

To interact with a pen-based computer, the user can point, tap, draw, and write on the unit's screen with a pen.

Touch Screens

Touch screens allow the user to point directly at the computer display, usually to select from a menu of choices on the screen. Most touch-screen computers use sensors in, or near, the computer's screen that can detect the touch of a finger, sensing either the finger's pressure or warmth.

Touch screens are appropriate in environments where dirt or weather would render keyboards and pointing devices useless, and where a simple, intuitive interface is important. They are well suited for simple applications such as automated teller machines or public information kiosks. Touch screens have become common in department stores, drugstores, and supermarkets, where they

When you receive a package via UPS, you sign your name on a pen-based computer, which stores a digital image of your signature.

A student obtains campus information at a public information kiosk.

are used for all kinds of purposes, from creating personalized greeting cards to selling lottery tickets. There are even computerized touch screens on slot machines in gambling casinos.

Bar Code Readers

The most widely used input device after the keyboard and mouse are **bar code readers**. The most common type of bar code reader is the flatbed model, which is commonly found in supermarkets and department stores. Workers for delivery services, such as Federal Express, also use handheld bar code readers to identify packages in the field.

These devices convert a **bar code**, which is a pattern of printed bars on products, into a product number by emitting a beam of light—frequently a laser beam—that reflects off the bar code image. A light-sensitive detector identifies

the bar code image by recognizing special bars at both ends of the image. After the detector has identified the bar code, it converts the individual bar patterns into numeric digits. The special bars at each end of the image are different, so the reader can tell whether the bar code has been read right-side up or upside down.

To enter prices and product information into a cash register, a cashier passes groceries over a bar code reader. The bar code reader projects a web of laser beams onto the bar code and measures the pattern of the reflected light.

After the bar code reader has converted a bar code image into a number, it feeds that number to the computer, just as though the number had been typed on a keyboard.

Image Scanners and Optical Character Recognition (OCR)

The bar code reader is actually just a special type of image scanner. **Image scanners** convert any image into electronic form by shining light onto the image and sensing the intensity of the reflection at every point. Figure 3.9 illustrates the process.

Color scanners use filters to separate the components of color into the primary additive colors (red, green, and blue) at each point. Red, green, and blue are known as primary additive colors because they can be combined to create any other color.

The image scanner is useful because it translates printed images into an electronic format that can be stored in a computer's memory. You can then use software to organize or manipulate the electronic image.

NORTON Online

For more detailed information on **scanning** and **OCR**, visit this book's Web site at **www.glencoe.com/norton/online**

Handheld bar code readers are used to track FedEx packages.

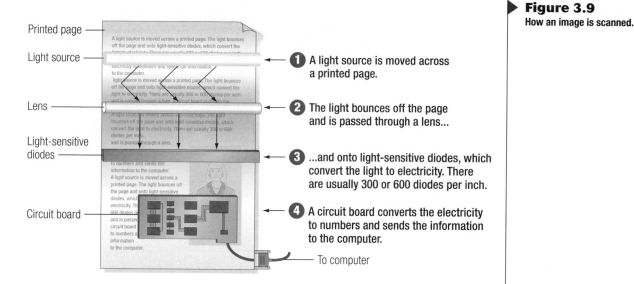

Printed page

Light source

Lens

Light-sensitive
diodes

Circuit board

To computer

1 A light source is moved across a printed page.

2 The light bounces off the page and is passed through a lens...

3 ...and onto light-sensitive diodes, which convert the light to electricity. There are usually 300 or 600 diodes per inch.

4 A circuit board converts the electricity to numbers and sends the information to the computer.

For example, if you scan a photo, you can use Adobe Photoshop—a graphics program—to increase the contrast or adjust the colors. If you have scanned a text document, you might want to use **optical character recognition (OCR)** software to translate the image into text that you can edit. When a scanner first creates an image from a page, the image is stored in the computer's memory as a bitmap. A **bitmap** is a grid of dots, each dot represented by one or more bits. The job of OCR software is to translate that array of dots into text (that is, ASCII codes) that the computer can interpret as letters and numbers.

To translate bitmaps into text, the OCR software looks at each character and tries to match the character with its own assumptions about how the letters should look. Because it is difficult to make a computer recognize an unlimited number of typefaces and fonts, OCR software is extremely complex. For example, Figure 3.10 shows a few of the many ways the letter g can appear on a printed page.

Despite the complexity of the task, OCR software has become quite advanced. Today, for example, many programs can decipher a page of text received by a fax machine. In fact, computers with fax

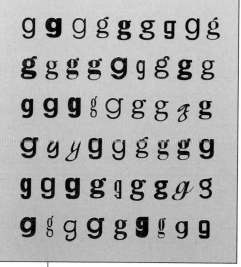

To use a handheld scanner, you roll the end of the scanner across the image. If the image is wider than the scanner, you can make multiple passes.

modems can use OCR software to convert faxes they receive directly into text that can be edited with a word processor.

Scanners come in a range of sizes, from handheld models to flatbed scanners that sit on a desktop. **Handheld scanners** are less expensive but typically require multiple passes over a single page because they are not as wide as letter-size paper. They do, however, have the advantage of portability.

Flatbed scanners are more expensive than handheld scanners but offer higher-quality reproduction, and they can scan a page in a single pass. (Multiple scans are sometimes required for color, however.) To use a flatbed scanner, you place the printed image on a piece of glass similar to the way a page is placed on a photocopier.

There are also medium-size scanners that are sheet-fed. That is, you feed the sheet through the scanner, in a manner similar to the way a page is fed through a fax machine.

Microphones and Voice Recognition

Now that sound capabilities are a standard part of computers, microphones are becoming increasingly important as input devices. Sound is used most often in multimedia, where the presentation can benefit from narration, music, or sound effects. In software, sounds are used to alert the user to a problem or to prompt the user for input.

For this type of sound input, a digitized recording is all that is required. All you need to make such a recording are a microphone (or some other audio input device, such as a CD player) and a **sound card** that translates the electrical signal from the microphone into a digitized form that the computer can store and process. Sound cards can also translate digitized sounds back into analog signals that can then be sent to the speakers.

There is also a demand for translating spoken words into text, much as there is a demand for translating handwriting into text. Translating voice to text is a capability known as **voice recognition** (or **speech recognition**). With it, you can speak to the computer instead of typing, and you can control the computer with simple commands, such as "open" or "cancel."

Voice-recognition software takes the smallest individual sounds in a language, called *phonemes*, and translates them into text or commands. Even though English uses only about 40 phonemes, a sound can have several different meanings ("two" versus "too," for example) making reliable translation difficult. The challenge for voice-recognition software is to deduce a sound's meaning correctly from its context and to distinguish meaningful sounds from background noise.

Voice-recognition software has been used in commercial applications for years but traditionally has been extremely costly, as well as difficult to develop and use. Low-cost commercial versions of voice-recognition software are now available and promise to be a boon to users who cannot type or have difficulty using a keyboard. Commercial voice-recognition software packages have large stored "vocabularies" or words they can recognize. However, users often need to spend a great deal of time learning to use the software (speech must be clear and each word succinctly pronounced) and "training" the software to recognize their pronunciation. This process involves dictating to the software, stopping, and then going back and correcting the software's errors.

NORTON Online

For information on **digital video cameras** and how they work, visit this book's Web site at www.glencoe.com/norton/online

Video Input

With the growth of multimedia and the Internet, computer users are adding video input capabilities to their systems in great numbers. Applications such as videoconferencing enable users to use full-motion video images, captured by a **PC video camera**, and transmit them to a limited number of recipients on a network or to the world on the Internet.

The video cameras used with computers are similar to those used in production studios. PC video cameras, however, **digitize** images by breaking them into individual pixels. Each pixel's color and other characteristics are stored as digital code. This code is then compressed (video images can be very large) so that it can be stored on disk or transmitted over a network.

Many PC video cameras attach to the top of the PC screen, enabling the user to "capture" images of himself or herself while working at the computer. This arrangement is handy for videoconferencing, where multiple users see and talk to one another in real time over a network or Internet connection.

Using **video cards**, the user can also connect other video devices, such as VCRs and camcorders, to the PC. This enables the user to transfer images from the video equipment to the PC, and vice versa. Affordable video cards are enabling home users to edit their videotapes like professionals.

Using a PC video camera system, such as Intel's Create & Share system, you can conduct online video-conferences and include full-motion video in your documents or e-mail.

Digital Cameras

Digital cameras work in much the same way as PC video cameras, except digital cameras are portable, handheld devices that capture still images. Whereas normal film cameras capture images on a specially coated film, digital cameras capture images electronically. To do this, the digital camera digitizes the image, compresses it, and stores it on a special disk or ROM card. The user can then copy the information onto a PC, where the image can be edited, copied, printed, embedded in a document, or transmitted to another user. A wide range of digital cameras is available, from inexpensive home-use models to professional versions costing several thousand dollars.

THE MONITOR

Although there are many kinds of input devices, there are currently just three common types of output devices: monitors, printers, and sound systems. Of the three, monitors are the most important because they are the output devices with which users interact most often.

Indeed, users often form opinions about a computer just from the look of the monitor alone. They want to know: Is the image crisp and clear? Does the monitor display colorful graphics? Two important elements determine the quality of the image a monitor displays: the monitor itself and the video controller. In this section, you will learn about both of these elements in detail and find out how they work together to display text and graphics.

Two basic types of monitors are used with PCs. The first is the typical monitor that you see on a desktop computer—it looks a lot like a television screen and works the same way. This type uses a large vacuum tube, called a **cathode ray tube (CRT)**. The second type, known as a **flat-panel display**, is used with notebook computers. Either of these types can be **monochrome**, displaying only one color against a contrasting background (often black); **grayscale**, displaying varying intensities of gray against a white background; or **color**, displaying anywhere from four to millions of colors. Today, most new monitors display in color.

How a CRT Monitor Displays an Image

Figure 3.11 shows how a typical CRT monitor works.

Near the back of a monochrome or grayscale monitor housing is an electron gun. The gun shoots a beam of electrons through a magnetic coil, which aims the beam at the front of the monitor. The back of the monitor's screen is coated with phosphors, chemicals that glow when they are struck by the electron beam. The screen's phosphor coating is organized into a grid of dots. The smallest number of phosphor dots that the gun can focus on is called a **pixel**, a contraction of *pi*cture *el*ement. Modern monochrome and grayscale monitors can focus on pixels as small as a single phosphor dot.

Actually, the electron gun does not just focus on a spot and shoot electrons there. It systematically aims at every pixel on the screen, starting at the top-left corner and scanning to the right edge, and then dropping down a tiny distance and scanning another line, as shown in Figure 3.12.

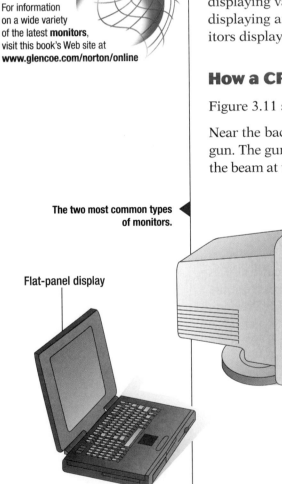

The two most common types of monitors.

Flat-panel display

CRT

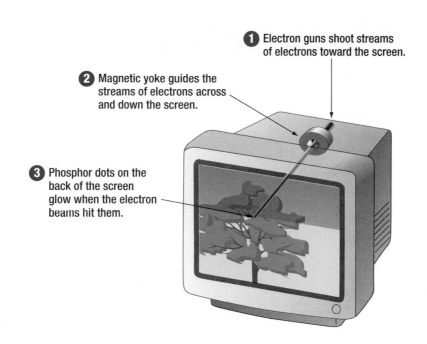

① Electron guns shoot streams of electrons toward the screen.

② Magnetic yoke guides the streams of electrons across and down the screen.

③ Phosphor dots on the back of the screen glow when the electron beams hit them.

▶ **Figure 3.11**
How a CRT monitor creates an image.

Like human eyes reading the letters on a page, the electron beam follows each line of pixels from left to right until it reaches the bottom of the screen. Then it starts over. As the electron gun scans, the circuitry driving the monitor adjusts the intensity of each beam to determine whether a pixel is on or off or, in the case of grayscale, how brightly each pixel glows.

A color monitor works just like a monochrome one, except that there are three electron beams instead of just one. The three guns represent the primary additive colors (red, green, and blue), although the beams they emit are colorless. Each pixel on the screen is made up of three tiny red, green, and blue phosphors arranged in a triangle. When the beams of each of these guns are combined and focused on a point on the screen, the phosphors at that point light up to form a tiny spot of white light. Different colors can be displayed by combining various intensities of the three beams. All monitors use masks with holes in them to align the beams. The holes in most monitors are arranged in triangles. Taking a slightly different approach, Sony Trinitron monitors, another popular model, use a single gun and a mask with parallel slots to align the beam on the colored phosphors.

① The electron gun scans from left to right,

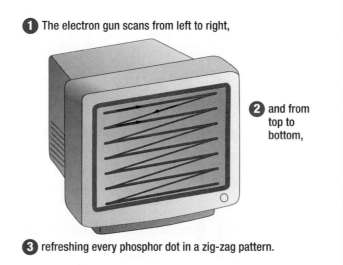

② and from top to bottom,

③ refreshing every phosphor dot in a zig-zag pattern.

▶ **Figure 3.12**
The scanning pattern of the CRT's electron gun.

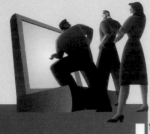

NORTON *Notebook*

Making the Web Accessible

If you have access to the Internet, you have unbelievable resources at your disposal. You can read newspapers, listen to music, or watch video clips.

The key word, however, is *access*. The Internet is not terribly useful for people who cannot access its resources. For persons with physical disabilities, the Internet is not always the user-friendly resource that its proponents claim.

For persons who are visually impaired, navigating the Web is a special challenge. Discerning text-based links can be difficult or impossible, and highly stylized Web sites can be hard to read unless they are modified in some manner. The color-blind user may have difficulty telling hyperlinked text from normal text if the designer has styled links to appear without underlining or some other obvious formatting feature.

The Web can also be a frustrating place for the deaf or hearing-impaired. Many sites feature audio content, but few provide a text or graphical version (or description) of their audio content.

By taking advantage of new technologies, however, and applying some common-sense design strategies, Web designers are opening up the Internet to users who might not ordinarily have access to it. Like many other public areas, the Internet is becoming more accessible to everyone. Here are some of the tools that are making the Web more accessible:

■ *Universal Web pages.* In addition to stylish, highly designed versions of Web pages, designers are adding universal versions of the pages to their sites. The universal versions are stripped of formatting enhancements. These basic pages provide more control to the user; vision-impaired users can enlarge the fonts in their browser, for example, to make these pages easier to read. Hyperlinks are also easier to see.

■ *User-definable style sheets.* Cascading style sheets enable designers or users to customize the appearance of any Web page. Style sheets are called "cascading" because the user can create a style sheet that overrides the page's existing formatting. Vision-impaired users can create style sheets that automatically apply large, highly contrasting fonts to any page they visit, making them easier to view.

■ *Screen readers.* Although they are not new technology, screen readers are finding new applications on the Internet. A screen reader "reads" the contents of the computer screen, converting text to audio output for blind or visually impaired users.

■ *Audio clips.* Most browsers support audio players or plug-ins, and although audio capabilities are not new to the Web, designers are using audio files in new ways to provide information or instructions to blind or visually impaired users.

■ *Document-conversion technology.* At the Adobe, Inc. site, users can convert files from Adobe's Portable Document Format (PDF) into HTML format. The resulting document can be viewed in a browser, giving the user more control over font sizes. Other sites can convert HTML files into Braille or perform other types of conversions.

■ *Captioning.* Microsoft's new Synchronized Accessible Media Interchange (SAMI) format enables designers to embed on-screen captions in audio content. When an audio file is playing from a Web page, SAMI enables the user to view its text or even a musical score.

Although these technologies may seem unique to the Internet, many of them are also being used in other areas of computing. SAMI, for example, is being used in multimedia applications, where audio content can be augmented by captions for the deaf or hearing impaired.

Many Web sites provide audio files containing descriptions or instructions, for blind and visually impaired users.

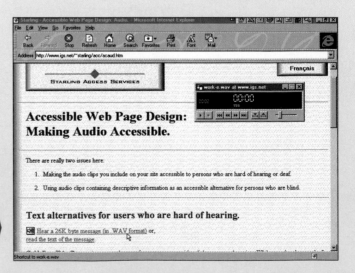

Comparing CRT Monitors

When buying a monitor, it is important to do some comparison shopping first. More than just being aesthetically pleasing, a good monitor is easier on your eyes, allowing you to work longer and more comfortably. A poor monitor will cause eyestrain and headaches and can even cause long-term vision problems.

The first thing to do when shopping for a monitor is to take a close look at the display. Look at a screenful of text and examine how crisp the letters are, especially near the corners of the screen. Also, if you are going to work with graphics, display a picture with which you are familiar and see whether the colors look accurate.

Even if the monitor looks good (or if you are buying it through the mail), you need to check several specifications. These are the most important specifications:

- Size
- Resolution
- Refresh rate
- Dot pitch

NORTON Online

For more information on **monitor manufacturers'** Web sites, visit this book's Web site at **www.glencoe.com/norton/online**

Monitor Size

The physical size of the picture tube has an obvious bearing on how well you can see everything. With a large monitor, as shown in Figure 3.13, you can make the objects on the screen appear bigger, or you can fit more of them on the screen. In other words, bigger is better. Naturally, though, bigger costs more.

Monitors, like televisions, are measured diagonally, in inches across the front of the tube. For example, a 15-inch monitor measures 15 inches from the lower-left to the upper-right corner. Actually, the picture that appears on a monitor is smaller than is indicated by the monitor size because the image cannot extend too far into the corners of the CRT without becoming distorted. The picture on a 15-inch monitor, for example, usually measures about 13 inches diagonally.

Today, most new desktop systems are sold with monitors that measure about 15 inches. Over time, this measurement has gradually increased, so the norm may soon creep up to 17 inches.

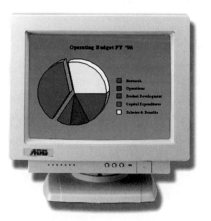
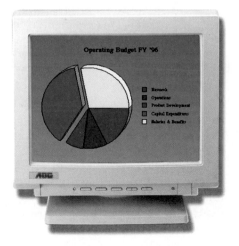

Figure 3.13
Comparison of a 17-inch monitor to a 15-inch monitor.

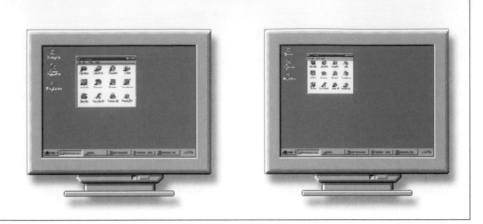

Figure 3.14 ◀
Windows uses this picture of a monitor to show how screen items appear at different resolutions. (a) shows the monitor at a resolution of 640x480. (b) shows it at 800x600. (c) shows it at 1024x768. Notice that more items can fit on the screen at higher resolutions, but the items appear smaller.

Resolution

The **resolution** of a computer monitor is classified by the number of pixels on the screen, expressed as a matrix. For example, a resolution of 640x480 means there are 640 pixels horizontally across the screen and 480 pixels vertically down the screen. Because the actual resolution is determined by the video controller, not by the monitor itself, most monitor specifications list a range of resolutions. For example, most 15-inch monitors have pixel grids that allow for three settings: 640x480, 800x600, and 1024x768, as shown in Figure 3.14.

In the mid-1980s, IBM established the **VGA (Video Graphics Array)** standard of 640x480 pixels. The **SVGA (Super VGA)** standard expanded the resolutions to 800x600 and 1024x768. A few 15-inch monitors, and any good monitor bigger than 15 inches, will include even higher settings. Higher settings are not always better, however, because they can cause objects on screen to appear too small, and this can result in squinting and eyestrain. Most users with 15-inch monitors set them to display either 640x480 or 800x600. Users with 17-inch monitors will often use the higher settings.

Refresh Rate

When shopping for a monitor, the size and resolution are simple choices. The size is likely to be determined by your budget (although you may want to spend more on a big monitor if you are working with graphics). The resolutions tend to be standard. The **refresh rate** of the monitor, however, is neither obvious nor standard. Refresh rate is the number of times per second that the electron guns scan every pixel on the screen. Refresh rate is measured in Hertz (Hz), or in cycles per second. This means that the monitor is refreshing itself at least several dozen times each second.

The refresh rate is an important concern because phosphor dots fade quickly after the electron gun passes over them. Therefore, if the screen is not refreshed often enough, it appears to flicker, and flicker is one of the main causes of eyestrain. The problem is compounded because you may not even detect the flicker; nevertheless, in the long run, it can still cause eyestrain.

Opinions vary as to what is an acceptable refresh rate. In general, a refresh rate of 72 Hz or higher should not cause eyestrain. However, note that some monitors have different refresh rates for different resolutions. Make sure the refresh rate is adequate for the resolution you will be using.

Dot Pitch

The last critical specification of a color monitor is the **dot pitch**, the distance between the phosphor dots that make up a single pixel (see Figure 3.15).

Recall that, in a color monitor, there are three dots—one red, one green, and one blue—in every pixel. If these dots are not close enough together, the images on the screen will not be crisp. Once again, it is difficult to detect slight differences in dot pitch, but blurry pixels will cause eyestrain anyway. In general, when you are looking for a color monitor, look for a dot pitch no greater than 0.28 millimeter.

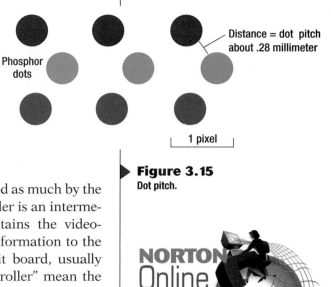

Distance = dot pitch about .28 millimeter

Phosphor dots

1 pixel

Figure 3.15
Dot pitch.

The Video Controller

The quality of the images that a monitor can display is defined as much by the **video controller** as by the monitor itself. The video controller is an intermediary device between the CPU and the monitor. It contains the video-dedicated memory and other circuitry necessary to send information to the monitor for display on the screen. It consists of a circuit board, usually referred to simply as a card ("video card" and "video controller" mean the same thing), which is attached to the computer's motherboard. The processing power of the video controller determines, within the constraints of the monitor, the refresh rate, resolution, and number of colors that can be displayed.

During the 1980s, when most PCs were running DOS and not Windows, the screen displayed ASCII characters. Doing so took little processing power because there were only 256 possible characters and 2,000 text positions on the screen. Rendering each screen required only 4,000 bytes of data.

Windows, however, is a graphical interface, so the CPU must send information to the video controller about every pixel on the screen. At the minimum resolution of 640x480, there are 307,200 pixels to control. Most users run their monitors at 256 colors, so each pixel requires one byte of information. Thus, the computer must send 307,200 bytes to the monitor for each screen.

If the user wants more colors or a higher resolution, the amount of data can be much higher. For example, for the maximum amount of color (24 bits per pixel will render millions of colors) at 1024x768, the computer must send 2,359,296 bytes to the monitor for each screen.

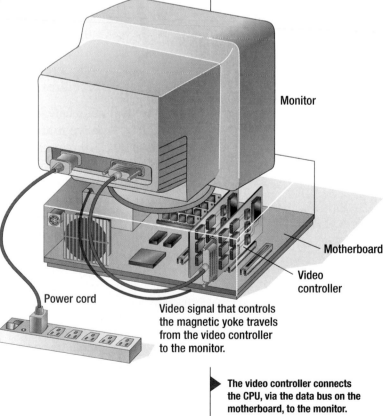

Monitor

Motherboard

Video controller

Power cord

Video signal that controls the magnetic yoke travels from the video controller to the monitor.

The video controller connects the CPU, via the data bus on the motherboard, to the monitor.

The result of these processing demands is that video controllers have increased dramatically in power and importance. There is a microprocessor on the video controller, and the speed of the chip limits the speed at which the monitor can be refreshed. Most video controllers today also include at least 2 MB of **video RAM**, or **VRAM**. (This is in addition to the RAM that is connected to the CPU.) VRAM is "dual-ported," meaning that it can send a screenful of data to the monitor while at the same time receiving the next screenful of data from the CPU. It's faster and more expensive than **DRAM** (Dynamic RAM), the type of memory chip used as RAM for the CPU. Users with large monitors or with heavy graphics needs usually will want even more than 2 MB of VRAM.

Flat-Panel Monitors

CRT monitors are the standard for use with desktop computers because they provide the brightest and clearest picture for the money. There are, however, two major disadvantages associated with CRT monitors. They are big, and they require a lot of power. CRT monitors are not practical for notebook computers, which must be small and need to run off a battery built into the computer. Instead, notebooks use flat-panel monitors that are less than one-inch thick.

Flat-panel monitors for desktops are becoming increasingly popular.

There are several types of flat-panel monitors, but the most common is the **liquid crystal display (LCD) monitor**. The LCD monitor creates images with a special kind of liquid crystal that is normally transparent but becomes opaque when charged with electricity. If you have a handheld calculator, it probably uses liquid crystal. One disadvantage of LCD monitors is that, unlike phosphor, the liquid crystal does not emit light, so there is not enough contrast between the images and their background to make them legible under all conditions. The problem is solved by backlighting the screen. Although this makes the screen easier to read, it requires additional power.

There are two main categories of liquid crystal displays: active matrix and passive matrix. **Passive matrix LCD** relies on transistors for each row and each column of pixels, thus creating a grid that defines the location of each pixel. The color displayed by each pixel is determined by the electricity coming from the transistors at the end of the row and the top of the column. The advantage of passive matrix monitors is that they are less expensive than active matrix, a major consideration in laptops, where the monitor can account for one-third the cost of the entire computer. One disadvantage is that the pixels can be seen only if you are sitting directly in front of the monitor. In other words, the monitor has a narrow viewing angle. Another disadvantage is that passive matrix displays do not refresh the pixels very often. If you move the pointer too quickly, it seems to disappear, an effect known as submarining. Also, animated graphics can appear blurry.

Most notebooks that use passive matrix technology now refer to their screens as **dual-scan LCD**. In dual-scan LCD, the problem of the refresh rate is lessened by scanning through the pixels twice as often. Thus, submarining and blurry graphics are much less troublesome than they were before the dual-scan technique was developed.

Active matrix LCD technology assigns a transistor to each pixel, and each pixel is turned on and off individually. This allows the pixels to be refreshed much more rapidly, so submarining is not a problem with these monitors. In addition, active matrix screens have a wider viewing angle than dual-scan screens. Active matrix displays are considerably more expensive than their passive matrix counterparts, but the performance gains are worth the cost for many users.

Although flat-panel monitors have so far been used primarily on portable computers, a new generation of large, high-resolution flat-panel displays is gaining popularity among users of desktop systems. These new monitors, while providing an equal or larger diagonal display area, take up less desk space and run cooler than traditional CRT monitors. Flat-panel displays for desktops, however, are expensive and produced only by a limited number of vendors. Prices are expected to fall as more manufacturers add flat-panel desktop displays to their product lines.

NORTON Online

For information on the new generation of **flat-panel monitors** for use with desktop PCs, visit this book's Web site at **www.glencoe.com/norton/online**

PRINTERS

Besides the monitor, the other important output device is the printer. Two principal types of printers have become the standard with PCs: laser printers and ink jet printers. In years past, the dot-matrix printer was also a popular choice because it was once far less expensive than the other types. However, ink jet printers now offer much higher quality for about the same price, so dot-matrix printers are used only when physical impact with the paper is important, such as when the user is printing to carbon-copy forms.

In evaluating printers, four criteria are most important:

1_ *Image quality.* Image quality, also known as print resolution, is usually measured in dots per inch (dpi).

2_ *Speed.* Printer speed is measured in the number of pages of text the computer can print each minute. Pages per minute is abbreviated as ppm. Most printers have different ppm ratings for text and graphics because graphics generally take longer to print.

3_ *Initial cost.* The cost of new printers has fallen dramatically in recent years, while their capabilities and speed have improved just as dramatically. It is possible to buy a good-quality personal laser or ink jet printer for $300 or less. Professional-quality, high-output systems can range in price from $1,000 to tens of thousands of dollars.

4_ *Cost of operation.* The cost of ink or toner, and maintenance, varies with the type of printer.

Ink Jet Printers

Ink jet printers create an image directly on paper by spraying ink through tiny nozzles (see Figure 3.16). Ink jet technology has been around since

Figure 3.16
How an ink jet printer creates an image.

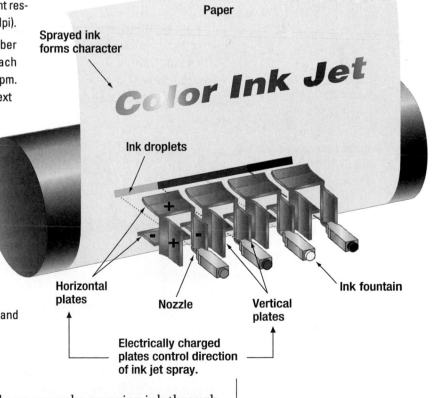

Paper

Sprayed ink forms character

Color Ink Jet

Ink droplets

Horizontal plates

Nozzle

Vertical plates

Ink fountain

Electrically charged plates control direction of ink jet spray.

before the PC boom, but the popularity of ink jet printers jumped around 1990 when the speed and quality improved, and the price plummeted. Today, good ink jet printers are available for as little as $200. These models typically attain print resolutions of at least 360 dots per inch, comparable to that of most laser printers sold before 1992, and they can print from two to four pages per minute (only slightly slower than the slowest laser printers). The operating cost of an ink jet printer is low. Expensive maintenance is rare, and the only part that needs replacement is the ink cartridge, which typically costs less than $20 for black (color cartridges cost slightly more).

Another improvement in ink jet printers has been in the paper they require. For many years, they needed a special paper, and each sheet had to dry before you could touch it. Today, you can run normal photocopy paper through most ink jet printers (although glossy paper looks slightly better), and the ink is dry within a few seconds.

Finally, ink jet printers offer by far the most cost-effective way to print in color. Color ink jet printers have four ink nozzles: cyan (blue), magenta (red), yellow, and black. These four colors are used in almost all color printing because it is possible to combine them to create any color in the visible spectrum. Notice, however, that the colors are different from the primary additive colors (red, green, blue) used in monitors. This is because printed color is the result of light bouncing off the paper, not color transmitted directly from a light source. Consequently, cyan, magenta, yellow, and black are sometimes called subtractive colors. For this reason, color printing is sometimes called four-color printing. Color ink jet printers continue to drop in price. "Last year's model" can be found for less than $250. Color ink jet printers have been a boon to home users and small offices, where cost is usually a more important consideration than speed.

Ink jet printers are now being combined with other technologies to create complete "all-in-one" office machines. Manufacturers such as Hewlett-Packard, Canon, and others are now offering combination printers, copiers, fax machines, and scanners based on ink jet technology. A basic all-in-one unit with black-and-white printing can be purchased for less than $800.

Ink jet technology is the basis for many new "all-in-one" office systems.

High-resolution color systems are considerably more expensive, starting at around $2,000.

Laser Printers

Laser printers are more expensive than ink jet printers, their print quality is higher, and most are faster.

As the name implies, a laser is at the heart of these printers. A separate CPU is built into the printer to interpret the data that it receives from the computer and to control the laser. The result is a complicated piece of equipment, using technology similar to that in photocopiers.

Figure 3.17 shows how a laser printer works.

Just as the electron gun in a graphics monitor can target any pixel, the laser in a laser printer can aim at any point on a drum, creating an electrical charge. **Toner**, which is composed of tiny particles of oppositely charged ink, sticks to the drum in the places the laser has charged. Then, with pressure and heat, the toner is transferred off the drum to the paper. Also like a monitor and its video controller, laser printers contain special memory to store the images they print.

A color laser printer works like a single-color model, except that the process is repeated four times, and a different toner color is used for each pass. The four colors used are the same as in the color ink jet printers: cyan, magenta, yellow, and black

Single-color (black) laser printers typically can produce between 4 and 16 pages of text a minute. However, if you are printing graphics, the output can be a great deal slower. The most common laser printers have resolutions of 600 dpi, both horizontally and vertically, but some high-end models have resolutions of 1200 or 1800 dpi. The printing industry stipulates a resolution of at least 1200 dpi for top-quality professional printing. It is difficult, however, to detect the difference between text printed at 600 dpi and 1200 dpi. The higher resolution is most noticeable in graphics reproduction, such as photographs and artwork.

The quality and speed of laser printers make them ideal for office environments where several users can share the same printer easily via a LAN.

Convenience is another advantage of laser printers. Most can use standard, inexpensive copy paper, which is loaded into a paper tray. The disadvantages of laser printers are the price and the cost of operation. Laser printers start at about $300 and go up dramatically if you want speed, high resolution, or color. In addition, laser printers require new toner cartridges after a few thousand pages, and toner cartridges cost from $40 to $80 for black toner.

On the other hand, the cost of laser printers has come way down. In 1990, a 300 dpi laser printer that printed four pages per minute cost about $1,000. Today, you can get 600 dpi and about the same speed for $500. At the same time, color laser printers have also become more affordable, although most still cost several thousand dollars.

NORTON Online

For information on **laser printers** and their operation, visit this book's Web site at www.glencoe.com/norton/online

Laser printers produce high-resolution output quickly and quietly. However, they tend to cost more than ink jet printers. Color laser printers, such as this HP Color LaserJet LJ, can cost several thousand dollars.

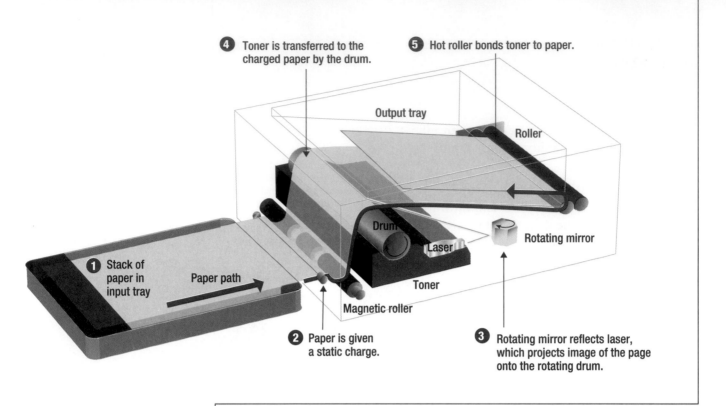

④ Toner is transferred to the charged paper by the drum.

⑤ Hot roller bonds toner to paper.

Output tray

Roller

Drum

Laser

Rotating mirror

① Stack of paper in input tray

Paper path

Toner

Magnetic roller

② Paper is given a static charge.

③ Rotating mirror reflects laser, which projects image of the page onto the rotating drum.

Figure 3.17
How a laser printer creates a printed page.

Other High-Quality Printers

Although most offices and homes use ink jet or laser printers, a variety of other types are used for special purposes. These printers are often used by publishers and small print shops to create high-quality output, especially color output. The last type discussed in this section, the plotter, is designed specifically for printing CAD documents.

Thermal-Wax Printers

Thermal-wax printers are used primarily for presentation graphics and handouts. They create bold colors and have a low per-page cost for pages with heavy color requirements. The process provides vivid colors because the inks it uses do not bleed into each other or soak the specially coated paper. Thermal-wax printers operate with a ribbon coated with panels of colored wax that melts and adheres to plain paper as colored dots when passed over a focused heat source.

Dye-Sub Printers

Desktop publishers and graphic artists get realistic quality and color for photo images using **dye-sub** (for *dye sub*limation) printers. In dye-sublimation technology, a ribbon containing panels of color is moved across a focused heat source that is capable of subtle temperature variations. The heated dyes evaporate from the ribbon and diffuse on specially coated paper where they form areas of different colors. The variations in color are related to the intensity of the heat applied.

Dye-sub printers create extremely sharp images, but they are slow and costly because the special paper required can make the per-page cost as high as $3 to $4.

NORTON Online

For more information on **printer makers**, visit this book's Web site at **www.glencoe.com/norton/online**

Fiery Printers

One high-quality form of printing takes advantage of digital color copiers. The **fiery print server** is a special-purpose computer that transmits documents to a digital color copier, where they are printed. Fiery printers are used in print shops as an alternative to press printing.

IRIS Printers

IRIS printers are used by print shops to produce high-resolution presentation graphics and color proofs that resemble full-color offset printed images. The IRIS is a high-tech form of ink jet printing in which individual sheets of paper are mounted onto a drum. The nozzles on the ink jet printing head pass from one end of the spinning drum to the other spraying minute drops of colored ink to form the image. This type of printer can produce an image with a resolution of 1800 dpi.

▶ A roller plotter uses a robotic arm to draw with colored pens on oversized paper. Here, an architectural elevation is being printed.

Plotters

A **plotter** is a special kind of output device. It is like a printer in that it produces images on paper, but the plotter is typically used to print large-format images, such as construction or engineering drawings created in a CAD system.

Early plotters were bulky, mechanical devices that used robotic arms, which literally drew the image on a piece of paper. Table plotters (or flatbed plotters) use two robotic arms, each of which holds a set of colored ink pens, felt pens, or pencils. The two arms work in concert with one another, operating at right angles as they draw on a stationary piece of paper. As well as being complex and large (some table plotters are almost as big as a billiard table), table plotters are notoriously slow; a large, complicated drawing can take several hours to print.

A variation on the table plotter is the roller plotter, which uses only one drawing arm but moves the paper instead of holding it flat and stationary. The drawing arm moves side-to-side as the paper is rolled back and forth through the roller. Working together, the arm and roller can draw perfect circles and other geometric shapes, as well as lines of different weights and colors.

In recent years, mechanical plotters have been largely displaced by thermal and ink jet plotters, as well as large-format dye-sub printers. These systems, which also produce large-size drawings, are faster and cheaper to use than their mechanical counterparts. They also can produce full-color renderings as well as geometric line drawings, making them more useful.

▶ Like desktop ink jet printers, an ink jet plotter uses a spray system to create either simple line drawings or detailed artistic renderings.

SOUND SYSTEMS

Just as microphones are now important input devices, speakers and their associated technology are key output systems. Today, when you buy a **multimedia PC**, you are getting a machine that includes a CD-ROM drive, a high-quality video controller (with plenty of VRAM), speakers, and a sound card.

The speakers attached to these systems are similar to ones you connect to a stereo. The only difference is that they are usually smaller, and they contain their own small amplifiers. Otherwise, they do the same thing any speaker does; they transfer a constantly changing electric current to a magnet, which pushes the speaker cone back and forth. The moving speaker cone creates pressure vibrations in the air—in other words, sound (see Figure 3.18).

The more complicated part of the sound output system is in the sound card. The sound card translates digital sounds into the electric current that is sent to the speakers. Sound is defined as air pressure varying over time. To digitize sound, the waves are converted to an electric current measured thousands of times per second and recorded as a number. When the sound is played back, the sound card reverses this process, translating the series of numbers into electric current that is sent to the speakers. The magnet moves back and forth with the changing current, creating vibrations.

With the right software, you can do much more than simply record and play back digitized sound. Utilities built into Windows 95/98 provide a miniature sound studio, allowing you to view the sound wave and edit it. In the editing, you can cut bits of sound, copy them, amplify the parts you want to hear louder, cut out static, and create many exotic audio effects.

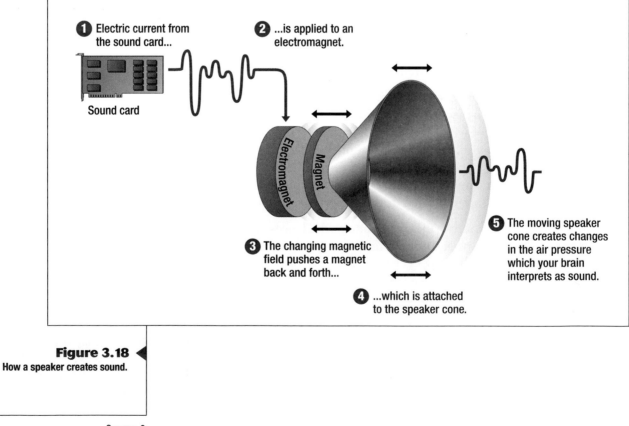

❶ Electric current from the sound card...

❷ ...is applied to an electromagnet.

Sound card

Electromagnet

Magnet

❸ The changing magnetic field pushes a magnet back and forth...

❹ ...which is attached to the speaker cone.

❺ The moving speaker cone creates changes in the air pressure which your brain interprets as sound.

Figure 3.18 ◀
How a speaker creates sound.

Techview

The Computer as an Aural Medium

Except for an occasional beep, computers were once mute. But the increasing demand for multimedia has made sound an important element in nearly every new computer and many software applications.

With the introduction of PC sound cards in the late 1980s, computers were able to play recorded sounds and music (from an application or a compact disk) and even synthesize sounds. Thanks to recent innovations in computer audio, sound has become an integral part of everyday computing, and computers have become an integral part of the audio industry.

Here are a few examples of the way audio and computer technologies are working together:

Embedded Audio Objects Business documents no longer need to be bland. Users can embed sound objects into word processing documents, spreadsheets, databases, e-mail messages, and other types of files. When the finished document is sent to another person on disk or via e-mail, he or she can open the sound file by double-clicking an icon; the file plays in a small, portable player. The process can even be automated so that the sound file plays immediately when the document is opened.

Multimedia Computer-Based Training (CBT) Using audio, video, text, and screen-capturing technologies, CD-ROM and online training tools are interactively teaching people a variety of skills, from preparing taxes to using computers. These programs can talk a user through a process—repeatedly, if necessary—to help the user master all sorts of tasks.

Real-Time Audio Conferencing Using inexpensive conferencing software, users can literally talk to one another through their computers. Only a sound card and microphone are required, along with a network connection. This type of conferencing can be done over local area networks (LANs), wide area networks (WANs), or the Internet.

Audio Chat Text-based chat systems have experienced explosive growth since 1994. Now many popular chat services and Web sites offer audio chat, as well. By using special communication software (which can be downloaded at no cost), a sound card, and a microphone, users can engage in real-time talks online. Little or no typing is required during these sessions.

Internet Phones A variety of software packages enable users to make long-distance phone calls over the Internet. The advantage is that the user can avoid paying long-distance charges. The disadvantages are poor sound quality, signal loss, and lack of full duplex (simultaneous two-way) communication.

Internet Radio A number of radio stations have taken their services online. This technology enables someone in Maine, for example, to listen to a radio station in Hawaii over an Internet connection. Web sites such as AudioNet and NetRadio act as clearinghouses for Internet-based audio resources.

Online Music Stores

Online music outlets, such as CDNow, enable Web users to select from a huge variety of albums. Users can listen to samples of music online and order the ones they like.

Today, it is virtually impossible to buy a new PC without a modem, speakers, sound card, microphone, and software. Considering the increasing use of audio in desktop applications and the Internet, these peripherals are now considered necessities.

Despite bandwidth problems that result in poor sound quality, streaming audio is extremely popular on the Internet. Online audio services, such as NetRadio, provide users with access to a variety of radio stations, as well as news, sports, talk, and other audio services.

CONNECTING I/O DEVICES TO THE COMPUTER

Earlier, you learned that all the components of a computer tie into the computer's CPU by way of the data bus. When you need to add a new piece of hardware to your computer, you need to know how to connect it to the bus. There are two basic ways. In some cases, you can plug the device into an existing socket, or **port**, on the back of the computer. Most computers have several types of ports, each with different capabilities and uses. The most common types are shown in Figure 3.19.

Figure 3.19
Standard ports on a PC.

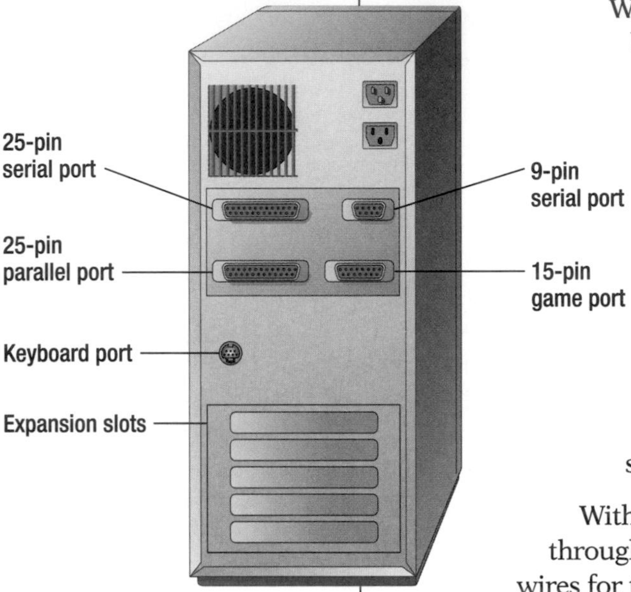

25-pin serial port

25-pin parallel port

Keyboard port

Expansion slots

9-pin serial port

15-pin game port

When a port is not available, you need to install a circuit board that includes the port you need.

Serial and Parallel Ports

Internally, a PC's components communicate through the data bus, which consists of parallel wires. Similarly, a **parallel interface** is a connection where there are eight or more wires through which data bits can flow simultaneously. Most computer buses transfer 32 bits simultaneously. However, the standard parallel interface for external devices like printers usually transfers eight bits (one byte) at a time over eight separate wires.

With a **serial interface**, data bits are transmitted one at a time through a single wire (however, the interface includes additional wires for the bits that control the flow of data). Inside the computer, a chip called a **UART** converts parallel data from the bus into serial data that flows through a serial cable. Figure 3.20 shows how data flows through a 9-pin serial interface.

Figure 3.20
Data moving through a serial interface.

Serial ports are most often used to connect a mouse or a modem. The current standard for serial communications is called **RS-232**, but there are many

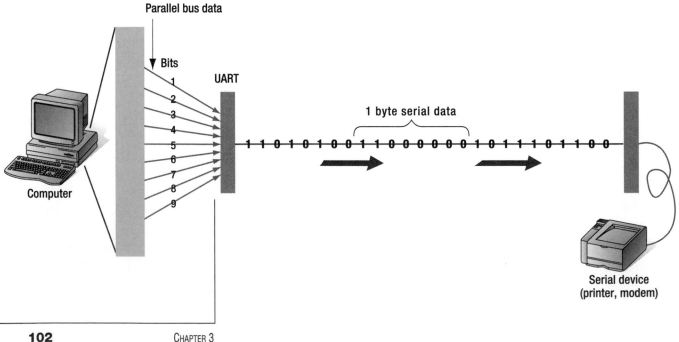

Parallel bus data

Bits

UART

1 byte serial data

11010100110000001011101100

Computer

Serial device (printer, modem)

variations. For instance, a serial port can have either 9 or 25 pins. The PC shown earlier in Figure 3.19 has two RS-232 serial ports, one 9-pin and one 25-pin. This is a common configuration. Most serial devices come with a cable and an adapter so that you can use whichever type of port is available.

As you would expect, a parallel interface can handle a higher volume of data than a serial interface because more than one bit can be transmitted through a parallel interface simultaneously. Figure 3.21 shows how data moves through a parallel interface.

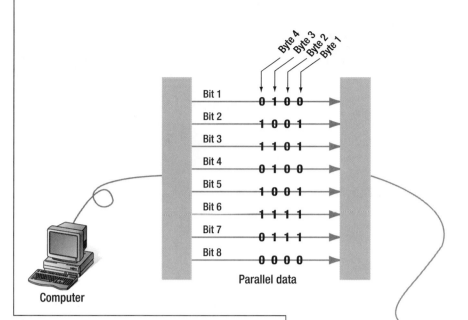

Figure 3.21
Data moving through a parallel interface.

Parallel device (printer)

Parallel ports are most often used for printer interfaces, although some other products use them as well. Parallel ports have a 25-pin connector at the computer end. The printer end of a parallel printer cable has a 36-pin **Centronics interface**, developed by the first manufacturer of dot-matrix printers.

Two serial ports, one parallel port, and one port for a mouse or other pointing device, and a joystick for playing games, is a typical rear-panel configuration.

Expansion Slots and Boards

PCs are designed so that users can adapt, or **configure**, the machines to their own particular needs.

PC motherboards have two or more **expansion slots**, which are extensions of the computer's bus that provide a way to add new components to the computer. The slots accept **expansion boards**, also called **cards**, adapters, or sometimes just boards. Modern notebook computers are too small to accept the same type of cards that fit into desktop models. Instead, new components for notebooks come in the form of **PC cards** (also called *PCM-CIA cards*), small devices—about the size of credit cards—that fit into a slot on the back or side of the notebook. Figure 3.22 shows a PC expansion board being installed. The board is being attached to the motherboard—the main system board to which the CPU, memory, and other components are attached.

The expansion slots on the motherboard are used for three purposes:

1_ To give built-in devices—such as hard disks and diskette drives—access to the computer's bus via controller cards.

2_ To provide I/O ports on the back of the computer for external devices such as monitors, external modems, printers, and the mouse (for computers that do not have a built-in mouse port).

NORTON
Online

For information on **installing** different types of **expansion boards** and **other devices**, visit this book's Web site at **www.glencoe.com/norton/online**

This small PC card is a modem that plugs into a notebook computer. The cord plugs into a standard telephone jack.

25-pin connector

9-pin connector

This modem cable has a 9-pin connector that plugs into the serial port on the back of the computer and a 25-pin RS-232 connector that plugs into the modem.

9-pin RS-232 connector

9-pin connector

This cable has two different 9-pin serial connectors, allowing the user to link a Macintosh and PC through their serial ports.

3_To give special-purpose devices access to the computer. For example, a computer can be enhanced with an **accelerator card**, a self-contained device that enhances processing speed through access to the computer's CPU and memory by way of the bus.

The first and second of these are I/O functions. Adapters that serve these purposes provide a port to which devices can be attached and serve as a translator between the bus and the device itself. Some adapters also do a significant amount of data processing. For example, a video controller is a card that provides a port on the back of the PC into which you can plug the monitor. It also contains and manages the video memory and does the processing required to display images on the monitor. Other I/O devices that commonly require the installation of a card into an expansion slot include sound cards, internal modems or fax/modems, network interface cards, and scanners.

Expansion card

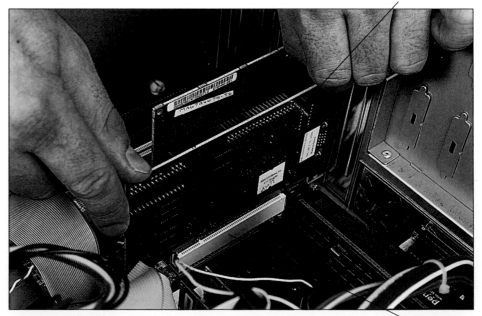

Expansion slots

Figure 3.22
An expansion card being inserted into an expansion slot.

The third type, the accelerator cards, are often installed to speed up the CPU or the display of video.

SCSI

One device interface that takes a different approach from those discussed so far goes a long way toward overcoming the constraints of a limited number of expansion slots on the motherboard. This device is called **small computer system interface** (**SCSI**, pronounced "scuzzy"). Instead of plugging cards into the computer's bus via the expansion slots, SCSI extends the bus outside the computer by way of a cable. In other words, SCSI is like an extension cord for the data bus. Just as you can plug one extension cord into another to lengthen a circuit, you can plug one SCSI device into another to form a daisy chain.

For information on **SCSI**, visit this book's Web site at www.glencoe.com/norton/online

IBM developed SCSI in the 1970s as a way to give mainframe computers access to small computer devices and vice versa. Since then, SCSI has undergone many changes. The emerging standard is SCSI-3, which far exceeds the SCSI-2 limit of six devices that could be daisy-chained on a single SCSI port. SCSI-3 can potentially link as many as 127 devices.

To provide a PC with a SCSI port, you insert a SCSI adapter board into one of the PC's available expansion slots. Many devices use the SCSI interface. Fast, high-end hard disk drives often have SCSI interfaces, as do scanners, tape drives, and optical storage devices such as CD-ROM drives.

Whereas SCSI is an option for PCs, a SCSI port is built as a standard interface into Macintosh computers and into many UNIX workstations. In fact, with some Macintosh models, you do not have any other access to the computer's bus. Ports for a mouse, modem, and monitor are all built into the computer. Any other devices you want to add—such as an external hard drive, scanner, or CD-ROM drive—can be daisy-chained on the built-in SCSI port.

▶ SCSI peripherals daisy-chained together.

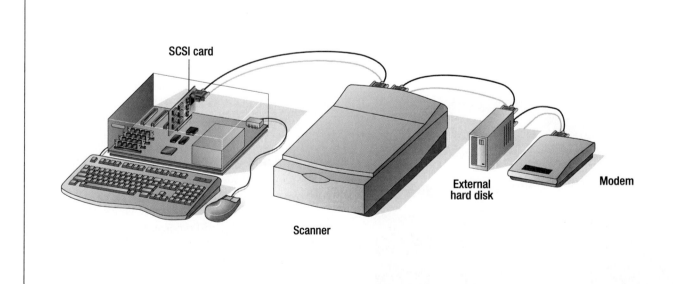

SCSI card

Scanner

External hard disk

Modem

Computers
In Your Career

The input and output devices you choose can have a tremendous impact on your computing productivity. That is just one of the reasons why there are so many input and output options available. Different devices are designed to accommodate different needs, and to make computing easier, safer, and more productive. The manner in which you interact with the computer may also depend on your profession. In fact, some professions rely a great deal on specific types of input and output devices. For example:

Programmers, accountants, bookkeepers If you are writing programming code or working with numbers, accuracy is critical to your success. In such professions, a good keyboard is a must. Some users prefer a standard 101-key keyboard, while others prefer ergonomically correct keyboards that more naturally fit the positioning of the hand, wrist, and forearm while typing. A worn-out or poorly designed keyboard can not only slow you down and cause typing errors, but also can result in injury.

Graphic artists, illustrators, designers Keyboarding is secondary for some people. If your job requires you to draw on the computer—or even to drag blocks around on the screen—then you may rely more on a pointing device than on a keyboard. Many graphic artists use large trackballs rather than mice because they are more comfortable and require less hand movement. CAD and high-end design applications frequently can work with digitizing tablets, which enable the user to draw and issue commands without touching the keyboard.

Secretaries, transcriptionists, writers Some professions require the computer user to enter endless streams of text. For these people, a keyboard may not be enough to handle the task. Scanners are handy for entering text from a printed source, as is required when old documents must be transcribed to disk. Speech-recognition software can be extremely helpful, as well, for users who need to type a great deal but don't know how to type or are unable to use a keyboard.

Many professionals have special output device requirements, as well. For example:

Architects, engineers, 3-D designers

Professional designers often need high-quality, large-format hard copies of their designs. This is especially true for architects and engineers, whose drawings are used in the construction of buildings or products. Many 3-D designers, who create elaborate still images of interiors or landscapes, also need high-quality color output for their projects. These professionals frequently use large-format plotters and thermal wax printers, which are expensive but indispensable.

Multimedia and game designers, animators For these developers, audio and video output is critical. Multimedia and gaming professionals often add high-end audio systems to their computers, which enable them to sample, record, edit, and mix sounds of all types, as well as play them back. These users also require video recording and playback capabilities, and install video cards, digital cameras, and video recording units to their systems.

WHAT TO EXPECT IN THE FUTURE

Among input devices, major advances of the future will probably be in the area of natural human-interface technologies, namely, voice recognition and handwriting recognition. The limitations here are in the realm of software rather than hardware because it is quite difficult to program handwriting- and voice-recognition software.

Handwriting-recognition software is already available, but it is not 100-percent reliable. Rapid progress is being made, however, because the makers of personal digital assistants need this technology for the PDA to become a successful product. Even when handwriting recognition becomes reliable, you still will not see many handwriting tablets attached to desktop computers. Once you know how to type, typing is faster than writing, so the keyboard will remain the input device of choice wherever there is room for a keyboard.

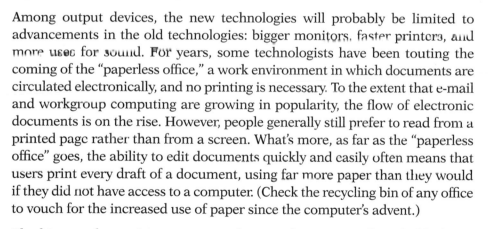

Voice recognition, on the other hand, will eventually make its way to the desktop. In fact, there are already programs that can understand simple commands and clearly enunciated speech (although still not with a high degree of reliability). It is only a matter of time before the reliability of the software becomes acceptable and the microphone becomes an input device to rival the keyboard.

Among output devices, the new technologies will probably be limited to advancements in the old technologies: bigger monitors, faster printers, and more uses for sound. For years, some technologists have been touting the coming of the "paperless office," a work environment in which documents are circulated electronically, and no printing is necessary. To the extent that e-mail and workgroup computing are growing in popularity, the flow of electronic documents is on the rise. However, people generally still prefer to read from a printed page rather than from a screen. What's more, as far as the "paperless office" goes, the ability to edit documents quickly and easily often means that users print every draft of a document, using far more paper than they would if they did not have access to a computer. (Check the recycling bin of any office to vouch for the increased use of paper since the computer's advent.)

The biggest change in output over the next few years will probably be in more elaborate and less expensive printing options, especially the use of color. Equally exciting changes are on the horizon for audio and video output. It will become easier and less expensive for home users to create, record, and edit their own audio and video content using the PC and then output the content to tape or CD-ROM.

Visual Summary & Exercises

VISUAL SUMMARY

The Keyboard

■ There are five parts to the standard keyboard: the alphanumeric keys, the numeric keypad, the function keys, modifier keys, and the cursor-movement keys.

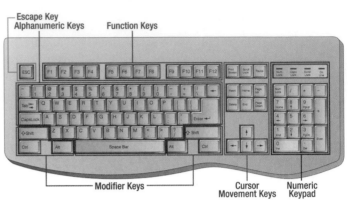

The Mouse

■ The mouse is a pointing device that lets you control the position of the pointer on the screen without using the keyboard.

■ Using the mouse involves a total of five techniques: pointing, clicking, double-clicking, dragging, and right-clicking.

■ Most mice operate with a ball that spins a set of rollers. If the mouse does not operate properly, you can clean it by removing the coverplate and ball and removing any debris, such as dust, from the ball itself and the rollers.

■ A trackball provides the functionality of a mouse but requires less space on the desktop.

■ A trackpad provides the functionality of a mouse but requires less space and less movement.

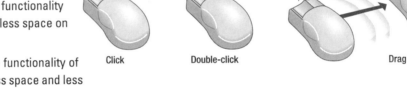

Click   Double-click   Drag

Other Input Devices

■ With pen-based systems, you use an electronic pen to write on a special pad or directly on the screen.

■ Touch-screen computers accept input directly through the monitor.

■ Bar code readers, such as those used in grocery stores, can read bar codes, translate them into numbers, and input the numbers.

■ Image scanners convert printed images into digitized formats that can be stored and manipulated in computers.

■ An image scanner equipped with OCR software can translate a page of text into a string of character codes in the computer's memory.

■ Microphones can accept auditory input and turn it into text and computer commands with voice recognition software.

■ PC video cameras and digital cameras can digitize full-motion and still images, which can be stored and edited on the PC or transmitted over a LAN or the Internet.

Visual Summary & Exercises

The Monitor

- Computer monitors are roughly divided into two categories: CRT and flat-panel monitors.

- A CRT monitor works with an electron gun that systematically aims a beam of electrons at every pixel on the screen.

- When purchasing a monitor, you must consider size, resolution, refresh rate, and dot pitch.

- The video controller is an interface between the monitor and the CPU.

- Most LCD displays are either active matrix or passive matrix (dual-scan).

Flat-panel display

CRT

Printers

- Ink jet and laser printers are the most commonly used printers in homes and business.

- Ink jet printers are inexpensive for both color and black printing, have low operating costs, and offer quality and speed comparable to low-end laser printers.

- Laser printers produce higher-quality print and are fast and convenient to use, but they are also more expensive than ink jet printers.

- Thermal-wax, dye-sub, fiery, and IRIS printers are used primarily by print shops and publishers to create high-quality color images.

- Plotters create large-format images, usually for architectural or engineering uses, using mechanical drawing arms, ink jet technology, or thermal printing technology.

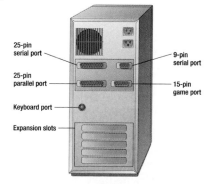

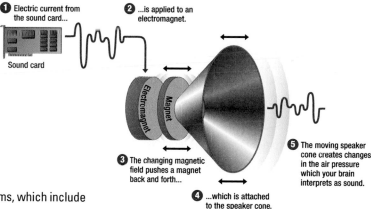

1 Electric current from the sound card...

Sound card

2 ...is applied to an electromagnet.

Electromagnet

Magnet

3 The changing magnetic field pushes a magnet back and forth...

4 ...which is attached to the speaker cone.

5 The moving speaker cone creates changes in the air pressure which your brain interprets as sound.

Sound Systems

- Multimedia PCs generally come with sound systems, which include a sound card and speakers.

- The sound card translates digital signals into analog ones that drive the speakers.

Connecting I/O Devices to the Computer

- External devices—such as those used for input and output—are connected via ports on the back of the computer.

- Expansion slots on a PC's motherboard give external devices access to the computer's bus via expansion boards and provide I/O ports on the back of the computer.

- Most computers come with both serial and parallel ports.

- A SCSI port extends the bus outside the computer by way of a cable, which allows devices to be connected to one another in a daisy chain.

25-pin serial port

25-pin parallel port

Keyboard port

Expansion slots

9-pin serial port

15-pin game port

Visual Summary & Exercises

KEY TERMS

After completing this chapter, you should be able to define the following terms:

accelerator card, 103
active matrix LCD, 95
alphanumeric key, 74
bar code, 84
bar code reader, 84
bitmap, 85
card, 103
cathode ray tube (CRT), 88
Centronics interface, 103
click, 78
color (monitor), 88
configure, 103
cursor, 75
cursor-movement key, 75
digitize, 87
dot pitch, 93
double-click, 78
drag, 78
drag and drop, 78
DRAM, 94
dual-scan LCD, 94
dye-sub printer, 98
expansion board, 103
expansion slot, 103
fiery print server, 99
flat-panel display, 88

flatbed scanner, 86
function key, 75
grayscale (monitor), 88
handheld scanner, 86
I-beam cursor, 75
image scanner, 84
ink jet printer, 95
insertion point, 75
integrated pointing device, 81
interrupt request, 76
IRIS printer, 99
keyboard buffer, 76
keyboard controller, 76
keyboarding, 74
laser printer, 97
liquid crystal display (LCD) monitor, 94
modifier key, 74
monochrome (monitor), 88
multimedia PC, 100
numeric keypad, 75
optical character recognition (OCR), 85
parallel interface, 102
passive matrix LCD, 94
PC card, 103
PC video camera, 87
pixel, 88

plotter, 99
pointer, 77
pointing device, 77
port, 102
QWERTY, 74
refresh rate, 92
resolution, 92
right-clicking, 78
RS-232, 102
scan code, 76
serial interface, 102
small computer system interface (SCSI), 105
sound card, 86
SVGA (Super VGA), 92
thermal-wax printer, 98
toner, 97
trackpad, 81
TrackPoint, 81
UART, 102
VGA (Video Graphics Array), 92
video card, 87
video controller, 93
video RAM (VRAM), 94
voice recognition (speech recognition), 86

KEY TERM QUIZ

Fill in the missing word with one of the terms listed in Key Terms:

1. The _____ indicates where the characters you type will appear on screen.

2. A(n) _____ image is stored in the computer's memory as a grid of dots.

3. The vacuum tube used in PC monitors is known as a(n) _____.

4. The number of pixels on the screen, expressed as a matrix, is called the _____.

5. The _____ is the number of times per second that electron guns scan every pixel on the monitor's screen.

6. A(n) _____ printer is used primarily for producing boldly colored presentation graphics and handouts.

7. A(n) _____ chip converts parallel data from the bus into serial data.

8. _____ are devices used to translate printed images into electronic format that can be stored in a computer's memory.

9. _____ software translates a scanned image into text that you can edit.

10. An intermediary device between the CPU and the monitor that sends information to the monitor for display on screen is called a(n) _____.

Visual Summary & Exercises

REVIEW QUESTIONS

1. Describe briefly how a parallel interface handles a higher volume of data than a serial interface.

2. Describe briefly how a sound card digitizes sounds.

3. List and describe at least three factors that have made ink jet printers so popular over the last ten years.

4. List and describe the most important specifications to consider when purchasing a monitor.

5. What is the primary difference between passive matrix LCD monitors and active matrix LCD monitors?

6. What are the important criteria for evaluating printers?

7. What device interface acts, in one sense, like an extension cord for the computer's data bus?

8. What input device significantly revolutionized the graphic design field, and how?

9. What is the biggest challenge facing developers of voice recognition software?

10. Why are pens currently not an optimal input device choice for word processing tasks?

DISCUSSION QUESTIONS

1. Despite the rapid advancements being made with handwriting recognition software, do you think that the keyboard will continue to be the preferred input device for generating text? Which alternative—voice recognition through a microphone or handwriting recognition through a pen and tablet—do you think has a better chance of ultimately replacing the keyboard as the primary device for inputting text?

2. Suppose that you are responsible for computerizing a gourmet restaurant's order-entering system. What type of input device do you think would be best-suited for the waitperson staff to input orders to the kitchen? What type of output device do you think would best serve the kitchen staff? What factors would you consider in your decision making?

3. When you think about the two most frequently used output devices for computers—monitors and printers—why do you think it stands to reason that color technology for printers will become more commonplace, more affordable, and more necessary to many users?

4. In your view, what primary factors led to the development of more sophisticated video controllers? Can you cite one or two current examples that indicate which video controller technology will continue to evolve?

*inte*NET Workshop

The following exercises assume that you have access to the Internet and a browser. If you need help with any of the following exercises, visit this book's Web site at **www.glencoe.com/norton/online**. This book's Web site also lists the URLs you need to complete many of these exercises.

1. Visit at least three sites on the World Wide Web. How accessible is each site to persons with physical disabilities? In what ways could the sites improve their accessibility?

2. Investigate the possibilities of audio on the Internet. How many Web sites can you find that offer ongoing audio content, such as radio programming, talk shows, sports shows, concerts, and so on? Also, see whether any of your local radio stations are broadcasting over the Web. (Hint: In your browser's address box, type **http://www.<*your station's call letters*>.com** and see what happens.) Overall, how would you rate the quality of sound produced by these sites? Were you required to download and install a plug-in to use any of these sites? If so, was the process of installing the plug-in worth the effort? Did you find the audio-enabled sites rewarding or compelling?

3. The Web is an excellent resource for current information on computer equipment and innovations. A good place to start for general product information is the Web sites provided by manufacturers. See whether you can find at least three manufacturers' Web sites, as well as one site offering objective product reviews, for the following items:

- Pointing devices
- Monitors
- PC video cameras

4. Do you know keyboarding? If not, your ability to use the computer could be hampered. Check the Web for information or tutorials on touch typing. Search on the keyword "typing." Are any programs or lessons available online?

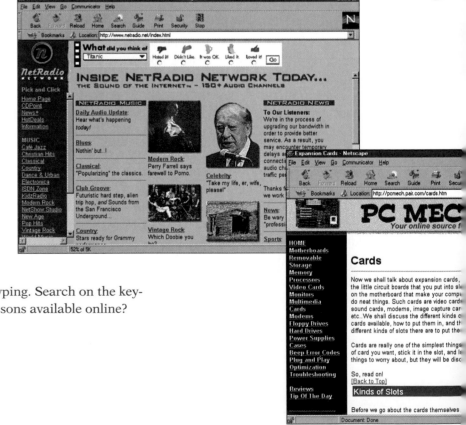

5. If you don't know keyboarding, speech recognition software may be a good idea for you, especially if you use the PC for writing large amounts of text. Several speech recognition products are available, from a variety of sources. Look for reviews at the University of Northumbria at Newcastle Web site. Do any of these products seem right for you? Why or why not?

6. Could you install an expansion card in your computer, for example, if you wanted to add a modem to your system? The Web is a good place to get information about expansion cards of all kinds, and helpful tips for doing the job yourself. Good starting points include PC Webopaedia's page on expansion boards, and the PC Mechanic's Expansion Card page. What advice can you find about selecting and installing expansion cards in a PC?

7. Will you need to select a printer for your home or business? The range of products is mind-boggling, but the Web is a great place to look for basic product information and reviews. For product specifications and dealer information, visit the product-information pages of printer manufacturers. For product reviews, check sites such as *PC Magazine Online's* Peripherals Review Index and *LAN Times Online's Printer Buyer's Guide.* Which type of printer seems right for your needs—laser, ink jet, dot matrix, or some other type? For your preferred type of printer, which brand and models have the options that appeal to you?

Storing Information in a Computer

CONTENTS

OBJECTIVES

When you complete this chapter, you will be able to do the following:

- List four common types of storage devices.
- Name three common uses of floppy disks.
- Name the four areas on floppy and hard disks.
- List three ways tape drives differ from disk drives.
- Identify four types of optical storage devices.
- Name and describe the four main disk drive interface standards.

The personal computers of the late 1970s and early 1980s generally included one or two diskette drives and no hard disk. This was true of the first IBM PC. Some early PCs also included attachments for tape drives, which could store data on ordinary audiocassette tapes.

It did not take long, however, before PC manufacturers found it necessary to include better storage technology that allowed users to keep most of their files and programs in one place. The solution was to build hard disks into the computers. In 1983, IBM recognized the need for bigger, faster, built-in storage, and added a 10 MB hard disk to its second-generation PC, the IBM PC XT.

The physical components or materials on which data is stored are called **storage media**. The hardware components that write data to, and read it from, storage media are called **storage devices**. For example, a diskette is a storage medium ("medium" is the singular form of "media"), whereas a diskette drive is a storage device. Storage media and devices have evolved dramatically since computers were in their infancy, and this pace has accelerated since the introduction and growing popularity of PCs.

Two of the most widely used storage devices and accompanying media have been around for at least 15 years. The first to appear on PCs, the diskette (or floppy disk), is a flat piece of plastic, coated with iron oxide, and encased in a vinyl or plastic cover. The computer reads and writes data on the diskette by using a diskette drive. A hard disk is like a diskette, but it consists of one or more rigid metal platters that are permanently encased in the hard disk drive.

Compared to the diskette drives of the day, those early hard disk drives were lightning quick and could store amazing amounts of data. The XT hard disk held the equivalent of almost thirty 360 KB diskettes. One of the basic truths of computing, however, is that there is never enough storage space. As soon as users began storing their files—and especially their programs—on their hard disks, they began to need hard disks with even more storage capacity. Soon 20 MB disks became the norm, then 40 MB. By the mid-1990s, new PCs came with hard drives that could store at least 1.6 GB of data. Now, many users want hard drives that store upwards of 10 GB. Today, the hard disk continues to be the data warehouse of the PC world, although the perpetual need for more storage has spawned the development of many new technologies. In this chapter, you will learn about the most important storage media and devices and find out what each is best suited for, how they work, and which offer the most speed and capacity.

TYPES OF STORAGE DEVICES

Two main technologies are used to store data today: magnetic and optical storage. Although devices that store data typically employ one or the other, some combine both technologies. The primary types of magnetic storage are:

■ Diskettes

■ Hard disks

■ Removable hard disks

■ Magnetic tape

The primary types of optical storage are:

■ Compact Disk Read-Only Memory (CD-ROM)

■ Write Once, Read Many (WORM) drives

■ Phase-Change Rewritable disks

■ Magneto-optical disks

■ Floptical drives

NORTON Online

For more information on **storage devices**, visit this book's Web site at www.glencoe.com/norton/online

Most new PCs come with a diskette drive, a hard disk drive, and a CD-ROM drive.

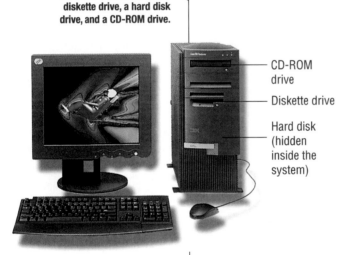

— CD-ROM drive

— Diskette drive

Hard disk (hidden inside the system)

The most common storage devices are diskette drives and hard disk drives. Both are referred to as **magnetic storage** because they record data as magnetic fields. The difference between diskette drives and hard disk drives is that diskettes are small and portable (they can be removed from diskette drives), but most store only 1.44 MB. Typically, hard disks are built into the computer, so they are not portable (unless the entire computer is). However, most hard disks can store at least 500 times as much data as a diskette. Hard disk drives are also much faster than diskette drives. Almost all PCs sold today come with a hard disk and at least one diskette drive.

The tape drive is another popular magnetic storage device. A tape drive is an add-on that is often used to create a backup copy of a hard disk, preserving the contents in case the hard disk is damaged.

The Seagate Sidewinder tape drive from Seagate is designed for backing up hard disks.

The removable hard disk combines the portability of diskettes with speeds and storage capacities comparable to hard disks.

Some storage manufacturers offer another type of device that combines some benefits of diskette drives and hard disks—the removable hard disk drive.

Optical devices are also gaining popularity. The best-known optical device is the CD-ROM (Compact Disk Read-Only Memory) drive, which uses the same technology as audio CD players. Other optical storage devices include write once, read many (WORM) drives, magneto-optical drives, phase-change rewritable, floptical, and recordable CD drives.

The Fujitsu DynaMO 640 disk drives can be used as CD-ROM drives and magneto-optical drives.

MAGNETIC STORAGE DEVICES

Because they all use the same medium (the material on which the data is stored), diskette drives, hard disk drives, and tape drives use similar techniques for reading and writing data. The surfaces of diskettes, hard disks, and magnetic tape are all coated with a magnetically sensitive material (usually iron oxide) that reacts to a magnetic field.

You may remember from high school science projects that one magnet can be used to make another. For example, you can make a magnet by taking an iron bar and stroking it in one direction with a magnet. The iron bar eventually becomes a magnet itself because its iron molecules align themselves in one direction. The iron bar becomes **polarized**; that is, its ends have opposite magnetic polarity (see Figure 4.1).

Magnetic storage devices use a similar principle to store data. Just as a transistor can represent binary data as "on" or "off," the orientation of a magnetic field can be used to represent data. A magnet has one important advantage over a transistor: It can represent "on" and "off" without a continual source of electricity.

NORTON Online

For more information on **Panasonic CD-ROM drives**, visit this book's Web site at **www.glencoe.com/norton/online**

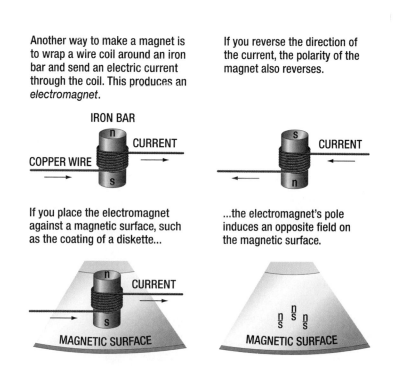

Another way to make a magnet is to wrap a wire coil around an iron bar and send an electric current through the coil. This produces an *electromagnet*.

If you reverse the direction of the current, the polarity of the magnet also reverses.

IRON BAR

CURRENT

COPPER WIRE

CURRENT

If you place the electromagnet against a magnetic surface, such as the coating of a diskette...

...the electromagnet's pole induces an opposite field on the magnetic surface.

CURRENT

MAGNETIC SURFACE

MAGNETIC SURFACE

Figure 4.1
How an electromagnet creates a field on a magnetic surface.

Productivity Tip

Backing Up Your Files

You have been working all week on a presentation, and it is due at noon. You take a break—confident that your work is done. When you return, you see that a disk error has corrupted your hard drive. You can forget about making that deadline.

It won't happen? If not a disk error, then software bugs, power surges, data corruption, fire, viruses, and myriad other unpredictable assailants can destroy your files in the blink of an eye. That's why backing up files should be as much a part of your routine as brushing your teeth.

Start your backup program by asking yourself these questions and then by making these decisions:

What kind of backup medium will I use?

Currently, the most popular options are floppy disks, tape drives, removable hard disks, magneto-optical (MO) disks, and recordable CDs. The medium you choose depends on how much storage you need and your budget. Floppy disks are a quick, convenient backup choice for small amounts of data. In most modern business settings, roomier media such as tape, removable hard disks, MO disks, or CDs are used. An emerging backup solution is to commission companies to back up desktop PC or network servers over the Internet.

Convenience is another factor. For example, tape drives are much less expensive than MO drives, but they are also slower and more cumbersome to use. For convenience and speed, many users opt for high-density removable disks, such as the

Iomega Jaz and Zip drives, or SyQuest SyJet drive. Although removable disks are more expensive than most tape drives, removable disks are easy to use and are fast.

What kind of software do I need? For backups onto a floppy disk, removable hard drive, or MO drive, the file-management program that comes with your operating system may be all you need. For greater convenience, programs like Microsoft Backup allow you to schedule backups ahead of time and back up either to disk or tape.

What will my backup procedures be? One thing is certain: your backup procedure should start with a full backup, which should be repeated once a week. Beyond that, you can do a series of partial backups—either incremental (files that have changed since the last partial backup) or differential (files that have changed since the last full backup).

Just how much backup is enough? Here are some suggestions for deciding:

- For a home computer used mainly for games and children's education, you might need backups only of your programs, made when first installed, plus occasional monthly backups of any drawings and reports your children made for school.

- If you have a home-office computer used for accounting, word processing, and some faxing, you could probably get by with weekly backups of your data.

- If you have a small office computer used every day for word processing, personal scheduling, and budgeting, you should back up incrementally every day, at the end of the day, with a second set of full backups weekly.

- If you have a network server computer handling the documents of a half-dozen people in a workgroup, you'll need a full backup every day.

Where will I store my data? Where will you keep your disks or tapes, so that when an unforeseen emergency like a fire, flood, or earthquake strikes, your data won't perish with your office? Some organizations routinely ship their media to a distant location, such as a home office or a commercial warehouse, or store them in weatherproof, fireproof, bombproof vaults. Home users may want to keep their backups in a safe-deposit box. Companies often keep three or more full sets of backups, all at different sites. Such prudence may seem extreme, but where crucial records are at stake, backups can mean the life or death of a business.

Windows 98's Backup program is used to back up desktop PCs.

118

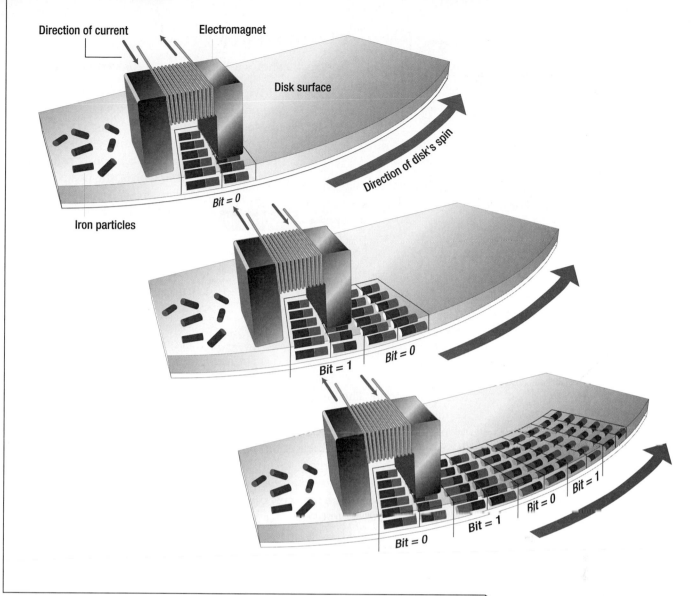

Direction of current

Electromagnet

Disk surface

Direction of disk's spin

Bit = 0

Iron particles

Bit = 1   Bit = 0

Bit = 0   Bit = 1   Bit = 0   Bit = 1

Figure 4.2
Data being recorded
by a read/write head.

The surfaces of disks and magnetic tapes are coated with millions of tiny iron particles so that data can be stored on them. Each of these particles can act as a magnet, taking on a magnetic field when subjected to an **electromagnet**. The read/write heads of a hard disk drive, diskette drive, or tape drive contain electromagnets, which generate magnetic fields in the iron on the storage medium as the head passes over the disk (hard disk or diskette) or tape.

As shown in Figure 4.2, the read/write heads record strings of 1s and 0s by alternating the direction of the current in the electromagnets.

To read data from a magnetic surface, the process is reversed. The read/write head passes over the disk or tape while no current is flowing through the electromagnet. Because the storage medium has a magnetic field but the head does not, the storage medium charges the magnet in the head, which causes a small current to flow through the head in one direction or the other depending on the polarity of the field. The disk or tape drive senses the direction of the flow as the storage medium passes by the head, and the data is sent from the read/write head into memory.

Diskette Drives

Figure 4.3 shows a diskette and a **diskette drive**.

The drive includes a motor that rotates the disk on a spindle and read/write heads that can move to any spot on the disk's surface as the disk spins. This capability is important because it allows the heads to access data randomly rather than sequentially. In other words, the heads can skip from one spot to another without having to scan through everything in between.

Diskettes, which are often called floppy disks or simply **floppies**, spin at around 300 revolutions per minute. Therefore, the longest it can take to position a point on the diskette under the read/write heads is the amount of time required for one revolution—about 0.2 second. The farthest the heads would ever have to move is from the center of the diskette to the outside edge (or vice versa). The heads can move from the center to the outside edge in even less time—about 0.17 second. Because both operations (rotating the diskette and moving the heads from the center to the outside edge) take place simultaneously, the maximum time to position the heads over a given location on the diskette—known as the **maximum access time** (or **seek time**)—remains the greater of the two times, or 0.2 second (see Figure 4.4).

Actually, though, the maximum access time for diskettes can be even longer, because diskettes do not spin when they are not being used. It can take as much as 0.5 second to rotate the disk from a dead stop.

The most common uses of diskettes are as follows:

Moving files between computers that are not connected through network or communications hardware. One of the easiest ways to move data between computers is to copy the data to a diskette, remove the diskette from the first computer's drive, and insert it in another computer's drive.

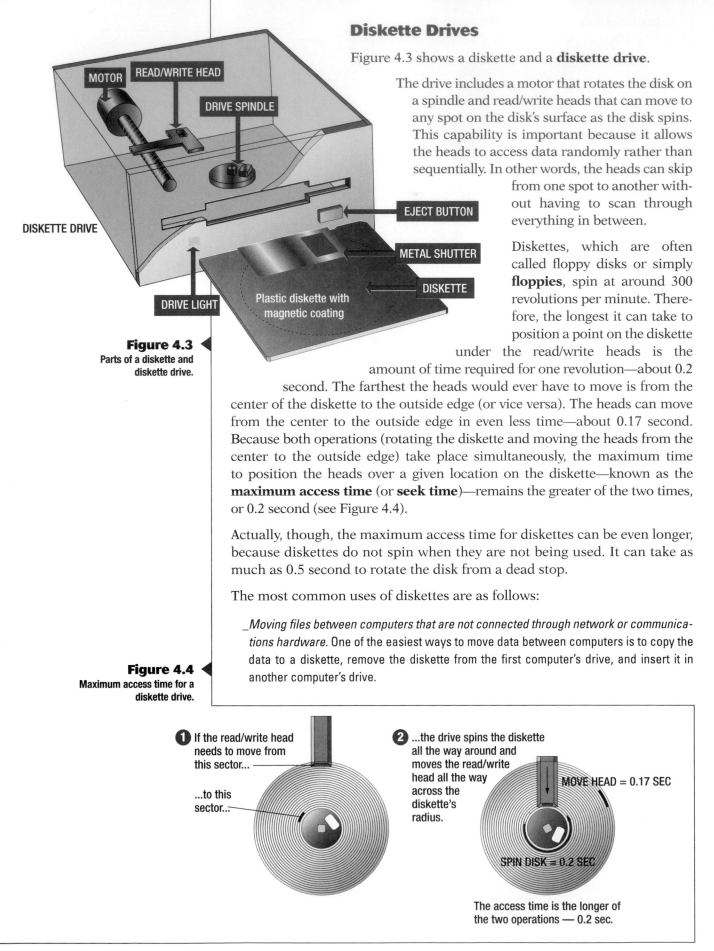

Figure 4.3
Parts of a diskette and diskette drive.

MOTOR
READ/WRITE HEAD
DRIVE SPINDLE
DISKETTE DRIVE
EJECT BUTTON
METAL SHUTTER
DISKETTE
Plastic diskette with magnetic coating
DRIVE LIGHT

Figure 4.4
Maximum access time for a diskette drive.

❶ If the read/write head needs to move from this sector...
...to this sector...

❷ ...the drive spins the diskette all the way around and moves the read/write head all the way across the diskette's radius.

MOVE HEAD = 0.17 SEC
SPIN DISK = 0.2 SEC

The access time is the longer of the two operations — 0.2 sec.

Loading new programs onto a system. Although large programs are often delivered on CD-ROM, many programs are still sold on diskettes. When you buy a program from a software retailer, you install it by copying the contents of the diskettes onto your hard disk drive, or by running a small program on the diskettes that installs the files on your hard drive automatically.

Backing up data or programs, the primary copy of which is stored on a hard disk drive. **Backing up** is the process of creating a duplicate set of programs and/or data files for safe-keeping. Most people rely on a hard disk drive for the bulk of their storage needs, but what if the hard drive malfunctions or is damaged? To protect against data loss, it is always wise to back up a hard disk. One common way to do so is to copy files onto diskettes (or tapes).

NORTON Online

For more information on **diskettes**, visit this book's Web site at www.glencoe.com/norton/online

Types of Diskettes

During the 1980s, most PCs used 5.25-inch diskettes. Today, though, the 3.5-inch diskette has largely replaced its 5.25-inch cousin. The size refers to the diameter of the disk, not to the capacity. The 5.25-inch type, shown in Figure 4.5, is encased in a flexible vinyl envelope with an oval cutout that allows the read/write head to access the disk.

The 3.5-inch type, shown in Figure 4.6, is encased in a hard plastic shell with a sliding metal cover. When the disk is inserted into the drive, the cover slides back to expose the diskette to the read/write head. It is important to realize that both these types are diskettes. The term _diskette_ refers to the disk inside, not to the square plastic protector.

Both types of diskette have evolved from lower to higher densities. The **density** of the disk is a measure of the capacity of the disk surface: The higher the density, the more closely the iron-oxide particles are packed, and the more data the disk can store. Thus, a diskette marked "high density" can store more data than one marked "double density." Table 4.1 shows the capacity, in bytes, of each kind of diskette.

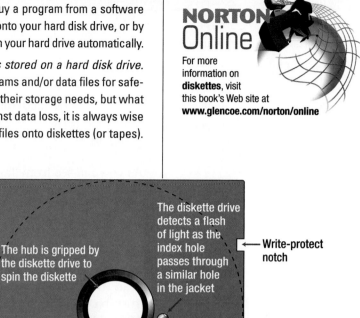

Figure 4.5
5.25-inch diskette.

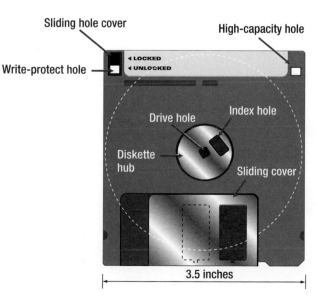

Figure 4.6
3.5-inch diskette.

Table 4.1	Diskette Capacities	
DIAMETER	TYPE	CAPACITY
5.25 inches	Double density	360 KB
5.25 inches	High density	1.2 MG
3.5 inches	Double density	720 KB
3.5 inches	High density	1.44 MB (most common)
3.5 inches	High density	2.88 MB

The sizes given in the table are for DOS- and Windows-based machines. The Macintosh never used 5.25-inch disks. A double-density diskette with a Macintosh format holds 800 KB, not 720 KB—a result of the different ways the two machines use the disks. A Macintosh high-density disk holds 1.44 MB, the same capacity as a DOS- or Windows-based diskette.

As you can see from Table 4.1, the physically smaller disks can actually hold more data than the larger ones, thanks to newer technology. Because of their hard plastic shell and the sliding metal cover, the 3.5-inch diskettes are also more durable. As a result, the 5.25-inch diskette has virtually disappeared.

Although the high-density 2.88 MB floppy disk holds more data than the standard high-density 1.44 MB floppy disk, you need a special floppy disk drive to read the higher-density disk. The 2.88 MB floppy disk drive was released by Toshiba Corporation in 1987 and was adopted by IBM for the PS/2 system in 1991. Most other PCs, however, do not include 2.88 MB floppy disk drives.

How Data Is Organized on a Disk

When you buy new diskettes (or a new hard drive), the disks inside are nothing more than simple, coated disks encased in plastic. Before the computer can use them to store data, they must be magnetically mapped so that the computer can go directly to a specific point on the diskette without searching through data. The process of mapping a diskette is called **formatting** or **initializing**. Today, many diskettes come preformatted for either PCs or Macs. If you buy unformatted diskettes, you must format them before you can use them. The computer will warn you if this is the case and will format the diskette for you if you want.

The first thing a disk drive does when formatting a disk is create a set of magnetic concentric circles called **tracks**. The number of tracks on a disk varies with the type (most high-density diskettes have 80). The tracks on a disk do not form a continuous spiral like those on a phonograph record; rather, each one is a separate circle, like the circles on a bull's-eye target. The tracks are numbered from the outermost circle to the innermost, starting from zero, as shown in Figure 4.7.

Figure 4.7
Tracks are concentric circles, numbered from the outside in.

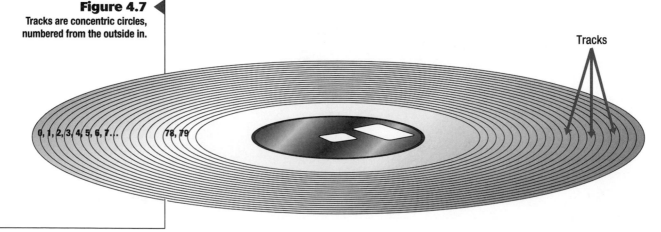

Tracks

0, 1, 2, 3, 4, 5, 6, 7... 78, 79

Each track on a disk is also split into smaller parts. Imagine slicing up a disk the way you cut a pie. As shown in Figure 4.8, each slice would cut across all the disk's tracks, resulting in short segments, or **sectors**. All the sectors on the disk are numbered in one long sequence so that the computer can access each small area on the disk with a unique number. This scheme effectively simplifies what would be a set of two-dimensional coordinates into a single numeric address.

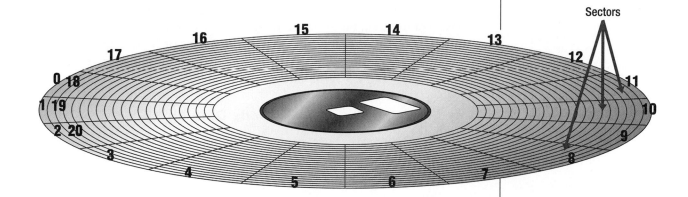

Figure 4.8
Sectors on a disk, each with a unique number.

When people refer to the number of sectors a disk has, the unit they use is sectors per track—not just sectors. If a diskette has 80 tracks and 18 sectors per track, it has 1,440 sectors (80 x 18)—not 18 sectors. This is true regardless of the "length" of the track. The disk's outermost track is longer than the innermost track, but each is still divided into the same number of sectors. Regardless of physical size, all sectors hold the same number of bytes; that is, the shortest, innermost sectors hold the same amount of data as the longest, outermost sectors.

Like any flat object, a disk has two sides. Some early drives could read data on only one side, but today, all disk drives can read and write data on both sides of a disk. To the computer, the second side is just a continuation of the sequence of sectors. For example, the 3.5-inch, 1.44-MB diskette has a total of 2,880 sectors (80 tracks per side x 2 sides x 18 sectors per track).

On most diskettes, a sector contains 512 bytes, or 0.5 KB. The different capacities of diskettes are generally a function of the number of sides, tracks, and sectors per track. Table 4.2 shows how the capacities of diskettes relate to the dimensions.

NORTON Online

For more information on **formatting a disk,** visit this book's Web site at **www.glencoe.com/norton/online**

Table 4.2			Formatting Specifications for Various Disks						
DIAMETER (INCHES)	SIDES	TRACKS	SECTORS/ TRACK	SECTORS	BYTES/ SECTOR	BYTES	KB	MB
5.25	2	40	9	720	512	368,640	360	.36
5.25	2	40	18	1440	512	737,280	720	.7
3.5	2	80	15	2400	512	1,228,800	1,200	1.2
3.5	2	80	18	2880	512	1,474,560	1,440	1.44
3.5	2	80	36	5760	512	2,949,150	2,880	2.88

A sector is the smallest unit with which any disk drive (diskette drive or hard drive) can work. Each bit and byte within a sector can have different values, but the drive can read or write only whole sectors at a time. If the computer needs to change just one byte out of 512, it must rewrite the entire sector.

Because files are not usually a size that is an even multiple of 512 bytes, some sectors contain unused space after the end of the file. In addition, the DOS and Windows operating systems allocate groups of sectors, called **clusters**, to each of the files they store on a disk. Cluster sizes vary, depending on the size and type of the disk, but they can range from 4 sectors for diskettes, to 64 sectors for some hard disks. A small file that contains only 50 bytes will use only a portion of the first sector of a cluster assigned to it, leaving the remainder of the first sector, and the remainder of the cluster, allocated but unused.

How the Operating System Finds Data on a Disk

A computer's operating system can locate data on a disk (diskette or hard drive) because each track and sector is labeled, and the location of all data is kept in a special log on the disk. The labeling of tracks and sectors is called performing a **logical format** or **soft format**. A commonly used logical format performed by DOS or Windows creates these four disk areas:

- The boot record
- The file-allocation table (FAT)
- The root folder or directory
- The data area

When a disk is formatted, these four areas are defined.

Boot record

FAT (copy 1)

FAT (copy 2)

Data area

Root directory

Unused area

The **boot record** is a small program that runs when you first start the computer. This program determines whether the disk has the basic components of DOS or Windows that are necessary to run the operating system successfully. If it determines that the required files are present and the disk has a valid format, it transfers control to one of the operating system programs that continues the process of starting up. This process is called **booting**—because the boot program makes the computer "pull itself up by its bootstraps."

The boot record also describes other disk characteristics, such as the number of bytes per sector and the number of sectors per track—information that the operating system needs to access the data area of the disk.

The **file-allocation table (FAT)** is a log that records the location of each file and the status of each sector. When you write a file to a disk, the operating system checks the FAT for an open area, stores the file, and then identifies the file and its location in the FAT.

The FAT solves a common filing problem: What happens when you load a file, increase its size by adding text to it, and then save it again? For example, say that you need to add 5,000 bytes to a 10,000-byte file that has no open space around it. The disk drive could move the surrounding files to make room for the 5,000 bytes, but that would be time-consuming. Instead, the operating system checks the FAT for free areas and then places pointers in it that link together the nonadjacent parts of the file. In other words, it splits the file up by allocating new space for the overflow.

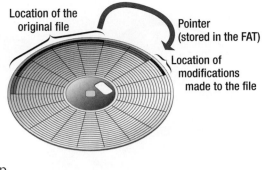

Location of the original file

Pointer (stored in the FAT)

Location of modifications made to the file

When new data needs to be added to a file and there is no more room next to the cluster where the original data is stored, the operating system records the new information in an unused cluster on the disk. The FAT lists both clusters, and a pointer at the end of the first cluster connects it to the second.

When the operating system saves a file in this way, the file becomes **fragmented**. Its parts are located in nonadjacent sectors. Fragmented files cause undesirable side effects, the most significant being that it takes longer to save and load them.

Users do not normally need to see the information in the FAT, but they often use the folder information. A **folder**, also called a **directory**, is a tool for organizing files on a disk. Folders can contain files or other folders, so it is possible to set up a hierarchical system of folders on your computer, just as you have folders within other folders in a file cabinet. The top folder on any disk is known as the root. When you use the operating system to view the contents of a folder, the operating system lists specific information about each file in the folder, such as the file's name, its size, the time and date that it was created or last modified, and so on. Figure 4.9 shows a typical Windows 98 folder listing.

The part of the disk that remains free after the boot sector, FAT, and root folder have been created is called the **data area** because that is where the data files (or program files) are actually stored.

Figure 4.9
A Windows 98 folder listing.

Hard Disks

Although a shift toward optical technology is occurring, the **hard disk** is still the most common storage device for all computers. Much of what you have learned about diskettes and drives applies to hard disks as well. Like diskettes, hard disks store data in tracks divided into sectors. Physically, however, hard disks look quite different from diskettes.

These two photos show the inside of a hard disk drive. The stack of platters is shown on the left. On the right is the circuitry that controls the drive. When they are installed in the computer, the circuitry is screwed to the top of the case that contains the hard disk.

NORTON Online

For more information on **hard disks**, visit this book's Web site at www.glencoe.com/norton/online

Figure 4.10
Parts of a hard disk.

Read/write head

Access arm

Spindle

Aluminum platters with magnetic coating

A hard disk is a stack of one or more metal platters that spin on one spindle, like a stack of rigid diskettes. Each platter is coated with iron oxide, and the entire unit is encased in a sealed chamber. Unlike diskettes, where the disk and drive are separate, the hard disk and drive are a single unit. It includes the hard disk, the motor that spins the platters, and a set of read/write heads (see Figure 4.10).

Because you cannot remove the disk from its drive (unless it is a removable hard disk, which you will learn about later), the terms *hard disk* and *hard drive* are used interchangeably.

Hard disks have become the primary storage device for PCs because they are convenient and cost-efficient. In both speed and capacity, they far outperform diskettes. A high-density 3.5-inch diskette can store 1.44 MB of data. Hard disks, in contrast, range in capacity from about 80 MB on up. Most PCs now come with hard disks of at least 1.6 GB.

Two important physical differences between hard disks and diskettes account for the differences in performance. First, hard disks are sealed in a vacuum chamber, and second, the hard disk consists of a rigid metal platter (usually aluminum), rather than flexible mylar.

The rigidity of the hard disk allows it to spin much faster—typically more than ten times faster—than diskettes; a hard disk spins between 3,600 rpm and 7,200 rpm, instead of a diskette's 300 rpm. The speed at which the disk spins is a major factor in the overall performance of the drive.

The rigidity of the hard disk and the high speed at which it rotates allow a lot more data to be recorded on the disk's surface. As you may recall, waving a magnet past an electric coil like the one in a drive's read/write head causes a current to flow through the coil. The faster you wave the magnet, and the closer the magnet is to the coil, the larger the current it generates in the coil. Therefore, a disk that spins faster can use smaller magnetic charges to make current flow in the read/write head. The drive's heads can also use a lower-intensity current to record data on the disk.

Not only do hard disks pack data more closely together, they also hold more data because they often include several platters, stacked one on top of another. To the computer system, this configuration just means that the disk has more than two sides; in addition to a side 0 and side 1, there are sides 2, 3, 4, and so on. Some hard disk drives hold as many as 12 disks, but both sides of the disks are not always used.

With hard disks, the number of sides that the disk uses is specified by the number of read/write heads. For example, a particular hard disk drive might have six disk platters (that is, 12 sides), but only 11 heads, indicating that one side is not used to store data. Often, this is the bottom side of the bottom disk, as shown in Figure 4.11.

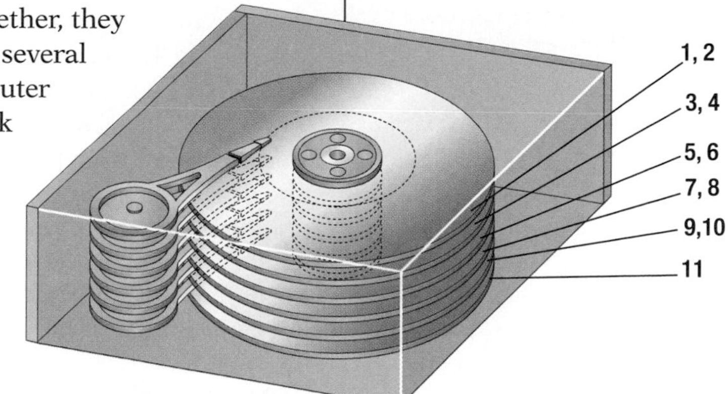

Because hard disks are actually a stack of platters, the term **cylinder** is used to refer to the same track across all the disk sides, as shown in Figure 4.12. For example, track 0 (the outermost track) on every disk is cylinder 0.

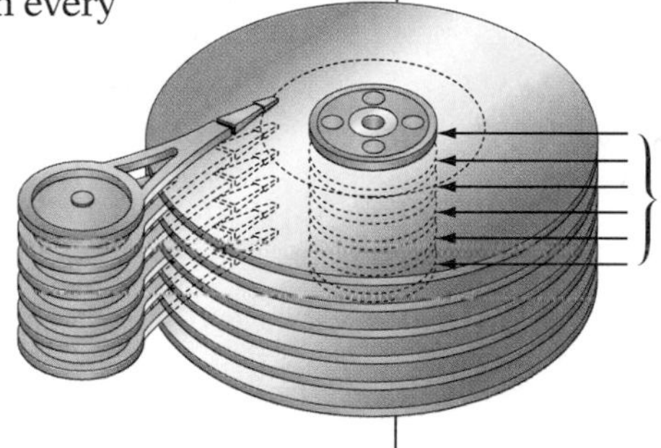

Like diskettes, hard disks generally store 512 bytes of data in a sector, but because of their higher tolerances, hard disks can have more sectors per track—54, 63, or even more sectors per track are not uncommon.

The computation of a hard disk's capacity is identical to that for diskettes—but the numbers are larger. Here's the breakdown for a disk that is sold as a 541 MB disk:

1,632 cylinders X 12 heads (sides)   = 19,584 tracks

19,584 tracks X 54 sectors/track   = 1,057,536 sectors

1,057,536 sectors X 512 bytes/sector = 541,458,432 bytes

Figure 4.11
Read/write heads on each side of each platter, except the bottom side of the bottom platter.

1, 2
3, 4
5, 6
7, 8
9, 10
11

Figure 4.12
A cylinder on a hard disk.

A cylinder consists of a vertical stack of tracks, one track on each side of each platter.

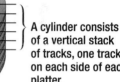

For more information on **hard disk capacity**, visit this book's Web site at **www.glencoe.com/norton/online**

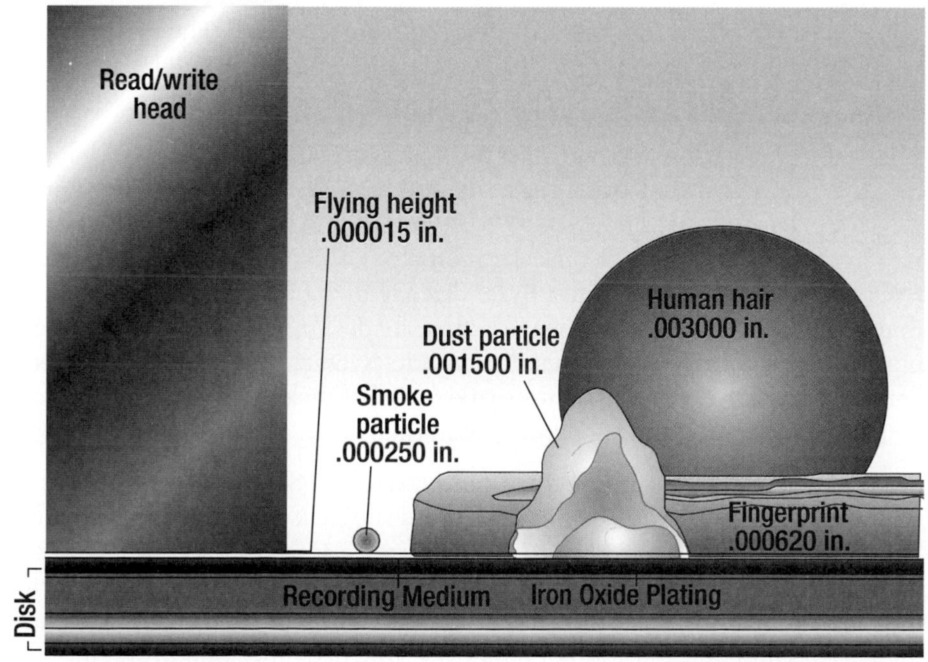

Read/write head

Flying height
.000015 in.

Human hair
.003000 in.

Dust particle
.001500 in.

Smoke particle
.000250 in.

Fingerprint
.000620 in.

Recording Medium   Iron Oxide Plating

Disk

Figure 4.13
Distance between a hard disk's read/write head and the disk's surface, compared to the size of possible contaminants.

In spite of all the capacity and speed advantages, hard disks have one major drawback. To achieve optimum performance, the read/write head must be extremely close to the surface of the disk. In fact, the heads of hard disks fly so close to the surface of the disk that if a dust particle, a human hair, or even a fingerprint were placed on the disk it would bridge the gap between the head and the disk, causing the heads to crash. A **head crash**, in which the head touches the disk, destroys the data stored in the area of the crash and can destroy a read/write head, as well. Figure 4.13 shows the height at which a hard disk head floats, compared to the sizes of dust particles, hair, and fingerprints.

Removable Hard Disks

NORTON Online

For more information on **removable hard disks**, visit this book's Web site at **www.glencoe.com/norton/online**

Removable hard disks and drives attempt to combine the speed and capacity of a hard disk with the portability of a diskette. There are many different types of devices in this category. Choosing the best type is usually a matter of balancing your needs for speed, storage capacity, compatibility (will it work in different computers?), and price.

Hot-Swappable Hard Disks

At the high end, in terms of both price and performance, are **hot-swappable hard disks**. These are sometimes used on high-end workstations that require large amounts of storage. They allow the user to remove (swap out) a hard disk and insert (swap in) another while the computer is still on (hot).

Hot-swappable hard disks are like removable versions of normal hard disks: the removable box includes the disk, drive, and read/write heads in a sealed container.

Hard Disk Cartridges

This SyQuest SyJet drive records and reads data from small cartridges that can store up to 1.5 GB.

Most removable hard disks used with PCs are different from the hot-swappable design. Most work a bit like a diskette, with a disk in a plastic case that is inserted into or removed from the drive. The disk and case are often called a hard disk cartridge. Some popular drives with removable hard disks are made by SyQuest.

The original SyQuest disk was the same diameter as an old floppy: 5.25 inches. During the early and mid-1990s, the standard storage capacity was 44 MB, 88 MB, and 200 MB. SyQuest also offers a smaller, 3.5-inch disk that can store 105 MB or 270 MB. Another SyQuest offering is the SyQuest SyJet drive, which offers a 3.5-inch cartridge that holds 1.5GB. SyQuest chose to license its design to other hardware manufacturers, so many companies have made SyQuest-type disks and drives. During the early 1990s, this factor made SyQuest disks highly compatible and helped to make the SyQuest a popular standard.

Price was also a factor that helped popularize the SyQuest drive. The drive typically costs between $200 and $300, and the disk cartridges cost between $60 and $90. The SyQuest SyJet runs between $360 and $500, with the cartridges costing around $125. The major drawbacks of the SyQuest disks are that the older models are noticeably slower than a built-in hard disk, and data errors and degeneration of data over time are more of a problem.

Although the storage medium is flexible, not hard, the Zip drive is a competitor to the SyQuest drive. It is manufactured by Iomega Corporation. The Zip drives are slower than SyQuests but have gained popularity due to low prices. Typically, the drive costs about $150, and the disks cost as little as $15 for a 100 MB cartridge.

The Iomega Jaz drive can store up to 1.0 GB of data on a removable cartridge.

NORTON Online

For more information on **SyQuest products**, visit this book's Web site at **www.glencoe.com/norton/online**

Iomega is also pushing up the storage capacity and speed of removable hard disks. Their Jaz drive, for example, is as fast as some internal hard disks and can store 1 GB of data. Its cost is slightly lower than the SyQuest SyJet drive, running between $260 and $400.

The Bernoulli Drive

Another technology that competes with the SyQuest drives is the Bernoulli drive, also made by Iomega. This drive, which dates back to 1983, is actually not a removable hard disk because the disk itself is made of plastic, similar to a diskette. When the disk spins, air pressure bends the disk up toward the read/write head but maintains a thin layer of air between the heads and the disk. The first Bernoulli disks held 5 MB, but more recent versions can store up to 230 MB and are almost as fast as internal hard disks.

Tape Drives

Tape drives read and write data to the surface of a tape the same way an audio cassette recorder does. The difference is that a computer tape drive writes digital data rather than analog data—discrete "1s" and "0s" rather than the finely graduated signals created by sounds in an audio recorder.

The best use of tape storage is for data that you do not use often, such as backup copies of your hard disk (which you will need only if your hard drive malfunctions or you accidentally delete a valuable file). Because a tape is a long strip of magnetic material, the tape drive has to write data to it sequentially—one byte after another. Sequential access is inherently slower than the direct access provided by media such as disks. When you want to access a specific set of data on a tape, the drive has to scan through all the data you do not need to get to the data you want. The result is a slow access time. In fact, the access time varies depending on the speed of the drive, the length of the tape, and the position on the tape to which the head wrote the data in the first place.

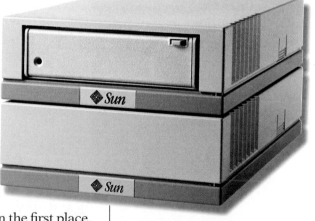

SPARCstorage UniPack Family— Tape and Hard Drive.

Despite the long access times, however, tape drives are well suited for certain purposes, especially for backing up your system's entire hard disk. Because hard disks usually have capacities much greater than diskettes, backing up or restoring a system with diskettes can be a long and tedious process requiring dozens or even hundreds of diskettes. Backing up using removable hard disks is usually expensive. Tape, however, offers an inexpensive way to store a lot of data on a single cassette.

Tape was one of the first widely used media for mass storage. Early mainframe computers used reel-to-reel tape systems, such as the one pictured in Figure 4.14.

Today, most tapes are housed in cassettes that contain both reels of the tape. The cassettes come in many sizes, but most are about the same size or smaller than an audio cassette. Oddly, you cannot tell much about the capacity of a tape from the cassette's size. Some of the largest cassettes have capacities of only 40 to 60 MB, whereas some of the smallest microcassettes can hold as much as 8 GB of data.

DAT Drives

Generally, the highest capacities are achieved by **digital audiotape (DAT)** drives. DAT drives typically have two read heads and two write heads built into a small wheel (or cylinder) that spins near the tape at about 2,000 rpm—at the same time, the tape itself moves past the wheel at a relatively slow speed (about 0.34 inch per second). The write heads on the spinning wheel each write data with opposite magnetic polarities on overlapping areas of the tape. Each read head reads only one polarity or the other. The result is a high data density per inch of tape. Although DAT cassettes are inexpensive (they usually cost from $5 to $10), the DAT drives often cost between $575 and $1,000 but can run as high as $2,700. Individual users are more likely to buy less expensive systems. Today, tape systems for backing up a 1 GB hard disk can be purchased for about $200.

Figure 4.14 ◀
An old reel-to-reel tape storage system.

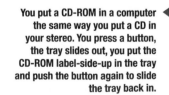

NORTON
Online

For more information on **tape drives**, visit this book's Web site at
www.glencoe.com/norton/online

OPTICAL STORAGE DEVICES

Because of the continuing demand for greater storage capacity, hardware manufacturers are always on the lookout for alternative storage media. Today, the most popular alternatives to magnetic storage systems are optical systems.

Optical storage techniques make use of the pinpoint precision possible only with laser beams. A laser uses a concentrated, narrow beam of light, focused and directed with lenses, prisms, and mirrors. The tight focus of the laser beam is possible because the light is all the same wavelength.

There are two common types of optical technology. The most widely used type is compact disk (CD) technology, which is used in CD-ROM, WORM, PhotoCD, and CD-Recordable. The other type, which has been steadily gaining in popularity over the past few years, is a hybrid that combines magnetic and optical technology. These devices are known as magneto-optical drives.

You put a CD-ROM in a computer the same way you put a CD in your stereo. You press a button, the tray slides out, you put the CD-ROM label-side-up in the tray and push the button again to slide the tray back in.

CD-ROM

The familiar audio compact disk is a popular medium for storing music. In the computer world, however, the medium is called compact disk, read-only memory (CD-ROM). CD-ROM uses the same technology used to produce music CDs. In fact, if you have a sound card and speakers connected to your computer, you can play CDs with your PC.

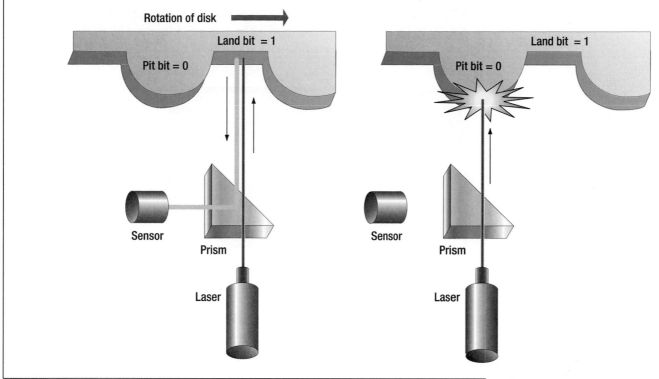

Figure 4.15
How data is read from
a CD-ROM.

The CD-ROM drive for music or data reads 0s and 1s off a spinning disk by focusing a laser on the disk's surface. Some areas of the disk reflect the laser light into a sensor, whereas others scatter the light. A spot that reflects the laser beam into the sensor is interpreted as a 1, and the absence of a reflection is interpreted as a 0.

Data is laid out on a CD-ROM in a long, continuous spiral that starts at the outer edge and winds inward to the center. Data is stored in the form of **lands**, which are flat areas on the metal surface, and **pits**, which are depressions or hollows. A land reflects the laser light into the sensor, and a pit scatters the light (see Figure 4.15). On a full CD-ROM, the spiral of data stretches almost three miles long!

CD-ROM Speeds

Compared to hard disk drives, CD-ROM drives are quite slow, in part because the laser reads pits and lands one bit at a time. Another reason has to do with the changing rotational speed of the disk. Like a track on a magnetic disk, the track of an optical disk is split into sectors. However, as shown in Figure 4.16, the sectors are laid out quite differently than they are on magnetic disks.

As you can see, the sectors near the middle of the CD wrap farther around the disk than those near the edge. For the drive to read each sector in the same amount of time, it must spin the disk faster when reading sectors near the middle, and slower when reading sectors near the edge. Changing the speed of rotation

For more
information on
CD-ROM drives, visit
this book's Web site at
www.glencoe.com/norton/online

SECTORS ON A MAGNETIC DISK

Sectors are wider at the edge
than they are near the middle.

SECTORS ON A CD-ROM

Sectors form a continuous spiral,
and each sector is the same width.

Figure 4.16
How sectors are laid out on a
CD-ROM versus a magnetic disk.

takes time—enough to seriously impair the overall speed of the CD-ROM drive. The first CD-ROM drives read data at 150 KBps (kilobytes per second)—"single speed." This is much slower than a typical hard drive at 5–15 MBps (megabytes per second). At the time this book was published, CD-ROM drives read data two (300 KBps) to 32 (4800 KBps) times faster than the first models. However, by the time you read this, the speed will undoubtably be higher.

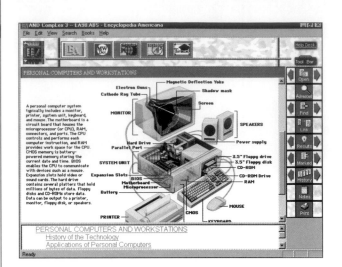

Even with the changing speed of the disk, though, reading data from an optical medium is a relatively simple undertaking. Writing data, however, is another matter. The medium is a foil disk that is physically pitted to reflect or scatter the laser beam. The disk is covered in a plastic coating, and it is difficult to alter the surface of the disk after it has been stamped.

CD-ROM Uses

The fact that you cannot write data to a CD-ROM does not mean that this storage medium is not useful. In fact, many applications rely on huge volumes of data that rarely change. For example, dictionaries; encyclopedias; professional reference libraries; music; and video all require tremendous amounts of data that you would not normally want to alter even if you could.

In addition to these uses, software companies can distribute their products on CD-ROM. Because of the high precision and data density possible with CD-ROM, a single CD typically can hold about 650 MB of data. Because of their high capacity and the fact that one CD is much cheaper to produce than a set of diskettes, many software publishers regard CDs as the distribution medium of choice. For example, the Microsoft Office suite of applications is available on a single CD that also includes an online version of the printed manuals. Instead of having to install the programs from a series of 22 diskettes (or more), the user needs to insert only a single CD.

DVD Media

CDs may soon take a new direction with the advent of DVD, digital versatile disk, a high-density medium capable of storing a full-length movie on a single disk the size of a CD. (Actually, it uses both sides of the disk.) In fact, DVDs look like CDs, and DVD-ROM drives can play current CD-ROMs. A slightly different player, the DVD Movie player, connects to your TV and plays movies like a VCR. The DVD Movie player will also play audio CDs.

Each side of a DVD can hold up to 4.7 GB. Therefore, these two-sided disks can contain as much as 9.4 GB of data.

CD-Recordable, WORM disks, and PhotoCD

For large quantities, CD-ROM disks can be produced by manufacturers with expensive duplication equipment. For fewer copies or even single copies, a **CD-recordable (CD-R) drive** can be attached to a computer as a regular peripheral device. CD-R drives allow you to create your own CD-ROM disks that can be read by any CD-ROM drive. After information has been written to a part of the CD, that information cannot be changed. However, with most CD-R drives, you can continue to record information to other parts of the disk until it is full.

One popular form of recordable CD is **PhotoCD**, a standard developed by Kodak for storing digitized photographic images on a CD. Many film developing stores now have PhotoCD drives that can store your photos and put them on a CD. You can then put the PhotoCD in your computer's CD-ROM drive (assuming that it supports PhotoCD, and most do) and view the images on your computer. Once there, you can also paste them into other documents. With a PhotoCD, you can continue to add images until the disk is full. After an image has been written to the disk using a field of lasers, however, it cannot be erased or changed.

▶ CD-R drives can record data on special CDs. The disks can then be read by any CD-ROM drive.

▶ After your pictures have been processed and stored on a PhotoCD, you can see them on your computer screen and copy them into documents.

Before CD-R and PhotoCD existed, the first ventures into developing a more flexible optical technology resulted in the **write once, read many (WORM) drive**. As with the CD, once data has been etched into the surface of a WORM disk, it cannot be changed. WORM is an ideal medium for making a permanent record of data. For example, many banks use WORM disks to store a record of each day's transactions. The transactions are written to an optical disk and become a permanent record that can be read but never altered.

Phase-Change Rewritable Drives

Phase-change rewritable drives are similar to the write-once, read-many (WORM) drives in that a field of lasers writes and reads data on the phase-change disk. With WORM drives, however, you can write only once to the disk. Phase-change disks can be written to more than once. This is due to the laser beam altering the molecular structure of the disk. One downside to phase-change disks is that they cannot be read by conventional CD-ROM drives. You must have a phase-change drive to read them. An example of a phase-change rewritable drive is the Micro Solutions backpack drive. It is similar in appearance to a CD-ROM drive and can accept regular CD-ROMs and audio CDs. It also can accept 650 MB data cartridges. The cost for the Micro Solutions drive is between $450 and $530, with the data cartridges costing about $45.

Phase-change rewritable drives can access CD-ROM and cartridge media.

Magneto-Optical Drives

Magneto-optical (MO) disks combine some of the best features of both magnetic and optical recording technologies. An MO disk has the capacity of an optical disk but can be rewritten with the ease of a magnetic disk.

The medium that MO disks use is unlike that of either an optical or a magnetic disk. The disk is covered with magnetically sensitive metallic crystals sandwiched inside a thin layer of plastic. In its normal state, the plastic surrounding the crystals is solid, preventing them from moving. To write data to the disk, an intense laser beam is focused on the surface of the medium, which briefly melts the plastic coating enough to allow a magnet to change the orientation of the crystals (see Figure 4.17). The magnet has an effect at only the precise focal point of the laser, where the heated coating allows the crystals to be reoriented.

When the magnet changes the orientations of the metallic crystals on the surface of an MO disk, some crystals are aligned so that they will reflect the laser beam into a sensor; others are oriented so that they will not reflect into the sensor. To read data from the disk, the MO drive focuses a less intense laser beam on the track of crystals. As the track spins under the

NORTON
Online

For more information on **phase-change rewritable drives**, visit this book's Web site at **www.glencoe.com/norton/online**

This magneto-optical drive can store up to 1.3 GB on a removable disk.

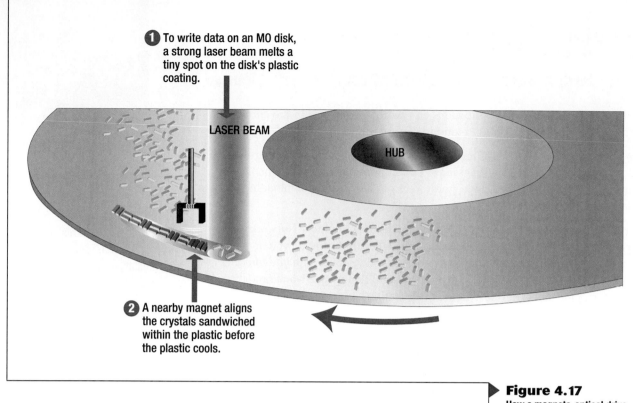

① To write data on an MO disk, a strong laser beam melts a tiny spot on the disk's plastic coating.

LASER BEAM

HUB

② A nearby magnet aligns the crystals sandwiched within the plastic before the plastic cools.

Figure 4.17
How a magneto-optical drive records data.

beam, some spots reflect light into the sensor, and others do not, creating the stream of 1s and 0s the computer recognizes as data (see Figure 4.18).

MO disks are available today in various sizes and capacities. Some of them look identical to 3.5 inch diskettes but have capacities of more than 1 GB and are comparable in speed to hard disks. Also, MO disks are portable, and the data on them cannot be corrupted by magnets, heat, or humidity.

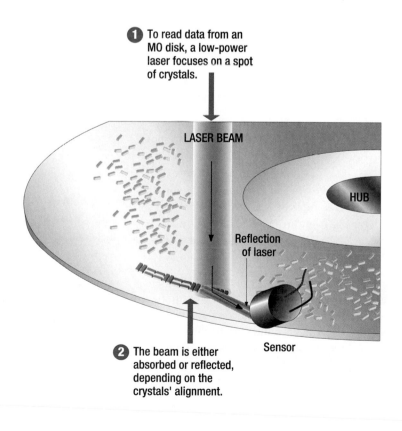

① To read data from an MO disk, a low-power laser focuses on a spot of crystals.

LASER BEAM

HUB

Reflection of laser

② The beam is either absorbed or reflected, depending on the crystals' alignment.

Sensor

Figure 4.18
How a magneto-optical drive reads data.

Techview

PC Card: A Hard Disk the Size of Your Driver's License

Today's gigantic software applications can seem like the bull in the china shop. They take up a lot of room and tend to disrupt things in small spaces.

Put just a few of them on your PC, and you may soon find yourself with barely enough room to store your e-mail messages and multimedia presentations, let alone all your everyday work and the storerooms of data you're downloading every day from the Internet.

On top of this, how do you share the gargantuan files they produce? Network access probably lets you share your projects in the office, but what do you do when you want to take that presentation for tomorrow's meeting home with you tonight to fine-tune on your home computer? Often a standard floppy disk won't hold even one modern graphic file, let alone a whole presentation.

Many types of removable mass storage devices are available to meet these challenges, and one of the most interesting is the PC Card. PC Cards, also referred to as PCMCIA (Personal Computer Memory Card International Association) cards, are credit-card-sized expansion devices that are inserted into slots in your personal computer (primarily portable models). Although PC Card adapters are available for desktop computers, the size of the PC Cards makes them ideal for portable computers.

PC cards provide varied add-on functionality to laptop computers.

PC Card hard disk storage capacities currently range from 170 MB to more than 1.45 GB of data. Considering that the capacity of the entire hard disk of a desktop PC starts where these cards leave off, at around 1.5 GB, the capacity of these tiny devices is astonishing. This means that you can carry an additional hard disk with you like a credit card in your wallet!

PC Cards are credit card size in their length and width; however, they tend to be thicker than a credit card. There are three types of PC Cards: Type I, II, and III, varying in thickness from about .16 inch to about .5 inch. Some companies even offer PCMCIA docks for both portable and desktop PCs. One product is the KanguruDock™ system from Interactive Media Corp. The KanguruDock™ is a removable hard drive system that connects directly to your PCMCIA socket and provides storage of up to 6.4 GB of data.

PC Card storage devices will serve adequately as either removable storage (you can take it with you) or secure removable storage (you keep a copy of your data separate from your computer as a backup or as an alternate storage site if your hard drive is full). PC Cards work well to share or transfer data because they can be unplugged from one computer and then plugged into another. You can even mail an entire hard drive to another person!

In addition to storage, PC Cards are available for a variety of other functions:

■ **Digital Video PC Cards** transform a laptop computer into a multimedia platform capable of recording, displaying, and transmitting real-time, full-motion video.

■ **Audio PC Cards** let you add music or sound to presentations or enjoy an audio environment with recording and playback capabilities.

■ **SCSI/Audio Multimedia Combo PC Cards** add 16-bit CD-quality sound and SCSI capabilities on a single card. This lets you listen to your favorite CD by connecting a CD-ROM drive to the SCSI interface. Or add music, sound, even voice annotation to your word processing documents and spreadsheet applications, all while you're on the road.

■ **Cellular-Ready Fax/Modem PC Cards** allow mobile executives and field professionals to use their cellular telephones to send and receive data and faxes, anywhere, anytime.

■ **Network PC Cards** in conjunction with remote access technology allow travelers instant access to their company network for sharing all kinds of files or communications.

■ **Global Positioning System PC Cards** (with appropriate software) allow mobile businesspeople to map their route, find addresses, trace a route, or determine their position and speed—ideal for remote field work.

Floptical Drives

Floptical drives are a combination of two technologies, including floppy disk and optical disk technologies. Floptical drives include an ultra-high density magnetic head that can write up to 20 tracks at a time, instead of just one. Examples of floptical drives include Imation SuperDisk LS-120 and the O.R. Technologies a:drive. They both accept conventional 3.5-inch floppy disks as well as 120 MB diskettes (SuperDisk) or cartridges (a:drive). You can use these devices instead of a standard floppy disk drive on your PC. The Imation SuperDisk costs about $200 and the diskettes about $18. The cost of the a:drive is about $210, with the cost of the 120 MB cartridge running $18.

▶ Floptical drives have the flexibility of reading conventional 3.5-inch disks and new high-capacity cartridges that hold 120 MB.

MEASURING DRIVE PERFORMANCE

When evaluating the performance of common storage devices, you need to be aware of two common measures: the average access time and the data-transfer rate. For random-access devices (all the storage devices discussed, with the exception of magnetic tapes), you generally want a low access time and a high data-transfer rate. With tape drives, all you really need to worry about is convenience and capacity. In addition to these factors, the drive interface is an important consideration.

Average Access Time

The **average access time** of a device is the amount of time it takes the device to position its read or read/write heads over any spot on the medium. It is important that the measurement be an average because access times can vary greatly depending on the distance between the heads' original location and their destination. To measure the access time of a drive effectively, you must test many reads of randomly chosen sectors—a method that approximates the actual read instructions a disk drive would receive under normal circumstances.

Access time is the combination of two factors: the speed at which a disk spins (revolutions per minute, or rpm), and the time it takes to move the heads from one track to another. In the section on diskettes, you saw that the longest it takes the head to access any point is about 0.2 second, which is the amount of time it takes the disk to complete one revolution at 300 rpm. Access times are measured in **milliseconds (ms)**, or 0.001 second. The maximum access time for diskettes—0.2 second—is 200 milliseconds. The average seek time is about one half the maximum, or 100 milliseconds.

Average access times for hard drives can vary, but most good ones generate rates of 8 to 12 milliseconds. If you compare these figures to those for diskette drives, you will see that access times for hard disks are generally at least 8 to 10 times faster than diskette drives.

Access times for CD-ROM and WORM drives tend to be quite slow by hard disk drive standards, ranging from 100 to 300 milliseconds.

With removable hard disks and magneto-optical disks, access times can vary greatly. The best models compete with good hard disks, whereas the mediocre ones are about half as fast as a slow hard disk.

NORTON Online

For more information on **floptical drives**, visit this book's Web site at **www.glencoe.com/norton/online**

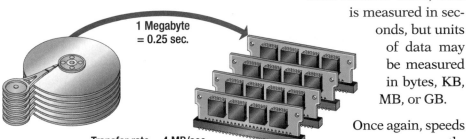

File Compression

Even with the large storage devices available, many users still find themselves pushing the limits of what they can store on their PCs. One solution to this storage problem, besides upgrading to larger devices, is to compress data. **File compression**, or **data compression**, is a technology of shrinking the size of a file, thereby opening up free space for more data and programs to reside on the disk. Entire hard disks, floppy disks, or individual files can be compressed by as much as a 3:1 ratio (a 300 MB of data fills only 100 MB of space, for instance). File compression is performed by software and uses **mathematical algorithms** to squeeze data into smaller chunks by removing information not vital to the file or data. When the file is returned to its original state, this data is reinserted so that your original data is reproduced exactly as it was before compression. These algorithms are copyrighted by companies, such as Stac Electonics' LZS compression algorithm. Two favorite compression programs for PCs include PKZIP and DriveSpace 3. DriveSpace 3 is part of the Windows 98 operating system. StuffIT is a favorite among Macintosh enthusiasts.

Data-Transfer Rate

The other important statistic for measuring drive performance is the speed at which it can transfer data—that is, how long it takes to read or write data. Speeds are expressed as a rate, or as some amount of data per unit of time. For **data-transfer rates**, time is measured in seconds, but units of data may be measured in bytes, KB, MB, or GB.

Once again, speeds can vary greatly. Speeds for hard disks are generally high, from about 5 MB per second (abbreviated MBps) up to 15 MBps for the high-end drives designed for networks. When buying a hard disk, the data-transfer rate is at least as important a factor as the access time.

Data-transfer rate is the time required to move a specific amount of data (for example, 1 MB) from one device to another, such as from the hard disk to memory.

1 Megabyte = 0.25 sec.

Transfer rate = 4 MB/sec.

CD-ROMs and diskettes are the slowest storage devices. CD-ROMs range from 300 KBps for a double-speed player, up to 900 KBps for a 6X drive (six times faster than a single speed drive). Diskette drives average about 45 KBps. Removable hard disks and magneto-optical disks range from about 1.25 MBps up into the hard disk range.

Note: Some drive manufacturers and dealers advertise their drive's data transfer rates in units of MBps, but others may express them in megabits per second, or Mbps. When comparison shopping, make sure that you notice whether the rate specified is "MBps" or "Mbps."

The speeds for various common storage devices are summarized in Table 4.3.

Drive-Interface Standards

Another important factor in determining how quickly a drive can read and write data is the type of controller that the drive uses. Just as a video monitor

NORTON Notebook
Storing All That Data: Data Warehousing and Data Mining

For many corporations, data is their lifeblood. For years, companies have collected, sorted, stored, and spit out vast amounts of data on their customers, products, inventories, employees, sales, and stores. They also store external data about their competitors and their industry. This data is crucial for managers, employees, and executives in better understanding their organization.

There are two major issues concerning all this collected data: where to store it and how to access it when you need it. This problem is known as *infoglut*.

The usual approach to battling infoglut is to maintain well-designed databases. At some point, however, the law of diminishing returns comes into play, and there is simply too much information. It simply is not practical to create a new database and a new database management system (DBMS) for each new problem that comes along. So the newest approach to the problem of infoglut is to build a **data warehouse** and then to mine the data warehouse for critical information.

A data warehouse is a massive collection of corporate information, often stored in gigabytes or terabytes of data. It can include any and all data that is relevant to the running of a company. All this data is stored in databases spread among many storage devices on computers running tens or even hundreds of central processing units.

Raid 7, 73 series, 70 series, and 72 series by Storage Computer.

However, setting up a data warehouse is much more complicated than simply dumping all kinds of data into one storage place. There are several factors to consider.

First, what types of processing scheme will be used? Generally, two types of technologies, Symmetrical Multiprocessing (SMP) or Massively Parallel Processing (MPP), are used. For smaller storage needs, such as between 50 GB to 300 GB, SMP is used. For data warehouses larger than 300 GB, many companies opt for MPP because of the ability to scale (or add) additional processors as the storage needs grow.

Second, how much storage space is needed and what type of backup plan is needed? One of the most popular storage schemes is RAID (Redundant Array of Independent Disks). RAID is a storage system that links any number of disk drives to act as a single disk. In this system, information is written to two or more disks simultaneously to improve speed and reliability, and to ensure that data is available to users at all times.

RAID's capabilities are based on three techniques: (1) mirroring, (2) striping, and (3) striping-with-parity. In a mirrored system, data is written to two or more disks simultaneously, providing a complete copy of all the information on a drive, should one drive fail. Striping provides the user with speedy response by spreading data across several disks. Striping alone, however, does not provide backup if one of the disks in an array fails. Striping-with-parity provides the speed of striping with the reliability of parity. Should a drive in such an array fail, the disk that stores the parity information can be used to reconstruct the data from the damaged drive. Some arrays using the striping-with-parity technique also offer a technique known as "hot swapping," which enables a system administrator to remove a damaged drive while the array remains in operation.

Third, what type of data scrubbing will be set up? Data scrubbing means sifting through data and performing such tedious tasks as eliminating duplications and incomplete records and making sure that similar fields in different tables are defined in exactly the same ways.

After the data warehouse has been set up, it can be an invaluable resource for serving the needs of customers, outsmarting the competition, discovering trends in the market, and developing new products.

Ultimately, the goal of data mining is to answer complex business questions. Regardless of the type of hardware and software a company uses for its data warehouse, the end result of data mining is that a company can put its vast storehouse of information to better business uses by finding out exactly what it knows, how to get to it, and what to do with it.

Table 4.3	Average Access Times and Data-Transfer Rates for Common Storage Devices				
	HARD DISKS	**REMOVABLE HARD DISKS**	**MAGNETO-OPTICAL**	**DISKETTES**	**CD-ROMS**
Avg. Access Time (ms)	8–12	12–30	15–20	100	100–300
Data-Transfer Rate (MBps)	5–15	1.25–5.5	2–6	0.045	0.3–0.9

requires a controller to act as an interface between the CPU and the display screen, storage devices also need a controller to act as an intermediary between the drive and the CPU. A disk controller is connected directly to the computer's bus. On most computers, part of the disk controller is an integral part of the computer's main motherboard, and the rest is built into the drive itself. On some older computers, the controller is an expansion board that connects to the bus by plugging into one of the computer's expansion slots.

The ST-506 Standard

In 1979, Shugart Technology, which would later become Seagate Technology, developed the first standard for interfacing hard disks with PCs. That interface became known as ST-506, after the original hard disk drive that used it. The first ST-506 drives used a **data-encoding scheme** called *modified frequency modulation* (MFM). A data-encoding scheme is the method that a disk drive uses to translate bits of data into a sequence of flux reversals (changes in magnetic polarity) on the surface of a disk.

Because of MFM's inherent limitations, ST-506 drives that used this scheme had a maximum capacity of 127.5 MB and a maximum data-transfer rate of about 655 KB per second.

The second generation of ST-506 drives employed a new data-encoding scheme called run-length limited (RLL). The RLL encoding scheme made more efficient use of the surface space on a hard disk. With RLL encoding, the maximum drive capacity of the ST-506 increased to 200 MB, and the data-transfer rate improved to almost 800 KB per second.

Integrated Drive Electronics

The **integrated drive electronics (IDE) interface** places most of the disk controller's circuitry on the drive itself to provide a simpler interface with the computer and more reliable operation than was possible with the older ST-506 drives.

In 1983, Compaq Computer came up with the idea of integrating the disk controller circuitry onto the hard disk drive itself. The result was IDE, a simpler and more reliable standard than ST-506. Originally, IDE was capable of providing data-transfer rates of about 1 MB per second under ideal conditions, but this capacity grew to 8.3 MBps, which was faster than the data-transfer rates of most hard disks at that time. Enhanced IDE (EIDE) upgraded the standard and currently supports rates up to 16.6 MBps. When you shop for a system, you can generally assume that IDE really means EIDE. Enhanced IDE is currently the most popular drive interface for PCs.

NORTON Online

For more information on **Compaq**, visit this book's Web site at www.glencoe.com/norton/online

Enhanced Small Device Interface

Also in 1983, the Maxtor Corporation developed its own improvement on the ST-506 interface. Like IDE, the **enhanced small device interface (ESDI)** (pronounced "es-dee") incorporates much of the circuitry of the controller directly into the drive.

Early ESDI controllers could transfer data at a rate of 1.25 MB per second, and the standard was improved to support transfers up to 3 MB per second—almost five times the rate of the earlier ST-506 drives. However, ESDI gradually lost market share to Enhanced IDE, and it has largely disappeared.

This kit includes the hardware and software necessary to install a hard disk in a PC.

Small Computer System Interface

The history of the small computer system interface (SCSI) goes back to the 1970s. SCSI (pronounced "scuzzy") was originally developed as a way to connect third-party peripheral devices to mainframe computers—specifically IBM mainframe computers. SCSI went through many transformations before the American National Standards Institute (ANSI) established a definition for the interface in 1986. Since then, the definition of SCSI continued to evolve, first with SCSI-2, and most recently with SCSI-3.

SCSI takes an approach that is different from IDE and ESDI. Because the original concept of SCSI was to provide peripherals (not just hard disk drives) access to the computer system's bus, one way to think of SCSI is as an extension of the computer's bus. As such, all interface circuitry needed by the device has to be on the device itself.

One benefit of SCSI is that bringing the computer's bus directly into the drive improves efficiency. It allows even higher data-transfer rates than are possible with Enhanced IDE. SCSI-2 began by supporting transfer rates up to 5 MBps, but variations allow up to 20 MBps. SCSI-3 raised the ante again to a range of 10–40 MBps.

Another benefit of SCSI is that it can accommodate multiple devices—as many as the bus can handle. SCSI-2 allows up to 7 devices, and SCSI-3 allows up to 127 devices. Also, because a SCSI interface is an extension of the bus, any type of device can be linked (or daisy-chained) on a single SCSI port. Remember, devices that use SCSI interfaces include not only hard disk drives but also optical drives, tape drives, removable hard drives, printers, plotters, and scanners.

Despite the capabilities of SCSI, there are certain pitfalls. If you add a SCSI device to a PC, you should make sure that the device driver is supported by the SCSI card in your PC. In addition, some SCSI devices must be placed at the end of a SCSI chain, so you cannot have more than one such device on a single chain.

NORTON Online

For more information on **SCSI-2**, visit this book's Web site at **www.glencoe.com/norton/online**

Computers
In Your Career

If you're interested in a career in which computers will play a large part, you need to become familiar, if not intimate, with the way computers store data. Careers that involve supporting, maintaining, and building computers rely heavily on storage device specifications and knowledge. Even if you don't plan to be an administrator or other support technician, you need to understand the basics of storing data. Every user who creates files, edits documents, and accesses a database must understand how a computer stores data. You may not need to know how often a hard drive is backed up (unless that task becomes your responsibility) or on which partition a file is stored. However, you do need to understand the difference between floppy disks, hard drives, CD-ROM drives, and removable storage.

A knowledge of storage devices plays an important role in the following careers, among others:

Network Administrators One of the network administrator's primary responsibilities is making backups of data stored on the network server(s) and on users' desktop PCs. This task involves knowing when to make the backups and what backup media and devices are the best for the job. Administrators also need to understand how each type of storage media—such as EIDE hard disks and removable hard drives—store data. This way, administrators will know how to best allocate storage resources on the network depending on the data that users create.

Help Desk Operators When a user calls the help desk for technical support on a hard disk problem, such as the inability to store or retrieve data, the operator must be able to quickly understand the problem and offer solutions. Help desk operators should become familiar with the different file systems that operating systems use (such as FAT or FAT32 for Windows 98) and how these operating systems work with different storage devices. In addition, help desk operators should become comfortable advising users on how to install and configure removable hard drives because many companies use these types of devices to share data between users.

Database Designers As database designers create databases, they need to know the type of storage media being used. Databases created for CD-ROMs, for instance, will allow users only the ability to access, not change, data. For databases created for hard disks, the designer must know the maximum size that the database can grow to (which includes the data already in the database as well as the data that will be added in the future) based on the size of the storage media. If, after assessing the existing storage requirements, a larger storage device is needed, the database designer must consider downgrading the database storage requirements or upgrading the existing storage hardware.

WHAT TO EXPECT IN THE FUTURE

Some of the most important changes in computer hardware over the next few years are likely to occur in the area of storage technology.

The first major change could result from removable hard disk and magneto-optical technologies that are finally competing with hard disk technology on three crucial fronts: speed, capacity, and price. If there were a device that was equal to a good hard disk in all three of these categories, most customers probably would prefer to have a device with a removable disk. That way, they could easily expand the total storage capacity of their systems, trade large data files with others, and replace drives when they malfunction.

Other changes will arrive soon in the form of new standards and new technologies. Recent improvements in CD technology are increasing the capacity of the disk to about 4.5 GB. Another new approach is to record multiple layers of information on CDs using holographic images that are recorded in a crystal. Also, holographic techniques are being developed for storing terabytes (thousands of gigabytes) in crystals the size of sugar cubes. This technology is still in the lab and probably will not appear in common use until after the end of the century.

Although the trend in storage technology for many years has been to bring ever-greater speeds and capacities to the desktop, there is also a groundswell of industry experts and companies that are advocating computers that do not include any storage devices at all. This idea has been driven by the popularity of the Internet. The theory is that people will buy inexpensive diskless machines, known as dumb Internet terminals, or network computers. These computers will include high-speed communication links to the Internet and will obtain most of their software from it each time they are turned on. Many other industry experts scoff at the notion of computers without storage capacity. Only time will tell whether this idea catches on.

VISUAL SUMMARY

Types of Storage Devices

■ Storage devices can be classified as magnetic or optical.

■ The most common magnetic storage devices are diskettes, hard disks, magnetic tape, and removable hard disks.

■ The most common optical devices are CD-ROM, WORM, and magneto-optical disks.

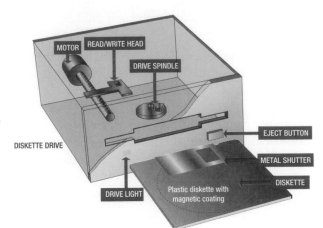

Magnetic Storage Devices

■ Magnetic storage devices work by polarizing tiny pieces of iron on the magnetic medium.

■ Read/write heads contain electromagnets that create magnetic charges on the medium.

■ Diskette drives, also known as floppy disk drives, read and write to diskettes.

■ Diskettes are most often used to transfer files between computers, as a means for distributing software, and as a backup medium.

■ Diskettes come in two common sizes: 3.5-inch and 5.25-inch.

■ Before a disk (diskette or hard disk) can be used, it must be formatted, or initialized—a process in which the read/write heads record tracks and sectors on the disk.

■ At the same time the physical formatting is taking place, the computer's operating system in a PC establishes the disk's logical formatting by creating the boot sector, the FAT, the root folder, and the data area.

■ Hard disks can store more data than diskettes because the high-quality media, the high rotational speed, and the tiny distance between the read/write head and the disk xsurface permit densely packed data and rapid access.

■ Removable hard disks combine high capacity with the convenience of diskettes.

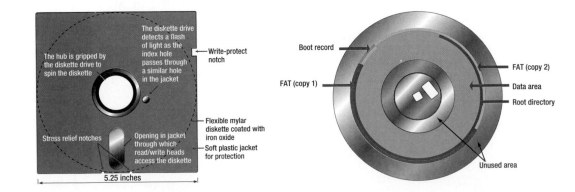

- The best removable hard disks are now as large and fast as good internal hard disks.

- Because data stored on magnetic tape is accessed sequentially, it is most appropriate for backup, when the cost and capacity of the medium are of concern, but speed is not.

Optical Storage Devices

- CD-ROM uses the same technology as a music CD does; a laser reads lands and pits from the surface of the disk.

- CD-ROM disks can store 650 MB, but they cannot be written to.

- WORM disks and CD-Recordable disks can be written to once, but not rewritten or erased.

- Phase-change rewritable drives enable you to write to a phase-change disk more than once.

- Magneto-optical drives write data with a high-powered laser capable of melting the plastic on the disk coating and a magnet that aligns the crystals under the melted area. A less powerful laser reads the alignment of the crystals.

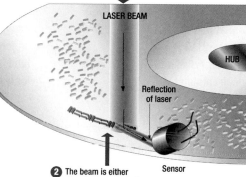

1 To read data from an MO disk, a low-power laser focuses on a spot of crystals.

LASER BEAM

HUB

Reflection of laser

2 The beam is either absorbed or reflected, depending on the crystals' alignment.

Sensor

Measuring Drive Performance

- When considering the performance capabilities of storage devices, you must know the average access time and the data-transfer rate.

- The average access time is the average time it takes a read/write head to move from one place on the recording medium to any other place on the medium.

- The data-transfer rate is a measure of how long it takes the device to read or write a given amount of data.

- The best access times and data-transfer rates are provided by hard disks and some of the latest removable hard disks and magneto-optical disks. CD-ROMs have the slowest access times. Diskettes have the slowest data-transfer rates by far.

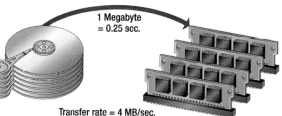

1 Megabyte = 0.25 sec.

Transfer rate = 4 MB/sec.

Drive-Interface Standards

- A disk controller, the interface hardware between the CPU and the disk drive, usually conforms to one of the common interface standards: IDE, ESDI, or SCSI.

- IDE has been upgraded to Enhanced IDE. The upgraded interface standards support data-transfer rates as high as 16.6 MBps.

- SCSI, the second most common drive interface, essentially extends the capacities of the computer's bus.

- The most recent versions of SCSI support data-transfer rates from 10 to 40 MBps.

Visual Summary & Exercises

KEY TERMS

After completing this chapter, you should be able to define the following terms:

average access time, 137
backing up, 121
boot record, 124
booting, 124
CD-recordable (CD-R) drive, 133
cluster, 124
cylinder, 127
data area, 125
data compression, 138
data-encoding scheme, 140
data-transfer rate, 138
data warehouse, 139
density, 121
digital audiotape (DAT), 130
directory, 125
diskette drive, 120
electromagnet, 119

enhanced small device interface (ESDI), 141
file-allocation table (FAT), 124
file compression, 138
floppy, 120
floptical drive, 137
folder, 125
formatting, 122
fragmented, 125
hard disk, 125
head crash, 128
hot-swappable hard disk, 128
initializing, 122
integrated drive electronics (IDE) interface, 140
land, 131
logical format, 124

magnetic storage, 116
magneto-optical (MO) disk, 134
mathematical algorithm, 138
maximum access time, 120
millisecond, 137
phase-change rewritable drive, 134
PhotoCD, 133
pit, 131
polarized, 117
sector, 123
seek time, 120
soft format, 124
storage device, 115
storage media, 115
track, 122
write once, read many (WORM) drive, 134

KEY TERM QUIZ

Fill in the missing word with one of the terms listed in Key Terms:

1. The process of mapping a disk is called _____.

2. A(n) _____ disk has the capacity of a CD-ROM, but it can be rewritten like a magnetic disk.

3. The amount of time it takes a device to position its read or read/write heads over any spot on the medium is known as _____.

4. _____ is the process of creating a duplicate set of programs and data for safekeeping.

5. You use a(n) _____ to organize files on a disk.

6. The internal process of starting up the computer is known as _____.

7. The _____ is the primary storage device for microcomputers.

8. A statistic for measuring how long a drive takes to read or write data is called the _____.

9. Because a hard disk is actually a stack of platters, the term _____ is used to refer to the same track across all the disk sides.

10. A(n) _____ is the smallest segment of a track on a disk.

Visual Summary & Exercises

REVIEW QUESTIONS

1. Name and describe briefly two widely used storage devices for PCs.

2. Describe how a removable hard disk offers the benefits of both diskettes and hard disks.

3. What is an important advantage that a magnet has over a transistor?

4. Describe briefly how a read/write head is able to pass data to and from the surface of a disk.

5. What is a diskette's density a measure of?

6. Describe briefly how a computer's operating system is able to locate data on a disk's surface.

7. Describe briefly the process in which new data added to an existing file is stored on disk. What important component makes this process seamless to a user?

8. Describe the functions of lands and pits on the surface of a compact disk.

9. List and describe some of the benefits and disadvantages of using compact disks rather than diskettes.

10. In what way is SCSI regarded as an extension of a computer's bus? What primary benefit does SCSI provide for storage drives?

DISCUSSION QUESTIONS

1. Why do you think a "basic truth" in computing is that one never has enough data storage space? To what factors do you attribute the need for storage devices that hold increasingly larger amounts of data?

2. Suppose that you are considering the best storage medium for backing up data on a hard disk. What important considerations must you take into account? Would serial, or sequential, data access be preferable, or would random access be better for this purpose?

3. Why is it necessary that access times be averaged to measure the performance of a storage device accurately?

inteNET Workshop

The following exercises assume that you have access to the Internet and a browser. If you need help with any of the exercises, please visit the book's Web site at **www.glencoe.com/norton/online**. This book's Web site also lists the URLs you need to complete many of these exercises.

1. Backing up data is a huge concern for most businesses and users. Some companies offer backup services over the Internet. Can you find two of these services by accessing a search engine? Try searching on terms such as "backup," and "backup service." What services can you find? What types of backup services do they offer?

2. Because of the relatively slow connection most users have to the World Wide Web, some companies offer data compression software to decrease download times. Data compression makes sense in offline uses, as well, because compressed files require less space on floppy disks, hard disks, tapes, and other storage media. Locate products on the Web that offer compression utilities for users and businesses? (HINT: Visit a search engine and search on the term "data compression.") How do these different compression products work? Which product appears to be the standard? Why would you use data compression in your work?

3. The Web offers a unique way to shop for hardware devices, including storage devices. Locate a site or group of sites where you can order the following devices:

- Hard drives
- Removable hard drives
- DVD drives
- CD-ROM drives
- CD-R drives

How many sites did you find? Which ones provided the best information about products? Which sites offered the best deals on hardware?

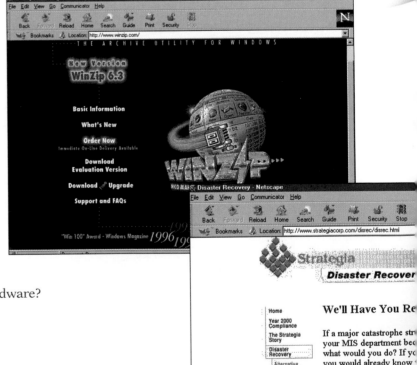

4. Sometimes a backup is not enough. When disaster strikes, data may be unrecoverable, resulting in losses for businesses. Disaster recovery, therefore, is a growing service as new technologies emerge to help businesses recover data from damaged systems, disks, and tapes. Using a search engine, search on the term "disaster recovery." What services can you find? Are any located in your area? What do such services cost? What steps can a business take to protect its data, to avoid the need for such a service?

5. Tape drives have long been a favorite means of backing up and storing large quantities of data. A number of tape standards exist, and a variety of products exist within each standard. What information can you find about tape drives on the Web? What sort of drive would be best suited for use in the home?

6. Optical drives are becoming increasingly popular as backup and storage solutions. Visit the Web sites of optical drive manufacturers. What product information can you find? Would an optical drive be a good purchase for you? Why or why not?

7. Simple methods of backing up and storing large files are constantly being developed. Visit the Web sites of several manufacturers for general information about these products. Can you find product reviews of storage devices? What do the reviewers say?

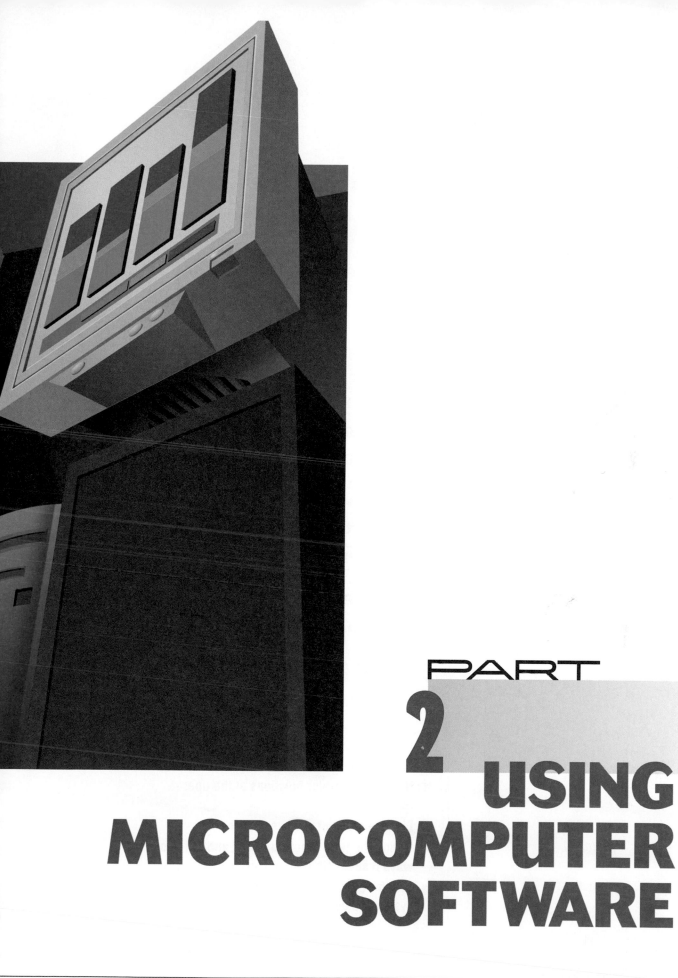

PART

2

USING MICROCOMPUTER SOFTWARE

CHAPTER **5**

The Operating System and the User Interface

CONTENTS

OBJECTIVES

When you complete this chapter, you will be able to do the following:

■ Define the terms "operating system" and "user interface."

■ Name three major functions of the operating system.

■ List five types of utility software.

■ Define the term "multitasking" and list two ways it saves time for a user.

■ List three other significant operating systems, aside from DOS and Windows.

Microsoft—backed by powerful allies such as Compaq and other industry giants—claimed that a delay would harm the entire American economy, even resulting in lost jobs. A national debate surrounded the release of a piece of software.

Although Windows 98 was released in June 1998, the debate continues. Operating systems are not just essential software for computers. They are also enormously important to the people who use them.

What is an operating system? Why should a user be familiar with the operating system? What is the Windows 98 operating system? How could the announcement of an operating system be what many considered to be "a shot heard round the world" for computers?

In this chapter, you will explore the operating system; you will learn what it does for you as you work and what it does in the background with other programs and hardware. You will look at the evolution of operating systems from Microsoft, the operating system leader. Then you will briefly review some of the other players in the operating system game: IBM's OS/2, Apple Computer's Macintosh operating system, and UNIX (originally developed by AT&T). You also will see how operating systems are used to manage files, load programs, and perform multitasking operations.

On August 24, 1995, Microsoft Corporation co-founder and CEO Bill Gates stepped up to the podium at Microsoft headquarters in Redmond, Washington, and announced that Microsoft Windows 95 was beginning to ship to customers. Within four days, the first million copies had already gone out. It was the biggest product announcement in the history of computers—notifying the public of a new operating system.

In the spring of 1998, even greater anticipation—and controversy—awaited the release of Windows 95's successor, Windows 98. As the new operating system's release date approached, the Department of Justice and members of Congress threatened to delay the product's release, claiming that Microsoft had broken an antitrust agreement by adding its Web browser (Internet Explorer) to the operating system.

WHAT IS AN OPERATING SYSTEM?

An operating system (OS) is a software program, but it is different from word processing programs, spreadsheets, and all the other software programs on your computer. The OS is the computer's master control program. The OS provides you with the tools (commands) that enable you to interact with the PC. When you issue a command, the OS translates it into code the machine can use. The OS also ensures that the results of your actions are displayed on screen, printed, and so on.

When you turn on a computer, the machine looks for an operating system to boot before it runs any other programs. After the OS starts up, it takes charge until you shut down the computer. The operating system performs the following functions:

■ Provides the instructions to display the on-screen elements with which you interact. Collectively, these elements are known as the **user interface**.

■ Loads programs (such as word processing and spreadsheet programs) into the computer's memory so that you can use them.

■ Coordinates how programs work with the CPU, RAM, keyboard, mouse, printer, and other hardware as well as with other software.

■ Manages the way information is stored on and retrieved from disks.

The functionality of the OS can be extended with the addition of utility software.

THE USER INTERFACE

When you start an operating system, you see and interact with a set of items on the screen; this is the user interface. In the case of most current operating systems, including Windows 98, Windows 95, and the Macintosh OS, the user interface looks like a collection of objects on a colored background. Figure 5.1 shows what you see when you start a computer running Windows 98.

The release of Windows 95 turned out to be a huge media event. Here, Bill Gates addresses the crowd.

Note: Most of the screens in this chapter show Windows 98 because it is the most current version of Windows at the time this book was being written. However, the concepts discussed and the terms defined in the first half of this chapter apply equally well to Windows 95, the Mac OS, OS/2, and to most versions of UNIX (except where specifically noted). Many operating system elements explained in this chapter are patterned after Windows 98 and are identical or similar in Windows 95. In many cases, descriptions in this chapter reference "Windows 95/98," indicating that the topic applies to both Windows 95 and Windows 98.

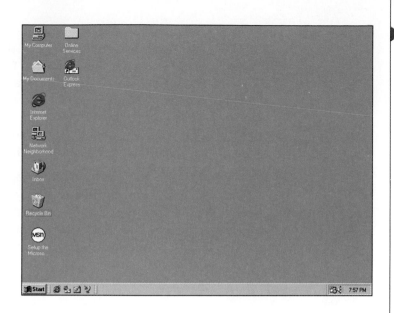

Figure 5.1
The screen you see when you
start Windows 98.

Parts of the Interface

Figure 5.2 shows the Windows 98 interface with the Start menu open, a program running, and a dialog box open. These features are discussed in the following sections.

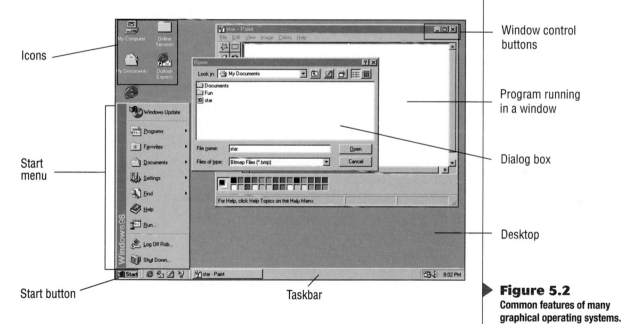

Icons

Start
menu

Start button

Taskbar

Window control
buttons

Program running
in a window

Dialog box

Desktop

Figure 5.2
Common features of many
graphical operating systems.

The Desktop

Software makers call the colored area you see on screen the desktop because they want you to think of it just as the surface of a desk. The pictures, too, stand for things you might have in your office—in the case of Windows, My Computer, a Recycle Bin, an Inbox, and a Briefcase. These pictures are called icons, a word that means *image*. In this context, an icon is an image that represents an object. In Figure 5.1, for example, the Internet Explorer icon represents the Internet Explorer program, which resides on the computer's disk. You can start the program simply by double-clicking its icon on the desktop.

Because you point at graphics on the screen, programmers sometimes refer to the interface as a **graphical user interface**, or **GUI** (pronounced "gooey"). People also refer to it as a *point-and-click* interface because you use a mouse to point at on-screen objects and then "click" them. Apple Computer introduced the first successful GUI with its Macintosh computer in 1984.

To perform tasks on the desktop, you control the icons by using the mouse and its on-screen pointer. Sometimes you simply point at the icons; sometimes you click them once; sometimes you double-click. Sometimes you slide an icon across the desktop by moving the mouse while holding down a mouse button—an operation known as dragging.

Icons

Icons represent the parts of the computer you work with—printers, fonts, document files, folders (a way to organize files into logical groups), disk drives, programs, and so on. Software designers try to make the icons look like what they represent, so it is easy to identify the icon you need.

These icons represent programs that you can launch from the Start menu in Windows 98.

There are fairly consistent rules for using the mouse to interact with icons:

■ You click an icon to **select** it. This indicates that you plan to work with it.

■ You double-click on an icon to **choose**, or **activate**, it. For instance, you double-click the icon of a word processing program to load that program into memory and start using it.

■ If you click an icon and hold down the mouse button, you can drag the mouse to move the icon to another location on the desktop. Sometimes you drag an icon to another icon to perform an action. For instance, you drag an icon for a file from one folder to another in order to move the file. You can also highlight the icon's text to select and edit it.

■ With Windows 95/98 operating systems, if you right-click many parts of the desktop, you will see a **context menu** containing the most common commands associated with that part. This menu is also sometimes called a *shortcut menu*.

Although icons generally look like the object they represent, another class of symbols, called buttons, generally look the same from program to program. **Buttons** are areas of the screen you can click to cause something to happen. Most buttons have a name or icon (or both) surrounded by a black border. The Start button in Figure 5.3 is one such button. When you click it, you cause the Start menu to appear.

The Taskbar and the Start Button

Whenever you start a program in Windows 95/98, a button for it appears on the **taskbar**—an area at the bottom of the screen whose purpose is to display the buttons for the programs you are running. When you have multiple programs running, you can shift from one to the other by clicking a program's button on the taskbar, as shown in Figures 5.4 and 5.5. The program in the foreground with the highlighted button in the taskbar is called the **active program**.

Figure 5.3
The Windows 95/98 Start button.

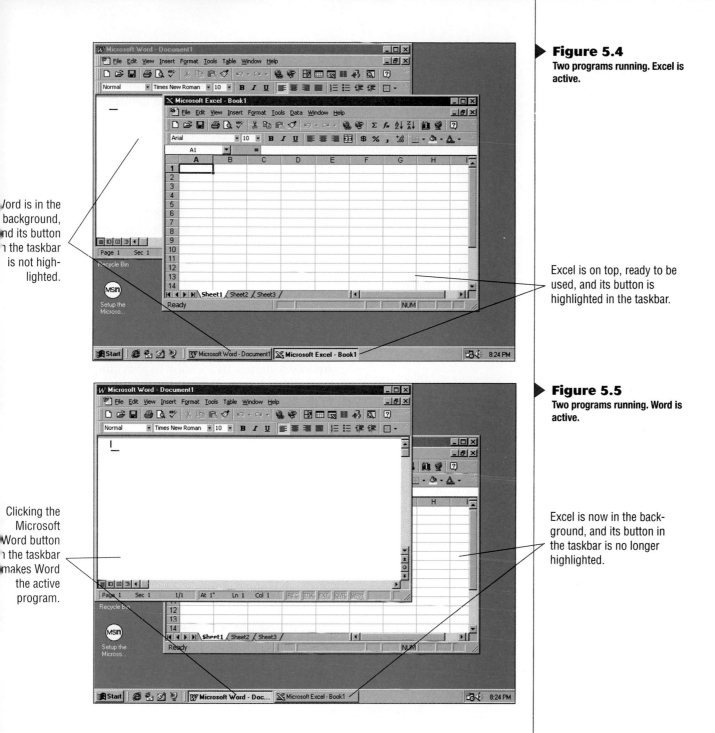

Figure 5.4
Two programs running. Excel is active.

Word is in the background, and its button in the taskbar is not highlighted.

Excel is on top, ready to be used, and its button is highlighted in the taskbar.

Figure 5.5
Two programs running. Word is active.

Clicking the Microsoft Word button in the taskbar makes Word the active program.

Excel is now in the background, and its button in the taskbar is no longer highlighted.

The **Start button** is a permanent feature of the taskbar. You click it to open the Start menu (see Figure 5.6). From the Start menu, you can click a program icon to start a program, choose Help to find information to assist you as you work, or choose Shut Down when you are ready to turn off your computer.

Note: The taskbar and the Start button are unique to Windows 95/98, and Windows NT version 4.0 or later. They do not appear in any other operating systems.

Programs Running in Windows

After you double-click a program icon to load a program into memory, when the program appears, it may take up the whole screen or it may appear in

Figure 5.6 ◀
Typical contents of the Start menu.

a rectangular frame on the screen, known as a **window**. By manipulating these windows on the desktop, you can see multiple programs that have been loaded into memory at the same time. For example, in Figure 5.7, you can see three open windows displaying three different programs.

Although each of the programs displayed in the different windows is running concurrently, you still need a way to tell Windows which one you want to use. (You can use only one window at a time, even though several may be open.) To do this, you simply click in the desired window, or click on its button on the taskbar. As shown in Figure 5.8, the window's title bar becomes highlighted to show that it is the **active window**—the window where your next actions will take effect. Most windows share many of the same characteristics. For example, all windows include a **title bar** across the top that identifies what the window contains. In addition to providing useful information, the title bar has another useful purpose; that is, you can move the entire window by clicking the title bar and dragging the window to a new location on the desktop.

Below the title bar, most programs contain a menu bar and toolbars that help you to tell the program what you want it to do.

In all versions of Microsoft Windows, OS/2, and the Macintosh operating system, windows also have adjustable borders and corners. If you drag the corners or sides of the windows, you can make the windows larger or smaller so that you see more or less of what is in them. As shown in Figure 5.9, many windows also have **scroll bars**, which enable you to view the different parts of the program or file that are longer or wider than what can be displayed in its window.

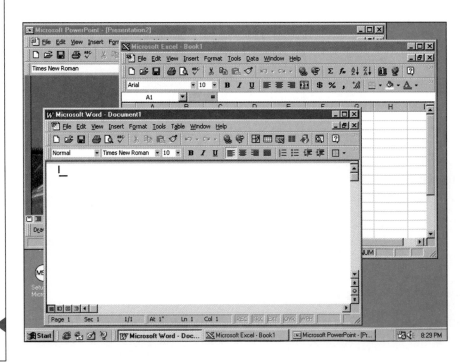

Figure 5.7 ◀
Three open windows.

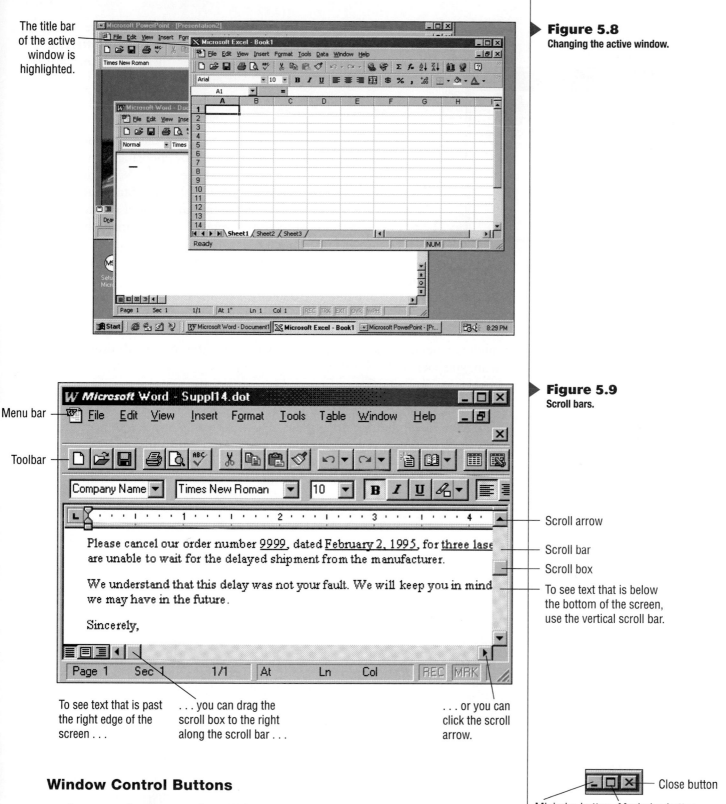

The title bar of the active window is highlighted.

► **Figure 5.8**
Changing the active window.

► **Figure 5.9**
Scroll bars.

Menu bar

Toolbar

Scroll arrow

Scroll bar

Scroll box

To see text that is below the bottom of the screen, use the vertical scroll bar.

To see text that is past the right edge of the screen . . .

. . . you can drag the scroll box to the right along the scroll bar . . .

. . . or you can click the scroll arrow.

Window Control Buttons

In the top-right corner of a window in Windows 95/98 are three buttons for manipulating the windows (see Figure 5.10).

- You click the single line—the Minimize button—to reduce the program to a button on the taskbar.

- You click the picture of a box—the Maximize button—to restore the window to its previous size.

- You click the X—the Close button—to close the window altogether.

Close button

Minimize button   Maximixe button

► **Figure 5.10**
The window control buttons for Windows 95/98, and Windows NT versions 4.0 and later.

Double-click here to close
the window. (Clicking once
opens a Control menu.)

Minimize
button

Maximize
button

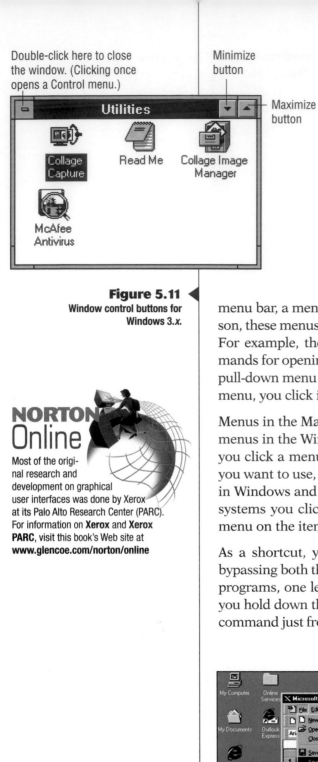

Figure 5.11
Window control buttons for
Windows 3.*x*.

In Windows 3.1, Windows for Workgroups, and versions of Windows NT prior to 4.0, these buttons look different. The window control buttons for these programs are shown in Figure 5.11.

Menus

Although you initiate many tasks by clicking icons and buttons, you can also start tasks by choosing commands from lists called **menus**. You have already seen the Start menu, which appears when you click the Start button in Windows 95/98. The more standard type of menu, however, appears at the top of many windows (in all the popular GUI operating systems) in a horizontal list of menus called the **menu bar**. When you click an item in the menu bar, a menu "drops down" and displays a list of commands (for this reason, these menus are sometimes called *pull-down menus* or *drop-down menus*). For example, the File menu in Windows programs typically contains commands for opening, closing, saving, and printing files. Figure 5.12 shows such a pull-down menu in Excel. To execute or run one of the commands listed in the menu, you click it.

Menus in the Macintosh operating system operate somewhat differently from menus in the Windows and Windows NT operating systems. On a Macintosh, you click a menu and hold down the mouse button, point to the menu item you want to use, and then release the mouse button. This same method works in Windows and Windows NT, but typically in these Microsoft GUI operating systems you click and release on the menu to open it and then click in the menu on the item you want to use.

As a shortcut, you also can execute many commands from the keyboard, bypassing both the mouse and the pull-down menus. For example, in Windows programs, one letter is underlined in the name of many menu commands. If you hold down the Alt key and type that underlined letter, you can activate the command just from the keyboard (see Figure 5.13). Once in an open menu, you

The user is selecting the Save As
command from the File menu.

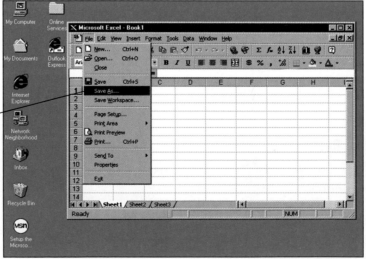

Figure 5.12
The File menu in Excel.

just press the underlined letter in the command you want to execute. For example, in Figure 5.13, you could just press Alt+O or O to display the Open dialog box, where you specify the file you want to open.

Dialog Boxes

Dialog boxes are special-purpose windows that appear when you need to tell a program (or the operating system) what to do next. For example, if you choose Find and then choose Files or Folders from the Windows Start menu, a dialog box appears, asking you to describe the file or folder you want to find. A dialog box is called that because it conducts a "dialog" with you as it seeks the information it needs to perform a task. Figure 5.14 shows a typical dialog box and explains how to use the most common dialog box features.

The underlined F indicates that you can press Alt + F to open the File menu.

With the File menu open, you can press Alt+O, or simply the letter *O*, to execute the Open command.

As a one-step shortcut, you can press Ctrl+O to execute the Open command without opening the File menu.

Figure 5.13
Shortcuts for initiating menu commands.

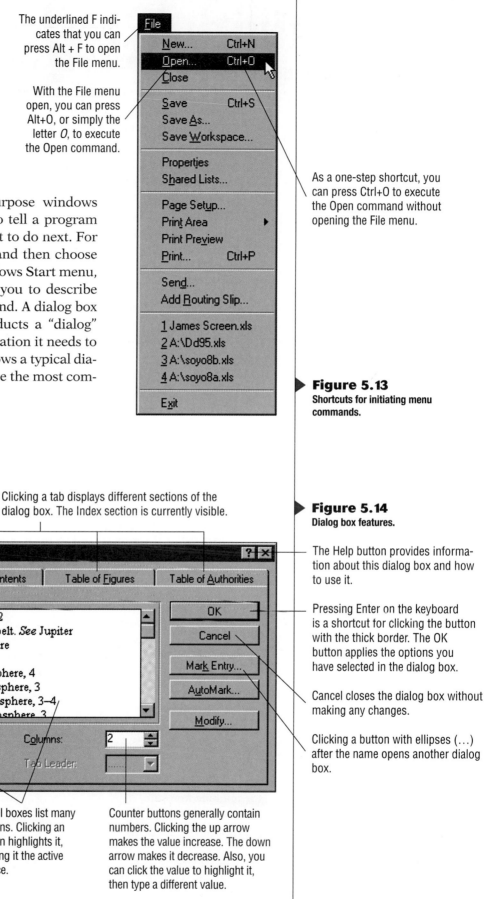

Radio buttons let you select one option from a set of choices.

Clicking a tab displays different sections of the dialog box. The Index section is currently visible.

Figure 5.14
Dialog box features.

The Help button provides information about this dialog box and how to use it.

Pressing Enter on the keyboard is a shortcut for clicking the button with the thick border. The OK button applies the options you have selected in the dialog box.

Cancel closes the dialog box without making any changes.

Clicking a button with ellipses (…) after the name opens another dialog box.

Clicking a check box turns a feature on or off. This box is empty, so the Right Align Page Numbers feature is currently off.

Scroll boxes list many options. Clicking an option highlights it, making it the active choice.

Counter buttons generally contain numbers. Clicking the up arrow makes the value increase. The down arrow makes it decrease. Also, you can click the value to highlight it, then type a different value.

Productivity Tip

Upgrading Your Operating System

There are several reasons to upgrade your operating system. Newer operating system versions typically offer better ease-of-use, new features, greater protection from buggy programs, and support for new hardware. In most cases, updating your operating system is not expensive, either. Before you rush off to buy that new version, however, do a little planning. In particular, check the following things:

■ *CPU type.* Is a specific CPU type required by the new version? On a PC, for example, if your computer contains a 386 or older processor, you cannot upgrade to Windows 95/98 because your CPU cannot run the new operating system.

■ *Memory.* How much RAM does the new version require? Windows 3.1 runs adequately on systems with 8 MB of RAM. Windows 95/98, however, require at least 16 MB to run adequately.

■ *Disk space.* Does your computer's hard disk contain enough free space to install the new version? The amount of free space varies widely with operating systems and the options you intend to install. A full upgrade can require 120 MB of disk space or more. If you are low on space, consider adding another hard disk to your system.

■ *Compatibility.* Is your hardware compatible with the new operating system? Make sure that the new operating system or version fully supports all the equipment in or connected to your computer.

After you have determined that your computer will handle the upgrade, you should follow a few general steps to make sure that the upgrade goes smoothly.

Making Backups Make a backup of your document files and any other files that you can't afford to lose. Backups are copies of files stored to floppy disks, tape drives, or other media that you can restore to your main system in the event of a system problem that destroys or corrupts the originals. It is unlikely that a problem will occur during the upgrade, but you should make sure that your files are backed up before starting the upgrade. In particular, if you decide to reformat the hard disk (see the next section), you should make a complete backup of your entire hard disk.

If you have a second physical hard disk in the system with enough available space, you can simply copy the files to the other hard disk. In most cases, though, you'll need to back up the files to floppy disk, tape, or writable CD (called CD-R). If you don't intend to reformat the hard disk, backing up your document files is sufficient. Unless you have many files, it usually is practical to back them up to floppy disk. If you want to back up your entire system, you'll need a tape drive or CD-R. Tape drives are somewhat less expensive than CD-R units and generally can hold more data than a CD, which is limited to about 650 MB.

If you are not comfortable performing the backups or upgrading the operating system, see whether a local computer technician will perform the upgrade for you and how much it will cost.

Reformat or Not? In most cases, you can simply upgrade the existing operating system with the new version. In some cases, though, it is a good idea to completely reformat your hard disk and start from scratch. If you have been using your computer for several years, you probably have many extra programs and files on the system that you no longer need. Although you could weed them out one-by-one, it's much easier to just reformat the hard disk and reinstall your programs from scratch. Think of this as a major spring cleaning.

If you decide to reformat the hard disk, you need to understand that doing so will erase every bit of information on the disk, including all your program and document files. So, it's vitally important that you have all your files backed up to tape or CD-R. After you format the drive, you will install the new operating system, install all your programs one at a time, and then restore your document files from the backup to the system.

Reformatting the hard disk is something of a radical procedure but one that will give you an optimum operating system installation and weed out all the unneeded files from your system. If you are a novice user, consider either upgrading without reformatting or having a computer technician perform the upgrade for you.

Becoming Familiar with the Interface

A well-designed GUI offers more than a set of easy-to-use, point-and-click tools. It also offers consistency and familiarity for the user because it forces the applications that run under the operating system to use the same tools.

For example, take a look at the two screens shown in Figures 5.15 and 5.16. They show different kinds of software. Figure 5.15 shows a spreadsheet program, and Figure 5.16 shows a programming environment. Notice how many elements of the interface are the same. Both screens have the same window dressing—window control buttons, menu bars, and toolbars. The names of some of the menus differ, and the buttons look different, but all the menus and buttons are accessed in the same way.

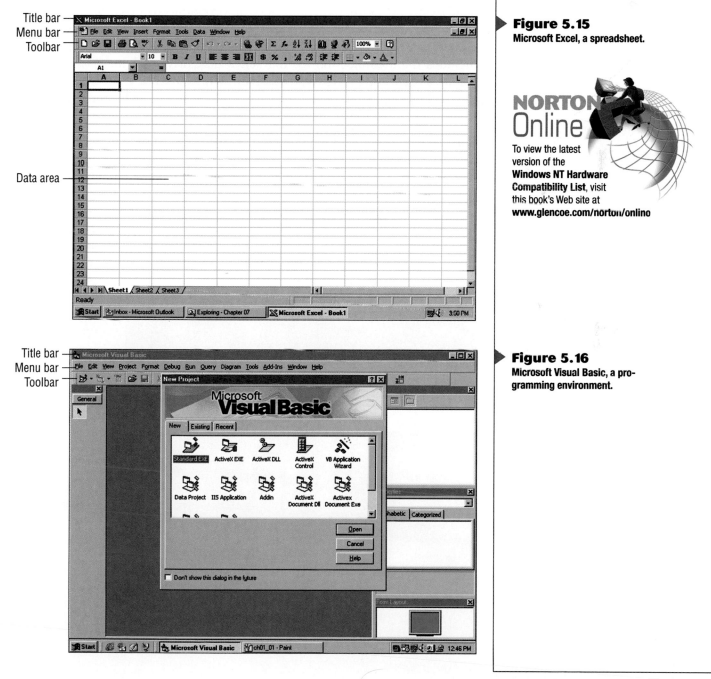

Figure 5.15
Microsoft Excel, a spreadsheet.

NORTON Online

To view the latest version of the **Windows NT Hardware Compatibility List**, visit this book's Web site at **www.glencoe.com/norton/online**

Figure 5.16
Microsoft Visual Basic, a programming environment.

NORTON Online

For a list of many **DOS commands** and their uses, visit this book's Web site at www.glencoe.com/norton/online

This level of consistency in the interface is an important part of making the computer system intuitive and easy to use. It is known as **common user access (CUA)**. Once users learn how to use the basic tools, they can move from one program to the next with much more ease than they could if all the aspects of the interface for each application were different.

The Command-Line Interface

The graphical user interface has become the standard because the Macintosh and Windows operating systems use it. However, for more than a decade, computer operating systems used command-line interfaces, which are environments that use type-written commands rather than graphical objects to execute tasks and process data.

During the 1980s, the most popular of these were Microsoft's MS-DOS and its near twin PC-DOS from IBM. "DOS" is pronounced "doss" and stands for "Disk Operating System." Users interact with a **command-line interface** by typing strings of characters at a prompt on screen. In DOS, the prompt usually includes the identification for the active disk drive (a letter followed by a colon), a backslash (\), and a greater-than symbol, as in C:>. Figure 5.17 shows the DOS prompt, which is still available in Windows 95/98 for those who want to run DOS programs or to work with DOS keyboard commands.

Some experienced users of command-line interfaces argue that they are simpler, faster, and provide better information than GUI operating systems. However, GUIs became the standard because most users preferred them, in part because they are easier to learn. Finding and starting programs from a command-line prompt can be compared to traveling at night with a road map in your head. Instead of pointing and clicking at icons, you type a series of *memorized* commands. For instance, in DOS, you type DIR at the prompt to see a list of the files in a particular "directory" (the equivalent of a folder), as shown in Figure 5.18.

Figure 5.17
The DOS prompt.

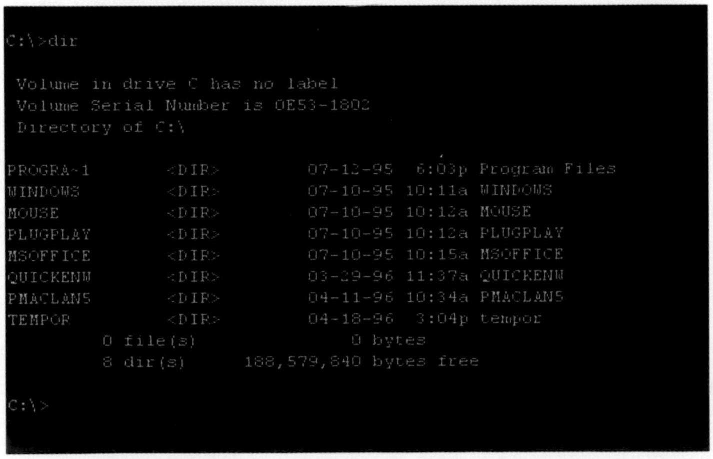

```
C:\>ver

Windows 95. [Version 4.00.950]
```

Figure 5.18
The results of the DIR command in DOS.

```
C:\>dir

 Volume in drive C has no label
 Volume Serial Number is 0E53-1802
 Directory of C:\

PROGRA~1      <DIR>        07-12-95   6:03p Program Files
WINDOWS       <DIR>        07-10-95  10:11a WINDOWS
MOUSE         <DIR>        07-10-95  10:12a MOUSE
PLUGPLAY      <DIR>        07-10-95  10:12a PLUGPLAY
MSOFFICE      <DIR>        07-10-95  10:15a MSOFFICE
QUICKENW      <DIR>        03-29-96  11:37a QUICKENW
PMACLANS      <DIR>        04-11-96  10:34a PMACLANS
TEMPOR        <DIR>        04-18-96   3:04p tempor
        0 file(s)              0 bytes
        8 dir(s)      188,579,840 bytes free

C:\>
```

RUNNING PROGRAMS

Just as the operating system can provide a consistent interface for running programs on the computer, it is also the interface between those programs and other computer resources (such as computer memory, a printer, or another program such as a spreadsheet application).

When programmers write computer programs, they build instructions into them—called **system calls**—that request services from the operating system. (They are "calls" because the program has to call on the operating system to provide some information or service.)

For example, when you want your word processing program to retrieve a file, you use the Open dialog box to list the files in the folder that you specify (see Figure 5.19).

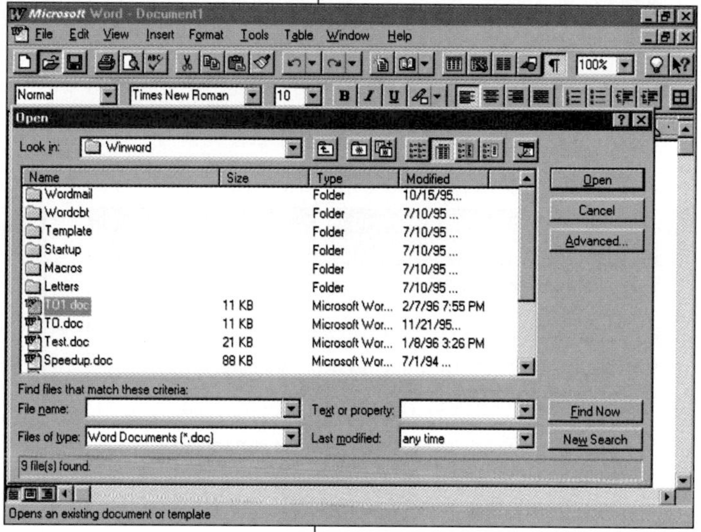

To provide the list, the program calls on the operating system. The OS goes through the same process to build a list of files whether it receives its instructions from you (via the desktop) or from an application. The difference is that when the request comes from an application, the operating system sends the results of its work to the application rather than the desktop.

Some other services that an operating system provides to programs, in addition to listing files, are:

Figure 5.19
The Open dialog box in Word.

- Saving the contents of files to a disk for permanent storage
- Reading the contents of a file from disk into memory
- Sending a document to the printer and activating the printer
- Providing resources that let you copy or move data from one document to another, or from one program to another
- Allocating RAM among various programs that you may have open
- Recognizing keystrokes or mouse clicks and displaying characters or graphics on the screen

Sharing Information

As soon as you begin using a word processing program—or almost any other type of application—you discover the need to move chunks of data from one place in a document to another. For example, you might look at a letter and realize that it would make more sense if the second paragraph were moved to page 2. One of the beauties of using a computer is that this type of editing is not only possible but simple.

Most operating systems, including Windows 95/98, Windows NT, and the Macintosh OS, accomplish this feat with an operating system feature known as the Clipboard. The **Clipboard** is a temporary storage space for data that is being copied or moved. For example, to move a paragraph in a word processed document, you perform the actions shown in Figure 5.20.

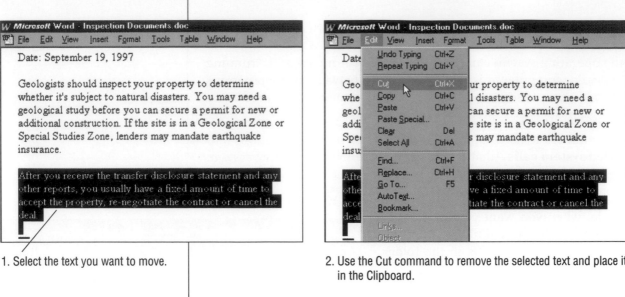

1. Select the text you want to move.

2. Use the Cut command to remove the selected text and place it in the Clipboard.

3. Move the insertion point to the text's new position in the document.

4. Use the Paste command to copy the text from the Clipboard to the new position in the document.

Figure 5.20
Using the Clipboard to move a paragraph to a different place in a document.

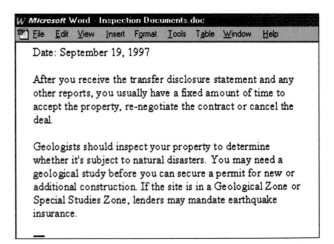

5. The moved text. A copy of the text remains in the Clipboard until the next time you use the Cut or Copy command.

NORTON Online

For information on **operating system Clipboards**, visit this book's Web site at **www.glencoe.com/norton/online**

Often, instead of using the **Cut** command, which removes data and places it on the Clipboard, you may want to use **Copy**, which makes a copy of the data and stores it on the Clipboard but does not remove the original. In either case, you use the **Paste** command to copy the contents of the Clipboard back into your document.

Note: The Clipboard stores only one set of data at a time, although the set of data can be almost any size or length. The contents of the Clipboard are cleared each time you select a new set of data and choose either the Cut or Copy commands again. This fact has two important consequences:

1_ You must be careful not to erase valuable data that has been placed in the Clipboard, or you will lose it.

2_ You can Paste data from the Clipboard as many times as you like (until you choose Cut or Copy again).

As you might imagine (or already know), the Clipboard also can be used to move data from one document to another. For example, you can copy an address from one letter to another and thereby avoid rekeying it.

The real versatility of the Clipboard, however, stems from the fact that it is actually part of the operating system, not a particular application. As a result, you can use the Clipboard to move data from one program to another. For example, say that you created a chart in a spreadsheet program and want to paste it into a report that you created with your word processing program. As shown in Figure 5.21, you can do it easily with the Clipboard.

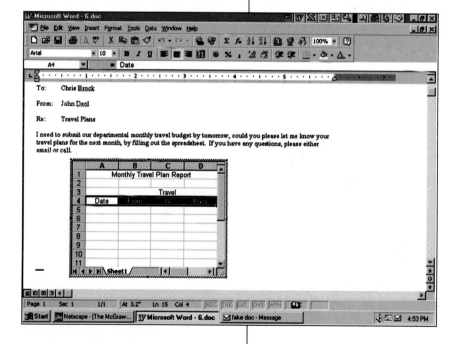

Figure 5.21
A spreadsheet chart pasted into a word processing document.

The versatility of the Clipboard has been further extended with a feature known in Windows as **OLE**, which stands for **Object Linking and Embedding**. A simple cut and paste between applications results in **object embedding**. The data, which is known as an object in programming terms, is embedded in a new type of document. It retains the formatting that was applied to it in the original application, but its relationship with the original file is destroyed—it is simply part of the new file.

Object linking, however, adds another layer to the relationship: The data that is copied to and from the Clipboard retains a link to the original document, so that a change in the original document also appears in the linked data. For example, suppose that the report shown in Figure 5.21 is generated weekly, and it always contains the same chart, updated with the correct numbers for the current week. With object linking, the numbers in the spreadsheet from which the chart is generated can be updated, and the chart in the report will automatically reflect the new numbers.

Multitasking

Besides being able to run programs and share data across applications, Windows and Macintosh operating systems have joined OS/2 and UNIX in achieving a long-sought goal of personal computers: multitasking, which is a computer's version of being able to "walk and chew gum at the same time." **Multitasking** means much more than the capability to load multiple programs into memory (although even that was difficult for earlier operating systems). Multitasking means being able to perform two or more procedures—such as printing a multipage document, sending e-mail over the Internet, and typing a letter—all simultaneously.

Software engineers use two methods to develop multitasking operating systems. The first requires cooperation between the operating system and application programs. Programs that are currently running will periodically check the operating system to see whether any other programs need the CPU. If any do, the running program will relinquish control of the CPU to the next program. This method is called **cooperative multitasking** and is used by the Macintosh and Windows 3.*x* operating systems to allow such activities as printing while the user continues to type or use the mouse to input more data.

The second method is called **preemptive multitasking**. With this method, the operating system maintains a list of programs that are running and assigns a priority to each program in the list. The operating system can intervene and modify a program's priority status, rearranging the priority list. With preemptive multitasking, the operating system can preempt the program that is running and reassign the time to a higher-priority task at any time. Preemptive multitasking thereby has the advantage of being able to carry out higher-priority programs faster than lower-priority programs. Windows 95/98, Windows NT, OS/2, and UNIX employ preemptive multitasking.

Multitasking lets you do more than one thing at a time. Here, the computer is starting the modem and printing a picture while the user composes an e-mail message.

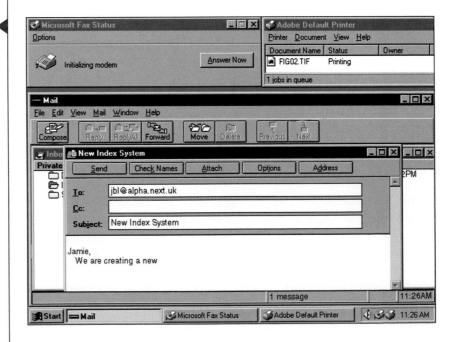

NORTON Notebook

How Will Operating Systems Evolve?

The meteoric rise of the World Wide Web in this decade is changing the way that people think about computer operating systems, and what they expect their operating systems to do.

An operating system manages a computer's processes, memory, files, and any external devices, such as a mouse, printer, or network interface.

With the rise of the biggest network of all, the Internet, people have come to expect more than just basic interfacing capabilities. They want the capability to access, retrieve, and display all the varieties of information available on the World Wide Web. These functions require a browser, special navigational software designed to access the Web through the network connections provided by the OS.

Currently, there is also a wide variety of "helper apps," software tools that enable the browser to display the many kinds of files encountered on the Web, such as graphics, sound, video, and program content like Java applets. Finding these tools—either by downloading them from the Web or by purchasing software—can be time-consuming. Once found, even helper apps must be configured to function with a user's browser, network connection, operating system, and hardware platform.

Microsoft's Internet Explorer is one of many available Internet browsers.

![Screenshot of Microsoft Internet Explorer showing Microsoft Internet Start page]

Microsoft Internet Start - Microsoft Internet Explorer

File Edit View Go Favorites Help

Address http://home.microsoft.com/

Links · Best of the Web · Microsoft · Product News · Today's Links · Web G

your start page · personalize · the internet · magazine · feedback · msn — Microsoft

start internet

Fox Sports — New in the Sports section

February 18 · Click these icons to add or remove content from this page.

news
msnbc news · U.S. war plans jarred by opposition · Irish court delays Sinn Fein ruling · N. Korean economic crisis deepens

video clips
bloomberg television · Hewlett Packard Earnings Out/Domain Name Equipment Stolen
fox news · U.S. Air Strike of Iraq May Be Imminent
msnbc · NBC?s Conan Nolan on California slide woes

stock quotes
microsoft investor

Symbol	Name	Last	Chg	%Chg
$INDU	Dow Industrials	8,451.06	52.56	0.62%
XAX	AMEX Market Value	688.50	1.07	0.16%
COMP	NASDAQ Composite	1,715.73	12.30	0.72%

Start · Microsoft Internet Sta... · 8:47 PM

But this is no longer the case.

Microsoft has released several utilities that make it easy to work with the Internet and Internet documents. For example, the latest version of its Office suite of applications all can save documents directly to HTML format, the most common format used for Web pages. This makes it easy to create your own Web documents.

Another utility from Microsoft is a program called Peer Web Services that allows users to convert existing documents to documents containing the HTML coding needed for Web viewing. It also allows users to set up their own small Web server using their desktop PCs.

Several software developers including Microsoft have available programs for creating Web content. The programs give you a WYSIWYG (What You See Is What You Get) interface for creating Web pages, just like you use a word processing program to create written documents.

Browser manufacturers are best exemplified by the Mountain View, California company Netscape, manufacturer of the Navigator browser. Netscape enables third parties to write software that plugs into Navigator's existing feature set, making new Web features such as sound, animation, and video easy to implement as they become available.

One of the Web's founding fathers, Tim Berners-Lee, suggested a broader perspective on the whole issue in a1996 interview published in the *San Francisco Examiner*. Berners-Lee (who now directs a consortium establishing technical standards for the Web), believes that it no longer makes sense to differentiate between operating systems and browsers.

"It is more logical to think of the local information [on a computer] as just one part of the world of information," he said. "That way, the browser and the desktop become one. Whether you think of that as the browser making the desktop obsolete or the desktop making the browser obsolete, that might depend on where you currently have a large market share." ("Battle of the Browsers," Evan Ramstad, *San Francisco Examiner*, March 17, 1996)

Microsoft has taken exactly that approach and integrated the Web browser into the operating system with Windows 98. With Windows 98, you browse local hard disk and other resources using the same interface you use to browse the Internet. In this way, Microsoft has blurred the distinction between local computer resources and remote resources on the Internet.

MANAGING FILES

The files that the operating system works with may be programs or data files. Most programs you purchase come with numerous files—some may even include hundreds. When you use the programs, you often create your own data files, such as word processing documents, and store them on a disk under names that you assign to them. A large hard disk often holds thousands of program and data files. It is the responsibility of the operating system to keep track of all these files so that it can copy any one of them into RAM at a moment's notice.

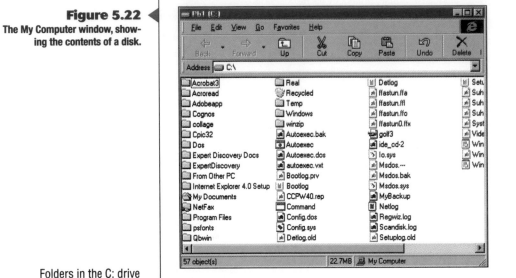

Figure 5.22
The My Computer window, showing the contents of a disk.

Folders in the C: drive

Files   File   File   Date and time when
         sizes   types   the file was last
                         saved

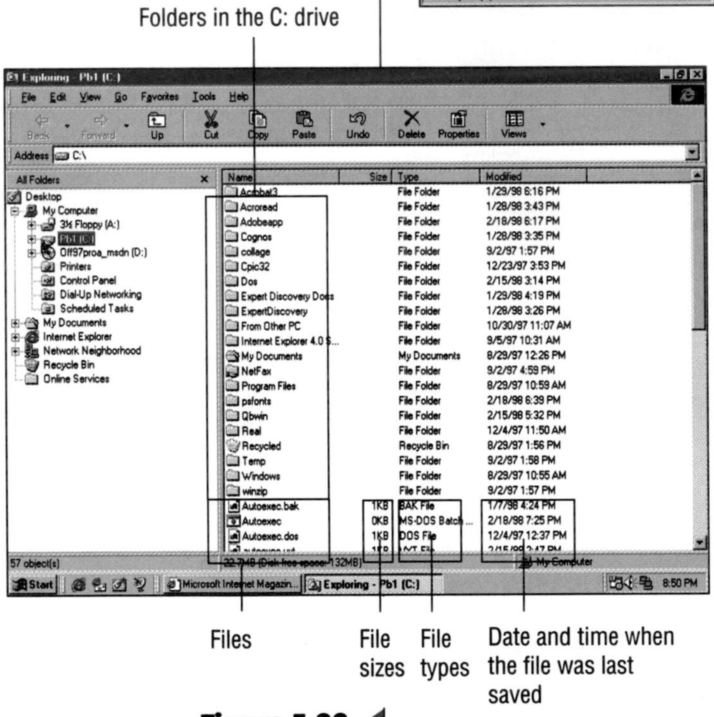

Figure 5.23
The Explorer window, showing the contents of the hard disk.

To accomplish this feat, the operating system maintains a list of the contents of a disk on the disk itself. As you may recall, there is an area called the File Allocation Table, or FAT, that the operating system creates when you format a disk. The operating system updates the information in the FAT any time a file is created, moved, renamed, or deleted. In addition, the operating system keeps track of different disks or disk drives by assigning names to them. On IBM and compatible computers, diskette drives are assigned the letters *A* and *B*, and hard disk drives are designated as the *C* drive and up. CD-ROM drives have the first available letter following the hard drives—often the letter *D*. Operating systems not created by Microsoft use slightly different schemes for keeping track of disks and their contents, but each of the different schemes accomplishes the same task.

In Windows 95/98, there are actually two different programs for viewing and managing the contents of a disk, the My Computer window and the Windows Explorer. In either one, you select the icon that represents a disk drive, and a window appears with the list of files on that disk (see Figure 5.22).

When there are hundreds of files on a disk, finding the one you want can be time-consuming. To find files quickly, you can organize them using folders. Figure 5.23 shows a listing of the main folder of a hard disk. Notice how file names are accompanied by the file sizes in bytes, and the date and time when the files were last modified.

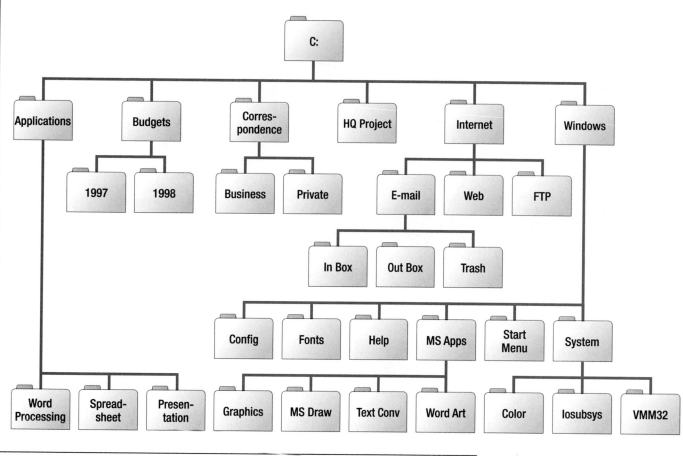

Figure 5.24
A hierarchical file system.

Also notice that there are several folders in the list. Folders can contain other folders, so you can create a structured system known as a **hierarchical file system**. A diagram for a hierarchical file system is shown in Figure 5.24.

MANAGING HARDWARE

When programs run, they need to use the computer's memory, monitor, disk drives, and other devices, such as a printer, modem, or CD-ROM drive. The operating system is the intermediary between programs and hardware. In a computer network, the operating system also mediates between your computer and other devices on the network.

In the next sections, you will see three ways in which the operating system serves as the go-between to keep hardware running smoothly.

Processing Interrupts

The operating system responds to requests to use memory and other devices, keeps track of which programs have access to which devices, and coordinates everything the hardware does so that various activities do not overlap and cause the computer to become confused and stop working. The operating system uses **interrupt requests (IRQs)** to help the CPU coordinate processes. For example, if you tell the operating system to list the files in a folder, it sends an interrupt request to the computer's CPU. The basic steps in this process are shown in Figure 5.25.

For information on **how the operating system uses interrupts to manage hardware**, visit this book's Web site at **www.glencoe.com/norton/online**

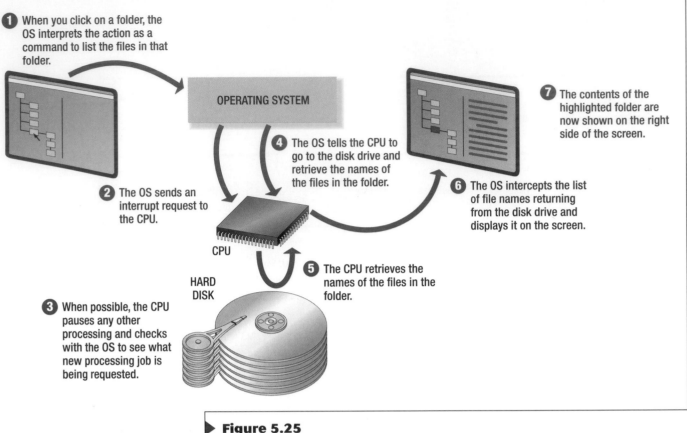

1 When you click on a folder, the OS interprets the action as a command to list the files in that folder.

OPERATING SYSTEM

4 The OS tells the CPU to go to the disk drive and retrieve the names of the files in the folder.

7 The contents of the highlighted folder are now shown on the right side of the screen.

2 The OS sends an interrupt request to the CPU.

6 The OS intercepts the list of file names returning from the disk drive and displays it on the screen.

CPU

HARD DISK

5 The CPU retrieves the names of the files in the folder.

3 When possible, the CPU pauses any other processing and checks with the OS to see what new processing job is being requested.

Figure 5.25
How the operating system communicates with the CPU.

The interrupt request procedure is a little like using parliamentary procedures in a large meeting. At first, it may seem like an extra layer of unnecessary formality. In fact, this formality is needed to keep everyone from talking at once—or in the case of interrupt requests, to keep the CPU from becoming overwhelmed with a barrage of possibly conflicting processing procedures.

Drivers

In addition to using interrupts, the operating system often provides complete programs for working with special devices, such as printers. These programs are called **drivers** because they allow the operating system and other programs to activate and use—that is, "drive"—the hardware device. In the days when DOS reigned, drivers had to be installed separately for each program used. With modern operating systems such as Windows 95/98, Windows NT, and the Macintosh OS, drivers are an integral part of the operating system. This means that most of the software you buy will work with your printer, monitor, and other equipment without requiring any special installation. For example, many modems use the same unified driver in Windows 95/98. All that is different is the setup information the operating system uses to configure the modem to accommodate specific capabilities of each modem.

Word processing program • Spreadsheet • E-mail • Presentation software • Graphics software

APPLICATION SOFTWARE

OPERATING SYSTEM

CPU

OTHER HARDWARE

Input • Output • Communications • Storage

The operating system acts as an intermediary between the application software and all the hardware.

Networking

Besides providing interrupt requests and drivers for working with individual devices, the OS also can allow you to work with multiple computers on a network.

On a network, usually each person has a separate PC with its own operating system. The network server also has its own operating system, which manages the flow of data on the file server and around the network. The leading network operating system for PCs today is a system dedicated just to networking—Novell IntranetWare. However, Windows NT seems to be rapidly overtaking IntranetWare (and its earlier versions, called NetWare) as the predominant network operating environment. As operating systems continue to advance and evolve, networking will become an integral part of all operating systems.

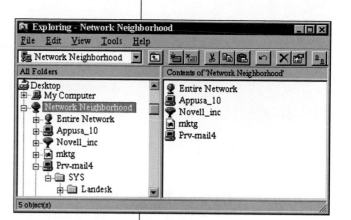

In Windows 95/98, other computers on a LAN appear as part of the Network Neighborhood.

ENHANCING THE OPERATING SYSTEM WITH UTILITY SOFTWARE

Operating systems are designed to let you do most of the things you normally would want to do with a computer—manage files, load programs, print files, multitask, and so on. These programs (actually, sets of programs) are sold by the behemoths of the software industry: Microsoft, Apple, IBM, Santa Cruz Operation (SCO), and Novell. However, many other talented software firms are constantly finding ways to improve operating systems. The programs they create to do this are called utilities. In the 1980s, when utilities for PCs first appeared, some of the most popular were those that helped the user to back up files, detect computer viruses (rogue programs that can destroy data files), and retrieve files that have been deleted. A few utility programs actually replace parts of the operating system, but the vast majority simply add helpful functionality.

Because they aid the inner workings of the computer system, utilities are grouped with the operating system under the category of system software.

Software makers began to provide utility programs to remedy perceived limitations in operating systems. However, over the years, makers of operating systems have integrated many utilities into the system itself. Generally, this year's utility programs become next year's operating system features.

Today, popular utilities range from programs that can organize or compress the files on a disk to programs that help you remove programs you no longer use from your hard disk. The categories of utilities covered in the following sections include file defragmentation, data compression, backup, data recovery, antivirus, and screen savers.

File Defragmentation

When you first copy a file to a disk, the operating system tries to put it all in one place, in one or more contiguous sectors. If you later go back and add

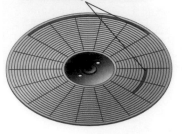

This file has been fragmented into noncontiguous sectors.

Figure 5.26
File fragmentation.

data to the file, however, the sectors next to the original may no longer be available. In this case, the operating system puts the new data somewhere else on the disk (see Figure 5.26).

A file that is split up this way is said to be fragmented because its parts are physically separated. Fragmented files cause the hard drive to take longer to read and write them because the disk must reposition its read-write heads several times while working with the same file.

A utility program that defragments files on a disk can speed up the disk drive noticeably. Windows 95/98 comes with a **defragmentation utility** called Disk Defragmenter. Before you use this or any other defragmentation utility, however, be sure to back up your data.

Data Compression

Data compression, the capability to reduce the storage requirements of a file by using mathematical algorithms, has several applications, including data communications and multimedia. As you may recall, data compression techniques are built into modems so that they can send files faster.

Another use for data compression is to fit more data on a disk. Doing so usually requires a **data compression utility**, a program specifically designed to abbreviate sequences of bits to make files as small as possible. Data compression utilities come in different types, depending on how they will be used. Some utilities compress files on demand, usually to fit data onto a disk, or to reduce the amount of hard disk space taken up by files that are rarely accessed. PKZip and WinZip for the PC and StuffIt for the Macintosh are some of the most popular data compression utilities.

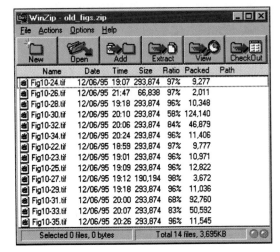

This dialog box shows the progress being made by the Disk Defragmenter utility as it defragments the files on the hard disk.

The files listed in this WinZip window have been compressed and stored in a new file with a ZIP extension. The Ratio column shows that the files have been compressed by as much as 98 percent. A file with a 98-percent compression ratio means that the data in the file now occupies only two percent of the disk space it required before it was compressed.

Another type of utility compresses all the data as it is stored on your hard disk, effectively doubling the capacity of the disk. The user need not even know that data compression and decompression are going on, except that in some cases opening files may be slower. DriveSpace, which is built into Windows 95/98, is an example of this type of utility. Windows NT also provides built-in disk compression, although NT's disk compression and DriveSpace in Windows 95/98 are not compatible with one another.

NORTON Online

For more information on **data compression utilities**, visit this book's Web site a www.glencoe.com/norton/online

Backup Software

Data compression is also built into backup software, another type of utility. **Backup software** is designed to help you copy large groups of files from your hard disk to some other storage media, such as diskettes, magnetic tape, removable hard disks, magneto-optical disks, or recordable CDs.

Once again, backup software was originally sold by independent software firms but is now often found as part of the operating system. For example, Microsoft Backup was originally developed by Symantec as a separate utility, but it is now packaged with all the different Microsoft operating systems, including MS-DOS, Windows 95/98, and Windows NT.

Users can and should back up their data. The real purpose of this utility is to make the backup process as painless as possible. For example, most backup software lets you set a timer and automatically copy the contents of your hard disk to magnetic tape or the network server when you are not using your computer, usually late at night.

Data Recovery Software

Once in a while, you may erase a file from a disk and then realize that you still need it. This is when you need a **data recovery utility**, also called an **unerase program**, which can recover data files that have been mistakenly deleted or somehow rendered unusable.

Both the Macintosh operating system and Windows 95/98 try to help with the problem of mistakenly erased files by providing the Trash (Mac) and the Recycle Bin (Windows 95/98); these are areas to which you can move files that you no longer need. The operating system does not actually erase the files until you give the command to Empty Trash or Empty Recycle Bin.

Even then, however, the computer does not actually destroy the data in the files. All it does is mark each file in such a way that the operating system can write over it. Until the operating system actually does copy a new file to that area on the disk, the old file cannot be seen by the user, but it can be resurrected. Data recovery software is designed to make files that have been erased but not written over visible to the user. The user can select them and then change their status back to a usable form.

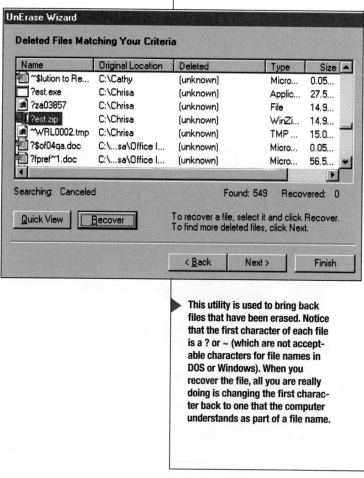

Here, Microsoft Backup is being used to create a backup copy of the hard disk.

This utility is used to bring back files that have been erased. Notice that the first character of each file is a ? or ~ (which are not acceptable characters for file names in DOS or Windows). When you recover the file, all you are really doing is changing the first character back to one that the computer understands as part of a file name.

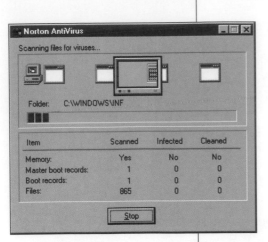

Antivirus utilities look at the boot sector and every executable file on a disk, and report how many are infected with viruses.

The same type of software also can be used to examine a disk and look for damaged files. Files can become unreadable if they are damaged by an error in software or the disk drive, or if the storage media itself is damaged. Data recovery software can sometimes piece together the readable parts of such files and make those parts available again.

Antivirus Utilities

A **virus** is a parasitic program buried within another legitimate program or stored in a special area of a disk called the *boot sector*. The boot sector is a part of the logical formatting of the hard disk and contains a program that runs when the computer is first turned on. It determines whether the disk has the basic components necessary to run the operating system successfully. Executing the legitimate program or accessing the disk activates the virus without the user's knowledge. Viruses can be programmed to do many things, including copy themselves to other programs, display information on the screen, destroy data files, or erase an entire hard disk. If you occasionally transfer files or trade diskettes with other computer users, you can spread the virus unknowingly.

Tracking viruses down, eradicating them, and preventing their spread is the major objective of **antivirus utilities**. Antivirus programs examine the boot sector and executable files on a disk, identify any viruses, and attempt to remove them. You can also configure antivirus programs so that they are active at all times, searching for infected files or suspicious programs.

Star Trek: The Screen Saver has been a long-time favorite. In addition to spaceships and exploding robots floating across your screen, other modules include scenes of Capain Kirk barking orders and security guards running away from creatures who drill through rocks.

Screen Savers

Another popular utility is the **screen saver**, a program that displays moving images on the screen if no input is received for several minutes. Screen savers originally gained popularity as a way to fight "ghosting," a hardware problem of computer monitors in the early 1980s in which an image that was displayed for many hours on the screen became "burned" into the phosphor dots and therefore was permanently visible on the screen's surface. However, even after the hardware was corrected and ghosting no longer took place, programmers had become so creative with the types of images displayed by screen savers that users began to buy them just for the sake of novelty and to protect their data from being seen when they are away from their desks. Today, you can find screen savers that display flying toasters, "Far Side" comic strips, bizarre mathematical color patterns, and scenes from TV shows like "Star Trek" and "The Simpsons."

MICROSOFT OPERATING SYSTEMS

Although many companies have offered operating systems over the years, Microsoft Corporation has dominated the market for microcomputer operating systems. Microsoft itself has supplied what may seem an alphabet soup of operating systems. In practice, however, Microsoft's products have evolved from one to another in a reasonably sequential fashion. The following is a brief summary.

MS-DOS

Microsoft's **MS-DOS** (which stands for Microsoft Disk Operating System), along with IBM's PC-DOS (Personal Computer Disk Operating System) and competitors like DR DOS (originally from Digital Research and later purchased by Novell), was once the most common of all the PC operating systems. An overwhelming volume of software was available that ran under DOS, and a large installed base of Intel-based PCs ran DOS.

Although it ruled throughout the 1980s, initially DOS did not gain the upper hand without a fight. Its toughest early competitor was an operating system called CP/M, which stood for Control Program for Microprocessors. However, DOS won the early operating system marketing wars because it was finally accepted by IBM as the standard operating system for the IBM PC. It therefore became the operating system for the huge market of IBM-compatibles.

DOS was adequate for the IBM-compatible PCs of the early 1980s, but it has certain limitations that became more noticeable as PCs became more powerful. For example:

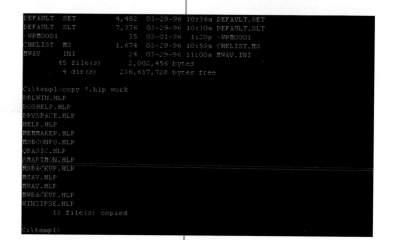

Most PCs during the 1980s and early 1990s ran DOS. This screen shows a set of help files being copied into a subdirectory named "work."

- Under DOS, you can load only a single program into memory at a time. To work with a second program, you have to close the first—a process that often hinders productivity.

- DOS was not designed to handle the large amounts of RAM that today's PCs typically use. As a result, you have to use utilities to access memory beyond the 640 KB limit imposed by DOS.

- DOS was designed for 8-bit and 16-bit CPUs; it cannot take advantage of the 32-bit architecture of the 486, Pentium, and later chips. DOS forces higher-performance computers to work at speeds below their capacity.

- DOS file names are limited to eight characters, plus a three-character "extension" following a period, as in the name "wordproc.doc". Windows 95/98 have remedied this situation by allowing file names up to 256 characters long. The UNIX and Macintosh operating systems, however, have long supported file names of up to 256 characters.

- Finally, as has been mentioned, the DOS command-line interface is more difficult to learn than a well-designed GUI. When Windows came along, most users were all too happy to stop typing commands and start clicking icons.

Microsoft Windows 3.x (3.0, 3.1, and 3.11)

In the mid-1980s, Microsoft accepted the popularity of the Macintosh computer and users' desire for a GUI. Microsoft's solution was Windows, a GUI that ran on top of DOS, replacing the command-line interface with a point-and-click system. Windows, therefore, was not originally an operating system but an **operating environment**, another term for an interface that disguises the underlying operating system.

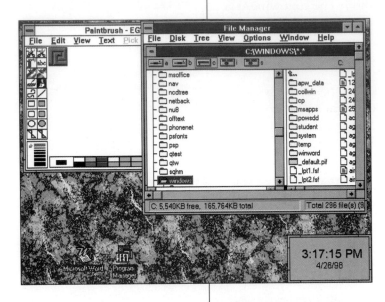

The first version of Windows did not work very well and did not sell very well either, and the second version also was not a success. Not until Microsoft released Windows 3.0 in 1990 did the program really take off.

Windows 3.0 was reasonably stable and succeeded in providing a GUI and the capability to load more than one program into memory at a time. During the early 1990s, **Windows 3.0**, **Windows 3.1**, and **Windows 3.11** (called Windows for Workgroups) became the market leaders. (DOS actually remained the most popular operating system because it was required to run these operating environments.) Windows for Workgroups was an important step for the Windows line of operating systems because it was network-enabled. This meant that two computers running Windows for Workgroups could be networked together without the need to purchase a separate network operating system like Novell NetWare. Further, it made connecting Windows for Workgroups computers to other networks (like NetWare and Windows NT) much less complicated.

The interface for Windows 3.0 and 3.1 has a lot in common with that of the Mac and Windows 95/98. Users work with files and programs by clicking desktop icons to open windows.

From time to time, you may see the term "Windows 3.x." This term is used when referring to more than one member of the Windows 3 family.

Microsoft Windows 95 (and Upgrades)

NORTON Online

For information on **Windows 95**, visit this book's Web site at **www.glencoe.com/norton/online**

In 1995, Microsoft released **Windows 95**, a complete operating system and a successor to DOS for desktop computers. Windows 95 is a 32-bit, preemptive multitasking operating system with a revised GUI. All the strengths of Windows 95, which followed the Windows 3.x series, had already existed in other operating systems—most notably the Macintosh and Windows NT. In fact, purists considered it a compromise because, unlike those 32-bit operating systems, Windows 95 contains a good deal of 16-bit code—needed to run older DOS and Windows programs. Though the 16-bit code may have represented a backward glance, it was probably Windows 95's greatest marketing strength.

As a result of the 16-bit code, Windows 95 can run almost any DOS or Windows program. Thus, if a company has already invested in many such programs, it can continue to use its familiar programs while migrating to the new operating system.

For users of Windows 3.*x*, Windows 95 has several attractions. First, it offers 32-bit processing. This means that for programs designed with 32-bit processing in mind, the operating system can exchange information with printers, networks, and files in 32-bit pieces instead of 16-bit pieces as in Windows 3.*x* and DOS. For information moving around in the computer, the effect is like doubling the number of lanes on an expressway.

Second, Windows 95, like Windows NT, offers preemptive multitasking and not the less efficient cooperative multitasking of Windows 3.1 and the Macintosh. The self-contained 32-bit preemptive multitasking means that, if one program fails, you still have access to all the other programs loaded into memory. In most cases, you do not have to restart the computer to work with those programs, as you did with earlier versions of Windows.

Third (and probably first in the eyes of users), Windows 95 has a graphical interface that is a welcome improvement over Windows 3.*x*. The Windows Explorer, for example, improves on earlier Microsoft operating systems for working with files. Windows 95 also allows users to type file names of up to 256 characters and to have spaces in those names—freedoms that had not been available on DOS-based PCs.

In addition, Windows 95 offers a plug-and-play standard for connecting new hardware. With Windows 3.*x*, users often faced nightmare-like complexities when installing disk drives, sound cards, modems, printers, CD-ROM drives, and other hardware. Under **plug-and-play**, the manufacturers do all the compliance work in advance. You simply connect a Windows 95-certified device to your computer, and the operating system does everything else to make sure that it works properly with the computer.

Another Windows 95 asset is compatibility with networking software such as IntranetWare and Microsoft Windows NT Server. With networks, too, you can simply identify the network operating system when you install Windows 95, and Windows 95 will be compatible with it.

As with any program, upgrades to Windows 95 will continue to improve on these advances, eliminating bugs from earlier versions and improving such features as network links, the Internet browser, and support for 3-D games.

DOS, running in a window.

▶ **Windows 95 is primarily designed to run 32-bit applications. However, it can also run the older, 16-bit applications designed for Windows 3.*x* and DOS.**

A 16-bit application, designed for Windows 3.*x*.

▶ **The Windows Explorer lists folders on the left side of the screen and the contents of folders on the right side.**

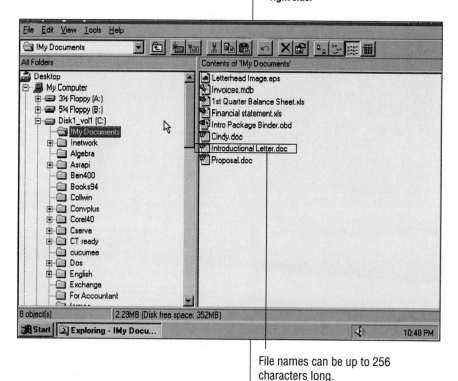

File names can be up to 256 characters long.

NORTON
Online

For information
on **Windows 98**,
visit this book's Web site at
www.glencoe.com/norton/online

Windows 98

The latest version of Windows is **Windows 98**. By and large, you can consider Windows 98 to be an upgrade from Windows 95, rather than a major Windows operating system upgrade. In other words, the differences from Windows 95 to Windows 98 are not as significant as the differences from, say, Windows 3.x to Windows 95. Indications are that Windows 98 will be the last iteration of the Windows family of operating systems. Microsoft's position appears to be that Windows 98 is a "consumer" operating system, and that Windows NT Workstation 5.0 will be the successor to Windows 98 on the consumer's desktop, as well as on the corporate desktop.

Windows 98 incorporates and builds on all the features found in Windows 95. In addition, Windows 98 adds several new features. These features are explored in the following sections.

Usability

One key change in Windows 98 is the inclusion of the Internet Explorer 4.0 (IE4) interface, including a new feature called the Active Desktop. This new IE4 interface provides a single user interface for browsing the Internet as well as local computer resources. For example, you can browse a local hard disk using the same interface you use to browse the Internet. Using a single interface essentially means that you only have to learn one means of browsing for resources. Active Desktop enables you to integrate Internet resources such as stock tickers and news information services directly on your Windows desktop. If you have an active Internet connection, the information will update automatically.

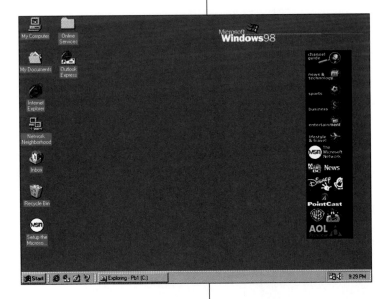

The Windows 98 Active Desktop.

Windows 98 also adds support for new and emerging technologies and expands other hardware support. These include Universal Serial Bus (USB) IEEE1394 devices, Digital Versatile Disk (DVD), and OnNow (which enables computers to be booted and ready to use almost instantly). One interesting feature is Windows 98's capability to support up to eight monitors at one time. This new feature is ideal for certain applications such as computer-aided design to provide large desktops and the capability to separate application and document windows. It's also a great feature for many online and interactive games.

Green PC and notebook users will find benefit in Windows 98's support for Advanced Configuration and Power Interface, or ACPI. ACPI enables easier device power management on these types of computers and makes possible better battery performance on new notebooks that support ACPI.

Speed and Reliability

Reliability is another area of improvement offered by Windows 98. In addition to fine-tuning in the core operating system, Windows 98 includes a new feature called Windows Update. This Web-based resource enables Windows to periodically connect to Microsoft via the Internet to update your operating system. This means that Windows can automatically update itself to add new features, drivers, and so on. Windows Update ushers in a new way to receive operating system updates without the need to go out and buy CD-ROM- or floppy disk-based upgrades. Scheduling has been expanded to enable Windows 98 to automatically perform routine maintenance such as disk scanning and repair and optimize the system in the background.

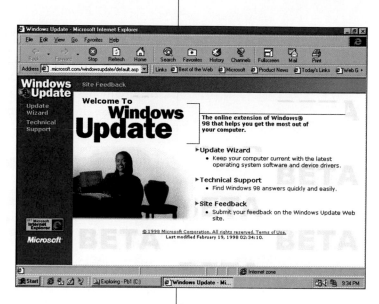

The Backup utility in Windows 98 has been improved as well, to incorporate support for additional tape drives and new backup hardware. These improvements make it easier for you to back up and restore your system, helping protect your system from catastrophic crashes.

The Windows 98 Update feature.

In addition, all the date-dependent components in Windows 98 have been updated to accommodate what has become known as the "Millenium Problem." This means that Windows 98 will accommodate dates in and after the year 2000.

Another feature that can improve performance is FAT32. FAT stands for File Allocation Table and refers to the way in which the operating system stores information on a hard disk. FAT32 is a 32-bit implementation of the FAT file system that in addition to other improvements, can improve file system performance. FAT32 is not compatible with DOS or Windows NT systems, however. If you use either of these operating systems on your computer in addition to Windows 98, you will not be able to access any FAT32 partitions from these other operating systems.

Other Changes

In addition to the enhancements described in the previous sections, Windows 98 includes several other changes and added features. Many of these new features relate to the Internet, intranets, and broadcast content such as television.

The broadcast features in Windows 98, for example, provide built-in software to support television reception devices such as TV/video card combinations that enable you to watch television on your PC. The broadcast features extend beyond TV reception to other data broadcast technologies that enable data to be pushed from the Internet to your computer. Multimedia streams, news, and stock quotes are just a few examples of these types of data.

Also, many features made available as add-ons to Windows 95 have been incorporated directly into Windows 98. For example, you can change video resolution and color depth without restarting your computer. Many features in the Plus! for Windows 95 add-on have also been incorporated into Windows 98, including on-screen font smoothing, the Task Scheduler, capability to customize desktop icons, and more.

Microsoft Windows NT

Although Windows 95 is considered the successor to DOS, Microsoft released **Windows NT**, a 32-bit operating system for PCs, in 1993. Windows NT was originally designed to be the successor to DOS, but by the time it was ready for release, it had become too large to run on most of the PCs in use at the time. As a result, Microsoft repositioned Windows NT to be a high-end operating system designed primarily for powerful workstations and network servers. With Windows NT released, Microsoft went back to the drawing board to create Windows 95.

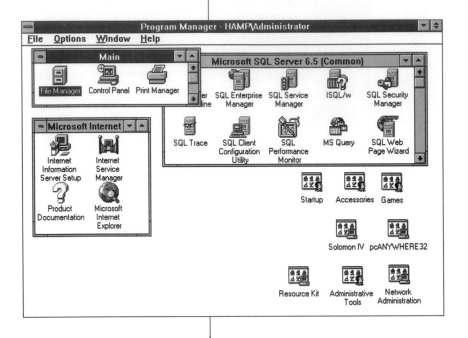

Windows 95 retained backward compatibility for users working with older machines and older programs. However, Windows NT addressed the market for the powerful 32-bit, networked workstations that use some of the most powerful CPUs on the market today. Because these types of computers fell into two primary categories, Microsoft separated Windows NT into two distinct products: Windows NT Workstation and Windows NT Server.

The interface for Windows NT started out looking a lot like Windows 3.1. More recent versions resemble Windows 95.

Windows NT Workstation

Although Windows NT Workstation looks almost identical to Windows 3.*x* and Windows 95, the underlying operating system is almost completely different. Windows NT Workstation is designed to take better advantage of today's computers and also runs on a broader range of CPUs than does Windows 98 and prior operating systems, which run only on Intel processor-based systems. Windows NT runs on systems that use Intel, Alpha, and PowerPC processors. As Windows NT has become more popular, indications have grown that it will find its way onto other hardware platforms, as well, including those that use Motorola processors. These systems include, among others, high-end workstations from Hewlett-Packard and personal computers from Apple.

NORTON Online

For information on **Windows NT Workstation** and **Windows NT Server**, visit this book's Web site at **www.glencoe.com/norton/online**

Windows NT also incorporates much greater security than do Microsoft's other operating systems. Windows NT requires a user to have an account either on the computer he is using or on a server on the network. Resources on the local computer, as well as resources on remote servers, can be configured to limit access to specific users and groups of users. For example, files can be protected on a file-by-file basis, granting access to a file to one person or group but not to another. This is achieved by using Windows NT's NT File System (NTFS), a high performance file system that replaces the older FAT file system introduced by MS-DOS. Users and administrators have the option of using NTFS or FAT on their Windows NT computer, but NTFS must be used to enable file-by-file access rights.

Windows NT is also more fault tolerant than other Microsoft operating systems. Because of the way the operating system isolates programs from one another, it is much less likely for one program to adversely affect another. Windows NT also integrates other advanced features that provide for disk mirroring, which is the capability to have online a backup hard disk that is a mirror image of another. If the primary hard disk fails, the mirrored drive takes over automatically.

Windows NT also turns in better performance figures. Although performance varies according to your hardware and application, you can expect roughly 50 percent better performance in many situations running Windows NT versus Windows 3.x.

Windows NT Server

Windows NT Server incorporates all the same features as Windows NT Workstation but also has other capabilities. Microsoft fine-tuned Windows NT Server to function as an operating system for file and print servers, and on other systems that provide services for other computers on the LAN or Internet. Windows NT Server offers expanded security features for grouping and authenticating users and controlling their access to network resources.

Windows NT Server also incorporates several features not found in Windows NT Workstation. For example, Windows NT Server supports several additional levels of RAID (Redundant Array of Independent Disks) for disk duplexing, disk striping, and disk mirroring. All these features make it possible for Windows NT Server to ensure disk and data security even in the event of a catastrophic failure of a hard disk. Features such as support for volume sets enable you to combine storage space on several different disks to look and function as a single drive.

NORTON Online

For information on **Windows CE**, visit this book's Web site at **www.glencoe.com/norton/online**

Windows CE is designed to run on many kinds of small computerized devices, such as handheld computers, PDAs, and others.

Windows CE

The newest member of the Miscrosoft family of operating systems is **Windows CE** (which stands for Consumer Electronics). Windows CE is a 32-bit operating system that offers many of the same features and functionality of full-fledged operating systems like Windows 98 and Windows NT. However, Windows CE has been miniaturized to run on small platforms, such as handheld PCs, personal digital assistants, television set-top boxes, and other types of consumer electronics.

Windows CE differs from other versions of Windows in that it can be stored completely in a hardware device's ROM, reducing the need for RAM or disk space, which can be used by applications and data required by the user. Further, because Windows CE is modular, hardware developers can use only the modules required by their specialized hardware devices. This means that developers can save precious system resources instead of devoting them to uneeded OS code.

Developers have been creating "pocket" versions of popular software products to run on Windows CE-based systems, including word processors, spreadsheets, calendars and scheduling software, Internet browsers, and more.

Microsoft hopes that Windows CE will become the operating system of choice for small computerized devices of all types that can use or require input from a user. The variety of hardware is wide-ranging, from entertainment hardware in the home (VCRs, televisions, stereo equipment) and home appliances (microwave ovens, alarm systems) to industrial equipment (such as industrial control devices, flow meters), and more.

OTHER OPERATING SYSTEMS FOR PERSONAL COMPUTERS

Although Microsoft has become the unquestioned market leader in operating systems, that has not always been the case. Other operating systems have been popular, and some continue to keep their staunch supporters' loyalty.

The Macintosh Operating System

The Macintosh is a purely graphical machine. In its early days in the mid-1980s, its tight integration of hardware, operating system, and its GUI made it the favorite with users who did not want to deal with DOS's command-line interface. Another big advantage of the Macintosh was that all its applications

NORTON
Online

For information on the **Macintosh operating system**, visit this book's Web site at www.glencoe.com/norton/online

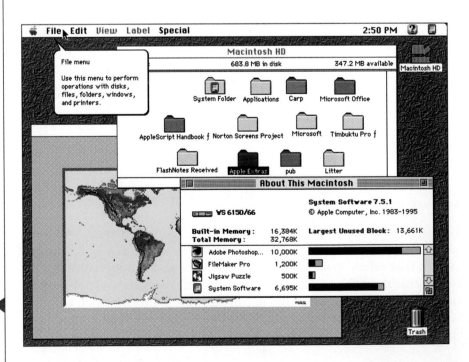

The Macintosh was the first commercially successful computer to come with a GUI operating system.

Techview

Crossing the Platform

The operating system basically determines what programs you can run on your computer. Applications must be compatible with the OS of the computer you use. Most applications are OS-specific, meaning that they run on one operating system only.

Most modern applications offer identical versions designed for different operating systems, but many do not.

Also, it can be frustrating trying to use files created in a different operating system from your own. Many major applications, such as Excel and Word, have built-in conversion capabilities, but these conversions are imperfect and sometimes alter formatting or introduce foreign characters.

In addition, many computers are platform-specific, which means, for example, that a PC computer may not be able to read a Mac disk.

For these reasons and more, it is necessary for the modern businessperson to learn to work in what are called cross-platform environments. This means that you must find ways to work with a variety of operating systems or with systems that are built to cross the boundaries of operating systems.

A simple example of a cross-platform environment that most computer users see every day is a network. A network can link certain functions of multiple operating systems over a local area or wide area network. For example, you can print files over a network from both Macintosh and Windows-based computers.

Users on different operating systems also can share files over a network. The computers must be equipped with utility programs that allow disks from other computers to be recognized in disk drives and with file formats that can be translated back and forth among operating systems and application programs.

Another option is to use applications that come in identical versions for each operating system. Then those applications can easily exchange files and the computer operators need learn only one application.

The Power Macintosh offers a cross-platform environment capable of reading this PC disk.

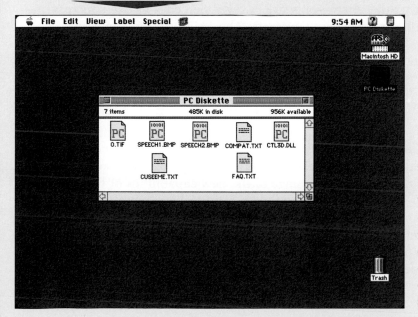

One recent development in cross-platform environments is called a hardware plug-in. Here, a computer is miniaturized to fit on a circuit board and then plugged into another computer. The plug-in computer doesn't need its own disk drives, monitor, or other such devices. It can share memory and hard drive space with the main computer.

Another common form of cross-platform environments is called software emulation. This involves a special kind of software program called an emulator, which makes one computer act like another and capable of running that other computer's operating system and applications. This is a relatively inexpensive way to get the benefits of more than one operating system and software library.

The latest wrinkle in cross-platform systems is a new hardware specification called Common Hardware Reference Platform, or CHRP. A hardware specification is a group of standards established for building a piece of hardware, most commonly the computer itself. Currently, the two most common standards are Mac OS and IBM- compatible or DOS- based.

CHRP is designed to support a variety of operating systems at once—for example, Windows, Macintosh, UNIX, and Windows NT. Computers based on CHRP certainly will earn points for flexibility; how easy they are to use, and how completely and consistently they will accommodate the various operating systems remains to be seen.

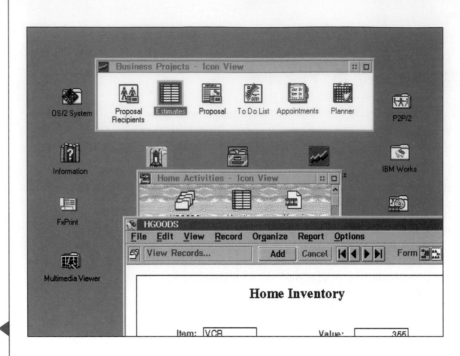

The interface for OS/2.

functioned similarly, applying the concepts of common user access and making them easier to learn than DOS applications. Now that GUIs have become the standard, it is difficult to appreciate just how big a breakthrough this really was.

The **Macintosh operating system** was also ahead of Windows with many other features, including plug-and-play hardware compatibility and built-in networking. Nevertheless, the Mac operating system works only on Macintosh and compatible hardware, whereas DOS and all the varieties of Windows work only on IBM-compatible computers (which account for about 85 percent of the PC market). Still, the Mac remains the first choice of many publishers, multimedia developers, graphic artists, and schools. As of the mid-1990s, Apple controlled about a ten percent share of the personal computer market—surpassing former rival IBM. Today, however, Apple controls a much smaller market share—only five to seven percent—as users increasingly migrate to Windows-based systems. This migration is one result of Apple's inability to update the Macintosh operating system to keep pace with competitors, a problem that has disillusioned both users and Macintosh software developers.

OS/2 Warp

Although they are now fierce rivals, IBM and Microsoft were once allies. After the introduction of the Intel 80286 processor in 1982, both companies recognized the need to take advantage of the new capabilities of this CPU. They teamed up to develop **OS/2**, a modern multitasking operating system for Intel microprocessors. The partnership did not last long. Technical differences of opinion and IBM's perception of Microsoft Windows as a threat to OS/2 (which proved to be accurate) caused a rift between the companies that ultimately led to the dissolution of the partnership.

IBM continued to develop and promote OS/2 as a strategic cornerstone of its System Application Architecture (SAA), a comprehensive plan for overall business computing.

Like Windows NT, OS/2 is a single-user multitasking operating system with a point-and-click interface. It is also a true multitasking system. Its designers claim that it is better than Windows 95 at running older DOS-based programs and that it performs more efficient multitasking.

UNIX

NORTON
Online

For information on **UNIX**, visit this book's Web site at www.glencoe.com/norton/online

UNIX is older than all the other PC operating systems, and in many ways it served as a model for them. Initially developed by Bell Labs and geared toward telecommunications, UNIX was sold to Novell in the early 1990s. Because of its early use in university settings, several versions were developed. The best known is Berkeley UNIX. Other versions include A/UX for the Mac and AIX for IBM high-end workstations.

UNIX was not just a multitasking system like the other operating systems in this chapter. It was also a multiuser and multiprocessing operating system. That is, it could allow multiple users to work from more than one keyboard and monitor attached to a single CPU, just as a mainframe with dumb terminals does. UNIX allowed for a PC with more than one CPU working at a time—an admirable feat by early PC standards.

UNIX runs on many different types of computers—on Cray supercomputers, PCs, and everything in between, including mainframes and minicomputers. Because of its capability to work with so many kinds of hardware, it became the backbone of the Internet. Thanks to its power and its appeal to engineers and other users of CAD and CAM software, UNIX has been popular for RISC workstations such as those from Sun Microsystems, Hewlett-Packard, IBM, and Silicon Graphics.

```
line:2> ls
Mail/           News/           brian/          mail/
Mailboxes/      ShopCart.dat    james.pl        public_html/
line:2> cd mail
line:2> ls
saved-messages          sent-mail            sent-mail-feb-1996
line:2> cd
line:2> ls
Mail/           News/           brian/          mail/
Mailboxes/      ShopCart.dat    james.pl        public_html/
line:2> ps
  PID TT STAT  TIME COMMAND
 3023 p8 S     0:00 -csh (csh)
line:2> ftp
ftp> open ftp.netscape.com
Connected to ftp20.netscape.com.
220 ftp20 FTP server (Version wu-2.4(17) Tue Feb 20 09:08:35 PST 1996) ready.
Name (ftp.netscape.com:swankman): anonymous
331 Guest login ok, send your complete e-mail address as password.
Password:
230-Welcome to the Netscape Communications Corporation FTP server.
230-
230-If you have any odd problems, try logging in with a minus sign (-)
230-as the first character of your password. This will turn off a feature
230-that may be confusing your ftp client program.
230-
230-Please send any questions, comments, or problem reports about
230-this server to ftp@netscape.com.
230-
230-*********** October 13, 1995 ***********
230-Private ftp is now only on ftp1.netscape.com. Anonymous is supported on
230-ftp 2 through 8. If you are accessing a named account please use ftp1
230-
230 Guest login ok, access restrictions apply.
ftp> bye
221 Goodbye.
line:2>
```

Command-line UNIX looks much like DOS, with typed commands and command prompts. In fact, DOS borrowed several commands and features from UNIX.

Although it is a robust and capable operating system, command-line UNIX is not for the faint of heart, because it requires many commands to do even simple things. A UNIX windowing system called X-Windows has brought a GUI to UNIX computers, but it has remained an operating system for engineers and technical users. Although some of its capabilities have become mainstream, UNIX has gradually lost ground to operating systems such as DOS, Windows, and the Mac, which generally have been perceived as easier to learn and use.

Computers
In Your Career

If you find yourself in a career that involves the use of computers—specifically, as a tool to get your job done—you probably will be working only with one operating system. In most general businesses, that operating system will probably be some variation of Windows or Windows NT. Many careers in the publishing industry will involve Apple computers and the Macintosh operating system. Specialized careers such as engineering and medicine will likely involve either Windows NT or some form of UNIX. In all these cases, however, your experience will probably be limited to a single operating system, which means you only have to learn one.

Network Administrators, Hardware Technicians Careers in data services, however, could likely require working with several different hardware platforms and operating systems. Network managers, for example, typically have to deal with Windows NT, Windows 95/98, and UNIX. Having a good understanding of one operating system usually means an easier time learning the next. And, the more you know about different systems, the more marketable your skills become, offering better growth potential within a company and more possibilities for moving on to other companies when the time comes.

Programmers Some specialized careers may require you to master—or at least understand—a variety of operating systems. Many programmers, for example, must write different versions of programs to run on different operating systems. This requires the programmer to know the many differences between operating systems, and sometimes to use various development tools and languages.

Graphic Artists, Desktop Publishers Similarly, in the world of computer graphics, astists and designers use many different hardware and software tools. This is because different platforms offer unique strengths and features. In digital studios, therefore, you can commonly find Windows, Macintosh, and UNIX systems all on the same network.

WHAT TO EXPECT IN THE FUTURE

Every 12 to 16 months, the manufacturers of PC operating systems—primarily Microsoft, IBM, and Apple—release new versions of their operating systems. In the operating systems market, the trend is definitely toward building ever more capabilities into operating systems, making some types of utilities (and perhaps even applications) unnecessary.

With the release of Windows 98, with its integrated copy of the Internet Explorer browser, the U.S. Department of Justice and a coalition of software companies began to scrutinize this trend. They claimed that by extending the functionality of the operating system, Microsoft was stepping on its competitors. If you have a Web browser built into your operating system, asked critics, then why should you buy or install a different browser made by another company? This debate may extend into other areas of the operating system, from the use of built-in compression and disk management features, to the use of "applets" such as Notepad. In short, where should the operating system end and other types of software begin?

For the foreseeable future, the debate may focus on the Internet-related capabilities of operating systems. Beyond that, however, developers have expressed interest in adding other features to their operating systems, such as:

- *Speech recognition.* Many developers believe the microphone will ultimately replace the keyboard as the primary input device. The OS is responsible for keystroke recognition; should it also be responsible for handling voice input? OS developers developers say yes, whereas developers of commercial speech recognition software certainly disagree.

- *Visual recognition.* Imagine a computer that reads hand signals, your expressions, or even your lips. Instead of pressing Enter or even saying "Yes," you simply nod your head. This technology may seem like a flight of fancy, but it is in development. Like speech recognition, it seems like the logical domain of the operating system.

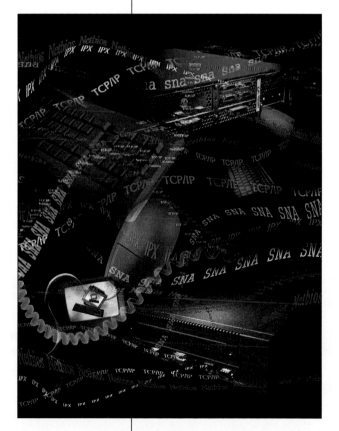

- *Enhanced plug-and-play.* Some day, you may be able to add any device to your computer without installing special software, such as drivers. When the plug-and-play standard is universal, the OS will recognize virtually any new piece of hardware, so you can use it right away.

- *Zero administration.* Network managers have long dreamed of a network operating system that is so intelligent it requires minimal human intervention. Backups, for example, would be automatic, and conflicts would be resolved in the background. New operating systems, such as Windows NT 5.0, promise a great step forward in reducing administration, and this functionality may someday hit the desktop, as well. This could mean less reliance on utilities and system-management products.

How big should the operating system become? The answer may lie only in our imagination—in the ultimate vision of computing power and ease-of-use. Developers, users, and the government may all need to work together to define the boundaries of the OS of the future.

VISUAL SUMMARY

What Is an Operating System?

- The operating system provides interfaces for the user, software, hardware, and for file management.
- The functionality of the operating system can be extended with the addition of utilities.

The User Interface

- Most modern operating systems employ a graphical user interface (GUI), in which users control the system by pointing and clicking on screen graphics.
- A GUI is based on the desktop metaphor, icons, sizable windows, menus, and dialog boxes.
- The applications designed to run under a particular operating system use the same interface elements, so users see a familiar interface or common user access (CUA) no matter what they are doing on the computer.
- Some older operating systems, such as DOS, use command-line interfaces, which the user controls by typing commands at a prompt.

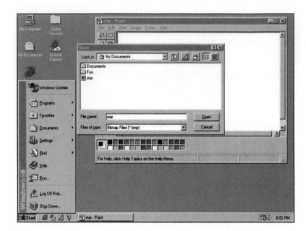

Running Programs

- The operating system manages all the other programs that are running.
- The operating system also provides system-level services to those programs, including file management, memory management, and printing.
- The operating system allows programs to share information. In Windows 3.1, 3.11, NT, 95, and 98, sharing is accomplished through the Clipboard and OLE.
- A modern operating system also makes multitasking possible.

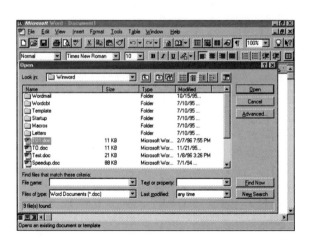

Managing Files

- The operating system keeps track of all the files on each disk. On a PC, Windows does this by constantly updating the FAT.
- Users can make their own file management easier by creating hierarchical file systems that include folders and subfolders.

Visual Summary & Exercises

Managing Hardware

■ The operating system uses interrupt requests to maintain organized communication with the CPU and the other pieces of hardware.

■ Each of the hardware devices is controlled by another piece of software, called the driver, which allows the operating system to activate and use the device.

■ The operating system also provides the software necessary to link computers and form a network.

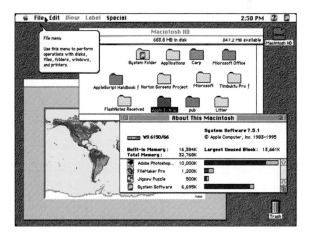

This file has been fragmented into noncontiguous sectors.

Enhancing the Operating System with Utility Software

■ Operating systems gradually have included more and more utilities.

■ The most common utilities are for file defragmentation, data compression, backup, data recovery, protection against viruses, and screen saving.

Microsoft Operating Systems

■ DOS dominated the operating system market during the 1980s but gradually became obsolete.

■ Windows 3.0, 3.1, and 3.11 are operating environments that provide a GUI for computers running DOS.

■ The strengths of Windows 95 are its simplified interface, 32-bit multitasking, and its capability to run older Windows and DOS programs.

■ Windows 98's features include advanced Internet capabilities, improved user interface called the Active Desktop, and enhanced file system performance.

■ Microsoft Windows NT offered true 32-bit architecture and excellent networking capabilities.

■ Windows CE brings many capabilities of Windows 95 to consumer electronics devices, such as personal digital assistants.

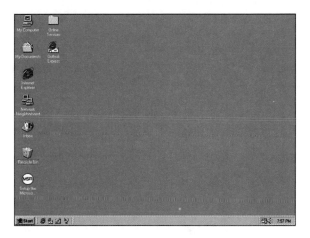

Other Operating Systems for Personal Computers

■ The Macintosh has long been a favorite among GUI fans, as well as publishers, multimedia developers, graphic artists, and schools, primarily because of its consistent interface, built-in networking, and plug-and-play hardware capability.

■ IBM's operating system is OS/2 Warp, a single-user, multitasking system for Intel-based machines.

■ UNIX was the first multiuser, multiprocessing operating system on personal computers, but it has been losing market share.

Visual Summary & Exercises

KEY TERMS

After completing this chapter, you should be able to define the following terms:

activate, 156
active program, 156
active window, 158
antivirus utility, 176
backup software, 175
button, 156
choose, 156
Clipboard, 165
command-line interface, 164
common user access (CUA), 164
context menu, 156
cooperative multitasking, 168
Copy, 167
Cut, 167
data compression utility, 174
data recovery utility, 175
defragmentation utility, 174
dialog box, 161
driver, 172

graphical user interface (GUI), 156
hierarchical file system, 171
icon, 156
interrupt request (IRQ), 171
Macintosh operating system, 186
menu, 160
menu bar, 160
MS-DOS, 177
multitasking, 168
object embedding, 167
object linking, 167
Object Linking and Embedding
   (OLE), 167
operating environment, 178
OS/2, 186
Paste, 167
plug-and-play, 179
preemptive multitasking, 168
screen saver, 176

scroll bar, 158
select, 156
Start button, 157
system call, 165
taskbar, 156
title bar, 158
unerase program, 175
UNIX, 187
user interface, 154
virus, 176
window, 158
Windows 3.0, 178
Windows 3.1, 178
Windows 3.11, 178
Windows 95, 178
Windows 98, 180
Windows CE, 183
Windows NT, 182

KEY TERMS QUIZ

Fill in the missing word with one of the terms listed in Key Terms:

1. When you double-click an icon, you _____ it.

2. The _____, _____, and _____ commands enable you to share information in different documents or applications, by using the operating system's Clipboard feature.

3. The _____ across the top of the window identifies the contents of the window.

4. The capability to perform two or more processes at the same time is known as _____.

5. When you copy or move data, it is stored temporarily on the _____.

6. _____ is the process of cutting and pasting between applications.

7. You can use the _____ to view different parts of a document that do not fit in the document window.

8. A(n) _____ utility is designed to locate and eradicate a parasitic program.

9. You use _____ to copy large groups of files from your hard drive to other storage media.

10. _____ is a full 32-bit operating system, miniaturized for use with small computing devices.

REVIEW QUESTIONS

1. Why is an operating system known as a master control program?

2. List and describe briefly the four functions performed by an operating system.

3. Why does the term *desktop* serve as a metaphor for the on-screen interface of an operating system?

4. Name the four mouse techniques commonly used to work with on-screen objects.

5. What does a window in a graphical-user interface represent?

6. What GUI feature conducts a "dialog" with a user to gather the information necessary to perform a task?

7. What are two important characteristics of a well-designed GUI?

8. List and describe briefly at least three services that an operating system provides to active applications.

9. Describe briefly what occurs when an object in one document is linked to another document. How does this process contrast with a simple cut-and-paste operation?

10. List and describe briefly the various types of system utility programs that are provided with today's operating systems.

DISCUSSION QUESTIONS

1. What does multitasking mean to a user? In what ways does the user benefit from the multitasking capabilities of an operating system?

2. In what ways have newer operating systems such as Windows 95/98, Windows NT, and the Macintosh OS simplified procedures such as managing files, hardware devices, and memory?

3. How can data that has been deleted from a disk still be recovered? Can erased data be recovered at any time, or is there variability to this process? What factors might render erased data unrecoverable?

4. Do you think that using an antivirus program is mandatory for anyone using a PC for business purposes? Are there any drawbacks to using antivirus software? Do you think such programs are 100 percent effective against all viruses? What do you think daily users of computers should do to ensure the best chances that their systems will remain clean?

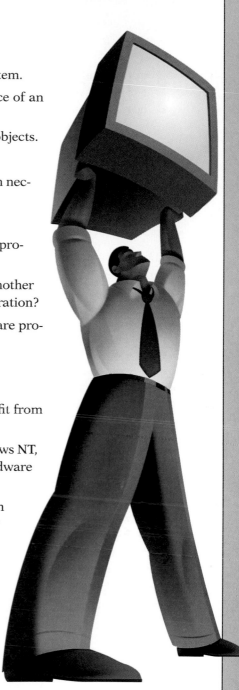

inteNET Workshop

The following exercises assume that you have access to the Internet and a browser. If you need help with any of the exercises, visit this book's Web site at **www.glencoe.com/norton/online**. This book's Web site also lists the URLs you need to complete many of these exercises.

1. Using a search engine, gather information regarding at least three products that enable files and disks to be shared between Macintosh and Windows-based computers. Briefly explain how these products are different and choose the one product you feel offers the best tools for sharing data between Macs and PCs.

2. Locate at least two resources on the Internet that discuss user interface design. Citing these resources, briefly summarize the type of role that a graphical user interface plays in simplifying computer use.

3. Using a search engine, locate on the Internet at least two sites that provide a library of shareware and utilities that expand the function of the MacOS operating system. Locate at least two additional sites that provide the same programs for the Windows 95/98 operating systems.

4. Find at least one site providing information about computing devices that run on the Windows CE operating system. What types of devices are discussed? What information can you find about those particular devices? How useful do you think such devices might be?

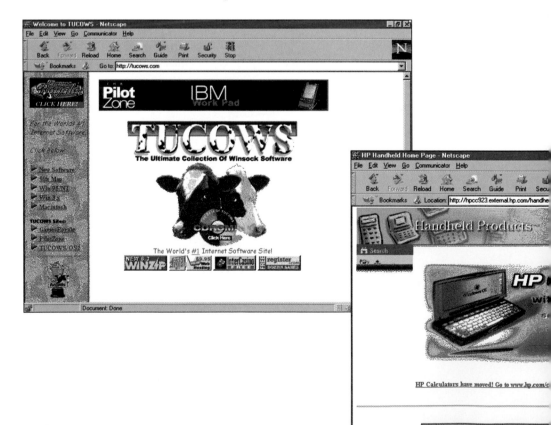

*inte*NET Workshop

5. Visit the AntiVirus Resources Web site. Using this site as a starting point, find information about the nature and development of viruses, how they work, how they are spread, and how they can be detected and removed from computer systems.

6. Many software developers and computer industry analysts believe that Java will emerge as the basis for the next significant operating system. Can you find any discussions of this on the Web? If so, what opinions can you find, and what facts support those opinions?

7. Visiting sites such as Amazon.com and the Barnes & Noble Web sites, search for information on books about operating systems. Considering your own need to master operating systems, do you find any current books that seem especially useful? Which ones appeal to you most, and why?

CHAPTER 6

Productivity Software

CONTENTS

OBJECTIVES

When you complete this chapter, you will be able to do the following:

- Name three types of documents you can create with word processing software.
- Name two types of editing and three types of formatting you can do in a word processor.
- Name and describe the four types of data that can be entered in a worksheet.
- Explain how cell addresses are used in spreadsheet programs.
- Name the two most common types of database structures and differentiate them.
- List six important data management functions that can be performed in a DBMS.
- List at least four types of formatting that can be done on slides in a presentation program.
- Describe three methods for presenting slides created in a presentation program.

or graphics, working with numbers, searching for data, or preparing a presentation. With the advent of window-based interfaces, these different applications now can work together in many ways, sharing data with one another and enabling users to perform multiple tasks simultaneously.

This chapter introduces you to the four most popular types of productivity software:

- *Word processing software.* This type of software provides tools for creating and formatting text-based documents. It is the most common type of software application found on PCs.

- *Spreadsheet programs.* Spreadsheets are specialized tools for working with numerical data and perform complex calculations with blazing speed. Spreadsheet software has become one of the most important financial tools for accountants, business managers, and anyone else who needs to create budgets, analyze statistics, or collect numerical research.

Early desktop computers had only one or two uses. Some people used the PC almost exclusively as a replacement for the typewriter, to generate letters, memos, and other documents. Many business professionals relied on the computer to "crunch numbers," and the PC began to replace the ledger book as the primary tool for tracking and analyzing revenues and expenses in business. One of the earliest uses for computers—tracking huge amounts of data—continues to be one of their primary uses today, as organizations and individuals use computers to maintain lists of contacts, products, sales, personnel, and countless other items.

Most computer users now have several types of **productivity software** on their computer. Just as the name implies, productivity software can be any application that helps the user accomplish a specific task, whether the task involves generating text

- *Database management systems.* Computerized databases help people keep track of things—from a salesperson maintaining a list of contacts, to government agencies tracking entire populations. The goal of these systems is to gather large volumes of data and process them into useful information.

- *Presentation programs.* Today, many businesspeople—especially sales and marketing professionals—would be lost without presentation software. This type of application enables the user to quickly create sophisticated presentations using text, graphics, numerical data, sound, and animations. The resulting presentations can be printed, displayed as slides or overheads, or played back on a computer screen.

WORD PROCESSING SOFTWARE

Word processing software (also called a *word processor*) provides an extensive set of tools for working with text. It is used to create all kinds of documents, from the simplest notes to complete books containing hundreds of pages. Every day, millions of people use word processing software to create and edit memos, letters, brochures, resumes, reports, and many other kinds of documents. It is estimated that between 80 and 90 percent of all personal computers have word processing software installed.

▶ Word processors are frequently used to create business letters and resumes. The formatting can be simple or elaborate.

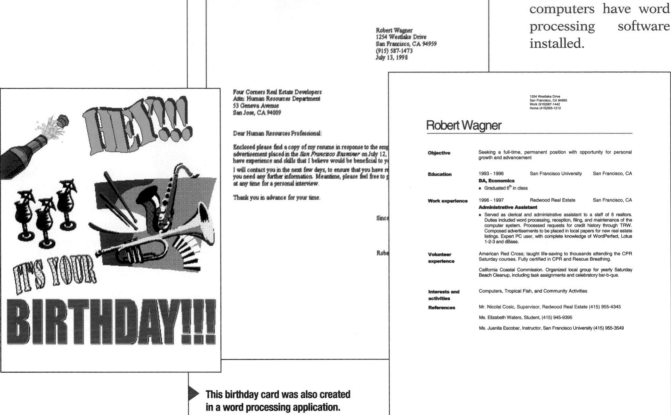

▶ This birthday card was also created in a word processing application. It features colors, rotated text, and clip art graphics.

The Word Processor's Interface

The word processor's main editing window displays your document and a number of tools.

Figure 6.1 shows Microsoft Word 97, commonly called "Word." In addition to a **document area**, which is where you view the document, a word processor provides several sets of tools. These tools include a menu bar, from which you can select hundreds of commands and options. Two **toolbars** provide tools that resemble buttons; these represent frequently used commands, such as those for printing and for selecting text styles. A **ruler** shows you the positioning of text, tabs, margins, and other elements across the page. Horizontal and vertical scroll bars let you "scroll" through a document that is too large to fit inside the document area. Most word processors also offer a **status bar** across the bottom of the window with information related to your position in the document, the page count, and the status of keyboard keys.

Modern word processors are highly *configurable,* meaning that you can customize them in any number of ways. You can set up the toolbars to display different tools, create macros, and much more. These capabilities enable you to personalize your word processor so that it functions perfectly for your needs. A medical transcriptionist, for example, probably will customize his word processor so that it looks and acts very differently from a student's word processor.

Some word processors operate under non-graphical operating systems, such as DOS or UNIX. The most popular word processors, however, are designed to work in graphical environments such as Windows or the Macintosh operating system. These graphical systems provide two advantages. First, they enable users to work with a mouse or other pointing device, greatly speeding up their work. Second, they display text on screen in a manner that closely resembles the document's printed appearance. This feature is called **WYSIWYG** (pronounced "wiz-ee-wig")—an acronym for "What You See Is What You Get."

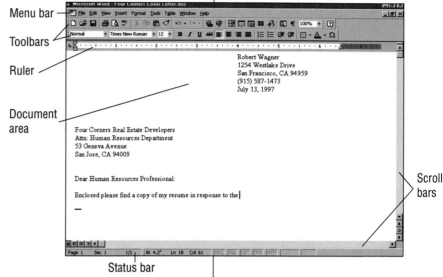

Menu bar

Toolbars

Ruler

Document area

Scroll bars

Status bar

Figure 6.1
Microsoft Word's interface features tools that are common to nearly all Windows and Macintosh word processing programs.

For information on **WYSIWYG,** visit this book's Web site at **www.glencoe.com/norton/online**

Entering Text

You create a document by typing text on the keyboard—a process known as *entering text.* In a new document, the program places a blinking insertion point (also called a *cursor*) in the upper-left corner of the document window. As you type text, the insertion point advances across the screen, showing you where the next character will be placed.

When your text reaches the right edge of the screen, you do not have to press Enter (or Return) to move the insertion point down to the next line. Instead, the word processor automatically moves the insertion point to the next line, as shown in Figure 6.2. This feature is called **word wrap**. The only time you need to press Enter is at the end of a paragraph. (In a word processor, you press Enter to start a new paragraph.)

When the insertion point reaches the end of a line . . .

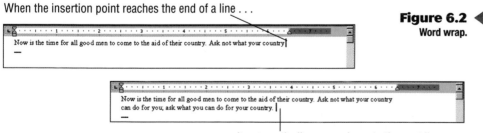

Figure 6.2
Word wrap.

. . . it automatically moves down to the next line.

Editing Text

Perhaps the greatest advantage of word processing software over the typewriter is that it enables you to change text without retyping the entire page. Instead, you retype only the text that needs to be changed. Changing an existing document is called **editing** the document. Word processing software provides several simple methods for quickly erasing and retyping text:

- *The Backspace and Delete keys.* The Backspace key moves the insertion point one character to the left, erasing each character as you go. If you mistakenly type "wetn" rather than "went," you can simply press Backspace twice to delete the last two characters and then retype them correctly—assuming that the insertion point is at the immediate end of the word. The Delete key works like Backspace but deletes each character to the right of the insertion point.

- *Overtyping.* All word processors let you work in **overtype mode**, in which the new text you type writes over existing text. Suppose that you write a sentence and then decide you don't like it. Using overtype mode, you can return the insertion point to the beginning of the sentence and simply type over it, without deleting it first. (Otherwise, you work in **insertion mode**, and the word processor inserts text wherever the insertion point is located, without overtyping existing text.)

- *Autocorrect.* Many word processors can automatically correct common misspellings, a feature called **autocorrect**. You can customize the Autocorrect feature to catch words that you typically misspell. Autocorrect can catch many other common mistakes, too, such as forgetting to capitalize the first word of a sentence, or capitalizing the names of days or months.

The word processor's real beauty is its capability to work with blocks of text. A **block** is a contiguous group of characters, words, lines, sentences, or paragraphs in your document that you mark for editing—including deleting, copying, moving, formatting, and more.

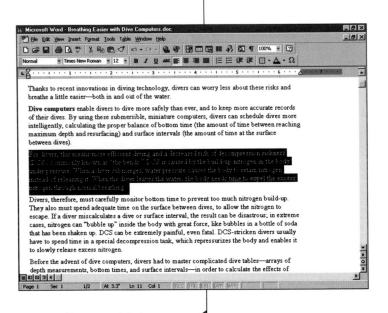

The paragraph that appears as white text against a black background has been highlighted; it is a selected block of text. With the text selected, the user can perform edits that affect the entire paragraph.

To mark the text for editing, you **select** it. You can select text by using the mouse (dragging, for example, to select several words or lines), the keyboard (using Shift and the arrow keys to select characters, words, or lines), or both (using Ctrl while clicking, for example, to select entire sentences). When you select text, it changes color—becoming **highlighted**—to indicate that it is selected.

After you select a block, you can do many things to it. You can erase the entire block by pressing the Delete key or by typing any other text over the selected block. You can change the formatting of the selection, by making it bold or underlined, for example, or by changing the font or font size.

You also can copy or move the block from one part of the document to another, or even from one document to another. With some word processors, moving text is as easy as dragging the block to a new location, a technique called **drag-and-drop editing**. The same effect can be accomplished by cutting or copying the block to the Clipboard and then pasting it to a new location.

To **deselect** a selected block of text, click the mouse anywhere on the screen or press any arrow key. The text is displayed again as normal.

FORMATTING TEXT

Most word processing features are used to **format** the document. The process of formatting a document includes controlling the appearance of text, the layout of text on the page, and the use of pictures and other graphic elements, such as tabs and indents, margins, tables, lines, boxes, and shading. Most formatting features fall into one of three categories:

- Character formats
- Paragraph formats
- Document formats

NORTON Online

For information on **fonts**, visit this book's Web site at www.glencoe.com/norton/online

Character Formats

Character formats include settings that control the attributes of individual text characters, such as font, type size, type style, and color.

Fonts

The term **font** or **typeface** refers to the style of the letters, symbols, and punctuation marks in your document. Fonts have names like Times, Helvetica, and Palatino. In addition to those that come with the operating system, most word processors provide at least a handful of built-in fonts.

> This is the Courier font, which is monospaced.
>
> This is the Arial font, which is proportional.

There are two general categories of fonts: monospace and proportional. Every character of a monospace font takes up exactly the same amount of horizontal space. Monospace fonts (such as Courier) resemble a typewriter's output. This is a useful characteristic if you need to line up columns of type.

Most fonts, however, are proportional fonts. With a proportional font (such as Times), each character may have a slightly different width. The letter *M*, for example, uses more horizontal space than *I* does.

▶ In a monospaced font, each character occupies the same amount of horizontal space. In a proportional font, characters take up only as much space as they need to be legible.

Typefaces also fall into two additional broad categories: **serif** and **sans serif**. Serif fonts have fancy curls or extra decorative lines at the ends of the strokes that make up each character; sans serif fonts do not (*sans* means "without" in French). According to general typesetting conventions, serif type is easier to read and therefore more suitable for body text, whereas sans serif type is better for display text or headings. The headings in this book are set in a sans serif face; the text in this sentence is set in a serif face.

> Times New Roman is a serif font.
>
> Arial is a sans serif font.

▶ Serif fonts have decorative lines and curls at the ends of strokes. Sans serif fonts do not.

Type Size

The size of a font is measured in **points**. One point equals .02 inch in height. Therefore, 12-point type, the most common size used in business documents, is .24 inch tall, from the top of the tallest letters to the bottom of the letters that descend below the baseline *(g, j, p, q, and y)*. Modern word processors let you work with type sizes from as little as one point, to as large as 1,638 points. The body text in this book, for example, is 10-point type.

In addition to the font and type size, the appearance of characters can be controlled with **type styles** (which are often referred to as *attributes* or *effects*). The most common styles used in documents are bold, italics, and underlining.

This is 10 point Times New Roman type.

This is 12 point Times New Roman type.

This is 14 point Times New Roman type.

This is 16 point Times New Roman type.

This is 18 point Times New Roman type.

This is 24 point Times New Roman type.

This is 36 point Times New Roman type.

You can make your text **bold**.

You can use *italics*, too.

Underlining is an old standby.

Sometimes you can use ~~strike through~~.

You can also use SMALL CAPS vs. LARGE CAPS.

Type styles. ◄

NORTON Online

For information on **fonts** you can purchase or download from the Internet, visit this book's Web site at **www.glencoe.com/norton/online**

Less commonly used style attributes include strikethrough, superscript, subscript, small caps, and many others.

Paragraph Formats

In word processing, the word *paragraph* has a slightly different meaning than it does traditionally. Word processing software creates a **paragraph** each time you press the Enter key. A group of sentences is a paragraph, but a two-word heading (like the one above this paragraph) is defined as a paragraph, as well.

Paragraph formatting includes settings applied only to one or more entire paragraphs. These settings include line spacing, paragraph spacing, indents, alignment, tab stops, borders, and shading.

Line and Paragraph Spacing

Word processing software provides precise control over the amount of space between each line of text in a paragraph, a setting known as **line spacing**. Lines can be single-spaced or double-spaced, or set to any spacing you want.

Paragraph spacing refers to the amount of space between each paragraph. By default, the paragraph spacing is the same as the line spacing. However, you can set the software so that extra space is automatically included before or after each paragraph. In many documents, paragraph spacing is roughly equivalent to one blank line between paragraphs.

Indents and Alignment

Margins are the white borders around the edge of the page where the text is not allowed to go. Every document has top, bottom, left, and right margins, and in any document all four margins can be the same or different. Many documents, such as business letters, require margins of a standard width. A word processor lets you set each margin as precisely as you want, usually to an accuracy of one-tenth of an inch.

Indents determine how close each line of a paragraph comes to the margins. In a report, for example, the body text lines may reach all the way to the left and right margins, whereas quoted material is indented by one inch from each margin, creating an inset.

Alignment refers to the orientation of the lines of a paragraph with respect to the margins. There are four alignment options: left, right, center, and justified (or full justification).

Alignment and indents are paragraph formats; the margins are part of the overall document format. Together, the indents and alignment control the shapes of paragraphs.

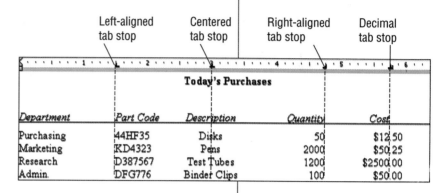

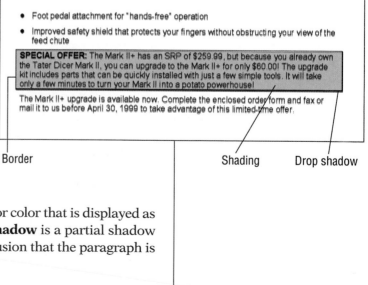

Tabs and Tab Stops

The keyboard's Tab key moves the insertion point forward (to the right) until it encounters a tab stop, inserting a fixed amount of space in the line. A **tab stop** is a position, both on screen and in the document, usually measured from the left margin of the document. When you create a new document, tab stops typically are defined at every fourth or fifth character, or at every .5-inch position. Most word processors allow you to change or remove the tab stops by displaying a ruler across the top or bottom of the screen that shows where tab stop positions are set.

Tabs are most often used to align columns of text accurately or to create tables; word processors provide at least four different types of tab stops so that you can align columns in different ways. For example, in Figure 6.3, the columns are separated by tab spacing (rather than by spaces inserted with the space bar). The first column is aligned along the page's left margin, the second column is aligned by a left-aligned tab stop, the third by a centered tab stop, the fourth by a right-aligned tab stop, and the fifth by a decimal tab stop.

Borders, Shading, and Shadows

Finally, paragraphs can be formatted with borders or shading. A **border** is a line, often called a *rule*, that is drawn on one or more sides of a paragraph. **Shading** consists of a pattern or color that is displayed as a background to the text in a paragraph. A **drop shadow** is a partial shadow around a bordered paragraph, which creates the illusion that the paragraph is "floating" above the page.

▶ **Figure 6.3**
Four kinds of tab stops.

▶ A paragraph formatted with a border, shading, and a drop shadow.

Portrait printing. ◀

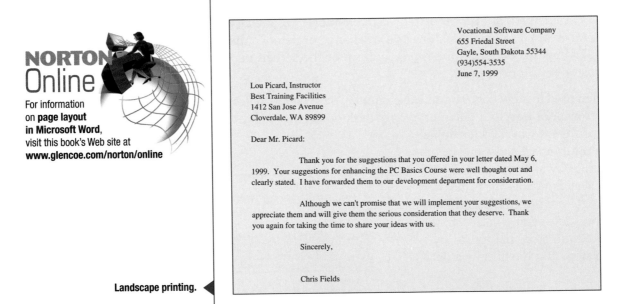

Vocational Software Company
655 Friedal Street
Gayle, South Dakota 55344
(934)554-3535
June 7, 1999

Lou Picard, Instructor
Best Training Facilities
1412 San Jose Avenue
Cloverdale, WA 89899

Dear Mr. Picard:

Thank you for the suggestions that you offered in your letter dated May 6, 1999. Your suggestions for enhancing the PC Basics Course were well thought out and clearly stated. I have forwarded them to our development department for consideration.

Although we can't promise that we will implement your suggestions, we appreciate them and will give them the serious consideration that they deserve. Thank you again for taking the time to share your ideas with us.

Sincerely,

Chris Fields
Account Representative

Document Formats

You already have been briefly introduced to margins, one of the most important of the **document formats**. In addition, the document formats include the size of the page, its orientation, and headers or footers. Word processing software also lets you apply special formats to documents, such as columns. You also can divide a document into sections and give each section its own unique format.

Page Size and Orientation

Normally, documents are set up to fit on 8.5 by 11-inch pieces of paper, a standard known as *letter-size* paper. You can, however, set up your word processor document for other standard sizes, such as *legal size* (8.5 by 14 inches), assuming that your printer can handle paper of that size. You can also set up your document for custom paper sizes.

The dimensions of the document are also determined by the orientation of the paper. By default, documents are set up with **portrait orientation**, where the document is taller than it is wide. However, you can always switch to **landscape orientation**, in which the paper is turned on its side.

NORTON Online

For information on **page layout** in **Microsoft Word**, visit this book's Web site at www.glencoe.com/norton/online

Vocational Software Company
655 Friedal Street
Gayle, South Dakota 55344
(934)554-3535
June 7, 1999

Lou Picard, Instructor
Best Training Facilities
1412 San Jose Avenue
Cloverdale, WA 89899

Dear Mr. Picard:

Thank you for the suggestions that you offered in your letter dated May 6, 1999. Your suggestions for enhancing the PC Basics Course were well thought out and clearly stated. I have forwarded them to our development department for consideration.

Although we can't promise that we will implement your suggestions, we appreciate them and will give them the serious consideration that they deserve. Thank you again for taking the time to share your ideas with us.

Sincerely,

Chris Fields

Landscape printing. ◀

Headers and Footers

Long documents generally include headers, footers, or both. **Headers** and **footers** are lines of text that run along the top and bottom of every page. They may include the document's name and the page number. The date on which the document was printed and the author's name might also be included. For

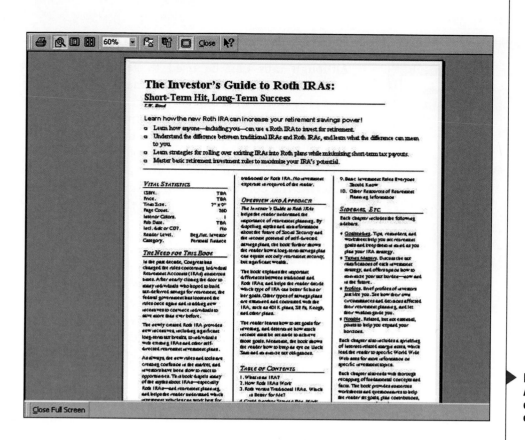

Figure 6.4
A two-section document, with different document formats in each section.

example, the footers in this book include the chapter number or the chapter name (depending on whether it is a left-facing page or a right-facing page) and the page number. There are no headers.

Columns and Sections

Columns are a popular and effective format for certain types of documents. Newsletters, for example, typically are laid out in a two- or three-column format. Columns make it easy to read a document quickly and open the door for other special formatting techniques.

Sometimes, a columnar layout is appropriate for only one part of a document, while a normal page-wide layout better suits the rest of the document. For this reason, word processors allow you to divide a document into **sections** and apply a different format to each section. In Figure 6.4, the document's top section is a heading followed by a page-wide list. The second section is a three-column format.

Special Features of Word Processing Software

All modern word processing programs are rich in features, many of which have nothing to do with formatting. Some of these features, such as mail merge, are utilities, giving you access to system-level features. Others, such as HTML scripting and the capability to add graphics or sounds to your document, add functions that are almost like adding new software programs.

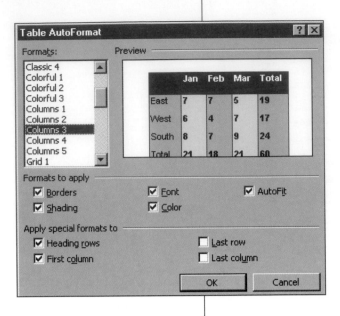

You can format tables manually by adding lines, borders, shading, and colors. Most word processors also let you select a variety of automatic table-formatting options.

Tables

Although tabs can be used to set up rows and columns of information in a document, word processors provide features that let you create **tables** in just a few steps. The size of a table is limited only by the amount of page space that can be devoted to it, and tables can be formatted in dozens of ways. Tables are typically set up with a header row across the top, to describe the contents of each column. Many tables also include a special first column that describes the contents of each row.

Mail Merge

A **mail merge** is the process of combining a form letter with the contents of a database, usually a name and address list, so that each copy of the letter has one entry from the database printed on it. The mail merge feature makes it easy to send the same letter to a list of different people with the correct name and address printed on each letter.

ADDRESS DATABASE

FORM LETTER

One row for each address

Codes in the form letter match the column headings in the database.

MERGED LETTERS

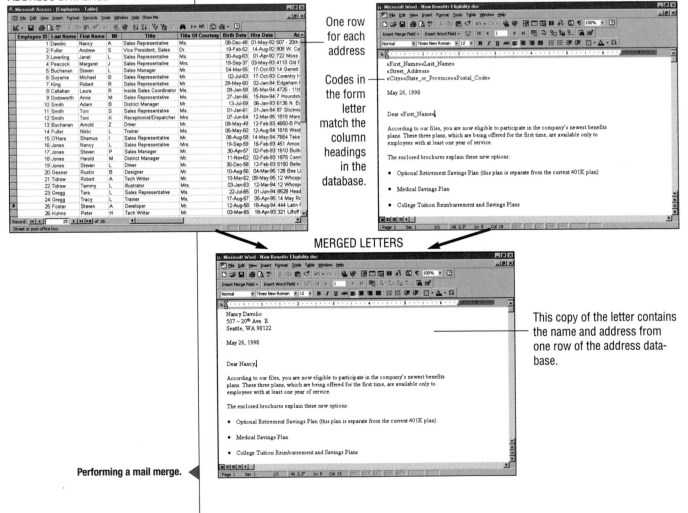

This copy of the letter contains the name and address from one row of the address database.

Performing a mail merge.

Adding Graphics and Sounds

Using a word processor, you can add graphic images—photos, drawings, or clip art—to your documents. In fact, the process is simple. You set the cursor where you want the graphic to appear, tell the word processing program that you want to insert a graphic, and then locate the graphic file. The only catch is that the graphic must be in a format that the word processing software can understand. However, most word processing software can readily import the standard types. After the graphic has been imported, you can move, size, crop, and add borders to it. You can even adjust the alignment so that your text flows around the picture.

In addition to graphics, some software now lets you embed sound files in your documents. You embed the sound file in much the same way that you embed a graphic file. The only difference is that an icon, displaying a speaker, appears in the document. Clicking the icon plays the sound file. Although sound files are of no value in printed documents, they can be useful in documents that are distributed electronically—on disk, online, or across a network.

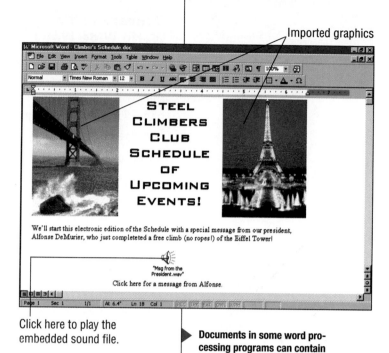

Imported graphics

Click here to play the embedded sound file.

▶ Documents in some word processing programs can contain both graphics and sounds.

Templates

Word processors provide **templates** to make document design easier. Templates are predesigned documents that are blank, except for preset margins, fonts, paragraph formats, headings, rules, graphics, headers, or footers. You can open a document template, type your text into it, save it, and you're

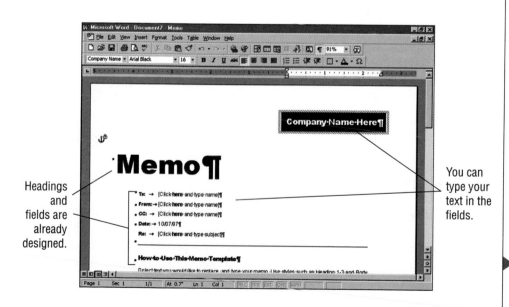

Headings and fields are already designed.

You can type your text in the fields.

NORTON Online
For information on **adding graphics to your documents**, visit this book's Web site at **www.glencoe.com/norton/online**

▶ Predesigned templates make it easy to create professional documents.

NORTON Online

For more
information on
the **HTML capabilities**
of popular word processors,
visit this book's web site at
www.glencoe.com/norton/online

done. Templates free users from manually formatting complex documents, such as memos, fax cover sheets, reports, resumes, and other types of business, legal, or academic documents. You can even create your own templates.

Converting Word Processed Documents into World Wide Web Pages

In 1994 and 1995, many companies and individuals began creating electronic documents that can be accessed on the part of the Internet known as the World Wide Web. These documents are known as Web pages. Creating a page for the Web requires formatting the page using Hypertext Markup Language, or HTML.

Some word processors, such as Word and WordPerfect, can even convert documents into HTML format for you. The resulting Web page contains not only the original text but is formatted with HTML tags so that headings, body text, bullet lists, and other elements will appear in a standard Web format. An example of a document coded with HTML is shown in Figure 6.5. The resulting page, as it appears on the Web, is shown in Figure 6.6.

Figure 6.5
A document coded with HTML tags. Word has actually converted this document from a normal DOC-format file to an HTML-format file, freeing the user from doing the HTML coding manually.

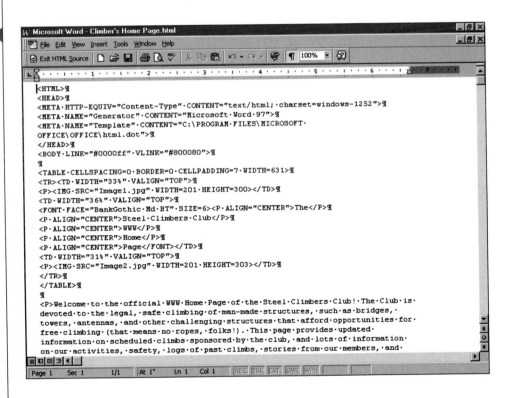

Desktop Publishing Software

The introduction of **desktop publishing (DTP) software** revolutionized the publishing and graphic arts industries, bringing to ordinary users the power to produce professional-quality documents and publications. Popular DTP software packages include Aldus PageMaker, QuarkXPress, and Adobe FrameMaker, among others.

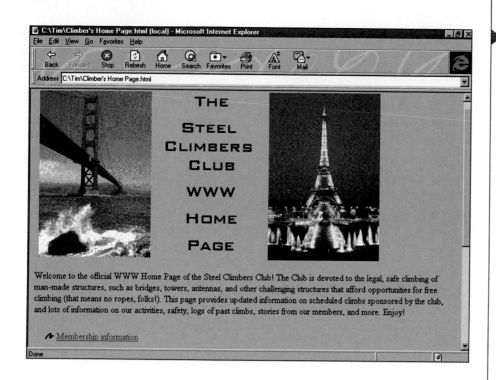

Figure 6.6
The HTML document, viewed in a browser.

Before DTP software, producing publications of any kind (from brochures to encyclopedias) was a complex process involving multiple people with different skills. DTP software enabled one person to perform all the required tasks—design, layout, typesetting, placement of graphics, and more—and create a document that was ready to go to the printer.

The impact of desktop publishing on the microcomputer market has influenced the ongoing development of word processing, spreadsheet, and database software, inspiring developers of the major business applications to include DTP features in their software. In fact, word processors now feature many capabilities once found only in DTP software, and most users find that their word processor more than satisfies their daily desktop publishing and page layout requirements.

Many features that were once found only in DTP software (graphics importing, font controls, and many others) are now commonly found in word processing packages. However, because DTP software is designed specifically to produce complex, multicolor, printer-ready documents, it is the better choice for professional document design. Here is a sampling of the advanced document-design features found in DTP software:

- *Type controls.* DTP software gives the user fine control over type, or alphanumeric characters. Because spacing is often a concern in page layout, DTP software enables the user to control **kerning** (the spacing between individual letters) and **tracking** (a general setting for character spacing for entire blocks of text). DTP software also provides nearly infinite control of **leading**, which is the amount of space between lines of text.

- *Graphics controls.* DTP software is sophisticated and flexible with graphics, giving the user direct control over the exact placement of the graphic on the page, the wrapping of text around the graphic, and the use of borders or shading with graphics. This book provides many excellent examples of the graphics capabilities of DTP software.

■ *Page layout and document controls.* Because DTP software was designed for the publisher, it offers sophisticated controls for setting up the format of documents and coordinating multiple documents in a publication. A magazine, for example, might contain several documents, with some laid out in slightly different styles. A common page layout control in DTP software is called **master pages**, which are special pages that are set aside for defining elements that are common to all pages in the document, such as page numbers, headers, headings, rules, and more.

■ *Prepress controls.* Perhaps the most unique characteristic of DTP software is its prepress controls—that is, its capability to prepare documents for the printing press. DTP enables the user to specify colors according to printing industry standards, for example, such as Pantone and TruMatch, so that the printer can understand precisely what colors to use. DTP software also prepares **color separations** for documents printed in color. Color separations are separate pages created for each color on each page of the document.

Kerning can be especially important in headlines. ◄

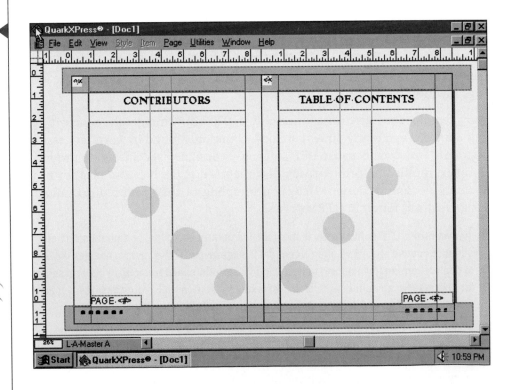

With kerning, these letters were moved closer together.

Shown here are two master pages. The design elements contained in these pages will be applied to certain pages of the final document, to ensure consistency. ◄

NORTON *Notebook*

Publish on the Internet

One of the most exciting aspects of the Internet is its openness. With the right software and an Internet account, you can go online and view a huge variety of materials that others have published—that is, posted on an Internet server. Add a little creativity to the mix, and you can publish your own materials for viewing by a worldwide audience. One of the easiest and fastest ways to publish your work online is to create your own page on the World Wide Web.

The Internet isn't limited to big business. Individuals, private organizations, and small companies actually publish the vast majority of materials on the Internet. The variety of online publishing opportunities is almost limitless, and people are using them to enhance their businesses, share information, entertain, and educate others.

Before it can be viewed in a Web browser, a document must be formatted with special tags—called Hypertext Markup Language (HTML) tags. These tags, which surround the text they affect, tell the browser how to display the text, whether as a heading, a table, a link, normal text, and so on.

Fortunately, you don't have to be a computer whiz to create HTML documents. In fact, you don't even need to know anything about HTML. With the right tools, you can quickly create attractive, interesting pages that are ready to be published on the Web.

Just about any newer word processor, spreadsheet, database, or presentation application can convert ordinary documents into HTML files. As you saw earlier in this chapter, these features let you create any type of document, save it in HTML format, and then immediately open it in a Web browser (such as Netscape Navigator or Microsoft Internet Explorer). You can even make changes to the documents in their native format (DOC, XLS, and so on), resave them in HTML format again, and view your changes a in browser—without typing a single HTML tag! Many desktop applications now have tools that let you embed graphics, create hotlinks, and add other special features to your HTML documents.

Many Web browsers provide editors that enable you to create feature-rich Web pages. Using a browser's editing tools, you can create new pages from scratch or use predesigned templates. A popular page-design method is to find a Web page you like, copy it to disk, and then open it in Edit mode in the browser. You then can use that page's HTML formatting as the basis for your page! Using a browser-based editor, you only have to work directly with HTML tags if you want to. If you prefer, the browser can do all the HTML formatting for you.

After you have created your pages, simply contact your Internet Service Provider (ISP). Your ISP can provide you with space on a Web server and an address where others can find your pages. Using your chosen HTML editing tools, you can update, expand, and refresh your Web site whenever you want.

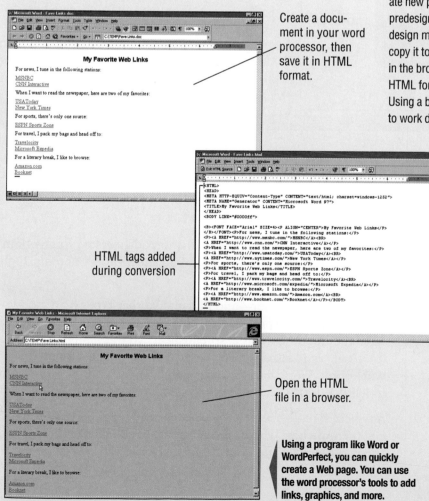

Create a document in your word processor, then save it in HTML format.

HTML tags added during conversion

Open the HTML file in a browser.

Using a program like Word or WordPerfect, you can quickly create a Web page. You can use the word processor's tools to add links, graphics, and more.

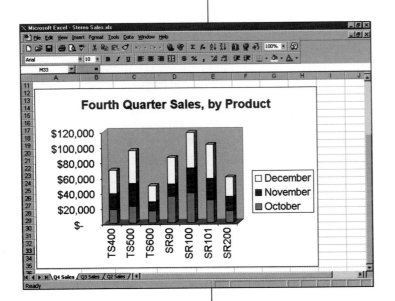

The following table appears within the spreadsheet image:

Fourth Quarter Sales, by Product				
		October	November	December
Amplifiers	TS400	$ 18,246	$ 20,647	$ 30,611
	TS500	$ 21,810	$ 30,446	$ 42,785
	TS600	$ 15,462	$ 12,454	$ 20,669
Tuner/Amps	SR90	$ 34,887	$ 15,799	$ 34,825
	SR100	$ 39,005	$ 32,647	$ 46,600
	SR101	$ 29,733	$ 28,320	$ 44,058
	SR200	$ 15,355	$ 18,810	$ 25,321

Spreadsheet users generally set up their information to display in a classic row-and-column format.

The latest spreadsheet programs, however, enable you to create elaborate reports from your data, including charts, text, colors, graphics, and much more.

Norton Online

For information on the most popular **PC spreadsheets**, visit this book's Web site at **www.glencoe.com/norton/online**

SPREADSHEET PROGRAMS

A **spreadsheet** is a software tool for entering, calculating, manipulating, and analyzing sets of numbers. Spreadsheets have a wide range of uses—from family budgets to corporate profit and loss statements.

You can set up a spreadsheet to show information in any number of ways, such as the traditional row-and-column format (which the spreadsheet takes from its predecessor, the ledger book), or a slick report format with headings and charts.

This book's Web site features several exercises designed to help you learn to use spreadsheet software. To find these exercises, visit **www.glencoe.com/norton/online**.

The Spreadsheet's Interface

Like a word processing program, a spreadsheet lets you work in a main editing window, which displays your data and a variety of tools. Figure 6.7 shows Microsoft Excel 97.

Like a word processor—and like many other types of Windows-based applications—modern spreadsheets provide a document area, which is where you view the document. In a spreadsheet, you actually work in a **worksheet** (or *sheet*, as it also is called), and you can collect related worksheets in a **workbook**. Worksheets can be named, and a workbook can contain as many individual worksheets as your system's resources will allow.

A typical spreadsheet interface also provides a menu bar, toolbars, and a special **formula bar**, where you can create or edit data and formulas in the worksheet. Scroll bars help you navigate a large worksheet, and at the bottom of

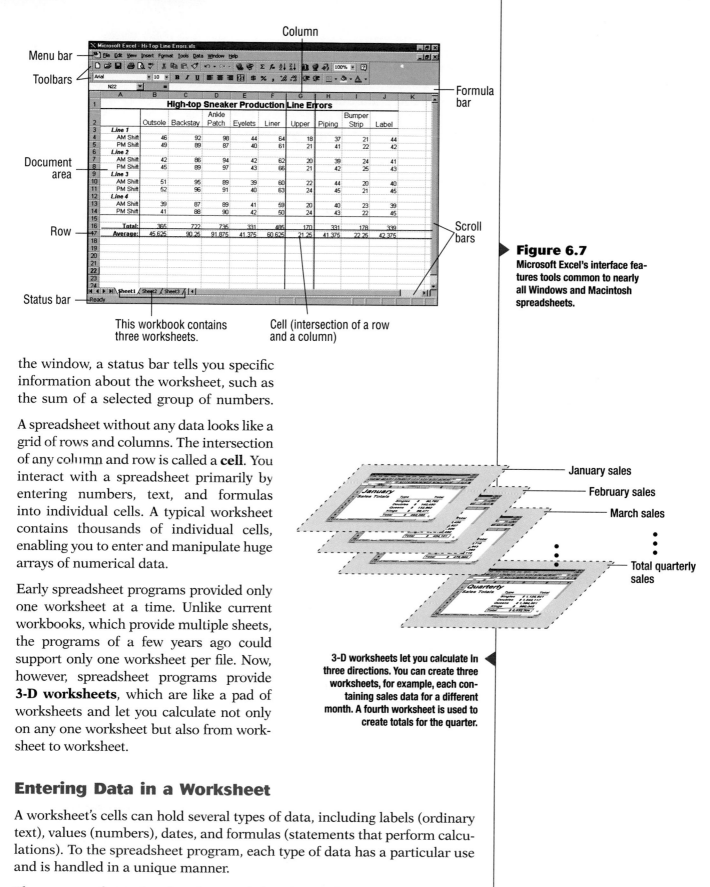

Menu bar

Toolbars

Column

Document area

Row

Status bar

Formula bar

Scroll bars

Figure 6.7
Microsoft Excel's interface features tools common to nearly all Windows and Macintosh spreadsheets.

This workbook contains three worksheets.

Cell (intersection of a row and a column)

High-top Sneaker Production Line Errors

	Outsole	Backstay	Ankle Patch	Eyelets	Liner	Upper	Piping	Bumper Strip	Label
Line 1									
AM Shift	46	92	98	44	64	18	37	21	44
PM Shift	49	89	87	40	61	21	41	22	42
Line 2									
AM Shift	42	86	94	42	62	20	39	24	41
PM Shift	45	89	97	43	66	21	42	25	43
Line 3									
AM Shift	51	95	89	39	60	22	44	20	40
PM Shift	52	96	91	40	63	24	45	21	45
Line 4									
AM Shift	39	87	89	41	59	20	40	23	39
PM Shift	41	88	90	42	50	24	43	22	45
Total:	365	722	735	331	485	170	331	178	339
Average:	45.625	90.25	91.875	41.375	60.625	21.25	41.375	22.25	42.375

January sales

February sales

March sales

Total quarterly sales

3-D worksheets let you calculate in three directions. You can create three worksheets, for example, each containing sales data for a different month. A fourth worksheet is used to create totals for the quarter.

the window, a status bar tells you specific information about the worksheet, such as the sum of a selected group of numbers.

A spreadsheet without any data looks like a grid of rows and columns. The intersection of any column and row is called a **cell**. You interact with a spreadsheet primarily by entering numbers, text, and formulas into individual cells. A typical worksheet contains thousands of individual cells, enabling you to enter and manipulate huge arrays of numerical data.

Early spreadsheet programs provided only one worksheet at a time. Unlike current workbooks, which provide multiple sheets, the programs of a few years ago could support only one worksheet per file. Now, however, spreadsheet programs provide **3-D worksheets**, which are like a pad of worksheets and let you calculate not only on any one worksheet but also from worksheet to worksheet.

Entering Data in a Worksheet

A worksheet's cells can hold several types of data, including labels (ordinary text), values (numbers), dates, and formulas (statements that perform calculations). To the spreadsheet program, each type of data has a particular use and is handled in a unique manner.

The process of entering data in a worksheet is simple. Using the mouse or arrow keys, you select a cell to make it active. The active cell is indicated by a **cell pointer**, a rectangle that makes the active cell's borders look bold.

To navigate the worksheet, you need to understand its system of **cell addresses**. All spreadsheets use the row and column identifiers as the basis for their cell addresses. If you are working in the cell where column B intersects with row 3, for example, you are in cell B3.

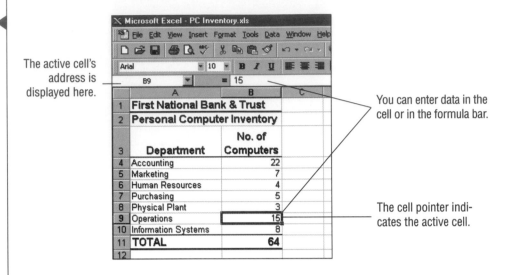

The cell pointer highlights the active cell, where you can enter and edit data.

The active cell's address is displayed here.

You can enter data in the cell or in the formula bar.

The cell pointer indicates the active cell.

NORTON
Online
For a wide variety
of information on
spreadsheets, visit
this book's Web site at
www.glencoe.com/norton/online

When you have selected a cell, you simply type the data into it. When a cell is active, you also can type its data into the formula bar. The formula bar is handy because it displays much more data than the cell can. If a cell already contains data, you can edit it in the formula bar, as well.

You also can use the spreadsheet's cut, copy, and paste features to duplicate and move data to various parts of the worksheet. These features work among the different sheets in a workbook, from one workbook to another, and between the spreadsheet and other applications.

Labels

Worksheets can contain normal text—called **labels**—as well as numerical and other data. In spreadsheets, text is referred to as a label because it usually is used to identify a value or series of values (as in a row or column heading) or to describe the contents of a specific cell (such as a total). Labels help you make sense of a worksheet's contents.

You can place labels in any cell in a worksheet and can easily move or delete labels. In fact, you can use spreadsheets to create and manage large lists that contain nothing but labels. The spreadsheet program recognizes labels as such and differentiates between labels and values or formulas, which might be involved in calculations.

Labels help organize the information in a worksheet.

These labels are used as titles for the worksheet.

These labels are column headings, labeling the contents of the cells below them.

These labels identify the data in the cells to their right.

You can format text in a spreadsheet by applying different fonts, font sizes, styles, alignments, and special effects to your labels. These formatting capabilities let you create professional, easily understood worksheets and reports.

Values

In a spreadsheet, a **value** is any number you enter or that results from a computation. You might enter a series of values in a column so that you can total them. Or you might enter several different numbers that are part of an elaborate calculation.

Spreadsheets can work with whole numbers, decimals, negative numbers, currency, and other types of values, including scientific notations. In fact, some spreadsheet programs are intelligent enough to understand the types of values you are entering. Most spreadsheets recognize currency entries easily, depending on the context of the values being entered.

The number formatting options in a spreadsheet are nearly endless.

Dates

Dates are a necessary part of most worksheets, and spreadsheet programs can work with date information in many ways. A date may be added to a worksheet simply to indicate when it was created, or a date function may be used, which updates whenever the worksheet is opened.

Spreadsheets can use dates in performing calculations, as well. An example might be when calculating late payments on a loan. If the spreadsheet knows the payment's due date, it can calculate late fees based on that date.

You can format date information in many ways, as normal calendar dates, serial dates, and so on.

Formulas

The power of the spreadsheet lies in **formulas**, which calculate numbers based on values or formulas in other cells. You can create many kinds of formulas manually, to do basic arithmetic operations, calculus or trigonometric operations, and so on.

Spreadsheets make it a simple matter to perform calculations on a set of numbers. Suppose, for example, that the manager of a real estate office wants to calculate the commissions paid to agents over a given time period. Figures 6.8 and 6.9 show a simple formula that takes the total sales amount for each agent and calculates the commission for that total. If any part of the formula (either the sales total or the commission percentage) changes, the formula can automatically recalculate the resulting commission.

You can format the cell to display the formula itself, or to display the formula's results.

Figure 6.8
An example of a formula used to calculate simple percentages.

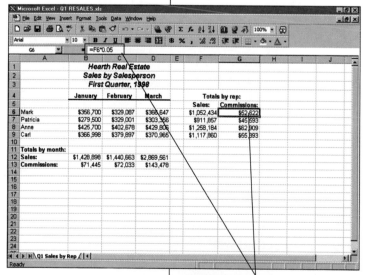

This cell contains a simple formula, which multiplies total sales by a commission percentage. Notice that the cell displays the results of the formula rather than the formula itself.

When this agent's sales total changes...

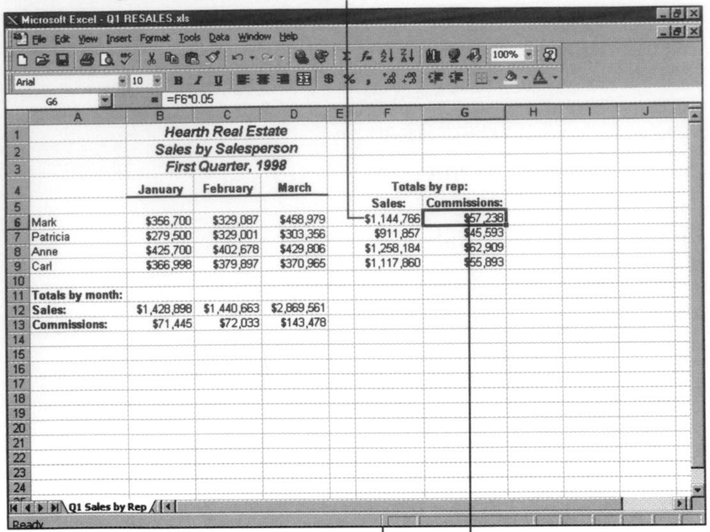

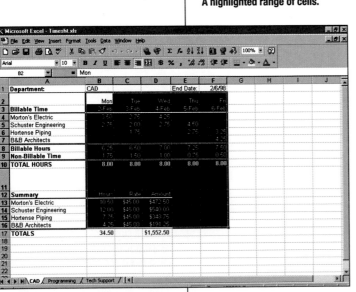

Figure 6.9
Spreadsheet formulas automatically recalculate if any of their base data changes.

... the commission is automatically recalculated.

As shown in the preceding example, the latter approach is more common. (You can easily select the cell and view the underlying formula in the formula bar.)

You can create formulas from scratch in a spreadsheet, to get specific results. This process requires an understanding of mathematical operations and the way spreadsheets function. Spreadsheet programs provide an array of tools to help users create custom formulas.

Cell References and Ranges

Formulas typically refer to the values in other cells throughout the worksheet. To reduce time and errors, you can use a **cell reference** in formulas. A cell reference tells the formula to look up the contents of the referenced cell; this saves you the trouble of typing the referenced cell's contents into the formula. The most common method is to refer to the cell by its address, such as A1, B10, or Y254. Therefore, if you want to add the values in cells B13 and C16, your formula might look like this:

=B13+C16

A cell reference can refer to one or more cells in the same worksheet, in a different worksheet from the same workbook, or in a different workbook. Sophisticated worksheets that draw data from many different sources may use dozens—or even hundreds—of formulas containing cell references.

If your formula uses cells that are contiguous, you can refer to all the cells at once, as a **range** (also called a *block*). For example, in Excel, the formula =SUM(B4,C4,D4) can be written =SUM(B4:D4). Ranges can consist of a group of cells in a column, a row, or even a group that includes several rows and columns. For example, a range of B2:F16 includes the whole block that has B2 as the upper-left corner and F16 as the lower-right corner, as shown in Figure 6.10.

Figure 6.10
A highlighted range of cells.

You can even give names to cells or cell ranges instead of using their row and column address. After you assign a name to a cell, you can include the name rather than the cell address in formulas. The formula =SUM(B4,C4,D4) might then appear as =SUM (April_Income, May_Income, June_Income). This makes the formula much more comprehensible because the words convey more meaning than the cell addresses.

Functions

Spreadsheets come with many built-in formulas, called **functions**, that perform specialized calculations automatically. You can include these functions in your own formulas. Some functions are simple, such as the COUNT function, which counts how many values are in a range of cells. Many functions, however, are complex. You may not know the mathematical equations for a loan payment or the depreciation of an asset using the double declining balance method, but by using spreadsheet functions, you can arrive at the answer.

You add **arguments** within the parentheses of the function. Arguments are the values (often cell references) that the function uses in its operation. The number and type of arguments used depend on the function.

The most commonly used function is the SUM function, which adds a list of numbers to get a total sum. In the following formula, the SUM function's argument is a range:

=SUM(B4:G4)

This formula adds the values in the six cells that comprise the range B4:G4.

The leading spreadsheets come with dozens of these functions. Table 6.1 lists some of the most commonly used ones.

This cell contains a SUM function, which adds the values in the cells above it.

An example of the SUM function in an Excel worksheet.

Table 6.1	Common Functions
FUNCTION NAME	**DESCRIPTION**
ABS	Absolute (positive) value of an argument
AVERAGE/AVG	Average of arguments
COUNT	Count of numbers in a range of cells
IF	Specifies a logical test to perform; then performs one action if test result is true, another if it is false
LEN/LENGTH	Number of characters in a string of characters
MAX	Maximum value of arguments
MIN	Minimum value of arguments
PMT	Periodic payment for a loan or annuity
PV	Present value of an investment
ROUND	Number rounded to a specified number of digits
SUM	Total value of arguments

NORTON Online

For information on the **history of spreadsheets**, visit this book's Web site at **www.glencoe.com/norton/online**

Editing the Worksheet

After a worksheet has been created, anything it contains can be edited. Like word processors, spreadsheet programs are extremely accommodating when you want to make changes. To change a label or a date, you simply select its cell and make the desired changes. You can manually edit any part of a formula or function simply by selecting its cell and making your changes in the formula bar.

Spreadsheet programs make it easy to move, copy, or delete the contents of cells. You can also insert or delete rows and columns. You can add new sheets to a 3-D file, or delete worksheets you no longer need.

When you move formulas and data to a new location, the spreadsheet automatically adjusts the cell references for formulas based on that data. In Figure 6.11, for example, the second-quarter totals in cells D7 and D8 can be copied to create third-quarter totals without having to reenter the cell references. In Figure 6.12, the second-quarter formulas were copied to create the third-quarter formulas. The spreadsheet program created the proper formulas automatically (based on the existing formulas), summing up the third-quarter months.

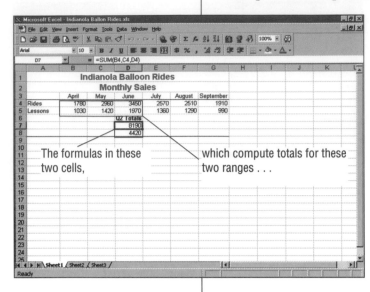

The formulas in these two cells,

which compute totals for these two ranges . . .

Figure 6.11
Copying formulas.

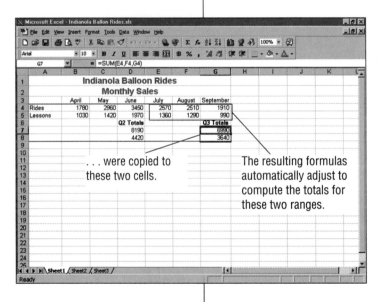

. . . were copied to these two cells.

The resulting formulas automatically adjust to compute the totals for these two ranges.

Figure 6.12
The copied formulas.

Relative and Absolute Cell References

The spreadsheet program changes the formulas when you copy them because it remembers that the formulas being copied will reference the same rows as the original but will automatically change the column reference when the formulas are moved to a new column. For this reason, when they are used in formulas, cell references such as B4 or D7 are called **relative cell references**. In Figure 6.12, cell D7 contains the formula =SUM(B4,C4,D4). When it was copied to cell G7, the program automatically changed the formula to =SUM(E4,F4,G4) so that it would add up the July, August, and September sales in row 4. This saved the time of having to type the formula. When you work with long lists of formulas, the time saved can be tremendous, and you will make fewer keyboard mistakes.

However, sometimes you don't want the formulas to change as you copy them. You want all the formulas, no matter where they are, to refer to a specific cell. For example, if the current interest rate is in cell A1 and several formulas are based on that rate, you want to be able to copy the formulas without the reference to A1 changing. In this case, you use an **absolute cell reference**, which is usually written using the dollar sign ($). For example, A1 is a relative cell reference, and A1 is an absolute cell reference. Figure 6.13 shows a projection

NORTON Online

For a comprehensive list of **questions about spreadsheets** and a **list of online resources** for spreadsheet users, visit this book's Web site at **www.glencoe.com/norton/online**

for third and fourth quarters. In this case, the user wanted to copy the formula from cell E8 to E9 to avoid retyping it and then edit it based on the previous years' experience. But both the projections for the third and fourth quarters needed to refer to cell E6. This was accomplished using absolute cell references.

Formatting Values, Labels, and Cells

Spreadsheet programs offer numerous formats specifically for numbers. Numbers can appear as dollars and cents, percentage, dates, times, and fractions. They can be shown with or without commas, decimal points, and so forth.

Dates and times are a special category of numbers. To calculate dates (for example, to find out how many days are between November 15, 1996, and March 2, 2002), spreadsheets turn dates into serial numbers, usually starting from January 1, 1900. A typical way to calculate time is to treat time as a fraction of a day. You can still enter and display a time or date using a standard format such as 3/9/99.

The formulas in these two cells are based on an absolute cell reference.

Figure 6.13
Absolute cell references.

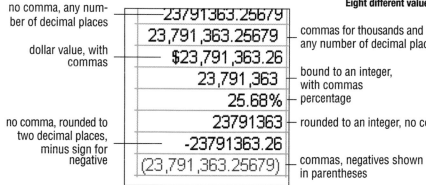

Eight different value formats.

Format description	Value
no comma, any number of decimal places	23791363.25679
	23,791,363.25679 — commas for thousands and millions, any number of decimal places
dollar value, with commas	$23,791,363.26
	23,791,363 — bound to an integer, with commas
	25.68% — percentage
no comma, rounded to two decimal places, minus sign for negative	23791363 — rounded to an integer, no commas
	-23791363.26
	(23,791,363.25679) — commas, negatives shown in red in parentheses

In addition to number formats, spreadsheets also offer a choice of fonts and type styles, shadowed borders, and more. You can create special effects by adding graphics, such as clip art, to your worksheets. The latest versions of Lotus 1-2-3 and Excel come with maps that you can use to create unique charts based on your data. In addition, you can now automatically dress up your charts using professionally designed, prepackaged formats.

Adding Charts

A popular feature of spreadsheet software is the capability to generate **charts** based on numeric data. Charts make data easier to understand—for example, when presenting data to an audience. You will often see charts in business presentations, yet you will rarely see the worksheets used to create the charts.

Figure 6.14
A spreadsheet containing
data about stereo sales.

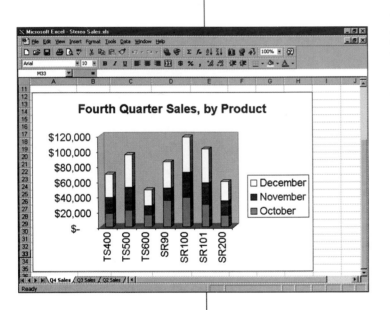

Figure 6.15 ◄
The same data, summarized
in a chart.

NORTON
Online

For more
information on
**spreadsheet analysis
tools**, visit this book's Web site at
www.glencoe.com/norton/online

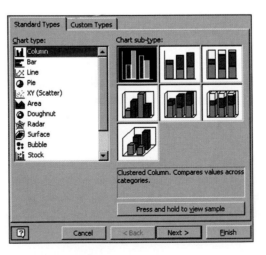

Figure 6.16 ◄
Chart types in Excel.

The worksheet in Figure 6.14 lists total sales of various stereo components over a three-month period. Making quick conclusions based on this data is difficult. You must look carefully and do some mental arithmetic to determine which products sold best and which month had the best sales. But when the information is displayed in a chart, as in Figure 6.15, it is obvious that the SR100 model is the best-selling product. Without too much analysis, you can also see that December was the best month for sales.

With modern spreadsheets, creating a chart is simple. The one in Figure 6.15 was created with just a few mouse clicks. You select the data you want to chart, click a chart button, and then interact with a series of dialog boxes. After the chart is created, you can continue to adjust its appearance, using a set of special chart tools.

The most important decision you make when creating a chart is the *type* of chart to create. The most popular types are bar charts, line charts, pie charts, and scatter charts. As you can see in Figure 6.16, these basic types can take many forms. In fact, depending on the program you use, you may be able to choose from more than a dozen different types of charts, and each type may further have several subtypes. The decisions you make are critical to how well the chart will illustrate your data.

Analyzing Data in a Spreadsheet

When your worksheet's basic format is complete, you can use the worksheet to analyze the data. Even adding up totals is a simple form of analysis, but you may need more. This section discusses three useful techniques: what-if analysis, goal seeking, and sorting.

What-if analysis is the process of using a spreadsheet to test how alternative scenarios affect numeric results. All spreadsheets allow you to do simple what-if analysis. You can easily change one part of a formula or a cell that it refers to and see how that affects the rest of the worksheet. A more sophisticated type of what-if analysis, however, is to create a table that automatically calculates the results based on any number of assumptions. Figure 6.17 shows such a table, which calculates the monthly mortgage payment for several possible interest rates.

B7		= =PMT(B4/12,B5*12,-B3)		
A	B	C	D	E
1 **Mortgage Payment Examples**				
2			Other Possible Interest Rates	
3 Total Mortgage	125000			
4 Interest Rate	8.25%		7.50%	$1,158.77
5 Years Paid	15		7.75%	$1,176.59
6			8.00%	$1,194.57
7 Monthly Payment	$1,212.68		8.25%	$1,212.68
8			8.50%	$1,230.92

B7		= =PMT(B4/12,B5*12,-B3)	
A	B	C	D
1 **Mortgage Payment Examples**			
2			
3 Total Mortgage	$ 123,693		
4 Interest Rate	8.25%		
5 Years Paid	15		
6			
7 Monthly Payment	$1,200.00		

What-if analysis is such an important tool that spreadsheets offer yet another way to do it. You can create several scenarios or versions of the same spreadsheet, each one containing different assumptions reflected in its formulas. In the mortgage loan example, you can create a best-case scenario that assumes you will find a house for $100,000 and an interest rate of 7.5%. Your worst-case scenario might be a house for $150,000 and an interest rate of 9%. Then you can create a report summarizing the different scenarios.

Goal seeking finds values for one or more cells that make the result of a formula equal to a value you specify. In Figure 6.18, cell B7 is the result of the Payment (PMT) formula. In this case, you know the maximum monthly payment you can afford is $1,200, so you want cell B7 to be your starting point. The bank is offering an interest rate of 8.25% over 15 years. The total mortgage, cell B3, can be calculated from the monthly payment, years paid, and interest rate. Figure 6.18 shows the result of this process—you can afford a mortgage of $123,693.

Spreadsheet programs offer the capability to create, arrange, and select data in lists. They do not offer the same database capabilities as relational database management programs, but they can handle many simple database tasks. You can **sort** the data—that is, arrange the records in a specific manner, based on certain criteria, such as by date, dollar amount, or alphabetically—then perform calculations on the results.

Productivity Tip

Making Complex Documents Simple

Productivity applications are increasingly being designed to work together. With a set of these applications on your computer, you can move data freely from one program to another, share different types of data among different applications, and add data from one application to documents created in a different application.

With these capabilities, you can create a report in your word processor and then insert a chart that you created in a spreadsheet. If you have a graphics package, you can create a logo and add it as part of the memo's letterhead. If you distribute the memo online or on disk, you also can add other types of files—such as audio, video, or animation files—that were created in other types of applications.

When you are finished, you have what is called a *complex document*—one that contains data from more than one application. The complex document's data comes from other files, called *source files*. Modern applications and operating systems offer several ways of creating complex documents:

■ *Cut, Copy, and Paste.* Suppose, for example, that you are writing a research paper in Word, and you want the paper to include data from a worksheet in Excel. You can open the worksheet, select the data you want to use, and then choose the Cut or Copy command. This places the data in a temporary storage area, called the Clipboard. Then, in Word, you place the insertion point where the data should go, choose the Paste command, and the worksheet's data is added to the research paper. Cut/Copy/Paste is fast and simple, but it is *static*. If the worksheet data changes, the copied data in the research paper remains the same, unless you copy and paste the new data over it.

■ *Dynamic Data Exchange (DDE).* This works in much the same way as Cut/Copy/Paste but gives you an extra option. That is, when you paste the copied data from Excel into Word, you can establish a link back to Excel. Then if the data in your worksheet ever changes, it can be updated in the Word document without copying and pasting again. Using DDE, you can set the data in Word to update itself automatically, or you can update it manually.

■ *Object Linking and Embedding (OLE).* OLE works like DDE, but instead of enabling you to update the shared data in the complex document, OLE inserts the shared data as an object. This lets you launch the shared data's source application within the complex document.

Suppose, for example, that you are reading your research paper in Word and see that you need to change the Excel data. Instead of opening Excel separately, changing the data, and then recopying it or updating it in the Word file, you simply double-click the Excel data in the Word document. A mini Excel window appears inside the Word document, enabling you to change the Excel data (and the original worksheet) on the spot. OLE provides other advantages, as well. Suppose, for example, that you want to embed a sound file in an e-mail message. When you do this, the recipient can just double-click the sound file's icon in the message. This action launches a player that plays the file, on the spot. This capability frees the document's user from opening different applications.

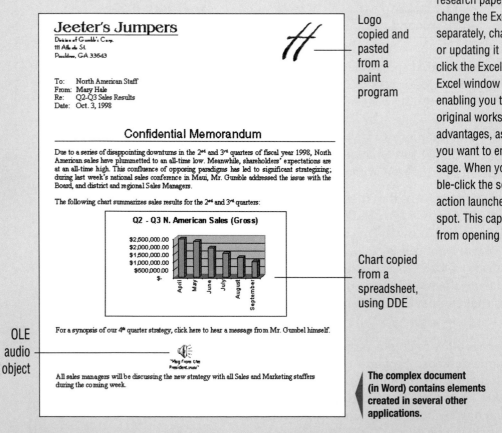

Logo copied and pasted from a paint program

Chart copied from a spreadsheet, using DDE

OLE audio object

The complex document (in Word) contains elements created in several other applications.

DATABASE MANAGEMENT SYSTEMS

To make large collections of data useful, individuals and organizations use computers and an efficient data management system. Like a warehouse, a **database** is a repository for collections of related data or facts. A **database management system (DBMS)** is a software tool that allows multiple users to access, store, and process the data or facts into useful information. The goal of database management software is to gather large volumes of data and process them into useful information.

DBMSs are one of the primary reasons that people use computers. Many large companies and organizations rely heavily on commercial or custom DBMSs to handle immense data resources. Organizations like these require sophisticated DBMSs to accommodate their data management needs. Often, these DBMSs are custom-made, proprietary, and programmed using standard programming languages such as COBOL and C. These programs are often designed to run on large, mainframe computers.

DBMSs are equally vital tools for people and organizations that use networks and stand-alone personal computers. In these cases, the DBMS is often a commercial product, sold by the same companies that offer popular spreadsheets and word processing software.

Personal computers have brought database management to the desktops of individuals in businesses and private homes. Although the average individual at home may not need an inventory-tracking system, home users use commercial DBMS products to maintain address lists of friends and business contacts, manage household purchases and budgets, and store data for home businesses.

A DBMS makes it possible to do many routine tasks that would be otherwise tedious, cumbersome, and time-consuming without the services of a computer. For example, a DBMS can do the following tasks:

- Sort thousands of addresses by ZIP code prior to a bulk mailing.
- Find all records of New Yorkers who live in boroughs outside Manhattan.
- Print a list of selected records, such as all real estate listings that closed escrow last month.
- Invoice a customer's new car lease, adjust the dealership's inventory, and update the service department's mailing list—merely by entering the data for a single sales transaction.

For exercises designed to help you learn to use database management systems, visit this book's Web site at **www.glencoe.com/norton/online**.

The Database

A database contains a collection of related items or facts, arranged in a specific structure. The most obvious example of a database is a telephone directory. In a computerized database, data is usually entered, and sometimes viewed, in a two-dimensional table consisting of columns and rows, similar to the structure of a spreadsheet (see Figure 6.19).

The entire collection of related data in the table is referred to as a file. Each row represents a **record**, which is a set of data for each database entry. Each table column represents a **field**, which groups each piece or item of data among the records into specific categories or types of data.

Notice that the table arrangement shown in Figure 6.19 consists of a set number of named columns and an arbitrary number of unnamed rows. The table organizes each record's data by the same set of fields, but the table can store any number of records. The only limit is the storage capability of the disk. Any one record in the table does not necessarily have data in every field. However, for a record to exist, it must have data in at least one field.

The order of fields in a table strictly defines the location of data in every record. A phone number field, for example, must contain a record's phone number—it cannot contain a person's name or ZIP code, for example. Similarly, the set of fields in any one table provides a sensible definition of the database for those who must access its data. For instance, you would expect to find the part number for a radiator in an inventory of auto parts, but you should not expect to view an employee's payroll record in the same table.

A database file that consists of a single data table is a **flat-file database**. Flat-file databases are useful for certain single-user or small-group situations, especially for maintaining lists such as address lists or inventories. Data that is stored, managed, and manipulated in a spreadsheet is another example of a flat-file database.

In a **relational database**, a database made up of a set of tables, a common field existing in any two tables creates a relationship between the tables. For instance, a Customer ID Number field in both a *customers* table and an *orders* table links the two tables (see Figure 6.20). The relational database structure is easily the most prevalent in today's business organizations and would likely contain data tables such as the following:

- Customer information
- Order information
- Vendor information
- Employee information
- Inventory information

Multiple tables in this kind of database make it possible to handle many data management tasks. For example:

- The customer, order, and inventory tables can be linked to process orders and billing.
- The vendor and inventory tables can be linked to maintain and track inventory levels.
- The order and employee tables can be linked to control scheduling.

NORTON Online
For comparisons of **different types of databases**, visit this book's Web site at
www.glencoe.com/norton/online

Although this chapter focuses on the relational structure, the other three types do bear mention:

- **Hierarchical databases.** In a hierarchical database, records are organized in a treelike structure by type. The relationship between record types is said to be a parent-child relationship, in which any child type relates only to a single parent type.

- **Network databases.** The network database is similar to the hierarchical structure except that any one record type can relate to any number of other record types. Like the hierarchical structure, the network database structure is used in older—primarily main-frame—systems.

- **Object-oriented databases.** An object-oriented database is a newer structure that recently has been generating a great deal of interest. This structure groups data items and their associated characteristics, attributes, and procedures into complex items called **objects**. Physically, an object can be anything: a product, an event, a house, an appliance, a textile, an art piece, a toy, a customer complaint, or even a purchase. An object is defined by its characteristics, attributes, and procedures. An object's characteristics can be text, sound, graphics, and video. Examples of attributes might be color, size, style, quantity, and price. A procedure refers to the processing or handling that can be associated with an object.

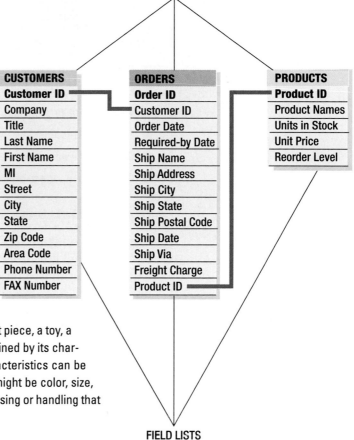

TABLE NAMES

FIELD LISTS

▶ **Figure 6.20**
Linked fields in relational database tables.

The DBMS

Computers make it possible to harness large data collections efficiently using a DBMS. A DBMS is a program, or collection of programs, that allows any number of users to access data, modify it (if necessary), and construct simple or complex requests to obtain and work with selected records.

Perhaps a DBMS's biggest asset is its capability to provide quick access and retrieval from large databases. Because database files can grow extremely large (many gigabytes on large systems), recalling data quickly is not a trivial matter. A DBMS, especially when it is running on powerful hardware, can find any speck of data in an enormous database in minutes—sometimes even seconds or fractions of a second.

Although there are many tasks you can perform with a DBMS, including creating and designing the database itself, data management tasks fall into one of three general categories:

- Entering data into the database
- Sorting the data; that is arranging or reordering the database's records (for example, arranging a list of customers by first name, or by last name, or by ZIP code)
- Obtaining subsets of the data

Equally important, DBMSs provide the means for multiple users to access and share data in the same database by way of networked computer systems.

Working with a Database

The DBMS interface presents the user with data and the tools required to work with the data. You work with the interface's tools to perform the important data management functions, including:

- Creating tables
- Entering and editing data
- Viewing data by using filters and forms
- Sorting the records
- Querying the database to obtain specific information
- Generating reports to print processed information

Creating Database Tables

The first step in building any database is to create one or more tables. The database tables hold the raw data that the DBMS will work with. To create a new database, you must first determine what kind of data will be stored in each table. In other words, you must define the fields. This is a three-step process:

1_Name the field.

2_Specify the field type.

3_Specify the field size.

Figure 6.21 ◄
Clearly named fields.

Field Names

When naming the field, indicate, as briefly as possible, what the field contains. Figure 6.21 shows a database table with clearly named fields.

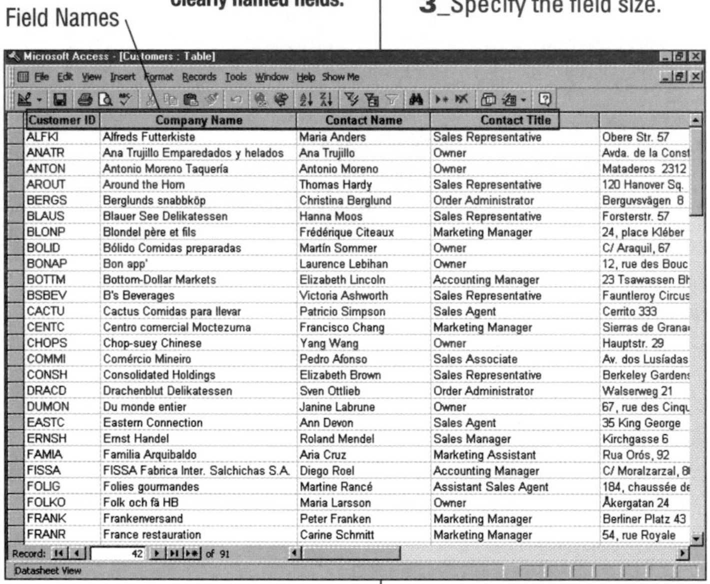

Specifying the field type requires knowledge of what kind of data the DBMS can understand. Most modern DBMSs can work with seven predefined field types. Figure 6.22 shows examples of each of these field types.

Text fields (also called *character fields* or *alphanumeric fields*) accept any string of alphanumeric characters such as a person's name, a company's name, an address, a phone number, or any other textual data. Text fields

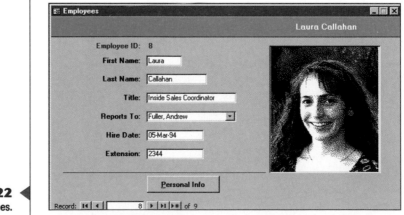

Figure 6.22 ◄
Field types.

also typically store entries consisting of numbers, like phone numbers or ZIP codes, that are not used in numeric calculations.

Numeric fields store purely numeric data. The numbers in a numeric field might represent currency, percentages, statistics, quantities, or any other value. The data itself is stored in the table strictly as a numeric value, even though the DBMS can display the value with formatting characters, like dollar or percent signs, decimal points, or comma separators.

A **date field** or **time field** stores date or time entries. This field type converts a date or time entry into a numeric value, just as dates and times are stored internally as serial numbers in spreadsheet cells. In most DBMSs, a date value represents the number of days that have elapsed since a specific start date. When you enter a date in a date field, the DBMS accepts your input, displays it in the format of a date, and converts it to a number that it stores in the database. Date and time fields typically include automatic error-checking features. For instance, date fields can verify a date entry's accuracy and account for the extra day in leap years. Date and time fields are quite handy for calculating elapsed time periods, such as finding records for invoices 31 days overdue.

Logical fields store one of only two possible values. You can apply almost any description for the data (yes or no, true or false, on or off, and so forth). For example, a Reorder field in a Products table can tell an inventory clerk whether a quantity has dipped below a certain value as a reminder to restock.

Binary field containing a video clip

Binary fields store binary objects, or BLOBs. A **BLOB (Binary Large OBject)** can be a graphic image file such as clip art, a photograph, a screen image, a graphic, or formatted text. A BLOB can also be a soundtrack, video clip, or other object.

Binary fields allow graphic images and other nontext items to be stored in a database.

In some DBMSs, **counter fields** store a unique numeric value that the DBMS assigns for every record. Because it is possible for two records to have identical data in some tables, a counter field ensures that every record will have a completely unique identification. Counter fields may also be used for creating records that number sequentially, such as invoices.

Because most field types have fixed lengths that restrict the number of characters in an entry, **memo fields** provide fields for entering notes or comments of any length.

Entering and Editing Data

After the table has been set up, data can be entered. In most cases, entering data is a matter of typing characters at the keyboard. Entering data in a database table is much like entering data in a spreadsheet program. However, the process can have more pitfalls than you might expect, especially if it is being carried out by someone other than the user who set up the tables. For example, the DBMS might not handle a number correctly if the user enters it with a dollar sign—even though the number will be displayed as a dollar amount.

Most DBMSs allow you to set up a device that validates or converts what is typed at the keyboard so that the data is properly entered in the field. Such devices have different names and different capabilities, depending on the specific DBMS product. Some products call them masks; others call them pictures or field formats. Regardless of the name, the device accepts only valid characters and controls the entry's display format.

For example, you can set up a State field so that a state's two-letter code appears uppercase (TN), no matter how the data is typed (tn, Tn, tN, or TN). A phone number field's entry can be controlled in a similar manner. Even though the user types only the phone number's ten digits, it appears with the area code enclosed in parentheses, a space, and a hyphen following the prefix—for example, (818) 555-1234.

Viewing Records

The way data appears on screen contributes to how well users can work with it. You have already seen examples of data presented in two-dimensional, worksheet-style tables. With many DBMS products, the table (sometimes called the *datasheet view*) is what you use to create a database table and to modify field specifications. This view is also suitable for viewing lists of records that you group together in some meaningful way, such as all customers who live in the same city.

This form lets the user work with all the information for a single order.

There are times, however, when viewing the entire table is unwieldy—there may simply be too many entries. **Filters** are a DBMS feature for displaying a selected list or subset of records from a table. The visible records satisfy a condition that the user sets. It is called a filter because it tells the DBMS to display those records that satisfy the condition, while hiding—or filtering out—those that do not. For example, you can create a filter that displays only those records that have the data "USA" in the Country field.

For many users, extensive data entry can be handled more conveniently with a customized form. A **form** is simply a screen that displays data for a single record. You can customize its appearance to your liking. A form can be associated with a single table or with multiple tables.

DBMSs also allow you to create forms to search out records that meet conditions that you specify. For instance, you can create a query to select records for products necessary to fill an order. Queries can perform other data-management operations, such as performing a calculation to deduct the order quantity from the Stock on Hand field in an inventory table.

Sorting Records

One of the most powerful features of DBMSs is their capability to **sort** a table of data rapidly, either for a printed report or for display on screen. Sorting arranges records according to the contents of one or more fields. For example, in a table of products, you can sort records into numerical order by product ID or into alphabetical order by product name. To obtain the list that is sorted by product ID, you define the condition for the Product ID field that tells the DBMS to rearrange the records in numerical order for this data (see Figure 6.23).

Product ID	Product Name	Supplier	Category	Quantity Per I ▲
1	Chai	Exotic Liquids	Beverages	10 boxes x 20 ba
2	Chang	Exotic Liquids	Beverages	24 - 12 oz bottle:
3	Aniseed Syrup	Exotic Liquids	Condiments	12 - 550 ml bottl(
4	Chef Anton's Cajun Seasoning	New Orleans Cajun Delights	Condiments	48 - 6 oz jars
5	Chef Anton's Gumbo Mix	New Orleans Cajun Delights	Condiments	36 boxes
6	Grandma's Boysenberry Spread	Grandma Kelly's Homestead	Condiments	12 - 8 oz jars
7	Uncle Bob's Organic Dried Pears	Grandma Kelly's Homestead	Produce	12 - 1 lb pkgs.
8	Northwoods Cranberry Sauce	Grandma Kelly's Homestead	Condiments	12 - 12 oz jars
9	Mishi Kobe Niku	Tokyo Traders	Meat/Poultry	18 - 500 g pkgs.
10	Ikura	Tokyo Traders	Seafood	12 - 200 ml jars
11	Queso Cabrales	Cooperativa de Quesos 'Las Cabras'	Dairy Products	1 kg pkg.
12	Queso Manchego La Pastora	Cooperativa de Quesos 'Las Cabras'	Dairy Products	10 - 500 g pkgs.
13	Konbu	Mayumi's	Seafood	2 kg box
14	Tofu	Mayumi's	Produce	40 - 100 g pkgs.
15	Genen Shouyu	Mayumi's	Condiments	24 - 250 ml bottl(
16	Pavlova	Pavlova, Ltd.	Confections	32 - 500 g boxes
17	Alice Mutton	Pavlova, Ltd.	Meat/Poultry	20 - 1 kg tins
18	Carnarvon Tigers	Pavlova, Ltd.	Seafood	16 kg pkg.
19	Teatime Chocolate Biscuits	Specialty Biscuits, Ltd.	Confections	10 boxes x 12 pi
20	Sir Rodney's Marmalade	Specialty Biscuits, Ltd.	Confections	30 gift boxes
21	Sir Rodney's Scones	Specialty Biscuits, Ltd.	Confections	24 pkgs. x 4 piec
22	Gustaf's Knäckebröd	PB Knäckebröd AB	Grains/Cereals	24 - 500 g pkgs.
23	Tunnbröd	PB Knäckebröd AB	Grains/Cereals	12 - 250 g pkgs.
24	Guaraná Fantástica	Refrescos Americanas LTDA	Beverages	12 - 355 ml cans
25	NuNuCa Nuß-Nougat-Creme	Heli Süßwaren GmbH & Co. KG	Confections	20 - 450 g glasse
26	Gumbär Gummibärchen	Heli Süßwaren GmbH & Co. KG	Confections	100 - 250 g bags ▼

Figure 6.23
Records arranged numerically by Product ID.

When sorting records, one important consideration is determining the **sort order**. An *ascending sort order* arranges records in alphabetical or numerical order according to the data on which the sort is based. For example, if you base an ascending sort on a Last Name field, the records will be arranged in alphabetical order by last name. Conversely, a *descending sort order* arranges records in the opposite order, that is, from Z to A or 9 to 0.

Querying a Database

In a manner similar to entering sort conditions, you can enter expressions or criteria that:

- Allow the DBMS to locate records
- Establish relationships or links between tables to update records
- List a subset of records
- Perform calculations
- Delete obsolete records
- Perform other data management tasks

Any of these types of requests is called a **query**, a user-constructed statement that describes data and sets criteria so that the DBMS can gather the relevant data and construct specific information. In other words, a query is a more powerful type of filter that can gather information from multiple tables in a relational database.

In this database, the records have been arranged alphabetically according to the contents of the Product Name field.

Product ID	Product Name	Supplier	Category	Quantity Per I ▲
17	Alice Mutton	Pavlova, Ltd.	Meat/Poultry	20 - 1 kg tins
3	Aniseed Syrup	Exotic Liquids	Condiments	12 - 550 ml bottl(
40	Boston Crab Meat	New England Seafood Cannery	Seafood	24 - 4 oz tins
60	Camembert Pierrot	Gai pâturage	Dairy Products	15 - 300 g rounds
18	Carnarvon Tigers	Pavlova, Ltd.	Seafood	16 kg pkg.
1	Chai	Exotic Liquids	Beverages	10 boxes x 20 ba
2	Chang	Exotic Liquids	Beverages	24 - 12 oz bottle:
39	Chartreuse verte	Aux joyeux ecclésiastiques	Beverages	750 cc per bottle
4	Chef Anton's Cajun Seasoning	New Orleans Cajun Delights	Condiments	48 - 6 oz jars
5	Chef Anton's Gumbo Mix	New Orleans Cajun Delights	Condiments	36 boxes
48	Chocolade	Zaanse Snoepfabriek	Confections	10 pkgs.
38	Côte de Blaye	Aux joyeux ecclésiastiques	Beverages	12 - 75 cl bottles
58	Escargots de Bourgogne	Escargots Nouveaux	Seafood	24 pieces
52	Filo Mix	G'day, Mate	Grains/Cereals	16 - 2 kg boxes
71	Fløtemysost	Norske Meierier	Dairy Products	10 - 500 g pkgs.
33	Geitost	Norske Meierier	Dairy Products	500 g
15	Genen Shouyu	Mayumi's	Condiments	24 - 250 ml bottl(
56	Gnocchi di nonna Alice	Pasta Buttini s.r.l.	Grains/Cereals	24 - 250 g pkgs.
31	Gorgonzola Telino	Formaggi Fortini s.r.l.	Dairy Products	12 - 100 g pkgs
6	Grandma's Boysenberry Spread	Grandma Kelly's Homestead	Condiments	12 - 8 oz jars
37	Gravad lax	Svensk Sjöföda AB	Seafood	12 - 500 g pkgs.
24	Guaraná Fantástica	Refrescos Americanas LTDA	Beverages	12 - 355 ml cans
69	Gudbrandsdalsost	Norske Meierier	Dairy Products	10 kg pkg.
44	Gula Malacca	Leka Trading	Condiments	20 - 2 kg bags
26	Gumbär Gummibärchen	Heli Süßwaren GmbH & Co. KG	Confections	100 - 250 g bags
22	Gustaf's Knäckebröd	PB Knäckebröd AB	Grains/Cereals	24 - 500 g pkgs. ▼

A sales manager, for example, might create a query to list orders by quarter. The query might include field names such as CUSTOMER and CITY from a "Customers" table, and ORDER DATE from an "Order" table. To get the desired information, the query requires the specific data or criteria that will isolate those records (orders received during a given period) from all the records in both tables. In this case, the sales manager includes a range of dates during which the orders would ship.

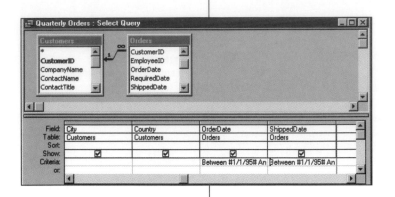

Some DBMSs provide special windows or forms for creating queries. Generally, this window or form provides an area for selecting the tables the query is to work with and columns for entering the field names where the query will get or manipulate data.

This query is being set up to display the orders received during a given time period. The results will show the customers that placed the orders and the dates the orders were placed and shipped.

SQL and QBE

Within every DBMS is a language similar to a programming language. This language is designed specifically for communicating with a database using statements that are closer to English than to programming languages. In many DBMSs, this standardized language is known as **SQL**. SQL was based on an earlier query language called SEQUEL, which was an acronym for "Structured English QUEry Language." It is used to structure query statements.

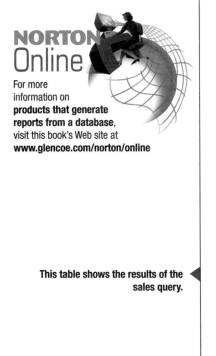

NORTON Online

For more information on **products that generate reports from a database**, visit this book's Web site at www.glencoe.com/norton/online

This table shows the results of the sales query.

Although SQL and query languages are an important part of a DBMS, few PC and Macintosh users who work with a DBMS ever actually write a SQL (or any other query language) statement. DBMSs commonly provide an interface, like a form or a grid, that collects the facts about a query from the user and composes the SQL or query statements behind the scenes. This feature allows a user to **query by example (QBE)**, or to perform "intuitive" queries. With QBE, you specify the search criteria by typing values or expressions into the fields of a QBE form or grid.

Generating Reports

Not all DBMS operations have to occur on screen. Just as forms can be based on queries, so, too, can reports. A **report** is printed information that, like a query result, is assembled by gathering data based on user-supplied criteria. In fact, report generators in most DBMSs create reports from queries.

Reports can range from simple lists of records to customized formats for specific purposes, such as invoices. Report generators can use selected data and criteria to carry out automated mathematical calculations as the output is being printed. For example, relevant data can be used to calculate subtotals and totals for invoices or sales summaries. Reports are also similar to forms in that their layouts can be customized with objects representing fields and other controls.

PRESENTATION PROGRAMS

If you have ever attended a seminar or lecture that included slides or overhead transparencies projected on a screen—or a series of slides displayed on a computer screen or video monitor—then you probably have seen the product of a modern presentation program. **Presentation programs** enable the user to create and edit colorful, compelling presentations, which can be displayed in a variety of ways and used to support any type of discussion. Popular presentation programs include Microsoft PowerPoint, Corel Presentations, and Lotus Freelance Graphics.

Presentation programs are used to produce a series of **slides**—single-screen images that contain a combination of text, numbers, and graphics (such as charts, clip art, or pictures), often on a colorful background. Slides can be simple or sophisticated. Depending on how far you want to go, you can turn a basic slide show into a multimedia event, using the built-in features of current presentation programs.

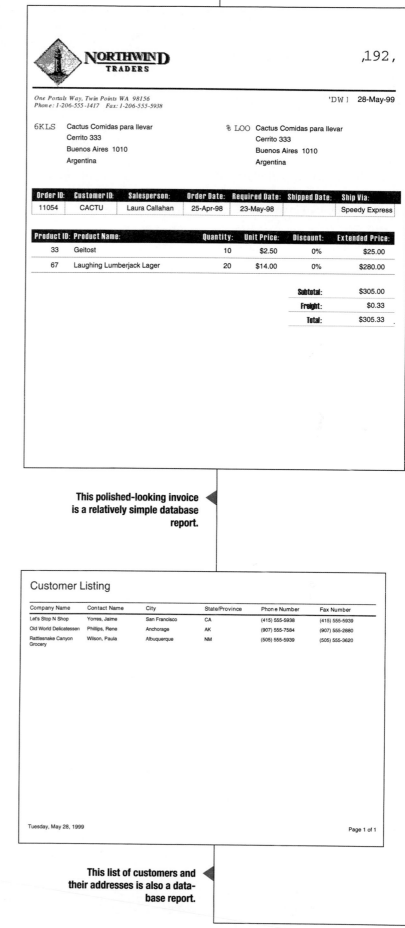

This polished-looking invoice is a relatively simple database report.

This list of customers and their addresses is also a database report.

Techview

Managing the SOHO

Because resources are so limited for the small business owner, application suites and a new breed of financial software are making it easy to run a small office/home office (SOHO). Instead of relying on outside accountants, marketers, designers, and other consultants, many SOHO workers are finding that they can do many nontraditional chores themselves—as well as their daily work—by using sophisticated software packages. These applications are helping small business owners solve a variety of problems about which they have little expertise, at a minimal investment.

Application suites (such as Microsoft Office, Corel PerfectOffice, and Lotus SmartSuite) include the following types of programs:

■ *Word processor.* Most word processors include professional templates to give documents a clean look and can help the user with spelling, grammar, and word choice. Word processors greatly simplify mass mailings and can print envelopes, brochures, and other complex documents. New versions even create HTML documents.

■ *Spreadsheet.* Spreadsheets help managers tackle crucial financial tasks; the resulting files can be imported into many financial or accounting programs, or can be useful to an accountant or consultant.

■ *Database.* These packages enable the small business to track products, orders, shipments, customers, and much more. When used as part of an application suite, the DBMS can provide much of the data required for invoices, receipts, letters, and so on.

■ *Presentation.* These programs help the user to quickly create impressive presentations for use in slide shows, overheads, and on the computer screen. Colorful graphics, animation, and concise text can help persuade clients and close sales.

■ *Contact and schedule management.* Even in a small office, time is valuable, and people cannot afford confused schedules. Programs such as Microsoft Outlook and Lotus Organizer help people (individually and in groups) manage and coordinate their schedules, set appointments and meetings, and manage lists of contacts.

The specialty software market for small businesses is rapidly growing. Here are some examples of the types of special business-oriented programs that are available:

■ *Financial.* These inexpensive yet powerful packages can track inventories, billings, expenses, and much more. They also can help the user categorize income and expenses and do tax planning.

■ *Business planning.* New business-planning programs provide templates to help with the creation of business plans, and let you customize documents by industry, product type, or customer type.

■ *Tax planning and preparation.* Tax software enables business owners to prepare their own taxes without using an accountant or consulting. You plug in the numbers; the software does the rest.

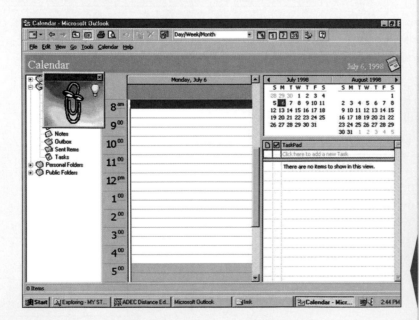

Microsoft Outlook provides contact management and scheduling capabilities, and includes a full-featured e-mail package.

232

Presentation software is an important tool for anyone who must present information to a group. Sales and marketing professionals, for example, maintain a variety of "stock" presentations, which they can customize for different clients or products. Managers use professional-looking slides to present information to employees, such as lists of benefits and responsibilities that are explained during new-hire orientation. Teachers and trainers commonly rely on slides in the classroom, to serve as a roadmap for discussion.

This book's Web site features several exercises designed to help you learn to use presentation programs. To find these exercises, visit **www.glencoe.com/norton/online**.

The Presentation Program's Interface

Until the early 1990s, presentation programs hardly existed and were difficult to use. Since the advent of Windows-based applications and WYSIWYG, however, they have become one of the simplest and most enjoyable types of productivity software to use.

The typical presentation program displays a slide in a large document window and provides a wide array of tools for designing and editing slides. Most presentation programs provide many of the features of word processors (for working with text), spreadsheets (for creating charts), and paint programs (for creating and editing simple graphics). You can add elements to the slide simply by typing, making menu or toolbar choices, and dragging. As you work on the slide, you see exactly how it will look when shown to an audience.

Figure 6.24 shows a slide being designed in Microsoft PowerPoint 97, a popular presentation program.

In Figure 6.24, note that the status bar says that the presentation contains ten slides. A presentation can contain a single slide or hundreds. Most presentation programs let you save a set of slides as a group in one file so that you can open the related slides and work with them together.

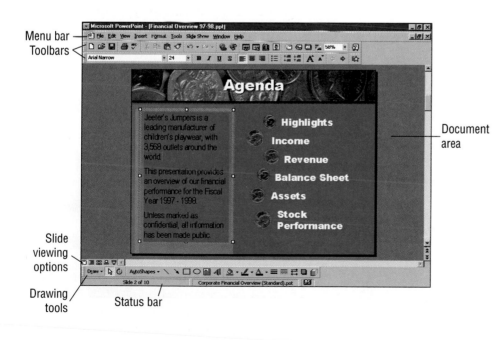

Figure 6.24
Creating a slide in Microsoft PowerPoint 97.

Creating a Presentation

Creating a presentation is simple; just choose the type of slide you want to create and then start adding the content. A complete presentation usually includes multiple slides, arranged in a logical series. As you go, you can insert new slides anywhere, copy slides from other presentations, and reorder the slides any way you want.

You can create slides from scratch (just starting with a blank slide), but it is easier and faster to work with one of the presentation program's many templates. Like a template in a word processor, a presentation template is a predesigned document, which already has finished fonts, a layout, and a background. Your presentation program should provide dozens of built-in templates.

After you select a template, you can quickly assemble a presentation by creating individual slides. To create a slide, you can choose a slide type, as shown in Figure 6.25. Presentation programs provide several types of slides, which can hold varying combinations of titles, text, charts, and graphics. You can choose a different type for each slide in your presentation, if you want.

After you have selected a slide type, the program provides special **text boxes** and **frames** (special resizable boxes for text and graphical elements) to contain specific types of content.

These special boxes often contain instructions, telling you exactly what to do. To add text to a text box, simply click in the box to place the insertion point there and then type your text. The text is automatically formatted, but you can easily reformat the text later, using many of the same formatting options available in word processors.

Most presentation programs provide a variety of templates.

▶ **Choosing a presentation template in PowerPoint.**

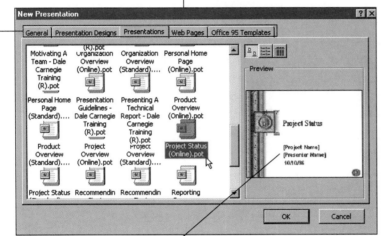

In preview mode, you can see what the selected template looks like before deciding whether to use it.

NORTON
Online

For information
on **choosing
slides for a presentation**,
visit this book's Web site at
www.glencoe.com/norton/online

▶ **Figure 6.25**
Choosing a slide type.

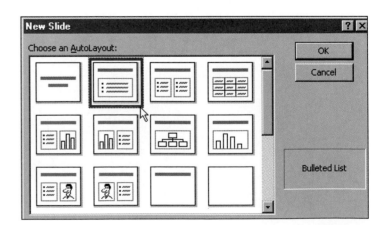

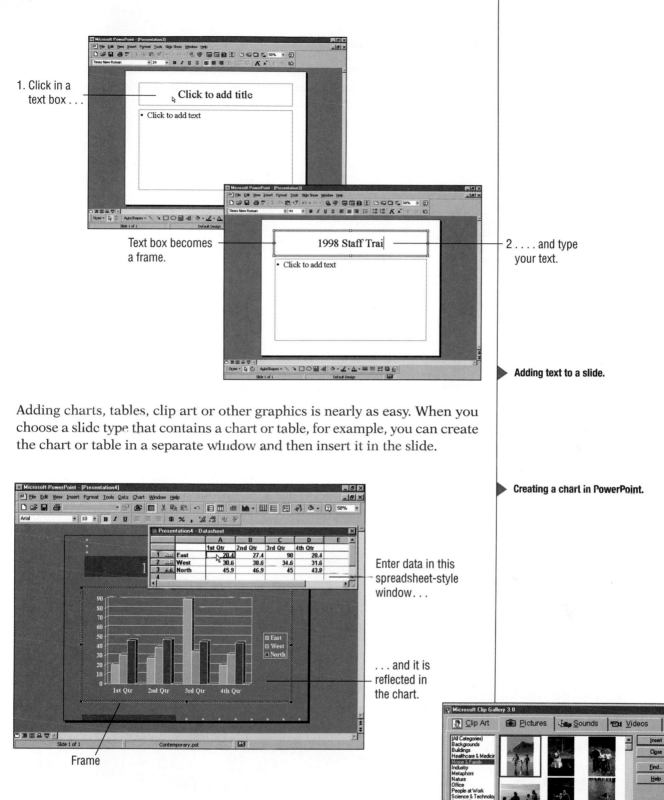

1. Click in a text box . . .

Text box becomes a frame.

2. . . . . and type your text.

Adding charts, tables, clip art or other graphics is nearly as easy. When you choose a slide type that contains a chart or table, for example, you can create the chart or table in a separate window and then insert it in the slide.

Enter data in this spreadsheet-style window . . .

. . . and it is reflected in the chart.

Frame

To insert clip art or another type of graphic in a slide, you can select the appropriate image from your software's collection of graphics, or import an image file. Built-in paint tools also enable you to draw simple graphics and add them to your slides. (These tools are handy if you want to add callouts to specific elements of a slide.)

Formatting Slides

Because presentation programs are like a combination of a word processor, spreadsheet, and paint program, you can easily format slides in many ways, including formatting text, resizing frames, adding color, and adding borders or shading.

Formatting text in a presentation program is just like formatting text in a word processor. Text in slides is usually in the form of titles, headings, and lists. Although a text box can hold multiple paragraphs, the paragraphs themselves are usually quite short.

To format text, you select it and then apply formats by using the toolbars or options from the Format menu.

When you add a chart or graphic to a slide, you may need to resize it to allow better spacings for other elements on the slide. Sometimes it is necessary to resize text boxes, too, if you type more or less text than the box can hold by default. Resizing is easy, using frames, which surround most of the elements in a slide. To resize a frame, drag one of its **handles**. The frame expands or shrinks depending on which direction you drag the handle.

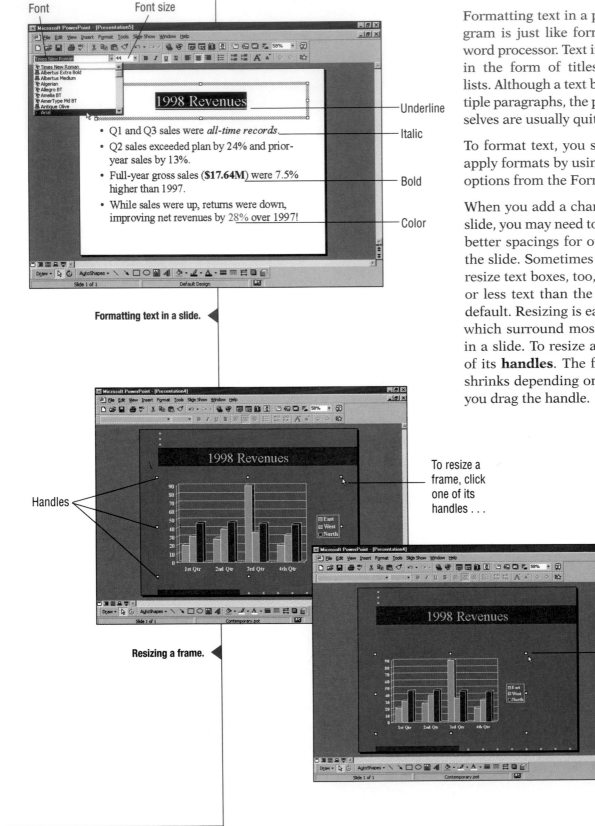

Font

Font size

Underline

Italic

Bold

Color

Formatting text in a slide.

Handles

To resize a frame, click one of its handles . . .

Resizing a frame.

. . . and drag to a new position.

Color can create a wide range of moods for your presentations, so choose colors carefully. Further, make sure that the slides' colors complement one another and do not make text difficult to read.

You can apply specific colors to fonts by using the Format menu. You also can create custom color schemes for an entire presentation, however, by using a dialog box and selecting a specific color for each element used in your slides.

You can add depth to a plain presentation by giving it a shaded background and by placing borders around certain elements. Borders separate different elements and help hold the viewer's attention on individual parts of the slide. Shaded backgrounds provide depth and can make static information appear dynamic. A gradient fill, as shown in Figure 6.26, changes color as it moves from one part of the slide to another. This effect can almost make the slide appear as if it is in motion.

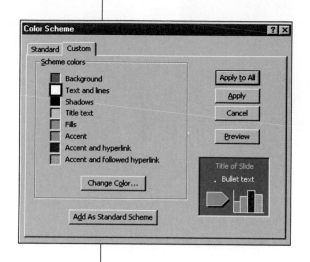

Setting a color scheme for a presentation.

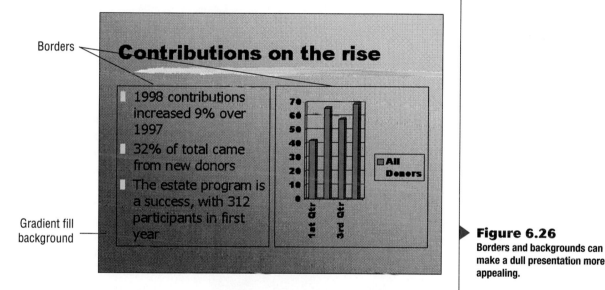

Borders

Gradient fill background

Figure 6.26
Borders and backgrounds can make a dull presentation more appealing.

Special Features of Presentation Programs

As well as enabling you to quickly create dynamic and detailed slides, a presentation program can help you make your presentations lively and engaging, to encourage your audience to pay attention and participate. Thanks to presentation programs, you can present your slides directly from disk, displaying them on the PC's screen or by connecting the PC to a video monitor or projection unit. You can display slides manually, clicking the mouse button or pressing Enter to display the next slide. Or, you can automate the presentation by setting a display time for each slide.

You can add special note text, called **annotations**, to each slide; use the animation tools to make text pop up or crawl onto the screen, or to make slides "build themselves" on the screen; or add multimedia components such as sounds and full-motion video to your presentations.

NORTON
Online

For information on **different tools for delivering a presentation**, visit this book's Web site at **www.glencoe.com/norton/online**

Computers
In Your Career

Regardless of your career choice, if your work involves the use of personal computers, then you probably will find yourself using one or more of the productivity applications described in this chapter. Word processors, spreadsheets, databases, and presentation programs are widely used in businesses and organizations, by employees of all kinds, with responsibilities of all types.

Secretaries, Writers, Editors, Journalists The word processor is probably the most essential of all productivity applications, and whether you are a secretary who types letters and memos or a scientist summarizing research data, you will find the word processor a required tool. Even if another type of computer program (such as a spreadsheet or CAD program) is your primary tool, you doubtlessly will find yourself using the word processor again and again.

Accountants, Bookkeepers, Business Managers, Financial Planners The spreadsheet program has become as essential to these professionals as the ledger book once was, so if your career path leads you into business or finance, spreadsheet skills are a must. If this is the case, be sure to develop skills with analytical tools such as what-if analysis, goal seeking, and others. Professional spreadsheet users also suggest mastering the software's page layout features and charting capabilities, to make your work look as polished as possible.

Database Developers, Data Processing Administrators, Data-Entry Specialists On a daily basis, most computer users do not work with a true DBMS. Instead, most work with a front-end program, such as a contact manager or order-entry system, which acts as an intermediary between the user and the actual database. But the call for experienced database professionals is strong, especially for high-end users who can develop custom forms and set up complex relational databases. Database developers are called on to develop custom tools for corporate databases, create special front ends and order-entry tools, generate complicated queries, develop report-generation macros, and more. These developers are skilled in database languages such as SQL and QBE and are familiar with powerful databases such as Sybase, Oracle, and others.

Sales and Marketing Professionals, Trainers, Intstructors Presentation software is proving its usefulness in a wide variety of professions, many of which require only minimal computer use or skills. If your chosen field is sales or marketing, you will find the presentation program to be your best friend because it enables you to format and present information in many ways. Teachers and instructors of all kinds—working in all types of subject areas—are using presentation software in class, replacing the static chalkboard with the dynamic PC and slide show. Business managers, recruiters, architects, and many other professionals use presentation software weekly or even daily.

WHAT TO EXPECT IN THE FUTURE

A few years ago, most computer users felt perfectly productive using only one type of software. As a result, word processors, spreadsheets, database programs, and presentation programs were typically purchased and installed as stand-alone applications. Increasingly, however, users are turning away from single applications in favor of application "suites." Suites—such as Microsoft Office, Lotus SmartSuite, and others—include a word processor, spreadsheet, database program, and several other productivity tools, such as presentation software, schedulers, organizers, Web browsers, and more.

As developers continually add new features to their products, however, suites are also growing in size, giving rise to the term "bloatware." A full installation of a leading suite can consume well over 50 MB of disk space, and the RAM required to run these packages has increased considerably, as well.

Users are caught in a tug of war; do they want more features with each new version of the software, or do they want software to be smaller, faster, and cheaper? The answer, ironically, is both. The future of productivity software, therefore, seems to be going in two directions at once: more features with less required overhead. Software developers are addressing these demands in a number of ways:

- **Code sharing.** If multiple software packages can be installed together and share the same interface, they can share other code, too. For example, your word processor, spreadsheet, database, and other packages can share a spell checker, dictionaries, thesaurus, clip art, formatting tools, and more.

- **Modularity.** A complete suite may be considerably less expensive than buying a word processor, spreadsheet, and database package separately. But what if you don't need a database package? Why pay for and install software you don't need? Software companies are addressing this by packaging suites differently. Microsoft, for example, makes its Office suite available in several editions, so you can choose only the tools you need. The future will probably bring you-build-it suites, which will enable the customer to order only the modules he or she needs. The ordering may be done on the Internet, by phone, or in stores.

- **New standards.** The OpenDoc standard, for instance, was designed to encourage software developers to reduce the size of software products. The standard is not universally accepted yet, but industry giants like IBM and Apple are committed to it.

- **New development tools.** Programming languages such as Java and object-based tools are enabling developers to write code that is not only smaller but that can be reused on multiple platforms. Unless developers get carried away and add unneeded features to their products, these new programming methods promise to streamline software, reducing its size.

- **Group computing.** It is not always necessary for every user in an office to have every piece of software installed. In networked environments, users can share programs from a central file server or application server. This technique saves the cost of buying multiple packages (although multiple-user licenses are often required). It also saves time and effort in support and maintenance. The network PC promises to take group computing to a new level, enabling businesses to cut storage costs even further while giving users access to software and documents from central, speedy servers.

Visual Summary & Exercises

VISUAL SUMMARY

Word Processing Software

■ Word processing software is used to create documents that consist primarily of text, from simple letters and memos to brochures, resumes, and long documents.

■ To edit or format blocks of text, you can select the block and then apply changes to the entire block (by making menu or toolbar choices; cutting, copying, and pasting; or by using drag-and-drop editing).

■ Character formats include fonts, type size, type styles, and color.

■ Paragraph formats include line and paragraph spacing, indents and alignment, borders, and shading.

■ Document formats include margins, page size and orientation, headers and footers.

■ Mail merge combines a form letter with contents from a database, creating a separate copy of the letter for each entry in the database.

■ Modern word processors enable you to add graphics and sounds to your documents.

■ Many word processing programs can create HTML documents for use on the World Wide Web.

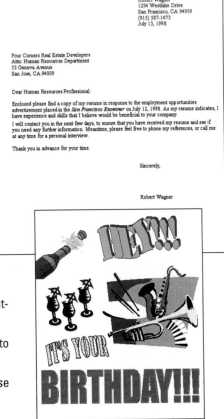

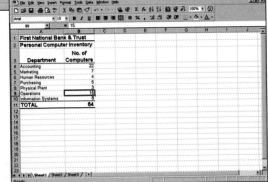

Spreadsheet Programs

■ A spreadsheet program is used to calculate and analyze sets of numbers.

■ A data file created with a spreadsheet is called a worksheet.

■ A worksheet is formatted in columns and rows of cells. Cells can contain values, labels, or formulas.

■ A formula lets you create a value in one cell that is calculated based on the values in other cells.

■ A cell's address is created by combining its column and row headings, as in B4.

■ Numbers can be formatted as dollars, percentages, dates, times, fractions, and decimals.

■ Charts are added to worksheets to make data easier to understand. The most common types of charts are bar charts, line charts, pie charts, and scatter charts.

■ Spreadsheets can perform many analytical operations, such as what-if analysis and goal seeking.

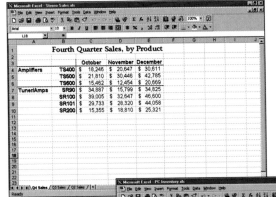

Database Management Systems

- A database is a repository for collections of related items or facts. A database management system (DBMS) is a software tool that enables users to create database tables and which provides multiple users with access to data.

- Flat-file databases are basically two-dimensional tables of fields and records. They cannot form relationships with other tables.

- Relational databases are powerful because they can form relationships among different tables.

- Forms are custom screens for displaying and entering data that can be associated with database tables and queries.

- Filters let you browse through selected records that meet a set of criteria.

- Sorting arranges records in a table according to specific criteria.

- Queries are user-constructed statements that set conditions for selecting and manipulating data.

Presentation Programs

- Presentation programs enable users to construct a series of slides, which can be used to support a discussion.

- A presentation can be saved as a single file containing one slide or many slides, which are used together.

- Slides can include different types of text (titles, headings, lists), charts, tables, and graphics.

- Most presentation programs provide templates, which are predesigned slides. The user needs only to insert the content into a template to create a presentation.

- Slides can be formatted with different fonts, colors, backgrounds, and borders. Using frames, the user can resize many of the elements in a slide.

- Presentation programs enable users to add animations, sounds, and other multimedia components to their presentations.

- Using presentation software, you can present a slide show "live" from the computer's disk on a PC or video screen.

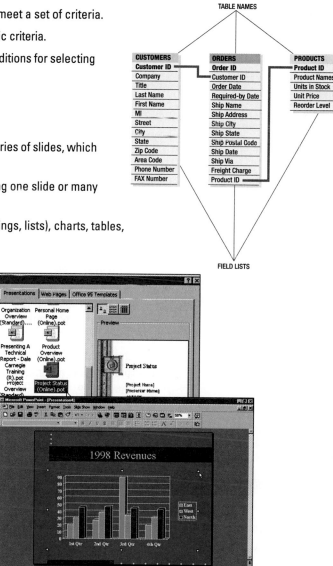

TABLE NAMES

FIELD LISTS

Visual Summary & Exercises

KEY TERMS

After completing this chapter, you should be able to define the following terms:

3-D worksheet, 213
absolute cell reference, 218
alignment, 203
annotation, 237
argument, 217
autocorrect, 200
binary field, 227
binary large object (BLOB), 227
block, 200
border, 203
cell, 213
cell address, 214
cell pointer, 213
cell reference, 216
character format, 201
chart, 219
color separation, 210
column, 205
counter field, 227
database, 223
database management system
   (DBMS), 223
date field, 227
deselect, 200
desktop publishing (DTP) software, 208
document area, 198
document format, 204
drag-and-drop editing, 200
drop shadow, 203
editing, 199
field, 223
filter, 228
flat-file database, 224
font, 201
footer, 204
form, 228

format, 200
formula, 215
formula bar, 212
frame, 234
function, 217
goal seeking, 221
handle, 236
header, 204
hierarchical database, 225
highlight, 200
indent, 203
insertion mode, 200
kerning, 209
label, 214
landscape orientation, 204
leading, 209
line spacing, 202
logical field, 227
mail merge, 206
margin, 202
master page, 210
memo field, 227
network database, 225
numeric field, 227
object, 225
object-oriented database, 225
overtype mode, 200
paragraph, 202
paragraph format, 202
paragraph spacing, 202
productivity software, 197
point, 201
portrait orientation, 204
presentation program, 231
query, 229
query by example (QBE), 230

range, 216
record, 223
relational database, 224
relative cell reference, 218
report, 231
ruler, 198
sans serif, 201
section, 205
select, 200
serif, 201
shading, 203
slide, 231
sort, 228
sort order, 229
spreadsheet, 212
status bar, 198
structured query language (SQL), 230
tab stop, 203
table, 206
template, 207
text box, 234
text field, 226
time field, 227
toolbar, 198
tracking, 209
type style, 201
typeface, 201
value, 215
what-if analysis, 221
word processing software, 198
word wrap, 199
workbook, 212
worksheet, 212
WYSIWYG, 199

KEY TERM QUIZ

Fill in the missing word with one of the terms listed in Key Terms.

1. Productivity software gives users the option of issuing commands by clicking buttons on a _____.

2. In a word processor, three types of formatting are _____, _____, and _____.

3. In a spreadsheet, a(n) _____ is the intersection of a row and a column.

4. A(n) _____ is a group of contiguous cells in a worksheet.

5. In a(n) _____, a common field in any two tables creates a relationship between the tables.

Visual Summary & Exercises

6. A(n) _____ is a DBMS feature for displaying a selected list or subset of records.

7. Most presentation programs provide a selection of _____, which are pre-designed slides.

8. A(n) _____ combines a form letter with the contents of a database.

9. Spreadsheets can perform analytical operations such as _____, _____, and _____.

10. A(n) _____ is a user-constructed statement that sets conditions for selecting data.

REVIEW QUESTIONS

1. In a word processor, what makes a block of text?

2. Which page orientation would you choose for a document containing a wide eight-column table?

3. Describe the advantages of using the templates provided by a word processor.

4. What is the difference between a spreadsheet and a worksheet?

5. Name the four types of data you can enter in a worksheet.

6. Describe the difference between an absolute cell reference and a relative cell reference.

7. What primary characteristic distinguishes a flat-file database from a relational database?

8. What does it mean to "filter" database records?

9. What is a presentation program used for?

10. What is the advantage of adding animated elements to a slide for use in a presentation?

DISCUSSION QUESTIONS

1. Do you think that using a spelling checker and a grammar checker for all your final documents is a sufficient substitute for proofreading? Explain why or why not.

2. What fundamental feature of spreadsheet software provides the real power behind its calculation capabilities? Briefly describe at least one kind of common operation that demonstrates this capability.

3. Describe a scenario in which a large organization might use a database management system. In the scenario you describe, what types of tables would the organization's database contain? What kinds of relationships would exist among the tables? What types of queries might be run on those tables, in the management of the organization?

4. Suppose that you were required to give a presentation on a topic that you understand well. To support your presentation, you are asked to prepare a slide presentation using a presentation program. Describe the slide presentation you would create. How large would it be? How would you organize the slides, and what types of content would you use in each? What features of the presentation program would you use to enhance your presentation?

inteNET Workshop

The following exercises assume that you have access to the Internet and a browser. If you need help with any of the exercises, visit this book's Web site at **www.glencoe.com/norton/online**. This book's Web site also lists the URLs you need to complete many of these exercises.

1. Using a newer version of a word processor (such as Word 97 or WordPerfect 8), create a basic document. Format the document any way you want, but be sure to include at least one heading and a list. If possible, insert a graphic or two. When you are finished, use the word processor's Save As or Save As HTML command to save the document in HTML format. Then view the document in your Web browser. How did the HTML conversion work?

2. Next, try the opposite. Find a Web page you like. Then use your browser's Save As command to save the page to your disk as an HTML file. Next, see if you can open the HTML file in your word processor. (If you are using a newer word processor, you should be able to select HTML files in the Open dialog box.) How does the HTML file look now? How does its appearance compare to the file you created in exercise 1?

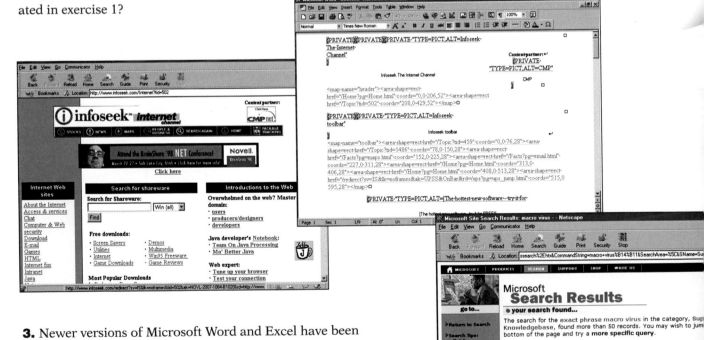

3. Newer versions of Microsoft Word and Excel have been plagued by a specific new type of virus, called a "macro virus." This type of virus, disguised as a macro, can ruin documents and other data on a user's disk. Visit Microsoft's Web site and search for two things: (1) information about macro viruses and (2) utilities you can download and install that will find and eliminate such viruses from your documents.

4. If you do not already own one, you probably will want to purchase a suite of applications at some time. Now is a good time to start doing your homework on these complex, expensive products. A good place to start is the World Wide Web. Search and visit the Web sites of major software vendors that offer application suites. What tools does each suite offer? Within each application, what options are available? What are the system requirements of each suite?

5. Some users resist the urge to invest in large, expensive software suites, opting instead for freeware or low-cost shareware packages. Search for and visit popular shareware and freeware sites on the Web where you can find a variety of full-featured shareware programs. Look for stand-alone word processors, such as Yeah Write and WordExpress, and spreadsheet programs like VistaCalc. You can download and evaluate these packages. How do they compare to the popular applications, such as Word and Lotus 1-2-3? Would you choose a shareware package over a commercial package? Why or why not?

6. While you are visiting the shareware and freeware sites, search on the term "template." Can you find any templates for use with popular desktop applications? For example, are any templates available for use with PowerPoint? Can you find any templates to create specialized documents (such as calendars or invoices) in Excel or 1-2-3?

7. If you have an interest in database management systems, and possibly a career in database management or development, look at some of the leading DBMS tools available. Check out the Web sites of major software firms that market DBMS tools. While you are visiting those sites, look for job listings or career opportunities. What can you find? What are these powerful systems used for? Who are some of the largest clients of these companies?

CHAPTER 7

Networks and Data Communications

OBJECTIVES

When you complete this chapter, you will be able to do the following:

■ List four major benefits of connecting computers to form a network.

■ Define the terms LAN, WAN, and MAN.

■ List the three types of networks.

■ Name the three physical topologies used to build networks.

■ Name four common media for connecting the computers in a network.

■ Give four reasons for connecting computers through the telephone lines.

■ List six common types of digital lines and the basic characteristics of each.

Sometimes, such as in the case of connecting a computer to the Internet via modem, a modem is used to connect a computer to a network. The process of connecting a computer to a network, either through a modem or a direct connection, is known as going **online**. Networking lets organizations maximize the value of computers, so it is not difficult to imagine a day when virtually every organization, large or small, will have some or all of its computers networked.

When PCs first began appearing in the business environment and software applications were simple and designed for a single user, the advantages of connecting PCs were not so compelling. As these machines spread throughout business, and as complex multiuser software appeared, connecting PCs became a goal for many organizations. **Data communications**, the electronic transfer of information between computers, became a major focus of the computer industry. The rapid growth of the worldwide computer network called the Internet further spurred the spread of data communications.

Computers communicate in two main ways: through modems and through networks. Modems enable computers to use telephone lines, cellular connections (the kind that mobile telephones use), or even satellite links to connect to other computers to exchange data. Networks connect computers directly (known as a **direct connection**) at higher speeds, either through special wiring or by some form of wireless transmission.

For these reasons, networking technology has become the most explosive area of growth in the entire computer industry. This is because the demand for larger, faster, higher-capacity networks has increased as businesses have realized the value of networking their computer systems.

Networks come in many varieties. When most people think of a network, they imagine several computers in a single location sharing documents and devices such as printers. Networks, however, can include all the computers and devices in a department, a building, or multiple buildings spread out over a wide geographic area. By interconnecting many individual networks into a massive single network (like the Internet), people around the world can share information as though they were across the hall from one another. The information they share can be much more than text documents. Many networks carry voice, audio, and video traffic, enabling videoconferencing and types of collaboration that were not possible just a few years ago.

THE USES OF A NETWORK

The word *network* has several definitions. The most commonly used meaning describes the methods people use to maintain relationships with friends and business contacts. Applied to computers, the term has a similar definition. A **network** is a way to connect computers together so that they can communicate, exchange information, and pool resources.

In business, networks have revolutionized the use of computer technology. Many businesses that used to rely on a centralized system with a mainframe and a collection of terminals (input/output devices that are connected to mainframes and do not have the same features as PCs) now use computer networks in which every employee who needs a computer has a personal computer connected to the network. Computer technology and expertise are no longer centralized in a company's mainframe and information systems departments. The technology and expertise are distributed throughout the organization among a network of computers and computer-literate users.

In education, schools have also shifted to strategies built around networked personal computers. These include LANs (local area networks), such as a network that connects the computers and printers in a computer lab, and WANs (wide area networks)—especially the Internet.

Whatever the setting, networks provide tremendous benefits. Four of the most compelling benefits are:

- Allowing simultaneous access to critical programs and data
- Allowing people to share peripheral devices, such as printers and scanners
- Streamlining personal communication with e-mail
- Making the backup process easier

The following sections examine each of these advantages in more detail.

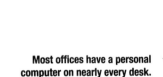

NORTON Online

For more information on the **basics of networks**, visit this book's Web site at www.glencoe.com/norton/online

Most offices have a personal computer on nearly every desk. The computers are connected to form a network.

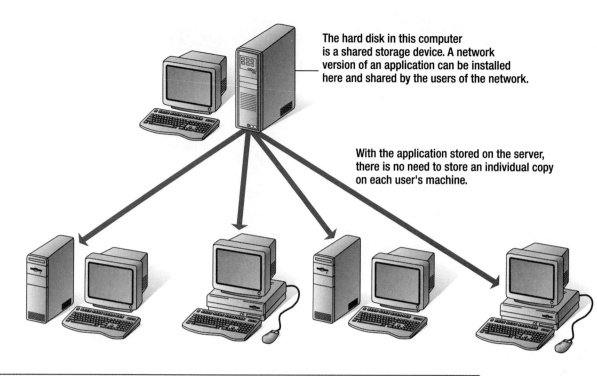

The hard disk in this computer is a shared storage device. A network version of an application can be installed here and shared by the users of the network.

With the application stored on the server, there is no need to store an individual copy on each user's machine.

Figure 7.1
Using a network version of an application.

Simultaneous Access

It is a fact of business computing that multiple employees, using a computer network, often need access to the same data at the same time. Without a network that enables file sharing, employees keep separate copies of data on different hard disks, and universally updating the data becomes very difficult. As soon as a change is made to the data on one machine, a discrepancy arises, and it quickly becomes difficult to know which set of data is correct. Storing data that is used by more than one person on a shared storage device makes it possible to solve the problem.

It is also true that most office workers use the same programs. One solution to purchasing separate copies of applications for every worker is to use **network versions** of programs. These programs are designed so that only one copy of the application needs to be stored on the **network server** (called an **application server**), with a minimum number of supporting files copied to each employee's computer. A network server is a large central computer. (If the server stores data files for users to access, it is commonly called a **file server**.)When employees need to use a program, they simply load it from a shared storage device into the RAM of their own desktop computers, as shown in Figure 7.1.

A network version of a software application is also a more efficient use of hard disk space because many users can access a single shared copy instead of storing separate copies on each user's hard disk.

Some software designed for networks is classified as **groupware**. This type of software includes scheduling software, e-mail, and document-management software. Groupware allows multiple users on a network to cooperate on projects. Users can work on the same documents, share their insights,

NORTON *Notebook*

What Do the FDA, the YMCA, and the Stock Market Have in Common?

Answer: A network. In this computer age, activities that seem as different as night and day often share the common thread of being network-based. Networks of all kinds connect our world today, and they provide the means to accomplish widely divergent tasks never before possible. Here are some interesting examples.

Global Dealing with the FDA One of the responsibilities of the FDA (Food and Drug Administration) is to review and approve new drugs for the market. Pharmaceutical companies looking to patent a new drug must conduct lengthy and costly research to determine the effectiveness and possible side effects of the new drug and then submit the research to the FDA for final approval.

Companies want to streamline and speed up the approval process to turn investment of research and development time into actual products, which will allow them to sell the drug. The cost and time associated with dealing with the FDA is high, involving huge volumes of reports and forms that get submitted to the FDA.

Stock brokers rely on real-time transactions over networks to ensure trading continues without a glitch.

Now, the FDA has introduced SMART (Submission Management and Review Tracking Program). The SMART initiative lets pharmaceutical companies submit forms and product applications electronically over the Internet.

The FDA's Center for Drug Evaluation and Research (DER) uses a client/server network system that is based on Documentum's document-management system, Adobe Acrobat documents, and an Oracle 7 database running on a Digital Equipment Alpha-based VMS and Microsoft Windows NT network server. For one company, Baxtor Hyland, the FDA electronic submission network has saved about 30,000 pages of reports. Now Baxtor Hyland needs to submit only three electronic copies of the primary report.

Network at the YMCA Networks help branches of the San Francisco YMCA stay in touch and share centralized information. The network uses 180 Wyse Winterm workstations to connect 13 sites via a frame-relay network. It uses a Hewlett-Packard LC 133 network server at the central YMCA office, plus HP servers at each site to provide access to centrally stored information.

In the past, each YMCA office connected to a central mainframe running UNIX. This resulted in redundant work processes as well as increased costs for maintenance. The new system runs Windows NT, Lotus Notes, and Microsoft Office. Not only will it save an estimated $1 million over the next five years, but the YMCA hopes the new and improved system will improve its point-of-sale service and enhance its image.

Stock Market Updates The Bank of Boston uses a network and special software to transfer live TV news coverage to its traders' PCs on the stock market trading room floor. This way, the traders can keep abreast of up-to-date news on TV via their PCs without the chaos and noise that would be caused by numerous TV monitors stationed in the trading room.

Until recently, TV monitors were mounted on the walls for traders to watch breaking news events that affect fast-changing markets. These TVs, necessary as they were, often created problems, including physical obstructions, logistical cable nightmares, and increases to the already deafening noise level.

Television-capable PCs with direct hookups to cable TV were introduced in 1994 and are now widely available. However, the Bank of Boston, a multinational banking firm, wanted to upgrade its present equipment instead of buying new computers.

The solution came in the form of a unique software program called InSoft Network Television (INTV). This program transfers either live or recorded digital video from a server to client machines over a network, allowing traders to watch cable TV in a small window on their monitors while simultaneously running other programs.

Now, traders have their own private TVs at their fingertips, complete with remote control to select channels and adjust volume. Traders say they usually have the news running all the time and are able to respond to market changes immediately.

and keep each other abreast of their schedules so that meetings can be set up easily. Lotus Notes and Microsoft Exchange are perhaps the best-known examples of groupware, although there are many competitors.

Shared Peripheral Devices

Perhaps the best incentive for small businesses to link computers in a network is to share peripheral devices, especially expensive ones such as laser printers, large hard disks, and scanners, as shown in Figure 7.2.

Many high-quality laser printers cost more than $2,000, so it is not very cost-effective for each user to have one. Sharing a laser printer on a network makes the cost much less prohibitive. By using a process called **spooling**, multiple users can send multiple print jobs to a printer. (Spooling can also occur when a computer is not connected to a network, and multiple print jobs are sent to a non-networked printer.) When users print a document or other file to a networked printer (known as a **print job**), each job is stored in a temporary spool file on the file server. As

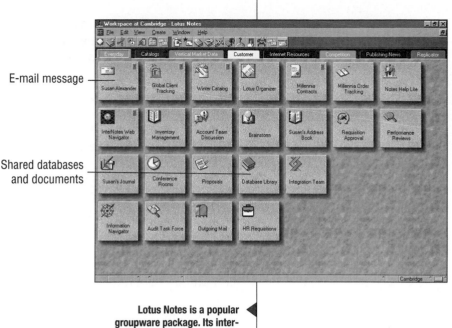

E-mail message

Shared databases and documents

Lotus Notes is a popular groupware package. Its interface gives users access to shared documents, e-mail, and other resources.

For more information on **Microsoft Exchange**, visit this book's Web site at www.glencoe.com/norton/online

Figure 7.2
Computers on a LAN sharing a laser printer, scanner, and large hard disk.

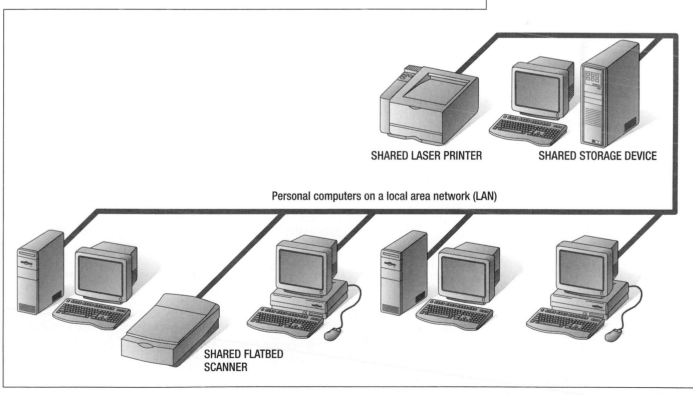

SHARED LASER PRINTER   SHARED STORAGE DEVICE

Personal computers on a local area network (LAN)

SHARED FLATBED SCANNER

the printer finishes printing a current job, the file server sends the next spooled job to the printer so that it can be printed. Typically, a **banner page** is printed at the beginning of a new job to separate print jobs.

Personal Communication

One of the most far-reaching applications of data communications is **electronic mail (e-mail)**, a system for exchanging written messages (and increasingly, voice and video messages) through a network. E-mail is something of a cross between the postal system and a telephone answering system. In an e-mail system, each user has a unique address. To send someone an e-mail message, you enter the person's e-mail address and then type the message. When you are finished, the message is sent to the e-mail address. The next time that user accesses the e-mail system, it reports that mail has arrived. Some systems notify the recipient as each message arrives by flashing a message on the computer screen or beeping. After reading the message, the recipient can save it, delete it, forward it to someone else, or respond by sending back a reply message. Figure 7.3 shows the process for sending and receiving e-mail.

NORTON Online

For more information on **electronic mail**, visit this book's Web site at **www.glencoe.com/norton/online**

In addition to sending a page or pages of mail text, many systems allow you to attach data files—such as spreadsheet files or word processed documents—to your message. This means that an e-mail system allows people to share files even when they do not have access to the same storage devices. For example, a local area network also may have a connection to a large information network, such as America Online, Microsoft Network, or the Internet. In this case, the person on the local network can share files with anyone on the large information network.

E-mail is both efficient and inexpensive. Users can send written messages without worrying about whether the other user's computer is currently running. On centralized networks, the message is delivered almost instantaneously, and the cost of sending the message is negligible. E-mail has provided the modern world with an entirely new and immensely valuable form of communication.

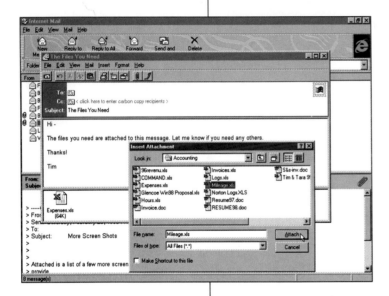

Attaching a document to an e-mail message is a simple way to trade files with coworkers.

In addition to e-mail, the spread of networking technology is adding to the popularity of teleconferencing and videoconferencing. A **teleconference** is a virtual meeting in which a group of people in different locations conducts discussions by typing messages to each other. Each message can be seen by all the other people in the teleconference. Teleconference software has become more sophisticated, gradually adding such features as a shared scratch pad where diagrams or pictures can be drawn or electronically pasted.

The spread of networking is adding to the popularity of collaborative software, which allows users to connect with one another over LAN or modem links so that they can see what's happening on other users' computers. It lets people send messages, exchange files, and sometimes even work on the same document at the same time. Figure 7.4 shows Timbuktu, a collaborative program, being used by a Windows computer to access a Macintosh through a LAN.

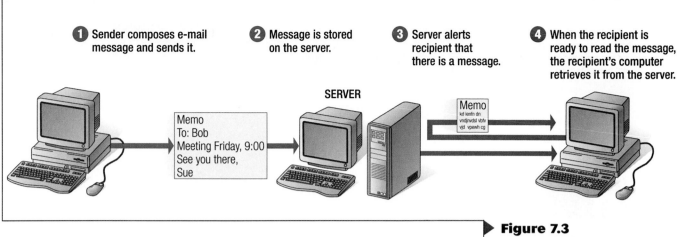

1 Sender composes e-mail message and sends it.

2 Message is stored on the server.

3 Server alerts recipient that there is a message.

4 When the recipient is ready to read the message, the recipient's computer retrieves it from the server.

Figure 7.3
Sending and receiving e-mail.

If users have the necessary hardware and software, they can actually see and speak to each other as they meet online (instead of merely typing messages). This is a process known as **videoconferencing**, as shown in Figure 7.5.

Easier Backup

In business, data is extremely valuable, so making sure that employees back up their data is critical. One way to address this problem is to keep all valuable data on a shared storage device that employees access through a network. Often the person managing the network has the responsibility of making regular backups of the data on the shared storage device from a single, central location. Network backup software is also available that enables backups to be made of files stored on employees' hard drives. This way, the files do not have to be copied to the central server to be backed up.

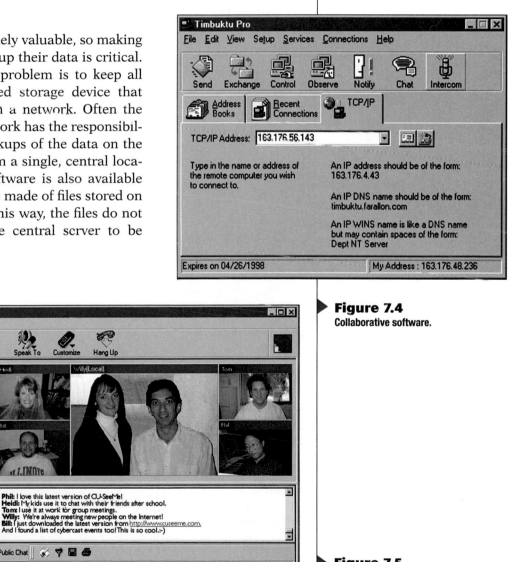

Figure 7.4
Collaborative software.

Figure 7.5
A group of people participating in an online videoconference.

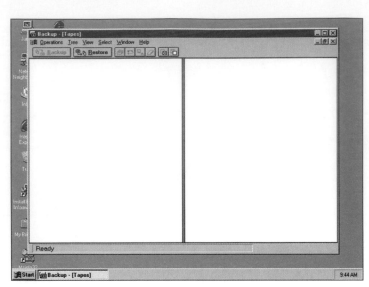

HOW NETWORKS ARE STRUCTURED

To understand the different types of networks and how they operate, it is important to know something about how networks can be structured. First, there are two main types of networks, distinguished mainly by geography: local area networks (LANs) and wide area networks (WANs). Second, any of these types can be classified according to the logical relationships among the computers. There are networks that use servers (such as file servers and application servers) and those that do not (called peer-to-peer networks).

Local Area Networks

A network of computers located relatively near each other and connected by a cable (or a small radio transmitter) is a **local area network (LAN)**. A LAN can consist of just two or three PCs connected together to share resources, or it can include several hundred computers of different kinds. Any network that exists within a single building, or even a group of adjacent buildings, is considered a LAN.

Figure 7.6
Accessing shared storage devices on a network.

A LAN permits all the computers connected to it to share hardware, software, and data. The most commonly shared resources are disk storage devices and printers. To LAN users, the network is (or should be) completely transparent, which means that the shared devices on it seem to be directly connected to the user's computer as if they were merely peripherals. For example, a file server should appear to the LAN user simply as another disk drive, as shown in Figure 7.6.

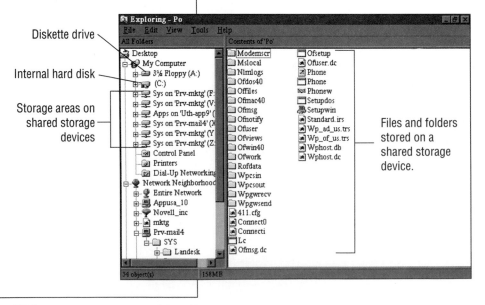

Diskette drive

Internal hard disk

Storage areas on shared storage devices

Files and folders stored on a shared storage device.

Techview

Remote Network Administration

One goal of a network administrator is to ensure that users have access to the networked data and resources they need to complete their jobs. For many companies, this is a 24-hour, 7-day-a-week process. Even when the administrator (or team of administrators) leaves for the night or weekend, the network must still operate.

There are many times, however, when the network fails to complete an operation, a user can't log on, or a similar failure occurs. The network administrator must then fix the problem—and fix it fast!

Remote Administration to the Rescue For those times when network administrators must be out of the office but still stay in contact with the network, **remote administration** technologies help the administrator keep in touch with the network without physically being in the same location. Remote administration enables administrators to fix server problems, add and remove clients, change passwords, and perform other administration tasks.

This administrator is connecting to the company network via an Internet connection and Web Administration for Windows NT Server.

Remote administration technologies include the hardware, software, and infrastructure necessary to administer and manage a network from a remote location. This remote location may be a remote office, a home office, a garage, or even a hotel room—any place where a phone line is accessible. Administrators can dial into their network using modems and common telephone lines. Or they can use Internet connections to connect to their servers and perform administration duties.

Web Administration for Window NT Server A popular remote administration tool for networks using Microsoft Windows NT 4.0 servers is the Web Administration for Microsoft Windows NT Server software. It enables administrators to remotely administer a Windows NT Server computer using a World Wide Web browser on a Windows, Apple Macintosh, or UNIX platform.

Web Administration for Windows NT Server works by creating Web pages on the server that include forms administrators can use to administer that particular server. The administrator simply needs to connect to the Internet, use a Web browser to connect to the server, and navigate through the Web-based forms to complete required administration tasks, including:

- Viewing/changing user properties
- Adding/removing user accounts
- Changing user passwords
- Managing individual and group accounts

A New Breed of Administrators Remote administration technologies have not only changed the way administrators manage their own network but also have created a new set of services for consulting firms to offer. With remote administration, small to medium sized businesses can have off-site, full-time administrators supervise their networks. The business does not have to hire a full-time employee to manage its LAN, saving money for other expenses.

Companies that offer off-site remote administration provide a wide range of remote-management services, including:

- Automated system backups
- Process and security monitoring
- Performance tuning
- Connectivity management

In the future, you may never see your network administrator unless you encounter a problem involving the physical layer of the network, such as a cable problem or network adapter failure.

In addition to shared hardware, LANs can provide all the other benefits of networks, including simultaneous access, enhanced personal communication, and easier backup.

Connecting Networks

It is often helpful to connect different LANs. For example, two different departments in a large business may each have its own LAN, but if there is enough need for data communication between the departments, then it may be necessary to create a link between the two LANs.

To understand how this can be accomplished, you must first know that, on a network, data is sent in small groups called packets. A **packet** is a group of bits that includes a header, payload, and control elements that are transmitted together (see Figure 7.7). You can think of a packet as one sentence or a group of numbers being sent at the same time.

The payload is the part that contains the actual data being sent. The header contains information about the type of data in the payload, the source and destination of the data, and a sequence number so that data from multiple packets can be reassembled at the receiving computer in the proper order.

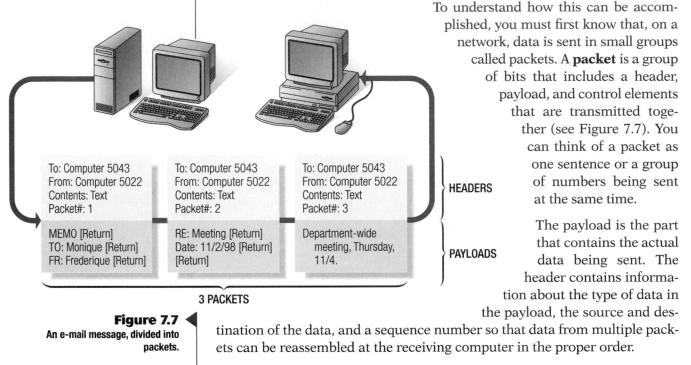

Figure 7.7
An e-mail message, divided into packets.

Each LAN is governed by a **protocol**, which is a set of rules and formats for sending and receiving data. If two LANs are built around the same communication rules, then they can be connected with a bridge or a router. A **bridge** is a relatively simple device that looks at the information in each packet header and rebroadcasts data that is traveling from one LAN to another. A **router** is a more complicated device that stores the addressing information of each computer on each LAN and uses this information to act like an electronic post office, sorting data and sending it along the most expedient route to its destination. Bridges forward data from one network to another but are not suitable in many large organizations because of the amount of packets bridges send to all networks connected to the bridge. Routers, on the other hand, send packets only to the desired network, reducing overall network traffic.

In some cases, a router can also be used to connect two different types of LANs. However, a router only "routes" data: it knows how to send it to the correct location, and that's all. If you need a more sophisticated connection between networks, you need a **gateway**, a computer system that connects two networks and translates information from one to the other. Packets from different networks have different kinds of information in their headers, and the information can be in different formats. The gateway can take a packet

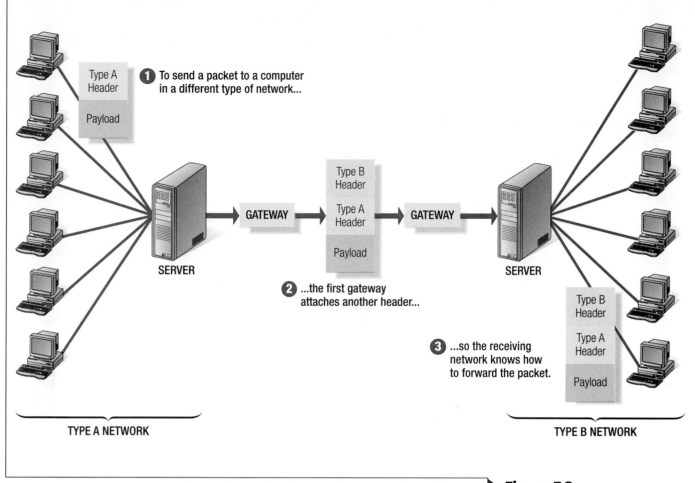

1 To send a packet to a computer in a different type of network...

Type A Header

Payload

Type B Header

Type A Header

Payload

GATEWAY

GATEWAY

2 ...the first gateway attaches another header...

3 ...so the receiving network knows how to forward the packet.

Type B Header

Type A Header

Payload

SERVER

SERVER

TYPE A NETWORK

TYPE B NETWORK

Figure 7.8
How a gateway forwards a packet from one type of network to a different type of network.

from one type of network, read the header, and then encapsulate the entire packet into a new one, adding a header that is understood by the second network, as shown in Figure 7.8.

Wide Area Networks

Typically, a **wide area network (WAN)** is two or more LANs connected together, generally across a wide geographical area using high-speed or dedicated telephone lines. For example, a company may have its corporate headquarters and manufacturing facility in one city and its marketing office in another. Each site needs resources, data, and programs locally, but it also needs to share data with the other site. To accomplish this feat of data communication, the company can attach a router to each LAN to create a WAN. Figure 7.9 shows a typical WAN connecting two LANs.

The Internet is the ultimate WAN because it connects many thousands of computers and LANs around the world. Most of the commercial online services and large bulletin boards were not WANs when they started out because, typically, users dialed in to a single computer or a group of computers housed at a single site. (Commercial online services are businesses you connect to via a modem that offer their own internal products and services, one of which may be Internet access.) However, today most of these systems provide connections to other specialized services and to the Internet, so they are now more like WANs.

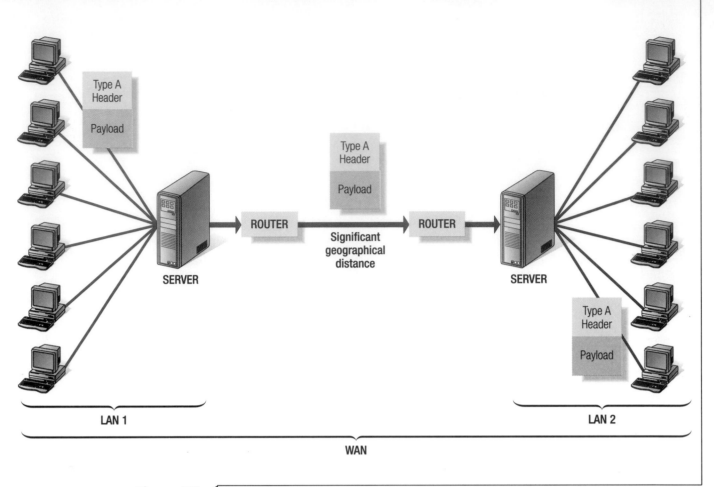

Figure 7.9
Combining two LANs to form a WAN.

File Server Networks

Describing a network as a LAN or a WAN gives a sense of the physical area the network covers. However, this classification does not tell you anything about how individual computers on a network, called **nodes**, interact with other computers on the network.

Many networks include not only nodes but also a central computer with a large hard disk that is used for shared storage. This computer is known as the file server, network server, or simply, server. Files and programs used by more than one user (at different nodes) are generally kept on the server.

One relatively simple implementation of a network with nodes and a file server is a **file server network**. This is a hierarchical arrangement in which each node can have access to the files on the server but not necessarily to files on other nodes. When a node needs information on the server, it requests the entire file containing the information. In other words, the file server is used simply to store and forward (send) files (see Figure 7.10).

Client/Server Networks

One popular type of server-based network is **client/server** computing, a hierarchical strategy in which individual computers share the processing and storage workload with a central server. This type of arrangement requires specialized software for both the individual node and the network

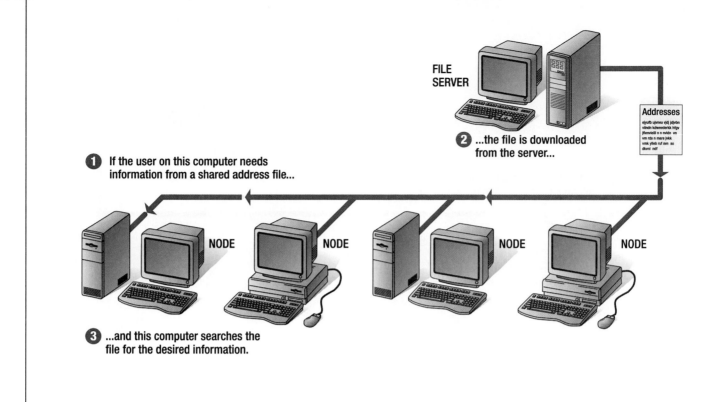

① If the user on this computer needs information from a shared address file...

② ...the file is downloaded from the server...

FILE SERVER

Addresses

③ ...and this computer searches the file for the desired information.

NODE NODE NODE NODE

Figure 7.10
A simple LAN with a file server.

server. It does not, however, require any specific type of network. Client/ server software can be used on LANs or WANs and a single client/server program can be used on a LAN where all the other software is based on a simple file server relationship.

The most common example of client/server computing involves a database that can be accessed by many different computers on the network. The database is stored on the network server. Also stored on the server is the server portion of the database management system (DBMS), the program that allows users to add information to, or extract it from, the database. The user's computer (which can be called the node, workstation, or client) stores and runs the client portion of the DBMS.

Now, suppose that the user wants information from the database. For example, suppose that the database is a list of customer purchases, and the user needs to know the names of customers in the Wichita area who made purchases of more than $500. The user uses the client software to describe the information that is needed and sends the request to the server. The server software searches the database, collects the relevant customer names, and sends them back to the client. The client software then presents the information to the user in a way that makes sense. This process is shown in Figure 7.11.

Client/server software is valuable to large, modern organizations because it distributes processing and storage workloads among resources efficiently. This means that users get the information they need faster.

Client/server computing is also a commonly used model on the Internet. Users typically have client software that provides an easily used interface for interacting with this giant WAN. Other types of processing, such as receiving,

NORTON Online

For more information on **client/server technology,** visit this book's Web site at **www.glencoe.com/norton/online**

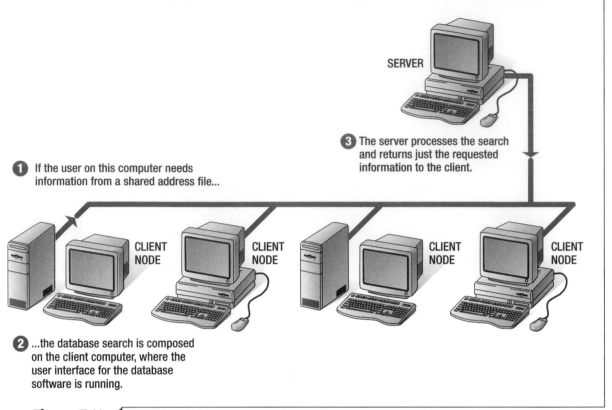

1 If the user on this computer needs information from a shared address file...

3 The server processes the search and returns just the requested information to the client.

SERVER

CLIENT NODE

CLIENT NODE

CLIENT NODE

CLIENT NODE

2 ...the database search is composed on the client computer, where the user interface for the database software is running.

Figure 7.11
Distribution of processing in a client/server computing model.

storing, and sending e-mail messages, are carried out by remote computers running the server part of the relevant software.

Peer-to-Peer Computing

A third arrangement is a **peer-to-peer network**, in which all nodes on the network have equal relationships to all others, and all have similar types of software. Typically, each node has access to at least some of the resources on all other nodes, so the relationship is nonhierarchical. If they are set up correctly, Windows 95 and its predecessor, Windows for Workgroups, give users access to the hard disks and printers attached to other computers in the network. A peer-to-peer network is shown in Figure 7.12.

In addition, some high-end peer-to-peer networks allow **distributed computing**, which enables users to draw on the processing power of other computers in the network. That means people can transfer tasks that take a lot of CPU power—such as creating computer software—to available computers, leaving their own machines free for other work.

Peer-to-peer LANs are commonly set up in small organizations (fewer than 50 employees) or in schools, where the primary benefit of a network is shared storage, printers, and enhanced communication. Where large databases are used, LANs are more likely to include client/server relationships.

A peer-to-peer network can also include a network server. In this case, a peer-to-peer LAN is similar to a file server network. The only difference between them is that the peer-to-peer network gives users greater access to the other nodes than a file server network does (see Figure 7.12).

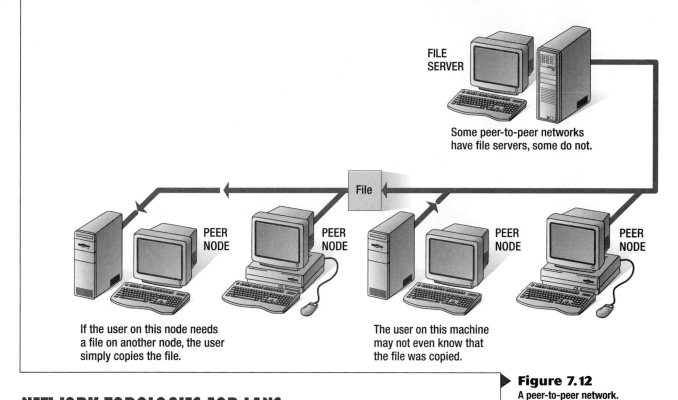

Some peer-to-peer networks have file servers, some do not.

FILE SERVER

PEER NODE

PEER NODE

PEER NODE

PEER NODE

File

If the user on this node needs a file on another node, the user simply copies the file.

The user on this machine may not even know that the file was copied.

▶ **Figure 7.12**
A peer-to-peer network.

NETWORK TOPOLOGIES FOR LANS

In addition to the size of a network and the relationship between the nodes and the server, another distinguishing feature among LANs is the **topology**—the physical layout of the cables that connect the nodes of the network. There are three basic topologies: bus, star, and ring. Network designers consider a number of factors in determining which topology, or combination of topologies, to use. Among the factors considered are the type of computers currently installed, the type of cabling currently in place (if any), the cost of the components and services required to implement the network, the distance between each computer, and the speed with which data must travel around the network.

The Bus Topology

A **bus network**, like the bus of a computer itself, is a single conduit to which all the network nodes and peripheral devices are attached (see Figure 7.13). Nodes on one type of bus network, Ethernet, transmit data at any time, regardless of any data being sent by other nodes. If one set of data happens

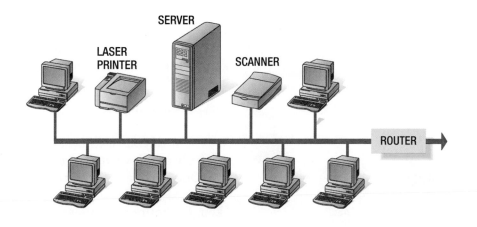

SERVER

LASER PRINTER

SCANNER

ROUTER

NORTON Online

For more information on **cabling design**, visit this book's Web site at **www.glencoe.com/norton/online**

▶ **Figure 7.13**
A LAN with bus topology.

Figure 7.14 ◀
A LAN with star topology.

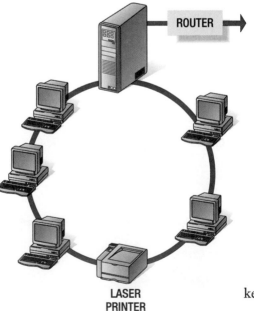

to collide with another set of data transmitted by other nodes—that is, if two nodes try to send data at the same time—each node waits a small, random amount of time and then attempts to retransmit the data.

Although the bus topology is one of the most common, it has inherent disadvantages. Keeping data transmissions from colliding requires extra circuitry and software, and a broken connection can bring down (or "crash") all or part of the network, rendering it inoperable so that users cannot share data and peripherals until the connection is repaired.

The Star Topology

A **star network** places a hub in the center of the network nodes. Groups of data are routed through the central hub to their destinations. This scheme has an advantage in that the hub monitors traffic and prevents collisions, and a broken connection does not affect the rest of the network. If you lose the hub, however, the entire network goes down. Figure 7.14 shows the star topology.

The Ring Topology

The **ring topology** connects the nodes of the network in a circular chain in which each node is connected to the next. The final node in the chain connects to the first to complete the ring, as shown in Figure 7.15.

With this methodology, each node examines data that is sent through the ring. If the data is not addressed to the node examining it, that node passes it along to the next node in the ring.

The ring topology has a substantial advantage over the bus topology. There's no danger of collisions because data always flows in one direction. One drawback to the ring, however, is that if a connection is broken, the entire network goes down.

NORTON
Online

For more information on the different types of cabling used in networks, visit this book's Web site at
www.glencoe.com/norton/online

Figure 7.15 ◀
A LAN with ring topology.

LASER
PRINTER

NETWORK MEDIA AND HARDWARE

No matter what their structure, all networks rely on **media** to link their nodes and/or servers together. You may recall that when referring to data storage, the term *media* refers to materials for storing data, such as magnetic disks and tape. In network communications, however, *media* refers to the wires, cables, and other means by which data travels from its source to its destination. The most common media for data communication are twisted-pair wire, coaxial cable, fiber-optic cable, and wireless links.

Twisted-Pair Wire

Twisted-pair wire normally consists of four or eight copper strands of wire, individually insulated in plastic, then twisted around each other in braided pairs and bound together in another layer of plastic insulation. (There were originally just two wires, rather than four or eight, hence the name *twisted-pair.*) Except for the plastic coating, nothing shields this type of wire from outside interference, so it is also called *unshielded twisted-pair (UTP)* wire. Some twisted-pair wire is further encased in a metal sheath and therefore is called *shielded twisted-pair (STP)* wire. Figure 7.16 shows what UTP and STP look like.

Indoor wiring for telephones uses twisted-pair wire, so twisted-pair is often called *telephone wire.* Because it was readily available and inexpensive, telephone wire gained early favor as a conduit for data communications. Today, however, some twisted-pair wire used for communication is made to more demanding specifications than voice-grade telephone wire.

Sometimes network media are compared by the amount of data they can transmit each second. The difference between the highest and lowest frequencies of a transmission channel is known as **bandwidth**. As more users transmit data over a network, the bandwidth reduces, thereby slowing down all transmissions. Bandwidth is expressed in cycles per second (hertz) or in bits per second. Twisted-pair wire was once considered a low-bandwidth media, but networks based on twisted-pair wires now support transmission speeds up to 150 megabits per second (Mbps), and even faster speeds are on the horizon.

Coaxial Cable

Coaxial cable, sometimes called **coax** (pronounced "co-axe"), is widely used for cable TV and is used in some networks (however, the connectors are different for TV and networks). There are two conductors in coaxial cable. One is a single wire in the center of the cable, and the other is a wire mesh shield that surrounds the first wire with an insulator in between (see Figure 7.17).

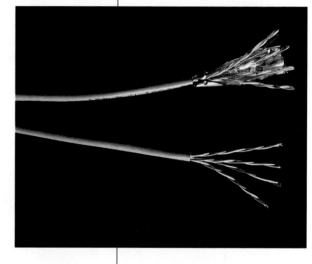

▶ **Figure 7.16**
Shielded (top) and unshielded (bottom) twisted-pair wire is the most common medium for computer networks.

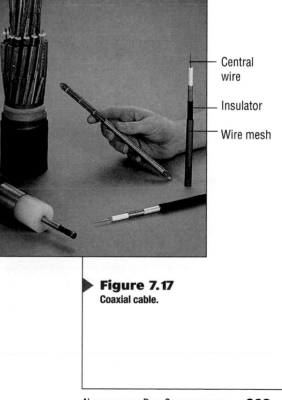

— Central wire

— Insulator

— Wire mesh

▶ **Figure 7.17**
Coaxial cable.

Coaxial cable can carry more data than older types of twisted-pair wiring, and it is less susceptible to interference from other wiring. However, it is also more expensive and has become less popular as twisted-pair technology has improved. Two types of coaxial cable are used with networks: thick and thin. Thick coax is the older standard and is seldom installed in new networks.

Fiber-Optic Cable

A **fiber-optic cable** is a thin strand of glass that transmits pulsating beams of light rather than electric frequencies (see Figure 7.18). When one end of the strand is exposed to light, the strand carries the light all the way to the other end—bending around corners with only a minute loss of energy along the way.

Figure 7.18
Fiber-optic cable.

Strands of glass

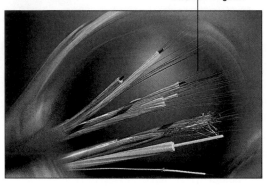

Because light travels at a much higher frequency than electrical signals, fiber-optic cable can easily carry data at more than a billion bits per second—usually 1300 Mbps. Fiber-optic cable is also immune to the electromagnetic interference that is a problem for copper wire.

The disadvantage of fiber-optic cable is that it is more expensive than twisted-pair and coax, and it is more difficult to install because it does not bend around corners as easily. As costs have come down, however, fiber-optic cable has become increasingly popular, and it is now revolutionizing a number of communications industries. Telephone and cable television companies, especially, have been moving from twisted-pair wire and coaxial cables to fiber-optic cables.

Wireless Links

Today, wireless communication is competing with twisted-pair, coaxial, and fiber-optic cable. The advantage of wireless communication is the flexibility that it offers in terms of the network layout. **Wireless communication** relies on radio signals or infrared signals for transmitting data. It is important to remember that radio frequencies form part of the electromagnetic spectrum, including X-rays, ultraviolet light, the visible spectrum, infrared, microwaves, and the longer waves that are used by commercial radio stations.

This device uses infrared light to connect a laptop computer to a LAN.

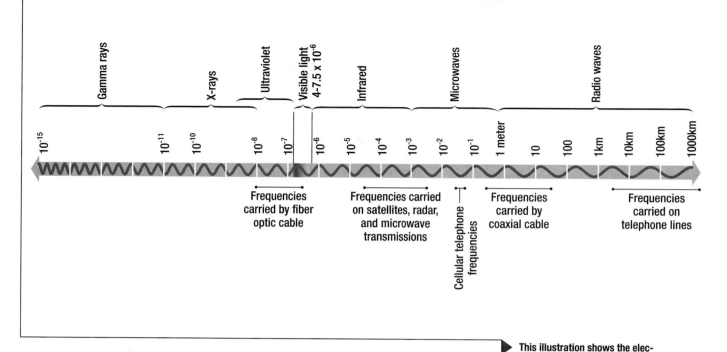

Gamma rays | X-rays | Ultraviolet | Visible light 4-7.5 x 10⁻⁶ | Infrared | Microwaves | Radio waves

10^{-15} 10^{-11} 10^{-10} 10^{-8} 10^{-7} 10^{-6} 10^{-5} 10^{-4} 10^{-3} 10^{-2} 10^{-1} 1 meter 10 100 1km 10km 100km 1000km

Frequencies carried by fiber optic cable

Frequencies carried on satellites, radar, and microwave transmissions

Cellular telephone frequencies

Frequencies carried by coaxial cable

Frequencies carried on telephone lines

There are four common uses of wireless communication in networks:

1_ Office LANs can use radio signals to transmit data between nodes.

2_ Laptops can be equipped with cellular telephone equipment and a modem so that business people can stay in touch with the office network, no matter where they travel.

3_ Corporate WANs often use microwave transmission to connect two LANs within the same metropolitan area. If a company has buildings on opposite sides of town, it can set up a microwave antenna on top of each one to move data back and forth quickly. This type of communication, however, requires an unobstructed line of sight between the two antennas.

▶ This illustration shows the electromagnetic spectrum, which includes not only the visible spectrum but also wavelengths longer than AM radio and up to Gamma rays.

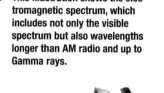

NORTON Online

For more information on **wireless networking**, visit this book's Web site at **www.glencoe.com/norton/online**

▶ This woman is logging on to her office network by attaching the modem in her notebook computer to a cellular phone.

Connecting LANs using microwave requires a direct line of sight between the two antennas. ◀

4_ WANs that cover long distances often use satellites and microwave communication. Television and telephone companies have used satellites for many years, but big businesses use them for their computer networks, as well.

The Network Interface Card, Network Protocols, and Cabling Specifications

Cables or radio waves may link a network together, but each computer on the network still needs hardware to control the flow of data. The device that performs this function is the network interface card (NIC). The NIC is a type of expansion board—a printed circuit board that fits into one of the computer's expansion slots and provides a port on the back of the PC to which the network cable attaches. The computer also requires network software, which tells the computer how to use the NIC.

Both the network software and the NIC have to adhere to a network protocol, which is a set of standards for communication. A **network protocol** is like a language computers use for communicating data. For computers to share data, they must speak the same language. As is often the case with computer technologies, protocols are in a continual state of flux. Whenever someone comes up with a new standard, someone else invents another that does the same job faster and more reliably. The most common protocols used in networks are TCP/IP, IPX/SPX, and NetBEUI.

Another specification of a network is to determine the network technology or cabling equipment used to create a LAN. The most common types of network technology include Ethernet (which also includes Fast Ethernet), Token Ring, and ARCnet. Each of these is designed for a certain kind of network topology and has certain standard features.

Ethernet

Currently, **Ethernet** is the most common network technology used. Ethernet was originally designed for a bus topology and thick coaxial cable. More recent implementations have moved to the star topology and twisted-pair wires.

Ethernet requires each computer or workstation on the network to wait its turn to send data. When a computer needs to send data to another computer or to a peripheral device, it must first determine whether the network is available. If the network is in use by another node, the computer waits a tiny fraction of a second and tries again. If two nodes inadvertently transmit simultaneously, the conflict is detected and they retransmit one at a time. This approach to network communication is called CSMA/CD (Carrier Sense Multiple Access/Collision Detection). As you might guess, when many computers are on an Ethernet network, access time can become noticeably delayed.

The original implementations of Ethernet, which used coaxial cable, were called 10Base-5 and 10Base-2. The most popular implementation of Ethernet currently is called **10Base-T**. It uses a star topology and twisted-pair wires and can achieve transmission speeds up to 10 Mbps.

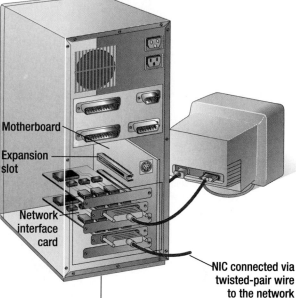

Motherboard
Expansion slot
Network interface card

NIC connected via twisted-pair wire to the network

Fast Ethernet

100Base-T, also known as **Fast Ethernet**, is available using the same media and topology as Ethernet, but different network interface cards are used to achieve speeds of up to 100 Mbps. The 3COM EtherLink XL 10/100 adapter is an example of a network interface card used to achieve 100 Mbps LAN speeds. Hewlett-Packard's 100Base-VG competes with 100Base-T. Still other implementations of Ethernet are pushing transmission speeds even higher.

Token Ring

IBM's network technology is the **Token Ring**. The controlling hardware in a Token Ring network transmits an electronic *token*—a small set of data that includes an address—to each node on the network many times each second. If the token is not currently in use, a computer can copy data into the token and set the address where the data should be sent. The token then continues around the ring. Each computer along the way looks at the address until the token reaches the computer with the address that was recorded in the token. The receiving computer then copies the contents of the token and resets the token status to empty.

Token Ring networks have the advantage of data traveling through the ring in one direction in a controlled manner. With this approach, data cannot collide, so a complex scheme like CSMA/CD is not necessary. However, the network hardware is not cheap; Token-Ring adapter cards can cost as much as five times more than other types of network adapters. Token Ring networks once operated at either 4 or 16 Mbits per second, but as with Ethernet, new technology has pushed the transmission rate up to 100 Mbits per second.

NORTON
Online

For more information on **Fast Ethernet**, visit this book's Web site at www.glencoe.com/norton/online

ARCnet

ARCnet (Attached Resource Computer network) has both a topology and networking technology all its own. ARCnet uses either twisted-pair wire or coaxial cable, and the star topology is formed with hubs attached to the network.

The original ARCnet protocol was very slow, but it became popular because it was inexpensive, reliable, and easy to set up and to expand. Fast ARCnet, like Fast Ethernet, increased the transmission rate to 100 Mbits per second and includes the capability to use fiber-optic cable.

NETWORK SOFTWARE

Most of the networking terms you have seen so far—with the exception of the protocols discussed in the previous section—have referred to hardware. As with every other part of the computer system, however, there must be software to control the hardware. The group of programs that manages the resources on the network is often called the **network operating system**, or **NOS**.

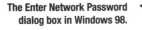

The Enter Network Password dialog box in Windows 98.

Enter Network Password

Enter your network password for Microsoft Networking.

OK

Cancel

User name: edulaney

Password:

One of the most popular NOS in terms of number of installations, NetWare (recently renamed IntranetWare), from Novell, can be used to run networks with different topologies, including Ethernet, Token Ring, and ARCnet. NetWare also includes support for various hardware platforms, such as Mac, PC, and UNIX hosts and servers.

Some of the other popular NOSs include:

■ *Microsoft Windows NT Server.* Windows NT Server provides a graphical user interface to administer small and large networks. Many companies that have invested in Microsoft Windows 3.11, Windows 95, and Windows 98 use Windows NT Server as their NOS. Windows NT Server also interoperates with many other NOSs, including IntranetWare, AppleShare, and Artisoft LANtastic.

■ *Banyan VINES.* The VINES NOS is commonly found in installations that have large network infrastructures, such as the U.S. Marine Corps. This is because VINES is good at updating user information on multiple servers connected to each other on the same network.

■ *AppleShare.* AppleShare is used by Apple Macintosh users to network each other. AppleShare provides access to shared resources, such as printers and storage devices, and to centralized servers. In many installations, you'll find networks comprising AppleShare networks along with servers running other NOSs, such as Windows NT Server.

■ *Artisoft LANtastic.* LANtastic has garnered a large share of the peer-to-peer market, including small businesses that cannot afford the overhead of network servers or do not need a large network infrastructure. LANtastic 7 enables computers to share files, applications, printers, modems, and Internet access over a peer-to-peer network.

DATA COMMUNICATION OVER TELEPHONE LINES

Network hardware and software offer a way to establish ongoing data communication, generally over media (twisted-pair wire, coaxial cable, fiber-optic cable, and so forth) specifically set up for the network and known as *dedicated* media. The alternative to using dedicated media is to use the telephone system for data communication. This is possible because the telephone system is really just a giant electronic network owned by the telephone companies.

Although it is designed to carry two-way electronic information, the network of telephone lines is significantly different from a typical computer network. Remember, the phone system was originally designed to carry voice messages, which are analog signals. Increasingly, however, phone lines are being used to send digital data.

The reason for this trend is simple. By connecting your computer to the telephone, potentially you can send data to anyone else in the world who has a computer and telephone service, and you do not need to set up a network to do it. You simply pay the phone company for the time you spend connected to the other computer. This trend has important implications for users as well as for phone companies. Typically, the analog lines that carry voice signals are not very well suited for carrying data because the limit for transmission speeds over analog lines is only about .005 as fast as a 10Base-T Ethernet network. As a result, the phone companies now offer digital lines specifically designed for data communication.

Soon after the introduction of the PC, users recognized the value of trading data and software over telephone lines. In response to this user demand, Hayes Microcomputer Products, Inc., developed the first modem for personal computers, the Smartmodem. Introduced in 1978, the modem connected a computer to a standard telephone line and allowed the transmission of data. This technological innovation started an explosion of digital connectivity for both businesses and individual users.

NORTON Online

For more information on **modems**, visit this book's Web site at **www.glencoe.com/norton/online**

Modems

Although digital telephone lines are gaining popularity, most people still have analog phone lines attached to their homes and businesses. Attaching a computer to an analog phone line requires a modem, so it is important to know a few things about how modems work and what to look for when you buy one.

How a Modem Works

In standard phone service, a telephone converts the sound of your voice into an electric signal that flows through the phone wires. The telephone at the other end converts this electric signal back into sound, so that the person you are talking to can hear your voice. Both the sound wave and the telephone signal are analog signals—they vary continuously with the volume and pitch of the speakers' voices. Because a computer's "voice" is digital—consisting of on/off pulses representing 1s and 0s—the device called a modem (short for *modulator-demodulator*) is needed to translate these digital signals into analog signals

Hayes created the first modem for personal computers in 1978. It transmitted data at about .01 the speed of today's modems.

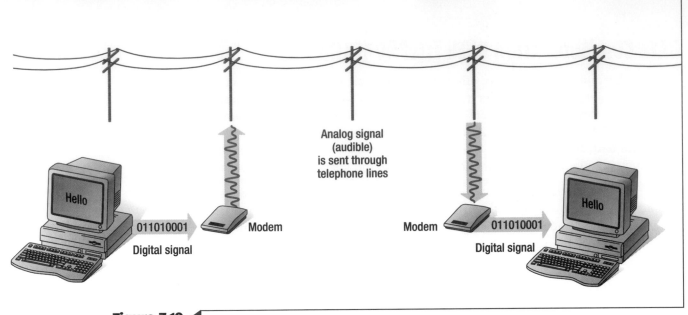

Analog signal
(audible)
is sent through
telephone lines

Hello

011010001

Modem

Digital signal

Modem

011010001

Hello

Digital signal

Figure 7.19
How modems connect computers
through telephone lines.

that can travel over standard phone lines. In its modulation phase, the modem turns the computer's digital signals into analog signals. In its demodulation phase, the reverse takes place. Figure 7.19 shows how computers communicate through modems and a phone connection.

Choosing a Modem

A modem can be a simple circuit board—an expansion card—that plugs into one of the PC's expansion slots, or it can be an external device that plugs into a serial port.

Choosing a modem is far from simple. The modem industry, like the computer telecommunications industry in general, is plagued by a bad case of alphabet soup addiction—a dizzying array of specifications, acronyms, and numbers that can confuse even the most experienced computer users. Terms such as V.22, V.32, V.32bis, V.34bis, V.34, V.42bis, CCITT, MNP4, and MNP5 are just a few that you will encounter. This confusion is due to the proliferation of new standards—telecommunications technology improves so swiftly that companies continually develop products that exceed the capabilities of existing ones.

When you buy a modem, there are four areas to consider:

■ Transmission speed

■ Data compression

■ Error correction

■ Internal versus external

By far the most important consideration is the transmission speed. With early modems, transmission speed was measured in baud rate, a measure of how fast the signal could modulate. However, the correct way to measure how fast data is transmitted is **bits per second**, or **bps**. Today, if you see a modem that lists a baud rate, it is really just a misnomer for bps.

The first modems transmitted data at 300 bps and then evolved to 1200 bps and 2400 bps. Then the makers of modems found ways to build data compression capabilities into their modems. Data compression uses mathematical algorithms to analyze groups of bits and represent them with shorter groups of bits. It soon became obvious that standards were necessary so that modems could understand the data compression schemes used by other modems. The first standard was called V.32, and it achieved transmission speeds of 9600 bps—four times the speed of a 2400 bps modem. A subsequent standard called V.32bis enabled modems to transmit at 14,400 bps. Following that came the V.34 standard, which allowed for 28,800 bps and 33,600 bps transmission rates. Two new competing protocols, Rockwell and Lucent's K56Flex and U.S. Robotics x2, provide speeds of 56,000 bps. Many companies support one of these protocols to provide modems that transmit at 56,000 bps. Because these protocols are incompatible with one another, you cannot reach maximum speeds when two modems not using the same protocol are communicating with each other. This means you must make sure that the modem with which you are communicating adheres to the same 56K protocol as the one you are using.

NORTON
Online

For more
information on
56K modems, visit
this book's Web site at
www.glencoe.com/norton/online

With modem communications, when bits per second are large numbers, they are abbreviated Kbps, which stands for 1,000 bits per second. Thus, 14,400 bps is abbreviated 14.4 Kbps. Today, 56.6 Kbps is the preferred standard for modems, especially among people who communicate over the Internet. Generally, you want your modem transmission speed to be as high as possible. Of course, with a fast modem, you can still connect to any slower modem—a fast modem just gives you the option to go faster when you can.

When computers communicate through telephone lines, data moves through the line so quickly that even the smallest amount of static can introduce significant errors. Noise you could not hear if you were using the telephone line for a conversation can wreak havoc with computer data. As a result, modems and communications software use **error-correction protocols** to recover from transmission errors.

When you purchase a modem, you will generally find the error-correction protocols listed. The common ones are MNP2, MNP3, MNP4, MNP5, and V.42bis, which incorporates the MNP protocols. Nearly all commercially available modems incorporate these standards, so consumers rarely need to concern themselves with the error-correction protocols supported by a particular modem.

▶ This is an external modem. On the back are connections for attaching it to the computer, a telephone jack, and a telephone. There is also a plug for a power cord because external modems require their own power supply.

One other issue to consider when buying a modem is whether to buy an internal or external modem. An **external modem** is a box that houses the modem's circuitry outside the computer. It connects to the computer using a serial cable connected through a serial port and to the telephone system with a standard telephone jack. An **internal modem** is a circuit board that plugs into one of the computer's expansion slots. An internal modem saves desktop space but occupies an expansion slot.

Deciding on which type of modem you buy often comes down to cost or convenience. Because of the added expense of the housing required for external modems, external modems generally cost more than equivalent internal modems. On the other hand, internal modems require users to open the PC cabinet to install them. For new users, external modems are easier to set up (just connect them to a serial port) than are internal modems.

Modems also come in the form of a PC card for use with laptop computers. Some use standard phone lines, but others include a cellular phone, which enables completely wireless transmissions.

Most modems used with personal computers can also emulate a fax machine. Called **fax modems**, these devices can exchange faxes with any other fax modem or fax machine. With the proper software, users can convert incoming fax files into files that can be edited with a word processor—something that stand-alone fax machines cannot do.

Connecting with a Modem

A computer equipped with a modem and connected to a standard telephone line can dial up and communicate with any other computer that has a modem and a telephone connection. These are some common uses for data communication over the phone lines:

- Direct connections with other users
- Connections with office LANs
- Connections with BBSs, online services, and the Internet

An internal modem plugs into one of the computer's expansion slots. When it is installed, all you can see is the metal edge with the two telephone jacks. One jack is used to attach the modem to the telephone jack on the wall. The other can be used to connect a telephone, so you can still use the telephone line for calls, even though the line goes through the modem.

NORTON Online

For more information on **PC card modems**, visit this book's Web site at **www.glencoe.com/norton/online**

Direct Connections with Other Users

Suppose that you are writing an article on commercial fishing in Puget Sound. Before you submit the article to *Field and Stream,* you want a friend to read what you have written. At first, you consider printing out the article, finding an envelope and stamps, and going to the post office to mail it. Fortunately, you remember that your friend has a computer and a modem, so it would be much easier to send the article electronically. You call your friend and explain that you want to modem the file. This is the process for sending it:

1_ You launch the software that controls your modem.

2_ You enter your friend's phone number, and your computer dials the number.

3_ Your friend's computer picks up the line, and the two computers establish a connection through the two modems.

4_ You use your modem software to send the file to your friend's computer.

5_ You tell your computer to hang up the phone.

The whole process takes a few minutes, and the cost is only the price of the phone calls. Your friend now has the file and can read it immediately.

Today, direct connections to other users are becoming less frequent because so many people have computers with the

Modems can be used to connect your computer to a friend's computer.

capability to attach files to e-mail messages and send them to friends and associates through the Internet or a commercial online service. This capability is often more convenient than a direct modem connection because the person receiving the file does not have to be connected at the same time as the sender. However, direct modem connections with other users is still a fast, easy, reliable, and inexpensive way to transfer files between computers.

File transfer is the general term used to describe sending a file to a remote computer whether the transfer occurs through the telephone lines or through a network. The act of sending a file to another user or to a network is known as **uploading** the file. Copying a file from a remote computer is known as **downloading** the file. For a file to be transferred from one computer to another through a pair of modems, both computers must use the same **File Transfer Protocol (FTP)**—the set of rules or guidelines that dictate the format in which data will be sent. The most common File Transfer Protocols for modems are called Kermit, Xmodem, Ymodem, and Zmodem.

One of the important functions of the File Transfer Protocol is to check for errors as a file is being sent. Normally, modem communication is **full-duplex**, which means data can travel in both directions at the same time. Sometimes, however, modem communication can be **half-duplex**, which means that data can be sent in both directions but only one direction

Normally, modern modem and network connections are full-duplex. However, computers are occasionally connected using half-duplex transmission.

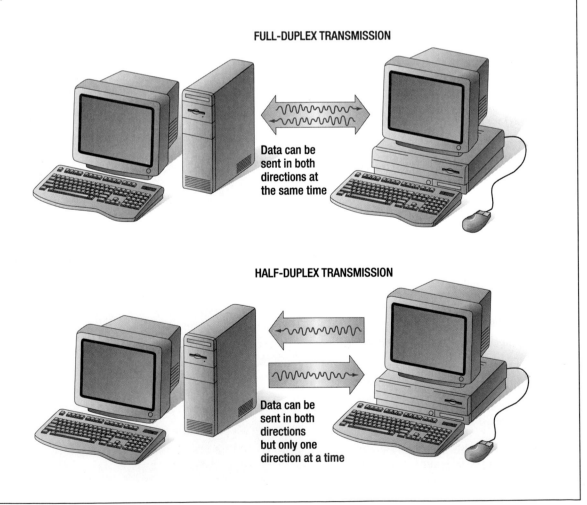

FULL-DUPLEX TRANSMISSION

Data can be
sent in both
directions at
the same time

HALF-DUPLEX TRANSMISSION

Data can be
sent in both
directions
but only one
direction at a time

at a time. In either type of communication, the receiving computer can respond to the sender and verify that the data it received contained no errors. If there are errors, the computer sending the data retransmits whatever portion is incorrect. Each File Transfer Protocol uses its own method to check for errors. Some are more efficient than others and therefore can transmit data faster.

Connections with Office Networks

These days, more and more people are **telecommuting**, working at home or on the road and using telecommunications equipment—telephones, modems, fax machines, and so forth—to stay in touch with the office.

The advantages of telecommuting over working in an office can be compelling. The telecommuter is spared the time and expense of traveling to work. This savings can include gas, automobile maintenance (or the cost of riding the bus or train), and sometimes the cost of insurance. As more workers telecommute, traffic congestion and air pollution are somewhat alleviated. Many companies and employees also find that telecommuters are more productive, presumably because there are fewer distractions at home during the day. As a result, many companies have instituted programs that encourage employees to work from home during part of the week.

For the telecommuter, setting up a home office almost always requires a computer and a modem. With the right software, the home user can then dial into the office network and upload or download files at any time. Dialing into the network has the same effect as logging into it at the office, except that transmitting files takes place more slowly. The home office computer should also be able to act as a fax machine unless the user has a stand-alone fax machine and a separate phone line for it. Finally, many people with home offices find it necessary to buy a copier.

Home offices now have access to multifunctional machines, such as this model from Panasonic, which can act as a printer, copier, fax machine, and scanner.

USING DIGITAL TELEPHONE LINES

As you learned in the modem section, standard telephone lines transmit analog signals, in which sound is translated into an electrical current. As a result, you need a modem to translate data into a form that can be sent over the phone lines. In addition, telephone lines operate at about 3100 Hz, which means that data has to be compressed to travel at more than about 2400 bps. Data compression has become quite sophisticated, so modems can often transmit data at rates as high as 56 Kbps (56,000 bps). Nevertheless, this can create a severe bandwidth bottleneck, considering that typical network transmission speeds are at least 10 Mbps (10,000,000 bps)—about 200 times as fast.

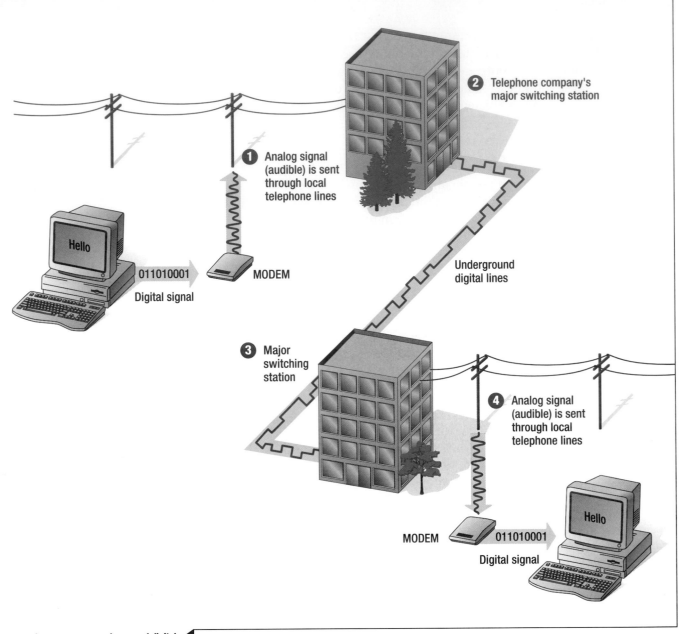

❷ Telephone company's major switching station

❶ Analog signal (audible) is sent through local telephone lines

Hello

011010001 ⟶ MODEM

Digital signal

Underground digital lines

❸ Major switching station

❹ Analog signal (audible) is sent through local telephone lines

MODEM 011010001 ⟶ Hello

Digital signal

In many areas, underground digital lines connect major telephone switching stations, but analog lines still connect the switching station to local houses and businesses. This mixture of lines makes for a confusing system. When sending data, a computer transmits a digital signal to a modem, which transmits an analog signal to the switching station, which transmits a digital signal to another switching station. The process is then reversed until it reaches the receiving computer.

The phone companies recognized this problem a number of years ago and began the long process of converting an analog system into a digital system. The massive data channels that connect major geographical regions are already digital, but the phone lines running under or above most city streets are still analog. This combination of digital and analog lines makes for an extremely confusing system, especially when you are transmitting data through a modem.

However, when the phone companies complete the transition and digital lines are installed to every building, the data transmission system will be a lot simpler.

The transformation from analog to digital lines will affect most users in three simple ways:

1_ You will need a different phone—a digital one that translates your voice into bits rather than an analog signal.

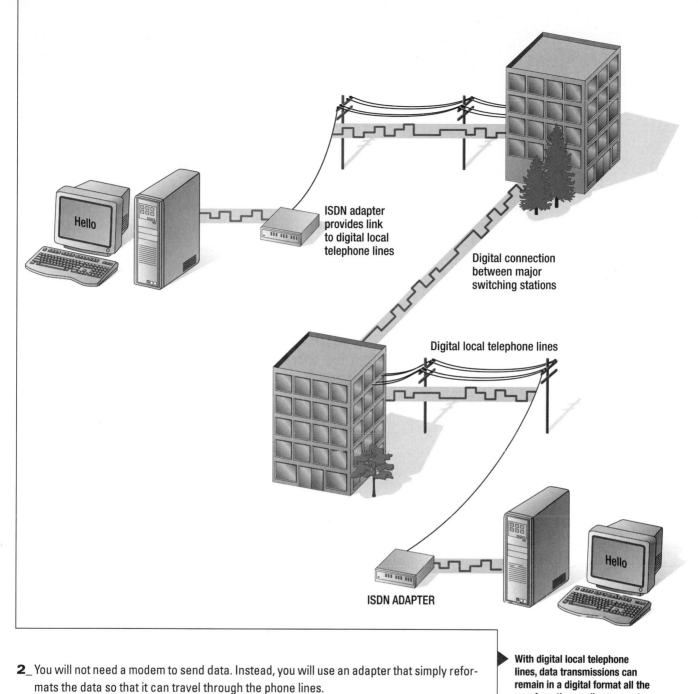

ISDN adapter provides link to digital local telephone lines

Digital connection between major switching stations

Digital local telephone lines

ISDN ADAPTER

2_ You will not need a modem to send data. Instead, you will use an adapter that simply reformats the data so that it can travel through the phone lines.

3_ You will be able to send data much more quickly.

ISDN, T1, and T3

Many different kinds of digital services are offered by the phone companies. The best known are called ISDN, T1, and T3.

Of the three, ISDN has received the most attention because it is the most affordable and the one most likely to make its way into homes and small businesses. **ISDN**, which stands for **Integrated Services Digital Network**, is a system that replaces all analog services with digital services.

When most people talk about ISDN, they are referring to a particular level of service called BRI (Basic Rate ISDN). BRI provides three communication

With digital local telephone lines, data transmissions can remain in a digital format all the way from the sending computer to the receiving computer.

NORTON Online

For more information on **ISDN**, visit this book's Web site at **www.glencoe.com/norton/online**

channels on one line—two 64 or 56 Kbps data channels and one 19 Kbps channel that is used to set up and control calls. The two data channels can carry voice or data, and they can be used simultaneously, so you can transmit data and carry on a conversation at the same time on the same line. Also, the channels can be combined so that BRI service can be used to transmit data at rates as high as 128 Kbps without compression.

Some phone companies now offer BRI service in some locations—especially in large metropolitan areas. Installation can be expensive, but the cost of service is slowly coming down to compete with the basic rates offered for analog lines.

A higher level of service for ISDN is called Primary Rate ISDN, or PRI. In this country, PRI provides 24 channels at 64 Kbps each, a total bandwidth of 1.544 Mbps. This level of bandwidth is also known as **T1** service. In Europe, PRI service provides 31 data channels.

Although not specified by the ISDN standard, it is also possible to purchase lines from telephone companies that offer even more bandwidth. For example, a **T3** line offers 672 channels of 64 Kbps each (plus control lines) for a total of 44.736 Mbps. Many phone companies also offer services between the levels of BRI and PRI. Different businesses have all kinds of different needs for bandwidth, so phone companies try to be as flexible as possible in their offerings. Table 7.1 summarizes some of the common digital services.

Table 7.1	Digital Telephone Services	
TYPE OF SERVICE	**SPEEDS AVAILABLE**	**DESCRIPTION**
ISDN	BRI = 128 Kbps PRI = 1.544 Mbps	BRI is a dial-up digital service, called *dial-up* because the line is open only when you make a call. Service is relatively inexpensive, but user pays for usage and long distance. PRI is a continuous, or dedicated, connection.
T1	1.544 Mbps	Can refer to several types of service, including PRI and private, leased lines between two points (usually to form a WAN).
T3	44.736 Mbps	Service equivalent to 28 T1 lines. Requires that fiber-optic cable be installed.
Frame Relay	Many speeds available, from 56 Kbps up to 1.536 Mbps.	A fast, packet-switching technology. Signal is carried to a frame relay circuit at the phone company's branch office. Groups of data are encapsulated in packets and forwarded to their destination. Frame relay service typically implies a permanent virtual circuit between two points (usually to form a WAN). However, frame relay switches can also be used with dial-up, ISDN lines.
SMDS	Many speeds, from 1.17 Mbps up to 34 Mbps	Switched Multimegabit Digital Service. Another fast, packet-switching technology, similar to frame relay service but catering to higher-end users.
ATM Cell Relay	51.84 Mbps up to about 10,000 Mbps now, with higher speeds in the future.	Yet another switching technology. Because it is fast, flexible, and well suited for all types of data (including sound and video), ATM may become the technology used for backbones in the telephone company branch offices.

ATM

ISDN, T1, and T3 can all be used effectively to set up WANs, as long as the networks are used primarily for transferring the most common types of data—files, e-mail messages, and so on. However, these types of services are not well suited for transmitting live video and sound. As a result, phone companies are beginning to offer a service called ATM, which stands for **Asynchronous Transfer Mode**.

ATM is a protocol designed by the telecommunications industry as a more efficient way to send voice, video, and computer data over a single network. It was originally conceived as a way to reconcile the needs for these different kinds of data on the telephone system, but the proponents of ATM argue that it can be implemented on computer LANs and WANs, as well. In fact, ATM is a network protocol—and therefore is similar to Ethernet and Token Ring.

ATM is one of the technologies that the telecommunications industry is examining for contributing to what is popularly known as the **information superhighway**, a worldwide network that will be capable of supporting high-bandwidth data communication to virtually every home, school, and business.

To understand the significance of ATM, you need to think about how most telephone lines work. With a **circuit-switched** line, you call a number, the phone system connects you, and you have complete access to that connection until you hang up. This arrangement is vastly different from most computer networks, which transmit packets of data and are therefore referred to as **packet-switched** systems. In circuit-switched lines, you and the person at the other end of the line have a fixed amount of bandwidth available. Even if you do not say anything to each other—or in the case of modem transmission, if you do not send any data—the bandwidth is still available.

This type of communication can be inefficient because data communication tends to be erratic. For example, consider two office LANs, connected using the telephone system. Every few minutes, a person in one office might send a file to a person in another office. During this time—maybe just a few seconds—the necessary bandwidth is high. During the remaining time, however, no bandwidth is required at all. Yet the phone line remains active, reserving the same amount of bandwidth.

Clearly, voice and data have different bandwidth requirements. Other types of communication, such as transmission of a digital video signal, have still different types of requirements. ATM addresses the needs of different kinds of communication by providing different kinds of connections and bandwidth on demand. Rather than reserving a fixed amount of bandwidth whether data is being transmitted or not, an ATM network transmits packets, known as cells, that include information about where they should go, what type of data is included, and what order the packets should follow. Cells can be sent in clumps, by different routes if necessary, even out of order (because the packet includes enough information to put the data back into proper order). Unlike standard phone transmission, which is based on circuit switching, ATM is based on cell switching.

NORTON Online

For more information on **ATM**, visit this book's Web site at **www.glencoe.com/norton/online**

Productivity Tip

Big Things Come in Small Packages: Network Computers

For many users, personal computers are a necessary part of their jobs. Computers help create information, store data, retrieve files, and entertain us. If you think you don't need your computer to complete your daily tasks, wait until there is a power outage or your hard disk crashes on you.

But in many companies, the PC is being taken away—and replaced with a new device. The **Network Computer (NC)** is hailed as the next big thing to come to many users' desktops.

Similar to the way terminals were commonly connected to large mainframe computers 30 years ago, NCs are being developed as a low-cost device that includes just the bare bones necessary to enable users to interact with network and Internet resources. Instead of companies investing in PCs that may cost thousands of dollars, companies can purchase NCs for under $1,000.

Network Computers (NCs) are perfect for dedicated applications, such as kiosks and call-center operations.

Thin Is In NCs are commonly referred to as **thin clients**. This is because they don't require much software to operate (mainly only software required for the BIOS and ROM) and they solve many of the problems associated with information technology dependent on PCs (or fat clients), namely reduction of technology costs, increase in productivity, greater flexibility, and ease of migration to new applications.

Thin clients are best suited for dedicated applications, such as accessing data on a database server or a call center operation application. NCs also are ideal for kiosks, such as you might see in retail settings.

Upgrades Are a Breeze An example of where NCs can reduce technology costs is seen when a company upgrades to new software. With PCs, most applications must be installed and configured on each computer to take advantage of or work around that computer's resources. Even with applications that can be installed from a network server, each computer has its own quirks and will often require the network administrator or IS professional to correct problems on a per-PC basis.

On the other hand, thin clients make upgrading to new applications a breeze. To upgrade, users simply log into the network, and the application is updated. The only place where the application is manually upgraded is on the network server.

Unlike PCs, NCs have fewer (if any) moving parts, such as hard drives, which may require upgrading or maintenance. If the NC fails, users spend very little downtime getting back online. Because data, applications, and personal files are not stored on the NC, there is no wasted time getting the user's environment back in order. The user simply gets a new or replacement NC, attaches to the network, and is up and running.

Specifications Not any old computer without a hard drive can be called an NC. In fact, several companies have developed a "reference profile" for NCs. Developed by Apple Computer, Microsoft, IBM, Netscape, Sun, and Oracle, an NC:

- Includes a pointing device
- Accepts text
- Provides audio output
- Operates in IP-based networks
- Has a minimum screen resolution of 640 x 480
- Supports VGA or equivalent monitors
- Supports HTML and HTTP Internet standards
- Supports Java

NCs also must support the SMTP e-mail protocol, JPEG multimedia format, and some type of security standard, such as the VISA or SmartCard specification.

Currently, NCs are available from Digital Equipment, NEC, Neoware Systems, NCI, Network Computing Devices, Sun Microsystems, and Wyse Technology.

Because the volume of cells being transmitted can vary with the bandwidth of the incoming signal, ATM is considered an ideal way to combine voice, data, and video transmission on the same high-bandwidth network. As a result, it is one of the most widely used industry buzzwords of the decade. Whether it will capture the telecommunications and data communications industries, however, is yet to be determined.

NETWORKING FOR THE NEW MEDIA

For companies specializing in new media applications (also referred to as multimedia), such as video and digital media creation and editing, data storage and retrieval is a daily concern. Many studios invest in networks to enable artists to store, retrieve, and share data with other users. These types of networks are commonly referred to as multimedia networks. **Multimedia networks** must provide high-speed access to large files, in addition to providing large repositories for new and modified files.

One major concern for companies investing in multimedia networks is the type of storage in which to invest. Media artists commonly create graphics, video, and 3-D animations using a variety of resources requiring a large amount of data to be shared over networks. When artists cannot retrieve or share their data, the work in a studio can grind to a halt, impeding results and possibly resulting in loss of contracts for the business. Use of removable hard drives is one way media artists share data but is not the most efficient way to do so. Networks built around Fast Ethernet is another way to create an environment in which multimedia data can be shared in a studio.

New protocols have emerged that enable multiple computers to share storage media. These include **Fibre Channel Arbitrated Loop (FC-AL)** and **Serial Storage Architecture (SSA)**. Both protocols provide large bandwidths to allow large amounts of data (80MBps for SSA and 100MBps for FC-AL) to be shared. Prices for SSA and FC-AL products are expensive, ranging from

For more information on **MegaDrive's Aria device**, visit this book's Web site at **www.glencoe.com/norton/online**

Today's mutimedia applications require fast, efficient networks.

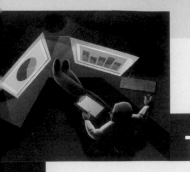

Computers
In Your Career

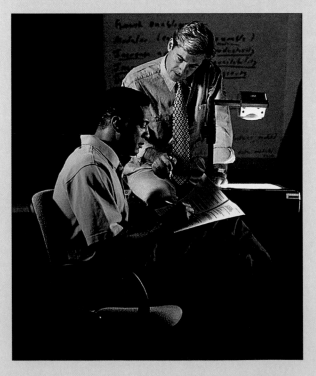

wo of the most popular (and best paying) computer-related fields are networking and data communications. Most large organizations have existing networks that must be maintained, repaired, and updated as the company grows or shrinks. Likewise, as companies merge, networks must be combined to create a seamless network for the organization. Many times this means combining two or more networks that use different topologies, network operating systems, and protocols into one large network. As these networks are merged, there must be a limited amount of downtime so that employees can continue processing data for the company. This means that people interested in careers relating to networking and data communications must be educated in a wide range of computing and networking topics.

Some of the careers relating to networking and data communications include:

Network administrators are responsible for managing a company's network infrastructure. Some of the jobs in this career field include designing and implementing networks, setting up and managing users' accounts, installing and updating network software and applications, and backing up the network. To succeed as a network administrator, you should gain experience in the major NOSs, including Novell IntranetWare and Windows NT 4.0 Server. You also should have experience with major operating systems, such as Windows 98, MS-DOS, Apple Macintosh, and UNIX. You might also consider becoming certified from Novell or Microsoft.

Information Systems (IS) managers are responsible for managing a team of information professionals, including network administrators, software developers, project managers, and other staff. Jobs in the IS management field differ according to the needs of the company, but many IS managers maintain project lists, oversee project management, perform database administration, and possibly do some programming. IS managers should possess experience and skills in a wide range of networking and computing areas, including network operating system experience, operating system experience, relational database knowledge, and staff management abilities.

Data communications managers are responsible for setting up and maintaining Internet, intranet, and extranet sites. Often data communications managers also are responsible for designing and establishing an organization's telecommuting initiative. This often requires experience with a number of technologies, including networking, data communications, remote access software, and Internet technologies. If you're interested in a career in data communications, you should learn as much as you can about these technologies.

$1,800-$3,000 per user plus the cost of storage drives. Some of the products available include MegaDrive's Aria, MountainGate's CentraVision, and Soci Solutions' MediaNet.

WHAT TO EXPECT IN THE FUTURE

It is probably safe to say that networking and data communications are the future of computing. Currently, we are witnessing a race toward global connectivity, with progress being made on almost every front:

■ Networking technology is growing more sophisticated, and transmission speeds are increasing rapidly.

■ All the telecommunications industries—telephone companies, cable companies, Internet service providers, online services, and so on—are working to offer high bandwidth to homes and businesses.

The last point is especially notable. Both the consumers of information and the telecommunications industry are rushing toward the common goal of massive connectivity. Each group sees a future where bandwidth will be cheap so that people can stay in touch no matter where they are, and the variety of available information will be virtually unlimited.

In the middle of all this enthusiasm, however, there is a missing link that some people find frightening and others find truly enchanting. People want connectivity, and the telecommunications industry wants to sell it to them, but people do not want to pay much just for bandwidth. They are only going to pay for information.

Well, what kind of information will people pay for? The more pessimistic pundits predict "500 channels and nothing on." Perhaps even worse, they see "infoglut," a world so saturated with information that it will be almost impossible to find the information you want.

On the other hand, the situation offers almost boundless opportunities for creative entrepreneurs with the vision to predict accurately and then supply the kinds of information for which people will pay.

Visual Summary & Exercises

VISUAL SUMMARY

The Uses of a Network

- Networks allow users simultaneous access to shared programs and data.

- Networks also allow users to share peripheral devices, such as printers and hard disks, and thereby prolong the usable life of many machines.

- Networks usually include the capability to send e-mail, and many e-mail systems let users attach files to their messages.

- Some networks also aid communication by providing tools for teleconferencing and videoconferencing.

- Connecting computers to form a network makes it easier to perform backups of the data on all the networked hard disks.

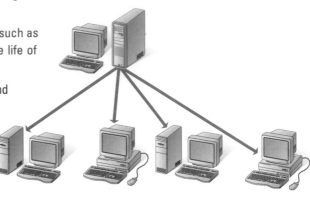

How Networks Are Structured

- LANs connect computers that are relatively close together, whereas WANs join multiple LANs that are spread over a large geographical area.

- LANs are connected using bridges, routers, and gateways.

- Nodes and a file server can be connected to create file server, client/server, and peer-to-peer networks.

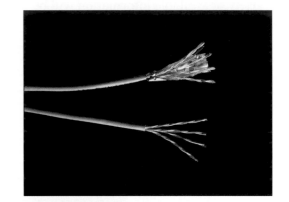

Network Topologies for LANs

- The physical layout of a LAN is known as the topology.

- LAN topologies can be a bus, star, or ring.

Network Media and Hardware

- The three most common wires used to connect computers are twisted-pair wires, coaxial cable, and fiber-optic cable.

- Increasingly, computers also communicate through wireless links; the most common types are cellular and microwave links.

- In addition to the media that connect the computers in a network, each computer also needs a network interface card.

- To communicate directly, the computers in a network must also use the same network protocol, the language used to communicate data.

- The most common network technologies are Ethernet, Token Ring, and ARCnet.

Network Software

■ The software that manages the resources on a network is called the network operating system, or NOS.

■ One of the most popular NOSs is IntranetWare, from Novell.

Analog signal (audible) is sent through telephone lines

011010001   Modem   Modem   011010001
Digital signal   Digital signal

Data Communication Over Telephone Lines

■ Increasingly, phone lines are being used to send digital data because the phone system is, in effect, a pre-existing network connecting a vast number of people around the world.

■ In 1978, Hayes Microcomputer Products, Inc., introduced the first modem that allowed PC users to transmit data through a standard phone line.

■ A modem is used to translate the computer's digital signals into analog signals that can travel over standard phone lines; a modem attached to the receiving computer translates the analog signal back into a digital one.

■ The most important consideration in choosing a modem is the speed at which it can send data, but other important considerations are the data compression and error-correction techniques it uses, and whether the modem is internal or external.

Using Digital Telephone Lines

■ Analog phone lines are slow and not well suited for sending data, so telephone companies have gradually been switching to digital service.

■ The best known type of digital service is called ISDN.

■ ISDN service is available in many urban areas, with the lowest-level service, BRI, providing a bandwidth of 128 Kbps.

■ T1 and T3 offer higher bandwidth: 1.544 Mbps and 44.736 Mbps, respectively.

■ The hottest buzzword in the telecommunications industry today is ATM, which promises a system designed to meet the needs of transmitting voice, data, and video data.

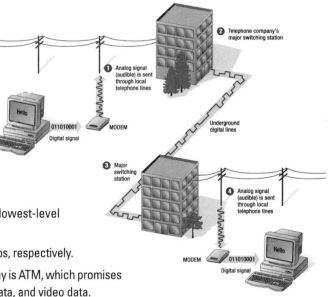

❷ Telephone company's major switching station

❶ Analog signal (audible) is sent through local telephone lines

011010001   MODEM   Underground digital lines
Digital signal

❸ Major switching station

❹ Analog signal (audible) is sent through local telephone lines

MODEM   011010001
Digital signal

Networking for the New Media

■ Multimedia networks provide high-speed access to large files, as well as provide large repositories for new and modified files.

■ New protocols have emerged that enable multiple computers to share a storage medium including Fibre Channel Arbitrated Loop (FC-AL) and Serial Storage Architecture (SSA).

Visual Summary & Exercises

KEY TERMS

After completing this chapter, you should be able to define the following terms:

10Base-T, 267
100Base-T, 267
application server, 249
ARCnet, 267
Asynchronous Transfer Mode (ATM), 279
bandwidth, 263
banner page, 252
bits per second (bps), 270
bridge, 256
bus network, 261
circuit-switched, 279
client/server, 258
coaxial cable (coax), 263
data communication, 247
direct connection, 247
distributed computing, 260
downloading, 274
electronic mail (e-mail), 252
error-correction protocol, 271
Ethernet, 266
external modem, 271
Fast Ethernet, 267
fax modem, 272
fiber-optic cable, 264

Fibre Channel Arbitrated Loop (FC-AL), 281
file server, 249
file server network, 258
file transfer, 274
File Transfer Protocol (FTP), 274
full-duplex, 274
gateway, 256
groupware, 249
half-duplex, 274
information superhighway, 279
Integrated Services Digital Network (ISDN), 277
internal modem, 272
local area network (LAN), 254
media, 263
multimedia network, 281
network, 248
network computer (NC), 280
network operating system (NOS), 268
network protocol, 266
network server, 249
network version, 249
node, 258
online, 247

packet, 256
packet-switched, 279
peer-to-peer network, 260
print job, 251
protocol, 256
remote administration, 255
ring topology, 262
router, 256
Serial Storage Architecture (SSA), 281
spooling, 251
star network, 262
T1, 278
T3, 278
telecommuting, 275
teleconference, 252
thin client, 280
Token Ring, 267
topology, 261
twisted-pair wire, 263
uploading, 274
videoconferencing, 253
wide area network (WAN), 257
wireless communication, 264

KEY TERM QUIZ

Fill in the missing word with one of the terms listed in Key Terms:

1. A system for transmitting written messages through a network is known as _____.

2. A(n) _____ is a network of computers that serves users located relatively near each other.

3. You can connect computers together to communicate and exchange information using a(n) _____.

4. The physical layout of the wires that connect the nodes of the network is the _____.

5. Copying a file from a remote computer is called _____.

6. A(n) _____ is a central computer that includes a large disk-storage device on a LAN.

7. The group of programs that manages the resources on the network is known as the _____.

8. A unit of measurement indicating how fast data is transmitted is called _____.

9. _____ are the individual computers on a network.

10. The act of sending a file to another user or to a network is called _____.

Visual Summary & Exercises

REVIEW QUESTIONS

1. List and describe briefly the benefits that networks provide.

2. How do networks help businesses save money?

3. How does groupware benefit users? Name and describe briefly at least three of its components.

4. Describe how an e-mail system emulates the postal system and a telephone-answering system.

5. List and describe briefly the four types of data communications media that link networks.

6. How is access time affected in an Ethernet network that links many computers?

7. List and describe the three most common network technologies.

8. Describe what takes place during a modem's demodulation phase.

9. What factors should you consider when purchasing a modem?

10. Describe the ways in which replacing analog phone lines with digital phone lines will simplify data communications.

DISCUSSION QUESTIONS

1. Describe at least two ways in which videoconferencing can save money for businesses.

2. Does a business save money by encouraging employees to telecommute? Despite the convenience aspects discussed in the chapter, are there any negative aspects to conducting business in this manner?

3. Suppose that a significant part of your job requires sending and receiving large-sized graphics files to different locations. What kind of features, hardware, and specifications should you consider in setting up a home office to handle this aspect of your job?

4. In what significant ways does asynchronous transfer mode affect data communications? Describe some possible changes people are likely to see over the next ten years, if ATM is implemented widely on the information superhighway.

inteNET Workshop

The following exercises assume that you have access to the Internet and a browser. If you need help with any of the following exercises, visit this book's Web site at **www.glencoe.com/norton/online**. This book's Web site also lists URLs you need to complete many of these exercises.

1. Many newer operating systems—such as the Macintosh OS 8.1, Windows 98, and Windows NT—feature built-in networking capabilities, which enable the user to set up a simple peer-to-peer network without installing additional software. Visit the Apple and Microsoft Web sites and search for information about the networking capabilities of these operating systems. What information can you find? Given the information available at these sites, can you conclude that this approach to networking is a good idea for some organizations? What types of organizations or businesses would benefit from a small peer-to-peer network?

2. A good understanding of networks requires a good understanding of topologies. Starting with PC Webopaedia's Network Topologies Web page, find out all you can about star, bus, and ring topologies. Which is in most common use today? Under what circumstances would you suggest installing one topology as opposed to the others?

3. In the past few years, network administrators have discovered the value of becoming certified in various networking technologies. This means following a course of study prescribed by the technology's manufacturer, taking a battery of tests, and earning a certification that proves a given level of expertise. The most highly sought-after certifications are offered by Microsoft and Novell, for their networking systems and other products. On the Web, locate information about the Microsoft and Novell certification programs. Can you find a course list for each certification program? What certifications are available? What are the costs and time commitments involved in earning a certification?

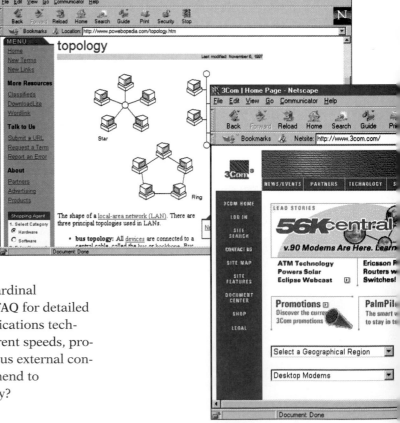

4. Check the Web sites of modem manufacturers, such as 3Com/US Robotics, Hayes, and Cardinal Technologies. Also visit the High-Speed Modem **FAQ** for detailed information on a variety of modem and communications technologies. Compare the features and cost for different speeds, protocols, compression techniques, and internal versus external connection. What type of modem would you recommend to someone who wanted to purchase a modem today?

5. What information can you find on the Web about cable modem technology?

6. ISDN is rapidly growing in popularity as a digital communication medium. This is because ISDN not only allows faster access to the Web and online services, but also businesses can use ISDN connections to improve transfer speeds between LANs in a wide area network, for teleconferencing, and other uses. Using the ISDN FAQ as a starting point, how much information can you find about ISDN on the Web? What are the benefits of having an ISDN connection? Can you determine whether any phone companies in your region provide ISDN service? If so, how much does ISDN service cost, compared to a typical home data line?

7. The most popular network operating systems are IntranetWare (formerlly called NetWare) from Novell and Windows NT from Microsoft. Explore the Novell and Microsoft Web sites to see how much specific information you can find about these products. More important, can you find information on any other Web sites that compares these two network operating systems? In reviews and performance tests, which one gets better grades? Based on your research, which NOS seems easier to work with? Which would you choose if you were running a business, and why?

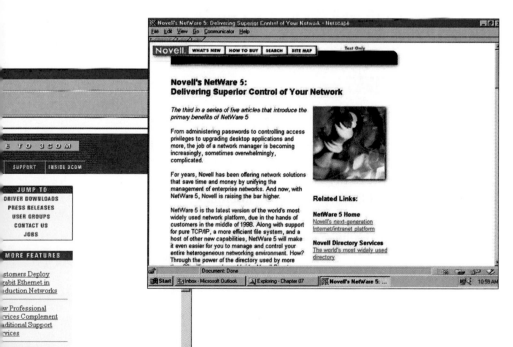

CHAPTER **8**

The Internet and Online Resources

CONTENTS

OBJECTIVES

When you complete this chapter, you will be able to do the following:

- Give two reasons why the Internet got started.
- Describe the two parts of an Internet address.
- Name the nine major features of the Internet.
- List two ways in which a PC can access the Internet.

Some

observers believe
that the Internet is having
the same kind of fundamental impact
on modern society as the invention of the printing press had
in the 15th century. The printing press expanded communication and the spread of information, making it possible to create
many copies of a document quickly and inexpensively. The
Internet, which is essentially a worldwide system of interconnected computer networks, is encouraging a giant leap forward
in the same process; it is increasing the availability of information and the ease and speed of communication.

By connecting millions of computers, the Internet makes
it possible for a computer user anywhere in the world to
exchange text, pictures, movies, sound, computer programs,
and anything else that can be stored in digital form with anyone
else in the connected world.

This worldwide con-
nectivity enables peo-
ple and organizations
to work together in
new ways and has
even resulted in the
creation of new busi-
ness models, such
as telecommuting and
virtual corporations.
Because they can work
from anywhere and
still be connected to
the office via the Internet, millions of workers—called telecommuters—are enjoying unprecedented freedom and flexibility.
They can work at home or on the road and still use the company's
resources, such as e-mail and networked data and software.
Companies can now create corporate relationships online
instead of physically moving people or equipment; in such
virtual corporations, businesses form partnerships online,
exchanging information, raw data, and even some types
of products (such as documents, software, and analysis) over
their networks while keeping travel and shipping to a minimum.
Using online capabilities such as real-time document sharing
and videoconferencing, workers can participate in meetings
online, regardless of their location.

This chapter focuses on the history and development of the
Internet, describes its most important functions and services,
and explains how you can connect your own computer to
the Internet.

BACKGROUND AND HISTORY: AN EXPLOSION OF CONNECTIVITY

The seeds of the Internet were planted in 1969, when the Advanced Research Projects Agency (ARPA) of the U.S. Department of Defense began connecting computers at different universities and defense contractors. The goal of this early network was to create a large computer network with multiple paths that could survive a nuclear attack or other disaster. ARPA also wanted users in remote locations to be able to share scarce computing resources.

Soon after the first links in **ARPANET** (as this early system was called) were in place, the engineers and scientists who had access to this system began exchanging messages and data that were beyond the scope of the Defense Department's original objectives for the project. In addition to exchanging ideas and information related to science and engineering, people also discovered that they could play long-distance games and socialize with other people who shared their interests. The users convinced ARPA that these unofficial uses were helping to test the network's capacity.

ARPANET started with a handful of computers, but it expanded rapidly. The network jumped across the Atlantic to Norway and England in 1973, and it never stopped growing. In the mid-1980s, another federal agency, the National Science Foundation (NSF), got into the act after the Defense Department dropped its funding of the Internet. NSF established five "supercomputing centers" that were available to anyone who wanted to use them for academic research purposes. NSF had expected that the people who used its supercomputers would use ARPANET to obtain access, but it quickly discovered that the existing network could not handle the load. In response, it created a new, higher-capacity network, called **NSFnet**, to complement the older and by then overloaded ARPANET. The link between ARPANET, NSFnet, and other networks was called the Internet. (The process of connecting separate networks is called *internetworking*. A collection of "networked networks" are described as being *internetworked*. This is where the Internet—a worldwide network of networks—gets its name.)

NSFnet made Internet connections widely available for academic research, but the NSF did not permit users to conduct private business over the system. Therefore, several private telecommunications companies built their own network backbones that used the same set of networking protocols as NSFnet. Like the trunk of a tree or the spine of a human being, a network **backbone** is the central structure that connects other elements of the network. These private portions of the Internet were not limited by NSFnet's "appropriate use" restrictions, so it became possible to use the Internet to distribute business and commercial information.

Interconnections (known as gateways) between NSFnet and the private backbones allowed a user on any one of them to exchange data with all the others. Other gateways were created between the Internet and other networks, large and small, including some that used completely different networking protocols.

The original ARPANET was shut down in 1990, and government funding for NSFnet was discontinued in 1995, but the commercial Internet backbone services have easily replaced them.

By the early 1990s, interest in the Internet began to expand dramatically. The system that had been created as a tool for surviving a nuclear war found its way into businesses and homes. Now, advertisements for new movies are just as common online as collaborations on particle physics research.

Today, the Internet connects thousands of networks and millions of users around the world. It is a huge, cooperative community with no central ownership.

HOW THE INTERNET WORKS

The single most important thing to understand about the Internet is that it potentially can link your computer to any other computer. Anyone with access to the Internet can exchange text, data files, and programs with any other user. For all practical purposes, just about everything that happens across the Internet is a variation of one of these activities. The Internet itself is the pipeline that carries data between computers.

TCP/IP: The Universal Language of the Internet

The Internet works because every computer connected to it uses the same set of rules and procedures (known as *protocols*) to control timing and data format. The set of commands and timing specifications used by the Internet is called Transmission Control Protocol/Internet Protocol, universally abbreviated as **TCP/IP**.

The TCP/IP protocols include the specifications that identify individual computers and exchange data between computers. They also include rules for several categories of application programs, so programs that run on different kinds of computers can talk to one another.

TCP/IP software looks different on different kinds of computers, but it always presents the same appearance to the network. Therefore, it does not matter if the system at the other end of a connection is a supercomputer that fills a room, a pocket-size personal communications device, or anything in between; as long as it recognizes TCP/IP protocols, it can send and receive data through the Internet.

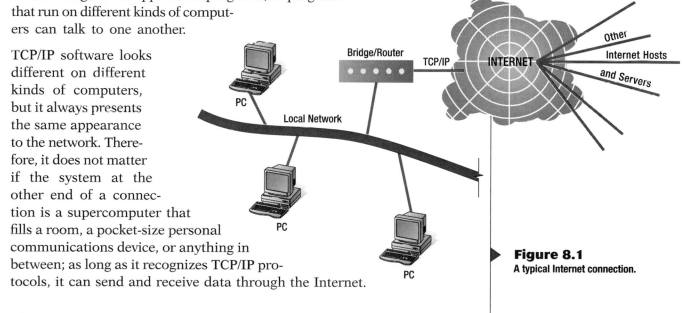

Figure 8.1
A typical Internet connection.

A Network of Networks—Backbones and Gateways

Most computers are not connected directly to the Internet—they are connected to smaller networks that connect through gateways to the Internet backbone. That is why the Internet is sometimes described as "a network of networks." Figure 8.1 shows a typical Internet connection.

The core of the Internet is the set of backbone connections that tie the local networks together and the routing scheme that controls the way each piece of data finds its destination. In most networking diagrams, the Internet backbone is portrayed as a big cloud because the routing details are less important than the fact that the data passes through the Internet between the origin and destination.

NORTON Online

For more information on **IP addresses**, visit this book's Web site at www.glencoe.com/norton/online

Addressing Schemes—IP and DNS Addresses

Internet activity can be defined as computers communicating with other computers using TCP/IP. The computer that originates a transaction must identify its intended destination with a unique address. Every computer on the Internet has a four-part numeric address, called the Internet Protocol address or **IP address**, which contains routing information that identifies its location. Each of the four parts is a number between 0 and 255, so an IP address looks like this:

205.46.117.104

Computers have no trouble working with big strings of numbers, but humans are not so skilled. Therefore, most computers on the Internet (except the ones used exclusively for internal routing and switching) also have an address called a **Domain Name System (DNS)**—an address that uses words rather than numbers.

DNS addresses have two parts: an individual name, followed by a **domain** (a name for a computer connected to the Internet) that generally identifies the type of institution that uses the address, such as *.com* for commercial businesses or *.edu* for schools, colleges, and universities. The University of Washington's DNS address is *washington.edu;* Microsoft's is *microsoft.com*.

Within the United States, the last three letters of the domain usually tell what type of institution owns the computer. Table 8.1 lists the most common types.

Table 8.1	Internet Domains
DOMAIN	**TYPE OF ORGANIZATION**
.com	business (commercial)
.edu	educational
.gov	government
.mil	military
.net	gateway or host
.org	other organization

Some large institutions and corporations divide their domain addresses into smaller **subdomains**. For example, a business with many branches might have a subdomain for each office—such as *boston.widgets.com* and *newyork.widgets.com*. You might also see some subdomains broken into even smaller sub-subdomains, like *evolution.genetics.washington.edu* (a contender for the Internet's longest DNS address).

Outside the United States (although many institutions and businesses in the United States are starting to use this same address scheme), domains usually identify the country in which the system is located, such as *.ca* for Canada or *.fr* for France. Sometimes, a geographic domain address will also include a subdomain that identifies the district within the larger domain. For example, Mindlink is a commercial Internet service provider in the Canadian province of British Columbia. Its DNS address is *mindlink.bc.ca*. Some United States institutions such as colleges and elementary schools use the same expanded address scheme. For example, some community colleges include *cc* in their DNS address, whereas some schools may include *K12* in their address.

DNS addresses and numeric IP addresses identify individual computers, but a single computer might have many separate users, each of whom must have an account on that computer. A user can set up such an account by specifying a unique user name. Some of the largest domains, such as America Online *(aol.com)* may have more than a million different user names. When you send a message to a person rather than a computer, you must include that person's user name in the address. The standard format is the user name first, separated from the DNS address by an "at" symbol (@). Therefore, John Smith's e-mail address might be:

jsmith@widgets.com

You would read this address as "J Smith at widgets dot com."

Clients and Servers

The basic model for most Internet tools is this: a client application on a user's computer requests information through the network from a server. A server is a powerful computer, generally containing a large hard disk, which acts as a shared storage resource. In addition to containing stored files, a server may also act as a gatekeeper for access to programs or data from other computers.

MAJOR FEATURES OF THE INTERNET

The technical details that make the Internet work are only part of the story—the reason that so many people use the Internet has more to do with content than connectivity. As it exists today, a huge amount of information is available through the Internet. For many users, it is a valuable source of news, business communication, entertainment, and technical information.

The Internet also has created hundreds of "virtual communities," made up of people who share an interest in a technical discipline, hobby, or political or social movement. There are online conferences of astronomers, toy train collectors, and house-bound mothers of two-year-olds. College students in Australia and Alabama come together on live Internet Relay Chat channels. Online conference services like the Well, based in northern California, resemble a kind of "cocktail party" where many interesting conversations are happening at the same time.

As a business tool, the Internet has many uses. Electronic mail is an efficient and inexpensive way to send and receive messages and documents around the world within minutes. The World Wide Web is becoming both an important advertising medium and a channel for distributing software, documents, and information services. As a channel for business research, the databases and other information archives that exist online are frequently better and more up-to-date than any library.

E-Mail

The single most common use of the Internet is for the exchange of electronic mail, or e-mail. Anyone with an e-mail account can send messages to other users of the Internet and to many networks connected to the Internet through gateways. Most e-mail programs also permit users to attach data files and program files to messages.

One popular Internet e-mail program is Eudora, which exists in versions for both Windows and Macintosh computers. Figure 8.2 shows a screen from the Windows version of Eudora.

Figure 8.2

An e-mail message in Eudora.

NORTON Online

For more information on **listserv systems**, visit this book's Web site at **www.glencoe.com/norton/online**

Besides one-to-one messages that are popular on both the Internet and LAN e-mail systems, Internet e-mail is also used for one-to-many messages, in which the same set of messages goes to a list of many names. One type of mailing list that uses e-mail is an automated list server, or **listserv**. Listserv systems allow users on the list to post their own messages, so the result is an ongoing discussion. Hundreds of mailing list discussions are in progress all the time on a huge variety of topics. For example, there are mailing lists for producers of radio drama, makers of apple cider, and members of individual college classes who want to keep up with news from their old friends.

News

In addition to the messages distributed to mailing lists by e-mail, the Internet also supports a form of public bulletin board called **News**. There are approximately 15,000 **news groups**, each devoted to discussion of a particular topic.

Many of the most widely distributed news groups are part of a system called **Usenet**, but others are targeted to a particular region or to users connected to a specific network or institution, such as a university or a large corporation.

A news reader program—the client software—obtains articles from a news server, which exchanges them with other servers through the Internet. To participate in News, you must run a news reader program to log onto a server.

To see messages that have been posted about a specific topic, you must subscribe to the news group that addresses that topic. News groups are organized into major categories, called domains, and individual topics within each domain. The name of a news group begins with the domain and includes a description of the group's topic, such as *alt.food*. Some topics include separate news groups for related subtopics, such as *alt.food.chocolate*.

Table 8.2	Common Usenet Domains

DOMAIN	DESCRIPTION
comp	Computer-related topics
sci	Science and technology (except computers)
soc	Social issues and politics
news	Topics related to Usenet
rec	Hobbies, arts, and recreational activities
misc	Topics that do not fit one of the other domains

The Most Important Alternative Topics Include	
alt	Alternative news groups
bionet	Biological sciences
biz	Business topics, including advertisements
clari	News from the Associated Press and Reuters, supplied through a service called Clarinet
k12	News groups for primary and secondary schools

There are six major domains within the Usenet structure and many more "alternative" domains. The major Usenet domains are listed in Table 8.2.

Anyone can contribute articles to a news group, and that is both the greatest strength and greatest weakness of the system. A good news group can have a strong spirit of community, where many people pitch in to work together. If you are looking for an obscure piece of information, there is a good chance that you can find it by asking the right group. There is no "fact-checking" in most news groups, however, so you cannot automatically assume that everything you read online is true. News groups are a relatively fast way to distribute information to potentially interested readers, and they allow people to discuss topics of common interest. They also can be a convenient channel for finding answers to questions. Many questions tend to be asked over and over again, so it is always a good idea to read the articles that other people have posted before you jump in with your own questions. Members of many news groups post lists of **Frequently Asked Questions**, or **FAQs**, every month or two.

As Figure 8.3 shows, subscribing to a news group is a three-step process.

You must download a list of available news groups from the server, choose the groups that interest you, and finally, select the articles that you want to read. In most news readers, you can choose to reply to an article by posting

Figure 8.3
Subscribing to a news group.

Step 1. Download of list of available news groups.

Step 2. Choose the group that interests you.

Step 3. Select the article you want to read.

This is the article.

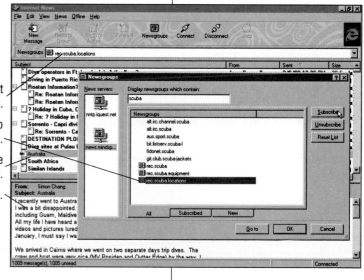

another article to the news group, or by sending a private e-mail message to the person who wrote the original article.

Telnet—Remote Access to Distant Computers

Telnet is the Internet tool for using one computer to control a second computer. Using Telnet, you can send commands that run programs and open text or data files. The Telnet program is a transparent window between your own computer and a distant host system—a computer that you are logging onto.

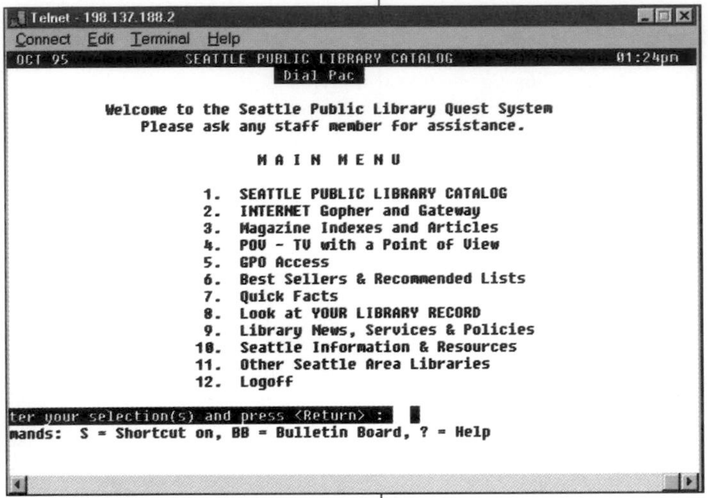

A Telnet connection sends input from your keyboard to the host and displays text from the host on your screen.

Connecting to a Telnet host is easy; enter the address, and the Telnet program sets up a connection. When you see a logon message from the host, you can send an account name and password to start an operating session. Access to some Telnet hosts is limited to users with permission from the owner of the host, but many other hosts offer access to members of the general Internet public.

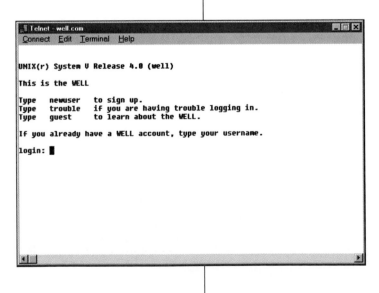

Figure 8.4
A Telnet connection to a library catalog.

Telnet connections are useful for many purposes. For example, Figure 8.4 shows a Telnet connection to a library's online catalog. You can obtain information about books in the library's collection over the Internet as easily as you could from the library's own reference room.

Another common use for Telnet is to provide access to online conferences that are not part of Usenet, such as the one in Figure 8.5.

FTP

Figure 8.5
A Telnet connection to an online conference service.

You can use Telnet to operate a distant computer by remote control through the Internet, but sometimes there is no substitute for having your own copy of a program or data file. File Transfer Protocol, or FTP, is the Internet tool used to copy files from one computer to another. When a user has accounts on more than one computer, FTP can be used to transfer data or programs between them.

There are also public FTP archives that will permit anyone to make copies of their files. These archives contain thousands of individual programs and files on almost every imaginable subject. Anyone with an FTP client program can download and use these files. Because these public archives require visitors to use the word "anonymous" as an account name, they are known as **anonymous FTP archives**.

Here are a few of the things that exist in FTP archives:

- Weather maps
- Programs for Windows, Macintosh, UNIX, and other operating systems
- Articles and reviews from scholarly journals
- Recipes
- Historic documents such as the United Nations Charter
- Digital images of paintings by Salvador Dali
- The collected poems of William Butler Yeats
- John von Neumann's 1945 report on the EDVAC, one of the earliest digital computing systems
- Maps from the United States Geological Survey

The list could fill this chapter four or five times over.

Using FTP is simple. Often, the hard part is locating a file that you want to download. One way to find files is to use **Archie**, the searchable index of FTP archives maintained by McGill University in Montreal. (Archie stands for *archives*.) The main Archie server at McGill gathers copies of the directories from more than a thousand other public FTP archives every month and distributes copies of those directories to dozens of other servers around the world. When a server receives a request for a "keyword search," it returns a list of files that match the search criteria along with the location of each file.

After you have an address and file name, it is simple to download a copy with an FTP client program.

Gopher

All kinds of information are available through the Internet, but much of it can be difficult to find without a guide. **Gopher** organizes directories of documents, images, programs, public Telnet hosts, and other resources into logical menus.

The first Gopher was created at the University of Minnesota (home of the Golden Gophers) to provide easy access to information on computers all over the university's campus. When a user selected an item from a Gopher menu, the Gopher server would automatically download that item to the user's computer. The system worked so well that other information providers

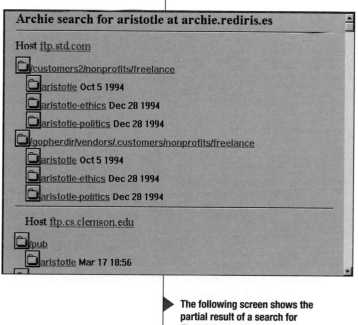

Up to higher level directory			
.cache	3 Kb	Wed Mar 02 00:00:00 1994	
.cap/		Tue Jul 11 11:15:00 1995	Directory
INDEX		Wed Sep 14 00:00:00 1994	Symbolic link
README	7 Kb	Mon Jul 10 21:00:00 1995	
agent046.zip	609 Kb	Wed Apr 05 00:00:00 1995	Zip Compressed Dat
bcgopher.zip	93 Kb	Sun Mar 27 00:00:00 1994	Zip Compressed Dat
col_12b1.zip	198 Kb	Sun Mar 27 00:00:00 1994	Zip Compressed Dat
cooksock.zip	105 Kb	Tue Jun 29 00:00:00 1993	Zip Compressed Dat
eudora14.exe	269 Kb	Thu Mar 24 00:00:00 1994	Binary Executable
fibsw130.zip	212 Kb	Mon Jan 30 00:00:00 1995	Zip Compressed Dat
fingd100.zip	113 Kb	Tue Aug 02 00:00:00 1994	Zip Compressed Dat
finger31.zip	66 Kb	Tue May 18 00:00:00 1993	Zip Compressed Dat
fingerd.zip	4 Kb	Tue Nov 09 00:00:00 1993	Zip Compressed Dat
gophbook.zip	867 Kb	Thu May 27 00:00:00 1993	Zip Compressed Dat
hgopher2.3.zip	185 Kb	Tue Sep 21 00:00:00 1993	Zip Compressed Dat

This is the index for an anonymous FTP archive at the University of North Carolina using an FTP program that displays subdirectories and files in a single list. The user clicks on the name of a file to download it. Other FTP programs use drag-and-drop graphic interfaces or separate text commands.

Archie search for aristotle at archie.rediris.es

Host ftp.std.com

/customers2/nonprofits/freelance
- aristotle Oct 5 1994
- aristotle-ethics Dec 28 1994
- aristotle-politics Dec 28 1994

/gopherdir/vendors/.customers/nonprofits/freelance
- aristotle Oct 5 1994
- aristotle-ethics Dec 28 1994
- aristotle-politics Dec 28 1994

Host ftp.cs.clemson.edu
/pub
- aristotle Mar 17 18:56

The following screen shows the partial result of a search for files related to "Aristotle." The search identified several public archives that contain copies of Aristotle's writings.

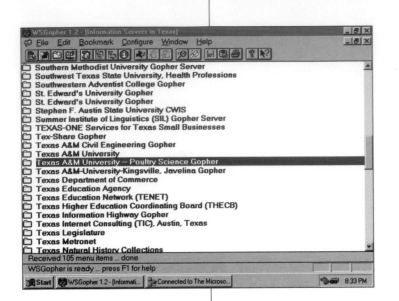

Figure 8.6
The top-level Texas Gopher menu.

created their own Gopher servers and linked them to the Minnesota menus.

A Gopher menu can include links to anything on the Internet, including files of all kinds, host computers, and other Gopher menus. Some menus and submenus are organized by subject, and others list resources in a particular geographical region. Most menus also include pointers to the local server's top-level menu or to the "Mother Gopher" in Minnesota that lists all the Gopher servers in the world. Therefore, it is possible to start on almost any Gopher menu and jump to any other Gopher with just a few intermediate steps.

As an example, let's follow a series of Gopher menus. Figure 8.6 shows a Gopher menu that lists Gopher servers in Texas.

When you select the Texas A&M Poultry Science Gopher from that menu, you get the menu in Figure 8.7, which lists specific services and additional menus.

The "Poultry Pictures" directory leads to more than a dozen GIF picture files, including the picture of a broiler in Figure 8.8.

Gopher goes a long way toward making the Internet more accessible, but with more than 15 million items in Gopher menus, there is still a lot of territory to search. Like the Archie search tool for FTP archives, **Veronica** (Very Easy Rodent-Oriented Net-wide Index to Computer Archives) is a keyword search tool that finds and displays items from Gopher menus.

Figure 8.7
The Texas A&M Poultry Science Gopher.

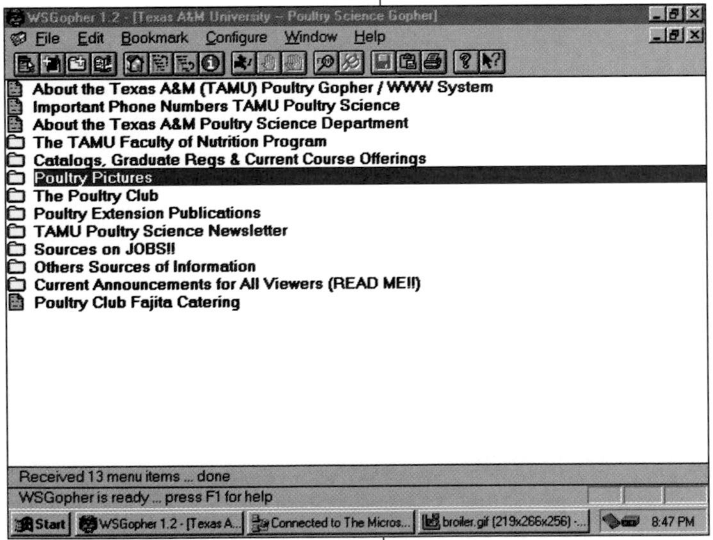

Figure 8.8
A picture from Texas A&M.

Internet Relay Chat (IRC)

Internet Relay Chat (IRC), or just **chat**, is a popular way for Internet users to communicate in real-time with other users. Real-time communication means communicating with other users right now. Unlike e-mail, chat does not require a waiting period between the time you send a message and the other person or group of people receives the message. IRC is often referred to as the "CB radio" of the Internet because it enables a few or many people join in a discussion.

IRC is a multiuser system where people join channels to talk publicly or in private. **Channels** are discussion groups where chat users convene to discuss a topic. Chat messages are typed on a user's computer and sent to the IRC channel, whereupon all users who have joined that channel receive the message. Users can then read, reply to, or ignore that message, or create their own message.

IRC became popular in the news during the 1991 Persian Gulf War. Updates from around the world came across the wire, and most IRC users who were online at the time gathered on a single channel to read those reports. Similarly, live reports of the coup attempt against Boris Yeltsin in September 1993 were communicated by Moscow IRC.

The World Wide Web

The **World Wide Web** (**the Web** or **WWW**) was created in 1989 at the European Particle Physics Laboratory in Geneva, Switzerland, as a method for incorporating footnotes, figures, and cross-references into online **hypertext** documents in which a reader can click on a word or phrase in a document and immediately jump to another location within the same document, or to another file. The second file may be located on the same computer as the original document or anywhere else on the Internet. Because the user does not have to learn separate commands and addresses to jump to a new location, the World Wide Web organized widely scattered resources into a seamless whole.

The Web was an interesting but not particularly exciting tool used by scientific researchers—until 1993, when Mosaic, a point-and-click graphic Web browser, was developed at the National Center for Supercomputing Applications (NCSA) at the University of Illinois. Mosaic, and the Web browsers that have evolved from Mosaic, have changed the way people use the Internet. Web pages are now used to distribute news, interactive educational services, product information and catalogs, highway traffic reports, and live audio and video, among many other things. Interactive Web pages permit readers to consult databases, order products and information, and submit payment with a credit card or other account number.

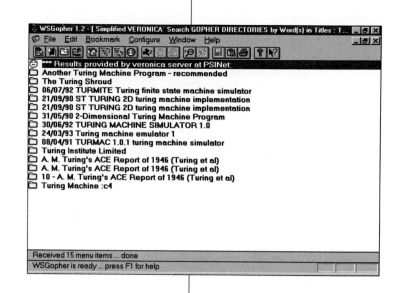

This screen shows the results of a Veronica search for items related to Alan Turing, the pioneer computer scientist.

NORTON Online

For more information on **IRC**, visit this book's Web site at **www.glencoe.com/norton/online**

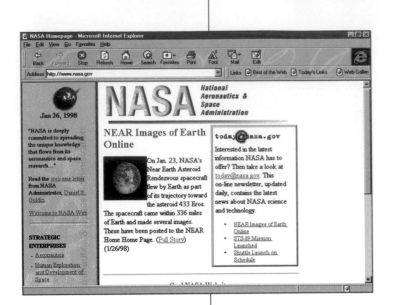

The latest generation of Web browsers, including Mosaic, Netscape Navigator, and Microsoft's Internet Explorer, can open file viewers and other application programs automatically when they receive graphic images, audio, video, and other files. Combined with distributed application languages, like Sun Microsystems' Java, browsers also can import live, interactive data (such as financial information that changes frequently) and executable programs from the World Wide Web.

Some observers currently think that Java, or something like it, will move many computing applications out of individual desktop computers and onto Internet servers.

A typical Web page. Here the user clicks on the underlined words to find out information about NASA's Near Earth Asteroid Rendezvous (NEAR) spacecraft.

The internal structure of the World Wide Web is built on a set of rules called **Hypertext Transfer Protocol (HTTP)** and a page-description language called **Hypertext Markup Language (HTML)**. HTTP uses Internet addresses in a special format called a **Uniform Resource Locator**, or **URL**. URLs look like this:

type://address/path

type specifies the type of server in which the file is located. *address* is the address of the server, and *path* is the location within the file structure of the server. So the URL for the University of Illinois is:

http://www.uiuc.edu

Files in other formats may also have URLs. For example, the URL for the SunSite FTP archive of PC software at the University of North Carolina is:

ftp://sunsite.unc.edu-/pub/micro/pc-stuff

Documents that use HTTP are known as **Web pages**. A typical Web page contains information about a particular subject with links to related Web pages and other resources. Many Web sites contain a top-level **home page** that has pointers to additional pages with more detailed information. For example, a university might have a home page with links to a campus guide, Telnet access to the library, and separate pages for individual departments and programs.

Hundreds of new Web pages appear every week, but they are not always easy to find. Unlike Gopher, which organizes information on the Internet into logical menus, the World Wide Web does not provide a basic structure for locating resources. As an attempt to fill this gap, an assortment of directories and search tools is available online. One of the best is Yahoo!, whose URL is *http://www.yahoo.com*. Yahoo! is an extensive directory with a menu that lists thousands of Web sites, organized by topic, and a search engine that looks for specified words in titles and addresses of the Web sites in the directories.

Productivity Tip

Finding Anything or Anyone on the Net

Searching for information and contact data on the Internet is enormously challenging because there is an astounding amount of information to sift through, and it's always changing. Also, it is organized in a chaotic and complicated interconnected system of Web sites, Gopher and FTP sites, news groups, and mailing lists.

The good news is that it is possible to find specific information on the Internet, and surprisingly quickly. A variety of different search engines are designed to access information specified by the user. However, finding what you want requires research techniques and a good command of how to use search engines.

Each search engine has its own Web page containing forms into which you type the string of text that describes what you want to find on the Web. Click a button, wait a little (hopefully) while, and the engine reveals its list of "hits," or information repositories that contain information that matches your string.

Search engines like AltaVista locate specific topics on the World Wide Web.

Becoming a Web researcher is a complex task. Here are some basic tips that can simplify your Web research right from the start:

Read instructions. Most engines provide a description of how they work and how to conduct a search.

Watch your language. Phrase your query string to maximize each particular search engine's capabilities. Some engines search on single words, others on phrases. Some accept wildcard characters, or Boolean characters, such as AND, OR, and NOT.

Use multiple engines. If one engine doesn't find what you want, another might. Some of the most popular engines include:

- Yahoo! (http://www.yahoo.com)
- Lycos (http://www.lycos.com)
- AltaVista (http://altavista.digital.com)
- Excite (http://www.excite.com)
- AOL NetFind a Person (http://www.aol.com/netfind/person.html)

Rewrite your query. If you don't get the results you want the first time, try rephrasing your query string to define more clearly what it is you want.

Spell correctly. Search engines don't correct typos.

Try, try again. After the first pass, go to the most promising sites and look for words you can use in your query to narrow or enlarge your search. Rephrase your text string, and try your search again.

Try synonyms. There are many different ways to say something. If "running" doesn't get what you want, try "races" or "jogging."

Try specialized engines. Some engines search only a specific group of sites, such as commercial sites, government-sponsored sites, or Usenet news groups. If you know where you want to look, these specialized engines can save you a lot of time.

Read the hit summaries. Most engines provide a summary of each "hit" they've found. These summaries can help you eliminate large numbers of entries without having to take the time to visit the pages.

Keep a trail of breadcrumbs. Use bookmarks to keep track of sites you want to visit again.

Keep up to date. Sites, engines, and the latest Web research tools change at least once every day. Stay informed.

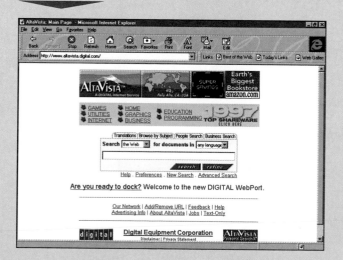

303

NORTON Online

For more information on **America Online**, visit this book's Web site at www.glencoe.com/norton/online

Online Services and BBSs

Today, many of the most exciting things you can do with a personal computer involve online services, bulletin board services (BBSs), and the Internet. In a world of information, these services are your passport.

An **online service** is a company that offers access, generally on a subscription basis, to e-mail, discussion groups, databases on various subjects (such as weather information, stock quotes, newspaper articles, and so on), and other services ranging from electronic banking to online games. Most online services also offer access to the Internet. Currently, the most popular online services are America Online, Microsoft Network, and Prodigy. In September 1997, America Online purchased the second most popular online service, CompuServe, raising the number of America Online subscribers to more than 13 million.

This is the home page of Yahoo!, an online search engine for finding information on the Web.

America Online offers a variety of information and services.

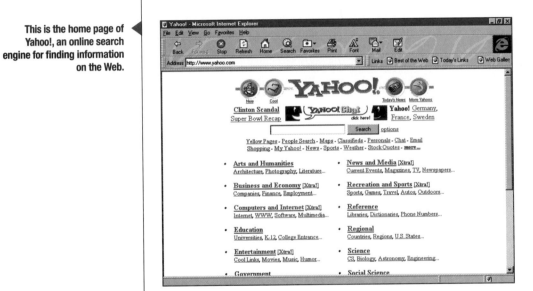

Users typically pay by the month; the subscription allows them to use the service for a limited number of hours per month. If they use the service for more time, they pay by the hour.

People subscribe to online services for all kinds of reasons. Many subscribe simply to have access to e-mail and the other kinds of communication that online services include, such as discussion groups and chat lines. A **discussion group** (also known as a **bulletin board** or a news group) is an electronic storage space where users can post messages to other users. The discussion group lets users carry on extended conversations and trade information. Figure 8.9 shows messages posted to a discussion group.

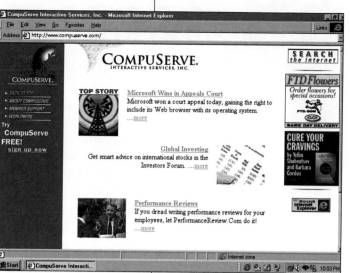

CompuServe, which is now part of America Online, is a favorite among technical and business users.

People tend to join discussion groups aimed at their professional or personal interests. Because different services have different kinds of discussion groups, the services tend to attract different kinds of users. For example, CompuServe (even after being purchased by America Online) attracts many computer professionals because there are discussions that relate to specific pieces of software or hardware. Prodigy, on the other hand, tends to attract home users. Like e-mail, discussion groups are an inexpensive, efficient means of communication. Online services such as America Online provide direct access to the Internet, for World Wide Web browsing, FTP file transfers, and news group support. With the acquisition of CompuServe, America Online plans to move the highly praised CompuServe forums to the Web, making them accessible for AOL members who prefer to stay on the Web to communicate in forums.

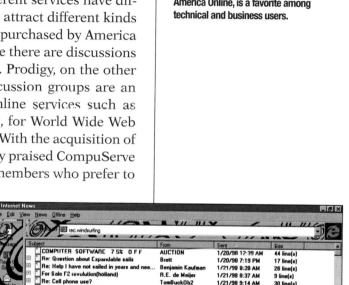

Many small services, usually known as bulletin board services, or **BBSs**, exist only to provide specific discussion groups or groups of discussion groups. BBSs gained popularity almost as soon as modems became popular. At first, most were run privately, out of people's homes. During the 1980s and early 1990s, they spread to the commercial services and the Internet. Today, the term **system operator**, or **sysop**, is used to describe the person who monitors group discussions.

Most of the online services also offer **chat lines**, which are similar to bulletin boards, except that they are live group discussions, more akin to a conference call than to a bulletin board. Although relatively new to computer networks (compared to bulletin boards), chat lines have a long history in the telephone system. In the early days of telephones, operators opened party lines where groups of people could have a "virtual" party without leaving their homes.

▶ **Figure 8.9**
Message posted to a discussion group.

Although the biggest online services are general in content and offer many features, others are much more specialized, offering access to specific databases.

One problem that has puzzled many Web content providers (companies or individuals who publish Web pages) is how to get and keep visitors. Much like a television show or any retail business, Web sites want a continuous stream of visitors. For commercial Web sites and Web sites featuring advertisements, the number of "hits" generated every day is critical to promoting and selling products.

Push Delivery Technology As a way around waiting for visitors to come, some Web sites have started delivering content to users automatically. This capability requires the use of **push delivery** technology.

The first company to offer push content was PointCast News (*http://www.pointcast.com*). PointCast delivers customized news to users' desktops at specified times. After downloading client software from PointCast, you choose the news, weather, sports, and business information you want to receive. Also, you can configure PointCast software to act like a screen saver and turn on the news for you whenever your PC is idle.

Because of the overwhelming popularity of PointCast (it's so popular among workers at some companies that management must regulate its use), many large software companies have begun to offer their own version of push. Netscape and Microsoft now offer products that enable users to receive automatic content from the Web.

Netscape's Netcaster, which is available with Netscape Navigator 4 or Netscape Communicator 4, uses Miramba's Java-based Castanet Tuner to subscribe to Web sites (called *channels*) that offer push information to a user's desktop. Push channels contain dynamic information that changes routinely, such as hourly, weekly, or as events occur. A news channel, for instance, may provide hourly updates, with late-breaking news being delivered as it happens. Netcaster also lets users subscribe to any Web site to download Web pages from it.

Netscape Netcaster provides automatic updates to Web pages you subscribe to.

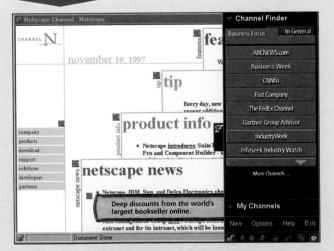

Netcaster users can control which channel they subscribe to, when the information is updated, and how the information is displayed. Netcaster can run as a windowed application or as a full-screen application, called the WebTop. When you run Netcaster in WebTop view, a channel is displayed in the background on your desktop as you are working in other applications. You also can run Netcaster to download information that you can then view offline. Offline viewing lets you read Web pages while not connected to the Internet.

Microsoft's Internet Explorer 4 also includes a push delivery application. Explorer's WebCasting technology supports Active Channel content, which can display on your computer as your desktop or screen saver, in full-screen mode, or as an e-mail message.

When a user subscribes to an Active Channel, content is delivered to the user's desktop automatically, based on the delivery schedule set by the user. Subscriptions can be set for specially designed Web pages that support the Channel Definition Format (CDF), a Microsoft technology that defines how push content is created and delivered. Internet Explorer 4 also enables users to subscribe to any page on the Web that they have saved as a favorite site. When changes are made to that site, Internet Explorer 4 will notify the user of the update.

Push Formats Push delivery documents are created based on proprietary formats (as in the case of PointCast) CDF, HTML, Java, and JavaScript. Microsoft has also developed the Open Software Definition (OSD), which software developers and corporate users can use to distribute new or updated software to users via Software Distribution Channels.

In the near future, you may be working at your computer and receive notification that a favorite Web site has been updated or automatically receive an update to your word processor.

Perhaps the best known is LEXIS-NEXIS, a company that sells access to its two databases. LEXIS © is a legal database that researchers can use to find specific laws and court opinions. NEXIS © is a bibliographic database that contains information about articles on a wide range of topics.

Internet Features in Application Programs

The Internet tools described up to this point usually appear as either separate, stand-alone applications or integrated programs that combine several Internet client functions into a single graphical interface. As the Internet continues to become part of daily life for more computer users, many other application programs have begun to integrate Internet functions. For example, WordPerfect, Microsoft Word, and other word processors and desktop publishing programs can import World Wide Web pages and other Internet files into documents. Many programs can also be used to create Web pages and browse the Web. Communications programs can send and receive messages through the Internet as easily as they use a telephone line. Spreadsheets and database managers can obtain information from Internet servers that they can analyze and display on a local computer. This trend is likely to continue and grow.

ACCESSING THE INTERNET

Because the Internet connects so many computers and networks, there are many ways to obtain access to it. Some methods are appropriate for computers attached to a local area network in a college or corporation, whereas others are better for an isolated computer in a home office or small business.

Direct Connection

In a direct connection, Internet programs run on the local computer, which uses the TCP/IP protocols to exchange data with another computer through the Internet. An isolated computer can connect to the Internet through a serial

data communications port using either **Serial Line Interface Protocol (SLIP)** or **Point to Point Protocol (PPP)**, two methods for creating a direct connection through a phone line.

Remote Terminal Connection

A remote terminal connection to the Internet exchanges commands and data in ASCII text format with a host computer that uses UNIX or a similar operating system. The TCP/IP application programs and protocols all run on the host. Because the command set in UNIX is called a shell, this kind of Internet access is known as a **shell account**.

Gateway Connection

Many networks that do not use TCP/IP commands and protocols may still provide some Internet services, such as e-mail or file transfer. These networks use gateways that convert commands and data to and from TCP/IP format.

Although it is possible to connect a local network directly to the Internet backbone, it is usually not practical (except for the largest corporations and institutions) because of the high cost of a backbone connection. As a general rule, most businesses and individuals obtain access through an **Internet Service Provider (ISP)**, which supplies the backbone connection. ISPs offer several kinds of Internet service, including inexpensive shell accounts, direct TCP/IP connections using SLIP or PPP accounts, and full-time high-speed access through dedicated data circuits.

With a remote terminal connection to a shell account, all information appears as text on the screen.

Connecting Through a LAN

If a local area network (LAN) uses TCP/IP protocols for communication within the network, it is a simple matter to connect to the Internet through a router, another computer that stores and forwards sets of data (called packets) to other computers on the Internet. If the LAN uses a different kind of local protocol, a bridge converts it to and from TCP/IP. When a LAN has an Internet connection, that connection extends to every computer on the LAN.

Connecting Through a Modem

If there is no LAN on site, an isolated computer can connect to the Internet through a serial data communications port and a modem, using either a shell account and a terminal emulation program, or a direct TCP/IP connection with a SLIP or PPP account. TCP/IP connections permit users to run application programs with graphical user interfaces instead of limiting them to ASCII text.

High-Speed Data Links

Modem connections are convenient, but their capacity is limited to the relatively low data-transfer speed of a telephone line. A 33.6 Kbps modem is fine for text, but it is really not practical for huge digital audio and video files. Furthermore, when many users are sharing an Internet connection through a LAN, the connection between the bridge or router and the ISP must be adequate to meet the demands of many users at the same time. Fortunately, dedicated high-speed data circuits are available from telephone companies, cable TV services, and other suppliers. Using fiber optics, microwave, and other technologies, it is entirely practical to establish an Internet connection that is at least ten times as fast as a modem link. All it takes is money.

For small businesses and individual users, ISDN (Integrated Services Digital Network) is an attractive alternative. ISDN is a relatively new digital telephone service that combines voice, data, and control signaling through a single circuit. An ISDN data connection can transfer data at up to 128,000 bits per second. Most telephone companies offer ISDN at a slightly higher cost than the conventional telephone service that it replaces.

Other Online Services

The Internet has overshadowed and absorbed some of the other online services, but it is not the only place to obtain information through a modem. Online information services such as America Online and the Microsoft Network provide their own conferences, live chat groups, news reports, online versions of magazines and newspapers, and huge libraries of downloadable files, along with Internet services such as e-mail, Usenet news, FTP file transfer, and access to the World Wide Web.

Access to the Internet through an online service usually costs a little more than an account with an ISP, but, so far, the added value of the online services, their conferences, news, and file libraries make them the preferred method for millions of users. All online services offer free trial memberships, so it is easy to sign up and look around without any risk.

CONNECTING A PC TO THE INTERNET

Connecting a desktop computer to the Internet actually involves two separate issues: software and the network connection. The industry has developed a standard interface called Windows Sockets, or **Winsock**, that makes it possible to mix and match application programs from more than one developer. Figure 8.10 shows how applications, the Winsock interface, and network drivers fit together.

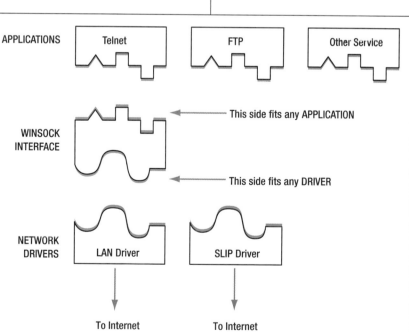

Figure 8.10
How Winsock provides an interface between applications and networks.

Integrated Internet Software Packages

Many companies offer suites of Internet access tools. These packages usually contain client programs for e-mail, Telnet, FTP, and other applications, along with a World Wide Web browser and software for connecting to a network using dial-up modem connections, connection through a LAN, or both. In addition, some packages include sign-up utilities that will work with one or more Internet service providers who offer modem access through local telephone numbers in most major metropolitan areas.

The all-in-one-box approach has several advantages. In most cases, the applications in a suite share a common interface design, so they are easy to learn and use. Additionally, because all the applications come from the same source, there is a single point of contact for technical support and product upgrades. If a suite includes an account with a particular ISP, it is a safe bet that the service provider has worked with the software developer to make sure that there are no incompatibilities between the software and the network.

NORTON Online

For more information on **firewalls**, visit this book's Web site at www.glencoe.com/norton/online

WORKING ON THE INTERNET

The increased use of the Internet and the World Wide Web places networks at even greater risk of undesired intrusion. Many organizations publish information on the Web, whereas others have employees who pass information to the Internet from the company network or download material from the Internet.

Not that long ago, the Internet was the exclusive province of educators, scientists, and researchers. That has changed, and today companies and individuals all over the world are eagerly stampeding into cyberspace. The legal, procedural, and moral infrastructure for this volume of activity simply does not yet exist. Both companies and individuals are taking it one step at a time while the standards are still being defined.

Businesses and Firewalls

With millions of Internet users potentially able to pass information to and take information from the network, the security of business networks is a huge concern. Most businesses set up **firewalls** to control access to their networks. Firewalls act as barriers to unauthorized entry into a protected network, allowing outsiders to access public areas but preventing them from exploring other proprietary areas of the network.

Today, many companies are exploring procedures for selling their products and services on the Web. Passing company information over the Internet and receiving payment, usually in the form of credit card numbers, are two of the major issues involved with commerce in cyberspace. The number of opportunities for stealing data is astronomical. Thus, security measures such as encryption must be further developed before there will be many companies selling their goods and services online. And there are, of course, legal ramifications to this change in business style. For example, who is liable if someone intercepts a credit card number?

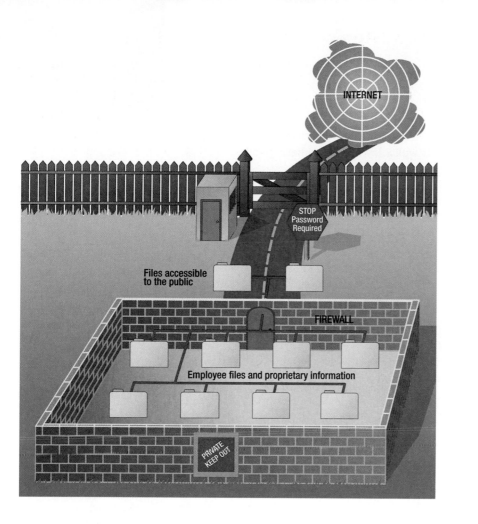

▶ Networks connected to the Internet use a firewall to prevent non-employees from accessing private or proprietary information. In many cases, portions of the network also are accessible to the public.

Issues for Individuals

Before you start publishing material or downloading material from other sites on the Internet, you need to think about what you are doing. Many people who use the Internet think that all the data available on it is free. Are you willing to have other people lift your material and use it as theirs?

Imagine that you have downloaded a gorgeous graphic from a site in Europe. Are you violating someone else's copyright? Do you know whether you have the right to import it into one of your documents and distribute it?

Another issue is the definition of libel in cyberspace. People are accustomed to voicing their opinions freely in a letter because letters are, presumably, private. On the Internet, however, "private" communications can be quickly forwarded far beyond their intended readership, which amounts to publication.

Another significant issue is the suitability of material for different audiences. Given that many children now are computer-literate, how do you feel about pornography distributed on the Internet? Would you even know whether a picture or document were pornographic according to the legal definition of that term?

If you do not know the answers to these questions, you are not alone. Most people do not, sometimes because the legal answers are still being formulated.

Techview

Emerging Internet Technologies

Over the past few years, several new Internet technologies have emerged. Some of these technologies, like push delivery, have received large amounts of press coverage. Others, such as XML, are not as well known to the general public.

To help you become savvy about these emerging technologies, here are descriptions of some of the most popular Web technologies you may encounter while online.

Java is a programming language, a set of codes used for creating cross-platform programs. It was developed by Sun Microsystems in the mid 1990s and enables Web page designers to include movement and interactivity in Web pages. Java programs included in Web pages are commonly referred to as **Java applets**. The two most popular Web browsers, Microsoft Internet Explorer 4 and Netscape Navigator 4, support Web pages that include Java applets.

ActiveX controls are programs that adhere to Microsoft's COM technology (which is the technology behind Microsoft's OLE capabilities found in Windows 98) to provide interoperability with other types of components and services that support COM. This means that a Web page can include ActiveX controls to activate other programs (such as applications in the Microsoft Office 97 suite) or to enable scripts, such as process viewer forms.

One misconception about ActiveX is that it is a competitor to Java. In fact, ActiveX is not as full-featured as Java and is only part of the entire set of COM services. On the other hand, Java is a programming environment that is akin to C++.

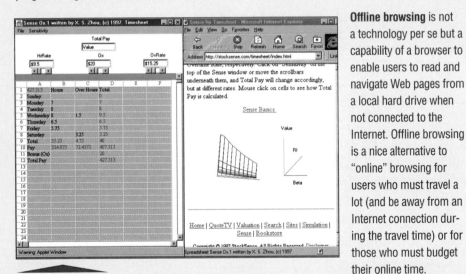

Java applets, like the Timesheet application shown here, provide a way for Web page authors to integrate interactive applications on their static Web pages.

Offline browsing is not a technology per se but a capability of a browser to enable users to read and navigate Web pages from a local hard drive when not connected to the Internet. Offline browsing is a nice alternative to "online" browsing for users who must travel a lot (and be away from an Internet connection during the travel time) or for those who must budget their online time.

HTML 4 is the latest proposal of the hypertext markup language. Currently HTML 3.2 is the recommended standard that new Web browsers should support. With HTML 4.0, Web sites will have advanced forms, improved frames, standards for handling scripts, and added features for users with disabilities.

Extensible Markup Language (XML) is a proposal for replacing HTML as the standard hypertext markup language for the Web. XML is built around the idea of letting anyone (which usually means software developers) define a way to describe information presented in a Web page.

XML is not a fixed markup language, as HTML is (that is, HTML has standardized how something coded should behave or look on screen). With XML, Web page authors can get closer to designing pages that mimic the way SGML (Standard Generalized Markup Language) defines the structure and content of electronic documents. SGML, for example, is used to display a formatted document that appears in word processors and desktop publishing applications.

WebView turns your desktop into a Web browser. With the release of Internet Explorer 4 and Windows 98, users have the choice of turning their desktop into a giant Web browser called the Active Desktop. All objects, such as files, documents, devices (such as printers and modems), and Web pages are accessible as hyperlinks. Users just need to single-click a document to open it instead of using the standard double-clicking method.

WebView technology also extends the user's desktop from a local desktop to one that "resides" on the Web. When a user wants a document, for example, she no longer needs to think about whether it resides on her hard drive, the network hard drive, or as a resource on the Net. She just clicks on a hyperlink that points to the document.

OVERVIEW OF BROWSERS

Deciding on the software you use to navigate the Internet usually comes down to which Web browser to choose. Today, two browsers have the majority of the market share: Netscape Navigator and Microsoft Internet Explorer. Navigator garners about 60 percent of the browser market, whereas Internet Explorer has 30-35 percent. Many other browsers are available, such as NCSA's Mosaic (which is the Web browser that initially introduced many Internet users to the Web), but none has a significant market share.

Netscape sells several versions of its Navigator product. The most recent release, Navigator 4x (released in 1997) is available in both a stand-alone version and as a component of Netscape's Communicator product. You can download either product for evaluation purposes at *http://home.netscape.com*. As a stand-alone product, Navigator 4x includes only the Web browser and NetCaster applications. On the other hand, Communicator is an all-in-one application that includes the following components:

- Navigator for Web navigation
- Composer for Web-page editing and creation
- NetCaster for receiving push documents
- Messenger for sending, receiving, and creating e-mail
- Collabra for joining news groups
- Conference for conducting online conferences

NORTON Online

For more information on **Netscape Navigator and other Netscape Internet products**, visit this book's Web site at **www.glencoe.com/norton/online**

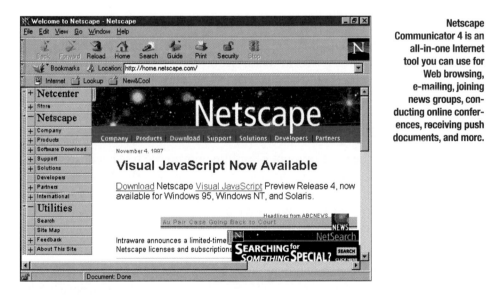

Netscape Communicator 4 is an all-in-one Internet tool you can use for Web browsing, e-mailing, joining news groups, conducting online conferences, receiving push documents, and more.

One advantage of Microsoft's Internet Explorer 4 is that it is free. Users can download full versions of Internet Explorer from the Microsoft Web site (*http://www.microsoft.com*) and use it indefinitely without a charge. (In early 1998, Netscape announced plans to make certain versions of its browser available for free, as well.) Like Communicator, Internet Explorer also supports e-mail, news groups, Web-page creation, and push technologies. You also can download NetMeeting 2.0 for online conferences.

Table 8.3	Web Browser Comparison Chart	
FEATURE	**INTERNET EXPLORER 4**	**COMMUNICATOR 4**
HTML 3.2	Yes	Yes
HTML editing	With FrontPage Express	With Composer
Cascading style sheets	Yes	Yes
E-mail	Yes	Yes
News reader	Yes	Yes
Online conferencing	No	Yes
Web view	Yes	No
VBScript	Yes	No
JavaScript	Yes	Yes
Plug-ins	As ActiveX Controls	Yes
Offline browsing	Yes	No
Java	Yes	Yes
ActiveX	Yes	Yes
Dynamic Web pages	Yes	Yes

To compare features and the type of Web page content each browser supports, see Table 8.3.

COMMERCE ON THE WEB

Would you buy flowers on the Internet? In 1994, the Flower Shop was the first "commercial" site on the World Wide Web. Now, there are an estimated 250,000 commercial Web sites. Commerce on the Web—called **e-commerce**— is in its infancy, but all signs point to an extremely short childhood. Web sales totaled more than $24 billion in 1997 (ActivMedia study), and sales are expected to hit $120 billion by the year 2000 (International Data Corp. study).

The big hurdle to the development of online commerce has been the lack of trusted security measures for transferring money over the Net. Businesses have routinely transferred money over networks for years (every time you make a transaction over your bank's ATM unit, for example), but these are secured private networks or point-to-point terminal connections—meaning that no one can jump online unnoticed from the outside.

The Internet is different. It is public and decentralized, and streams of information (like your credit card number) can be intercepted along its network by intelligent hackers. Various encryption systems and other security measures are on the drawing boards to make online commerce more private and secure.

In early 1996, Visa and Mastercard made financial history by announcing their intention to merge their rival security protocols into a single technological standard, called Secure Electronic Payment Protocol (SEPP). The new protocol, Secure Electronic Transactions (SET) is expected to be supported by the main Web browser developers, Microsoft and Netscape, as well as by other companies.

Electronic commerce advocates envision a world where business will be conducted online directly from business to consumer, unencumbered by costly middlemen and distribution channels.

A large amount of business is already being conducted online. For example:

To quickly access the sites described in this list, visit this book's Web site at www.glencoe.com/norton/online

- *Car buying via the Net.* General Motors created an online buying site, BuyPower (*http://www.gmbuypower.com*), that connects visitors to dealer inventories, vehicle features, pricing information, and more. When a shopper wants to make a purchase, he or she sends an e-mail message to a dealer asking for a price. Within 24 hours, the dealer responds with a price and availability. The shopper also can set up test-drive times and start the paperwork for a loan or lease agreement.

- *Mega-bookstore.* Amazon.com (*http://www.amazon.com*), a Net shopping pioneer, sells books online, offering more than 2.5 million different titles. You can "virtually" browse books, recommend books to other readers, and search for books by title, author, or subject.

- *Groceries at your door.* Approximately 40,000 subscribers in the San Francisco, Houston, Atlanta, Boston, and Chicago areas pay a monthly fee and a percentage of their grocery bill to order groceries from their computer keyboards via Peapod (*http://www.peapod.com*), an interactive online shopping and delivery service. Customers place their orders in an online form, filling their virtual shopping carts from a 20,000-item, constantly updated database. Trained Peapod personnel receive the orders online and then hand pick the groceries and deliver them to the customer. Peapod works with Jewel Food Stores in Chicago, Stop & Shop in Boston, Randalls in Houston, Brunos in Atlanta, and Safeway, Inc., in northern California.

Amazon.com is the largest bookstore on the Internet.

Computers
In Your Career

Many careers are associated with the Internet, including network administrators, IS (information systems) managers, and data communications managers. Besides careers that focus on the architecture and administration side of the Internet, the following are some other careers in which having a working knowledge of the Internet is important:

Multimedia Developers As more people get connected to the Internet, there will be a greater need for companies to provide highly visual content to capture and retain visitors. This need will drive up the demand for multimedia developers who can design content for the Internet, particularly the Web. To become marketable in this field, you need a thorough background in multimedia authoring and distribution skills, as well as a working knowledge of creating multimedia content for delivery over the Internet. Also look to acquire skills in one or more programming languages used on the Internet, such as the Java programming language.

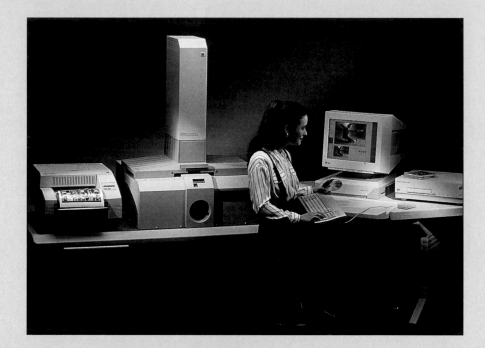

Librarians One of the goals of a library is to make materials readily available to its users. For this reason, many library systems have supplemented their on-shelf book system with electronic resources available over the Internet. Two areas of specialty in library information services include reference librarians and catalogers. Both of these specialists must become knowledgeable of the Internet and be able to categorize and retrieve information distributed over the Internet and other electronic media (such as CD-ROMs).

Writers and Editors Just as the Internet has changed the way multimedia content is delivered, so has it changed the way books, periodicals, and other printed media is delivered and viewed by consumers. Most publishing houses and newspapers require their writers and editors to work electronically and deliver manuscript and articles via the Internet or other network. Many writers must also know how to create content for the Internet and be familiar with creating HTML pages. Likewise, editors should have knowledge of how to work inside HTML pages and how to deliver these pages to an Internet site for delivery.

WHAT TO EXPECT IN THE FUTURE

The state of the Internet today is like broadcast radio in the early 1920s. It is still searching for the best way to evolve from a technical curiosity to a mass medium. The basic technology is in place, but the content and business models are still developing.

Over the next few years, the Internet will continue to expand and change in several important ways: faster connections, more users, new multimedia and "virtual reality" services, and distributed network-based applications. As cable TV and telephone companies provide affordable high-speed access, and as more homes and offices are connected, information providers will use the Internet to distribute digital audio and video services for education, entertainment, and business communication. Distributed application languages such as Java will enable information providers to supply interactive services such as multimedia newspapers, livestock market tickers, and games to millions of subscribers. Other programs will notify users automatically when predesignated events take place anywhere on the Internet.

Many businesses will find ways to make money online, whereas others will go bankrupt trying. Some Internet services will be surrounded by advertisements; others will require payment for access to their Web sites and FTP archives, or for individual downloads. Ten years from now, it is possible that the Internet will be as universal as radio and television are today.

VISUAL SUMMARY

Background and History: An Explosion of Connectivity

■ The Internet was created for the U.S. Department of Defense as a tool for military communications, command and control, and exchanges of data with defense contractors.

■ The Internet has continued to expand and grow by establishing interconnections with other networks around the world.

■ Today, the Internet is a network of networks interconnected through regional and national backbone connections.

■ The Internet carries messages, documents, programs, and data files that contain every imaginable kind of information for businesses, educational institutions, government agencies, and individual users.

How the Internet Works

■ All computers on the Internet use TCP/IP protocols to exchange commands and data.

■ Any computer on the Internet can connect to any other computer.

■ Individual computers connect to local and regional networks, which are connected together through the Internet backbone.

■ A computer can connect directly to the Internet, or as a remote terminal on another computer, or through a gateway from a network that does not use TCP/IP.

■ Every computer on the Internet has a unique numeric IP address, and most also have an address that uses the Domain Name System.

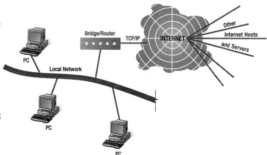

■ Most Internet application programs use the client/server model; users run client programs that obtain data and services from a server.

Major Features of the Internet

■ The Internet is a source of news, business communication, entertainment, and technical information. It also supports "virtual communities."

■ Electronic mail is the most popular use of the Internet.

■ Telnet allows a user to operate a second computer from the keyboard of his or her machine.

■ FTP is the Internet tool for copying data and program files from one computer to another.

■ News and mailing lists are public conferences distributed through the Internet and other electronic networks.

■ Gopher is a hierarchical menu system that helps users find resources that may be anywhere on the Internet.

■ Chats are public conferences conducted in real-time where people join channels to discuss topics of interest.

■ The World Wide Web combines text, illustrations, and links to other files in hypertext documents. The Web is the fastest growing part of the Internet.

- Online service companies and bulletin board services (BBSs) offer, in addition to Internet access, a wide variety of other features, such as e-mail, discussion groups, stock quotes, news, and online games.

- Other Internet tools and services can be integrated into word processors, database managers, and other application programs.

Accessing the Internet

- Users can connect to the Internet through local area networks (LANs), direct TCP/IP connections, and gateways from online information services.

Connecting a PC to the Internet

- The Winsock standard specifies the Windows interface between TCP/IP applications and network connections.

- Users can mix and match Winsock-compatible applications.

- Internet application suites are available from many suppliers; they combine a full set of applications and drivers in a single package.

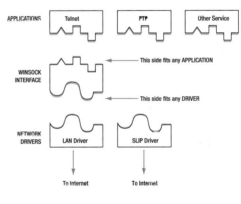

Working on the Internet

- Businesses that connect their networks to the Internet often set up firewalls to prevent unauthorized users from gaining access to proprietary information.

- Many legal issues related to using the Internet are still being formulated, including the use of encryption, copyright laws on the Web, the privacy of e-mail, and the availability of pornographic material to minors.

Overview of Browsers

- Web browsers are applications used to navigate and view documents on the Web.

- Netscape Navigator and Microsoft Internet Explorer are the two most popular Web browsers, with a combined market share of more than 90 percent.

Commerce on the Web

- Commerce on the Web has grown from a Web site selling flowers to an estimated 250,000-plus business sites devoted to selling products and services.

- Electronic commerce advocates envision a world where business will be conducted online directly from business to consumer, unencumbered by costly middlemen and distribution channels.

Visual Summary & Exercises

KEY TERMS

After completing this chapter, you should be able to define the following terms:

ActiveX control, 312
anonymous FTP archive, 298
Archie, 299
ARPANET, 292
backbone, 292
BBS, 305
bulletin board, 305
channel, 301
chat, 301
chat line, 305
discussion group, 305
domain, 294
Domain Name System (DNS), 294
e-commerce, 314
Extensible Markup Language (XML), 312
firewall, 310
Frequently Asked Questions (FAQs), 297

Gopher, 299
home page, 302
hypertext, 301
Hypertext Markup Language (HTML), 302
Hypertext Transfer Protocol (HTTP), 302
Internet Relay Chat (IRC), 301
Internet Service Provider (ISP), 308
IP address, 294
Java, 312
Java applet, 312
listserv, 296
News, 296
news group, 296
NSFnet, 292
offline browsing, 312
online service, 304

Point to Point Protocol (PPP), 308
push delivery, 306
shell account, 308
Serial Line Interface Protocol (SLIP), 308
subdomain, 294
system operator (or sysop), 305
TCP/IP, 293
Telnet, 298
Uniform Resource Locator (URL), 304
Usenet, 296
Veronica, 300
Web page, 302
Webview, 312
Winsock, 309
World Wide Web (the Web or WWW), 301

KEY TERM QUIZ

Fill in the missing word with one of the terms listed in Key Terms.

1. The central structure that connects elements of a network is known as the _____.

2. A(n) _____ is someone who monitors online group discussions.

3. The Hypertext Transfer Protocol uses Internet addresses in a special format, called a(n) _____.

4. There are thousands of _____ on the Internet devoted to different topics of discussion.

5. _____ lets you connect your computer to a distant host system.

6. You can use _____ to link to anything on the Internet.

7. _____ are documents that use HTTP.

8. A(n) _____ is a powerful computer that acts as a shared storage resource on a network.

9. A standard interface that makes it possible to mix and match applications from more than one developer is called _____.

10. Live group discussions online are carried out on _____.

Visual Summary & Exercises

REVIEW QUESTIONS

1. According to this chapter, what is the single most important aspect to understand about the Internet?

2. What are protocols? What do they do?

3. What allows any size computer to be able to send and receive data through the Internet?

4. Explain briefly why the Internet is sometimes described as "a network of networks."

5. What is Archie primarily used for?

6. Describe the differences between an IP address and a Domain Name System address.

7. Describe how e-mail uses listservs to let people communicate over the Internet.

8. What protocol is necessary for sharing data files between computers?

9. Describe how keyword search tools help users find information via the Internet.

10. What trend in application software is likely to continue to grow as the Internet grows in popularity?

DISCUSSION QUESTIONS

1. What do you think about the claim that new languages such as Java will move applications out of individual desktop computers to Internet servers? In what ways do you think such an occurrence might benefit businesses and other organizations? What do you think are some benefits to connecting a company's LAN to the Internet? Are there any detriments?

2. Based on what you read in this chapter about the Internet's history, what significant factor made it possible to conduct business and exchange commercial information over the Internet?

3. Despite the promise that the Internet will perhaps one day be as universal as radio and television, how do you feel about the growing "commercialization" of the Internet? Do you think the motive to use the Internet as a vehicle for profit will negatively impact it as a wealthy source of information?

4. Do you think that graphical Web browsers have changed significantly the way people use the Internet? Do you think that the graphical user interface programs for browsing the World Wide Web have contributed to the growing numbers of people who use the Internet?

inteNET Workshop

The following exercises assume that you have access to the Internet and a browser. If you need help with any of the exercises, visit this book's Web site at **www.glencoe.com/norton/online**. This book's Web site also lists the URLs you need to complete many of these exercises.

1. Many different Web sites are devoted to tracking and publishing facts and statistics about the Internet. One such service is the Open Market Internet Index. Locate two other sites that perform similar functions and discuss with the class how these sites may provide similar or different data about the Internet. In cases where you find contrasting data from these sites, what do you think accounts for the differences?

2. Every day, new Web pages, news groups, listservs, and FTP sites open up on the Internet. Using a sophisticated search engine such as Excite PowerSearch, find two different announcement services that provide links and information about new sites that appear each day or each week. (Note: engines such as Excite PowerSearch let you search based on multiple terms and apply specific constraints to get the most accurate results. Practice using this page.) Then rank five of your favorite new sites.

3. Many companies are investing in secure systems that will allow consumers to shop on the Internet. Locate at least one Web site that offers the following products or services and share those sites with the class. Also, note how each site handles transactions (for example, via telephone, e-mail, or online transaction).

- Books
- Music (CDs, cassettes, and so on)
- Shoes
- Investments

4. You do not need a news reader to use Internet news groups. Several Web-based services provide services that enable you to view and participate in thousands of news groups. Visit such a site and explore the world of news groups. Can you find any news groups that are of particular interest to you? How useful do you think news groups can be in your schoolwork or job?

5. Until recently, Internet users needed a special FTP client software package to download files from FTP sites. If you are using a recent version of a Web browser (such as Netscape Navigator 3 or later, or Microsoft Internet Explorer 3 or later), you can access FTP sites from the Web. This is handy if you need to download a file, such as a bug fix or a piece of shareware. Further, most software companies and many universities maintain large FTP sites, which are filled with files accessible by the public. Visit the FTP sites of some of the major software and hardware companies. Did you find any useful files or information? For a large list of official corporate-sponsored FTP sites, find and go to the Computer Companies FTP Sites Web page.

6. You no longer need a separate e-mail package to send and receive e-mail (although some might prefer a special e-mail package for its customizable features). Using Web-based services such as Hotmail, you can set up an e-mail account that can be accessed over the Web. This means that you do not need to access your ISP to send or receive mail; if you can get on the Web (from a friend's computer, for example), you can access e-mail service. Search for several Web-based e-mail services. How do these compare to typical e-mail systems provided by ISPs or online services?

7. Online privacy is a major concern among people who use the Internet regularly, especially those who use the Internet in their work. What online resources can you find that provide reliable information about privacy issues, such as current legislation, safeguards, computer crime, SPAM, and other online issues? Start with the Electronic Frontier Foundation's Web site and go from there.

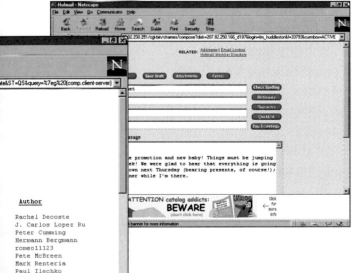

Computer Graphics and Design

CONTENTS

OBJECTIVES

When you complete this chapter, you will be able to do the following:

- List two significant uses for graphics software.
- List two significant differences between paint and draw programs.
- Name the five major categories of graphics software and list their differences.
- List five of the most common file formats for bitmap and vector graphics.
- Name three ways that computer animation is being used today.
- List and describe at least three possible applications for virtual reality technology.

computers, using specialized animation software.

With its capability to mimic traditional artists' media, graphics software also allows artists to do with a computer what they once did with brushes, pencils, and dark-room equipment. With a few keystrokes, the click of a mouse button, and some practice, a talented artist can create colorful and sophisticated images. Similarly, architects and engineers now do most of their design and rendering work on computers—even though most were trained in traditional paper-based drafting methods. By using the computer, they produce designs and renderings that are not only highly accurate, but aesthetically pleasing, as well.

Graphics software is used for many different purposes and by many different kinds of users. During a typical day, in fact, you may not realize how much of the imagery you see is created on a computer. For example, many stamps sold by the United States Postal Service were created with a draw program on a Macintosh computer. In the daily newspaper and popular magazines, many graphics are either created or retouched by draw or photo-manipulation programs. The titles of many popular television shows were produced by graphic artists using common 3-D modeling programs. Much of the animation you see in TV programs, commercials, and movies is created on

Although graphics software was a relative latecomer to the computer world, it has advanced a long way in a short time. In the early 1980s, most graphics programs were limited to drawing simple geometric shapes, usually in black and white. Today, graphics software offers advanced drawing and painting tools, and virtually unlimited color control. In newspapers and magazines, on posters and billboards, in TV and the movies, you see the products of these powerful tools. Their results can be subtle or stunning, obviously artificial, or amazingly lifelike.

WORKING WITH IMAGES

In today's publishing and design industries, it is not uncommon for an artist to take files created on a PC, convert them to Macintosh format, manipulate them with a whole series of graphics programs, and then convert them back to a PC format. It is also common to do just the opposite, converting images to a PC format and then back to a Macintosh format. Just as traditional artists must know the capabilities of their paints and brushes, today's computer-based artist must have a wide knowledge of graphics software, the hardware platforms on which it runs, and the formats in which the data can be stored.

Platforms

Many traditional artists have added one or more computers to their collection of tools.

In 1984, the introduction of the Apple Macintosh computer and a modest piece of software known as MacPaint ushered in the era of "art" on the personal computer. With a pointing device and a black-and-white monitor that displayed images just as they would print, the Macintosh computer allowed users to manipulate shapes, lines, and patterns with great flexibility.

Graphic artists also appreciated the Macintosh's easy-to-use graphical interface, with such enhancements as sophisticated typefaces and the capability to magnify images and undo mistakes. Within a few years, the graphics world had embraced the Macintosh as a serious production tool. With the release of more powerful graphics software and the advent of the **Postscript** page-description language—which enabled accurate printing of complex images—the Macintosh became the tool of choice for a new breed of computer artists.

In the late 1980s, Microsoft's Windows brought many of the same capabilities to IBM PCs and compatibles, greatly expanding that market for graphics software. Today, PCs have achieved relative parity with Macintosh systems in the area of graphics software. A wide array of graphics programs is now available for both platforms. Often, the same program comes in both Mac and PC versions. Now, creative decisions can involve more thought and discussion about "creative" issues and less worry about "computer" capability.

Another important platform for computer graphics is the class of machines known as workstations. These specialized single-user computers possess extremely powerful and fast CPUs, large-capacity hard disks, high-resolution displays, and lots of RAM. Many workstations use the UNIX operating system;

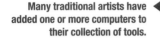

NORTON
Online

For information
on **Macintosh
computers**, visit
this book's Web site at
www.glencoe.com/norton/online

some use graphics software written especially for the workstation. Among professional graphic artists and designers, two popular models of workstations are the Sun SparcStation and the Silicon Graphics Indigo2.

NORTON Online

For information on **workstations being used in graphics**, visit this book's Web site at **www.glencoe.com/norton/online**

▶ A high percentage of printed advertisements are created using graphics software.

A workstation can be compared to a high-performance race car. Although it is fast and agile, its expense and complexity can make it seem impractical outside specialized arenas. Accordingly, workstations typically are reserved for the most demanding graphics projects, such as complicated animation, high-resolution mapping, technical drafting, and cinematic special effects.

In recent years, the price of workstations has dropped dramatically, making their power more accessible to the average graphics user. At the same time, however, Macintosh and Windows-based computers have become much more powerful, greatly shrinking the gap between workstations and personal computers. In fact, moviemakers are beginning to utilize PCs and PC-based software to create special effects and animations for movies—a domain once held exclusively by the workstation.

Often, the decision to purchase a particular type of computer rests as much on social or convenience factors as on what software you are going to use. If you are working as part of a team, and the rest of the team is using PCs, generally you will have an easier time trading files if you use a PC as well. On the other hand, if the work you plan to do can be done better and in one-third the time on a Sun workstation, then it is probably better to choose that platform and suffer the inconveniences of transferring files to other platforms when the need arises.

Types of Graphics Files

The issue of moving files between computers also brings up the topic of graphic file formats. As soon as you create or import an image and begin to work with it, you must determine the format in which you will save your file.

Many graphics programs save files in proprietary formats. For example, by default, Adobe Illustrator, CorelDraw, and Adobe Photoshop save files in a different format. Some programs can understand the proprietary formats of other programs, but some cannot. Fortunately, however, there are standard (nonproprietary) file formats used with graphic files on all types of computer systems. There are two basic groups into which these formats are divided: **bitmap** and **vector** formats.

Bitmaps Versus Vectors

Graphics files are composed of either:

- A grid of dots, called a bitmap. (Bitmap images are often referred to as raster images. Note that, even though the two terms are interchangeable, this book uses the term bitmap, for consistency.)

- A set of vectors, which are mathematical equations describing the positions of lines.

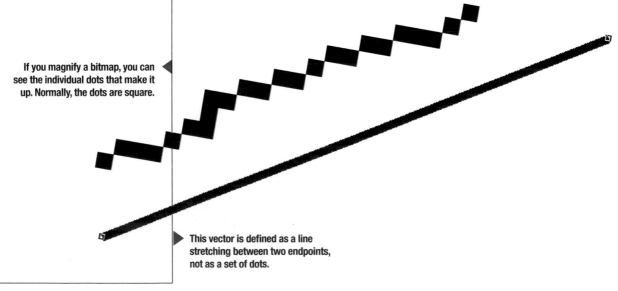

If you magnify a bitmap, you can see the individual dots that make it up. Normally, the dots are square.

This vector is defined as a line stretching between two endpoints, not as a set of dots.

In general, graphics programs fall into two primary categories along this division. Those that work with bitmaps are called **paint programs**. Those that work with vectors are called **draw programs**. Each category has advantages and drawbacks, depending on the kind of output needed.

When you use bitmap-based graphics software, you are using the computer to move pixels around. If you look closely at a computer screen, you can see the tiny dots that make up images—these are pixels. Manipulating pixels can become complex. For example, an 8 x 10-inch black-and-white image—if displayed at a typical screen resolution of 72 pixels per inch (ppi)—

Congratulations!

▶ This text has been generated with a paint program, so the text is actually composed of tiny dots, called pixels. This is a simple bitmap image.

is a mosaic of 414,720 pixels, as shown in Figure 9.1. That means that the computer must remember the precise location of each and every one of those pixels as they are viewed, moved, or altered. If it is decided that the same 8 x 10-inch piece of artwork must have up to 256 colors in its makeup (which is considered minimal with today's technology), then the computer must keep track of the 414,720 pixels multiplied by the 8 bits per pixel that are necessary to identify 256 different colors. That equals 3,317,760 bits that the computer must keep track of for one image (see Figure 9.2).

▶ **Figure 9.1**
An 8 x 10 image, displayed at standard screen resolution.

Unlike paint programs, which manipulate bitmaps, draw programs work their magic through mathematics. By using equations rather than dots to represent lines, shapes, and patterns, vector-based graphics software can represent highly detailed images with only a fraction of the computing power required by bitmaps.

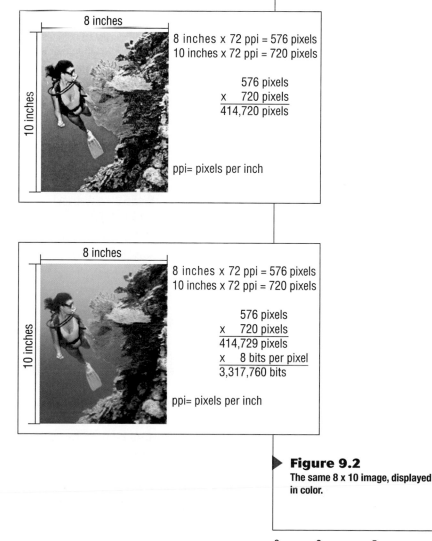

8 inches

10 inches

8 inches x 72 ppi = 576 pixels
10 inches x 72 ppi = 720 pixels

576 pixels
x   720 pixels
414,720 pixels

ppi= pixels per inch

8 inches

10 inches

8 inches x 72 ppi = 576 pixels
10 inches x 72 ppi = 720 pixels

576 pixels
x   720 pixels
414,729 pixels
x   8 bits per pixel
3,317,760 bits

ppi= pixels per inch

Strictly speaking, the vectors used by draw programs are lines drawn from point to point. Vector-based software can use additional equations to define the thickness and color of a line, its pattern, and other attributes. Although a line on the screen is still displayed as a series of pixels (because that is how all computer screens work), to the computer it is an equation. Thus, to move the line from Point A to Point B, all the computer does is substitute the coordinates for Point A with those for Point B. This saves the effort of calculating how to move thousands of individual pixels.

▶ **Figure 9.2**
The same 8 x 10 image, displayed in color.

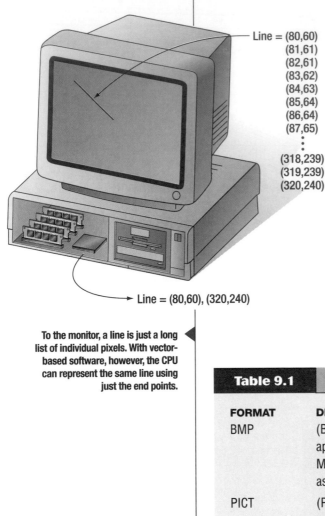

Line = (80,60)
(81,61)
(82,61)
(83,62)
(84,63)
(85,64)
(86,64)
(87,65)
⋮
(318,239)
(319,239)
(320,240)

Line = (80,60), (320,240)

To the monitor, a line is just a long list of individual pixels. With vector-based software, however, the CPU can represent the same line using just the end points.

NORTON Online

For information and examples of **graphic file formats**, visit this book's Web site at www.glencoe.com/norton/online

Whether you use a bitmap- or vector-based program depends on what you are trying to do. For example, if you want to be able to retouch each pixel in a photo, you will choose bitmap-based software. If you are making a line drawing of a car and want the capability of repositioning its wheels without having to redraw them, you will probably choose vector-based software. Or, if you need both capabilities, some graphics software allows you to create art that takes advantage of each kind of program.

Standard File Formats

If you need to share files with other users or move files between programs (artists and designers almost always do), you should be familiar with the standard file formats for graphics files, as shown in Table 9.1. These common formats apply only to bitmap images and can be used by nearly any newer software that creates or edits bitmap graphics.

Table 9.1	Standard Formats for Bitmap Graphics
FORMAT	**DESCRIPTION**
BMP	(BitMaP) A graphics format native to Windows and the Windows applications created by Microsoft. Widely used on PCs, less so on Macs, although the Macintosh can read BMP files with programs such as Photoshop.
PICT	(PICTure) The native format defined by Apple for the Mac. Widely used on Macs but not PCs.
TIFF	(Tagged Image File Format) Bitmap format defined in 1986 by Microsoft and Aldus. Widely used on both Macs and PCs.
JPEG	(Joint Photographic Experts Group) A bitmap format common on the World Wide Web and often used for photos that will be viewed on screen. JPEG is more than just a file format; it is a widely used standard that incorporates specific algorithms to ensure optimum image quality while keeping file size to a minimum. JPEG is often abbreviated as JPG.
GIF	(Graphic Interchange Format) A format developed by CompuServe. Like JPEG images, GIF images are often found on World Wide Web pages.
PNG	(Portable Network Graphics) A format developed as an alternative to GIF. The PNG format is still emerging, but gaining popularity on World Wide Web pages. It provides greater color quality and more color attributes than GIF or TIFF files, but smaller file sizes than JPEG.

Most vector draw programs create and save files in a proprietary file format, which usually cannot be used by other programs. This lack of commonality has forced developers to create "universal" file formats, which enable users of one program to work with files created in other programs. Only a handful of common file formats exist for vector graphics, such as DXF (Data Exchange Format) and IGES (Initial Graphics Exchange Specification). These "universal" formats enable you to create a vector file in one program, such as AutoCAD, and use it in another program, such as CorelDRAW or Visio. The most common format by far is **Encapsulated Postscript (EPS)**. This format is based on the Postscript printing language, the most common standard for Macs and PCs communicating with laser printers and high-end reproduction equipment.

Getting Existing Images into Your Computer

The majority of graphics programs allow the user to create images from scratch, building simple lines and shapes into complex graphics. However, when using high-end graphics software, it is probably more common to begin with an existing image. If the image you start with is already a graphic file, then getting it into your computer is a matter of importing the file into the program that you want to use. Doing so simply requires that your program understand the file format in which the graphic is stored. There are, however, other building blocks with which you can start. The most common are clip art and printed images that you digitize (convert from a printed format to a digital one) using a scanner. If you do not have an image, you can use a digital camera to capture something in the real world quickly and import it into your computer.

▶ A scanner is a valuable tool for graphic artists because it allows them to convert printed images into bitmap files that can be stored on a computer and manipulated with graphics software.

Scanners and Digital Cameras

A scanner is a little bit like a photocopy machine, except that instead of copying the image to paper, it transfers the image directly into the computer. If the image is on paper or a slide, a scanner can convert it into a digital file that a computer can manipulate. The scanner is attached to the computer by a cable and controlled by software that is often included with the graphics program. The result of scanning an image is a bitmap file (although software tools are available for translating these images into vector formats).

Digital cameras are another way to import images into a computer. These devices store digitized images in memory for transfer into a computer. Many are small and easy to use and include software and cables for the transfer process. Once again, the resulting file is generally a bitmap.

Advanced digital cameras have become useful to a number of creative professionals mostly because they save the time, expense, and inconvenience of developing film and creating prints in a darkroom. Newspaper photographers use expensive models to take pictures of late-breaking events, thereby saving the time it would take to develop film. Catalog photographers use digital cameras to record and store images of products directly into the same computers that are used to create their catalogs. Less expensive digital cameras are great for artists who need a quick picture for an illustration.

▶ A digital camera takes pictures in much the same manner as a traditional camera. The difference is that the digital camera stores the image as a bitmap file rather than an exposed piece of film.

Digital cameras are rapidly finding their way into the home, as well. New low-cost systems by Kodak, Panasonic, Hewlett-Packard, and others include not only a high-quality digital camera but also a printer that quickly prints full-color images on photo-quality paper. Such systems can be purchased for less than $500 and enable the home user to import digital photographs directly into a PC. Once on disk, digital images can be copied, edited, printed, or used on World Wide Web pages or other documents.

NORTON
Online
For information on **digital cameras**, visit this book's Web site at **www.glencoe.com/norton/online**

Electronic Photographs

Today, graphic artists use traditional photos translated into digital formats more often than they use photos from digital cameras. Digitizing a photo always involves some type of scanner, but the process has become sophisticated in recent years.

Most often, professional-quality photos that need to be digitized are sent to special processing labs that scan the image and save the resulting file in a format called PhotoCD. Kodak created the PhotoCD, or PCD, format as a standard means for recording photographic images and storing them on a compact disk.

The PhotoCD offers many advantages. First, it provides a convenient storage medium for photos. Second, PhotoCD software makes it easy to quickly view and select photos from disk. Third, many PhotoCDs store the images at several different resolutions, making them available for different purposes. (A magazine, for example, requires much higher-resolution images than a newspaper or a Web page.)

The computer shown here is used to convert pictures into a digital format and store them on PhotoCDs.

When you shoot a roll of film, you can take the roll to almost any film developer, who can send it out to be stored on a PhotoCD. In a few days, you can pick up the CD, take it home, and see the images on your computer (assuming you have a CD-ROM drive that is PhotoCD-compatible, which most are). Then you can paste the photos into your electronic documents or manipulate the images with graphics software.

Today, many professional photographers use PhotoCD, and many businesses sell or distribute photos or samples of photos.

Clip Art

For the nonartist, or for the artist looking for an easy way to start or enhance digital artwork, **clip art** is available from many vendors. The term "clip art" originated with the existence of large books filled with page after page of professionally created drawings and graphics that could be cut out, or "clipped," from the pages and glued to a paper layout.

Today, clip art is commonly available on CD-ROM, diskettes, or via commercial online services. Many word processing and presentation programs also feature a selection of clip art, although the choices may be limited unless the program came on a compact disk. Clip art can be found in both bitmap and vector formats. The variety of clip art is huge, ranging from simple line drawings

and cartoons to lush paintings and photographs. People, animals, plants, architecture, maps, borders, patterns, textures, and business symbols are but a few of the many categories.

Clip art is valuable because it is relatively inexpensive, readily available, easy to use with graphics software, and generally of high quality. For example, if you are looking for a picture of a truck and you lack the skills or time to draw one yourself, you can simply copy a clip art drawing into your file. Clip art also can be used as a basis for larger pieces of artwork. When you need a map of Florida, which would you rather do—draw it by hand, or import a professionally rendered image with your graphics software? Answer this question, and you will understand why computerized clip art is so popular.

Copyright Issues

The ease with which computer users can acquire and manipulate images has brought another issue to the fore—copyright. Although clip art is often licensed for unlimited use, most images that you see in print or on screen are not.

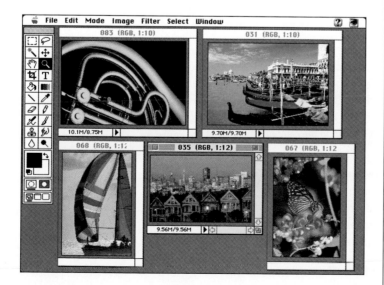

Digital photography is taking the modern graphics industry by storm. Digital photos can be seen in just the minutes it takes to upload the image from your camera to your computer. Plus, you can alter the picture you just took—instantly!

A digital camera, also called a filmless camera, records images on a stamp-sized photosensitive semiconductor chip called a charge-coupled device (CCD) instead of the light-sensitive silver halide crystals of traditional photography. Physically, the structure of the camera is similar to a film-based camera, with lens, shutter, and diaphragm.

Currently, digital cameras are more expensive than film-based cameras, and the image quality they produce is generally far less satisfactory, especially with entry-level models. High-end digital cameras can produce excellent image quality with higher resolution and greater color depth.

Although prices of digital cameras are falling as digital technology advances, basic consumer models still have a way to go before they match film cameras in quality. Enlarged digital images often exhibit artifacts (stray marks) and pixelization (blotchy patches and sawtooth edges).

So why would the general consumer want to use a digital camera? One big reason is to make Web pages. Web publishing does not require high-quality imaging, and it's a lot of fun to post your own pictures on your Web page. Motion video digital cameras are on the market that allow you to post your home videos (saved in a format like QuickTime) on your Web site, too.

Another big use of digital photography is for business applications where immediacy is important. For example, law-enforcement personnel, insurance field agents, building inspectors, real estate agents, and security personnel all use digital cameras to obtain visual records of particular scenes. Images for all sorts of documents such as newsletters, brochures, presentations, and school projects can also be done quite well with a digital camera.

Taking a digital picture is easy; most digital cameras are simple point-and-shoot devices. However, the image-saving process is quite different. In a digital camera, light strikes the CCD cells inside the camera and activates them electronically. Digital data is then created by the circuitry in the camera. This data is compressed and saved to the camera's memory in the form of pixels.

The digital images can then be uploaded electronically to your PC. This is a fairly straightforward process of connecting camera and computer via a serial cable. Then you use the software program that comes bundled with the camera to send your images to your hard disk, where you can open the files and see your pictures immediately. The process currently takes from 5 to 20 minutes.

One of the most startling aspects of digital photography is that you can alter your images. You can cut and paste, crop or resize, change perspective and colors, and create all kinds of special effects. To do all this, you need an image editor software program. These programs vary in sophistication from simple editors that come bundled with the digital camera or your computer operating system, to extremely sophisticated professional graphics programs such as Adobe Photoshop.

Digital video cameras are beginning to replace videotape-based cameras.

Instead, they are owned by the creator or publisher of the image and are licensed for publication in a specific place for a set number of times.

This means, for example, that if you scan a photograph from a magazine, place it in your work, and sell it to someone else, you are infringing on a copyright and could be fined or prosecuted. This applies even if you edit the image; making changes to someone else's work does not make it your own.

If you want to use an image you did not create solely on your own, and it is not part of a clip art package, you must contact the copyright holder for permission. Copyright law is complicated, and there are many gray areas. If you are ever unsure, it is best to contact a lawyer or the person who created the image.

NORTON Online

For information and a shareware version of **PaintShop Pro**, visit this book's Web site at **www.glencoe.com/norton/online**

GRAPHICS SOFTWARE

Creating a digital image, or manipulating an existing one, can involve a huge variety of processes. No single piece of graphics software is capable of performing all the possible functions. In fact, there are five major categories of graphics software:

- Paint software
- Photo-manipulation software
- Draw software
- Computer-aided design (CAD) software
- 3-D modeling and animation software

Of the five, the first two are bitmap-based paint programs, and the rest are vector-based draw programs. Grasping this difference will help you understand how artists use each type of program and why.

Paint Programs

With software tools that have names like paintbrush, pen, chalk, watercolors, airbrush, crayon, and eraser, paint programs have a familiar feel. However, because paint programs keep track of each and every pixel placed on a screen, they also can do things that are impossible with traditional artists' tools—for example, erasing a single pixel or creating instant copies of an image.

Paint programs lay down pixels in a process comparable to covering a floor with tiny mosaic tiles. Changing an image created with a paint program is like scraping tiles off the floor and replacing them with different tiles. This dot-by-dot approach allows a high degree of flexibility, but it has a few drawbacks. For example, once you create a circle or make an electronic brush stroke, you can erase or tinker with the individual pixels, making minor adjustments until the image is exactly what you want. On the other hand, you cannot change the entire circle or stroke as a whole, especially if you have painted over it. That is because the software does not think of bitmaps as a circle or brush stroke after they are created. They are simply a collection of pixels.

Although there are exceptions, most paint programs are also not well suited to

This circle was created using a paint program. As a result, the program has stored each tiny dot as separate information. The dots are not associated with each other, so the circle cannot be selected and moved.

handling text. Even though many provide an easy way to add text to an image, after that text is placed it becomes just another collection of pixels. This means that if you misspell a word, you cannot simply backspace over the faulty text and retype it. You must erase the word completely and start over.

These limitations aside, paint programs provide the tools to create some spectacular effects. As shown in Figure 9.3, some programs can make brush strokes that appear thick or thin, soft or hard, drippy or neat, opaque or transparent.

Some programs allow you to change media with a mouse click, turning your paintbrush into a chalk or a crayon, or giving your smooth "canvas" a texture like rice paper or an eggshell.

This text has been converted to a bitmap. Consequently, you cannot erase it letter by letter. You have to erase the group of pixels that form each letter. The pencil pointer shown here is erasing each dot that makes up the T.

Pencil pointer

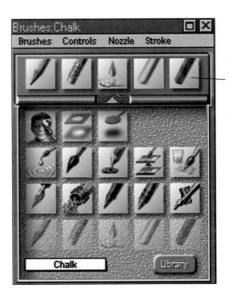

Each of the buttons on this palette gives the artist a different tool, and therefore a different effect. There are pencils, pens, chalk, crayons, and an airbrush.

Figure 9.3
Painting tools in Fractal Design Painter.

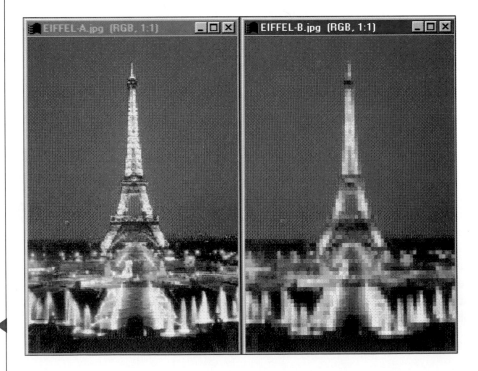

Figure 9.4
A photographic image, distorted by the Mosaic filter in PaintShop Pro.

Unusual special effects abound in paint programs. For example, you can convert an image in any number of bizarre ways. Paint programs let you distort a person's features, break a statue into hundreds of tiles, swirl an image as though it's being pulled into a whirlpool, and much more. Figure 9.4, for example, shows an image of the Eiffel Tower before and after the Mosaic effect is applied in PaintShop Pro.

Many different paint packages are available, including PaintShop Pro, Adobe SuperPaint, and Fractal Design Painter, to name a few.

Photo-Manipulation Programs

When scanners made it easy to transfer photographs to the computer at high resolution, a new class of software was needed to manipulate these images on the screen. A cousin of paint programs, **photo-manipulation programs** now take the place of a photographer's darkroom for many tasks. Although most often used for simple jobs such as sharpening focus or adjusting contrast, photo-manipulation programs are also used to modify photographs in ways far beyond the scope of a traditional darkroom. The picture shown in Figure 9.5, for example, has obviously been subjected to electronic manipulation.

Because photo-manipulation programs edit images at the pixel level, just as paint programs do, they can control precisely how a picture will look. They are also used to edit nonphotographic images and to create images from scratch. The advent of photo-manipulation programs has caused an explosion in the use of computers to modify images. Adobe Photoshop, Corel Photo Paint, and Micrografx Picture Publisher are some popular photo-manipulation programs.

This image was created using software tools that mimic the use of chalk.

This image was created using software tools that mimic the use of watercolors.

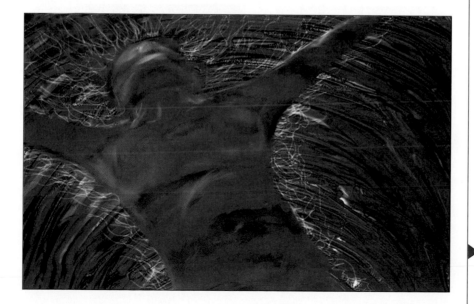

The texture in this image was created with a software tool that seems to repaint images with a blurring brush.

Figure 9.5 ◄
This image demonstrates how a photo-manipulation program can be used to combine a traditional photograph with computer-generated graphic effects.

Photo-manipulation programs can accomplish some amazing things. After a photograph has been brought into the computer, usually by scanning or from a PhotoCD, the user can change or enhance the photo at will, down to individual pixels. For example, if a photo has dust spots, or someone's eyes look red from a flash, the airbrush tool can draw just the right number of appropriately colored pixels delicately into the affected areas to correct the problem (see Figure 9.6).

Small or large color corrections can be made in seconds or minutes—for an entire photo or just a part of it. If someone's face appears too dark or too washed out, software tools can reveal hidden details—a job that formerly required minutes or hours in a darkroom.

Photo-manipulation programs also contain tools that can alter the original image drastically, in effect causing photos to lie. For example, if a photograph of a group of people has been scanned into the computer, special tools can erase the pixels that form the image of one of these people and replace them with pixels from the background area—effectively removing the person from the photo. There are even tools that can move objects in a scene or create a collage of several different images. Architects and planners use these kinds of tools to illustrate how a new building can change a city's skyline.

Today, almost every photograph you see in print has been scanned into a computer and enhanced by photo-manipulation programs. Most of the time, these changes are restricted to slight color corrections or to the removal of dust, but the potential for larger alterations is still there. The adage "photos don't lie" has become a relic of the past. In a society where image is everything, photo-manipulation programs represent genuine power. How far photo illustration artists will go, and in what direction, is limited only by their imagination and

White lines come from scratches on the original film.

The airbrush tool can be used to smooth over sharp lines.

Figure 9.6 ◄
Repairing a scratched image with an airbrush tool.

Notice that the keyhole in this photo has been partially erased and replaced with parts of a new background—the cow.

tempered only by their desire for credibility. Many newspapers and magazines have established written guidelines that limit the kinds of changes a photograph can undergo to include only the removal of dust spots or the correction of an unnatural cast of color.

Photo-manipulation programs are capable of outputting images at high resolutions, producing output that is indistinguishable from a darkroom-produced photograph. This means that to make best use of most photo-manipulation programs, you need a powerful computer—one with a fast microprocessor, lots of **RAM** and storage space, and a high-quality display. All this hardware does not come cheap, and many people who have photo-manipulation programs are not capable of using the programs to their fullest extent.

Draw Programs

Draw programs are well suited for work where accuracy and flexibility are as important as coloring and special effects. Although they do not possess the pixel-pushing capability of paint programs, they can be used to create images with an "arty" look and have been adopted by many designers as their primary tool. You see their output in everything from cereal box designs to television show credits, from business cards to newspapers. Macromedia FreeHand, Adobe Illustrator, and CorelDraw are some popular draw programs.

The original photograph used to create this image was under-exposed. As a result, the balloon appears very dark. However, the top part of the balloon has been manipulated with a dodge tool that brightens some of the colors.

Draw programs work by defining every line as a mathematical equation, or vector. Sometimes, draw programs are referred to as *object-oriented programs* because each item drawn—whether it be a line, square, rectangle, or circle—is treated as a separate and distinct object from all the others. For example, when you draw a square with a draw program, the computer remembers it as a square of a fixed size at a specific location, and not as a bunch of pixels that are in the shape of a square.

The hardware illustrations in this book were created using a draw program called Adobe Illustrator.

Draw programs offer two big advantages over paint programs. First, when objects are created, they remain objects to the computer. After you draw a circle, you can return to it later and move it intact by dragging it with the mouse, even if it has been covered over with other shapes or lines. You can change the circle's shape into an oval, or you can fill its interior with a color, a blend of colors, or a pattern.

The other big advantage draw programs have is the capability to resize images easily so that they match the dimensions of the paper on which they will be printed. Because bitmap images are a grid of dots, the only way to control the size of the image is to adjust the resolution, the number of dots per inch. However, lowering the resolution to make an image larger can make the image visibly rougher. This is why paint programs are often described as being **resolution-dependent**; the image's appearance may change depending on the resolution at which it is displayed.

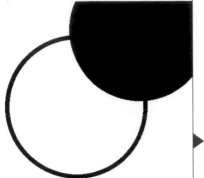

Because this circle was created with a draw program, it can be filled with a color (black, in this case), moved, and copied.

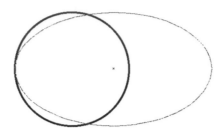

Simply by clicking and dragging in a draw program, you can change a circle into an oval. You can use similar techniques to change squares to rectangles and to modify other shapes.

Draw programs make it easy to color text.

Congratulations!

Vector graphics, on the other hand, are much easier to resize. The software mathematically changes all the objects so they appear larger or smaller. Similarly, many draw programs can scale objects—increasing or reducing size by a certain factor or in relation to other objects in the drawing. When this is done, there is no change in the resolution, so there is no loss in the image's quality. For this reason, vector-based draw programs are described as being **resolution-independent**, meaning the image looks the same no matter what resolution it is displayed at.

HAPPY BIRTHDAY!

Lines of text can be bent or distorted with draw programs.

For similar reasons, draw programs are also superior to paint programs in their handling of text. Because the computer treats text characters as objects rather than collections of dots, the text can be colored, shaded, scaled, tilted, or even joined to a curvy line with little effort.

the road less traveled, and that has made all the difference.

Text can also be forced to follow a curvy line.

Today, however, the distinction between draw programs and paint programs is blurring quickly. Attributes of paint programs have been incorporated into draw programs and vice versa, producing

Productivity Tip

Drawing Tools for Everyone

A popular piece of computing wisdom tells us: "Having a word processor does not make you a writer." Similarly, having a draw or paint program cannot make you an artist. But it won't hurt any, either, especially if you need to create or edit graphics for use in reports, Web pages, or other projects.

Even if you have no artistic skill, you can create simple but effective graphics using some basic, inexpensive software. In fact, paint and draw programs have become so sophisticated and simple to use, you really don't need to be an artist to get good results. But it does help to practice and to know the result you want to achieve before you start any drawing or painting project.

So, if you need to create graphics, you may want to start by trying out some inexpensive software or **shareware** programs. (You get a shareware program for free, initially, and can easily download them from many online services or the Internet. If you decide to keep a shareware program after the initial trial period, you should register your copy and pay the fee required by the developer. Fees for shareware products are usually low—much less expensive than comparable off-the-shelf products.) After practicing a bit, you may be ready to graduate to a full-featured package.

For quick, simple drawings (such as plain geometric shapes and line drawings), start with Windows Paint, which comes with every copy of Windows. If you use a word processor such as Word or Corel WordPerfect, you should find simple paint programs built into it, as well.

If your needs are a bit more complex, try a low-cost or shareware paint program, such as LView or PaintShop Pro (both can be downloaded from the Internet). These programs are easy to use but are also packed with features, including:

■ *Rich drawing tools.* Many inexpensive programs provide a wide array of drawing tools, including different brush types, chalk, pencils, airbrushes, and other special tools.

■ *Photo-manipulation features.* If you can save your scanned photos or digital pictures in a common file format (such as JPEG or TIFF), you can open and edit them in a number of ways, change color settings, make gamma corrections, hide flaws, and much more.

■ *Support for multiple file formats.* Paint programs used to support only basic formats but now can open and edit just about any commonly used file format, such as JPEG, GIF, TIF, PCX, and many others.

If you need to create more accurate drawings and want the capability to edit lines and shapes by dragging, then a draw program probably is called for. Instead of spending several hundred dollars for a sophisticated draw package, however, try a low-cost draw program such as Visio or an older version of a popular program, such as CorelDRAW 3. These programs make it possible to draw practically anything, with tools such as:

■ *Drag-and-drop editing.* You can move, copy, reshape, scale, and distort shapes simply by clicking and dragging. This eliminates the need to navigate menus and provides instant results.

■ *High resolution and color depth.* Even inexpensive draw programs can save files at high resolutions and in full color.

■ *Sophisticated text-handling capabilities.* Most draw programs provide outstanding text features, enabling you to create special text effects, shadows, 3-D text, and more. Because the text is made of vectors, edges are clean when viewed on the screen and in print.

There are even low-cost and shareware CAD and 3-D modeling programs available. If you are just beginning to experiment with computer graphics, however, you may want to delay installing or purchasing such programs until later. Start with the basics and work your way up from there. You'll be amazed at the results you can achieve with a little practice and patience.

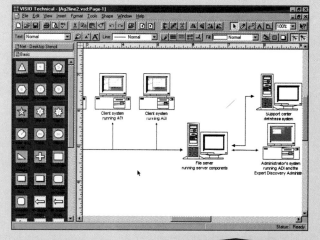

Visio is a popular low-cost drawing package that makes it easy for nonartists to create professional-looking illustrations. The program's strengths are its collections of predrawn objects, which you simply drag into your drawing, and the ease with which you can edit your drawings and text.

341

some software packages that can be used to handle almost any task involving graphic images. For example, most draw programs now include the capability to import photos or art created with paint programs, although for the most part they lack the capability to edit them at the pixel level.

Computer-Aided Design Programs

Computer-Aided Design (CAD), also known as Computer-Aided Drafting or Computer-Aided Drawing, is the computerized version of the hand drafting process that used to be done with a pencil and ruler on a drafting table. Over the last 15 years, the drafting process has been almost completely computerized, as CAD programs have become easier to use and offer an increasing array of features. CAD is used extensively in technical fields, such as architecture, and in mechanical, electrical, and industrial engineering. CAD software is also used in other design disciplines, as well, such as textile and clothing design, package design, and others.

Unlike drawings made using paint or drawing programs, CAD drawings are usually the basis for the actual building or manufacturing process—a house, an engine gear, or an electrical system. To satisfy the rigorous requirements of manufacturing, CAD programs provide a high degree of precision. If you want to draw a line that is 12.396754 inches long or a circle with a radius of .90746 centimeters, a CAD program can fulfill your needs. CAD programs are so precise, in fact, that they can actually produce designs that are accurate down to the micrometer—or one-millionth of a meter.

This accuracy extends to the other end of the scale, as well. Not only can you design the tiniest object in a CAD program, you can also design the largest objects, as well, in full scale. This means that in the CAD program's database, each line's measurements are identical to their actual measurements in real life. Therefore, if you want to draw a full-scale, three-dimensional version of the Earth, you can do it. (In fact, it has already been done!)

NORTON
Online

For information on **AutoCAD** and the many uses for **CAD products**, visit this book's Web site at www.glencoe.com/norton/online

You can't tell it on the computer screen, but in the AutoCAD database, this three-dimensional image of Earth is in full scale. If you had a sheet of paper large enough, you could print this drawing, and it would be the same size as the Earth. For more realistic applications, however, the CAD program can scale down the image so that it is smaller, yet its components are still in proportion to each other.

CAD programs achieve such a degree of accuracy through various means. First, CAD programs are vector-based. As you learned earlier in the chapter, this means that the CAD system recognizes objects not just as a fixed series of pixels, but according to variable starting and ending points, thickness, weight, and other attributes. Second, CAD programs generally do not store objects as objects; rather, they store the object's attributes in a database. (In fact, CAD programs are actually database programs; the information in the database tells the program how to re-create objects on screen and on paper.) Third, CAD programs are math-based and take advantage of the computer's floating-point math processor to perform calculations. As a result, CAD programs can easily recognize large or small objects and instantly scale the image to fit on the screen or on paper, and in proportion to other objects.

Another important feature of CAD programs is their capability to define layers, which are like transparent layers of film that you can place on top of each other. Layers permit CAD users to organize complex drawings. For example, a structural engineer designing an office building might create layers such as Electrical, Plumbing, Structural, and so on. The engineer can then show and hide these individual layers while different parts of the building are designed. The concept of layering has become so useful to designers, that many paint and draw programs now provide layering capabilities, which function in much the same manner as CAD layers.

CAD programs enable designers to create incredibly complex, detailed drawings. In this drawing, the objects on any layer are indicated by a unique color. By using layers, designers can more easily manage the many objects in a large drawing.

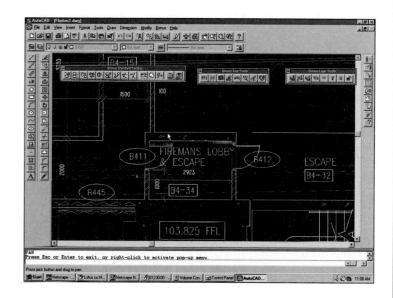

CAD programs can produce precise dimensions of any object you draw.

All CAD programs have the capability to add dimensions to a drawing. Remember, this is because the CAD program stores information about each object in the drawing, including its size and scale. Dimensions are notations showing the measurements of an object and are usually placed on their own layer. Dimensioning is essential to the process of actually building or manufacturing the object being drawn. Most CAD programs can also perform calculations on drawings. For example, they can calculate the area of a living room or the volume of a storage tank.

Finally, because CAD drawings are created from a database of attributes, designers can use the information in other ways. If you design a complete building in a CAD program, for example, you can use the database to create lists of materials required for construction. Special software enables contractors to use this database information to create cost estimates and schedules.

Hard copies of CAD drawings are usually created on plotters rather than on printers. Plotters can handle the large sheets of paper used for technical drawings and may use a different pen for each layer of the drawing.

CAD and 3-D Design

You can also thank the CAD world for the 3-D craze that has swept through the design industry since the early 1990s. Three-dimensional design got its start in CAD programs during the late 1980s, as a way to enable designers to view their designs from all possible angles on screen. Today, most CAD programs provide different ways to design, display, animate, and print 3-D objects, called **models**. For example, **wireframe models** represent 3-D shapes by displaying their outlines and edges. Figure 9.7 shows an example of a three-dimensional wireframe model. Many CAD programs also provide **solid models**. This type of modeling works by giving the user a representation of a block of solid material. The user can then use different operations to shape the material, cutting, adding, combining, and so on, to create the finished model.

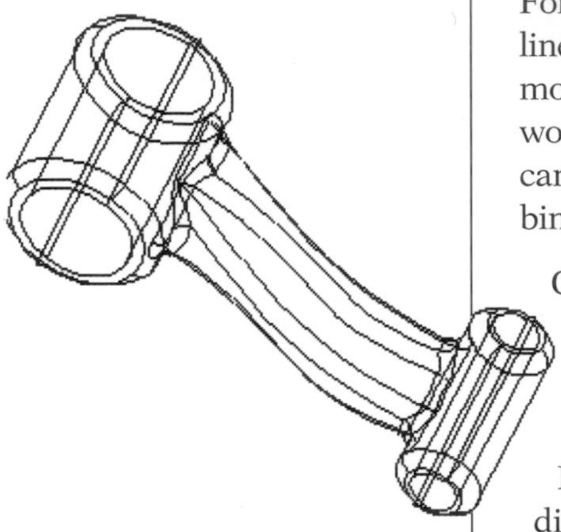

Once a model is finished, CAD programs can **render** the image, shading in the solid parts and creating output that looks almost real. Figure 9.8 shows a rendered image of the wireframe model from Figure 9.7. A solid model would look the same.

In the early days of 3-D design, the designer would create the raw three-dimensional models in a CAD program and then export the files into a special rendering and animation program (such as 3D Studio) to add lighting, shading, surface features, and more. Now, however, some CAD programs include many of these capabilities, freeing the user from relying on multiple programs—except when special effects or complicated animations are required.

Further, many of the 3-D features of CAD programs have been duplicated in 3-D draw and modeling programs. These programs are covered later in this chapter.

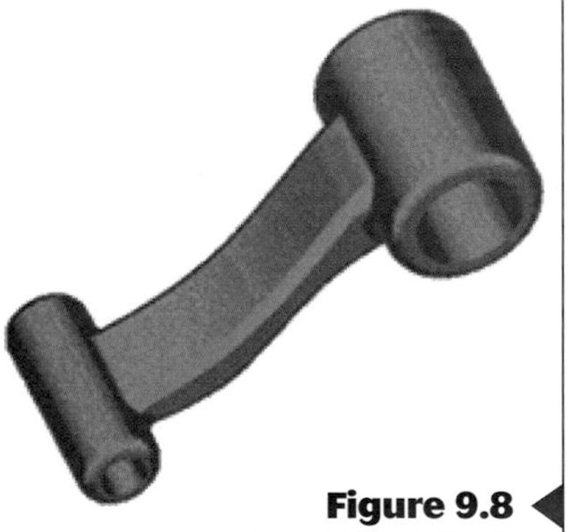

There are several different PC-based CAD programs, as well as CAD software for use on workstations. Depending on features, PC CAD programs can cost $2,000 or more, but the less expensive versions may fulfill your needs, and they start at about $100. The most popular program for professional CAD designers is Autodesk's AutoCAD. It is a full-featured program with 3-D rendering, programming language, and database capabilities. Other CAD programs include Drafix, AutoCAD LT, CADKEY, and MicroStation.

3-D Modeling Programs

Whether you are aware of it or not, you are constantly exposed to elaborate 3-D imaging in movies, television, and print. Many of these images are now created with a special type of graphics software, called **3-D modeling software**, which enables users to create electronic models of three-dimensional objects without using CAD software. Fast workstations or PCs coupled with 3-D modeling programs can lend realism to even the most fantastic subjects. Professional 3-D designers use sophisticated, expensive 3-D modeling programs such as

Figure 9.7
A 3-D wireframe model.

Figure 9.8
A rendering of the wireframe model. If the model had been solid rather than wireframe, the rendering would look virtually the same.

3-D Studio MAX, Electric Image, SoftImage, Ray Dream Designer, and Light-Wave 3D.

There are four different types of 3-D modeling programs: surface, solid, polygonal, and spline-based. Each uses a different technique to create three-dimensional objects. **Surface modelers** build objects by stretching a surface—like a skin—over an underlying wireframe structure. **Solid modelers** do the same thing as surface modelers but also understand thickness and density. This can be important if you need to punch a hole through an electronic object. **Polygonal modelers** combine many tiny polygons to build objects—similar to the way one would build a geodesic dome out of many perfectly fitted triangles. **Spline-based modelers** build objects, either surface or solid, using mathematically defined curves, which are rotated on an axis to form a 3-D shape.

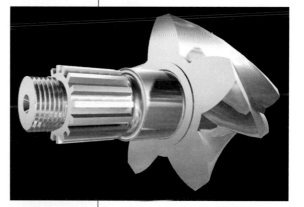

Regardless of their method of creation, 3-D objects can be modified to any shape using electronic tools akin to those used in woodworking. Just as wood can be cut, drilled, shaped, and sanded, objects created with a 3-D modeling program can be changed or molded with the click of a mouse. For example, holes can be drilled into computer-based 3-D objects, and corners can be made round or square by selecting the appropriate menu item. 3-D objects also can be given realistic textures and patterns, animated, or made to fly through space.

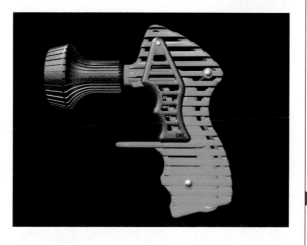

This model demonstrates how polygonal modeling techniques can be used.

NORTON Online

For a general introduction to **computer-based animation**, visit this book's Web site at **www.glencoe.com/norton/online**

Because 3-D modeling places high demands on hardware, it has long been the province of those who can afford workstations or ultra-high-end personal computers. Creative professionals believe that 3-D modeling programs are the wave of the future. As capable computers become less expensive, making the leap from realistic 2-D drawing to more realistic 3-D modeling will become even easier.

Animation

An outgrowth of the 3-D explosion is computer-based animation. Since the creation of filmmaking, animation was possible only through a painstaking process of hand-drawing a series of images, and then filming them one by one. Each filmed image is called a **frame**. When the film is played back at high speed (usually around 30 frames per second for high-quality animation), the images blur together to create the illusion of motion on the screen. The process of manually creating a short animation—even just a few seconds' worth—can take weeks of labor. A five-minute cartoon or a feature-length animated movie can take months or even years to produce.

Computer-generated imagery (CGI) has changed the world of animation in many ways. Although computer animation works on the same principles as traditional animation (a sequence of still images displayed in rapid succession), computer animators now have highly sophisticated tools that take the drudgery out of the animation process and allow them to to create animations more quickly than ever. Computer animators also have the advantage of being able to display their animations on the computer screen, or output them to CD-ROM, videotape, or film.

  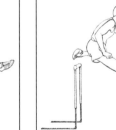  

Images from a traditional, manually drawn animation. Although computers speed up the animation process tremendously, they still work on the same old idea: generate hundreds or thousands of individual images, and then display them in rapid succession to create the illusion of motion.

An added bonus of computer animation is the capability to animate three-dimensional characters and create **photorealistic** scenes. (This means that the computer-generated image looks so realistic that it could be mistaken for a photograph of a real-life object.) These capabilities make computer-generated characters difficult to distinguish from real ones. Good examples are the dinosaurs in *Godzilla,* the space ships in *Lost in Space,* or the tornadoes in *Twister.*

Computer-generated animations are often so lifelike that it's hard to distinguish them from the real thing. The tornadoes in *Twister* are an excellent example. These "digital characters" were created on high-end graphics workstations, using specialized software. The swirling creations were then composited by computer, one frame at a time, onto film to create the final effect.

Using computers and special animation software, artists and designers can create many types of animations, from simple perspective changes to complex full-motion scenes that incorporate animated characters with real-life actors and sound.

Fly-Bys and Walk-Throughs

Architects and engineers frequently use the computer to take clients on a "virtual tour" of construction projects long before the actual construction has started. Using three-dimensional computer models created in a CAD program or in 3-D modeling software such as 3D Studio MAX, designers can create lifelike simulations of the finished project—whether it's a hotel or a factory—complete with finishing touches such as carpeting, lighting, landscaping, and people.

One of the simplest forms of computer animation is the **fly-by**. In a fly-by, the designer sets up an exterior view of a three-dimensional model, which may be of a building, a stadium, or some other structure. The view is provided by one of the software "cameras" in the CAD or 3-D software. (This type of software can provide many cameras, so the user can change views of a project at any time during the design process, or even see multiple views at once on the screen.) The designer then plots a motion path for the camera—that is, a line along which the camera travels. The motion path may take the camera around, over, or through the building, providing a "flying" effect, as though the building is being viewed by a bird on the wing. The designer then sets the camera in motion; as the camera travels along its path, the software captures still images (frames) of the scene, just as if it were being recorded by a real camera.

DISCUSSION TIPS

Discuss movies that students have seen that used computer animation. Which parts/objects looked realistic? Were there any parts/objects that were obviously computer-generated? What are the advantages/disadvantages of using computer animation to make movies?

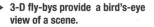

3-D fly-bys provide a bird's-eye view of a scene.

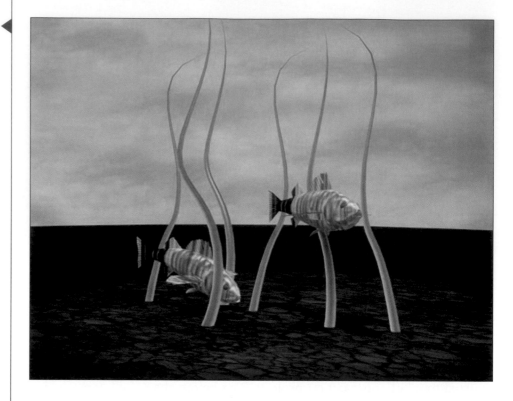

A **walk-through** operates on the same principle as a fly-by but is used to capture moving interior shots of a building or scene. If you have ever played a video game in which you control a character's movements through a 3-D scene (as in *Doom* or *Riven*), you are basically controlling a walk-through.

Walk-throughs and fly-bys can be preset by the designer. Using sophisticated software, however, designers can also do free-form walk-throughs and fly-bys in real time, controlling the camera's motion and angle as they go.

Fly-bys and walk-throughs can be output from the computer onto videotape or compact disk, but this is a static method of giving a virtual tour; that is, you can't deviate from the tour's route after it has been recorded. Therefore, many designers like to conduct virtual tours at the computer, enabling the "virtual visitor" to take charge of the tour. This way, the visitor can wander through the design freely, enter any room at will, take the elevator or the stairs, and even open drawers and cabinets in the virtual furniture!

Fly-bys and walk-throughs are considered simple forms of animation because the character (in this case, the building) does not move. Instead, the camera's ever-changing perspective creates the sense of motion through the scene.

Character Animation

The type of computer-based animation receiving the most attention today is **character animation**. This is the art of creating a character (such as a person, an animal, or even a nonorganic thing, such as a box or a car) and making it move in a lifelike manner.

The basic techniques of character animation have not changed much from the drawing board to the computer. The process still involves drawing the

character in a sequence of positions—one position per frame of film, and each one at a slightly more advanced position than the preceding one—until the entire movement is achieved.

If a character must walk from point A to point B, for example, the designer will start by drawing the character at the starting point, and then again at the ending point of the walk. These two points are called the **keyframes** because they represent the most important focal points in the action. Next, the designer creates all the frames that show the character moving between points A and B; these frames are called **tweens** (short for *in-between* because these frames are positioned between the keyframes).

▶ This animation cycle shows the beginning and ending keyframes, and some of the tweens that fall in between them.

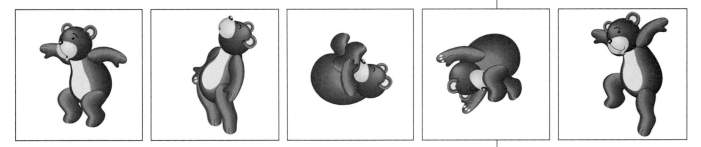

Computers have greatly simplified character animation in several ways. First, instead of drawing the character multiple times, the computer animator needs to draw it only once; the computer can duplicate the character as often as required. Instead of drawing a flat, two-dimensional character, however, many computer artists create complete three-dimensional characters that can be bent, twisted, and viewed from any angle.

To create a motion sequence, the animator needs only to create the keyframes. To do this, the character is set up in the beginning position and the ending position. The computer can then perform all the "tweening," by calculating the types of movements required to get the character from the first position to the last one. The animator can tweak individual tweens to get just the right effect.

▶ Computer-generated animation is used extensively by the National Oceanic and Atmospheric Administration.

Animation software offers a variety of tools to assist in the animation process and make the results more realistic. These tools include motion paths, inverse kinematics, boning, motion capture, and others.

To create full-length animated features or sophisticated special effects, many animation houses use workstations and high-end or proprietary software. Many current PC-based 3D packages offer a full array of animation capabilities, however, including 3D Studio MAX, LightWave 3D, SoftImage, and Electric Image, to name a few. Many powerful dedicated animation products are also available, such as Kinetix' Character Studio and Alias/Wavefront's PowerAnimator.

Computer Graphics in Film and Games

As in the movies, it comes as no surprise that the majority of modern video games are filled with computer-generated imagery, animation, backgrounds, and special effects. Large studios now exist at companies such as Sega, Nintendo, and other interactive game designers, where artists and animators use the latest technology to create the most realistic, action-packed gaming experiences.

Game designers and filmmakers use many of the same techniques to create characters and backgrounds for viewing. Using 3-D modeling software, animation tools, and scripting software, these designers create not only the graphics but also the action sequences through which the characters and players move. Using tools such as Macromedia Director and Authorware, game designers can create scripts that tell the computer which graphics to display, which user commands to accept, and much more.

Game makers and filmmakers rely heavily on computer-aided **compositing** techniques, to blend computer-generated imagery and filmed or videotaped images of real characters and objects. Using compositing tools, designers can add characters and objects to scenes that did not originally contain them. In the recent re-release of the *Star Wars* movies, for example, special effects artists at LucasFilms used these techniques to add familiar characters to previously unused scenes, enhancing the movies' plot and extending its length.

NORTON Online

For more information on **Director** and **AuthorWare**, visit this book's Web site at www.glencoe.com/norton/online

Using compositing techniques, game makers and filmmakers can add characters and objects where they previously didn't exist.

Techview

Animating the Inanimate

The demand for sophisticated, photorealistic character animation in television and film has led to some amazing innovations in the last few years. Computer-generated characters now look so lifelike and move so realistically that it's difficult to believe that they are not living—or at least real.

Computer-generated characters fall into two categories: organic and inorganic. Organic characters are representations of living things, including humans, animals, fish, trees, and so on. Inorganic characters are representations of non-living objects, such as cars or soda cans.

By developing a variety of software programs and special techniques, animators have become adept at making organic characters mimic the real thing. Human and animal characters can be animated to walk, move, talk, and change expressions in realistic ways. Facial and hand gestures are incredibly complex, and animators have been studying them intensively for years; decades of practical wisdom are now being applied to computer animation, with amazing results.

Consider the talking dragon in the film *Dragonheart,* or the futuristic characters of television's *Reboot.* The quality of their movements is realistic, making them much more believable than characters created by stop-motion photography or puppets.

In recent years, however, animators have found that computers can help them animate inorganic objects, as well, but not just to move like typical inanimate objects. Using special animation techniques, animators can create inorganic objects that move like humans or animals. Obvious examples include the dancing, boxing, vine-swinging Listerine® bottle, the dancing cars and gas pumps in the Shell® commercials, and the walking, talking M&Ms®.

How is it done? Here are some of the basic, nonproprietary techniques being used on PCs and workstations:

Inverse Kinematics Introduced in the early 1990s, inverse kinematics (IK) allows animators to take full advantage of their fully jointed 3-D characters (with elbow joints, knees, knuckles, and so on). Using complex algorithms, IK enables the animator to move a character by literally pulling parts of its body. If you pull a hand forward (a primary motion), for example, the rest of the arm and shoulder will follow (secondary and tertiary motions). IK software calculates all the related motions and assists in animating them.

Boning Special software enables animators to add "bones" to a 3-D character. The bones are embedded in the character, and are jointed at their intersections. By using IK-style techniques, the animator can manipulate the bones; the rest of the character follows, resulting in natural, fluid motion. To get more accurate movements, animators can simply add more bones. Bones can also be used to give human motion to inorganic characters. Add a set of bones (just a waist, knees, and shoulders, for example) to a cereal box, and you can make the box bend and twist in a human way.

Motion Capture This technique is being used a great deal in film and gaming. In motion capture, a puppet, animal, or person is outfitted with motion sensors. As the model moves, the sensors detect the movements and relative positions of the model's limbs. This data is transferred to a computer, where it can be applied to a 3-D character. The resulting movements are astoundingly realistic. Motion capture has been used to animate characters in movies such as *Men in Black* and video games such as *Donkey Kong Country.*

Using motion-capture technology (sometimes called "performance animation"), animators can transfer the real movements of a human or puppet to an animated character.

Virtual Reality

Virtual reality (VR) is a leap beyond typical computer-generated graphics and is viewed by many to be the future of computer interfaces, education, and entertainment. Virtual reality provides the user with an immersive multimedia experience by combining 3-D graphics, animation, video, audio, and sense-based media (goggles, headphones, and gloves or body suits equipped with motion and pressure sensors). Relying on systems with incredible computing horsepower, virtual reality developers can create fully immersive, fully interactive multimedia experiences.

Imagine, for example, your favorite video game or Web site. In its current form, it is displayed on a flat screen, and you interact with it from a distance, through a mouse or some other control device. In a true virtual reality environment, you move inside the game or the page and are surrounded by it, becoming part of the virtual environment. Wearing goggles and gloves, you can turn around, look up or down, and move about the environment, enjoying six degrees of freedom (the ability to look or move up, down, forward, backward, left, and right) without ever leaving the virtual environment.

Although the most obvious use of VR is in the gaming world, the technology began as a scientific application. Using VR environments, pilots can learn to fly in dangerous situations without even leaving the ground, military training can be done in the safety and security of a VR facility, businesses can train employees to perform difficult tasks without involving real products, and surgeons can learn to perform delicate surgery without practicing on real patients. The possibilities of VR are staggering.

The technology, however, still is in development, and it may be some time before commercial VR systems for business or home use become commonplace or affordable. Meantime, the best way to experience virtual reality is through gaming or the World Wide Web.

Graphics and the World Wide Web

Perhaps even more than 3-D design and animation, the World Wide Web has aroused intense curiosity and interest in computer graphics. This is because nearly anyone can create and post a Web page, and the World Wide Web can support many types of graphics.

Further, by using basic paint and draw software as described earlier in this chapter, it is easy to create or edit graphics for use on a Web page. Such graphics include simple items such as bullets and horizontal rules, more complicated images such as logos, and complex artwork and photographs. If you have spent any time surfing the Web, you may agree that graphic elements truly enhance the viewing experience and can make even a simple page look elegant.

Adding Graphics to a Web Page

Although a Web page might look like one big graphic, remember that most pages are actually collections of graphics and text elements combined by the browser according to HTML tags embedded in the page's content. If any navigation buttons, icons, bullets, bars, or other graphics appear on the page, they are separate graphics files that are being displayed at the same time.

When a Web page designer creates a Web page, he or she usually begins by adding the text elements to an HTML-format file. By surrounding the text elements with special codes—called HTML tags—the designer can cause different pieces of text to be displayed in different ways by the Web browser. Tags tell the Web browser what information to display and how to display it.

The designer can also add tags that tell the browser to display graphics, and a single Web page can hold many individual graphics. On the Web server,

▶ Graphics can make nearly any Web page easier to use, or simply more appealing to look at.

▶ These two screens show a Web page's source code and the results in a browser. On the left, you can see the tags that format text and display graphics. On the right, you can see how the browser interprets the tags and displays the information.

This tag in the HTML file . . .

. . . causes the browser to display this image on the screen

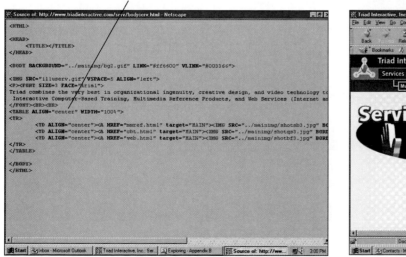

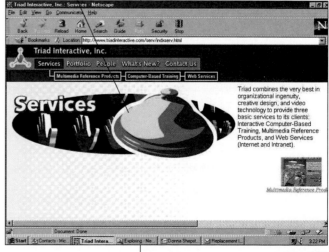

the designer must store all the graphics files required by the Web page. When the user's browser encounters the tags for a graphic, the server sends the graphic file to the browser. At the user's end, the HTML tags help the browser organize the graphics, text, and other design elements on the page.

The designer can use a variety of methods to incorporate graphics in a Web page. They can be placed virtually anywhere on the page, aligned in different ways, sized, incorporated in tables, and used as backgrounds. Graphic files are used to create buttons and bullets, horizontal rules, navigational tools, and much more.

Image Quality

As you learned earlier in this chapter, computers can display graphics at various resolutions and color depths. Whenever possible, designers use graphics of the highest possible resolution and color depth. On an interactive medium such as the World Wide Web, however, image quality often must be sacrificed to reduce file size and download times.

Remember that whenever your browser encounters a graphic in a Web page, it must download the graphic file from the Web server to your disk and then display it on screen. If the file is large or if the page contains many graphics, download time can be annoyingly slow. Web users frequently exit from a site before the page finishes downloading because the page is so graphics-intensive that it takes a long time to download.

Therefore, Web designers have adopted a few standards to ensure that their pages download as quickly as possible from the server to the user's disk:

- *Resolution.* Web graphics are generally saved and displayed at a resolution of 72 pixels per inch (ppi). Although much higher resolutions are possible, the improvement in visual quality is not necessarily obvious when the image is being viewed in a browser.

- *Color depth.* Although most computer screens can display colors of up to 24 bits (called true color), such files can be large. Generally, Web designers try to limit their color depth to 8 bits, or 256 colors. In some images, that can result in some loss of image quality, but because most computer monitors are set to display 256 colors anyway, the loss is minimal.

These three images were saved at different resolutions: 72 ppi, 144 ppi, and 244 ppi, from left to right. Note that the image's quality does not improve much with the change in resolution.

- *Image size.* Although it is possible to save images that are larger than the user's display space, Web designers try to avoid this practice. When a Web page requires a large graphic, designers try to ensure that the graphic is not so large that it will run off the edge of the user's screen at 800 x 600 screen resolution.

File Formats

To keep things consistent, designers create Web graphics in just two file formats: GIF and JPG. Although just about any graphic file format can be used on a Web page, browsers only support a few file formats without requiring the use of special plug-in software. Generally, browsers can open and view images in JPG and GIF formats directly in the browser window. (For descriptions of various file formats, refer back to Table 9.1.) For this reason, Web designers limit their graphics to JPG and GIF formats, as follows:

- *JPG.* The JPG format works well with complex images, that require many colors or contain subtle gradients, such as photographs or sophisticated logos. For this reason, most photographs and complex images appearing on the Web are in JPG format.

- *GIF.* The GIF format works well with simpler images that do not contain shading or subtle color changes. GIF also enables designers to use a single image many times over (such as buttons or backgrounds) because GIF files are relatively small and fast-loading.

Another graphic format that is gaining popularity on the Web is PNG. PNG can support higher resolutions and colors, like JPG, but is smaller and faster-loading, like GIF. At this point, however, most browsers do not support PNG files directly. To view a PNG file, you must use a plug-in program in the browser. When the browser encounters a PNG file, it opens the PNG viewer in a separate window to display the image.

Other Types of Graphics on the Web

Still images and buttons are not the only kinds of graphics that can be displayed from within a Web page. Emerging technologies are enabling designers to provide full-motion video and audio, animation, and interactive visual elements on the Web.

Animation

Using a variation of the GIF file, designers can easily add variety and movement to Web pages. The **animated GIF** file is simply a set of images, saved together in a single GIF-format file. When opened in a browser, the file's different images are displayed one after another, in a cycle. The designer can set the order for the images to display and the amount of display time for each image. The result is a mini-animation.

When displayed in succession, these images create a simple animation. They are saved together in a special animated GIF file, which a browser can display.

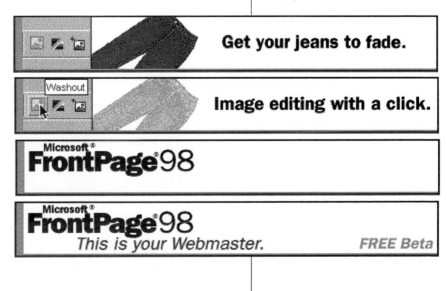

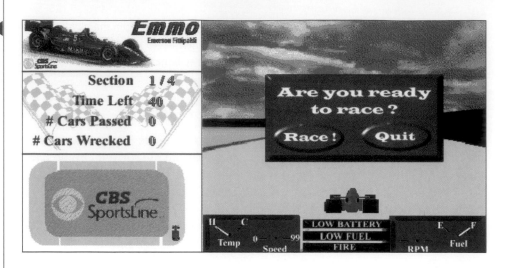

NORTON Online

For information on **Shockwave** and links to "Shocked" sites, visit this book's Web site at **www.glencoe.com/norton/online**

Animated GIFs are frequently used in advertising banners and other graphic elements where the user's attention is desired.

Designers also can make animations available through plug-ins. Macromedia's Shockwave plug-in, for example, has become a popular method for viewing animations in Web pages. The user must install the Shockwave plug-in software. Then, when the browser encounters a Shockwave-format file in a Web page, it can download the file and play it back. Plug-ins such as Shockwave provide additional capabilities; for example, designers can create interactive animations, such as games, which allow the user to interact with the animation and change its direction or outcome.

Streaming Video

There are several methods for incorporating full-motion video into Web pages. If the video is not an essential part of the page, the designer may choose to make the video file available in one of several formats, such as a QuickTime file or Movie file. The user can then download the file and play it by using the appropriate software, such as the QuickTime movie player.

Emerging technologies, however, are enabling Web designers to actually incorporate real-time video—called *streaming video*—into their pages. Using a special player, such as RealPlayer by RealNetworks, designers can incorporate video clips (complete with audio and animations) into their pages. Using a video plug-in, you can view videos as part of a Web page, with minimal download times. Further, the plug-ins free you from opening a separate window to view video content.

Streaming video and audio technologies are opening new doors for designers and making new types of content available on the Web. The technology is currently being used to transmit real-time news broadcasts over the Web to the user's computer screen, using standard phone lines and modem connections.

VRML

Just as virtual reality is the future of graphics in general, it is also the future of the Internet. Using new languages such as **Virtual Reality Modeling Language (VRML)**, Web designers can create nearly immersive 3-D sites—called *virtual worlds* or *moving worlds*—which include full 3-D graphics, animation, video, and audio. Many current VRML sites also provide real-time chat capabilities, so users can talk to one another using their computer's microphone and speakers. When you visit such a site, using a special browser, you find yourself moving through an animated 3-D world, interacting with other visitors and exploring computer-generated environments.

VRML gives developers a simple programming language with which to define three-dimensional shapes and paths. By creating and combining VRML objects, the developer can build a virtual world of endless possibilities, filled with buildings, rooms, furniture, landscapes, and 3-D characters. Developers are also making preconstructed VRML objects available on the Web so that others can use them in creating their own virtual worlds.

NORTON Online
For information on **VRML** and to get a **VRML browser**, visit this book's Web site at **www.glencoe.com/norton/online**

A VRML Web site.

Many 3-D Web sites invite users to enter online virtual chat rooms and don alternative identities or to become characters, called *avatars*. When you join in the activities at such a site, you not only can move through the 3-D environment by using your mouse, but you also can chat and interact with other avatars. Some sites currently offer customizable avatars, which you can design to suit your tastes.

Although VRML has found a home with gamers on the Web, it also has serious applications for business and education. Imagine someday learning how to repair your car over the Web, practicing in a 3-D environment, working on a computer-generated engine. At the NASA Web site, using a VRML-enabled browser, you can even try your hand at driving the Mars rover, Pathfinder.

Computers
In Your Career

Few areas of computing are as wide open as the field of computer graphics. If you are an artist or aspire to be a designer, consider adding computer-based design tools to your list of skills. By transferring their manual drawing and design skills to the computer, many of today's professional graphic artists have greatly expanded their portfolios and list of clients. Here are just a few areas where computer-based graphics are routinely employed:

World Wide Web Page Designers No Web site can compete unless it is graphically rich and filled with "cool" navigational tools. Web designers use packages such as Photoshop, Illustrator, and many others to illustrate their pages. Good designers bring a sense of color and balance to the Web page and use graphics to enhance the site's message, as well as make it more appealing.

Architects and Engineers If you have studied manual drafting, you can apply those skills to CAD and find a career in the architectural or engineering disciplines as a designer or drafter. CAD is used in a huge array of design fields, from building and construction design to aerospace design and product packaging. In the CAD world, you are limited only by your imagination and willingness to learn, as you can work in 2-D, 3-D, animation, programming, and many other vertical areas of computer-aided design.

Product Designers From shampoo bottles to automobiles, from initial specifications to modeling and visualization, more and more product design is being done at the computer.

Advertising Designers CGI has exploded in popularity among advertising agencies, which use computers to create everything from magazine ads to program-length television infomercials. Advertisers are continually pushing the envelope in computer-based and character animation as they seek to bring products to life and give personality to the items they hope to sell.

Game Designers and Filmmakers These fields are perhaps the pinnacle of computer graphics today, using the most sophisticated tools available to create complex effects for use in video games and movies. These designers use every tool available to get the desired results, from simple paint packages to advanced particle-generating effects software, as well as high-end workstations.

WHAT TO EXPECT IN THE FUTURE

Computer graphics is probably one of the fastest-moving fields in technology today. An explosion of new products (both hardware and software) and techniques has enabled computer artists at all levels to create imagery and effects that were impossible just two years ago. The future will continue to bring rapid innovations as designers bring new ideas to the table and developers work rapidly to create tools to bring those ideas to reality.

At the PC level, paint and draw packages will continue to merge, share features, and ultimately become more alike. It will become common for home users and casual users to have powerful yet inexpensive graphics software on their systems, just as word processors and browsers are common now. Do-it-yourself 3-D graphics, animation, and PC-based video are also becoming a reality as products with these capabilities reach the consumer and become almost effortless to use. Further, PC-based graphics software will continue to move toward the high end, duplicating the sophisticated capabilities now available only in workstation-based or proprietary graphics software.

Innovations in graphics and delivery technologies will also change the face of the Internet. The World Wide Web will become more like television in the coming few years, as new technologies are perfected for compressing, downloading, and playing a full range of multimedia content within the browser. Although it may not soon be possible for home users or casual users to create this content on a basic PC, any user with an Internet connection and browser will soon be able to enjoy streaming audio and video, and sophisticated animation. These processes will not simply be one-way viewing experiences but will become increasingly interactive, enabling the user to modify or direct the content as it appears on the screen.

Visual Summary & Exercises

VISUAL SUMMARY

Working with Images

■ Most graphics software is available for different computer platforms, including both Macs and PCs. Some software is available only for workstations.

■ Paint programs work with bitmaps. Draw programs work with vectors.

■ The most common bitmap formats are BMP, PICT, TIFF, JPEG, and GIF. The most widely used vector format is Encapsulated Postscript, or EPS.

■ Scanners, digital cameras, and clip art are three ways to input art into the computer.

■ Professional-quality photographs are often stored on PhotoCD.

■ Copyright issues are an important concern if artwork produced by someone else is to be used.

Graphics Software

■ The five main categories of graphics software are paint programs, photo-manipulation programs, draw programs, CAD software, and 3-D modeling programs.

■ Paint programs include tools like paintbrushes, ink and felt pens, chalk, and watercolors.

■ Paint programs are not well suited to applications that require a lot of text.

■ The specialty of paint programs is natural and realistic effects that mimic art produced via traditional methods.

■ Photo-manipulation programs have replaced many tools a photographer uses.

■ Photo-manipulation programs can exert pixel-level control over photographs and images.

■ With photo-manipulation programs, photographs can be altered with no evidence of alteration.

■ Draw programs are well suited to applications where flexibility is important.

- Objects created with draw programs can be altered and changed easily.

- Draw programs work well with text.

- Computer-Aided Design (CAD) software is used in technical fields, such as architecture and engineering, to create models of objects that are going to be built.

- CAD software allows users to design objects in three dimensions.

- Output from CAD software can appear as a wireframe model or as a rendered object, which appears solid.

- 3-D modeling programs are used to create spectacular visual effects.

- 3-D modeling programs work by creating objects via surface, solids, polygonal, or spline-based methods.

- Computers are now being used to create animations of organic and inorganic objects.

- Fly-bys and walk-throughs are basic types of computer animations.

- Character animation is the art of creating a character and making it move in a lifelike manner.

- Compositing tools let game makers and filmmakers add characters and objects to scenes that did not originally contain them.

- Virtual reality provides an immersive multimedia experience.

- Using HTML tags and simple graphics, you can easily add images to a Web page.

- The JPG and GIF image formats are the most widely used formats on the World Wide Web.

- Animation can be added to a Web page by using simple animated GIF files or plug-in software, such as Shockwave.

- Emerging technologies are making it possible to add streaming video to Web pages, making them much like television.

- The VRML programming language enables designers to create immersive 3-D Web sites, filled with computer-generated landscapes, buildings, and more.

the road less traveled, and that has made all the difference.

Visual Summary & Exercises

KEY TERMS

After completing this chapter, you should be able to define the following terms:

3-D modeling software, 344
animated GIF, 355
character animation, 348
clip art, 332
compositing, 350
Computer-Aided Design (CAD), 342
computer-generated imagery (CGI), 346
draw program, 329
Encapsulated Postscript (EPS), 331
fly-by, 347
frame, 346

keyframe, 349
model, 344
paint program, 329
photo-manipulation program, 337
photorealistic, 346
polygonal modeler, 345
Postscript, 326
render, 344
resolution-dependent, 340
resolution-independent, 340
shareware, 341
solid model, 344

solid modeler, 344, 345
spline-based modeler, 345
surface modeler, 345
tween, 349
vector, 328
virtual reality (VR), 352
Virtual Reality Modeling Language (VRML), 356
walk-through, 348
wireframe model, 344

KEY TERM QUIZ

Fill in the missing word with one of the terms listed in Key Terms.

1. Graphics programs that work with bitmaps are called _____.

2. A 3-D modeling program that also understands thickness and density is known as a(n) _____.

3. With CAD programs you can produce various types of _____ to represent 3-D objects.

4. You can also _____ a solid-looking representation of an object using a CAD program.

5. A non-artist can use _____ as an easy way to start or enhance digital artwork.

6. _____ is software you can try for free, then register and purchase if you decide to keep it.

7. Graphics files are composed of either bitmaps or a set of _____.

8. A(n) _____ graphics program displays images the same way regardless of the monitor you are using.

9. A _____ environment is one that immerses the user in 3-D animation, video, sound, and other types of media.

10. A computer-generated image that looks like a real object is said to be _____.

Visual Summary & Exercises

REVIEW QUESTIONS

1. According to the chapter, what two products "ushered" in the era of art on personal computers?

2. What kind of computers are the Sun SparcStation and the Silicon Graphics Indigo2, and in what ways do they benefit commercial graphic artists and designers?

3. Which kind of graphics program allows a user to work with vector images?

4. What device can be used to convert images on paper into a digital file format?

5. What factors have contributed to the popularity of clip art?

6. What limitations are there with bitmap-based paint programs?

7. Why are CAD programs so accurate?

8. Name the four types of 3-D modeling software described in this chapter.

9. What is the difference between a fly-by and a walk-through?

10. What are compositing tools used for?

DISCUSSION QUESTIONS

1. What tools and techniques, which were not required by graphic artists and illustrators in the past, do you think today's graphic artists must know and understand to be productive?

2. Discuss some of the implications that electronic retouching of photographs through the use of photo illustration software might create in today's society.

3. As cheaper and more powerful computers are developed, in what areas of our lives do you think we will see more sophisticated graphics imaging?

4. Suppose that you want to be able to build a collection or library of images as you work that you can use again and again to save time when creating new images. What kind of graphics software do you think would best accomplish this? What kind of hardware requirements do you think you would need?

5. What impact can technologies such as virtual reality and VRML have on education and business in the future? In what ways do you imagine this technology being used, not only in stand-alone applications but also in multiuser environments such as the World Wide Web? Support your answer.

*inte*NET Workshop

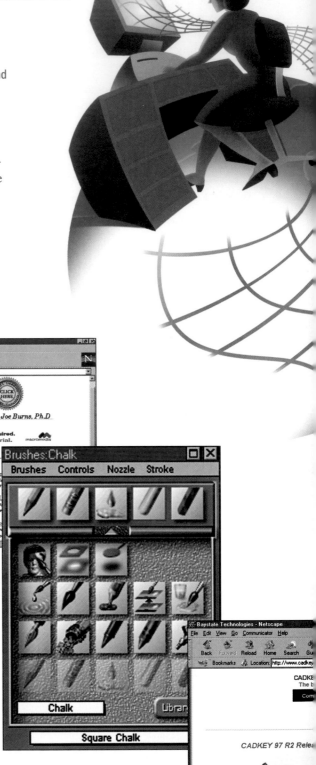

The following exercises assume that you have access to the Internet and a browser. If you need help with any of the exercises, visit this book's Web site at **www.glencoe.com/norton/online**. This book's Web site also lists the URLs you need to complete many of these exercises.

1. The Internet is the single richest resource of current information on computer graphics. Using a search engine such as Excite or Webcrawler, search on *one* of the following terms:

- Graphics
- Paint program
- Draw program
- 3-D design
- CAD
- Computer animation
- Web page design
- Virtual Reality (VR)
- Virtual Reality Modeling Language (VRML)

How many Web pages are listed as the result of your search? Choose five pages that appear most interesting or informative (based on the description provided by the search engine) and visit them. What information can you find that was not presented in the class discussion of the topic? Share this information with the class.

2. If you are interested in graphics, design, or marketing, you may want to consider a career in Web page design. Many Web sites provide tutorials, tips, prewritten HTML code, scripts, graphics, and free advice for designers of all levels of experience. A good place to start is by searching on "Web page design" in your favorite search engine, or visit a resource site on the Web, such as The Web Developer's Virtual Libaray or the HTML Goodies Home Page. Can you find other pages that provide useful information for beginning Web designers? Which aspect of Web design appeals most to you: HTML, graphics, style sheets, site layout, navigation, scripting? Why?

3. Macromedia's Shockwave and Flash products have changed the face of the Web by enabling designers to incorporate interactive animations and sounds in their pages. The emergence of "Shocked" technologies has led to a new level of interactivity on the Web, from gaming, to marketing, to the presentation of news stories. To take advantage of Shockwave- or Flash-based content, your browser must have either the Shockwave or Shockwave Flash plug-in installed. To install the plug-in, visit the Macromedia Web site and follow the links to install Shockwave, Shockwave Flash, or the newest Java-based Flash plug-in. Then visit the Macromedia Shockzone and explore some of the "Shocked" sites listed in their gallery of Shockwave-enabled sites. What can you do at these sites that you cannot do at other Web sites? How does the presence of the Shockwave plug-in affect your browsing?

4. Virtual Reality Modeling Language (VRML) has enabled Web designers to create full 3-D environments at their Web sites. Browsing these sites is like walking through a building or mall. In some VRML spaces, you can take on the identity of a 3-D character (called an "avatar") and interact with other visitors to the site. Your browser, however, must be VRML-enabled, meaning that you must use a VRML-based browser or install a VRML plug-in. To find a list of VRML plug-ins and browsers, visit The VRML Repository. Assuming that your classroom's Web browser has a VRML plug-in installed, visit at least two different VRML sites. (You can find a wide variety of VRML sites by conducting a search on the term "VRML.") How do the different sites make use of VRML? Do the virtual environments enhance your use of the Web? What possible uses can you think of for VRML in the future?

5. Computer-Aided Design is a rapidly expanding field, as computer technology continues to be applied to design disciplines that once used only manual techniques. Visit the Web sites of companies that produce popular CAD products, such as Autodesk (maker of AutoCAD), DataCAD LLC (maker of DataCAD), Bentley Systems (maker of MicroStation), and Baystate Technologies (maker of CADKey). For general information on CAD technologies and their applications, use your favorite search engine to search on the term "CAD." Do you find CAD being used in ways you did not expect? If so, what are they? What potential uses do you think can be found for CAD technologies? What benefits do you think CAD technologies have brought to the design disciplines? List these benefits with your classmates.

CHAPTER **10**

The New Media

CONTENTS

OBJECTIVES

When you complete this chapter, you will be able to do the following:

- Define the term "interactive media" and describe its role in new communications technologies.
- List three ways consumers receive multimedia content.
- Give one example of multimedia applications in each of these three areas: schools, businesses, and the home.
- Define the term "hypermedia" and describe its role in multimedia presentations.
- Name three ways in which you might use virtual reality.
- Explain one way in which digital convergence has affected the media being produced for mass consumption.

Today's high-powered yet affordable personal computers have encouraged businesses to examine the way they deliver information and entertainment to their customers. Computers invite people to explore new ways to communicate, get information, or be entertained.

For much of history, information was presented via a single, unique medium. A **medium** is simply a means of conveying information. Sound, such as the human voice, is one type of medium, and for centuries prior to the invention of written languages, it was the primary way of conveying and receiving information. The creation of written language gave people a new medium for expressing their thoughts. Text, graphics, animation, and video all are different types of **media** ("media" is the plural of "medium"), and each has traditionally been used to present certain types of information.

People long ago discovered, however, that messages are more effective—that is, the audience understands and remembers them more easily—when they are presented through a combination of different media. This is why teachers began using chalkboards in the classroom, so they could use written text to support their spoken lectures. Movies and television enabled people to combine different media (sound, moving photography, animation, and text) to create different types of messages, to inform and entertain in unique and meaningful ways. In practice, you can say that even the simplest speech-and-text presentation is a **multimedia** event because it uses more than one unique medium to deliver a message.

The computer, however, has taken multimedia to a new level, by enabling us to use many different media simultaneously. Think, for example, of an encyclopedia; it can be much more than just pages of text and pictures. In a multimedia edition, the pictures can move, and a narrator's recorded voice can speak to the user while entertaining music or informative sounds play in the background. By combining different types of media to present the message, the encyclopedia's developer improves the chances that everyone in the audience will understand the message. If the multimedia encyclopedia is interactive—that is, if it can also entice the reader to participate by clicking the mouse or typing on the keyboard—this multimedia experience involves its audience unlike any book, movie, or TV program.

Interactivity, however, involves more than just a computer or a mouse. The **new media** (a term encompassing all types of interactive multimedia technologies) bring into play different communication technologies, such as cable TV, telephone lines, the Internet, and others. As you will see throughout this chapter, the new media are actually a convergence of many types of technology, enabling individuals and large groups to communicate and convey information using computers and computerized systems.

THE POWER OF INTERACTIVITY

The last time a new electronic medium captured the public's attention was in the late 1940s and early 1950s with the rapid and widespread popularity of television. Television was a new way to convey information and entertainment to a mass audience—adding moving pictures to the sounds of radio that had been coming into people's homes for decades.

When television was introduced (and even today), critics said that presenting pictures along with sounds deprived viewers of their powers of imagination. Instead of allowing the audience to visualize and imagine what the characters and scenes looked like, as in a radio drama or a book, TV programs left little to the imagination. By passively watching hour after hour of ready-to-digest material, people can become "couch potatoes," sitting silent and motionless on the sofa as programs pour out of the picture tube.

Interacting with Television

Today, the prevalence of inexpensive computers offers a way to change our passive response to electronic media. Computers make it possible to create **interactive media**, which enable people to respond to—and even control—what they see and hear. Instead of passively accepting every sound bite, story line, or advertisement that appears on the video screen, viewers can become active participants, searching for items of particular interest, digging deeper into a news story, or even choosing to view an alternative plot line for a situation comedy.

Part of the public's interest in interactivity can be directly related to the success of home video games. As millions of children and adults around the world have demonstrated, it is possible to turn off spoon-fed television programming, and instead guide a character through a three-dimensional maze, manage a sports team on the field, or solve a computerized puzzle.

Figure 10.1
Traditional media with one-way communication.

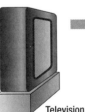

Information

Television

In a television broadcast, information flows in one direction, from the TV to the viewer.

These home video games are called **interactive** because they include a feedback loop that does not exist in most commercial media such as television, print, and radio. Most media offer only one-way communication, as shown in Figure 10.1.

Interactive media, however, put a computer in the hands of the viewer and thereby establish two-way communication—also known as a feedback loop. For an example, see Figure 10.2.

With a TV-based video game, the user has a computer (for example, a Nintendo 64 or Sony Playstation system) and some type of controller, such as a joystick. As a result, the information that comes out of the television is constantly changing in response to the information coming from the user.

In the world of television broadcasting, however, the transition from one-way communication to two-way, interactive communication is slow. Traditional broadcast companies such as the popular television networks and cable television companies are currently wrestling with major decisions about their futures. For example, should they continue to produce programs that appeal only to the couch potato? Or should they instead develop new kinds of programming and media aimed at a generation of viewers whose appetite for interactivity has been whetted by playing with video games or personal computers? The problem of accommodating the interactive communication with the cable company is still a technical hurdle to be solved. Few cable systems today are equipped to handle such two-way communication.

Figure 10.2
Interactive media with feedback loop.

Television

Video information to the user

Game system

Joystick information back to the game system

Joystick

One exception to this is pay-per-view. Some cable systems provide pay-per-view services only by telephone (for instance, you can call and order a recently released movie), which isn't exactly interactive. Others, however, such as satellite systems, hotel systems, and an increasing number of home systems, let you order a pay-per-view movie or event by using your remote control or special set-top box. This is one step toward making TV interactive.

One example of television and computers converging to provide an interactive setting is Cable News Network's (CNN) "TalkBack Live" show. "TalkBack Live" mixes several communications technologies to enable viewers to participate in discussions. These technologies include the conventional—telephone and fax—as well as the unconventional—electronic message boards, Internet chat, and e-mail.

NORTON Online

For more information on "TalkBack Live," visit this book's Web site at www.glencoe.com/norton/online

CNN's "TalkBack Live" television show enables viewers at home to communicate with the show's guests via the Internet.

Interacting with Computers

While consumers wait for the deployment of interactive television networks, many other multimedia content-delivery vehicles are already in place. Due to the large amount of information typically presented in an interactive production, the large electronic storage capacity of the CD-ROM has become popular for use with desktop personal computers.

Usually, each CD-ROM disk is a self-contained interactive program—a game, a self-paced learning program, or a course of instruction, such as one that shows you how to add a redwood deck to your house. More interactive than just play-only videocassettes, these programs usually ask viewers to use a mouse or keyboard to enter customized information about themselves or the problem they are trying to solve (like how to design the redwood deck to wrap around a corner of your house). The computer then uses programs and other materials on the CD-ROM disk to produce custom information just for the viewer (such as how much redwood deck planking to order).

Another increasingly popular delivery method for interactive material is a connection to the Internet or an online service, such as America Online (AOL). Unlike the broadcast world, commercial online services and the Internet are designed for high-volume, two-way information transfer. When a computer user connects to such a service, the service rarely does anything without some interaction—such as the user telling the service "where" to go by clicking an on-screen button or typing a command. The user is entirely in control of navigating through the information. These services also are being linked to television programs, such as the previous example of CNN's "TalkBack Live" show, as well as the Food Network's "Cooking Live" broadcast.

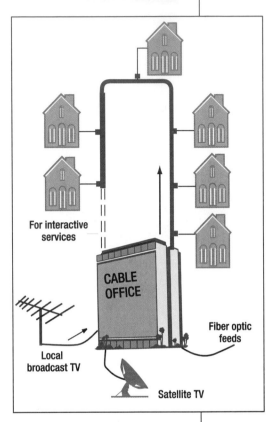

For cable companies to provide interactive programming, they will have to extend the wiring that connects all the homes back to the cable office.

Interactive video games are made for both computers and television, such as the Sonic the Hedgehog line of games.

Also, remember that interactivity includes interaction among real people; it is not just one individual interacting with a world of faceless computers. The most familiar form of electronic interactivity is a phone conversation. It is easy to forget, though, that a personal computer is also a communications device, letting people share ideas in a variety of forms. Connected to online services or the Internet, millions of people interact each day either in "live" conversations typed on the keyboard or via electronic mail.

For decades, different media have been used in various combinations in film, theater, and television. But the interactive component—where the viewer participates in the direction of action—distinguishes today's multimedia offerings from the past. Although interactive multimedia is a relatively new field, people have already identified a huge variety of potential uses.

Interactivity and Education

Education has embraced this new technology and is one of the first and best consumers of multimedia. In today's schools, multimedia computers are an integral part of many classrooms and bring a new level of interactivity to learning.

One major reform movement in education promotes active and cooperative learning. Computers and multimedia help students and teachers make the transition to this new mode of learning. In the classroom, visual presentations that include animation, video, and sound motivate students to become active participants in the learning process. Interactive multimedia programs bring concepts to life and help students integrate critical thinking and problem-solving skills.

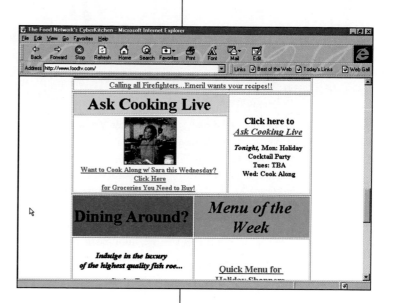

Viewers of Food Network's "Cooking Live" show can send e-mail questions to host Sara Moulton, who will answer them on the air.

This is funschool's World Wide Web page on the Internet. Children can click on the characters to look for related information.

Productivity Tip

Creating Multimedia Presentations for the Web

Creating Web pages is fairly simple, particularly if you have the right applications that help you create Web pages and you want to keep the page simple.

But if you plan to incorporate sophisticated multimedia elements into your Web pages, you need to know how to put them together. This is especially true if you want to offer your pages to the largest number of users, who will be connecting to your site using a mixture of different browsers, connection speeds, and platforms.

Here are some suggestions on building Web pages that offer multimedia content so that a large percentage of visitors can enjoy your content—and keep returning for more.

Track Your Visitors If you already have a Web page up, you should track who is visiting the page to create an audience profile. You can ask your Web site administrator or Internet Service Provider to provide you with a log (a file that records information about the users visiting your Web page) of your Web site activity. Some of the items you'll want to watch include the types of browsers and operating systems accessing your site. From this information, you may gather that your typical visitor uses Netscape Navigator residing on a Macintosh. Using this data, you can construct a multimedia page that caters to the Macintosh user (knowing they typically have built-in Apple QuickTime audio and video support). You can also include JavaScript elements (if users have Navigator 3.0 or later) and content that uses plug-ins, such as Vxtreme streaming video files.

On the other hand, if your visitors are predominantly Windows users, you may need to offer several different formats for your multimedia content. This may include video saved in AVI (Windows Video) and QuickTime for Windows. You may also consider creating scripts using Microsoft's ActiveX language rather than JavaScript. This way, users of Internet Explorer 3.0 or higher will have fewer problems running them.

Poll Your Audience If you're not getting enough information about the users of your site, set up a form in which you ask users for additional information about their system and content preferences. Ask for the following data:

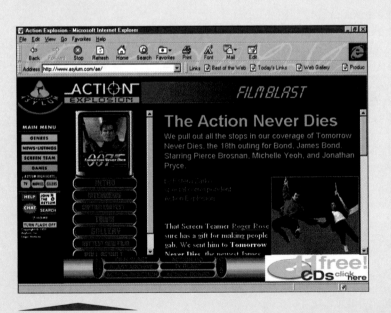

Designing multimedia Web pages means knowing your audience's likes and dislikes.

■ *Monitor size and resolution.* The size and resolution of a user's video display are important when creating Web pages, particularly those that include graphics and video. If the majority of visitors have 13-inch monitors and run at 640x480 resolution, build your Web pages for that resolution.

■ *Connection speed.* By far, slow connection speeds limit the type of multimedia content you can provide to your visitors. Although you can offer large video files to visitors to download, many users connecting at speeds of 33.3 Kbps will not download the files. It simply takes too much time. In these cases, offer video or audio in streaming format, using RealSystem format from Real Networks, Inc. (http://www.realaudio.com). Visitors then can start hearing and seeing content before the entire file downloads to their system.

■ *Content preferences.* Everyone has likes and dislikes. Don't assume that everyone likes frames, for instance. Some people love them; others refuse to return to sites that have them. In the same sense, don't assume that everyone likes audio or video files. Ask visitors whether they would like to see animated site maps, chat rooms, or Java applets added to your site.

Test Your Pages Always test your pages in different browsers, on multiple platforms, and in different viewing situations. In some cases, you may need to create different versions of your pages so that visitors can choose the one they prefer.

One common interactive multimedia application for education is an electronic encyclopedia contained on a CD-ROM. If students have an assignment to write a report on a region of Africa, they can read about the history and geography, and with the click of the mouse button, they can see video clips of the hustle and bustle of a city and hear audio clips of African languages or the sounds of tribal music. As a result, the information comes to life, and students may even have the software tools to produce their reports in the form of a multimedia presentation.

Interactive simulations can also involve the student in contemporary environmental and political issues. For example, an educational game called SimSafari lets the player run his or her own African wildlife refuge. Players populate the refuge with the animals and plants they want, as well as make decisions about ecological issues and the food chain that affect the entire park. Screen graphics show the effects of good and bad judgments immediately. A student can try out many different scenarios to find how to balance various issues pertaining to the park.

SimSafari enables students to set up and run their own African wildlife refuge.

Students in the same classroom and in classrooms separated by thousands of miles can collaborate on projects with the help of c o m m u n i c a tions networks such as the Internet. They can share video files, or see each other in a videoconference to review and expand their reports. The technology exists today for students to use an electronic camera to create virtual versions of their classrooms. Students and friends elsewhere can "move" around the electronic rooms while watching the view on a computer screen.

Virtual universities are also popping up on the Web to offer **distance learning (DL)**. These are sites that enable students to take classes, interact with instructors, send in homework and projects, and complete exams while online. Some DL sites provide Web-based learning, CD-ROM instruction, and live classroom instruction available over television broadcast. Some DL sites offer full degrees over the Internet, although the best solution for using DL is combining DL techniques with conventional classroom experiences.

One company that has been on the cutting edge of DL and Web-based learning is Jones Education Company. Jones provides courses and degrees from recognized universities (such as George Washington University and University of Colorado at Colorado Springs) straight to the student's desktop using videotape and the Internet. Students receive the same instructions that students who attend classes do but have the flexibility of learning on their own schedule. One downside to DL and Web-based learning is the limited interaction between students and instructors.

Interactive technology is enabling students to communicate with scientists conducting research in remote areas of the world, or even in outer space. Students at Oaklandon Elementary School in Oaklandon, Indiana, corresponded with astronaut David Wolf while he was aboard the space station Mir in 1997. Students exchanged e-mail messages and photographs with the astronaut while Wolf was stationed on Mir.

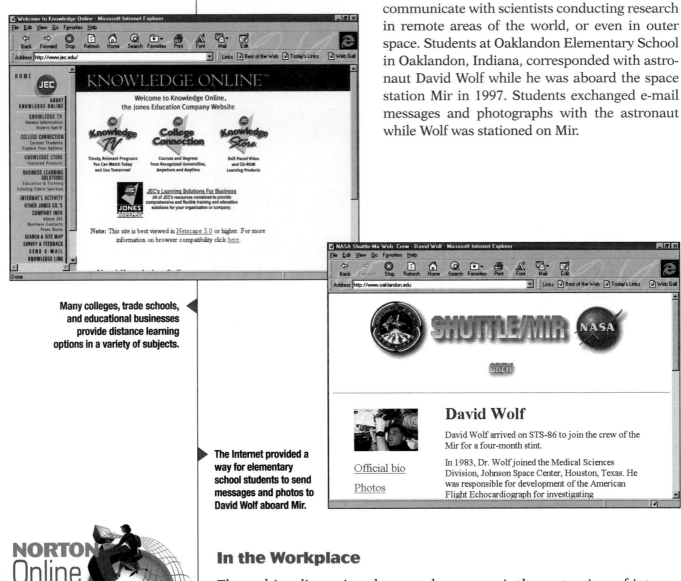

Many colleges, trade schools, and educational businesses provide distance learning options in a variety of subjects.

The Internet provided a way for elementary school students to send messages and photos to David Wolf aboard Mir.

NORTON
Online

For more information on **NASA** and **Mir**, visit this book's Web site at **www.glencoe.com/norton/online**

In the Workplace

The multimedia-equipped personal computer is the centerpiece of interactive multimedia applications in the workplace. At first, it may seem odd that media such as animation, sound, and video would play a role in business, but there is an unstoppable trend occurring to enlist these media in many business activities.

For example, training is a never-ending task in large corporations, especially as companies expect their employees to master the latest computer technologies. As a replacement for—or supplement to—classroom training, many companies have developed customized interactive training materials. These materials fall into a category of products called **computer-based training (CBT)**. Training courses on company policies, customized computer systems, and customer contact are of particular interest.

One company interested in keeping its workers up to date is Ernst & Young. By using a combination of CD-ROM-based and Web-based CBTs, Ernst & Young can deliver education to its employees any place the user has a computer, such as a remote office, a client setting, even a hotel room. Ernst & Young's CBT is called LEAP (Learning Environment to Accelerate Performance) and enables employees to access a host of information from different databases. Another company, JC Penney, trains its sales associates by using intranets to enable associates to collaborate with other associates to solve problems, share information, and discuss case studies.

Sales and marketing are taking on new meaning in the age of multimedia. Information that used to be distributed only in printed catalogs may now be available in an interactive electronic catalog, mailed to customers in CD-ROM format, or presented on a company's World Wide Web site. A department store or shopping network, such as the QVC shopping network, can use the Web to show products and let the viewer read about the features of a product. Companies are also beginning to allow customers to preview merchandise from an interactive catalog on the World Wide Web. Customers can place orders for merchandise by completing an on-screen order form.

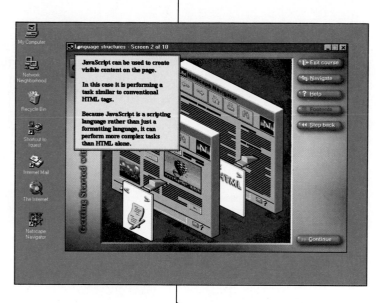

This computer-based training program is designed to teach JavaScript.

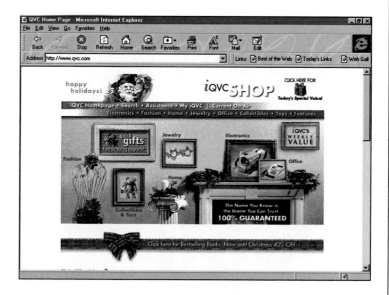

This screen shows the QVC shopping network's companion Web site.

NORTON Online

For more information on **Microsoft Knowledge Base**, visit this book's Web site at www.glencoe.com/norton/online

Companies also rely on the Web and CD-ROMs to deliver technical support to customers. Instead of providing large, seldom-used documentation to customers, businesses provide electronic documentation for customers looking for information or solutions relating to a number of problems. One of the most helpful Web sites for customers of Microsoft products is the **Microsoft Knowledge Base (KB)**. The Knowledge Base, which is also available on CD-ROM, provides a search engine to enable users to enter a keyword or phrase describing a problem. The Knowledge Base then displays links to documents that describe possible solutions to the problem.

Many companies that provide technical support, such as the Microsoft Knowledge Base, use CD-ROM and Web technology.

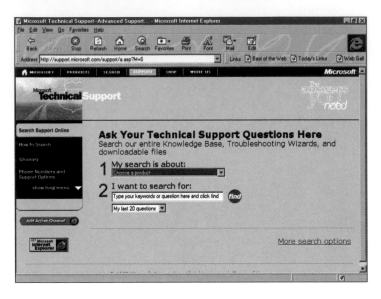

However, the primary focus of multimedia in business is on communication—both within the corporation and in getting the company's message out to the rest of the world. Multimedia is also helping employees to work together, even when their locations or schedules prevent face-to-face contact. Videoconferencing is no longer only the province of specially equipped meeting rooms and studios. Compact, inexpensive cameras and microphones can sit atop the desktop computer monitor, allowing two or more people to see and speak with each other by means of their screens. Other kinds of software allow two people to view the same document simultaneously on two computers in different parts of the world.

The two people in the windows on the right side of this screen are using videoconferencing to discuss the information shown in the spreadsheet.

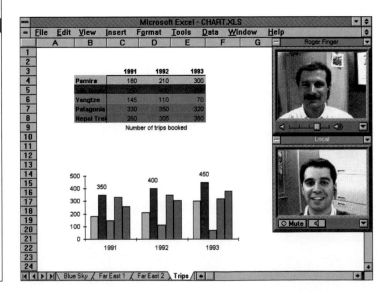

At Home

Reference materials, self-help instruction, and entertainment packages offer many opportunities for enhancement via multimedia productions. Regardless of the content, the goal is to engage the audience—to get the viewers to participate in the activity.

Perhaps you want some help in selecting a movie rental for the evening. Of course, you can read about a film you know by name in any of dozens of printed movie guides. However, an interactive guide such as The Internet Movie Database lets you search for movies by genre, performers, and other criteria that might interest you. For most of the films listed, you can view clips or trailers, read reviews from multiple sources, and find out which other films might be related.

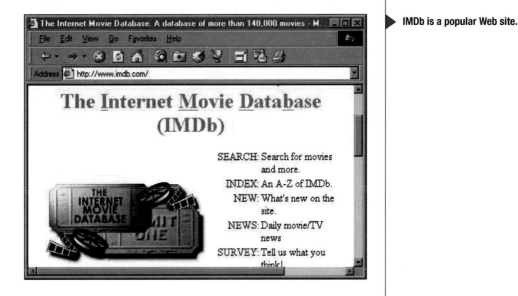

▶ IMDb is a popular Web site.

By far, the largest application for commercial multimedia is in the entertainment field. Video games sold on cartridges and CD-ROMs for dedicated game machines or for desktop computers are very popular. The large storage capacity of CD-ROMs often allows higher-quality animation, embedded video, digital-quality sound, and a broader variety of game play.

Multimedia packages for managing money are becoming popular. For example, financial planning for retirement is not easy for most families. Today, you can use the Internet to connect to investment firms such as Fidelity Investments to get some guidance about planning a retirement portfolio. At Fidelity's World Wide Web site, you enter information about your current financial status, how much risk you are willing to take, and your retirement financial goals. While you are still connected, the Fidelity computer displays a report that recommends the right mix of investments to meet your requirements.

Another interactive service is a technology called **interactive television**. In conjunction with a specially made computer connected to your television set, the remote control is used for more than just switching channels. On-screen menus allow you to select from vast libraries of movies stored in computers at your cable company office. Instead of going to the movie rental store or waiting for a cable TV movie to start at a certain time, you will be able to begin watching the movie of your choice when you want it.

NORTON *Notebook*

Anytime, Anywhere Learning

A growing trend in education is providing online learning opportunities. In the past, colleges have offered correspondence courses via regular mail. Today, students can take courses by television, videotape, or computer. In some cases, a convergence of all these technologies provides students with a virtual classroom, right in their own home.

Learn from Home Anytime, anywhere learning is the term often used to describe how technology and new media have opened the doors for educational opportunities that involve computers, the Internet, and other technologies. Another term used is distance learning (DL).

The University of Colorado in Colorado Springs began offering courses in 1997. Students taking a course in Fantasy Literature, for example, had access to weekly multimedia lectures. These lectures comprised 5-15 Web pages of comments from the professor, along with graphics and audio clips. Students were required to post homework, such as writing about dreams, to the course's Web site. Some assignments even let students respond to homework posted by other students, providing a group collaboration often found in traditional classrooms.

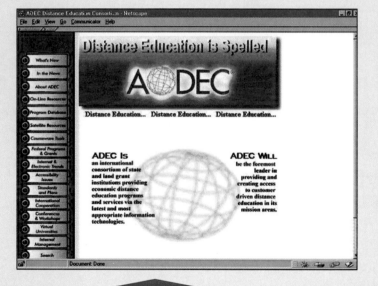

Multimedia studies programs are becoming more popular and necessary as new media technologies continue to converge on people's everyday lives.

To provide feedback to students, professors mark up papers using editing tools available in many word processors, such as Microsoft Word's revision marks. Instructors can also correspond by e-mail to students, or offer electronic chat rooms for real-time conversations.

No Commute Necessary Learning online is still in its infancy, and many institutions use it as a supplement to their normal classroom settings. But a trend in offering full degree programs online is growing. Now, many institutions offer online classrooms and distance learning courses using new media technologies, including:

■ *The Multimedia Studies Program Online at San Francisco State University College of Extended Learning.* SFSU provides classes in multimedia and certificate programs, programs in Digital Design and Production, 3-D Arts, and Web Design and Production. Find out more information at http://www.cef.sfsu.edu/msp/MSP2.html.

■ *Stanford Online at Stanford University.* Engineers and computer science professionals are offered distance learning courses in many different areas. Stanford Online delivers video with audio, text, and graphics over the Internet to students. Visit Stanford Online at http://arum.stanford.edu/.

■ *University of Phoenix Online Campus.* The Online Campus program offers full degree programs online and enables students to "gather" online using a specially designed software, called AlexWare. AlexWare provides a group mailbox that serves as an electronic classroom. Classes are not structured around semesters or quarters, so students can begin a class any month of the year. Some of the courses you can take include Project Management, Critical Thinking, and Philosophy. Visit the Online Campus at http://www.uophx.edu/online/index.htm.

■ *Massachusetts Institute of Technology (MIT) Center for Advanced Educational Services (CAES).* MIT's CAES offers distance learning-based non-degree programs in Advanced Marketing Management, Modeling and Simulation of Dynamic Systems, and Dynamic Strategic Planning. CAES mixes interactive multimedia, the World Wide Web, videoconferencing, satellite TV, and videotapes to deliver to students enrolled in distance learning courses.

In the future, you may be able to receive a certification or full degree by completing courses online. You may never need to attend a classroom or fight traffic getting to class.

THE NEW MEDIA

Traditional media companies—print publishing, music publishing, and broadcasting—have been in the business of delivering information and entertainment for a long time. Because the popularity of consumer-priced multimedia computers has increased, these companies have begun to search for ways to repackage their existing content to take advantage of the new technologies. Many companies are also developing content in a form that better matches the capabilities of the new computers. It is, therefore, not uncommon to hear multimedia frequently referred to as *new media*.

New media is a young industry, still groping to find the kind of material that will capture the imagination of millions of consumers. Another challenge in establishing new media as a mainstream entity is the frequent conflict of cultures between the traditional media companies (publishers, movie studios, and others) that own a lot of content and the computer software world. However, large new media products, such as an educational CD-ROM, often involve both kinds of companies: a publisher develops the content, and a software company combines it into a cohesive multimedia product.

At the core of new media is a concept known as **digital convergence**. As computers are used to create all kinds of content, from plain text to video, more and more of the content is in digital form. All digital information, regardless of its content, can travel to the consumer along the same path—perhaps via a CD-ROM disk or a cable TV wire. Rather than delivering movies on film or videotape, music on tapes or compact disks, and books on the printed page, different kinds of content now can reach the computer or cable TV box in the same way. Thus, a variety of content comes together, converging into one digital stream.

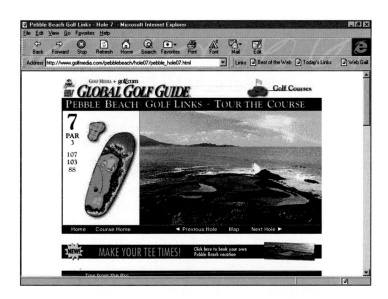

On this multimedia Web site, the Global Golf Guide offers visitors information about golf packages, resorts, courses, and employment. The site utilizes video, audio, text, and virtual reality to guide visitors around courses.

Multimedia: Beyond Words

Print publishers were among the first to explore the possibilities of delivering their content in digital form for display on a personal computer. Consumers, however, quickly rejected the simple conversion of the printed page to the computer screen, perhaps because reading extensive amounts of text on a screen is not as convenient or as comfortable as reading the printed page.

The task, then, was to make the electronic version of the content more engaging, utilizing the special powers that computers have to offer.

Adding Sound, Graphics, Animation, and Video

One way to make plain text and pictures inviting to an audience is to add time-based content, such as audio, cartoon animation, and video. It is, however, very important that the added media do more than merely mimic the static text and graphics content. It would be very boring indeed to watch a video of someone reading a passage of text that appears on the screen. But if the text is a scene from *Hamlet,* and the video displays that same scene with Sir Laurence Olivier's film portrayal, then the video enlivens the printed text.

The multimedia encyclopedia, such as the one included in the Encyclopedia Britannica software, adds a number of sound, animation, and video clips to enliven several subjects. For example, in an article about rocketry, a click of the mouse on the cross-section diagram of a rocket's components starts a narrated animation that demonstrates the process of mixing the fuel components to cause propulsion. Many interactive multimedia products, such as this, also allow the viewer to examine different slices of the content. Instead of searching for a particular word or phrase, users can scan through all the sound clips or animations, stopping to listen to or view any item that stimulates the imagination.

A focus on the *content* of a multimedia program or presentation is essential. It is the content that the consumer pays for, or the audience comes to see. For example, the first feature-length computer-animated film, *Toy Story,* would have had limited appeal for just its technical wizardry. Because it also had an appealing story and strong character development, the film attracted children and adults alike. Likewise, live-action films using computer animation and graphics to enhance or create objects or environments on the screen, such as the sinking ship in *Titanic,* would have limited appeal if the story was flat.

Platform Considerations for Multimedia

The way in which content reaches its audience is a separate issue from the content itself. Because of the intensive amount of digital information that goes into building every second of a program, multimedia publishers must always consider the user's equipment—the platform on which the content will be displayed.

Along with a fast CPU and plenty of RAM, a multimedia PC needs a CD-ROM drive, speakers, and a sound card.

The Apple Macintosh line of computers has been configured for multimedia since the early 1990s, when a CD-ROM drive and audio capabilities were included. For the most part, users who purchased Macintosh computers would not need extra equipment to play back multimedia applications. On the other hand, PCs (that is, IBM-compatible computers) did not come equipped with multimedia hardware until a few years ago.

Today, PCs often come with all the necessary multimedia components already installed. These computers ease the startup time for computer novices and home computer users because the users are not faced with complicated hardware issues, such as configuring a new CD-ROM player or installing a sound board. For older computers, however, it may be necessary to add one or more of the following components to turn the PC into a multimedia PC:

- Sound card
- Speakers
- CD-ROM drive

Additionally, a multimedia computer requires enough processing horsepower (a fast CPU chip) and memory (RAM) to accommodate multimedia programs.

To help multimedia developers predict how much multimedia power should be in users' computers, an industry group has defined minimum standards for multimedia PCs. As the capabilities of computers have increased over the years and costs to the consumer have come down, the standards have become more rigorous. In 1995, the latest upgrade to the **Multimedia Personal Computer (MPC) standard**, called MPC Level 3, was announced to software and hardware makers. Table 10.1 shows a summary of hardware features specified in the most recent standard for MPC computers.

Many hardware and software manufacturers, however, publish multimedia requirements for their products that are more demanding than those listed by the MPC 3 standard. Microsoft, for instance, publishes the *Hardware Design Guide* with a list of system requirements for hardware vendors designing hardware to be used with Microsoft Windows 98 and Windows NT. One

NORTON
Online

For more information on the **MPC standard**, visit this book's Web site at www.glencoe.com/norton/online

Table 10.1	Multimedia PC Level 3 Specification
CPU (Min.)	75 MHz Pentium or equivalent for hardware MPEG or 100 MHz Pentium for software MPEG or equivalent
Operating System	Windows 95
RAM (Min.)	8 MB
Floppy Drive	Yes
Hard Drive (Min.)	540 MB
Video Playback	MPEG
Two-Button Mouse	Yes
101-Key Keyboard	Yes
CD-ROM Drive	Quad speed; 600 KB per sec transfer rate; 250 ms average access time
Audio	Compact audio disk playback 16-bit digital; 44.1, 22.05, and 11.025 kHz sampling rates; microphone input; wavetable support; internal mixing of four sources
Serial Port	Yes
Parallel Port	Yes
Midi I/O Port	Yes
Joystick Port	Yes
Speakers	Two-piece stereo; 3 watts per channel

Source: Software Publishers Assn. Multimedia PC Working Group

difference between MPC 3 and Microsoft's core system requirements is CPU speed. Microsoft's list requires a 200 MHz CPU with Intel MMX technology, whereas MPC 3 requires only a 90 MHz CPU.

Even though a modern multimedia PC is capable of displaying multimedia content, other factors must be considered by the multimedia developer. Perhaps the most important is the issue of data compression.

The problem is that high-quality digital video requires that millions of bits be transmitted to the monitor every second. Remember, the monitor is attached to a video controller, which assigns 24 bits to each pixel on a full-color monitor. Monitors display a grid of pixels that measures at least 640x480, and video requires at least 15 image frames per second. If you multiply all these numbers together, you get the number of bits it takes to display digital video:

	24	bits per pixel
x	480	pixels vertically
x	640	pixels horizontally
x	15	frames per second
=	110,592,000	bits per second

It does not matter whether the information comes from a CD-ROM and is being displayed on a monitor, or comes through a cable box and is being displayed by the television—the wires connecting the components of the system usually are not capable of transmitting the digital information fast enough. The capacity for data transmission is known as *bandwidth*. Somewhere in a computer system, there is almost always a bottleneck in the bandwidth. When it comes to video, one potential solution is data compression.

Data compression typically uses mathematical analyses of digital source material to strip away unnecessary bits of data prior to sending it across the wire. At the receiving end (for example, inside a modern cable TV converter or direct-broadcast satellite receiver), the missing bits are quickly reinserted to produce a copy that is extremely close to the original in quality and detail.

Among the most common multimedia compression schemes currently being used are **JPEG** (pronounced "jay-peg," for Joint Photographic Experts Group), **MPEG** (pronounced "em-peg," for Motion Picture Experts Group), MPEG-2, and MPEG-3. Each scheme is sponsored by an industry consortium whose goal is to achieve high rates of compression and industry-wide agreement on standards. The push for standards is important because it means that multimedia-equipped cable TV boxes and other hardware will have the requisite decompression facilities built in (usually requiring special integrated circuit chips and software—all of which work behind the scenes). The standards also allow multimedia developers to choose the right compression scheme for the target audience.

Networking Multimedia

An increasing number of companies and organizations that use and develop multimedia

NORTON
Online

For more information on **MPEG**, visit this book's Web site at www.glencoe.com/norton/online

Multimedia LANs must handle large amounts of data in the most efficient manner. The PacketShaper 1000 device is one product that serves this purpose.

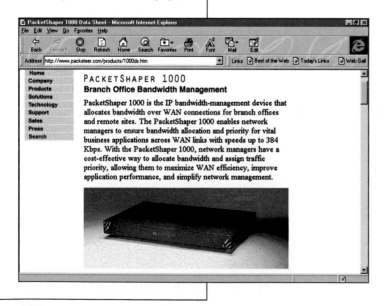

PacketShaper 1000 Data Sheet - Microsoft Internet Explorer

File   Edit   View   Go   Favorites   Help

Address http://www.packeteer.com/products/1000ds.htm

Home
Company
Products
Solutions
Technology
Support
Sales
Press
Search

PACKETSHAPER 1000
Branch Office Bandwidth Management

PacketShaper 1000 is the IP bandwidth-management device that allocates bandwidth over WAN connections for branch offices and remote sites. The PacketShaper 1000 enables network managers to ensure bandwidth allocation and priority for vital business applications across WAN links with speeds up to 384 Kbps. With the PacketShaper 1000, network managers have a cost-effective way to allocate bandwidth and assign traffic priority, allowing them to maximize WAN efficiency, improve application performance, and simplify network management.

applications and files encounter the problems of where to store the gigantic files associated with multimedia applications as well as how to let users access the files. One solution has been to build LANs to distribute and store multimedia files and applications. Some of the types of traffic that a multimedia LAN might carry include transaction-oriented data (such as customer orders), real-time data (such as videoconferencing), and bulk transfers (such as streaming multimedia and large files).

Multimedia LANs provide the same connectivity and resource sharing that normal LANs do, only with higher bandwidth capacity. **Bandwidth capacity** is the amount of traffic that a network can handle. Too much traffic, and the network slows down, and users become impatient. In worst case scenarios, a LAN can be brought to its knees, creating a gridlock effect on the LAN.

To prepare LANs for multimedia content, administrators must identify the types of data traffic that the LAN will carry, as well as give preferential treatment to essential information over nonessential traffic. This last point is important because not all LAN traffic is equally important for every business. One business, for instance, may deem videoconferencing traffic highly important and streaming multimedia rates on a lower scale. Solutions are available that help manage bandwidth usage. These solutions are called **bandwidth-management tools**. Some of these tools include PacketShaper from Packeteer, FloodGate-1 from CheckPoint, and IPath from Structured Internetworks.

NORTON Online

For more information on **bandwidth-management tools**, visit this book's Web site at **www.glencoe.com/norton/online**

Hypermedia: User-Directed Navigation

A major challenge accompanies the large volume of multimedia content that arrives via a CD-ROM or through an online service: finding your way through the text, pictures, and other media available in the presentation. This is where the interactivity component comes into play. The user is responsible for deciding where and when to go to a particular place within the collection of data.

Wending your way through electronic information is commonly called **navigation**. The person who wrote the information is responsible for providing the user with on-screen aids to navigate. In software that mimics the old format of books, the navigation aid might be a simple palette of left- and right-facing arrow icons to navigate backward or forward one page. Because authors of digital content are not bound by the physical constraints of pages, they also can provide buttons that allow you to jump to locations outside the normal, linear sequence.

Figure 10.4 illustrates navigation buttons that resemble the buttons on a tape deck—one of the many commonly used navigation methods.

Figure 10.4
This product displays a popular method of navigation in multimedia programs.

Techview

How to Choose a Multimedia PC

There's no question that multimedia expands the horizons of any product. A dance video becomes a personalized lesson. A dry encyclopedia becomes an audio-visual documentary. A game becomes Saturday afternoon at the movies.

But only if you have the right equipment. To view the eye-catching graphics, full-motion videos, and lively animations that come alive to the accompaniment of symphonic-quality scores, special sound effects, and crystal clear dialog, you need state-of-the-art equipment.

MechWarrior II from Activision. ▶

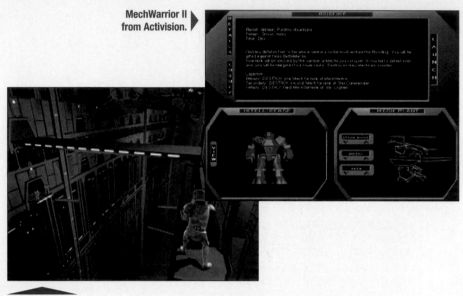

Rebel Assault II from Lucas Arts.

At a minimum, here is what to look for in a multimedia computer:

■ *System:* Pentium PC (or a Pentium Pro or Pentium II, if you can afford it), 200 megahertz or higher, 32 MB RAM or higher. Multimedia applications demand a lot of CPU power and storage space. The more you have, the quicker and smoother your CD-ROMs will perform.

■ *Hard disk:* 2 GB is preferable, larger if you can afford it.

■ *Sound card:* 16-bit with 44.1-KHz stereo sampling frequency. This allows you to achieve genuine CD-quality sound on all kinds of multimedia audio.

■ *Video Card:* Super Video Graphics Array (SVGA). This will put those gorgeous graphics in a full spectrum of 65,000 colors with clear, sharp detail. Also, to play streaming video or 3-D files, look for systems with over 2MB of video RAM installed.

■ *Display:* 17- or 20-inch monitor, SVGA compatible, with local bus graphics adapter. A large monitor will lessen eyestrain and allow you to work with more windows open on your screen.

■ *CD-ROM Drive:* 12X speed or faster is preferable.

■ *Speakers:* Good-quality right- and left-channel speakers or surround-sound speakers.

■ *Headphones:* Yes, especially if you have roommates or family whom you might disturb.

There are several ways to acquire a multimedia system. The easiest is to buy a new complete multimedia PC system, in which all the above components come bundled together. Installation and setup time is minimal, and you will not have to mix and match components. Plus, many multimedia systems come with a wide sampling of software worth hundreds of dollars.

The second approach is an upgrade. Upgrade kits come with varying arrays of components. You must be careful that every component in the upgrade is compatible with your system. And, unless you are an electronics whiz, you will probably need to have the upgrade installed by a computer retailer.

The last approach is to buy components individually and piece together a custom system with the setup you already have. This approach is generally advisable for technical wizards only, or for those with considerable amounts of time for tinkering and technical support phone calls.

Each button along the top row of icons leads to a different electronic book (a label pops into view when the pointer is on each icon). In the text, there are linked words (in small capital letters and colored differently). When you click a word, the program zips you to the page referring to that word. At the bottom right is a palette of navigation buttons that take you forward or backward by one page, or jump back to the previous page you viewed. In other programs, a click on a picture may turn that picture into a video or an audio track that explains the picture.

A new term has evolved to describe the environment that allows users to click on one type of media to navigate to the same or other type of media: that term is **hypermedia**. The word is a more modern version of a concept called hypertext.

In a 1945 *Atlantic Monthly* article, computing science pioneer Vannevar Bush wrote about the concept of associative links between ideas. At the time, crude computing power hindered the development of working models using this concept. It was not until the 1960s that computer scientists were able to experiment with working prototypes of associative links. In 1965, futurist Ted Nelson, writing in his book *Literary Machines,* coined the term "hypertext," defining it as "a body of written or pictorial material interconnected in a complex way that could not be conveniently represented on paper." Nelson's scheme predicted a world of interlinked computers and vast storage available to everyone. A click on a reference to a magazine article, for example, might bring up a display of the article from another computer halfway around the planet.

In some respects, the highlighted links you see in the World Wide Web pages on the Internet hint at hypertext and hypermedia as envisioned by Bush and Nelson. A click on such a link may automatically connect you to a related item on a computer in another country—and it appears on your screen as if it were coming from across the street.

Hypermedia can also exist on a smaller scale. You may have already used hypermedia in the Windows Help system or some of the programs designed for Windows. Figure 10.5 shows a screen from Microsoft Word's Help system.

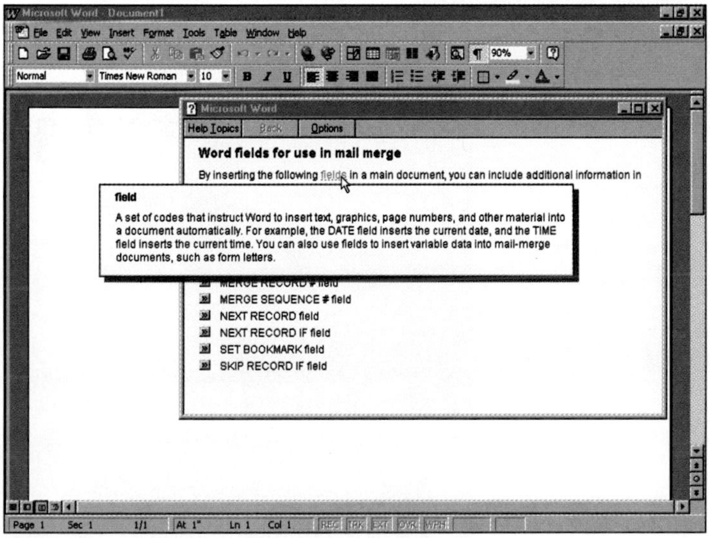

Figure 10.5
The Help system in Microsoft Word contains many hypertext links. Clicking a green, underlined word displays the definition for that word.

The word "fields" is underlined (and also displayed in a different color). Clicking that link displays the popup window, which shows a definition of the term. Clicking a button displays an entirely different screen from the Help system that explains how to use specific mail merge fields. At the top of the Help window is a button labeled "Back," which steps you backward along your trail through the help process; the Help Topics button takes you all the way out to the Help system's table of contents.

Authors of interactive multimedia must be conscious that while hypermedia links often can be helpful, there are times when it is undesirable to let the user wander off to other locations, perhaps never to return. Some content must continue to exist in a linear fashion, at least for part of the time. Steps in a tutorial or a carefully crafted story, for example, must be told in an unalterable sequence for accuracy or the most dramatic impact. The author must decide when it is acceptable for the viewer to take control of the navigation process.

Virtual Reality: Adding the Third Dimension

It could be said that the most effective computer navigation is when you have the feeling of traveling through a three-dimensional world. Imagine, for example, that every chapter of a reference book were a room off a corridor. Then, if you use the computer to move the view down the corridor and turn into a particular room, you would have a unique spatial sense of that chapter of information. The re-creation on a computer display of what appears to be physical space is called *virtual reality*. The images and sounds exist only in the RAM of the computer, but a user can enter this world using special devices such as head-mounted displays, stereoscopic glasses, data gloves, and sensor seats. These devices with motion sensors are connected to the computer. When a user walks or moves a hand, the sensors detect the motion and send data to the virtual reality program. The program processes the user's movements and projects the action into the virtual space.

These pictures are two different views of the same room. The computer assembles them (and several more) so that you can move through the virtual room and see how it would look from different perspectives.

Until recently, it was possible to experience virtual reality only with the help of mini- and mainframe computers. Increased personal computing power and clever software techniques now make it possible to see the effects at home. Presenting virtual reality is still difficult because it is the ultimate in user-directed navigation. With some of the wearable devices, a slight tilt of the head requires the computer to interpret the angle of movement, and recalculate and redraw a complex graphical scene based on the new point of view. To accomplish this in realistic animation at an acceptable speed is a significant engineering challenge.

At the moment, virtual reality is used predominantly for entertainment software. However, the time could come when you will travel by virtual reality links through space to jump from one piece of information to another.

NORTON
Online
For more information on VRML software, visit this book's Web site at www.glencoe.com/norton/online

► Each of these images was created with the help of trueSpace, a VRML authoring and 3-D graphics program from Caligari Corporation, which also makes Pioneer.

Many of the virtual reality environments in use today create artificial, cartoon-like virtual worlds. Another technique, called QuickTime VR (developed by Apple Computer) takes the concept of virtual reality and applies it to the real world. To prepare a QuickTime VR scene, a digital camera on a special tripod takes a number of photographs in all directions from the same point. The QuickTime VR software then blends the individual photos into a continuous, 360-degree scene. As the viewer maneuvers the mouse around the window, the point of view changes as if the person were standing in that spot and turning around or looking upward or downward—not in jerky shifts but in smooth movements. With another mouse action, the view magnifies, as if the person were walking toward the center point of the screen. In this case, the scene is virtual, but the photos are of real space.

Virtual reality is also invading the online world. Virtual Reality Modeling Language (VRML) is an authoring language used to create three-dimensional environments on the World Wide Web. This tool allows the user to navigate through 3-D worlds, create or edit 3-D objects, and link them to other Web objects. Pioneer, made by Caligari Corporation, is one of the most widely used VRML authoring programs.

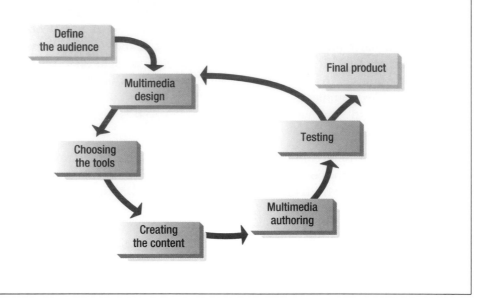

Figure 10.6
The multimedia development
process involves a number of
distinct steps before achieving
a final product.

CREATING MULTIMEDIA

Because of the different types of media and the flexibility in navigation, creating effective multimedia is difficult. The development team usually involves people with a variety of skills, and the development process is complex. Figure 10.6 shows an overview of the multimedia development process.

Defining the Audience

Because a multimedia presentation or program can offer so much in the way of content, it is valuable to understand precisely who the audience is. Imagine you are about to compose a multimedia program. Then imagine yourself as someone using or viewing that program. Then ask yourself the following questions:

- How much should users know about the subject before the presentation or program begins?

- What do users expect to gain from their experience with the program? Is the goal to learn something? To be entertained?

- How much time will users want to spend going through this content?

- Will users get more out of this content if it is predominantly text, graphics, sound, animation, or video?

- What kind of interaction will users want with the program? Is their feedback via a touch screen, a keyboard and mouse, or a game controller?

- Will the content or presentation be engaging enough to make users want to linger and to come back again?

Having answers to these questions will help the multimedia author focus on the result.

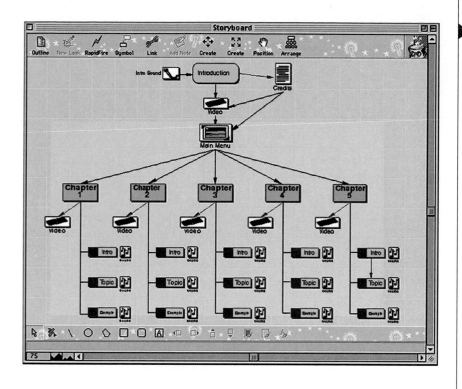

Some programs, such as Scene Slate Storyboard, can guide the user through the process of creating a storyboard for a multimedia product.

Design and Storyboarding

Planning the overall design is often the longest part of the development process. Much of this work goes on without any computers.

A common way to start is by composing an outline of the sequences and blocks of information that will appear on the screen. This is the time to determine how much information—text, graphics, clickable objects—will be presented on each screen. It is also the time to establish a navigation methodology for the user. Will there be a navigation bar with arrows leading from scene to scene, or will there be text or graphic objects that the user will click on to jump around the entire program?

When a program includes a great deal of animation or many different scenes, the best design aid is the storyboard. Used by film directors for productions ranging from 30-second television commercials to feature-length motion pictures, the **storyboard** consists of sketches of the scenes and action. Mapping out a storyboard helps the author to recognize gaps in logic. Some multimedia authoring programs provide facilities for drawing and organizing the frames of a storyboard.

Choosing the Tools

Because multimedia includes different kinds of content, creating it involves many types of software. Creating text often requires a word processor; working with digital images requires graphics software; using video requires a video-capture program and editing software; sound often requires its own editing software. All this software is used to generate the content. When the content is ready, it needs to be assembled in a process called **multimedia authoring**. This process requires still another type of software, which can understand all the different types of media, combine them, control the sequences in which they appear, and create navigational tools and an interface for the user.

It would be a mistake to select the tools before designing a multimedia extravaganza. It is better to imagine the ideal presentation in the design stage, and then locate the tools that let you come as close to that ideal as possible.

The variety of tools used for multimedia depends largely on the variety of media to be included. For a simple text-and-graphics slide show presentation, a presentation software program should suffice. You could enliven the offering by adding existing graphics from the hundreds of commercially available CD-ROM collections of clip art, clip sound, and clip video. These clip collections store small files in the proper file formats for use in a wide range of multimedia programs.

Adding animation, sound, or video that you need to create from scratch expands the number of tools you need. Although most multimedia PCs come equipped with basic hardware and software for sound recording, you may want to use a more sophisticated sound editing program, which allows you to splice together segments or add sound effects to the sounds you record. You can do the same kind of electronic editing for video by transferring the video from the camcorder to the computer via a video digitizer. This way, you can create exciting, professional video presentations.

Other, even more specialized tools allow you to perform such multimedia tricks as morphing (developing a video sequence that appears to transform one scene into another via smooth stretching and contorting) and creating fractal art for screen backgrounds. Note that the editing of time-based media generally requires significant amounts of hard disk storage and computer RAM.

Macromedia Director is one of the most popular programs for combining all the elements of a multimedia presentation. In Director, the multimedia author assembles each element—text, graphics, sound, and video—into separate "tracks." The program helps the author to synchronize all the elements, so that, for example, a crash sound effect is heard precisely when two animated objects collide. Macromedia Director is a powerful program for creating sophisticated presentations. These presentations are versatile enough to be distributed through various media. The file that Director generates is the one that contains the entire multimedia presentation, ready for distribution on disk or CD-ROM, or to be played over an interactive television linkup or through the Internet.

Another line of authoring products that is emerging is for DVD (Digital Versatile Disc) devices, including DVD-ROM drives and DVD-Video players. These devices play back video and audio at very high resolutions. For DVD-ROM titles, available authoring software includes premastering software, which is used to test a disc image of a title on a PC before outputting it to a premaster tape or DVD-R recorder. One premastering package is the CDMotion. For DVD-Video titles, however, many authoring system tools are needed, including audio and MPEG-2 video encoding system with DVD-Video emulation capabilities and expensive DVD authoring tools.

NORTON Online

For more information on **CDMotion**, visit this book's Web site at www.glencoe.com/norton/online

Multimedia Authoring

After all the content has been created (and converted to a digital form, if necessary), it is time to put it all together. For a complex product created with the use of a sophisticated tool such as Director, the multimedia authoring generally is performed by a skilled computer user, often referred to as the programmer.

Authoring proceeds more quickly and is more successful if the programmers have access to all the content at the outset, and there is a clear and detailed storyboard telling the programmers how the content fits together. If programmers begin a project without having the final content, they may have to make expensive and time-consuming changes. This could also affect the quality of the final product in a negative way.

Testing

If the multimedia program is to be used by other people—perhaps in a freestanding information kiosk in the lobby of a building or at various stations around a shopping mall—it is vital that the program be tested by the kinds of people who will be using it. By going through this testing, the programmer can locate any flaws ahead of time and repair them before unleashing the finished product on the world.

Just as with the testing of any software product, it is helpful for the program's author(s) to watch users navigate through the product. The kinds of problems to watch for are any locations in the product where the user does not know what to do next. Is the user struggling to read a font size too small for descriptive text? Are there sufficient controls to stop a video or audio clip if the user wants to move on without going through the entire clip? Is the user following navigational paths that lead quickly to the desired information, or do there appear to be times when the user seems lost in the multimedia maze?

Before a program is ready for release, it may need to go through several testing-and-revision cycles so that everyone is comfortable with the finished product. As part of the planning process, sufficient time must be built into the schedule for the testing cycles. Most software developers and programmers employ firms to test the software, or they have their own in-house testing departments.

A program's author and the final user often have different points of view. What the author believes to be simple to use—having designed the interface and used it for weeks or months during development—might be totally bewildering to someone seeing the interface for the first time. The author must learn to regard any problems the user detects with the program as constructive criticism. Testing is so valuable because it is all too easy to lose sight of the audience after the heavy-duty authoring starts.

Computers
In Your Career

Careers in multimedia are as varied and as numerous as the medium itself. The sheer variety and range of what can be done in multimedia is astonishing. This can be both enlivening and overwhelming to the multimedia professional.

How is the enormity of work involved in a multimedia product accomplished? Multimedia work is usually done by teams.

At the helm of a multimedia project is the creative director, who is responsible for developing and refining the overall design process from start to finish. The creative director is also responsible for integrating that design process into the developmental process of the company.

The team members of a multimedia project usually include some or all of the following. In fact, some members of the team may possess a combination of these skills:

Art Director Directs the creation of all art for the project. This involves a variety of original media, which winds up in digital form for manipulation on the modern artist's "canvas," the computer.

Technical Lead Ensures that the technological process of a project works and that it accommodates all project components and media.

Documentation Specialist Creates documentation for end-users as well as administrators of a product.

Interface Designer Directs the development of the user interface for a product, which includes not only what users see but also what they hear and touch.

Instructional Designer Designs the pedagogy, or instructional system for how material is taught, if the product is educational.

Visual Designer Creates the various art forms, usually within a specialized area such as graphic design, calligraphy, illustration, photography, image manipulation, or typesetting.

Game Designer Designs interactive games. A game may be an independent project, or part of a larger whole.

Interactive Scriptwriter A writer who weaves the project content among various media and forms of interactivity. A multimedia scriptwriter is part writer and part interactive designer.

Animator Creates the animation you see on screen. Animators used to work from models, but many use 2-D and/or 3-D computer programs to create their animation sequences.

Sound Producer Part manager, part creative artist, and part programmer. A sound producer designs and produces all sounds within a product, including musical scores, vocals, voice-overs, and sound effects, and makes sure that each sound interacts correctly with all the other media.

Videographer Creates the video footage that interfaces with the interactive technology of the product. Video is often the most complex, time consuming, and resource-demanding media to create.

Programmer/Software Designer Designs and creates the underlying software that runs a multimedia program and carries out the user's commands.

WHAT TO EXPECT IN THE FUTURE

New media will not be new forever. Interest in multimedia software will certainly increase in the near future, but it may no longer appear as a separate software category. Rather, the elements of multimedia—sound, video, interaction—will be integrated into all kinds of documents and programs. What is new media today will be the standard media in the not too distant future.

Additional improvements in the type and breadth of information available from distance learning institutions will help shape the future of education. Higher education institutions are so committed to providing online education that a new Internet infrastructure—called Internet2—is being developed by more than 100 U.S. universities. Internet2 (or I2) will provide fast connections for educators and researchers to share and transmit information around the world. Internet2 will be built around a multimedia broadband (high-capacity bandwidth) network to provide an architecture for the deployment of digital libraries, tele-immersion (similar to virtual reality environments), and virtual laboratories.

Where the most rapid advances will occur, however, will be in the delivery of content containing multiple media and interaction. Sophisticated cable TV networks will beckon some households to join their interactive services. A convergence of the Internet, CD-ROM, DVD-ROM, and television will become more prevalent as users will want to spend less time waiting for large graphics, videos, and audio files to download over the Internet. The importance of the CD-ROM could recede as more people are wired to the Internet. Multimedia reference material will become readily available with up-to-the-minute changes; computers will be able to categorize video, audio, and graphics so that you can search for time-based media as you now search for text; game opponents will be real humans elsewhere on the Internet; you will use the Internet to conduct international long-distance telephone calls via computerized videoconferencing; and you will be able to hear the most recent hour's BBC World Service news program whenever you want.

Visual Summary & Exercises

VISUAL SUMMARY

The Power of Interactivity

- Interactivity allows viewers to participate in the action on the screen.
- The popularity of video games demonstrates a widespread interest in interacting with content.
- Broadcast and cable TV companies are still determining how best to produce and deliver interactive material.
- The CD-ROM for personal computers and video games is the most popular interactive content delivery medium today.
- Online delivery via commercial services and the Internet is growing rapidly.
- Interactivity includes interaction between people as well as between people and computers.
- Multimedia is the combination of text, still graphics, animation, video, sound, and interactivity.
- In education, interactive multimedia can enrich the learning experience by engaging students in the content, connecting students in different locations, and simulating real-world actions and their consequences.
- Businesses use interactive multimedia for training, videoconferencing, and reaching customers with catalogs and customer support.
- Home reference and how-to books come alive in interactive multimedia form.
- Entertainment is the widest application of multimedia in the home today, but interactive television will allow the viewing of any content when you want it.

The New Media

- Existing media companies are looking to new media for new markets.
- Digital convergence implies that different kinds of data (voice, sound, video) can be delivered via a single medium, such as CD-ROM or the Internet.
- Adding animation, video, and sound to what is normally print media makes it easier for many users to understand concepts.

- Technical wizardry is not enough to sell a multimedia program: there must be content that the audience considers valuable.

- Data compression allows more information—higher-quality content—to reach users via existing delivery vehicles such as CD-ROM, telephone wires, and TV cable.

- There is an industry standard for what constitutes a multimedia-capable personal computer: the Multimedia PC (MPC) standard, which is currently in its third revision.

- Designing a multimedia product requires designing a navigation system for users to find their way around the content.

- A hypermedia link (derived from hypertext) connects one piece of media on the screen with perhaps a different kind of media, which may even be located on another computer along the network.

- Highlighted links of World Wide Web pages exemplify hypermedia.

- Software tools for creating presentations allow users to generate colorful and animated presentations by selecting ready-made art, video, and sounds from clip collections.

- Personal computers are becoming powerful enough to create virtual reality—scenes and sounds that make you believe you are in a different place.

Creating Multimedia

- Planning is the most time-consuming part of creating a multimedia program or presentation.

- Understanding your audience is of paramount importance.

- Before turning to the computer, sketch out an outline or storyboards of key scenes planned for the program.

- Select authoring tools that best meet the needs of your planned program.

- If possible, divide the content authoring among those with the most experience in writing, photography, video production, sound recording, and graphic design.

- Test the program on small audiences before releasing it to the world.

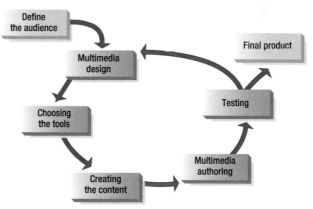

Visual Summary & Exercises

KEY TERMS

After completing this chapter, you should be able to define the following terms:

bandwidth capacity, 383
bandwidth management, 383
computer-based training (CBT), 375
digital convergence, 379
distance learning (DL), 374
hypermedia, 385
interactive, 368
interactive media, 368

interactive television, 377
JPEG, 382
MPEG, 382
media, 367
medium, 367
Microsoft Knowledge Base (KB), 376
multimedia, 367
multimedia authoring, 389

Multimedia Personal Computer (MPC)
    standard, 381
navigation, 383
new media, 367
storyboard, 389
virtual university, 374

KEY TERM QUIZ

Fill in the missing word with one of the terms listed in Key Terms.

1. Computers make it possible to create _____ in which people can respond to—and even control—what they see and hear.

2. The _____ standard helps computer makers and users ensure that current-model PCs can play the newest types of multimedia content.

3. Used by film producers for productions, a(n) _____ consists of sketches of the scenes and action.

4. _____ and _____ are popular file formats among multimedia developers.

5. Wending your way through electronic information is commonly called _____.

6. _____ is a new term that has evolved to describe the environment that allows users to click on one type of media to navigate to the same or other type of media.

7. _____ technology enables users to learn directly from the computer, without necessarily attending classes.

8. Text, graphics, animation, video, and sound can be combined to produce an engaging _____ presentation for any audience.

9. _____ describes the process by which a variety of content converges into one digital stream.

10. It is not uncommon to hear multimedia referred to as _____.

Visual Summary & Exercises

REVIEW QUESTIONS

1. What does the term "interactive media" mean?

2. What benefits can interactive multimedia bring to education?

3. List and describe at least three ways in which multimedia and communications have made significant contributions to businesses.

4. In what area is the biggest application of multimedia software?

5. Describe briefly what is meant by digital convergence.

6. List the basic steps involved in developing multimedia.

7. What are the key hardware components in a multimedia PC system?

8. Define data compression. Why is it such an important consideration for multimedia software developers?

9. Explain briefly how hypermedia allows a user to navigate through digital content without necessarily following a linear sequence.

10. Explain why a multimedia developer should not select software tools before beginning the design process.

DISCUSSION QUESTIONS

1. Why do you think animation, video, and audio are all described as "time-based media?" What problems might a multimedia developer face when integrating time-based media into a product?

2. Think about the issues that must be addressed by television and cable networks as interactivity becomes part of television broadcasting. What types of interactive programming can you envision? Will television programs and movies as we know them still exist in 30 years? To what extent should the government regulate the types of interactive programs that can be broadcast?

3. You have probably been exposed to some examples of multimedia educational software. Describe the examples you have seen. What were the strengths and weaknesses of this software? What suggestions can you make for improving educational multimedia? Can you suggest any specific products that would benefit students?

4. This chapter states that virtual reality is predominantly used for entertainment applications. Do you think virtual reality has practical applications in other areas, such as engineering, science, business, and education? Provide at least two examples in which you envision virtual reality technology being applied to other, nonentertainment sectors of the economy.

*inte*NET Workshop

The following exercises assume that you have access to the Internet and a browser. If you need help with any of the exercises, visit the book's Web site at **www.glencoe.com/norton/online**. This book's Web site also lists the URLs you need to complete many of these exercises.

1. The Web has taken the idea of interactivity to a new level. Not only can users interact with one another via chat rooms and news groups, but they also can participate in live national discussions online, as part of radio and television programs. Visit the chat/opinion pages of broadcast companies such as CNN, MSNBC, and National Public Radio. Do these broadcasters offer links that enable you to participate via e-mail in live discussions? Examine the manner in which the online discussions are promoted and operated, and monitor at least one online discussion, if possible. What sorts of comments do you find in such discussions? Do you feel they provide much value to the debate of important issues?

2. Currently, the most interactive products available are CD-ROM-based games and edutainment products. To experience demos of some popular interactive programs, search and visit the sites of game manufacturers and developers. How does the interactivity of games compare to the interactivity of the Web?

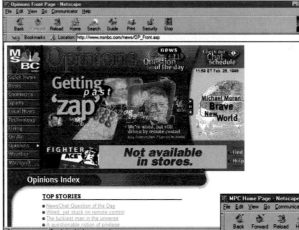

3. Is your computer multimedia-ready? To find out, visit the Software Publishers Association MPC Working Group Web page and review the current version of the MPC standard (MPC3). Does you system include all the components recommended by the standard? Make a list of these components; then visit the Web sites of some popular PC manufacturers. To purchase a new computer with all the components required to meet the latest MPC standard, how much would you have to spend? Do you think all these components are necessary to meet your personal computing needs? Which components could you live without?

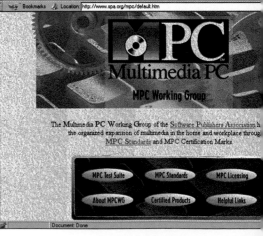

4. An understanding of hypermedia (hypertext, hyperlinks) is essential to a mastery of the Web and other interactive products, such as online help systems, computer-based training, and others. This is especially true if you want to create Web pages. For an interesting primer on hypermedia, hypertext, and the Web, visit the following pages:

- Entering the World Wide Web: A Guide to Cyberspace
- Hypertext and HTML
- Hypertext Terms
- Review on Hypermedia Issues and Applications

5. Many multimedia design shops list job openings on the Web. Use the Web to locate three different design shops that offer employment. (Hint: Using your favorite search engine, search on the terms "multimedia design." The results should include several Web sites of commercial design firms that design multimedia products, such as CD-ROMs, Web pages, and so on.) Compare these listings. How are they different? How are they the same? Are there any skills common to all of them?

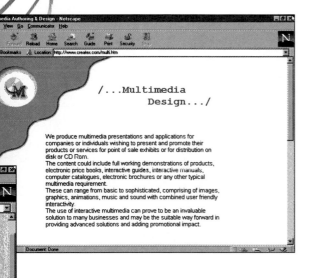

6. For information on a variety of multimedia authoring tools, visit the following sites:

- Macromedia (maker of Director and Authorware)
- TenCORE (maker of high-level authoring and language tools)
- InverVista Software (maker of WorldChart and WorldView)

Which tools appear to set the standard for multimedia authoring? Which tools do you think are more important to multimedia authors and designers? If you were considering a career in multimedia design, which tools would you want to master first or most completely?

3

OUR
TECHNOLOGICAL
SOCIETY

Development of Information Systems

CONTENTS

OBJECTIVES

When you complete this chapter, you will be able to do the following:

■ List at least six jobs that exist in an information systems department.

■ Name the five different types of information systems.

■ List the five different phases in the systems development life cycle (SDLC).

■ Define the term "computer program" and name five categories of computer programs.

■ List the two types of programming.

■ List the three major phases of program control flow.

■ Name at least four major programming languages.

■ List four tools that make programming more productive.

Ultimately, the information system is computer technology's reason for being. Because there are so many types of information—and uses for it—many kinds of information systems have been developed. For example, if you think of a bank's database of customers and accounts as an information system, you are correct. But would you think of a factory's computer-controlled machining system, or the system NASA uses to launch and control the space shuttle? If so, you would be correct again.

Information systems do much more than store and retrieve data. They help people use information in countless ways, whether that involves sorting lists, printing reports, matching a single fingerprint against a national database of millions of prints, or tracking the locations of planes in the night sky.

Information systems also help us derive greater value from data by applying it to different purposes. For example, an engineer

can use a CAD system to design a mechanical part, such as an engine block. The data from the CAD system can be used to perform cost analyses, stress tests, and other tests. It can also be used to control a computerized machining system, which cuts the finished product from a block of raw material.

A great deal of planning goes into the creation of any information system; a complex system can take months to develop and draw on the talents of dozens of skilled professionals.

In this chapter, you will learn first about the people who create and maintain these systems. You will read about the different types of systems that businesses implement and the systems development life cycle. Because software is such a critical part of any information system, you will learn what a computer program is and how it works. You also will learn how computer programs are created and the major programming languages used to create programs.

WHAT IS AN INFORMATION SYSTEM?

Information systems are not new. Long before computer automation, companies were collecting, storing, and updating information in the normal course of doing business. In the past as today, information systems consisted of the procedures and rules established to deliver information to the people in an organization. Different people require different information to perform their jobs, and the rules of the system govern what information should be distributed to whom, when, and in what format.

Working with manual information systems is time-intensive, even for small companies. Imagine, for example, that you have agreed to maintain a list of 200 clients for a flower shop. You start by buying 200 index cards and then, on each card, writing the name, address, and favorite flower choice of a client. When you finish, you sort the cards alphabetically by the clients' last names.

However arduous, this initial step of creating the card database is not nearly as difficult as maintaining it. To provide timely and accurate information to the store owner, the list must be continually updated. For example, clients move away; others change names or addresses. New clients are added, or a client's preference changes from yellow roses to dahlias. Soon, many of your cards will be dog eared and covered with crossed-out information. You need to identify these cards, create new ones, and then sort them again. To figure out the quantities of a specific flower to order, you thumb through all 200 index cards, every day, counting how many clients prefer that flower.

Now consider the following scenario. The store manager agrees to invest in a computer system for the store. You enter relevant information for each customer, such as name, address, and each floral arrangement purchased. When customers call for flowers, you can tell them instantly what they sent to their parents last year for their anniversary, or what kind of flowers their aunt in Colorado likes. Every week you run a report to determine which flowers sold well that week. Eventually you have enough information to predict how many flowers of each type to buy each month. Due to the improved service, the customer base increases until the store expands into three locations. The employees of the other stores enter data regarding the flowers sold, so you can continue to improve your trends analysis on flower preferences at different times of the year. In addition, you set up a system so that you can check on the availability of flowers at the different stores by checking the database.

Automated information systems have streamlined the manufacturing process.

The Information Systems Department

In large companies, the automation of business tasks encouraged the development of separate departments to service the emerging computer information systems. Initially, these departments—and the people who worked in them—were isolated from the rest of a company's operations. These departments were creating systems that collected data from the operations level and turned it into information for managers. Then, the rise of the PC and its nearly universal acceptance changed these departments along with the systems they serviced. As people other than managers became information workers, the information systems departments started serving entire organizations and became integral parts of the business operation.

The size of a company's information systems department typically correlates with the size of the company it supports. In very large companies, these departments may employ hundreds or even thousands of people. The names of these departments vary as well as their size. The organization chart of one company may include an Information Systems (IS) department, for example, while another company may use the name Management Information Systems (MIS), Information Technology (IT), or even Data Processing (DP). In this chapter, the department responsible for creating and maintaining information systems in a company is called the **IS department**.

Systems analysts spend much of their time interviewing and listening to users.

Building and supporting computer systems is complex work, requiring a wide range of skilled professionals:

- **Computer scientists** study the theory of computers by undertaking research, developing new computer designs, and attempting to achieve the next technological leap in the industry. They apply their high level of theoretical expertise to complex problems. Within academia, computer scientists undertake projects such as designing new hardware or developing new languages. They also work on multidisciplinary projects such as artificial intelligence. In private industry, computer scientists apply theory, develop specialized languages, and design knowledge-based systems (such as the expert systems you will read about later in this chapter).

- **Systems analysts** are responsible for thinking of possible solutions when an information system needs to be updated, modified, or completely revamped. After users or managers identify a need, systems analysts discuss the business, scientific, or engineering problem with them. Systems analysts spend a significant amount of time at the beginning of projects defining the goals and issues of a new information system. With the goals and issues defined, the systems analysts, sometimes working with computer scientists, start designing solutions. They must provide enough detail in the design so that other members of the project team can perform the work. For example, systems analysts typically are responsible for specifying the exact files and records that must be accessed by the system and the format of the information produced by the system.

Analysts, programmers, and engineers train and provide information to technical writers on the new system. The writers help to distill this information into manuals and instructional materials for all the other users.

- **Programmers** create computer programs, either as commercial products or as part of a company's information system. In some information system projects, programmers are called on to modify or expand existing programs. In these situations, the programmers must analyze the existing code before making any modifications. In other projects, programmers create an entire system from scratch. Due to the complexity of information systems, this work is usually performed in teams, with each team responsible for specific components.

- **User assistance architects** determine the organization of documentation and its structure, designing the instructional materials before the technical writers write the content. In the past, documentation was distributed on paper. Now, much of the information on systems is provided

User assistance architects
design and develop Help
systems for users.

Router Statistics

Statistics last reset at: 3/16/97   2:48 PM
Graphs show data for the past: 5 minutes ▼

Packets Routed: 10,787,408
Network Activity:

Throughput
(packets/sec)
10 ▼

10
Minutes: 5 4 3 2 1 0

Network Reliability: 100.0%
Network Errors:

Errors
(percent)

10
Minutes: 5 4 3 2 1 0

These router statistics show
network managers how much
data has been routed around
the network.

---

online, in Help systems or tutorials. The challenge in developing a Help system is to ensure that users can find the information they seek with minimal effort. Meeting that challenge requires an understanding of how users look for information online. User assistance architects also decide how material should be presented: in class as part of a short presentation, or in the online help.

■ **Technical writers** explain in writing how an information system works. Typically, technical writers produce a set of documentation for a system, which can be available in printed form or as part of an online Help system. This documentation includes materials intended for the different audiences who use or support the information system, including end users, network managers, and system administrators.

■ Hardware or software **purchasing agents** choose suppliers for system components and negotiate the necessary terms. Companies rely on agents because information systems are created from a variety of components, including hardware and software. Because some percentage of these components will be bought rather than built from scratch, IS departments need purchasing agents to bring all the pieces together within a certain time-frame.

■ **System managers** or **network managers** are responsible for keeping an information system up and running. Individual systems are linked in networks. Companies maintain their own internal networks, with links to outside networks such as the Internet. Today, practically every business and organization, from the Fortune 500 to very small companies, relies heavily on LANs. Although most PC-based LANs do not require full-time attention, they do need occasional maintenance, and any problems that arise must be solved by someone who knows what to do when things go wrong. In organizations with multiple LANs, wide area networks (WANs), bridges, and gateways to other systems, the system or network manager typically has a staff of full-time technicians, analysts, and programmers. Some of the key concerns of network managers include controlling unauthorized access, protecting the integrity of data on the network, and recovering data after computer disasters.

- **Trainers** to prepare users to accept the new information system even before it is put in place. Users should be comfortable with a system before they start using it to do their work. Through classes, trainers give users the opportunity to explore the new system, ask questions, and try out common tasks. IS personnel also provide day-to-day ongoing support to a system's users. Users may forget a procedure they learned in a training class or encounter a problem they do not know how to solve.

- **Hardware maintenance technicians** are needed to maintain the hardware components of an information system. Surprisingly, one of the most common problems for which technicians are called is a paper jam in a printer. Other problems, however, can be far more serious. Often, technicians are required for upgrading PCs with new peripherals, diagnosing problems with PCs and servers, and maintaining the network.

Note that IS departments may not employ individuals in all these different roles. Large companies often hire other companies or individuals to provide specialized skills, such as the development of a Help system. This approach to getting work done, in which freelance workers or outside companies are hired as contractors to do specific jobs, is called **outsourcing**. In addition, a single IS employee may provide more than one skill set, especially in a small company. A technical writer, for example, may be able to develop the Help system for a program, and a systems analyst may undertake a programming role in a project.

TYPES OF INFORMATION SYSTEMS

As more and more business functions have been automated, information systems have become increasingly specialized. One of a company's systems, for example, may be designed to help users gather and store the company's sales orders. Another

Summary reports that give a bird's-eye view of the company are generally produced for executives. This sales analysis, for example, compares sales and back orders for two months.

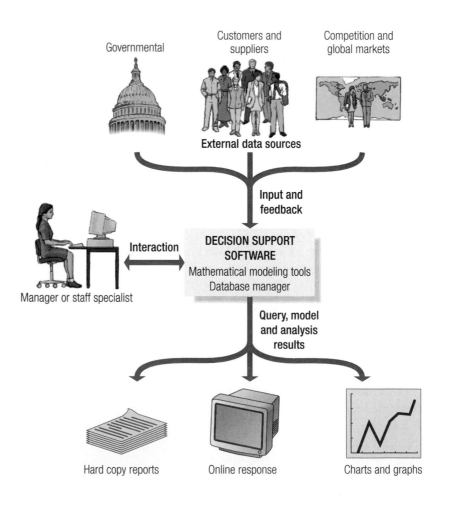

Milltown Manufacturing, Inc.
Sales Analysis
As Of 11/30/96

Month	Sales	Backorders	Shipments
Dec-96	$ 87,542	$ 13,992	$ 73,550
Jan-97	$ 66,452	$ 17,491	$ 48,961
	$153,994	$ 31,483	$ 122,511

Sales Analysis

system may be needed to send mail between company personnel. These individual systems are considered components or subsystems of a company's overall information system. Types of specialized information systems include:

- *Office automation systems.* Routine office tasks, such as sending letters or tracking schedules, are now automated by computer systems. Information workers use a range of applications, including word processors, spreadsheets, and communications programs, to help them with these tasks. To a large extent, office automation systems can be built from **off-the-shelf applications**, like those found in any computer store, rather than from customized applications.

Figure 11.1
Decision support systems.

Governmental

Customers and suppliers

Competition and global markets

External data sources

Input and feedback

Interaction

Manager or staff specialist

DECISION SUPPORT SOFTWARE
Mathematical modeling tools
Database manager

Query, model and analysis results

Hard copy reports

Online response

Charts and graphs

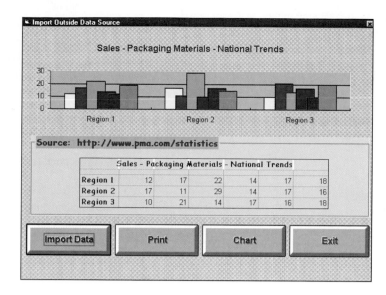

Figure 11.2
A decision support system using data imported from the Internet.

NORTON
Online

For more information on **expert systems**, visit this book's Web site at www.glencoe.com/norton/online

■ *Transaction processing systems.* **Transactions** are events, such as taking an order or paying an invoice. A business transaction typically begins with the collection of information, such as a client's name and address. The company stores this information and then performs the action required by the event. Often this action can be broken down into a series of steps. After an order has been taken, for example, the activity required is to fulfill the order. To do so, the order must be passed to the appropriate department, the items must be taken from inventory, missing items must be back-ordered, and then the materials must be shipped to the client. Processing business transactions means filing, retrieving, and tracking data about events.

Figure 11.3
A decision support system for analyzing market research.

■ *Decision support systems.* As shown in Figure 11.1, **decision support systems** often give managers direct access to data in the company's transaction processing system. In addition, these systems can include or access other types of general data (see Figure 11.2), such as stock market reports or geological data. Many decision support systems are spreadsheet applications that have been customized for specific businesses. Two examples of decision support systems built using spreadsheets are shown in Figures 11.3 and 11.4. Marketing managers, for example, use spreadsheets to analyze market research data, to size up the competition, and to plan effective strategies for penetrating their markets. Engineers and researchers use spreadsheets to perform complex calculations.

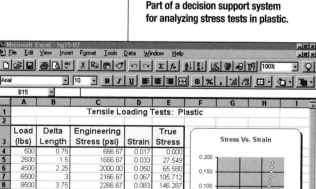

Figure 11.4
Part of a decision support system for analyzing stress tests in plastic.

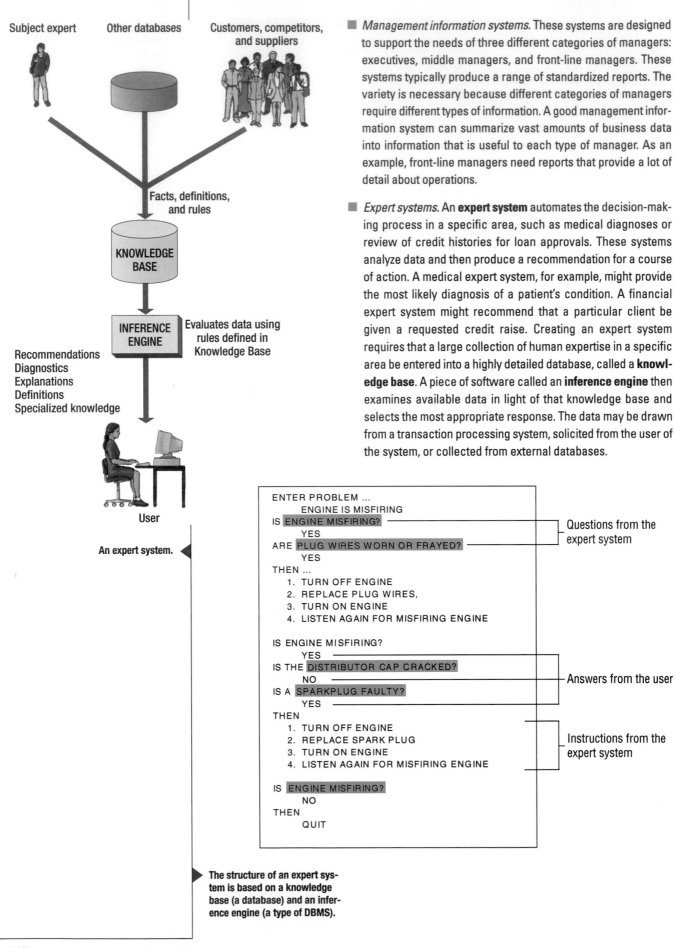

■ *Management information systems.* These systems are designed to support the needs of three different categories of managers: executives, middle managers, and front-line managers. These systems typically produce a range of standardized reports. The variety is necessary because different categories of managers require different types of information. A good management information system can summarize vast amounts of business data into information that is useful to each type of manager. As an example, front-line managers need reports that provide a lot of detail about operations.

■ *Expert systems.* An **expert system** automates the decision-making process in a specific area, such as medical diagnoses or review of credit histories for loan approvals. These systems analyze data and then produce a recommendation for a course of action. A medical expert system, for example, might provide the most likely diagnosis of a patient's condition. A financial expert system might recommend that a particular client be given a requested credit raise. Creating an expert system requires that a large collection of human expertise in a specific area be entered into a highly detailed database, called a **knowledge base**. A piece of software called an **inference engine** then examines available data in light of that knowledge base and selects the most appropriate response. The data may be drawn from a transaction processing system, solicited from the user of the system, or collected from external databases.

Subject expert   Other databases   Customers, competitors, and suppliers

Facts, definitions, and rules

KNOWLEDGE BASE

INFERENCE ENGINE — Evaluates data using rules defined in Knowledge Base

Recommendations
Diagnostics
Explanations
Definitions
Specialized knowledge

User

An expert system.

```
ENTER PROBLEM ...
        ENGINE IS MISFIRING
IS ENGINE MISFIRING? ─────────────────── Questions from the
        YES                                expert system
ARE PLUG WIRES WORN OR FRAYED? ────────┘
        YES
THEN ...
    1. TURN OFF ENGINE
    2. REPLACE PLUG WIRES,
    3. TURN ON ENGINE
    4. LISTEN AGAIN FOR MISFIRING ENGINE

IS ENGINE MISFIRING?
        YES ───────────
IS THE DISTRIBUTOR CAP CRACKED?
        NO ──────────────────── Answers from the user
IS A SPARKPLUG FAULTY?
        YES ───────────
THEN
    1. TURN OFF ENGINE
    2. REPLACE SPARK PLUG          Instructions from the
    3. TURN ON ENGINE              expert system
    4. LISTEN AGAIN FOR MISFIRING ENGINE

IS ENGINE MISFIRING?
        NO
THEN
        QUIT
```

The structure of an expert system is based on a knowledge base (a database) and an inference engine (a type of DBMS).

Techview

Intranets and Extranets: Private Webs

Currently, the terms "intranet" and "extranet" are two of the most popular buzzwords in the world of electronic global communications and information systems.

Intranet refers to a private, secure network, usually within a company or organization, that contains proprietary company data and restricts access to designated persons only.

On an intranet, users can do the same tasks they can on the Web—send e-mail, post documents, update material, and chat with other users. Intranets also permit workgroup collaboration on documents and graphics, videoconferencing, and continuous updating of company databases. The big difference is that an intranet is faster and more secure than the vast Internet.

Extranets enable remote users to access a company's internal network (or intranet) over the Internet. These remote users may be employees, suppliers, partners, or customers. By setting up an extranet, a company can, for instance, enable customers to access inventory data stored on an internal server within a firewall while also maintaining security of sensitive information.

Both intranets and extranets use the same tools and techniques, protocols and products, drawing heavily on the standard computer protocol of the Internet (TCP/IP—Transmission Control Protocol/Internet Protocol). The same HTML (Hypertext Markup Language) programming methods used on Internet home pages are used to create many of the interfaces to intranets and extranets.

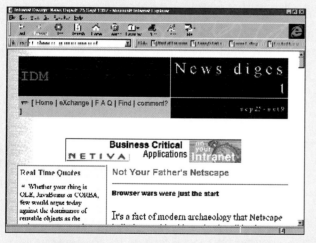

This is an example of an intranet. Employees can access various documents and services from the intranet.

Often a company intranet is a main means of intra office communication. Updates to business policies and procedures can be posted, as can job openings, information on health insurance and other benefits, profiles of various employees, the company's organizational structure, as well as in-house training for employees.

Extranets differ from intranets in the way users access them. With an extranet, a user is off-site—in a remote location—and must access the Internet first and then gain entry into the intranet. Some or all of the same privileges given to intranet users are given to the extranet user. For example, a sales engineer may work out of a branch office in Phoenix. His main office is in Chicago. Instead of dialing up the main office with a modem and incurring long distance charges, the engineer simply connects to the Internet via his local area network (LAN), enters the URL for the main office's intranet, and connects.

The main goal of intranets and extranets is to organize and disseminate organizational intelligence. This intelligence can include projects, schedules, customer data, budgets, and so forth. Although intranets and extranets can provide many employee services, such as electronic directory services, network-wide calendar systems, and electronic chat rooms, one growing trend in medium- and large-sized companies is to use these technologies to gather mission-critical information. This information is available instantly so that decision makers can analyze business processes, opportunities, and goals much faster. It also enables companies to have more employees become involved in decisions.

By connecting intranets and extranets to decision-support applications, for example, a manager can access raw data from a transaction system and summarize the data into reports. The reports can then be distributed to key employees, consultants, and other colleagues via the intranet or extranet for business decisions to be modified accordingly. Because the intranet and extranet offer a common environment for all users, reports can be constructed using templates to create a common look and feel among all documents. Also, with searching tools added to the intranet and extranet, users can quickly find the report they need (rather than sift through long pages of information).

THE SYSTEMS DEVELOPMENT LIFE CYCLE

Creating an information system can be a complex task. It involves several distinct phases, each of which often must be completed before a subsequent task can begin. To help create successful information systems, the **systems development life cycle (SDLC)** was developed. SDLC is an organized way to build an information system. As you can see from Figure 11.5, the SDLC is composed of a series of five phases.

Together, the phases are called a life cycle because they cover the entire "life" of an information system, as illustrated by the phased approach shown in Figure 11.6.

Phase 1: Needs Analysis

During **needs analysis**, the first phase of the SDLC, teams focus on completing three tasks:

1_ Defining the problem and deciding whether to proceed

2_ Analyzing the current system in depth and developing possible solutions to the problem

3_ Selecting the best solution and defining its functionality

Phase 1 begins when a need is identified for a new or modified system. Users may complain, for example, that the current system is difficult to use. Simple procedures require too many steps, and the system crashes repeatedly, resulting in a loss of data. Alternatively, a manager may approach the IS department, requesting a report that is not currently produced by the system.

Systems analysts then begin a preliminary investigation, talking with users and the managers of the departments that are to be affected. The first challenge is to define the problem accurately. With the problem accurately defined, the IS department can decide whether to undertake the project (the "go/no go" decision).

Figure 11.5
The systems development life cycle.

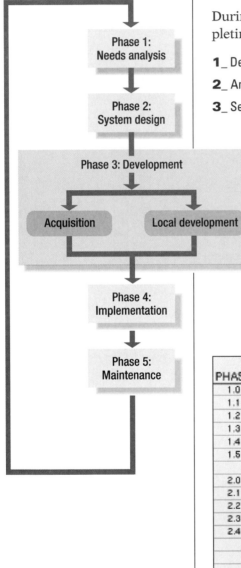

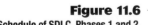

Figure 11.6
Schedule of SDLC, Phases 1 and 2.

PHASE TASK		BEGIN DATE	END DATE	3/1	3/15	3/29	4/12	4/26	5/10	5/24	6/7	6/21
1.0	Needs Analysis											
1.1	Problem Definition	1-Mar	15-Mar									
1.2	Go/No Go Decision	19-Mar	19-Mar									
1.3	Analysis of Current System	22-Mar	23-Apr									
1.4	Develop Alternative Solutions	29-Mar	30-Apr									
1.5	Best Alternative Decision	3-May	4-May									
2.0	System Design											
2.1	Data Flow Diagram	5-May	21-May									
2.2	Data Modeling	12-May	28-May									
2.3	Functional Design	24-May	18-Jun									
2.4	Make/Buy Decision	21-Jun	22-Jun									

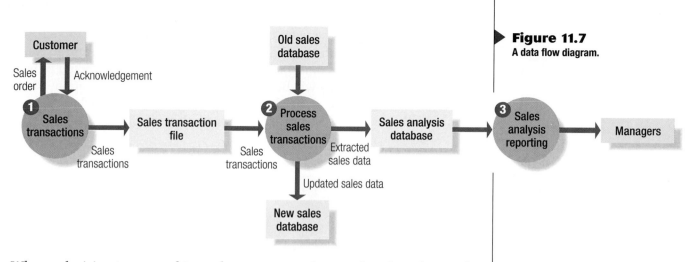

Figure 11.7
A data flow diagram.

When a decision to proceed is made, systems analysts undertake a thorough investigation of the current system and its limitations. They work with the people directly involved with the problem to document how it can be solved.

The knowledge gathered regarding the current system is documented in a number of different ways. Some analysts use data flow diagrams, which show the flow of data through a system (see Figure 11.7). They may use structured English to describe alternatives and actions (see Figure 11.8). Another option is to present the actions taken under different conditions in a decision tree (see Figure 11.9). The graphical representation is easier to understand than a list.

With this foundation, the analysts are ready to consider various solutions to the problem. They may call on computer scientists in the IS department to help them identify different approaches. Each is evaluated on the basis of project constraints, primarily budget and schedule. If a solution must be provided quickly, the IS team may consider solutions that are less than ideal but have the advantage of quick turnaround.

If item is received and
    the invoice date is over 30 days old
        If supplier is on payment hold status
            indicate status on invoice
            issue pending/future payment transaction

        Else issue payment voucher transaction

    Else calculate payment date
        issue pending/future payment transaction

Else issue invoiced/not received transaction

Figure 11.8
Structured English.

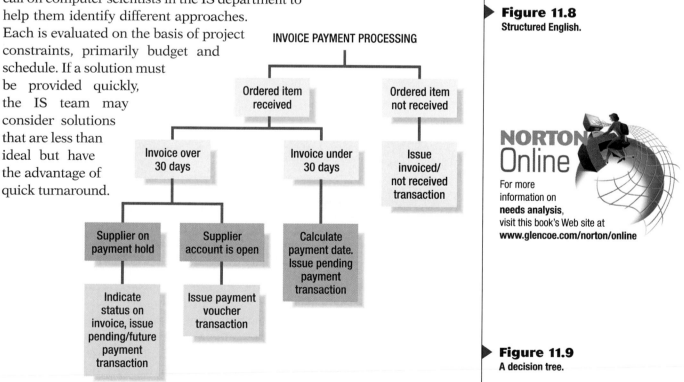

INVOICE PAYMENT PROCESSING

For more information on **needs analysis**, visit this book's Web site at **www.glencoe.com/norton/online**

Figure 11.9
A decision tree.

At the end of Phase 1, the team recommends a solution to be adopted. The analysts use information they have already gathered from system users to determine what features must be in the solution (what reports should be generated, in what form they will be output, and what special tools are needed). Throughout the needs analysis phase, they remain focused on "what" the system must do, not "how" the features will be implemented.

System designers frequently need to meet with the managers of the departments that will be affected by the new system.

NORTON Online

For more information on **CASE tools**, visit this book's Web site at **www.glencoe.com/norton/online**

Phase 2: Systems Design

During the second phase, **systems design**, the project team tackles the "how" of the selected solution. For example, a database application must be able to accept data from users and store it in a database. These are general functions, but how will the team implement them? How many input screens are necessary, for example, and what will they look like? What kind of menu options must there be? What kind of database will the system use?

The analysts and programmers involved at this point often use a combination of top-down and bottom-up design to answer these questions. In **top-down design**, the team starts with the large picture and moves to the detail. They look at major functions that the system must provide and break these down into smaller and smaller activities. Each of these activities will then be programmed in the next phase of the SDLC.

In **bottom-up design**, the team starts with the details (for example, the reports to be produced by the system) and then moves out to the big picture (the major functions or processes). This approach is particularly appropriate when users have specific requirements for output—for example, payroll checks, which must contain certain pieces of information.

Designers use many techniques to develop a good plan for a new system.

Throughout Phase 2, the manager of the project team reviews progress on the design of different system components. At the end of the phase, a larger review is conducted, typically involving the department that will be affected and top management. If the design passes inspection, development begins. In some instances, the review highlights problems with the overall solution, and the team must return to analysis or terminate the project.

Many tools are available to help teams through the steps of system design. Most of these tools also can be used during the development phase (Phase 3), or even during analysis (Phase 1). Many teams, for example, use working models called **prototypes** to explore the look and feel of screens with users. They also use special software applications for creating these prototypes quickly, as well as for building diagrams, writing code, and managing the development effort. These applications fall in the category of **computer-aided software engineering (CASE) tools** (see Figure 11.10). In other words, computer software is being used to develop other computer software more quickly and reliably.

Figure 11.10
Moving a button simply by dragging it on a screen in a CASE tool.

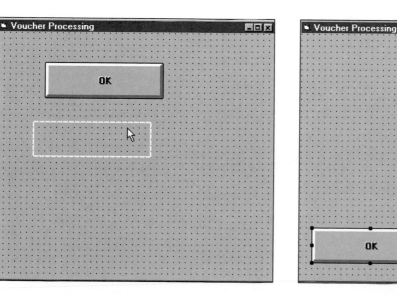

Phase 3: Development

During the **development** phase, programmers play the key role, creating or customizing the software for all the various parts of the system. Typically, the programmers on the team are assigned to specific components of the overall system. If a component is being built, the programmers write the necessary code or use CASE tools (if possible) to speed the development process. For purchased components, the programmers must customize the code as necessary to make the component fit into the new system.

There are two alternative paths through Phase 3: the acquisition path or the local development path. As early as Phase 1, needs analysis, the team may realize that some or all of the necessary system components are available as off-the-shelf hardware or software and decide to acquire, rather than develop, these components. Acquiring off-the-shelf components means that the system can be built faster and cheaper than if every component must be developed from scratch. Another advantage of acquired components is that they have already been tested and proven reliable, although they may need to be customized to fit into the overall information system. In many cases, project teams buy (or acquire) some components and build (or develop) others. Thus, they follow both acquisition and local development paths through the SDLC at the same time.

Technical writers work with the programmers to produce the technical documentation for the system. Technical documentation is vastly different from the **user documentation**, which describes to end users how to use the system. The **technical documentation** includes information about software features and programming, about the flow of data and processing through the system, and about the design and layout of the necessary hardware. These materials provide an overall view of the system and thus serve as a reference for team members focused on individual components. In addition, the technical documentation is vital for support personnel and programmers in charge of the system during the maintenance phase.

Other writers begin work on the user documentation, and user assistance architects start to lay out the architecture of the online Help system. These efforts are usually not finished until the early stages of the implementation phase.

Testing is an integral part of Phases 3 and 4 (development and implementation). The typical approach to testing is to move from the individual component

All three of these parts are created or acquired during Phase 3.

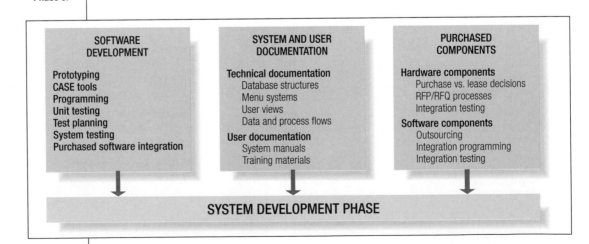

out to the system as a whole. The team tests each component separately (unit testing) and then tests the components of the system with each other (system testing). Errors are corrected, the necessary changes made, and the tests are then run again. Next comes installation testing, when the system is installed in a test environment and tested with other applications used by the business. Finally, acceptance testing is carried out, when the end users test the installed system to make sure that it meets their criteria.

Project teams often test systems or system components with real transactions—sometimes called "live data." This helps to ensure that the system can handle the flow of data expected on a daily basis after the system goes online. Programmers, however, should also test the system with invalid data or exception conditions. What happens, for example, when a user mistypes "1x33345" instead of "1333345" into a field that accepts only numerical data? These kinds of errors may not exist in the data normally used to test the system, but they are bound to occur when the system is used by real employees.

Phase 4: Implementation

In the **implementation** phase, the project team finishes buying any necessary hardware for the system users and then installs the hardware and software in the user environment. Then the users start using the system to perform work, not just to provide feedback on the system's development.

The process of moving from the old system to the new is called **conversion**. IS professionals must handle this process carefully, to avoid losing or corrupting data or frustrating users trying to perform their work. As shown in Figure 11.11, there are a number of different ways to convert a department or an organization, including the following:

■ **Direct conversion**. All users stop using the old system at the same time and then begin using the new. This option is fast, but it can be disruptive. Furthermore, pressure on support personnel can be excessive.

■ **Parallel conversion**. Users continue to use the old system while an increasing amount of data is processed through the new system. The outputs from the two systems are compared; if they agree, the switch is made. This option is useful for further live testing of the new system, but it is fairly time-intensive because both systems are operating at the same time.

■ **Phased conversion**. Users start using the new system component by component. This option works only for systems that can be compartmentalized.

■ **Pilot conversion**. Personnel in a single pilot site use the new system and then the entire organization makes the switch. Although this approach may take more time than the other three, it gives support personnel the opportunity to test user response to the system thoroughly, and they will be better prepared when many people make the conversion.

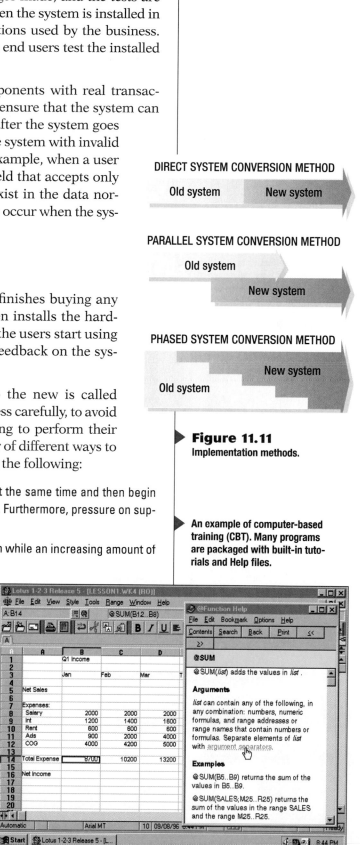

Figure 11.11
Implementation methods.

An example of computer-based training (CBT). Many programs are packaged with built-in tutorials and Help files.

Trainers and support personnel have a significant role during the conversion. Training courses usually involve classroom-style lectures, hands-on sessions with sample data, and computer-based training (CBT), which users can work with on their own time.

Phase 5: Maintenance

After the information systems are implemented, IS professionals continue to provide support during the **maintenance** phase. They monitor various indices of system performance, such as response time, to ensure that the system is performing as intended. They also respond to changes in users' requirements. These changes occur for a variety of reasons. As users work with the system on a daily basis, they may recognize instances where a small change in the system would allow them to be more effective. Or the manager of a user department might request changes due to a change in state or federal regulations of the industry.

Errors in the system are also corrected during Phase 5. Often, systems are installed in a user environment with known programming or design errors. Typically, these errors have been identified as noncritical, or not important enough to delay installation. Programmers have lists of such errors to correct during the maintenance phase. In addition, daily use of the system may highlight more serious errors for the programmers to fix.

Changes, or upgrades, to the system are made regularly during the remaining life span of the system. At some point, however, patch repairs to the system no longer meet user requirements, which may have changed radically since the system was installed. IS professionals or managers in a user department start calling for a major modification or new system. At this point, the SDLC has come full circle, and the analysis phase begins again.

CREATING COMPUTER PROGRAMS

If hardware is the muscle of an information system, and if network media act as the spinal cord, then software provides the intelligence that enables these components to process and distribute data and information. No information system—whether a stand-alone PC, a small peer-to-peer network, or a WAN—is complete without software.

Software requirements are an enormous consideration in the development of any information system. What tasks will users need to perform? What type of output is expected? Will different types of software work together? These questions, and many others, must be answered before any information system can function as intended.

Sometimes, developers can resolve these issues by using commercial software, purchased off the shelf. This solution works well when the users' needs are typical and require little or no customization of the software—as is often the case in small businesses or office automation systems.

Otherwise, the solution may involve creating new software or customizing existing software. This can be a

Even if effective online training has been developed for the new system, users always have many questions. Trainers and support personnel share the job of providing answers.

complex process—so complex, in fact, that software developers follow a development life cycle that mirrors the information systems development life cycle.

The first step in this process involves identifying the type or types of software needed to run the information system—regardless of whether the software must be purchased, created, or customized. Software products generally fall into one of the following categories:

- Operating systems
- Utilities
- Word processors
- Spreadsheets
- Database managers
- Communications and Internet browsers
- Graphics and publishing applications
- CAD software
- Multimedia and presentation software
- Education and entertainment software
- Software development systems
- Networking and network-management systems

▶ SB7, a business accounting application that lets a business maintain detailed records on its customers.

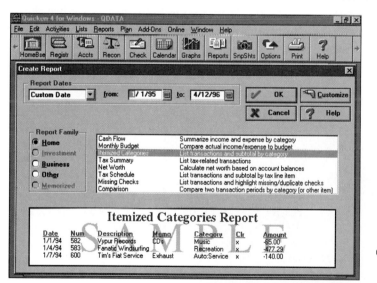

◀ Quicken is a financial management program designed especially for home users and small businesses.

▶ Games like this one are some of the most technically challenging programs to write.

Within these general categories, there are hundreds of specialized categories of software (sometimes called *vertical applications*) including the following:

- Accounting systems
- Bank management systems
- Retail point-of-sale systems
- Financial planning software
- Legal and medical office management systems
- Medical diagnostic software
- Insurance claims processing systems
- Software development accessories

The following sections explain how software programs function and describe the processes and tools that developers use to create software.

What Is a Computer Program?

A **computer program** is a collection of instructions, or statements (also called *code*) carried out by the computer's CPU. These instructions can be written in many different languages. Except for operating systems and utilities, all the categories of programs listed in the preceding section are application programs. These programs are developed to help users solve problems or perform tasks, such as sending mail messages, editing text, or finding a specific article in a library.

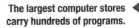

The largest computer stores carry hundreds of programs.

Application programs are usually composed of many files. Some of these files contain instructions for the computer, whereas other files contain data. On DOS- or Windows-based PCs, some common extensions for program files are .exe (executable), .dll (dynamic link library), .ini (initialization), and .hlp (help). These extensions define the type of file.

By default, most program files are stored in the folder that bears the application's name or an abbreviation of it. To view a list of the files needed to run an application, you can open that application's directory or folder (see Figure 11.12 for an example).

NORTON
Online

For more information on **vertical applications** in the financial and accounting market, visit this book's Web site at www.glencoe.com/norton/online

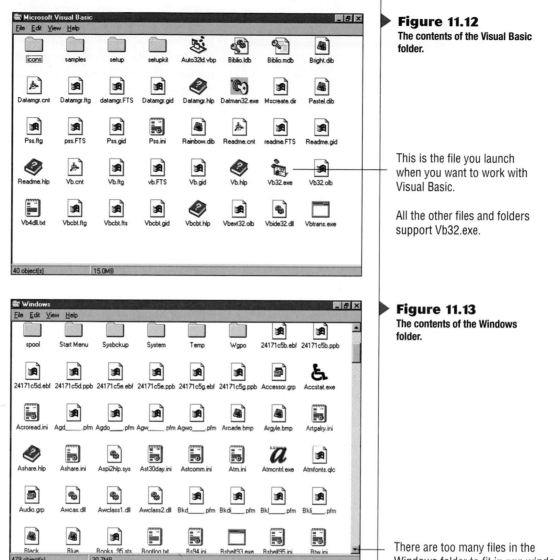

Figure 11.12
The contents of the Visual Basic folder.

This is the file you launch when you want to work with Visual Basic.

All the other files and folders support Vb32.exe.

Figure 11.13
The contents of the Windows folder.

There are too many files in the Windows folder to fit in one window.

The system software that controls your computer also includes many files. The folder in Figure 11.13 shows just a few of the ones used by Windows 98.

Program Control Flow

Although all the files in the program's folder are considered parts of the program, usually one file represents the core. This file is often called the **executable file** because it is the one that the computer executes when you launch the program. On PCs running DOS or Windows, the executable file has the same name as the program (or an abbreviation of it), plus the extension .exe.

When you launch a program, the computer begins reading and carrying out statements at the executable's main entry point. Typically, this entry point is the first line (or statement) in the file, although it may be elsewhere. After execution of the first statement, program control passes, or flows, to another statement, and so on, until the last statement of the program has been executed. Then the program ends. The order in which program statements are executed is called program **control flow**.

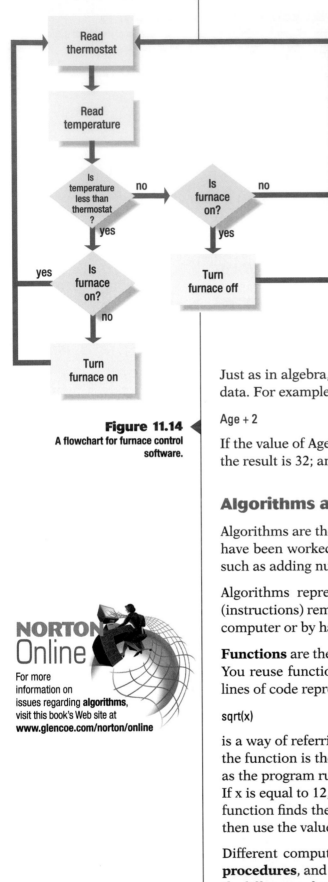

Figure 11.14 ◀
A flowchart for furnace control software.

The example in Figure 11.14 shows the flow of a small program that controls a furnace. The program constantly checks the thermostat setting and current temperature. If the current temperature is at or above the thermostat setting, the program executes the statements that turn off the furnace. If the current temperature is below the thermostat setting, the program executes the statements that turn on the furnace.

Variables

One element that most computer languages have in common is **variables**—placeholders for data being processed. For example, imagine you are writing a program that prompts users to enter their ages. You need a placeholder, or variable, to represent the data (different ages) they enter. In this case, you might choose to name the variable Age. Then, when a user enters a number at the prompt, this data becomes the value of the variable Age.

Just as in algebra, you can use variables in programs to perform actions on data. For example, consider the instruction:

Age + 2

If the value of Age is 20, the result of this instruction is 22; if the value is 30, the result is 32; and so on.

Algorithms and Functions

Algorithms are the series of steps by which problems are solved. Algorithms have been worked out for solving a wide range of mathematical problems, such as adding numbers or finding a square root.

Algorithms represent solutions to problems. The steps to the solution (instructions) remain the same, whether you are working out the solution by computer or by hand.

Functions are the expression of algorithms in a specific computer language. You reuse functions when you need them. You do not have to rewrite the lines of code represented by the function each time. For example:

sqrt(x)

is a way of referring to the square root's function. The (x) after the name of the function is the argument. You use arguments to pass input to functions as the program runs. In this example, x is a variable representing a number. If x is equal to 12, then the function will find the square root of 12. After the function finds the square root, it returns this value to the program. You can then use the value in other calculations.

Different computer languages use different names, such as **subroutines**, **procedures**, and **routines**, for these blocks of reusable code. There are subtle differences between these terms, but for now, the term "function" will be used for all of them.

TWO APPROACHES TO PROGRAMMING

Until the 1960s, relatively little structure was imposed on how programmers wrote code. As a result, following control flow through hundreds or thousands of lines of code was almost impossible. Programmers, for example, often used goto statements to jump to other parts of a program. A **goto statement** does exactly what the name implies. It identifies a different line of the program to which control jumps. (It goes to.) The issue with goto statements is identifying how program control flow proceeds after the jump. Does control return to the jumping-off place, or does it continue at the new location?

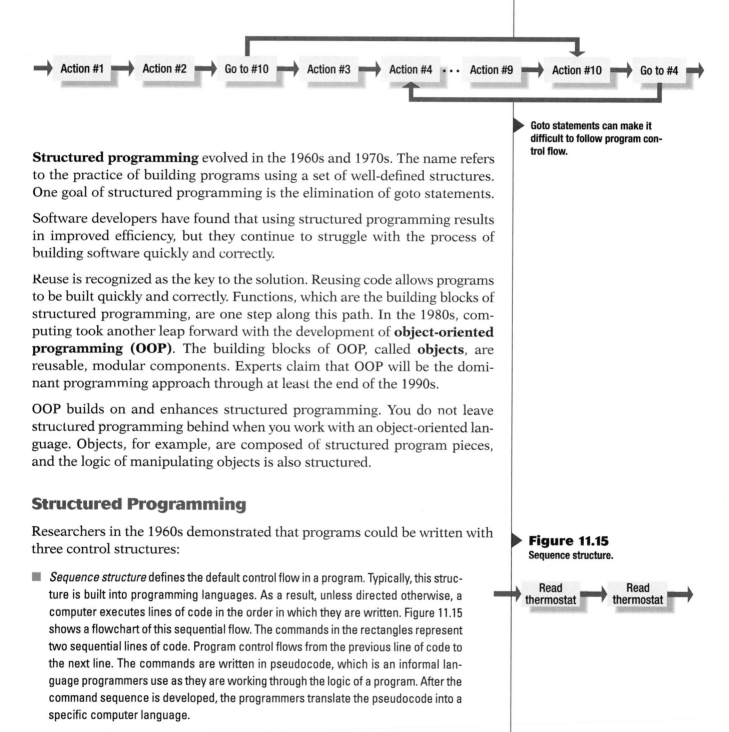

Goto statements can make it difficult to follow program control flow.

Structured programming evolved in the 1960s and 1970s. The name refers to the practice of building programs using a set of well-defined structures. One goal of structured programming is the elimination of goto statements.

Software developers have found that using structured programming results in improved efficiency, but they continue to struggle with the process of building software quickly and correctly.

Reuse is recognized as the key to the solution. Reusing code allows programs to be built quickly and correctly. Functions, which are the building blocks of structured programming, are one step along this path. In the 1980s, computing took another leap forward with the development of **object-oriented programming (OOP)**. The building blocks of OOP, called **objects**, are reusable, modular components. Experts claim that OOP will be the dominant programming approach through at least the end of the 1990s.

OOP builds on and enhances structured programming. You do not leave structured programming behind when you work with an object-oriented language. Objects, for example, are composed of structured program pieces, and the logic of manipulating objects is also structured.

Structured Programming

Researchers in the 1960s demonstrated that programs could be written with three control structures:

Figure 11.15
Sequence structure.

- *Sequence structure* defines the default control flow in a program. Typically, this structure is built into programming languages. As a result, unless directed otherwise, a computer executes lines of code in the order in which they are written. Figure 11.15 shows a flowchart of this sequential flow. The commands in the rectangles represent two sequential lines of code. Program control flows from the previous line of code to the next line. The commands are written in pseudocode, which is an informal language programmers use as they are working through the logic of a program. After the command sequence is developed, the programmers translate the pseudocode into a specific computer language.

- *Selection structures* are built around a **condition statement**. If the condition statement is true, certain lines of code are executed. If the condition statement is false, those lines of code are not executed. The two most common selection structures are: If-Then and If-Else (sometimes called If-Then-Else). Figures 11.16 and 11.17 illustrate these types of structures.

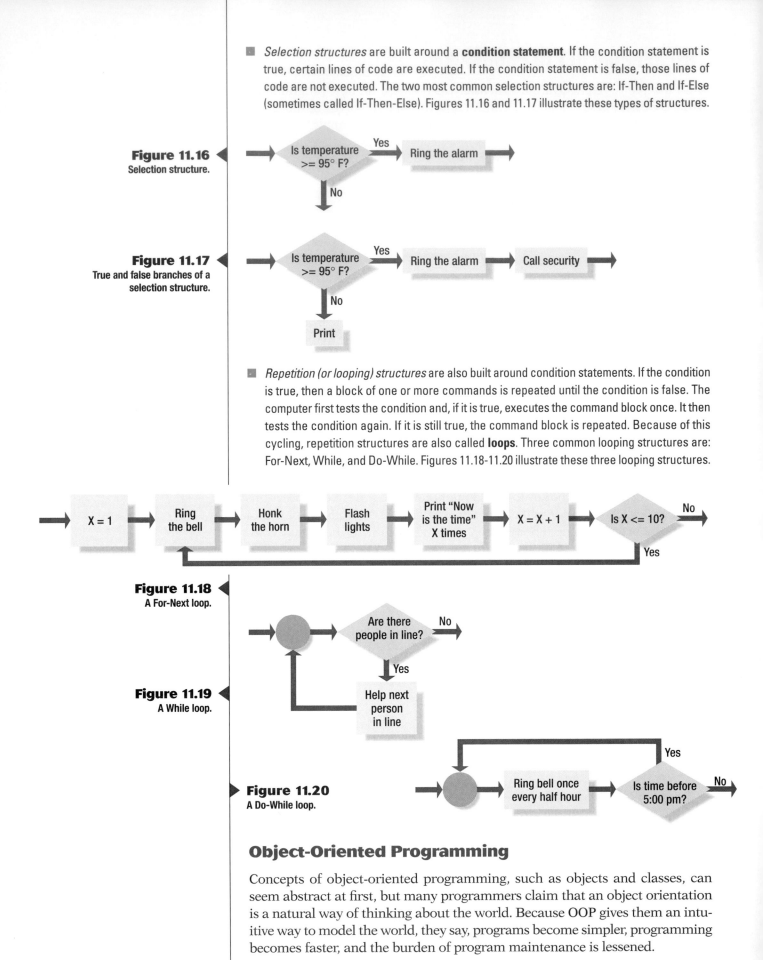

Figure 11.16
Selection structure.

Figure 11.17
True and false branches of a selection structure.

- *Repetition (or looping) structures* are also built around condition statements. If the condition is true, then a block of one or more commands is repeated until the condition is false. The computer first tests the condition and, if it is true, executes the command block once. It then tests the condition again. If it is still true, the command block is repeated. Because of this cycling, repetition structures are also called **loops**. Three common looping structures are: For-Next, While, and Do-While. Figures 11.18-11.20 illustrate these three looping structures.

Figure 11.18
A For-Next loop.

Figure 11.19
A While loop.

Figure 11.20
A Do-While loop.

Object-Oriented Programming

Concepts of object-oriented programming, such as objects and classes, can seem abstract at first, but many programmers claim that an object orientation is a natural way of thinking about the world. Because OOP gives them an intuitive way to model the world, they say, programs become simpler, programming becomes faster, and the burden of program maintenance is lessened.

Objects

Look around you—you are surrounded by objects. Right now, the list of objects around you might include a book, a computer, a light, walls, plants, pictures, and so forth.

For more information on **object-oriented programming**, visit this book's Web site at **www.glencoe.com/norton/online**

Think for a moment about what you perceive when you look at a car on the street. Your first impression is probably of the car as a whole. You do not focus on the steel, chrome, and plastic elements that make up the car. The entire unit, or object, is what registers in your mind.

Now, how would you describe that car to someone sitting next to you? You might start with its color, size, and shape. A car, like all objects, has attributes. You might then talk about what the car can do. It can accelerate from 0 to 60 mph in 9.2 seconds, for example, it turns on a dime, and so forth. Again, like all objects, a car has certain things it can do, or functions. Together, the attributes and the functions define the object. In the language of OOP, every object has attributes and functions and encapsulates other objects.

When you look more closely at the car, you may begin to notice many smaller component objects. The car, for example, has a chassis, a drive train, a body, and an interior. Each of these components is, in turn, made up of other objects. The drive train includes an engine, transmission, rear end, and axle. An object, then, can be either a whole unit or a component of other objects. Objects can include other objects.

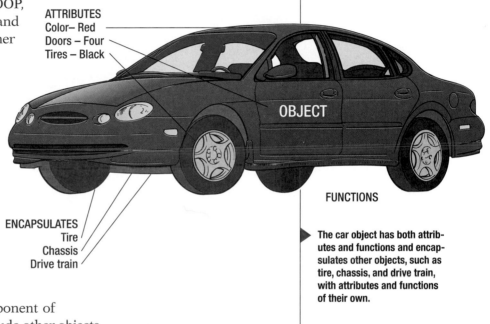

ATTRIBUTES
Color– Red
Doors – Four
Tires – Black

OBJECT

FUNCTIONS

ENCAPSULATES
Tire
Chassis
Drive train

The car object has both attributes and functions and encapsulates other objects, such as tire, chassis, and drive train, with attributes and functions of their own.

Classes and Class Inheritance

As you contemplate the objects around you, you will find that you naturally place them in abstract categories, or classes, with other similar objects. For example, the Porsche, Infiniti, and Saturn you see on the road are all cars. In OOP, therefore, you would group these into a car class.

A **class** consists of attributes and functions shared by more than one object. All cars, for example, have a steering wheel and four tires. All cars can drive forward, reverse, park, and accelerate. Class attributes are called **data members**, and class functions are represented as **member functions** or **methods**.

Classes can be divided into **subclasses**. The car class, for example, could have a luxury sedan class, a sports car class, and a pickup truck class. Subclasses typically have all the attributes and methods of the parent class. Every sports car, for example, has a steering wheel and can drive forward. This is called **class inheritance**.

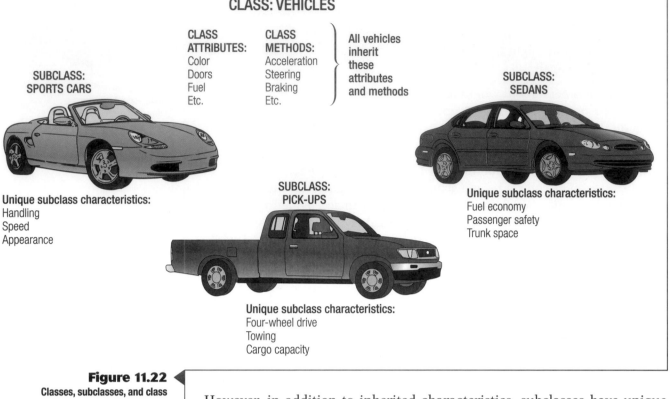

CLASS: VEHICLES

CLASS ATTRIBUTES:
Color
Doors
Fuel
Etc.

CLASS METHODS:
Acceleration
Steering
Braking
Etc.

All vehicles inherit these attributes and methods

SUBCLASS: SPORTS CARS

Unique subclass characteristics:
Handling
Speed
Appearance

SUBCLASS: PICK-UPS

Unique subclass characteristics:
Four-wheel drive
Towing
Cargo capacity

SUBCLASS: SEDANS

Unique subclass characteristics:
Fuel economy
Passenger safety
Trunk space

Figure 11.22
Classes, subclasses, and class inheritance.

However, in addition to inherited characteristics, subclasses have unique characteristics of their own. For example, pickup trucks have four-wheel drive and trailer hitches, as shown in Figure 11.22.

All objects belong to classes. When an object is created, it automatically has all the attributes and methods associated with that class. In the language of OOP, objects are **instantiated** (created).

Messages

Objects do not typically perform behaviors spontaneously. After all, many of these behaviors may be contradictory. A car, for example, cannot go forward and in reverse at the same time. You also expect that the car will not drive forward spontaneously either!

Figure 11.23
The flow of messages among objects.

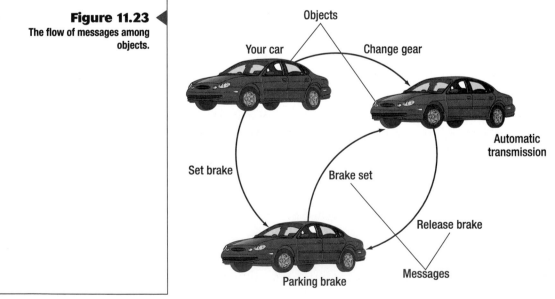

Objects

Your car

Change gear

Automatic transmission

Set brake

Brake set

Release brake

Parking brake

Messages

You send a signal to the car to move forward by pressing on the accelerator. Likewise, in OOP, **messages** are sent to objects, requesting them to perform a specific function. Part of designing a program is to identify the flow of sending and receiving messages among the objects (see Figure 11.23).

THE EVOLUTION OF PROGRAMMING LANGUAGES

Programming is a way of sending instructions to the computer. To be sure that the computer (and other programmers) can understand these instructions, programmers use defined languages to communicate. These languages have many of the same types of rules as languages people use to communicate with each other. For example, information must be provided in a certain order and structure, symbols are used, and punctuation is often required.

The only language that a computer understands is its **machine language**. People, however, have difficulty understanding machine code. As a result, researchers first developed assembly languages and then higher-level languages. This evolution represents a transition from strings of numbers (machine code) to command sequences that you can read like any other language. Higher-level languages focus on what the programmer wants the computer to do, not on how the computer will execute those commands.

Hundreds of programming languages are now in use. These languages fall into the following categories:

- **Machine languages** are the most basic of languages. Machine languages consist of strings of numbers and are defined by hardware design. In other words, the machine language for a Macintosh is not the same as the machine language for a PC. A computer understands only its native machine language—the commands of its instruction set. These commands instruct the computer to perform elementary operations such as loading, storing, adding, and subtracting. Ultimately, machine code consists entirely of the 0s and 1s of the binary number system.

- **Assembly languages** were developed by using English-like mnemonics for commonly used strings of machine language. Programmers worked in text editors, which are simple word processors, to create **source files**. Source files contain instructions for the computer to execute, but the files must first be translated into machine language. Researchers created translator programs called **assemblers** to perform the conversion. Assembly languages are still highly detailed and cryptic, but reading assembler code is much faster than struggling with machine language. Programmers seldom write programs of any significant size in an assembly language. (One exception to this rule is found in action games where the speed of the program is critical.) Instead, they use assembly languages to fine-tune important parts of programs written in a higher-level language.

- **Higher-level languages** were developed to make programming easier. These languages are called higher-level languages because their syntax is closer to human language than assembly or machine language code. They use familiar words instead of communicating in the detailed quagmire of digits that comprise the machine instructions. To express computer operations, these languages use operators, such as the plus or minus sign, that are the familiar components of mathematics. As a result, reading, writing, and understanding computer programs is easier with a higher-level language—although the instructions must still be translated into machine language before the computer can understand and carry them out.

Commands written in any assembly or higher-level language must be translated back into machine code before the computer can execute the commands. These translator programs are called **compilers**. Typically, then, a program must be compiled, or translated into machine code, before it is run. Compiled program files become executables.

The next section outlines a few of the more important higher-level programming languages.

Higher-Level Languages

Programming languages are sometimes discussed in terms of generations, although these categories are somewhat arbitrary. Each successive generation is thought to contain languages that are easier to use and more powerful than those in the previous generation. Machine languages are considered first-generation languages, and assembly languages are considered second-generation languages. The higher-level languages began with the third generation.

Third-Generation Languages

Third-generation languages have the capability to support structured programming, which means that they provide explicit structures for branches and loops. In addition, because they are the first languages to use English-like phrasing, sharing development between programmers is also easier. Team members can read each other's code and understand the logic and program control flow.

These languages are also **portable**. As opposed to the assembly languages, programs in these languages can be compiled to run on multiple CPUs.

Third-generation languages include:

- **FORTRAN** (FORmula TRANslator) was specifically designed for mathematical and engineering programs. The language, which enjoyed immediate and widespread acceptance, has been enhanced several times, most recently in 1990. The current version is often referred to as FORTRAN-90. Because of its almost exclusive focus on mathematical and engineering applications, FORTRAN has not been widely used with personal computers. Instead, FORTRAN remains a common language on mainframe systems, especially those used for research and education.

- **COBOL** (COmmon Business Oriented Language) was developed in 1960 by a government-appointed committee. Under the leadership of retired Navy Commodore and mathematician Grace Hopper, the committee set out to solve the problem of incompatibilities among computer manufacturers. Partly because of the government's backing, COBOL won widespread acceptance as a standardized language. Although COBOL had lost most of its following over the past five to ten years, the Year 2000 problem has required many COBOL programmers to come out of "retirement" to help reprogram millions of lines of programs written in COBOL to work after the year 2000.

- **BASIC** (Beginners All-purpose Symbolic Instruction Code) was developed by John Kemeny and Thomas Kurtz at Dartmouth College in 1964 and started out largely as a tool for teaching programming to students. Because of its simplicity, BASIC quickly became popular, and when personal computers took off, it was the first high-level language to be implemented on these new machines. Versions of BASIC were included with early personal computers, even before IBM PCs came on the market. Although BASIC is an extremely popular and widely used language in education and among amateur programmers, it has not caught on as a viable language for commercial applications—mostly

because it just does not have as large a repertoire of tools as other languages offer. In addition, BASIC compilers still do not produce executable files that are as compact, fast, or efficient as those produced by other languages.

- **Pascal** was introduced in 1971 by a Swiss computer scientist named Niklaus Wirth. Named after the 17th-century French inventor Blaise Pascal, Pascal was intended to overcome the limitations of other programming languages and to demonstrate the proper way to implement a computer language. Pascal is often considered an excellent teaching language. Beginners find it easy to implement algorithms in Pascal. In addition, the Pascal compiler enforces rules of structured programming, thus ensuring that errors are caught early. Because the compilers of other languages do not necessarily enforce these rules, finding errors in other programs may require a lengthy debugging process. Almost all early Macintosh applications were written in Pascal. Lately, Pascal has become well known for its implementation of object-oriented principles of programming but currently does not have the following it once had.

- **C**, which is often regarded as the thoroughbred of programming languages, was developed in the early 1970s at Bell Labs by Brian Kernighan and Dennis Ritchie. Ritchie, with Ken Thompson, had also developed the UNIX operating system. Kernighan and Ritchie needed a better language to integrate with UNIX so that users could make modifications and enhancements easily. Programs written in C produce fast and efficient executable code and are portable. C is also a powerful language—with C, you can make a computer do just about anything it is possible for a computer to do. Because of this programming freedom, C has become extremely popular and is the most widely used language among professional software developers for commercial applications. The disadvantage of such a powerful and capable language is that it is not particularly easy to learn.

- **C++** was developed by Bjarne Stroustrup at Bell Labs in the early 1980s. Like C, C++ is an extremely powerful and efficient language. Learning C++ means learning everything about C, and then learning about object-oriented programming and its implementation with C++. Nevertheless, more C programmers move to C++ every year, and the newer language is now replacing C as the language of choice among software development companies.

- **Java** is a programming environment that creates cross-platform programs. It was developed in 1991 by Sun Microsystems for TV set-top boxes for two-way interactive cable systems. When the Internet became a popular communications network in the mid-1990s, Sun redirected Java to become a programming environment in which Webmasters could create interactive and dynamic programs (called applets) for Web pages. Java is similar in complexity to C++. Nevertheless, many programmers and computer professionals are learning Java in response to the growing number of companies looking for Java applications. In the future, Sun is hoping Java will be the de facto programming environment, knocking off C++ as the number one programming environment.

NORTON Online

For more information on **Microsoft C++** and other Microsoft programming information, visit this book's Web site at **www.glencoe.com/norton/online**

Fourth-Generation Languages

Fourth-generation languages (4GLs) are mostly special-purpose programming languages that are easier to use than third-generation languages. With 4GLs, programmers can create applications rapidly. As part of the development process, programmers can use 4GLs to develop prototypes of an application quickly. Prototypes give teams and clients an idea of how the finished application will look and operate before the code is finished. As a result, everyone involved in the development of the application can provide feedback on design and structural issues early in the process.

A single statement in a 4GL accomplishes a much more than was possible in a similar statement from an earlier-generation language. In exchange for this capability to work rapidly, programmers have proved willing to sacrifice some of the flexibility available with the earlier languages.

Many 4GLs are database-aware, which means that you can build programs with them that work as front ends to databases. These programs include forms and dialog boxes for inputting data into databases, querying the database for information, and reporting information. Typically, much of the code required to "hook up" these dialog boxes and forms is generated automatically.

Fourth-generation languages include:

- **Visual Basic** is the newest incarnation of BASIC from Microsoft. VB, as it is often called, supports object-oriented features and methods. With this language, programmers can build programs in a visual environment. To place a box on a form, for example, Visual Basic programmers simply drag the box from a toolbox onto the form, as shown in Figure 11.31 In other languages, the programmers would have to write code to specify the exact placement of the box on the form, as well as its size. With Visual Basic, a programmer places the box visually and then drags the edges of the box with the mouse until it is the right size. The necessary code for the box's placement and size is written automatically. Using this visual environment, programmers find it easy to write programs quickly.

Figure 11.31
Creating a form using visual tools.

The length of this text box can be adjusted simply by dragging its borders.

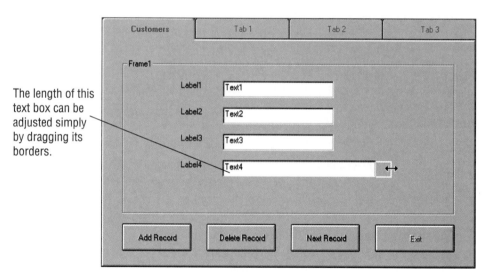

- **Application-specific macro languages** are built into many applications. These languages give users the capability to write commands and integrate applications. For Microsoft Excel, for example, the macro language is Visual Basic for Applications (VBA). Using a spreadsheet macro, you can write a sequence of commands to perform a task automatically, such as bold every entry of more than $10,000 in a spreadsheet. Macros can be created automatically or you can type in the macro yourself.

- **Authoring environments** are special-purpose programming tools for creating multimedia, computer-based training, Web pages, and so forth. One example of an authoring environment is Macromedia Director (which uses the Lingo scripting language) that you can use to create multimedia titles combining music clips, text, animation, graphics, and so forth. Like Visual Basic, these development environments are visual, with much of the code written

Macromedia Director is an authoring environment for creating multimedia software.

Many HTML authoring tools, such as FrontPage, ease the job of creating HTML pages.

automatically. However, most of the robust authoring environments also include their own languages, called scripting languages, which provide tools for added control over the final product. The programs used to create World Wide Web pages fall into another category of tools that are often lumped together with authoring environments. Some of these programs include Microsoft FrontPage, Netscape Visual JavaScript, and NetObjects Fusion.

Fifth-Generation Languages

The fifth generation of computer languages includes artificial intelligence and expert systems. These systems are intended to think and anticipate the needs of their users, instead of just to execute a set of commands. Although artificial intelligence systems are turning out to be harder to develop than originally expected, experts claim that systems such as neural networks will soon be able to take in facts and then use a set of data to work out an appropriate response—just as humans do.

NORTON *Notebook*

Creating a User-Centric Environment—Visual Programming

The object-oriented, event-driven environment of modern programming has changed how information flows through a program. It has given the control of a program's actions to the user.

In the past, programmers created program-centered processing in which the flow of action was totally dictated by the program. Even in an interactive program, where information flowed in two directions, the central focus was always the program with its preset logic and processing path.

Object-oriented, event-driven programming has changed that by putting the user in control. The user now chooses which actions are used, chooses how each action is started, and directs the flow of the entire activity. As a result, the programmer cannot presume which objects the user will choose, or the order in which they will be chosen.

Event-driven programs are designed around the interface options available to the user. An event is initiated by the user. When the user uses the mouse to click on an icon, presses the Enter key, or moves the pointer on the screen, an event occurs. Each event causes an object to gather its data, structure it, and process it through its method statements.

Event-driven programs are created in a visual WYSIWYG environment that uses a visual programming language (VPL). A VPL allows the programmer to visually create the graphical images the user will see and use. The programmer combines graphical icons, forms, diagrams, and expressions to create 2- or 3-dimensional programs to run in a graphical user environment.

Several visual languages are available for a number of processing environments. For instance, there is Prograph CPX for the Apple Macintosh; TCL/TK and Python for the OSF/MOTIF X-Windows environment; Borland's Delphi and Microsoft's Visual Basic; and Visual C++ for the Windows environment.

Recently, visual programs for Java and scripting environments—JavaScript and VBScript—have emerged. Some of the products you can find for these environments include Netscape Visual JavaScript and Microsoft FrontPad.

These languages use graphical objects, such as icons, forms, or diagrams to create programs that run in a visual environment. Programming in a visual language involves placing controls in the graphical presentation in such a way that users can interact with them. Controls are the various tools through which the user could enter data, begin a process, or indicate a choice.

For example, in the Windows Open File dialog box pictured, the Open, Find Now, Cancel, and Advanced buttons; each of the boxes that display the drive, directory, and file lists; all the other buttons and text boxes; and the window itself, are all controls.

Placing controls on a graphical environment typically is done using the "drag-and-drop" technique. The programmer chooses the control to be made available to the user for an event and places it on the window form. Usually, the available controls are contained in a menu, list, or dialog box for the programmer's ease of access and use, such as Visual Basic's "toolbox" shown below.

The Windows Open dialog box.

Visual programming is much easier for the programmer because it is based on how a programmer (and the user) sees things, rather than on the structure of the program. As in many other areas of computer software, the visual interface is making highly complex functions accessible to the everyday user.

The Visual Basic toolbox.

THE PROCESS OF PROGRAMMING

Programs are the building blocks of information systems. Thus, teams use the same process, or "life cycle," to create individual programs as they do to build systems. This process, called the systems development life cycle (SDLC), is detailed earlier in this chapter. The steps in the programming SDLC are as follows:

- *Needs analysis* is where a need or problem is identified and understood. In the current marketplace, the window of opportunity in which a company can take advantage of an opportunity is often quite small. Companies must respond immediately, or lose the chance to a competitor. With such increased time pressure, programmers look first to see whether someone else has faced the same problem already and developed a solution. Programming begins when no such solution is readily available.

- *Systems design* is the stage at which programmers work through the internal design of each program component as well as the interfaces between each component and other components in the program. Many tools are used in this process, although often they rely on whiteboards and the backs of napkins. Three of these design tools are flowcharting (for structured programming), circles and message pipes (object-oriented programming), and pseudocode. Examples of these tools are shown in Figures 11.32-11.34.

- *Development* involves writing the instructions to the computer, called source code, as well as testing those statements after they are written. Most of the time required to complete a project is spent here. Programmers also make extensive use of code they

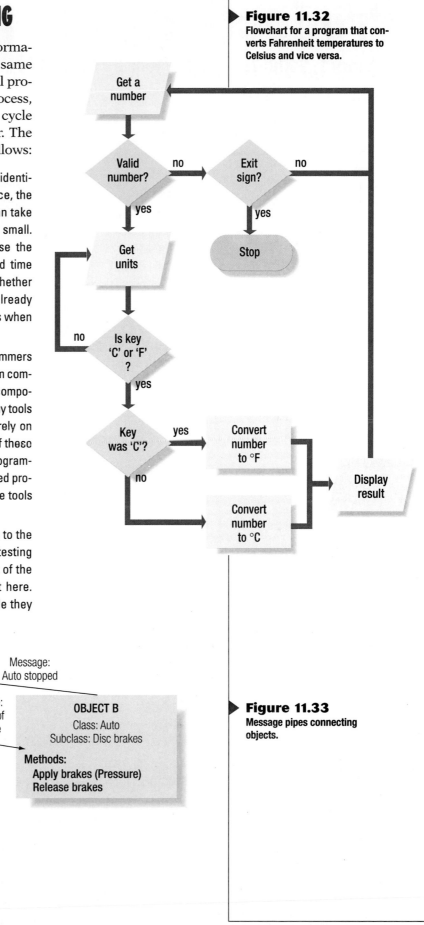

Figure 11.32
Flowchart for a program that converts Fahrenheit temperatures to Celsius and vice versa.

Figure 11.33
Message pipes connecting objects.

Productivity Tip

January 1, 2000: The Day the Your PC Stood Still

Did you know that many computer programs must be reconfigured to enter the 21st century? Right now, programmers are hard at work upgrading programs and computer systems to ensure that computers' internal clocks, and the hundreds of thousands of programs based on them, will make a smooth transition into the year 2000.

Programmers are trying to make sure that computers don't make these kinds of mistakes when 1999 becomes the year 2000:

- Record a phone call as lasting for 100 years if you happen to be on the phone when the century closes.

- Wipe out records of payments you have made on your home loan.

- Render some—or all—of your PC applications worthless.

These scenarios and others like them could occur at the turn of the century if programmers do not rewrite literally billions of lines of code in programs now being used by computers everywhere—in companies, governments, organizations, and by individuals around the world.

The "Millennium Bug," as this projected malfunction is being called, is the result of the common practice over the last several decades of referencing years with two digits rather than four in programming code. To reference the year 1998, a program stores only the 98 and assumes the 19. Unless corrected, these programs will store 2000 as 00, and assume it is 1900! This custom of date abbreviation was designed to conserve data storage and memory space on the early mainframe computers when even a small savings like two digits

made a difference. Back then, most programmers never dreamed that their code would still be in use 20 or 30 years later. But it is.

Two-digit date-sensitive computer programs, if not updated to four-digit date code by the turn of the century, will cause incorrect arithmetic operations, comparisons, or sorting of data fields when working with years beyond 1999.

This phenomenon may seem insignificant until you remember the vast reaches of computer programs these days. Automobile loans, mortgages, insurance policies, investments, bank accounts, billings from almost any business or service, financial and employee records, government services, and much more all rely on databases that are date-sensitive.

The Millennium Bug (sometimes called the Y2K problem) is not just a future challenge. Computer applications are now encountering problems. For example, some programs issue error messages when attempting to figure amortization tables that extend beyond the year 2000. As each month passes, more and more programs are beginning to yield incorrect, unreliable data.

What about your personal computer? Does it need updating? For the basic user, here are some tips:

- Updating for the year 2000 may simply mean checking that the computer's internal clock rolls over correctly. Many newer models will do this automatically, but some older models may need an instruction or a command to be executed to update the century. Contact your vendor or check your user manual for your computer's centennial updating procedure.

- Contact the vendors of your applications and hardware to inquire about bugs that may surface when the year 2000 hits. Some operating systems, for example, have trouble working with dates after 1999. Also, some applications, such as spreadsheets, interpret two-digit years differently and may report data as being in the wrong century. Check their Web pages for information, as well.

- Make a complete and up-to-date inventory of your system, including your hardware and software. This way, when you encounter an article or receive year 2000 information about a product, you can check it against your list.

Netscape - [Year 2000]

File Edit View Go Bookmarks Options Directory Window Help

Back | Forward | Home | Reload | Images | Open | Print | Find | Stop

Location: http://www.software.ibm.com/year2000/perspect.html

What's New? | What's Cool? | Handbook | Net Search | Net Directory | Software

IBM   Software

© 1996 IBM Corporation

Year 2000: A Perspective

If your computer system or its applications use two digits to represent the year, and many do, the change to dates of 1999, 2000 and beyond may skew the accuracy of the data created by every application from word processors to databases.

If it is not addressed quickly, this date change could affect calculations, comparisons and data sorting in applications from the desktop on up to the largest server. The price tag for potential errors could be high and could have a major impact on commercial, industrial, educational and governmental operations of all types.

This is a challenge for a world economy that depends on information technology. The problem can exist in any level of hardware or software, in the microcode, in new and old applications, in files and databases and on any computing platform.

100% of 3K

Start | Connecte... | Netsca... | Exploring - | 12:01 AM

IBM uses its Web site to educate people about how to update their computers for the year 2000.

434

Figure 11.34
Pseudocode of the temperature conversion program.

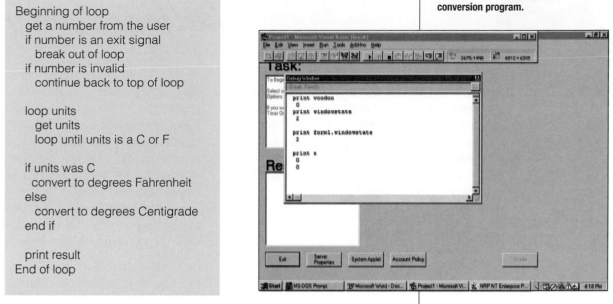

```
Beginning of loop
  get a number from the user
  if number is an exit signal
    break out of loop
  if number is invalid
    continue back to top of loop

  loop units
    get units
    loop until units is a C or F

  if units was C
    convert to degrees Fahrenheit
  else
    convert to degrees Centigrade
  end if

  print result
End of loop
```

Stepping through a program is useful in the debugging process.

have written before—especially when programming with an object-oriented language. Integrating and adapting existing code for a new application can save programmers a great deal of time. Inevitably errors, or **bugs**, find their way into programs. There are two main types of errors, **syntax errors** and **logic errors**. Syntax errors violate the rules of the programming language. A good compiler will locate and identify most syntax errors automatically. Logic errors are mistakes that cause the program to run in unexpected or incorrect ways. The process of identifying and eliminating these errors is called **debugging**.

■ *Implementation* involves installing the hardware and software, training, and so forth. This stage is primarily a systems rather than a programming concern. Still, during implementation, the programming team may recognize changes that are needed to individual programs in the system. Furthermore, at this stage, programmers are often called on to provide expertise to trainers and technical writers.

■ *Maintenance* starts as soon as the product is released. Work continues on products for any of a number of reasons. Some minor bugs may not have been fixed at the time the program was released. Also, the programmers may add major new functionality, either in response to market demands or user requests.

Comments, written when the program was originally developed, help programmers maintain the code.

Comment

Computers
In Your Career

As you have read throughout this chapter, information systems and software development require the expertise of many different professionals. From the computer scientist who dreams up new algorithms to the purchasing agent who buys components, dozens of specialists contribute to the creation of an information system or software program.

As a result, you can have a career in one of many IS fields. In fact, many IS professionals have successfully combined multiple areas of expertise (programming, network management, and systems analysis, for example) to become leaders in their industry.

Remember, too, that information systems do not exist for their own sake; they exist to support the efforts of an enterprise. The truly successful IS manager not only understands computer systems, but also understands the business they support. Therefore, if you can build expertise in a business—such as banking, human resources, insurance, or some other field—you can enhance your career even further. (Many top-level IS professionals have a masters degree in business.) The same is true of software development; if you fully understand the reasons a program is required and the way it will be used, your value as a programmer is substantially increased.

Here are a few basic IS and software-related careers you may want to consider. Once established in a basic position, you may want to further specialize in one or more specific aspects of your field:

Programmer   From operating systems to games, software is the key component of any information system. The demand for programmers continues to rise. In fact, the need for talented programmers has become so great that many U.S. software companies are looking to other countries for help. The variety of programming jobs is incredible, including database management systems, network operating systems, multimedia, and many others. Similarly, programmers use a tremendous number of tools, from assemblers to Java, so the more programming languages you know, the more successful you can be.

Network Administrator   From the small business to the worldwide enterprise, organizations of all kinds are looking for knowledgeable people to run and maintain their networks. Demand is high for administrators who understand a variety of network operating systems, communications software, protocols, and hardware. Highly successful administrators also understand the needs of the system's users, and the organization's need for quality control, security, and cost containment.

Technical Writers   If your studies focus more on the humanities than technology, take heart: the demand for talented writers is strong and growing in the world of information systems. Software developers and IS specialists generally lack the time and skills required to create software or system documentation. Technical writers must be able not only to write clear, concise text, but to learn about systems and translate their understanding into helpful reference and tutorial information.

Hardware Maintenance Technicians   Many IS professionals got their start focusing on basic hardware technology. The maintenance technician is a highly prized specialist with many opportunities for growth and advancement. These professionals take care of many of the hardware needs in an organization, whether installing new peripherals, repairing broken systems, or building new systems from the ground up. Often called *configuration specialists*, these technicians frequently customize hardware to meet special needs and are essential in keeping businesses on the cutting edge of technology.

WHAT TO EXPECT IN THE FUTURE

In the future, information systems will become more intelligent to process a wide range of data that a company amasses. Computer scientists are examining ways to move from passive to "actively intelligent" databases. In this scenario, data warehouses would collect a company's data, which would then be "mined" by the database. In other words, a software agent or some other mechanism would be used to find trends in the data before the manager starts looking for them.

As companies continue to downsize, they will outsource more IS functions. Distributed networking will become even more prevalent. As a result, communications and messaging software is an expanding market. Companies are looking for improved compatibility and performance in these software products.

On the programming front, the quality of application programs available to users improves every year. One developing trend in the programming industry today is an increasing reliance on reusable software components. In the near future, programmers or development teams will be able to buy most of the program component objects they need from providers, as they now do with hardware components like printers and workstations. At that point, the focus of programmers' work will become the integration of the objects, not the custom development of programs from scratch.

A second trend in programming is the result of the expanding presence of the Internet in our personal and business lives. Soon, programmers may be using the Internet for far more than looking up and sending files or messages. They may be using the Internet to run programs. Programs run on the Internet will have access to the vast, worldwide resources.

Visual Summary & Exercises

VISUAL SUMMARY

What Is an Information System?

- An information system is a set of rules and procedures for delivering information to the people in an organization.

- IS departments initially served managers' needs only. However, because of the PC explosion, IS departments began to serve entire organizations.

- IS departments include computer scientists, systems analysts, programmers, user assistance architects, technical writers, hardware or software purchasing agents, system or network managers, trainers and support personnel, and hardware maintenance technicians.

Types of Information Systems

- Office automation systems automate routine office tasks.

- Because transaction (event) data is stored in databases for easy retrieval, transaction processing systems are primarily database applications.

- Management information systems produce reports for different types of managers.

- Decision support systems give information workers the opportunity to run "what-if" scenarios.

- Expert systems include the knowledge of human experts in a particular area, such as medicine, in a knowledge base.

The Systems Development Life Cycle

- The systems development life cycle (SDLC) is an organized methodology for building an information system.

- The SDLC includes needs analysis, systems design, development, implementation, and maintenance phases.

- Project teams may decide to buy and then customize some components of an IS, or they may design and develop those components from scratch.

- At the beginning of needs analysis, systems analysts try to separate the problem from the solution.

Creating Computer Programs

- A computer program is a collection of instructions that a computer's CPU can interpret and carry out.

- Most of the different types of programs are application programs, which are designed to help users perform specific tasks, such as mailing messages.

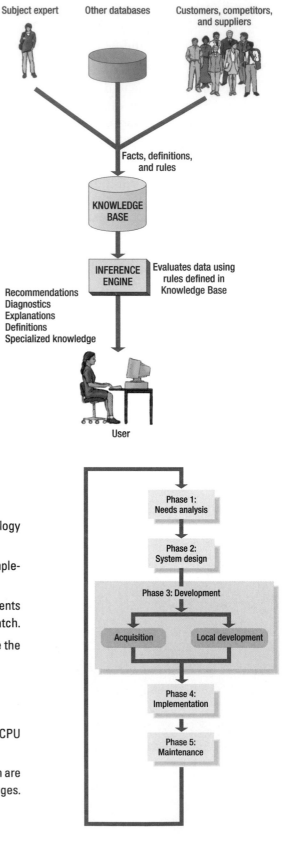

- The order in which program statements are executed is called program control flow.

- Variables are placeholders for data being processed.

- Algorithms are the series of steps by which problems are solved; functions are the expression of algorithms in a specific programming language.

Two Approaches to Programming

- Structured programming is an approach to software development whereby a program is defined as a set of logical processes, which may not be carried out sequentially. By taking the structured approach to programming, developers create software that is efficient in its execution.

- Structured programming languages are based on functions, subroutines, or procedures.

- Object-oriented programming allows a programmer to think modularly because programs are assembled into components called objects.

- An object is a self-contained unit containing functions and attributes.

The Evolution of Programming Languages

- The only real computer language is machine language, a series of digits unintelligible to people, but understood by the computer.

- The first languages to be developed after machine languages were assembly languages.

- Higher-level languages were developed to act as intermediaries between the programmer and the machine.

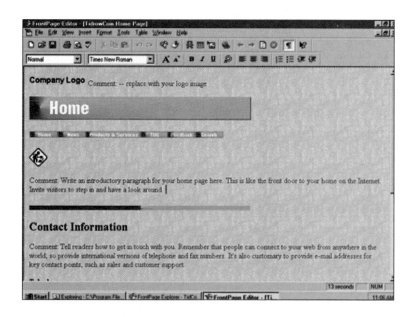

- Fourth-generation languages are more specialized than third-generation languages but are generally easier to use.

- 4GLs include Visual Basic, application-specific macro languages, and authoring environments.

The Process of Programming

- Analyzing user needs takes place while a program is being planned, but it should also continue as the program is designed and built.

- During system design, programmers use flowcharts, pseudocode, and message pipes to plan the programming process.

- Development includes coding, compiling, and debugging.

- After implementation, programs must be maintained with bug fixes and updated versions.

KEY TERMS

After completing this chapter, you should be able to define the following terms:

application-specific macro languages, 430

assembler, 427

assembly language, 427

authoring environment, 430

BASIC, 428

bottom-up design, 415

bug, 435

C, 429

C++, 429

class, 425

class inheritance, 425

COBOL, 428

code, 420

compiler, 427

computer-aided software engineering (CASE) tool, 415

computer program, 420

computer scientist, 405

condition statement, 424

control flow, 421

conversion, 417

data member, 425

debugger, 435

decision support system, 409

development, 416

direct conversion, 417

executable file, 421

expert system, 410

extranet, 411

FORTRAN, 428

fourth-generation language (4GL), 429

function, 422

goto statement, 423

hardware maintenance technician, 407

higher-level language, 427

implementation, 417

inference engine, 410

information system, 404

instantiated, 426

intranet, 411

IS department, 405

Java, 429

knowledge base, 410

logic error, 435

loops, 424

machine language, 427

maintenance, 418

member function (method), 425

message, 427

needs analysis, 412

network manager, 406

object, 423

object-oriented programming (OOP), 423

off-the-shelf application, 408

outsourcing, 407

parallel conversion, 417

Pascal, 429

phased conversion, 417

pilot conversion, 417

portable, 428

procedure, 422

programmer, 405

prototype, 415

purchasing agent, 406

routine, 422

source file, 427

structured programming, 423

subclass, 425

subroutine, 422

syntax error, 435

system manager, 406

systems analyst, 405

systems design, 414

systems development life cycle (SDLC), 412

technical documentation, 416

technical writer, 406

top-down design, 415

trainer, 407

transaction, 409

user assistance architect, 405

user documentation, 416

variable, 422

Visual Basic, 430

KEY TERM QUIZ

Fill in the missing word with one of the terms listed in Key Terms.

1. The people responsible for defining the goals and issues of a new information system are called _____.

2. When freelance workers or outside companies are hired for a project rather than full-time employees, the practice is known as _____.

3. The _____ in a company is responsible for creating and maintaining information systems.

4. New software is typically created by teams of _____.

5. An _____ is designed to automate the analysis of data in a specific area.

6. The order in which program statements are executed is called program _____.

7. A collection of instructions or statements that can be understood and carried out by the computer's CPU is called a _____.

8. Beginners who want to implement algorithms often find _____ an easy language to learn.

9. An If-Else selection structure is a _____.

10. Repetition structures are also called _____.

REVIEW QUESTIONS

1. What is an information system? What does one consist of?

2. What primary factor contributed to ending the isolation of information systems departments from the rest of a company's operations?

3. Describe briefly the general duties of the systems analyst.

4. What is the primary responsibility of the system or network manager?

5. List and describe the five types of specialized information systems.

6. Define a computer program.

7. What does a computer do when it launches a program?

8. Describe what an algorithm is and how it is used in programming.

9. Define an object.

10. What primary characteristic distinguishes programming languages as higher-level languages?

DISCUSSION QUESTIONS

1. Discuss the issues addressed during the needs analysis phase of an SDLC. What are the biggest challenges during this phase?

2. Suppose that a company is developing a system for tracking the important details of a variety of warranties that cover products returned for repair by customers. Depending on the product, some warranties cover parts only, some labor only, and others parts and labor for different time periods. During the systems design phase, which type of design, top-down or bottom-up, do you think the project team should use to approach the task?

3. Do you think it would be easier to write programs with a structured or an object-oriented programming language? Which language would allow you to recycle instructions to build applications?

4. Create a flowchart for a program that replaces all occurrences of a particular word in a document with a graphic.

The following exercises assume that you have access to the Internet and a browser. If you need help with any of the exercises, visit the book's Web site at **www.glencoe.com/norton/online**. This book's Web site also lists the URLs you need to complete many of these exercises.

1. Employment opportunities for IS personnel are an ever-increasing market. Some of the many jobs available include system analysts, programmers, and system or network managers. There are several job-posting and placement Web sites, where you can find many job openings for these skilled professions. Visit these three job-related sites:

■ NationsJob Network listing of computer software and systems job openings

■ Digital Station

■ EDP Professionals

Can you find any IS-related job openings in your geographic area, or in another where you would be interested in living? Write down your findings and share them with the class.

2. An excellent online example of an expert system is the Microsoft Knowledge Base, which can be accessed at the Microsoft Web site. (Choose the Support option; then register for online technical support. This takes only a moment and is free.) Using this expert system, you can describe a problem with a Microsoft product (for example, "cannot generate a table of contents"). The system returns at least one possible cure for the problem. Visit the Microsoft Knowledge Base and try to get an answer to a problem related to a Microsoft product. What type of response did you get from the system?

3. A great deal of information relating to programming is available from the Internet. Locate Web pages devoted to the following products:

■ JavaBeans

■ Visual J

■ Visual C++

■ Visual Basic

■ COBOL

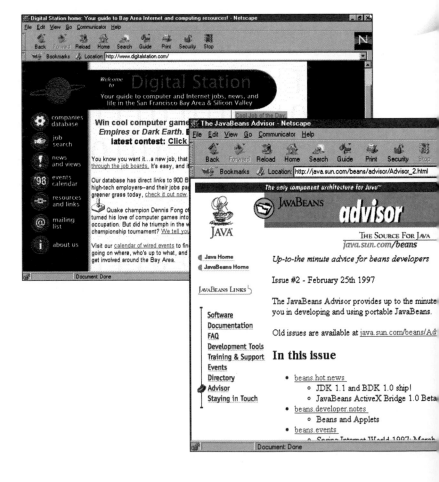

4. Many application developers have switched to object-oriented programming. One reason for this is the availability of object libraries that speed up development time and reduce design time. Use the Web to locate three companies that distribute object libraries.

5. Because systems development can be a time-consuming and expensive process, many organizations outsource their system development projects to consultants. Using your favorite search engine, locate at least three companies that provide systems development services. These services can include both information systems development and software development. Can you find at least one such company in your geographic area?

6. If you want to learn to do any type of programming, there are many resources to help you, including hundreds of books. Visit an online bookstore, such as Amazon.com or Barnes & Noble and search for titles related to programming. Can you find any books that teach programming skills in an area that interests you, such as Java programming or BASIC programming?

7. If you want to start learning to program right away, there are several hands-on tutorials for programming languages on the Web. Visit these tutorial sites:

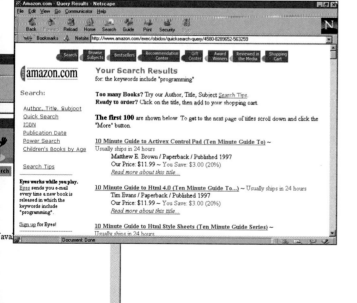

- The Java Tutorial
- The CGI Tutorial
- The HTML Tutorials

How helpful did you find these sites to be? Did you come away knowing more about programming than you did before? How do you think such online tutorials compare to learning from a book or in a class?

Living with Computers

CONTENTS

OBJECTIVES

When you complete this chapter, you will be able to do the following:

- List three basic ways to ensure that a computer workspace is ergonomically correct.
- Name two ways obsolete computer systems can negatively affect the environment and describe solutions to these problems.
- Define the term "software piracy" and explain why it is illegal.
- List two strategies being used to combat software piracy.
- Name two ways in which computer viruses can be transmitted and list at least three ways viruses can harm a computer system.
- List two types of damage caused by computer hackers and two methods used by network administrators to protect their networks from hackers.
- Define the terms "spamming" and "spoofing," and list two measures that computer users can take to avoid being victimized by junk e-mailers.
- List four reasons why a corporation might want to monitor employees' use of its computer systems.
- Name two ethical issues currently being debated in the fields of computing and the Internet.

It may be hard to believe that a computer can pose a threat to its user, but think of the caution people must exercise when using any other appliance or tool. We carefully choose the television programs that children watch, to ensure that they don't view inappropriate programs. When operating a vehicle, we are cautious to protect not only ourselves but those around us, as well.

An ever-growing number of professional and personal activities requires people to interact with computers—to live and work in **cyberspace**, an electronic frontier where data is stored, processed, and moved through vast data communications networks. As computers take on an ever-increasing role in our lives, we must learn to adapt to them.

This adaptation, however, means more than developing the skills required to use computers. Those skills—as basic as typing, or as complex as programming—are just one part of the equation. Computer users also must be aware of other aspects of computing, not just to ensure success with them but to protect themselves from the dangers that have become such a prevalent part of working and playing in cyberspace.

Like many other tools, the computer should be treated with respect and users should consider both the advantages and disadvantages that come with it. Although the computer can help people be more productive, and even provide a source of income or entertainment, certain risks are also inherent. Overuse may cause physical injuries. Carelessness online can invite viruses or even criminals. Junk e-mail is an increasing drain on resources and privacy. As users continually upgrade software and hardware, electrical usage rises and landfill space shrinks.

This chapter focuses on some of the practical, physical, environmental, and ethical issues involved in computer use. These are issues that affect computer users every day, whether they work with computers in business or use them at home or school.

ERGONOMICS AND HEALTH ISSUES

Much is being done to make computers easier, safer, and more comfortable to use. **Ergonomics**, the study of the physical relationship between people and their tools—such as their computers—addresses these issues.

Any office worker will tell you that sitting at a desk all day can become very uncomfortable. Sitting all day and using a computer can be even worse. Not only does the user's body ache from being in a chair too long, but wrist injuries can result from keyboarding for long periods of time or eyes can become strained by staring at a monitor. Thanks to the publicity these problems have received over the years, most people now recognize the importance of ergonomically designed computer furniture and proper techniques for using the computer.

Choosing the Right Chair

An important piece of ergonomic computer furniture is a good, comfortable chair like the ones shown in Figure 12.1.

You can avoid fatigue and strain by choosing the proper furniture. Look for three characteristics in any office chair: adjustable height, lower-back support, and arm rests. The chairs shown in the figure also feature adjustable arm rests. Your desk should also hold your keyboard and mouse at the proper height. Make sure that your desk has a built-in keyboard shelf; this helps you keep your arms parallel to the floor while typing, instead of reaching upward for the keyboard.

Figure 12.1
Ergonomic chairs.

Preventing Repetitive Stress Injuries

Office workers have been demanding comfortable chairs for a long time. The field of ergonomics, however, did not receive much attention until **repetitive stress injuries (RSIs)**—a group of ailments caused by continually using the body in ways it was not designed to work—began appearing among clerical personnel who spend most of their time entering data on computer keyboards. One injury that is especially well documented among these workers is **carpal tunnel syndrome**, a wrist or hand injury caused by extended periods of keyboarding.

The carpal tunnel is a passageway in the wrist through which a bundle of nerves passes. In carpal tunnel syndrome, the tunnel becomes misshapen because the victim has held the wrists stiffly for long periods, as people tend to do at a keyboard. When the tunnel becomes distorted, it can pinch the nerves that run through it, causing numbness, pain, or an inability to use the hands. Carpal tunnel syndrome is the best-known repetitive stress injury. It can become so debilitating that employees suffering from it have to take weeks or even months off work.

According to the Occupational Safety and Health Administration (OSHA), in 1993 alone, American companies paid more than $20 billion in worker's

NORTON Online

For more information about **repetitive stress injuries**, visit this book's Web site at **www.glencoe.com/norton/online**

compensation claims resulting from repetitive stress injuries. That year, nearly three million claims were made.

Several solutions have been proposed to make working at a keyboard more comfortable and to help prevent carpal tunnel syndrome. The first is to set the keyboard at a proper height. When setting up their computer systems, most people just put their keyboards on their desks. The problem is that most desks are too high for good keyboard placement. Ideally, your hands should be at the same height as your elbows, or several inches lower,

▶ **Figure 12.2**
Using a wrist support.

when they hover above the keyboard. To solve this ergonomic problem, many computer desks are slightly lower than traditional desks. Others are equipped with retractable shelves that position the keyboard at the correct height.

Another solution to wrist fatigue is to use a wrist support. The support can be built onto the keyboard or just placed in front of it, as shown in Figure 12.2. A wrist support allows you to rest your hands comfortably when not keyboarding. Remember, however, that you should never rest your wrists on anything—even a comfortable wrist support—when you are actually keyboarding. Use the support only when your fingers are not moving over the keyboard.

▶ The split layout of this keyboard allows the user's wrists to remain relaxed because the hands remain in line with the forearms.

One designer, Tony Hodges, realized that a flat keyboard is not well suited to the shape of our hands. After all, if you relax your arms, your thumbs tend to point up. Logically, then, keyboards should be designed with two sides, one for each hand. Hodges created just such a keyboard. Other manufacturers have followed his lead and designed ergonomic keyboards that allow the user's hands to rest in a more natural position. Many of these keyboards are fixed so that the user's hands must remain in one position; other designs actually break the keyboard into two or more separate parts, which the user can adjust for a customized fit.

A final solution is behavioral. You should take frequent breaks during an extended work period at a computer. Get up, walk around, stretch in your chair, and change positions frequently.

Protecting Your Eyes

Another area of ergonomic concern is protecting people's vision. Staring at a computer screen for long periods can strain or even injure the eyes. Many users have found their vision deteriorating as a result of prolonged computer use. In fact, eyestrain is the most frequently reported health problem associated with computers.

If looking at the screen for fewer hours is not an option, here are some ways to reduce eyestrain:

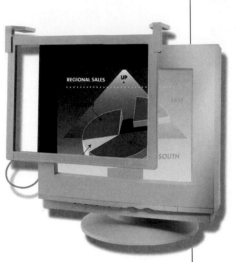

Anti-glare screens cut down on light reflecting off the surface of the monitor, so they are useful in bright offices or where there is a window that faces the monitor.

- Avoid staring at the screen for long stretches of time. Maintaining your focus at the same distance for long periods tends to distort the shape of your eye's lens.

- Remember to blink. It may seem strange, but studies indicate that people blink less often than normal when focusing at a fixed point for long periods of time. This causes dryness of the eye and eyestrain.

- Position your monitor between 2 and 2.5 feet away from your eyes. This is close enough for you to see everything on the screen but far enough away to let your eyes take in the whole screen at once.

- Try to position your monitor so that no bright lights, including sunlight, reflect off the screen. If you cannot avoid reflections, get an anti-glare screen. Also, keep your screen clean.

- When shopping for a monitor, remember that most people prefer a relatively large screen (at least 14 inches, measured diagonally). A small screen encourages you to get too close.

- Look for a monitor that holds a steady image without appearing to pulsate or flicker. Make sure that the dot pitch is no greater than .28 mm, and the refresh rate is at least 72 Hz.

Electromagnetic Fields

Electromagnetic fields (EMFs) are created during the generation, transmission, and use of low-frequency electrical power. These fields exist near power lines, electrical appliances, and any piece of equipment that has an electric motor. Currently, there is no convincing evidence to link EMFs with cancer. There is enough data, however, to raise suspicion. Given the pervasiveness of EMFs in our homes and workplaces, the issue cannot be ignored.

EMFs are composed of an electrical and a magnetic component. Of the two, the magnetic field is the one that raises the health concern. Electrical fields lose strength when they come in contact with barriers such as clothing and skin. A magnetic field, however, will penetrate most materials, even concrete or lead.

Populations deemed to be at greatest risk include children, pregnant women, and anyone who spends many working hours near a piece of electrical equipment. This latter category, of course, includes many computer users.

Magnetic fields lose strength rapidly with distance. Options to reduce your risk from EMFs include:

- Taking frequent breaks away from the computer.
- Sitting at arm's length away from the terminal.
- Using a monitor with a liquid crystal display (LCD), which does not radiate EMFs.

NORTON Online

For more information on **EMFs and health**, visit this book's Web site at **www.glencoe.com/norton/online**

Productivity Tip

Tips for Healthy Computing

Each year, thousands of people suffer repetitive stress injuries believed to be caused by computer use. Although they may sound like minor ailments, RSIs can be serious, even crippling. Severe cases of carpal tunnel syndrome, for example, have been known to end their victims' careers.

Even so, there is still much debate over whether RSIs can actually be attributed to computer use. Some companies and insurers are resisting claims that such injuries are job-related, saying that RSIs can be caused by a number of non-job-related activities, such as pushing a lawn mower or playing sports. Therefore, if you develop an RSI, there is no guarantee that your employer will agree with your claim that the injury is a result of your job or computer use.

No matter who is right on that issue, prevention is the best course of action. If you use a computer frequently, you can avoid RSIs by taking a few precautions, adjusting your workspace, and adopting good habits.

Choose a good chair and computer desk. Look for a chair that provides back support and armrests. The chair should have adjustable height. Your computer desk should hold the keyboard at a height that is level with or slightly below your hands, and the desk should allow you to change the keyboard's height. You should not have to reach up, forward, or down to touch the keyboard.

Make sure your workspace is ergonomically correct. Set up your computer and chair so that your forearms and thighs are parallel to the floor when you type. This may require you to raise or lower your chair and your keyboard.

Position your monitor correctly. Place your monitor directly in front of you, about 2 to 2.5 feet away, and a little below eye level. Tilt the monitor's face upward, about 10 degrees. This will enable you to view the monitor comfortably without bending your neck.

Sit up straight. Do not slouch as you type, and keep your feet flat on the floor in front of you. Do not cross your legs in front of you or under your chair for long periods of time.

Keep your wrists straight. Your hands should be in a straight line with your forearms as you type, when viewed either from above or from the side. If you keep your wrists bent in either direction, you can cause muscle fatigue and increase your risk of carpal tunnel or tendon injuries.

Do not rest your wrists on anything as you type. If you have a wrist support, use it only when you are resting your hands, not as you are actually typing. Resting the wrist while typing disables the forearms from moving the hands, and puts undue strain on the hands and fingers. Think of a pianist; pianists do not rest their wrists on anything as they play, and they keep their wrists straight.

Be gentle. Avoid pounding the keys or gripping the mouse too tightly. They do not require much pressure to operate.

Rest your eyes occasionally. Eyestrain develops from staring at a fixed distance for too long. Even if you cannot get up, look around you and focus on different objects at various distances. Close your eyes for a minute or so and let them relax.

Set your monitor for healthy viewing. Even if your monitor can operate at very high resolution (Super VGA, 1024 x 768 resolution, for example), this does not mean it's the best setting for your eyes. At higher resolutions, text and icons appear smaller on the screen, and can lead to squinting and eyestrain. If you find yourself straining to read your monitor, try lowering the resolution or changing the color setting.

Take frequent breaks. Get up and move around, and stretch occasionally during the day.

An example of an ergonomically correct computer setup. The forearms and thighs are parallel to the floor, the keyboard is in easy reach without bending or flexing the wrists, and the monitor is positioned to reduce eye and neck strain.

When typing, your hands should be in a straight line with your forearms at all times, when viewed from any angle. A split keyboard layout can help maintain the proper position.

COMPUTERS AND THE ENVIRONMENT

The sheer number of computers in homes and businesses today means that they must have a considerable impact on the environment. The environmental concerns include planned obsolescence and the use of power.

Planned Obsolescence

NORTON Online
For information on **computer recycling**, visit this book's Web site at www.glencoe.com/norton/online

A computer system that is bought today will be obsolete in, at most, two to three years. During that period of time, you may need to upgrade several parts of the machine, such as memory, the battery (in the case of a portable computer), or software. Compare that computer to a typewriter, which lasted a decade or more with occasional servicing and a change of ribbon, and the effect on the environment is obvious.

For example, every software release is accompanied by computer manuals, sales brochures, junk mailings, and computer books. Every time that software is updated, the disks, manuals, and books from the previous release can end up in a landfill.

As computers become faster, software is produced to take advantage of each increase in power. The introduction of new operating systems has had a particularly noticeable impact on the volume of discarded hardware and software. The migration to Windows 95, for example, caused some companies to buy new hard drives, throw out older machines, and acquire 32-bit versions of all the software they use on a regular basis.

Every year billions of dollars worth of obsolete hardware and software are thrown away.

Reducing the environmental impact is easier with software than with hardware. Already, much software is available online. Soon, you may be downloading virtually all new applications from the Internet rather than buying them (and their packaging) in a store. Windows 98, for example, features an automatic update capability, which enables the user to download operating system enhancements over the Internet.

In addition, documentation is now frequently viewed online rather than in hard copy. Even if you have old manuals, you generally can recycle them with the rest of your office paper.

Getting rid of old hardware is a little trickier. You should not throw old computers into the garbage, because many of them contain nickel-cadmium (nicad) batteries, and cadmium is a toxic heavy metal. To address this problem, some hardware manufacturers have begun programs to collect and properly dispose of old computers. Some companies now donate their old computers to nonprofit organizations, which can use them because they often do not need the latest technological advances to stay competitive. The donors get tax write-offs for their generosity, the recipients get usable computers, and the environment gets a nice break.

Use of Power

Another environmental concern relating to computers is a direct result of how we use them. If you visit a typical office, you will find many computers running but not being used. If you come back to the same office at night, you might find all the computers still on. In some cases, leaving computers running is justified because employees use modems to access their systems at night, and some automatic backup systems are used only at night. In other cases, the problem is old-fashioned computer wisdom that says it is cheaper and less damaging to leave the computer running than to turn it on and off every day.

The newest solution to energy consumption is using monitors, printers, and CPUs sporting the Energy Star logo. The logo indicates that the equipment meets standards set by the U.S. Environmental Protection Agency's Energy Star program. When this equipment is unused for a set number of minutes, it automatically reduces its power consumption. Some operating system software, such as Windows 95/98, also can be used to control the energy use of hardware. Windows 95/98 can stop your system's hard drive and power down the monitor after a specified period of non-use.

NORTON Online

For information on the **Energy Star program**, visit this book's Web site at www.glencoe.com/norton/online

The Energy Star logo tells you that the equipment has been designed to reduce power consumption, especially when the device has been left on but is not being used.

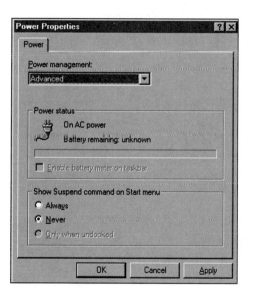

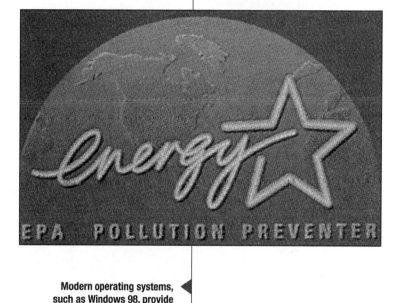

Modern operating systems, such as Windows 98, provide users with some control over the power usage of their systems.

COMPUTER CRIME

Not all computer-related problems are of a physical nature, occurring outside the machine. Many of the most troublesome computer-related problems actually originate within the machine—or, more significantly, within cyberspace.

The Internet has been compared to a big and rapidly growing city. As it attracts more people to work and play, it also attracts online predators who seek to prey on others. The profusion of online hooligans has led to myriad problems for typical computer users, including invasions of privacy, the spread of viruses, theft, e-mail abuse, and more. Even offline, computer users are threatened by the spread of viruses, and software companies lose millions each year because of software piracy.

Many events that occur in cyberspace are not addressed by the traditional body of law. For example, physical location has always been a fundamental concept in law: different laws govern according to the jurisdiction of community, state, or country. In cyberspace, however, physical location is not always relevant, so it is difficult to determine which laws govern certain transactions. Suppose, for example, that someone in Paris downloads an interesting short story from a computer in New York. He then distributes copies of the story to several friends. Has that person broken the law if the material is protected by copyright in the United States, even if it is the public domain in France?

To deal with questions like these, our legal system is currently developing or redefining the laws that govern the ownership of software and data, trespassing, and sabotage. This is the first step toward civilizing cyberspace—the creation of a standard set of rules by which acceptable behavior can be maintained.

Government officials and legal professionals, however, are finding it extremely difficult to define laws that deal with the intangible issues most prevalent in computing today. A good example is the question of **intellectual property**—that is, the ownership of ideas. As ideas are exchanged by the thousand and spread over the Internet, governments are hard-pressed to find clear-cut ways to protect (and in many cases, even to define) intellectual property rights.

As you use a computer, either alone, in an organization, or on the Internet, be aware that the programs, documents, images, and even ideas you encounter are probably the property of someone else.

Using the Internet, you can obtain documents from host computers all over the world. Therefore, it is possible to download files that are protected by the copyright laws of the U.S. but not by the laws of the country where the host computer is located. Similarly, you can upload a document to the Internet, and while it is protected under U.S. law, users in other countries may be able to copy the document and use it without violating any laws in their country.

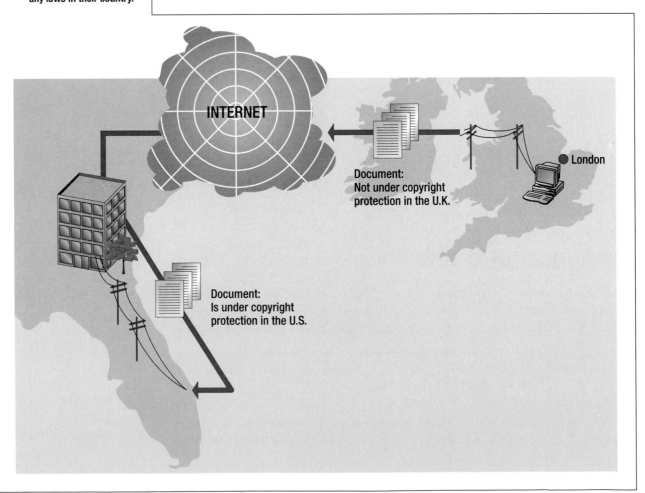

INTERNET

Document:
Not under copyright
protection in the U.K.

London

Document:
Is under copyright
protection in the U.S.

Software Piracy

The biggest legal problem affecting the computer industry is **software piracy**, which is the illegal copying or use of programs. Piracy is a huge problem because it is so easy to do. In most cases, it is no more difficult to steal a program than it is to tape a music CD that you have borrowed from a friend. Software pirates give up the right to receive upgrades and technical support, but they gain the use of the program without paying for it. Many **commercial software** programs—software you must purchase before using—cost as little as $20 to $50, but most applications cost between $100 and $500. Highly specialized or complex applications can cost several thousand dollars.

NORTON Online

For more information on **software piracy**, visit this book's Web site at www.glencoe.com/norton/online

Even **shareware**—software you can use for free on a trial basis and then register and pay for if you decide to use it—suffers from a high piracy rate. Each year, thousands of computer users install shareware programs and use them with no intention of registering or paying for them.

In May, 1997, the Software Publisher's Association reported that software publishers lost more than $11 billion worldwide because of software piracy in 1996. The report also estimates that in 1996, nearly half of all applications used by businesses were pirated copies.

Piracy is not a significant problem for publishers of **freeware**. Freeware is software that is available free of charge and that can be copied and distributed by anyone. Freeware publishers usually require that users not change any of the program's files before distributing the program to other users; freeware publishers also restrict other persons from charging a fee for distributing a freeware program, or including the program in a package being sold commercially for profit. Many useful freeware programs are available, and many can be downloaded from special Internet sites (such as SHAREWARE.COM and TUCOWS), which serve as clearinghouses for shareware and freeware products.

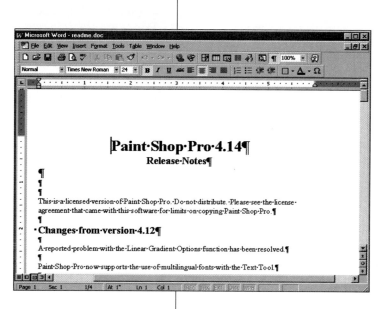

This is a portion of a README file from PaintShop Pro, a popular program that is available in both commercial and shareware forms. README files often define shareware and explain how the user can try out the software, distribute it to other users, and register it.

Software is pirated in many ways. The simplest method is to copy the software from its original floppy disks or compact disk. Users on a network can easily copy certain types of software directly from the server, or even exchange programs over their organization's e-mail system. The Internet has become the biggest hotbed of piracy, however, as pirates distribute programs by mail, across rogue sites on the World Wide Web, on FTP servers, and in newsgroups. Certain newsgroups—most notably the **Warez news groups**—have become notorious for blatantly posting entire operating systems, beta software, upgrades, and commercial applications for anyone to download and use.

Copyright Laws Regarding Software

The principal law governing software piracy is still the Copyright Act of 1976. In 1983, a Software Piracy and Counterfeiting Amendment was added. More recently, commercial software piracy was elevated from a misdemeanor to a felony.

The justification for these laws is that software is an intellectual property, usually created for the purpose of making money. Commercial software firms range in size from a single, self-employed programmer to huge corporations like IBM and Microsoft. Creating a complex program is an expensive process that can take highly trained programmers thousands of hours. The laws against software piracy were created to protect the interests and investments of these software developers.

Protections from Piracy

Part of the reason that piracy is so difficult to stop is that some kinds of copying are legal, a fact that tempts some people to gloss over the distinctions. For example, it is generally legal to copy software that you own so that you have a backup copy in case your original is damaged. In fact, installing a new piece of software means copying the program disks to your computer's hard disk. After the program is installed, however, you are generally reminded of its copyrighted status each time you start it, as shown in Figure 12.3.

Copyright notice

Figure 12.3

A splash screen, which appears each time this program is started. Many commercial and shareware programs automatically display such screens (sometimes called "nag screens") to remind the user of copyright and trademark information and to encourage unregistered users to register their software.

In the past, software companies manufactured their programs with safeguards that prevented illegal copying but made installation and backup difficult. For example, program disks were set up such that they could be copied to the purchaser's hard disk only a few times. Most companies found that this kind of **copy protection** caused more problems than it solved.

True copy protection is still used occasionally, but other antipiracy schemes are more common. One is to require that a password be entered the first time a program is installed. The password is recorded on the installation diskettes, so subsequent installations require the same password to be entered. This scheme can work well, but it cannot be used with programs sold on CD-ROM because the password cannot be recorded on the CD. A similar scheme is to print a code or serial number on the packaging in which the CD-ROM is sold. Anyone who does not have the original packaging, or who has not received the code or serial number from the original owner, cannot install the software. On the other hand, you cannot easily copy a CD-ROM and give it to a friend (unless you want to invest in a CD-R system), so piracy of CD-ROM-based software is less of a problem.

Some software publishers allow the purchaser to install the program without a password but require the purchaser to contact the publisher and obtain a password within a given time period. For example, some programs can be installed without a password but can be used only a limited number of times before they become inoperable and must be reinstalled. To avoid this, the user must contact the publisher, demonstrate proof of purchase, and obtain a password for the software.

None of these anti-piracy schemes is completely secure. Consequently, many software developers simply rely on the law and on people's respect for the law. They hope that most of their customers have sufficient integrity not to copy programs illegally.

FileMaker Pro Installation

Even if piracy cannot be stopped before it happens, there is an increasing movement by software publishers to catch pirates after the fact. Organizations like the Software Publishers Association and Business Software Alliance—which represent software developers of all types and sizes—not only lobby lawmakers for tougher antipiracy laws but also take proactive steps to stop pirates. The organizations offer rewards to persons who report pirates or acts of piracy, help businesses perform voluntary software audits, and work with law enforcement officials to conduct involuntary audits.

Many programs require you to provide a password, special code, or serial number during installation. This reduces piracy to a certain extent; would-be users who do not have the required information cannot install the software.

Ads such as this one from a computer magazine warn of the consequences of software piracy.

Network Versions and Site Licenses

Businesses and organizations are the biggest purchasers of computer hardware and software. As a result, the greatest potential loss of revenue caused by piracy is from their abuse of the copyright laws.

The temptation is significant. Imagine that you are a high school teacher in charge of a laboratory of 25 computers. You want your students to learn Lotus 1-2-3 but your school cannot afford to buy the software at several hundred dollars per copy for each computer. What do you do? Buy a single copy of the software and load it onto every computer? Your cause might be a noble one, but you could still get into serious trouble with the law.

Software companies recognize this temptation, as well as the costs associated with equipping multiple computers in an organization with the same application. They have developed two solutions based on volume discount—site licenses and network licenses. A **site license** is an agreement through which a purchaser buys the right to use a program on a given number of machines for less than the price of buying a separate copy of the program for each computer. Organizations that have many computers but no network generally opt for this solution.

The **network license** is based on the same principle as the site license but is intended for networked machines. The company buys a network license for commonly used applications and then loads these applications onto the network server.

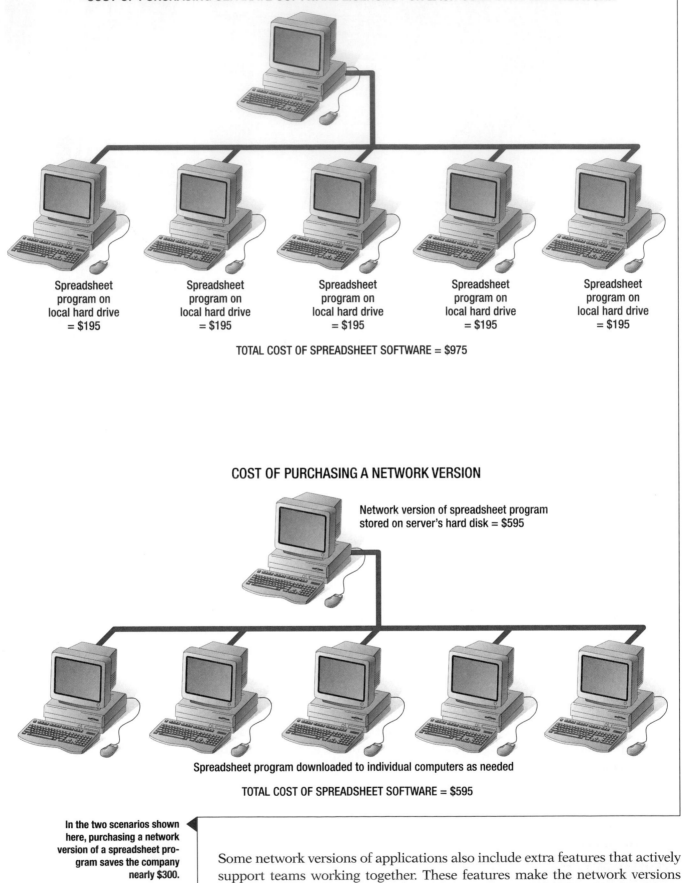

COST OF PURCHASING SEPARATE SOFTWARE LICENSES FOR EACH COMPUTER ON A NETWORK

Spreadsheet program on local hard drive = $195

Spreadsheet program on local hard drive = $195

Spreadsheet program on local hard drive = $195

Spreadsheet program on local hard drive = $195

Spreadsheet program on local hard drive = $195

TOTAL COST OF SPREADSHEET SOFTWARE = $975

COST OF PURCHASING A NETWORK VERSION

Network version of spreadsheet program stored on server's hard disk = $595

Spreadsheet program downloaded to individual computers as needed

TOTAL COST OF SPREADSHEET SOFTWARE = $595

In the two scenarios shown here, purchasing a network version of a spreadsheet program saves the company nearly $300.

Some network versions of applications also include extra features that actively support teams working together. These features make the network versions more attractive than a pirated single-user copy distributed over the network.

Software Forgeries

Sharing software illegally with friends or within a company is one issue. Blatant forgery with the intent to sell is another problem altogether. This concept is similar to selling clothes or leather goods as designer labels when they are really cheap imitations. Copying software, however, is far easier than copying designer clothing.

Although aggressive new treaties are forcing some countries to ensure more protection against pirating and forging of software, forgery is big business in some parts of the world, most notably Europe and Asia. In many countries, software products and other types of intellectual property do not enjoy the same copyright or trademark protection as other types of products.

No publisher is immune from forgeries and black-market sales. Software giant Microsoft provides an excellent example. In 1995 and 1996, as the Windows 95 operating system was being developed and tested for commercial release, black marketers in Asia were busily making illegal duplicates of the Windows 95 beta software and selling the copies to anyone who would purchase them. (**Beta software** is software that is in the developmental stage and not ready for commercial sale. Publishers often provide copies of beta software to independent testers and other software developers, who work with the program to find bugs and test for compatibility with other products. Beta software is usually protected by strict contractual agreements between the publisher and beta testers, who agree never to copy or distribute the software.) Even though Microsoft later created international versions of the operating system for sale in Asia, the company lost an unknown number of sales due to the black-market activities.

Forged software can look uncannily like the original product.

Computer Viruses

Although software piracy is by far the most prevalent computer crime, for many users the creation of a computer virus is perhaps a more disturbing crime. A virus, as you may recall, is a parasitic program buried within another legitimate program or stored in a special area of a disk called the *boot sector*. Executing the legitimate program or accessing the disk activates the virus without the user's knowledge.

Viruses can be programmed to carry out the following tasks, as well as many others:

- Copy themselves to other programs
- Display information on the screen
- Destroy data files
- Erase an entire hard disk
- Lie dormant for a specified time or until a given condition is met and then become active

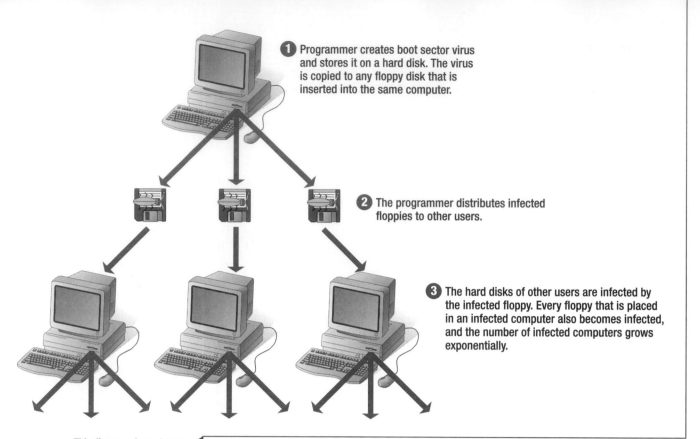

① Programmer creates boot sector virus and stores it on a hard disk. The virus is copied to any floppy disk that is inserted into the same computer.

② The programmer distributes infected floppies to other users.

③ The hard disks of other users are infected by the infected floppy. Every floppy that is placed in an infected computer also becomes infected, and the number of infected computers grows exponentially.

This diagram shows how a boot sector virus spreads from a single computer to many computers via an infected floppy disk. Viruses also can spread from one machine to another across computer networks and can be distributed over the Internet and online services.

The Birth of Viruses

As far back as the 1950s, computer scientists first discussed the possibility of software capable of replicating itself and spreading among computers. But, an actual software virus was not created until 1983, when a student at the University of California, Fred Cohen, wrote a doctoral dissertation on the subject.

Unlike the viruses that cause colds and diseases in humans, computer viruses do not occur naturally—each one must be programmed. There are no beneficial viruses. Sometimes, they are written as a prank, perhaps to needle people by displaying a humorous message. In such cases, the virus is little more than a nuisance. However, when a virus does real damage, who knows the purpose behind it? Anger? Revenge? Intellectual challenge? Whatever the motivation, it is clear that people creating viruses do not have much respect for other people's hard work.

Preventing Infection

Until viruses can be eradicated at their source—that is, until there comes a day when they are no longer written—users will need to protect their computers from viruses. Fortunately, safeguarding a system against viruses is not difficult, given a little knowledge and some handy utility software. The first thing you need to know is when your system is in danger of infection.

There are two common ways to pick up a virus:

1_ Receiving a disk (a diskette, a CD created by someone with a CD-R system, a removable hard disk, and so on) from another user. In this case, the virus could be in the boot sector of the disk or in an executable file (a program) on the disk.

2_ Downloading an executable file from another user, an online service, or the Internet.

Even programs purchased in shrink-wrapped packages from a reputable store have been known to harbor viruses. The best precaution is to treat all disks as potential carriers of infection.

Checking for viruses requires **antivirus software**, which scans disks and programs for known viruses and eradicates them. Figure 12.4 shows an antivirus program at work.

Most antivirus programs are easy to use. After it is installed on your system and activated, a good antivirus program checks for infected files automatically every time you insert any kind of disk or use your modem to retrieve a file. A few antivirus programs can even scan files as you download them from the Internet and can instantly alert you when you download an infected file. Several excellent antivirus programs are available, and some are even free. Some common antivirus programs are:

▶ **Figure 12.4**
McAfee VirusScan, one of several popular antivirus programs, at work. The program lets you choose which disk or directories to scan for viruses and then reports its findings. If a virus is found, the program can walk you through the process of eradicating it from the disk.

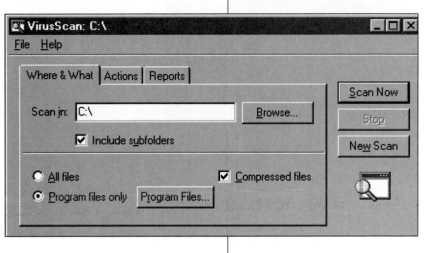

- McAfee VirusScan
- IBM AntiVirus
- Dr. Solomon's Anti-Virus
- Symantec Antivirus for the Macintosh
- Norton Antivirus
- VIrex
- Disinfectant

A note of caution: New viruses are constantly appearing, so no program can offer absolute protection against them all. However, virus utilities are constantly being updated to handle these new viruses. You can purchase subscriptions to receive the newest versions of the utilities automatically, or you can purchase the latest version every year or so. Some antivirus software vendors—such as McAfee, Symantec, and IBM—allow registered users to download updates to their programs over the Internet.

Hardware Theft

The crimes relating to software piracy and virus creation are well-known and publicized. Software, however, is not the only part of the computer that is vulnerable. Simple burglary is also a problem.

Although hardware theft has been going on for years, the problem was not particularly serious before PCs came along—it is a little difficult to make off with a mainframe. However, the introduction of the microcomputer in the 1970s made valuable equipment much easier to move. The problem has skyrocketed with the popularity of small portable computers. When powerful microcomputers worth several thousand dollars can be folded down to the size of a pad of paper and then slipped into a briefcase, it is not surprising that they occasionally disappear.

Expensive notebook and laptop computers are now the most common objects of hardware theft, but they are not the only ones. Company-owned desktop computers are frequently stolen, as are peripheral devices such as printers and modems. Parts manufacturers are at risk as much as individual companies. A truckload of computer chips can be worth more than its weight in gold.

Many schools, businesses, and other organizations now secure their computer equipment with steel cables like the one shown in Figure 12.5. Even relatively inexpensive items such as keyboards are often locked to the desk or to the rest of the computer. If you own a portable computer, or use one of your employer's, never leave it unattended in a public place.

Software products, such as CyberAngel, are now available to help prevent thieves from using stolen computers. CyberAngel protects computers with authorization codes. If a thief steals a computer protected by such software and attempts to use it, CyberAngel locks the computer's modem and ports, and forbids the unauthorized user to access specified programs, folders, and access to online accounts. If the stolen computer's modem is plugged in, CyberAngel can silently dial out to a commercial security system, notifying it of the telephone number from which the computer is dialing. Using this information, security specialists can locate the computer.

Figure 12.5 ◀

Steel cables, similar to those used to secure bicycles, are used to lock computers to desks at many schools and businesses.

Data Theft

In businesses and government, the theft of data can be far more serious than the theft of hardware, which can be replaced fairly easily. Data theft can occur in four ways:

1_ A person with access to the computer where the data is stored can copy the data to a diskette or to some other storage device.

2_ Someone can steal the storage device or media on which the data is stored.

3_ Someone can steal the whole system—the computer and its built-in hard disk.

4_ Someone can use a modem to enter an organization's computer system, gain access to sensitive files, and download them.

Valuable Data on Portable Computers

Once again, the advent of portable computers has contributed greatly to the problem of data theft. As users become accustomed to the convenience of carrying their computers with them wherever they go, they also may be jeopardizing the security of the data stored on their machines.

There are reports of thieves earning as much as $10,000 for stealing a portable computer from a corporate executive. The motive in such cases is clearly not the computer itself because most portables are not worth even half that amount. Instead, it is the data on the computer's hard disk that is valuable. After all, a company's strategic plans or trade secrets can be worth millions of dollars to its competitors.

Portable computers can be protected by many of the same techniques used for networks, including passwords. Today, many people use their portable computers to access their companies' networks while they are away from the office.

In these cases, the security measures built into the network (including passwords, automatic dial-back, and others) prevent thieves from obtaining valuable information using a stolen laptop.

Hackers

Hackers are experts in computer technology who take great pleasure in solving software problems, frequently by circumventing the established rules. Often, these experts are tempted by the power of their skills and become criminals. They can steal money or crash computer systems intentionally.

Colorful examples of computer crime abound. Using a personal computer, credit card thieves broke into a database at TRW, a company that keeps credit histories, and gained access to the confidential credit records of 90 million people. Using a computer in his bedroom, a 17-year-old high school student broke into AT&T's computer network and stole $1 million worth of software before he was caught. Several employees of an East Coast railroad manipulated data to show that 200 railroad cars had been destroyed, and then they sold the cars.

One scheme devised by hackers is just a computerized twist on the crime of embezzlement, usually from an employer. Computer embezzlers manipulate a company's computerized accounts to divert funds for their own use. For example, a bank embezzler might instruct a computer system to round down all interest payments on customer accounts to two decimal places and then enter the difference into the embezzler's account. Although the amount of each fraudulent transaction always would be minuscule, making that transaction several million times a day would add up to quite a lot of money. FBI records show that, whereas a bank robber steals an average of $1,600 per heist, a computer embezzler steals an average of $600,000.

Often, curious hackers are the ones who catch the criminals. In one celebrated case, a graduate student named Clifford Stoll followed up on a tiny account discrepancy at the Lawrence Berkeley Laboratory. He wound up tracking a computer intruder across international networks and uncovered a high-tech spy ring.

No one really knows the full extent of data theft that is occurring now, in part because companies do not want to admit that their computer systems have been breached. They fear the liability associated with that admission. By some estimates, though, the losses are huge, possibly as much as 5 percent of gross sales in some large companies. For the United States as a whole, a 1994 FBI estimate suggested the losses lie between $164 million and $5 billion. That range is as large as it is because only 1 percent, or less, of computer crime is even *detected*, much less solved.

There is no easy solution to the problem posed by computer crime. Data security is becoming more and more sophisticated, but so are criminals. To illustrate that point to the experts, a Dutch engineer first explained that computers emit TV-like signals that can be reconstructed with standard equipment and displayed. Then, to demonstrate his point, he set up his equipment in a basement and read the data from a PC located on the eighth floor of a neighboring office building.

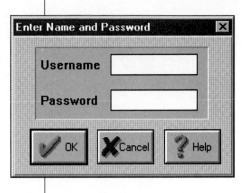

▶ Laptops can be protected with logon screens.

NORTON Online

For more information on the **Electronic Frontier Foundation**, visit this book's Web site at **www.glencoe.com/norton/online**

Although stiff penalties can be imposed to guard against computer crimes, catching the culprits can be extremely difficult, and the methods used to do so sometimes carry their own set of ethical dilemmas. Crackdowns on suspected hackers have occasionally resulted in the arrest and prosecution of people engaged in perfectly legal activities.

For example, after an unexplained, nine-hour crash of AT&T's long-distance network in 1990, Secret Service agents arrested Craig Neidorf, a Georgia college student. Neidorf had once published an illicit copy of a telephone company document in his electronic newsletter as an amusing example of bureaucratic nonsense. Later, the government's case collapsed when it was discovered that the information Neidorf had published could be ordered for about $20.

Organizations Devoted to Computing Issues

Incidents like these alarm people concerned about personal and legal freedoms in the age of electronic communications. One result has been the formation of the **Electronic Frontier Foundation (EFF)**. Two of the EFF's founders are Mitch Kapor, who founded Lotus Development Corporation, and Steve Wozniak, computer wizard and cofounder of Apple Computer.

Since its founding in 1990, EFF has maintained three primary goals: research, policy development, and legal services. In the area of research, EFF strives to understand and keep abreast of developments in the field of computers. In public policy, the EFF advocates laws and policies that promote openness in communications. Finally, EFF devotes a large part of its resources to defending computer users against overzealous law enforcement—the reason for which the EFF was founded.

Protecting Networks

Most companies and government agencies use security measures to limit access to their computer systems. One common method is to provide user identification codes and passwords to authorized employees. Before an employee can **log on**, or access a computer's files, the employee must enter a **user identification code** that identifies that person to the system. Usually, employees also need to enter a **password**, a word or symbol, usually chosen by the user, which verifies the user's identity. If a user's identification code or password does not match the records in the computer's security software, the user is locked out of the system. The screen shown in Figure 12.6 illustrates a typical logon procedure for a network computer system.

Passwords and user ID codes often are used to establish access privileges for employees. These can vary by employee. For example, a network manager

Figure 12.6
Network logon screen.

Enter Network Password

Enter your network password for Microsoft Networking.

User name: john_deol

Password:

Domain: etc_abs_domain

OK   Cancel

could set up access so that top-level employees have access to all directories on the network while other employees have access only to certain data.

Perhaps the most effective form of security is **encryption**, which is a method of encoding and decoding data. Encryption is used most often in messaging systems such as electronic mail. The most common encryption method, known as **DES (Data Encryption Standard)**, can encode a message in more than 72 quadrillion ways. Because a special software key is used to decode the message, unauthorized interception of the message is less of a threat. In many messaging systems, DES encryption takes place without users even knowing it.

Finding a workable encryption standard, however, is proving difficult. There are a number of encryption methods, and a message encrypted by one method may not be capable of being decoded by another. Patents are held on some encryption methods, limiting their availability. Finally, much encryption technology has been developed by governments to protect military data, and as a result, that technology is jealously guarded. In fact, some governments, including the United States, are currently seeking the right to decode private messages sent by company employees if those messages are thought to affect national security.

NORTON
Online
For more
information on
encryption and cryptography,
visit this book's Web site at
www.glencoe.com/norton/online

Currently, debate continues over the U.S. government's policies regarding encryption. Some federal agencies oppose the widespread use of encryption technologies, unless encryption keys are made available to enable agencies to decrypt certain types of files. Many government officials say this is necessary to guard national security and trade secrets, but privacy advocates claim that such policy would enable the government to open and search any file, regardless of its relevance to security or trade.

PRIVACY

Once laws governing cyberspace are established, computer crime becomes relatively easy to define: piracy, theft, and certain types of hacking are simply illegal. However, many legal uses of computer technology are nonetheless still controversial. In fact, legal uses that encroach on individual privacy anger most people more than actual crimes.

The crimes discussed earlier in this chapter are generally perpetrated by individuals, often at the expense of business or government. In this section, the tables are turned. Invasions of privacy are most often carried out by organizations that collect and trade information about individuals.

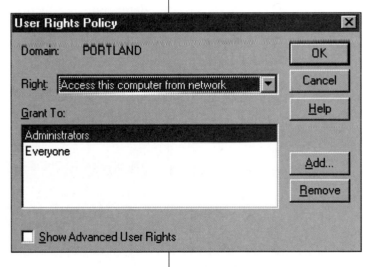

▶ Network software normally allows the network manager to establish access privileges for each individual or group using the network.

When people learn what kinds of data have been gathered about them, they are often outraged. Aren't these practices against the law? Usually, they are not. There is, after all, no explicit constitutional right to privacy. However, such protection may soon be necessary, given the computer's power to collect, organize, and sort data about people, and the power it gives people to contact one another.

Junk Faxes and E-Mail

Junk mail has been an ongoing problem in the 20th century. Each week, most of us find dozens of unsolicited pieces of mail in our mailboxes. As annoying as this problem is, it is for the most part perfectly legal for organizations and individuals to send unsolicited items through the mail. Technological advances, however, have taken the problem from the mailbox at the front door and moved it to the fax machine and computer.

Junk Faxes

During the mid-1980s, as faxes gained popularity in homes and offices, people found their machines printing "junk faxes"—unsolicited and unwanted messages received from unnamed senders. Junk faxes, like junk mail, usually invite the recipient to purchase a product or service, to call a salesperson, or to consider a get-rich-quick scheme of some sort.

Unlike the problem of junk mail, recipients have little recourse with junk faxes. Junk faxes tie up the recipient's resources, including paper, ink, and online time (when the fax is busy receiving an unwanted fax, the recipient cannot use the machine for a legitimate purpose). Further, senders of junk faxes frequently program their machines to send the faxes during business hours and not to include the sender's identification or fax number. These tactics interfere with the normal business use of many busy fax machines and leave the recipient helpless to identify or respond to the sender.

For these reasons, a new law was passed banning unsolicited fax messages. The law will remain in effect until 1999, when lawmakers will revisit it to determine its effectiveness. Meantime, the law prohibits anyone from sending a fax without including an identifier and return phone number.

Junk E-Mail

Junk e-mail, on the other hand, is a problem that is perplexing not only to computer users of all kinds but to lawmakers, as well. Junk e-mail is a lot like

Any user of an Internet or online e-mail service runs the risk of receiving junk e-mail, or spam.

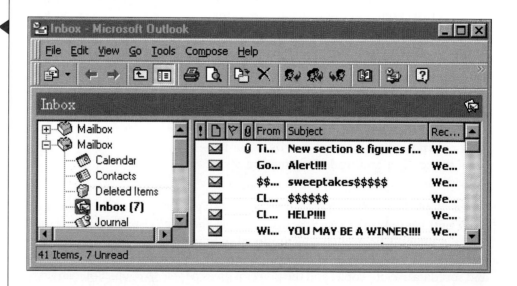

old-fashioned junk mail; that is, you open your electronic mailbox and find that it contains unwanted messages from a variety of senders. Like traditional junk mail, junk e-mail usually includes solicitations to purchase a product or service, but junk e-mail often is filled with lewd—even obscene—material.

NORTON Online

For more information on **spam** and **junk e-mail**, visit this book's Web site at www.glencoe.com/norton/online

The two most popular tricks used by junk e-mailers are spamming and spoofing. In **spamming**, the sender (called a *spammer*) sends hundreds, thousands, or even tens of thousands of messages (called *spam*) at the same time, to recipients across a wide geographic area. Spammers are extremely creative when it comes to procuring e-mail addresses of their recipients. Some rely on mailing lists purchased or hacked from the databases of legitimate marketers or service providers. Others simply use programs that generate addresses randomly, based on the domain names of known service providers.

Regardless of how they get an address, spammers are notorious for sending messages repeatedly, operating under the age-old marketing premise that if only a handful of recipients respond to the message, then the effort has shown a positive result. Therefore, spammers frequently sell their services to both legitimate and illegitimate organizations, which hope the huge mailings will generate sales or responses.

A more difficult technique, called **spoofing**, enables the junk e-mailer to hide his or her identity from the recipient. In spoofing, the sender places a false return address on the junk message. When spoofed, the recipient has no idea who sent the message, and no way of responding or stopping the problem. Spoofing can even fool e-mail service providers when they attempt to help their customers stem the flow of junk e-mail.

Using another technique, many spammers take advantage of free trial accounts from ISPs such as America Online. (Many service providers offer a free trial service period, complete with full Internet and e-mail use, before requiring users to establish a paid account.) Using the temporary free service, a spammer uses the new e-mail account to distribute spam, using a spoofed originating address. After spreading the junk e-mail, the spammer then quietly cancels the trial account. Such activities are forcing service providers to rethink their policies regarding free trials and have led to much stronger efforts to find and stop spammers.

The debate continues about whether junk e-mail should be outlawed, and the practice's future does not look bright. Like junk faxes, junk e-mail ties up resources—not just the recipient's but also the resources of the recipient's Internet service provider. Many people complain that they spend too much time downloading and sorting through junk e-mail, creating a loss of productivity and computing resources.

While lawmakers discuss the issue, many ISPs have taken actions of their own to minimize junk e-mail, ranging from the use of filtering software to massive lawsuits. In a recent case, America Online (whose servers process an estimated 30 million pieces of e-mail daily) won a lawsuit against a spammer who relentlessly clogged the mailboxes of customers with junk e-mail. Although the action got some relief for AOL customers, the spammer continued to operate, claiming that the practice is perfectly legal, and pledged to focus on other service providers' customers.

Techview

Beating Spammers at Their Own Game

Recent legal actions have slowed some spammers, but while the legality of junk e-mail and spam are being debated in courtrooms, newsgroups, and the media, computer users and Internet service providers are taking matters into their own hands.

If you have an e-mail account and receive unwanted or unsolicited e-mail messages, there are some strategies you can try, which may eliminate—or at least reduce—the junk in your mail box.

Start by working with your Internet service provider. Check the ISP's Web site or call a customer service representative, and check the company's policy dealing with spam and junk e-mail. If the ISP does not have such a policy, encourage the provider to adopt one quickly, or start looking for a new provider.

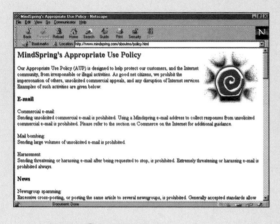

Your ISP should post its policies for appropriate uses of its services. This document, found at MindSpring's Web site, explains the ISP's policies regarding the use of e-mail, news groups, and other services.

Some ISPs—such as MindSpring, a regional ISP in Atlanta—provide users with access to services such as Spaminator, a program that can filter out spam at the e-mail server. Using a database of known spammers, the filtering service looks for incoming messages from known spammers and programs that send bulk messages. These mailings—as well as messages with no originating address—are refused by the server and do not make it to the customer's mailbox.

You can also use other Web-based services to minimize junk e-mail. Services such as Zero Junk Mail and NoThankYou enable you to register your e-mail address and, for a fee, will notify known junk e-mailers that you want to be removed from their mailing lists. Zero Junk Mail can also help you get your name removed from telemarketing lists and regular junk mail lists.

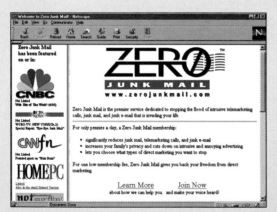

For a fee, online services such as Zero Junk Mail can help you reduce the amount of junk e-mail you receive.

As an added precaution, you may be able to use filters in your e-mail program to manage junk e-mail. Mail clients such as Microsoft's Internet Mail and Outlook, Netscape Messenger, Eudora Pro, and other e-mail clients provide simple filtering tools.

Assume, for example, that you frequently receive junk messages with Subject lines such as "Make Big $$$" or "Earn $$$ Now!!!" that peddle get-rich-quick schemes. Using filtering tools, you can tell your e-mail client to look for incoming messages with characters such as $$$ or !!! in the Subject line. You can set the filter to look for messages from certain domains or from specific persons, and set a variety of different filtering criteria, depending on your e-mail client's options. Many e-mail clients can utilize multiple filters.

When a message is received that matches the filter's criteria, your e-mail program can automatically save the message in a special folder, such as the Trash folder or a Spam folder, which you create, rather than your Inbox or the folder you use for normal mail.

A word to the wise, however: If you create your own e-mail filters, don't set your client to automatically delete messages. Instead, move them to a special folder and review them periodically before deleting them. This way, you can catch any legitimate messages that might be inadvertently filtered out (such as a message from a friend with the Subject line "I got the job!!!").

Mailing Lists

If you receive much junk mail, it is probably because data about you is first stored in a mailing list. Mailing lists can be created for many reasons but are most often used by marketers looking for trends in people's purchasing habits.

Junk mail has exploded in the past two decades because more and more information is being stored in mailing lists, which are now almost totally computerized. By storing these lists in huge databases, organizations can easily collect, sort, filter, and query the lists quickly and accurately. Because the lists are computerized, different organizations can easily exchange them or sell portions of them.

Perhaps the two most common ways to be put on a mailing list are to subscribe to a magazine or buy goods through the mail. Magazine companies know that if you subscribe to one magazine, you are likely to subscribe to other, similar ones. Magazine publishers frequently buy subscription lists from other magazines. Likewise, mail-order companies know that if you buy something by mail once, you are likely to buy again. Data on mail-order clients can be merged with census data to target individuals by household income and education.

There are, of course, other ways to get on mailing lists. Filling out a warranty registration is another guarantee to receive junk mail. Many people believe they have to fill out a warranty card for a new product to be guaranteed. In fact, your bill of sale, or receipt, is your proof of purchase. The warranty registration card is usually just a way for companies to find out who their customers are so their marketing departments can target the same people for

▶ In response to specified criteria, a mailing list company can generate a set of addresses, preformatted for mailing labels.

Nancy Davolio
507 - 20th Ave. E.
Apt. 2A
Seattle, WA98122

Andrew Fuller
908 W. Capital Way
Tacoma, WA98401

Janet Leverling
722 Moss Bay Blvd.
Kirkland, WA98033

Margaret Peacock
4110 Old Redmond Rd.
Redmond, WA98052

Steven Buchanan
14 Garrett Hill
London, SW1 8JR

Bill Dole
11423 Pine Street
New York, NY10310

Bob Hillary
9349 White Lane
Washington, NY10410

Roberto Nicks
44 Bernie Court
San Francisco, CA94959

Sean Wattenberg
1 Livermore Ave.
Dublin, NC03403

▶ Most junk mail is generated from mailing lists—databases— of potential customers.

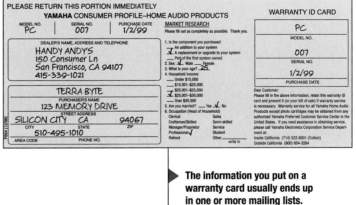

▶ The information you put on a warranty card usually ends up in one or more mailing lists.

future products. After a company has collected such data, it can make additional money by selling it.

Credit Histories

NORTON
Online

For more information on **credit histories**, visit this book's Web site at www.glencoe.com/norton/online

In addition to data about your purchasing or subscription habits, there are also records about your credit history. A credit history is a list of accounts you have held and information about whether you have ever been seriously delinquent in payment. A typical credit history is shown in Figure 12.7.

Before any company opens an account in your name, it will probably check your credit record. This is true of telephone companies, credit card companies, banks, and even prospective landlords. Companies that keep these records, such as TRW and Equifax, work just like mailing list companies. They buy account data about other companies' customers and sell it back whenever a company needs someone's credit history.

If, for some reason, your credit history contains erroneous data, the results can be disastrous. In one famous case, an elderly man was somehow registered as dead on a corporate database, even though he was very much alive. The incorrect data quickly spread from one database to another, and before long the man found that his Social Security and Medicaid benefits had been cut off without any notice.

There are many other kinds of databases. Before they accept you as a patient, doctors can find out whether you have ever filed a malpractice suit. Before accepting you as a tenant, landlords can see whether you have ever filed a complaint against another landlord. Are all these databases legal? They are. Are they morally acceptable? That is a more difficult question.

Corporations and Their Employees

Another threat to privacy can occur between a company and its employees. Electronic communications systems such as e-mail and voice mail are controlled by corporate computer systems. The company has access to the contents of communications, even if employees intend their messages to be private.

Although some people contend that businesses have no right to monitor employees' use of communications systems, the opposite may in fact be true. In a business setting, the computers, network, communications equipment, and software usually are the property of the company. This means that all information contained on the system or carried by the system is also the property of the company.

In fact, many companies routinely monitor their employees' communications. Why would a company institute such a policy? There are several compelling reasons:

■ To protect trade secrets

■ To prevent the distribution of libelous or slanderous messages

■ To prevent the system's users from downloading or copying data that is illegal, pornographic, or infected by computer viruses

■ To ensure that organizational resources are not being wasted or abused

TRW

THIS IS YOUR TRW CONSUMER IDENTIFICATION NUMBER. PLEASE REFER TO THIS NUMBER WHEN YOU CALL OR WRITE TRW. **ID# 6030929418361222**

JONATHON QUINCY CONSUMER
10655 NORTH BIRCH STREET
BURBANK, CA 91502

HOW TO READ THIS REPORT:

AN EXPLANATORY ENCLOSURE ACCOMPANIES THIS REPORT. IT DESCRIBES YOUR CREDIT RIGHTS AND OTHER HELPFUL INFORMATION. IF THE ENCLOSURE IS MISSING, OR YOU HAVE QUESTIONS ABOUT THIS REPORT, PLEASE CONTACT THE OFFICE LISTED ON THE LAST PAGE.

YOUR CREDIT HISTORY:

THIS INFORMATION COMES FROM PUBLIC RECORDS OR ORGANIZATIONS THAT HAVE GRANTED CREDIT TO YOU. AN ASTERISK BY AN ACCOUNT INDICATES THAT THIS ITEM MAY REQUIRE FURTHER REVIEW BY A PROSPECTIVE CREDITOR WHEN CHECKING YOUR CREDIT HISTORY. IF YOU BELIEVE ANY OF THE INFORMATION IS INCORRECT, PLEASE LET US KNOW. INSTRUCTIONS FOR REINVESTIGATION ARE INCLUDED ON THE LAST PAGE OF THIS REPORT.

AT YOUR REQUEST:

TRW INCLUDES THE FOLLOWING STATEMENT IN ALL REPORTS OF YOUR CREDIT HISTORY.

"MY IDENTIFICATION HAS BEEN USED WITHOUT MY PERMISSION ON APPLICATIONS FOR CREDIT. PLEASE CHECK WITH ME AT 213.999.0000 OR 714.555.0000 BEFORE APPROVING ANY CREDIT IN MY NAME."

ITEM		ACCOUNT NAME	DESCRIPTION	STATUS/PAYMENTS
1	*	CO SPR CT SANTA ANA 123 MAIN STREET SANTA ANA, CA 92765 CASE# 7505853	THE ORIGINAL AMOUNT OF THIS COURT ITEM IS $1,200. THE PARTY THAT BROUGHT THIS ACTION AGAINST YOU OR THE COURT REFERENCE NUMBER IS ALLIED COMPANY.	THIS JUDGMENT WAS FILED IN 10/88 AND PAID IN FULL ON 10/19/89.
2	*	BAY COMPANY 98 PIER BLVD SAN FRANCISCO, CA 94041 DEPARTMENT STORES ACCT# 4681123R101	THIS CHARGE ACCOUNT WAS OPENED 05/85 AND HAS REVOLVING REPAYMENT TERMS. YOU HAVE CONTRACTUAL RESPONSIBILITY FOR THIS ACCOUNT AND ARE PRIMARILY RESPONSIBLE FOR ITS PAYMENT. THE CREDIT LIMIT OF THIS ACCOUNT IS $1,600. THE HIGH BALANCE AMOUNT OF THIS ACCOUNT IS $1,285.	AS OF 01/95 THIS ACCOUNT IS CURRENT AND PAYMENTS ARE BEING PAID ON TIME BUT WAS PAST DUE 60 DAYS IN 04/93. YOUR BALANCE AS OF 01/21/95 IS $0. THE LAST PAYMENT REPORTED TO TRW WAS MADE ON 09/13/94. PAYMENT HISTORY: NNNCC1CCCCCC/CCCCCCCC21CC
3	*	CENTRAL BANK 1456 E. RANGER DR DALLAS, TX 75221 BANKING ACCT# 4590345859403	THIS CREDIT CARD ACCOUNT WAS OPENED 07/88 AND HAS REVOLVING REPAYMENT TERMS. YOU ARE OBLIGATED TO REPAY THIS JOINT ACCOUNT. THE CREDIT LIMIT OF THIS ACCOUNT IS $6,000. THE HIGH BALANCE AMOUNT OF THIS ACCOUNT IS $1,624.	AS OF 12/94 THIS ACCOUNT IS PAID IN FULL BUT WAS 30 DAYS PAST DUE IN 07/94. THE LAST PAYMENT REPORTED TO TRW WAS MADE ON 12/22/94. PAYMENT HISTORY: CCCC1CCCCCCC/CCCCCCCCCCCC

CONSUMER CREDIT REPORT (CDI) TRW – FORM 1.05W 03/15/95 16:42:19 PAGE 1

Figure 12.7
This printout shows the first page of a typical credit history from TRW.

NORTON *Notebook*

Protecting Your Online Privacy

Information about our private lives is available to a degree unimaginable just a few years ago. With the Internet's explosion in popularity, people are revealing more about themselves than ever before. Some examples:

- If you purchase an item over the World Wide Web, you not only provide the seller with your e-mail address but often with your credit card number. Some sites also request your Social Security number, mother's maiden name, and other personal information.

- Many Web sites that offer special services—such as travel planning, job hunting, or car buying services—require clients to complete forms, which store vast amounts of information about them.

- If you post a message to an Internet news group or participate in a chat room discussion, you reveal your e-mail address and interests to anyone who happens to be in the group at that time.

As an online consumer, you leave a trail of information about yourself wherever you go. This trail can be followed by marketers, spammers, hackers, and thieves right to your door. There is not a lot you can do after your information has fallen into the wrong hands. You can, however, take measures to prevent too many people from getting that information, especially if you regularly use the Internet or an online service.

- *Avoid being added to mailing lists.* When you fill out a warranty, subscription, or registration form— either on paper or online—make sure that it includes an option that keeps you from being added to a mailing list. If the option is available, check it; if not, do not return the form. If there's any doubt, contact the organization and learn its policies regarding mailing lists.

- *Make online purchases only through secure Web sites.* Before you purchase anything over the Web, make sure that the transaction is secure. By using an encryption method or a separate transaction server, the seller can ensure the privacy of the transaction and your personal information. You can do this in two ways. First, if you use a current browser, such as Internet Explorer 4.0 or Netscape Navigator 4.0, the browser can tell you whether the server is secure. Check the security settings before proceeding with a transaction. Second, read the Web site's information and see whether you have the option to switch to a secure server before making the transaction. If this option is available, take it.

- *Never assume that your e-mail is private.* Watch what you say, especially when using your company's or school's e-mail system. Never respond to an unsolicited e-mail message, especially if you do not recognize the sender. Be careful when giving out your e-mail address.

- *Be careful when posting to news groups.* Many Internet news groups and chat rooms are unsupervised. If you post a message to a group, your e-mail address and interests can make you easy prey for spammers and pranksters. Before posting a message to any group, watch the group for a few days, to determine whether its users are trustworthy. Try to determine whether the group is supervised by a sysop and get that person's address, if possible.

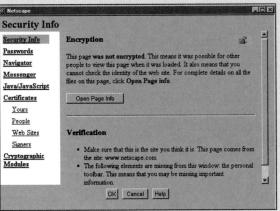

Current browsers can tell you whether a Web site is secure. In Netscape Navigator, for example, the Security tool displays a window of information about the currently open Web page.

- *Don't flame.* An online argument can have disastrous results. There are many documented cases of ISPs being shut down by spam as a result of a **flame**—a critical or insulting message—posted by one of the ISP's users. This can result not only in a total loss of online privacy but in your Internet service being cut off by the ISP, as well. Resist the urge to be critical or argumentative online, especially when participating in newsgroup or chatroom exchanges.

ETHICAL ISSUES IN COMPUTING

Advances in computer and communications technologies have placed tremendous new capabilities in the hands of everyday people. We can do things with information, sounds, and images that once could be done only by specially trained professionals using highly sophisticated tools. With these new capabilities, however, comes a set of responsibilities. As our technology gives us wonderful new powers, we are faced with troubling ethical questions. At the heart of the ethics dilemma is one simple question that almost defies answer: "Just because we can do something with computers, does that mean we *should* do it?"

In many cases, the answer plainly seems to be "yes." Should we use technology to assist in curing disease, or to enhance the lives of people who are isolated or have physical ailments? Certainly. Other cases merit an automatic "no," such as whether we should use technology for personal gain at any cost. Of course not.

But when the issue does not fall clearly on one side of the moral line, the answers are not so clear or easily found. Further, these perilous issues do not affect just the powerful, the wealthy, or the persons responsible for creating new technologies. Some of the most troublesome questions, in fact, apply to everyone who uses computers in the course of daily life.

In this chapter, for example, you have read about the manner in which computers can be use to send massive numbers of e-mail messages to persons who may not want them. The laws prohibiting such acts are vague and poorly enforced, but does that make it right to spam unsuspecting computer users? What if the messages are sent with good intentions (say, to warn computer users of a possible virus)? Does that make the act of spamming ethically acceptable? Or, if we decide to ban spam, should there be no exceptions whatsoever to the rule?

Similarly, we can use the Internet to share information and files with other users around the world. But at what point does this capability become unethical? When the information is libelous? Stolen? Obscene?

Computer hackers, to take another example, are generally seen as technological outlaws bent on wreaking havoc in cyberspace. They search out security weaknesses in networks and operating systems, create viruses, and demonstrate how vulnerable important data is. But we also learn a tremendous amount from many hackers' exploits, and operating systems, security methods, and programming techniques become stronger as we try to defend ourselves from them. Does this make their "work" any more or less ethical? Where do we draw the line on hacking?

Imagine finding a point on the ethical spectrum. As long as computer users do not go beyond that point, everything is fine. But when they exceed that limit, what do we do? Can that point be clearly defined? If so, can our action be clearly defined in dealing with those persons?

Lawmakers, activists, and everyday computer users will ponder these questions for some time. Laws will certainly be passed (such as the Telecommunications Act of 1996), challenged, enacted, and struck down. But until a set of laws is created that establishes guidelines for ethical computer use, personal ethics and common sense must guide us in our daily work and play.

NORTON Online

For more information about **ethical issues in computing**, visit this book's Web site at **www.glencoe.com/norton/online**

▶ **Computer student Robert Morris planted a virus in the national defense computer system, bringing the Internet to its knees in a matter of hours. He was arrested and charged with a federal offense. Computer experts say the episode taught them a great deal about security, the nature of viruses, and weaknesses in the Internet. Does that make Morris's actions any less unethical?**

Computers
In Your Career

The topics discussed in this chapter may not seem like obvious career opportunities, but a surprising number of people are working on these kinds of issues—people in different professions and disciplines, with a wide range of computing skills and expertise.

Physicians, Medical Researchers, Insurance Professionals The health and safety of people in the workplace is receiving more focus than ever in the healthcare community. If your career takes you into the medical or insurance industries, then you may become concerned with the prevention and cure of computer-related health issues, from RSIs to the effects of EMFs on pregnant women. Medical professionals are helping more people than ever to recover from RSIs, especially those involving the hands, wrists, and arms. Insurance professionals are actively working to verify the causes of workplace injuries and are helping government agencies and hardware manufacturers understand the importance of ergonomically correct hardware and equipment safety.

Environmentalists, Ecologists, Community Activists Either as a professional or volunteer, you may want to get involved with efforts in your area to reclaim and recycle old computer hardware and software. The benefits to the community are tremendous, from reducing waste in landfills to helping schools and nonprofit organizations find badly needed computer equipment. Most charitable organizations also maintain databases of their contributors. You may wish to consider volunteering your time to organize and update such files, gaining valuable experience in the process.

Law Enforcement Professionals, Security Specialists, Programmers If your professional goals involve a career in law enforcement, computer expertise is a valuable addition to your resume. Law enforcement and government agencies are devoting more resources than ever to tracking down computer criminals of all kinds. Especially in demand are high-level computer users with skills in networking, programming, and security. This type of expertise is essential in tracking down computer crooks who ply their trade on the Internet.

Perhaps, as in our noncomputing lives, we should adopt a simple set of rules to help us maintain our ethical balance as we work and play with computers, both online and offline. One such set of guidelines, suggested by the Computer Ethics Institute, takes a familiar format:

The Ten Commandments of Computer Ethics

1_ *Thou shalt not use a computer to harm other people.*

2_ *Thou shalt not interfere with other people's computer work.*

3_ *Thou shalt not snoop around in other people's computer files.*

4_ *Thou shalt not use a computer to steal.*

5_ *Thou shalt not use a computer to bear false witness.*

6_ *Thou shalt not copy or use proprietary software for which you have not paid.*

7_ *Thou shalt not use other people's computer resources without authorization or proper compensation.*

8_ *Thou shalt not appropriate other people's intellectual output.*

9_ *Thou shalt think about the social consequences of the program you are writing or the system you are designing.*

10_ *Thou shalt always use a computer in ways that ensure consideration and respect for your fellow humans.*

WHAT TO EXPECT IN THE FUTURE

Inevitably, the freedoms of cyberspace will be curbed by new rules and laws for interacting with each other. Writers' unions, for example, are working on methods to bill and receive payment when their members' works are requested over the Internet. Because online services run the risk of being sued for libel due to materials published on their bulletin boards and news-groups, such services will monitor their members more closely in the future. Some online services may begin limiting the types of ser-vices they offer to subscribers, to discourage users from trafficking in stolen or libelous materials, exchanging pornography, or using obscene language online.

In a backlash against pornography and antisocial materials online, many organizations (including the U.S. Congress) are considering how to regulate the material posted to the Internet. Software has been developed, for example, that can be used to block the delivery of offensive messages. There may soon come a time when every new computer will carry a mandatory chip that will allow parents to block access to pro-grams or networks they do not want their children to use. Meantime, private companies offer software that enable par-ents to lock their children out of certain types of Web sites and chat areas to protect them from encountering online smut and predators. This software will become much more flexible and secure in the next few years, which will be neces-sary with the proliferation of online sources of pornography.

VISUAL SUMMARY

Ergonomics and Health Issues

- Ergonomics is the study of the physical relationships between humans and their tools, such as computers.

- Office chairs should be adjustable in height and should have lower-back support and arm rests.

- Desks that allow proper keyboard height and special ergonomic keyboards have been developed to prevent carpal tunnel syndrome, a type of repetitive stress injury.

- To avoid damaging your eyes, avoid staring at the screen for long periods, position your monitor between 2 and 2.5 feet from your eyes, make sure no bright lights reflect off your screen, and use a monitor that has a relatively large screen without noticeable flicker.

Computers and the Environment

- The computer industry has become known for planned obsolescence, with both hardware and software being replaced every couple of years.

- Some of the leading toxic wastes coming from homes and offices are heavy metals used extensively in batteries, such as cadmium.

- Although some experts recommend leaving computers on all the time, the practice consumes more than the necessary amount of electricity. One response has been the development of Energy Star equipment, which conserves electricity even when left on.

Computer Crime

- Our legal system is gradually developing a code of laws to provide a legal framework for working with computers and on the Internet.

- The most prevalent breach of law in cyberspace is software piracy, the illegal copying or use of a program.

- Copyright laws relevant to computers and software are covered by the Copyright Act of 1976 and the Software Piracy and Counterfeiting Amendment of 1983.

- Instead of building copy protection into their programs, most software developers discourage piracy among organizations by offering site licenses and network versions.

- Software viruses are parasitic programs that can replicate themselves, infect computers, and destroy data. Users can protect their data and software by using an antivirus program.

- Hardware is sometimes stolen for the value of the data stored on it rather than for the value of the machine itself.

- Data is stolen by hackers who use their skills to break into computer systems, to access data or to embezzle funds.

- The Electronic Frontier Foundation (EFF) was created in response to government arrests of computer hackers; the EFF also advocates policies that promote openness in communication.

- Most corporate computer systems discourage unauthorized access with a logon procedure that requires a user identification code and a password.

Privacy

- Computer databases have allowed corporations to collect and sort massive amounts of data about individuals.

- Using information collected in various databases, both legitimate marketers and illegitimate pranksters deluge people with junk mail, junk faxes, and junk e-mail.

- Junk e-mailers, known as spammers, often send out huge mailings to thousands of computer users over the Internet. Using a tactic known as spoofing, a spammer can conceal his or her own e-mail address from the persons being spammed.

- Two well-known types of databases that are kept about people are the mailing list, which includes data about consumer behavior, and the credit history, which lists information about accounts and debts.

- Threats to privacy also occur between companies and their employees, especially with respect to company-owned channels of communication, such as e-mail.

Ethical Issues in Computing

- The many capabilities given to people by computers have created numerous ethical dilemmas.

- Practices such as excessive e-mailing, sharing objectionable or illegal material, and theft of intellectual property all create ethical questions for everyday computer users.

- Government, legal professionals, and computing professionals continue to debate computer-related ethical questions and attempt to develop laws that protect the freedoms of computer users while limiting immoral or illegal use of computers. Few actual laws, however, have been created or enforced, requiring computer users to let their own sense of ethics guide them.

Visual Summary & Exercises

KEY TERMS

After completing this chapter, you should be able to define the following terms:

antivirus software, 461

beta software, 459

carpal tunnel syndrome, 448

commercial software, 455

copy protection, 456

cyberspace, 447

Data Encryption Standard (DES), 467

electromagnetic field (EMF), 450

Electronic Frontier Foundation (EFF), 466

encryption, 467

ergonomics, 448

flame, 474

freeware, 455

hacker, 465

intellectual property, 454

log on, 466

network license, 457

password, 466

repetitive stress injury (RSI), 448

shareware, 455

site license, 457

software piracy, 455

spamming, 468

spoofing, 469

user identification code, 466

Warez news group, 455

KEY TERM QUIZ

Fill in the missing word with one of the terms listed in Key Terms.

1. The illegal copying or use of programs is called _____.

2. A(n) _____ gives the purchaser the right to use a program on a given number of computers.

3. Criminals who use their computer skills to intentionally steal data or crash computer systems are known as _____.

4. The act of sending unsolicited e-mail messages is called _____.

5. The study of the physical relationship between people and their tools—such as computers—is called _____.

6. Low-frequency electrical power creates _____.

7. _____ is the electronic frontier where data is stored, processed, and moved through vast communications networks.

8. A common injury among clerical personnel who spend most of their time entering data on computer keyboards is called _____.

9. In many businesses, an employee must enter a(n) _____ to access a computer's files.

10. _____, which is a method of encoding and decoding data, is perhaps the most effective form of data security.

Visual Summary & Exercises

REVIEW QUESTIONS

1. Describe briefly how your name and address end up being added to more than one mailing list.

2. Describe the methods used to protect networked systems from unauthorized access.

3. List four primary ways in which the theft of data can be accomplished.

4. List and describe at least three ways in which you can avoid eyestrain when using the computer.

5. List the ways in which software developers can project themselves against software piracy.

6. The use of what input device is likely the most common cause of carpal tunnel syndrome?

7. What are the three characteristics you should look for in an office chair?

8. How can the average computer user protect against junk e-mail?

9. What is your best precaution against infecting your computer system with a virus?

10. How does computer obsolescence contribute to pollution and environmental problems?

DISCUSSION QUESTIONS

1. How do you feel about the use of the Internet for marketing products and services? Do you believe that unsolicited e-mail is ever warranted? How would you react if you frequently received large numbers of e-mail messages from unknown sources, containing information that did not interest you—or that even offended you?

2. Suppose that you are responsible for acquisition and disposal of computer equipment for a small business. List and describe briefly as many possibilities as you can for performing this function in an "environmentally responsible" manner.

3. How do you feel about the online transmission of "questionable" materials, such as graphics that might be defined as pornography or documents that support so-called extremist positions? Do you feel that such materials should be regulated in some way? If so, how? Whom do you feel is qualified to regulate such materials?

4. Discuss the issue of intellectual property and the impact that computers and the Internet can have on an individual's or corporation's intellectual property rights? Do you feel that current laws adequately protect these rights?

inteNET Workshop

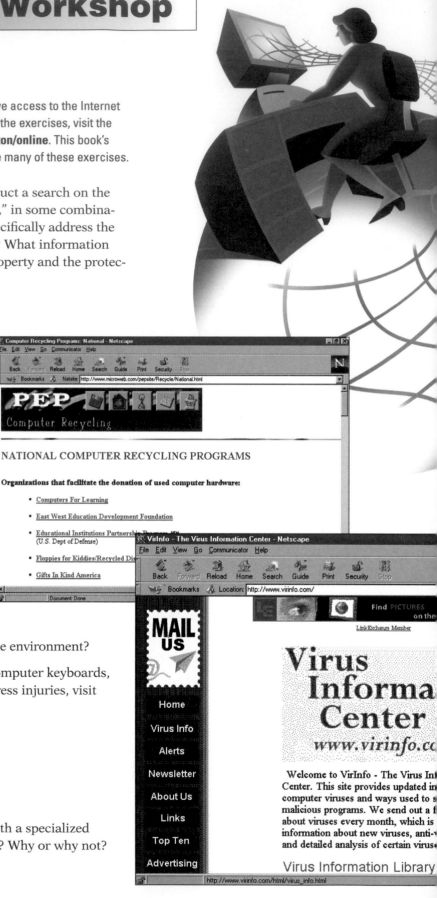

The following exercises assume that you have access to the Internet and a browser. If you need help with any of the exercises, visit the book's Web site at **www.glencoe.com/norton/online**. This book's Web site also lists the URLs you need to complete many of these exercises.

1. Using your favorite search engine, conduct a search on the terms "ethics," "computers," and "Internet," in some combination. How many sites can you find that specifically address the issues of computer ethics and cyberethics? What information can you find on the topic of intellectual property and the protection of intellectual property rights?

2. Find the home page of at least one Internet service provider in your area (start by getting a listing of local providers from the phone book and then check their Web sites), and see whether you can find information regarding the ISP's policies on privacy and spam. What protections does the ISP provide? Do you feel they are adequate? Find the Web site of a second ISP and compare its policies to the first ISP's policies. How do they compare?

3. Visit the PEP National Directory of Computer Recycling. Can you find an organization in your area that recycles computers, perhaps for worthy causes? What options do these organizations provide for discarding obsolete or used computers without harming the environment?

4. For information on different types of computer keyboards, designed to reduce the risk of repetitive stress injuries, visit the following sites:

- Workplace Designs
- Kinesis Corp.
- Microsoft Natural Keyboard
- Introducing the Dvorak keyboard

Do you think you would prefer working with a specialized keyboard rather than a standard keyboard? Why or why not?

5. If you want to avoid the damage that viruses can cause to your computer, you need to stay up-to-date on antivirus products. This means not only using the product that is aware of the most current viruses but also knowing how and when to upgrade the product so that it stays current. For general information on viruses and a listing of the most recently discovered ones, visit the following sites:

■ The Virus Bulletin Home Page

■ The Antivirus Resources Page

■ The Virus Information Center

Compare a few antivirus products at their Web sites. Which product do you think would work best for you? Why? What features or capabilities do you think are most important in an antivirus utility?

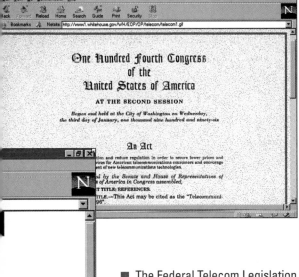

6. In 1996, Congress pass the Telecommunications Act of 1996. This multifaceted legislation was designed to enhance competition in the telecommunications industry, reduce regulations, and protect minors from indecent materials on the Internet. This bill is considered an important step in the development of the Internet for many reasons, but the Act was challenged in court immediately after its passage. Visit the following sites and do some research on the Telecommunications Act of 1996:

■ The Federal Telecom Legislation Home Page

■ The White House overview of the Telecommunications Act

■ The Telecommunications Act of 1996 Protest Site

■ The Benton Foundation's Telecommunications Act of 1996 Information Site

What are the specific stated goals of the Act? What actions did the Act propose to protect minors from indecent materials on the Internet? How was the bill supposed to foster competition among telecommunications providers? What ultimately happened to the bill? What is its current status?

APPENDICES

CONTENTS

THE HISTORY OF MICROCOMPUTERS

In the Beginning

In 1971, Dr. Ted Hoff put together all the elements of a computer processor on a single silicon chip slightly larger than 1 square inch. The result of his efforts was the Intel 4004, the world's first commercially available microprocessor. It sold for $200 and contained 2,300 transistors. It was designed for use in a calculator, and Intel sold more than 100,000 calculators that ran on the 4004 chip. Almost overnight, the chip found thousands of uses. It paved the way for today's computer-oriented world, and for the mass production of computer chips now containing millions of transistors.

The first microprocessor, Intel's 4004, was a 4-bit computer containing 2,300 transistors that could perform 60,000 instructions per second. By contrast, the modern 64-bit PC microprocessors contain 7.5 million transistors and are capable of more than a million operations per second.

1975

The first commercially available microcomputer, the Altair 880, was the first machine to be called a "personal computer". It had 64 KB of memory and an open 100-line bus structure. It sold for about $400 in a kit to be assembled by the user.

Two young college students, Paul Allen and Bill Gates, wrote the BASIC language interpreter for the Altair computer. It took them eight weeks, working night and day, to write the several thousand lines of code. During summer vacation they formed a company called Microsoft, now the largest software company in the world.

At Bell Labs, Brian Kernighan and Dennis Ritchie developed the C programming language, which became the most popular professional application development language.

1976

Steve Wozniak and Steve Jobs built the Apple I computer. It was less powerful than the Altair, but also less expensive and less complicated. Jobs and Wozniak formed the Apple Computer Company together on April Fool's Day, naming it after their favorite snack food.

Bill Millard, recognizing that people would rather buy pre-assembled computers in stores than put computers together themselves from kits, founded Computerland, the retail computer chain.

1977

In the 1970s, computer chips were designed by etching circuits in clay models with X-Acto knives. Today's chip designers use the latest in CAD computer software and photo-lithography to develop their prototypes.

The Apple II computer was unveiled. It came already assembled in a case with a built-in keyboard. Users had to plug in their own TVs for monitors. Fully assembled microcomputers hit the general market, with Radio Shack, Commodore, and Apple all selling models. Sales were slow because neither businesses nor the general public knew exactly what to do with them.

Datapoint Corporation announced ARCnet, the first commercial local area network (LAN) intended for

use with microcomputer applications. It transmitted data over a coaxial cable at 3 million bits per second.

Early commercial microcomputers were sold in kits and assembled by users, putting them in the domain of the electronic hobbyists. In the late 1970s, pre-assembled computers began to be sold in retail outlets, making them convenient for the average consumer.

1978

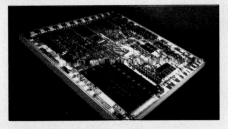

Intel released the 8086 16-bit microprocessor, setting a new standard for power, capacity, and speed in microprocessors.

The first major microcomputer bulletin board, run by Ward

Christensen and Randy Seuss, went online in Chicago, Illinois. Epson announced the MX-80 dot matrix printer, coupling high performance with a relatively low price.

1979

Intel introduced the 8088 microprocessor, featuring 16-bit internal architecture and an 8-bit external bus.

Motorola introduced the 68000 chip, used in early Macintosh computers. Software Arts, Inc. released VisiCalc, the first commercial spreadsheet program for personal computers, developed by Dan Bricklin and Bob Frankston. VisiCalc is generally credited as being the program that paved the way for the personal computer in the business world.

Bob Metcalf formed 3Com Corporation in Santa Clara, California, to develop Ethernet-based networking

products. Metcalf developed Ethernet while at Xerox Corporation's Palo Alto Research Center (PARC), and it later evolved into the world's most widely used network protocol. MicroPro International, founded by Rob Barnaby and Seymour Rubenstein, introduced WordStar, the first commercially successful word processing program for microcomputers. IBM released the IBM 3800, the fastest printer to date, which could print 20,000 lines per minute.

THE HISTORY OF MICROCOMPUTERS

1980

IBM chose Microsoft (co-founded by Bill Gates and Paul Allen) to provide the operating system for its upcoming PC, then under wraps as top secret "Project Acorn." Microsoft bought a program developed by Tim Patterson of Seattle Computer Products called Q-DOS (for Quick and Dirty Operating System), and modified it to run on IBM hardware, Q-DOS became PC-DOS, one of two operating systems eventually released with the IBM PC.

Bell Laboratories invented the Bellmac-32, the first single chip micro-processor with 32-bit internal architecture and a 32-bit data bus.

The Hercules Corporation introduced a graphics card allowing text and graphics to be combined on a display monitor at the same time.

Lotus Development Corporation unveiled the Lotus 1-2-3 integrated spreadsheet program combining spreadsheet, graphics, and database features in one package. The program was developed by Lotus president and founder, Mitch Kapor.

1981

IBM introduced the IBM PC, with a 4.77 MHz Intel 8088 CPU, 16 KB of memory, a keyboard, a monitor, one or two 5.25-inch floppy drives, and a price tag of $2,495.

Hayes Microcomputer Products, Inc., produced the SmartModem 300, which quickly became the industry standard.

Ashton-Tate developed dBase II, which set the standard for database programs.

Xerox unveiled the Xerox Star computer. Its high price doomed it to commercial failure, but its features inspired a whole new direction in computer design. Its little box on wheels (the first mouse) could execute commands on screen (the first graphical user interface).

1982

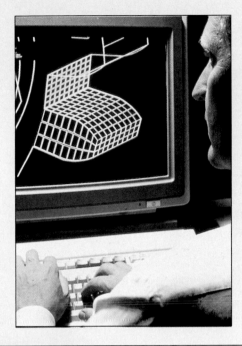

Intel released the 80286, a 16-bit microprocessor.

Peter Norton introduced Norton Utilities, a collection of software tools for the PC to help users recover corrupted files, clean up disk space, and increase the security of programs and data files.

AutoCAD, a program for designing 2-D and 3-D objects, was released. AutoCAD revolutionized the architecture and engineering industries.

1983

Time magazine featured the computer as the 1982 "Machine of the Year," acknowledging the computer's new role in society.

Apple introduced the Lisa, the first commercial computer with a purely graphical operating system and a mouse. The industry was excited, but its $10,000 price tag discouraged buyers.

IBM unveiled the IBM PC XT, essentially a PC with a hard disk and more memory. The XT was able to store programs and data on its built-in 10 MB hard disk drive.

The first version of C++ programming language was developed, allowing programs to be written in reusable independent pieces called objects.

The Compaq Portable was released, the first successful 100 percent compatible PC clone. Despite its 28 pounds, it was the first computer to be lugged through airports.

Apple announced its "Kids Can't Wait" program, donating Apple II computers to 10,000 California schools.

THE HISTORY OF MICROCOMPUTERS

1984

Apple introduced the "user-friendly" Macintosh microcomputer.

Adobe Systems released its Postscript system, allowing printers to produce crisp print in a number of typefaces, as well as elaborate graphic images.

IBM shipped the PC AT, a 6 MHz computer using the Intel 80286 processor, which set the standard for personal computers running DOS.

Satellite Software International introduced the Word-Perfect word processing program on several platforms.

Early PC operating systems used text commands, requiring the user to know dozens of command sequences. The graphical user interface, which became popular after the introduction of the Macintosh in 1984, made computing simpler and more accessible to the nontechnical user.

1985

Intel released the 80386 processor (also called the 386), a 32-bit processor with the capability to address more than 4 billion bytes of memory—ten times faster than the 80286.

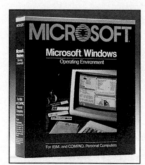

Microsoft released the Windows 1.0 operating system, which featured the first graphical user interface for PCs.

Aldus released PageMaker for the Macintosh, the first desktop publishing software for microcomputers. Coupled with Apple's LaserWriter printer and Adobe's PostScript system, the desktop publishing industry was born.

Hewlett-Packard introduced the Laser Jet laser printer featuring 300 dpi resolution.

Microsoft sold its first public stock for $21 per share, raising $61 million in the initial public offering.

The First International Conference on CD-ROM technology was held in Seattle, hosted by Microsoft.

Apple Computer introduced the Macintosh Plus, with increased memory and the capacity to connect an external hard drive.

IBM delivered the PC convertible, IBM's first laptop computer and the first Intel-based computer with a 3.5-inch floppy disk drive.

1987

IBM unveiled the new PS/2 line of computers featuring a 20-MHz 80386 processor at its top end.

IBM introduced its Video Graphics Array (VGA) monitor offering 256 colors at 320x200 resolution, and 16 colors at 640x480.

The Macintosh II computer, aimed at the desktop publishing market, was introduced by Apple Computer. It featured an SVGA monitor. Apple Computer introduced HyperCard, a programming language for the Macintosh, which used the metaphor of a stack of index cards to represent a program—a kind of visual programming language.

Motorola unveiled its 68030 microprocessor.

Novell introduce its network operating system called NetWare.

THE HISTORY OF MICROCOMPUTERS

1988

IBM and Microsoft shipped OS/2 1.0, the first multi-tasking desktop operating system. High price, steep learning curve, and incompatibility with existing PCs contributed to its lack of market share.

Apple Computer filed the single biggest lawsuit in the computer industry against Microsoft and Hewlett-Packard claiming copyright infringement of its operating system and graphical user

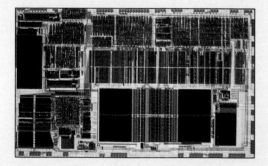

interface. Ashton-Tate sued Fox Software and Santa Cruz Operations alleging copyright infringement of dBase.

Hewlett-Packard introduced the first popular ink jet printer, the HP Deskjet.

Steve Jobs' new company, NeXT, Inc., unveiled the NeXT computer featuring a 25-MHz Motorola 68030 processor. The NeXT was a pioneer computer introducing several "firsts" to the industry. It was the first computer to use object-oriented programming in its operating system and an optical drive rather than a floppy drive.

Apple introduced Apple CD SC, a CD-ROM storage device allowing access to up to 650 MB of data.

1989

Intel released the 80486 chip (also called the 486), the world's first one-million-transistor microprocessor. The 486 integrated a 386 CPU and math coprocessor onto the same chip.

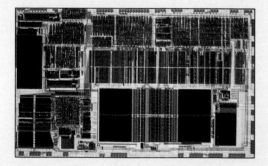

Tim Berners-Lee developed software around the hypertext concept, enabling users to click on a word or phrase in a document and jump either to a another location within the document or to another file. This software laid the foundation for the development of the World Wide Web.

The World Wide Web was created at the European Particle Physics Laboratory for use by scientific researchers.

1990

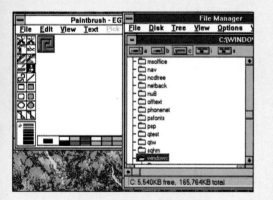

A multimedia PC specification setting the minimum hardware requirements for sound and graphics components of a PC was announced at the Microsoft Multimedia Developers' Conference.

Microsoft released Windows 3.0, shipping 1 million copies in four months.

The National Science Foundation Network replaced ARPANET as the backbone of the Internet. Motorola announced its 32-bit microprocessor, the 68040, incorporating 1.2 million transistors.

1991

Symantec released Norton Desktop for Windows, a software package giving the user an improved desktop environment. The ban on commercial business on the Internet was lifted.

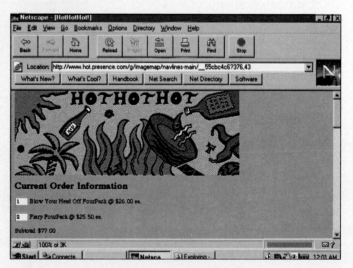

Apple Computer launched its new System 7.0 operating system and a product line featuring its new PowerBook series of battery-powered portable computers.

Apple, IBM, and Motorola signed a cooperative agreement to:

- Design and produce RISC-based chips.
- Integrate the Mac OS into IBM's enterprise systems.
- Produce a new object-oriented operating system.
- Develop common multimedia standards.

THE HISTORY OF MICROCOMPUTERS

1992

With an estimated 25 million users, the Internet became the world's largest electronic mail network.

Microsoft acquired Fox Software, including the popular Foxbase database management system.

In Apple Computer's five-year copyright infringement lawsuit, Judge Vaughn Walker ruled in favor of defendants Microsoft and Hewlett-Packard, finding that the graphical user interface in dispute was not covered under Apple's copyrights.

Microsoft shipped the Windows 3.1 operating system, including improved memory management and TrueType fonts. IBM introduced its ThinkPad laptop computer.

1993

Mosaic, a point-and-click graphical Web browser was developed at the National Center for Supercomputing Applications (NCSA), making the Internet accessible to those outside the scientific community.

Intel, mixing elements of its 486 design with new processes, features, and technology, delivered the long-awaited Pentium processor. It had a 64-bit data path and more than 3.1 million transistors.

Apple Computer expanded its entire product line, adding the Macintosh Color Classic, Macintosh LC III, Macintosh Centris 610 and 650, Macintosh Quadra 800, and the Powerbooks 165c and 180c.

Apple introduced the Newton MessagePad at the Macworld convention, selling 50,000 units in the first ten weeks.

Microsoft shipped its Windows NT operating system. IBM shipped its first RISC-based RS/6000 workstation, featuring the PowerPC 601 chip developed jointly by Motorola, Apple, and IBM.

1994

Apple announced its decision to license its System 7 operating system to other companies, opening the door for Macintosh clones.

Apple introduced the Power Macintosh line of microcomputers based on the PowerPC chip. This line introduced RISC to the desktop market. RISC was previously available only on high-end workstations.

Netscape Communications released the Netscape Navigator program, a World Wide Web browser based on the Mosaic standard, but with more advanced features.

Online service providers CompuServe, America Online, and Prodigy added Internet access to their services.

After two million Pentium-based PCs had shipped, a flaw in the Intel Pentium floating-point unit was found by Dr. Thomas Nicely. His report was made public on CompuServe.

1995

Microsoft released its Windows 95 operating system with a massive marketing campaign, including prime time TV commercials. Seven million copies were sold the first month, with sales reaching 26 million by the end of the year.

Netscape Communications captured more than 80 percent of the World Wide Web browser market, going from a start-up company to a$2.9 billion company in one year.

Power Computing shipped the first-ever Macintosh clones, the Power 100 series with a PowerPC 601 processor.

Intel released the Pentium Pro microprocessor.

Motorola released the PowerPC 604 chip, developed jointly with Apple and IBM.

THE HISTORY OF MICROCOMPUTERS

1996

Intel announced the 200 MHz Pentium processor. Microsoft added Internet connection capability to its Windows 95 operating system.

Digital Equipment Corp. launched Alta Vista, a Web search engine claimed to be the fastest online, with 36 million Web pages indexed.

Several vendors introduced VRML authoring tools that used simple interfaces and drag-and-drop editing features to create three-dimensional worlds with color, texture, motion video, and sound on the Web.

The U.S. Congress enacted the Communications Decency Act as part of the Telecommunications Act of 1996. The act regulated fines of up to $100,000 and prison terms for transmission of any "comment, request, suggestion, proposal, image or other communication which is obscene, lewd, lascivious, filthy, or indecent" over the Internet. The day the law was passed, millions of Web page backgrounds turned black in protest. The law was immediately challenged on Constitutional grounds and was consequently deemed unconstitutional.

1997

Intel announced MMX technology, which increases the multimedia capabilities of a microprocessor. Also, Intel announced the Pentium II microprocessor. It has speeds of up to 333 MHz and introduced a new design in packaging, the Single Edge Contact (SEC) cartridge. It has more than 7.5 million transistors.

The U.S. Justice Department charges Microsoft with an antitrust lawsuit, claiming Microsoft was practicing anti-competitive behavior by forcing PC makers to bundle its Internet Explorer Web browser with Windows 95.

AlterNIC founder, Eugene Kashpureff, is wanted by the FBI and arrested in Canada for wire and computer fraud by hijacking InterNIC's URL, http://www.inter-nic.net, and redirecting visitors to his home page at http://www.alternic.net. InterNIC, run by Network Solutions, is responsible for assigning and maintaining Internet domain names. AlterNIC is an organization protesting the monopoly InterNIC holds on the domain naming system.

Netscape Communications and Microsoft release new versions of their Web browser. Netscape's Communicator 4 and Microsoft's Internet Explorer 4 provide a full suite of Internet tools, including Web browser, news reader, HTML editor, conferencing program, and e-mail application.

> The number of Internet hosts has doubled every year since 1993. The number of hosts in 1993 was 1.1 million; 2.2 million in 1994; 4.8 million in 1995; 9.5 million in 1996; and an estimated 19.5 million in 1997.

Today

The pace of change in the computer industry has not slowed down in recent years and shows little sign of slowing in the future. To help you stay in touch with current developments in software and hardware, this book's Web site features frequently updated industry events, trends, products, and technological advances. For more information, visit this book's Web site at **www.glencoe.com/norton/online**

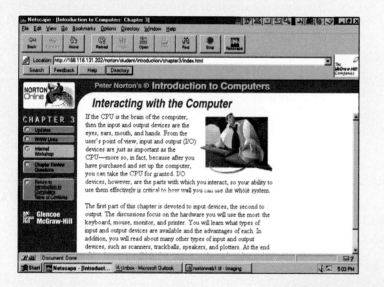

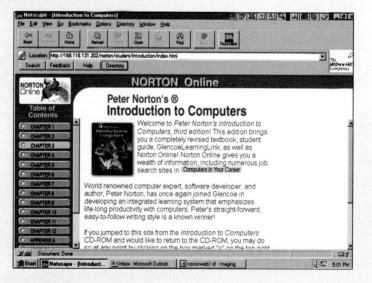

APPENDIX B

OBJECTIVES

When you complete this appendix, you will be able to do the following:

- Name two means of connecting to the Internet.
- Name at least six important tools in a browser and describe their purpose.
- List four methods for navigating within a Web page or among multiple Web sites.
- Name one source of online assistance for using a browser or locating Web sites.

This book features many Internet-related discussions, as well as exercises and review questions that require you to use the World Wide Web. Chapter 8, "The Internet," provides a detailed look at many aspects of the Internet. This appendix is designed to help you learn the basic steps required for using a browser and navigating the Web.

Whether you are an experienced netizen or a first-time surfer, you should read this appendix carefully and follow the steps outlined here. The following sections not only describe a variety of methods for navigating the Web but also introduce this book's own Web site—which you will use as the starting point for the "Internet Workshop" sections of each chapter and to link to other sites described throughout this book.

This appendix assumes that you have access to a PC with an installed Web browser and an Internet connection. Note that there are many ways to access and browse the Internet, and your system may differ from the one demonstrated in this appendix. If so, don't worry; the tools and techniques described here are common to nearly all Web browsers, and your instructor can assist you with any issues specific to your system.

CONNECTING TO THE INTERNET

There are many aspects to using the Internet, and unfortunately, the first thing you must do is also the most confusing. That is, you must establish a connection to the Internet. This process ensures that your PC is linked to another computer, which acts as an Internet server. The server, in effect, acts as your gateway to the Internet.

Chapter 8 describes the many different ways to connect to the Internet. This appendix assumes that your organization provides one of the following two types of connections:

- LAN connection
- Dial-up connection

This appendix also assumes that your school has already set up an Internet account for your PC, if necessary, and installed and configured the software needed to establish a connection. If this is not the case, ask your instructor for assistance.

BROWSER BASICS

A Web browser is software that enables you to view specially formatted Web pages. As you read in Chapters 6 and 8, a Web page is simply a document formatted with Hypertext Markup Language (HTML) tags, which your PC downloads from another computer across the Internet. The browser can interpret the HTML tags, which tell the browser how to display the page's contents. By using the tags, the browser can display the page on your screen as the page's designer intended, complete with images, hypertext links, and special formatting.

When you navigate the Web, you simply move from one Web page to another. That is, you tell your browser to find different Web pages, download them

onto your PC, and display them on your screen. You'll learn more about navigation in the next section. Before you can navigate the Web, you must launch your Web browser (open it on your screen) and become familiar with some of its basic tools.

This appendix's examples and illustrations are based on Netscape Navigator 4, running under Windows 95/98. If you are using a different browser—such as Microsoft Internet Explorer, Mosaic, or another version of Navigator—don't worry. The tools and features described here are common to most browsers and will enable you to navigate the Web with no problems.

GETTING STARTED ON THE WORLD WIDE WEB

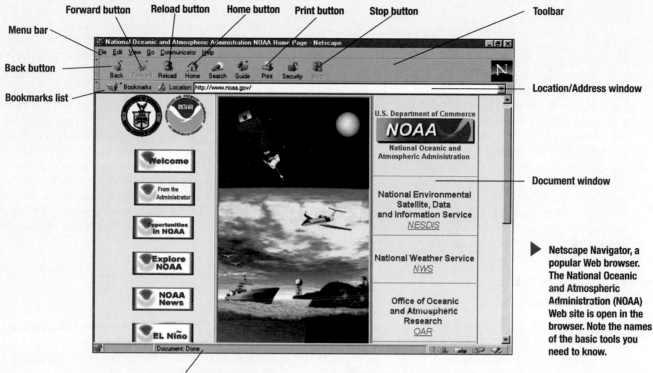

Menu bar
Back button
Bookmarks list
Forward button
Reload button
Home button
Print button
Stop button
Toolbar
Location/Address window
Document window
Status bar

▶ Netscape Navigator, a popular Web browser. The National Oceanic and Atmospheric Administration (NOAA) Web site is open in the browser. Note the names of the basic tools you need to know.

To launch your browser:

1. On the Windows 95/98 taskbar, click the Start button. The Start menu appears.

2. Point to Programs, and the Programs menu opens.

3. Choose your browser from the Programs menu. The browser opens on your screen. Your browser should provide the following basic tools, to help you navigate the Web and find the information you are looking for:

■ *Back button.* Returns you to the previously opened Web page. When you view several pages in succession, this button lets you move back through the pages without retyping their URLs. It's like flipping backward through a magazine, through pages you have already read.

■ *Forward button.* After you use the Back button to return to a previously opened Web page, you can use this button to move forward again, returning to the last page you opened. If you compare this feature to reading a magazine, it's like returning to the page where you stopped reading when you started flipping backward.

■ *Reload button.* Sometimes Web pages do not open correctly, for a variety of reasons. This button (called Refresh on some browsers) reloads the current page, ensuring that all its elements are on screen. This button is also helpful if you are viewing a page that changes frequently, such as a page of "live" stock quotes or sports scores. You can use this button to make sure that the content is updated.

■ *Home button.* You can set your browser so that it always opens to the same page, which can be a favorite Web site or a page stored on your local disk. This button returns you to that page—called the home page—any time, no matter where you are on the Web.

■ *Print button.* If your PC is connected to a printer, you can choose this button to print out the current page. In most browsers, the Print function prints the contents of the entire Web page, even if it is more than one screen in length.

■ *Stop button.* Choose this button to stop the current page from downloading any further. This button is handy if you realize that you have chosen the wrong page and want to stop it from fully displaying, or if a page is taking too long to load. When you stop a transfer, your browser will "idle"—that is, do nothing—until you issue a new command or go to another page.

- *Location/Address window.* Use this window to type the URL of any page you want to visit. When you type the URL here and press Enter, your browser will find the desired page and download it to your PC. In most browsers, this window stores the last few URLs you typed in a *history list,* so that you can return to them without retyping them. This window is called the Location window in some browsers, the Address window in others.

- *Bookmarks list.* If you find a Web page that you want to visit often, you can *bookmark* it; that is, you can save its URL. To quickly return to the site, you just open the Bookmarks list and select the desired site. Most browsers let you save an unlimited number of bookmarks and provide ways to categorize them and automatically update them.

NAVIGATING THE WEB

You navigate the Web by moving from one Web page to another. Often, you move from one point to another on the same Web page. Sometimes, you move from one page to another within the same Web site, such as when you move from the Netscape site's home page to its Products page. Other times, you move from one Web site to another, such as when you move from the Netscape site's home page to the Microsoft site's home page. All these moves work the same way; that is, you give your browser a uniform resource locator—called a URL for short—for the desired page, and the browser loads the page onto your PC.

You can move from one page to another in the following ways:

- *Type a URL in the Location window; then press Enter.* For example, to go to the White House Web site, click in the Location window, and type http://www.whitehouse.gov; then press Enter.

- *Click hyperlinked text.* Web designers make it easy to move to other pages, by providing hyperlinks in their Web pages. A hyperlink is simply a part of the Web page that is linked to a URL. When text has a hyperlink assigned to it, you can click it and "jump" from your present location to the URL specified by the hyperlink. Hyperlinked text looks different from normal text in a Web page; it is usually blue and

- *Status bar.* This part of the browser window shows you the progress of pages and graphics as they download and displays the URL behind any hyperlink that your mouse pointer touches. Most browsers let you hide the status bar to make the document window larger; experienced Web users, however, like to keep the status bar visible because it provides important information.

Your browser probably provides a number of other tools, as well, such as a Search tool, which takes you to a search engine or index site somewhere on the Web, such as Yahoo! or Lycos. Most browsers also feature a variety of pull-down menus. These menus provide all the same features found on the browser's toolbar, and many others. These features, however, are not necessary right now, as you focus on the basics of Web browsing.

underlined, but can be formatted in any number of ways. When your mouse pointer touches hyperlinked text, the hyperlink's URL appears in the browser's status bar.

- *Click a hyperlinked navigation tool or image map.* Many Web pages provide pictures or graphical buttons—called navigation tools—that direct you to different pages, making it easier to find the information you need. Another popular tool is the image map; a single image that provides multiple hyperlinks. You can click on different parts of the image map to jump to different pages. When your mouse pointer touches a navigation tool or image map, it turns into a hand pointer, and the hyperlink's URL appears in the status bar of your browser.

- *Use the Back and Forward buttons.* As described in the preceding section, these buttons return you to recently viewed pages, similar to flipping through a magazine.

- *Choose a bookmark from your Bookmarks list.* If you have saved any bookmarks to pages you have visited earlier, you can open the Bookmarks list, select a page, and quickly return to that page.

- *Choose a URL from the History list.* When you type URLs into the Location window, your browser saves them, creating a history list for the current session. You can choose a URL from this list and return to a previously opened page without having to use the Back button or any other tools.

GETTING STARTED ON THE WORLD WIDE WEB

The URL of the currently open Web page

When you click this hyperlinked text…

…you will move to the Web page at this URL.

The browser has moved to the URL specified by the hyperlikked text.

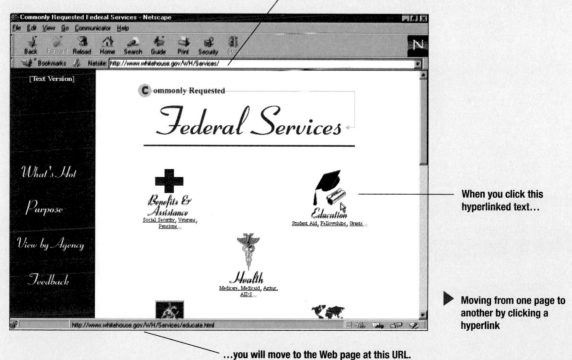

When you click this hyperlinked text…

▶ Moving from one page to another by clicking a hyperlink

…you will move to the Web page at this URL.

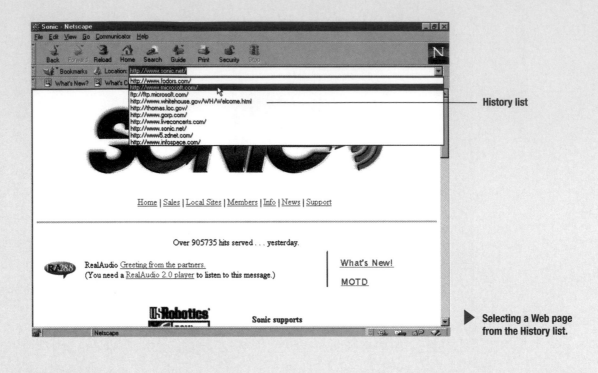

History list

Selecting a Web page
from the History list.

USING THIS BOOK'S WEB SITE

At the Glencoe/McGraw-Hill site on the World Wide Web, you will find a set of pages designed for use with this book. You can use these pages as resources to find more information on various topics discussed in this book, and as your base for searching the Web.

To get to this book's Web site, type the following URL in your browser's Location window; then press Enter:

http://www.glencoe.com/norton/online

The site uses the same structure as this book and is divided using the same chapters. Simply follow the links on the site to the appropriate chapter. In each chapter's pages, you will find hyperlinks to other sites. Use these hyperlinks to visit the Web sites listed in this book's margin notes and "Internet Workshop" sections.

In some cases, you may find additional information relating to the chapter's topics, which cannot be found in this book. For example, you may find online exercises in some chapters, links to still more Web sites, updated information about new technologies, and more.

The site uses the same structure as this book and is divided using the same chapters. Simply follow the links on the site to the appropriate chapter. In each chapter's pages, you will find hyperlinks to other sites. Use these hyperlinks to visit the Web sites listed in this book's margin notes and "Internet Workshop" sections.

In some cases, you may find additional information relating to the chapter's topics, which cannot be found in this book. For example, you may find online exercises in some chapters, links to still more Web sites, updated information about new technologies, and more.

GETTING STARTED ON THE WORLD WIDE WEB

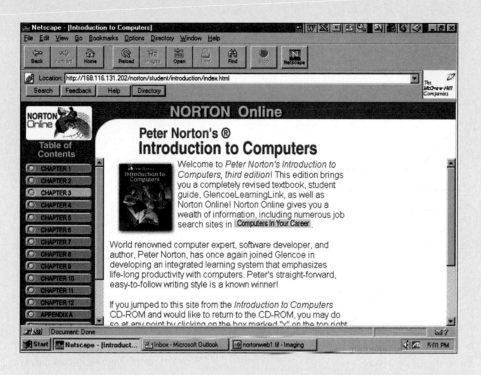

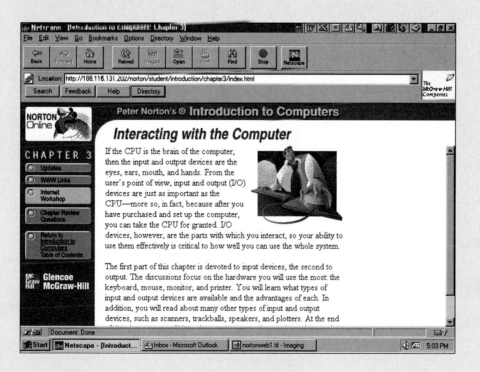

GETTING HELP

Although most browsers are easy to use, you may need help at some point. Because it is beyond the scope of this book to give you detailed instructions on your browser, you should be aware of other sources of information and help.

There are literally hundreds of books and magazines available devoted to the Internet, the Web, and various browsers. The fastest and easiest source of help, however, can be found online, in your browser's built-in Help system, or on the Web itself.

GETTING HELP FROM YOUR BROWSER

Newer browsers provide comprehensive Help systems, which can answer many of your questions

about browsing and the World Wide Web. To access your browser's Help system:

1. On the browser's menu bar, choose Help. A pull-down menu of help options should appear.

2. From the Help menu, choose Contents. A Help dialog box appears, listing all the topics for which help or information are available.

3. Look through the list of topics and choose the one that matches your interest.

Some Help systems are more sophisticated than others, providing search features, graphics, and even context-sensitive help, which can help you through the specific task you are trying to perform.

▶ The Netscape Communicator Help system. This dialog box opens when you choose Contents from the Netscape Navigator Help menu.

GETTING STARTED ON THE WORLD WIDE WEB

GETTING HELP ONLINE

If you use a popular browser, such as Microsoft's Internet Explorer, Netscape Navigator, or one of the browsers used by an online service such as America Online or CompuServe, you can find much information about the product on the company's Web site.

To find the information, just point your browser to the appropriate Web site. When the Web page opens, search the site for references to your specific browser. When you find the desired pages, you can save them to disk or print them. If you are have registered your copy of the browser, you also should find out how to contact the manufacturer's technical support staff, which can help you overcome specific problems with the software.

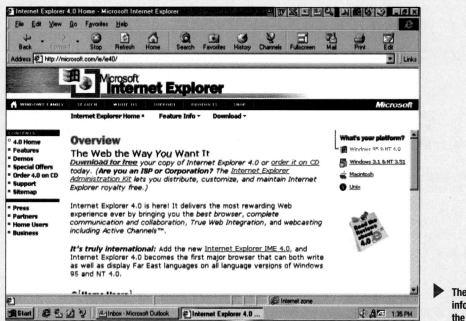

▶ The Internet Explorer information page, on the Microsoft Web site.

Glossary

10Base-T An Ethernet network standard that uses twisted-pair wires to achieve data transfer speeds of up to 10 Mbps.

100Base-T An Ethernet network standard, also known as Fast Ethernet. 100Base-T uses the same media and topology as typical Ethernet, but uses different network interface cards to achieve data transfer speeds of up to 100 Mbps.

3-D modeling software Graphics software used to create electronic models of three-dimensional objects. Types of 3-D modeling software include surface, solid, polygonal, and spline-based modelers.

3-D worksheet In a spreadsheet, a workbook that contains multiple individual worksheets. The user can "layer" the individual sheets and perform calculations that include data from any or all sheets.

5x86 A line of microprocessors produced by Advanced Micro Devices (AMD), which competes with Intel's Pentium series of microprocessors. The 5x86 line has a clock speed of 133 MHz and is roughly equivalent to the 75 MHz Pentium chip.

A

absolute cell reference A spreadsheet cell reference that does not change when copied to a new cell.

accelerator card A circuit board that fits into an expansion slot and enhances the processing speed of the CPU.

activate (1) To initiate a command or load a program into memory and begin using it. (2) To choose.

active desktop A Windows 98 interface option that sets your screen up to work like a web page and to receive and display information from Internet content providers.

active matrix LCD A liquid crystal display (LCD) technology that assigns a transistor to each pixel in a flat-panel monitor, improving display quality and eliminating the "submarining" effect typical of a flat-panel monitor.

active program See *active window*.

active window The program or area on the computer screen in which the next action taken by the user will occur. The active window's title bar is highlighted, while the title bars of inactive windows appear dimmed.

activeX control Program that allows interoperability with other technologies that support Microft's COM technology..

address bus A set of wires connecting the computer's CPU and RAM, across which memory addresses are transmitted. The number of wires determines the amount of memory that can be addressed at any one time.

Advanced Micro Devices (AMD) One of several chip manufacturers that makes processors that mimic the functionality of Intel's chips.

Advanced Research Projects Agency Network (ARPANET) An early network developed by the Department of Defense to connect computers at universities and defense contractors. This network eventually became part of the Internet.

algorithm A set of ordered steps or procedures necessary to solve a problem.

alignment The orientation of the lines of a paragraph with respect to the margins. In word processors, alignment options include left, right, center, and justified (also called *full justification*).

alphanumeric field A database field that stores a string of alphanumeric characters (also called a *text field or character field*).

alphanumeric keys On a computer keyboard, the keys that include the letters of the alphabet and other keys commonly found on a typewriter.

ALU See *arithmetic logic unit*.

American Standard Code for Information Interchange (ASCII) A 7-bit binary code developed by ANSI to represent symbols and numeric and alphanumeric characters. The ASCII character set is the most commonly used character set in PCs.

animated GIF A special type of graphics file (in GIF format) that contains several slightly different versions of the same image. When viewed in a Web browser that supports animated GIFs, the images "play back" in rapid succession, creating a simple animation. Animated GIF images are often used in banner ads in Web pages.

annotation In presentation programs, a feature that enables the user to embed notes in individual slides. The notes can be made visible only to the presenter, or can be printed out for distribution to the audience.

anonymous FTP archive A compilation of programs and data files accessible to the public on the Internet. Any Internet user can download a file from an FTP archive, using the account name "anonymous."

antivirus utility A program that scans a computer's disks and memory for viruses, detects them, and removes them. Some antivirus utilities can help the user recover data and program files that have been damaged by a virus.

applet Operating system program or software that supplements Windows 98 with application features, such as editing, drawing,and communications.

application server A network server that hosts shared application files, enabling multiple users to use a network version of a software program.

application software Any computer program used to create or process data, such as text documents, spreadsheets, graphics, and so on. Examples include database management software, desktop publishing programs, presentation programs, spreadsheets, and word processing programs.

application specific macro language A language that provides users the capability to write commands and integrate applications.

Archie A catalog of file names maintained by McGill University in Montreal. Internet users can search and locate a file among thousands of directories listed on this service.

ARCnet see *Attached Resource Computer Network*.

argument (1) In a spreadsheet, the values or cell references within a formula on which the function performs its operation. (2) In programming, an item of information needed by a function or subroutine to carry out its instructions.

arithmetic logic unit (ALU) The component of the CPU that handles arithmetic and logic functions. Instructions are passed from memory to the ALU.

arithmetic operation One of two types of operations a computer can perform, which are handled by the arithmetic logic unit (ALU). Arithmetic operations include addition, subtraction, multiplication, and division.

ARPANET See *Advanced Research Projects Agency Network*.

ascending sort order Alphabetical (A-Z) or numerical (0-9) order. This type of order is often used when arranging data, such as a list of items.

ASCII See *American Standard Code for Information Interchange*.

assembler A computer program that converts assembly language instructions into machine language.

assembly language A second-generation programming language that uses simple phrasing in place of the complex series of switches used in machine language.

Asynchronous Transfer Mode (ATM) A network protocol designed to send voice, video, and data transmissions over a single network. ATM provides different kinds of connections and bandwidth on demand, depending on the type of data being transmitted.

Attached Resource Computer Network (ARCnet) A LAN network standard that uses twisted-pair wire or coaxial cable to achieve data-transfer speeds of up to 20 Mbps.

attribute Enhancement or stylistic characteristic applied to text characters in a font; for example, bold, italic, and underlining.

authoring environment A fourth-generation programming tool used to create multimedia software, such as computer-based training programs.

autocorrect In word processing software, a feature that recognizes certain types of mistakes and corrects them automatically. This feature can be configured to recognize many specific misspellings, to capitalize the first word of a sentence, and so on.

average access time The average amount of time a storage device requires to position its read/write heads over any spot on the medium; usually measured in milliseconds (ms).

B

backbone The central structure that connects other elements of the network and handles the major traffic in the system.

backing up The process of creating a duplicate set of program or data files in case the originals become damaged. Files can be backed up individually, in whole directories, and in entire drives. Backups can be made to many types of storage media, such as diskettes, optical disks, or tape.

backup software A program that enables the user to copy large groups of files from a hard disk to another storage medium for safekeeping or use in case the originals become damaged.

bandwidth The amount of data that can be transmitted over a network; measured in bits per second (bps).

bandwidth capacity The amount of traffic that a network can handle.

bandwidth-management tool A software program that helps manage the use of a network's available bandwidth, to ensure maximum efficiency.

banner page A special page printed between multiple print jobs, enabling users to differentiate among different print jobs that have been spooled to the same network printer. Banner pages are automatically printed by the network software.

bar code A pattern of bars printed on a product or its packaging. A device called a *bar code reader* can scan a bar code and convert its pattern into numeric digits. After the bar code reader has converted a bar code image into a number, it feeds that number to the computer, just as though the number had been typed on a keyboard.

bar code reader An input device that converts a pattern of printed bars (called a *bar code*) into a number that a computer can read. A beam of light reflected off the bar code into a light-sensitive detector identifies the bar code and converts the bar patterns into numeric digits. These devices are commonly used in retail stores.

BASIC See *Beginners All-purpose Symbolic Instruction Code*.

BBS See *bulletin board service*.

Beginners All-purpose Symbolic Instruction Code (BASIC) A popular programming language used primarily as an educational tool.

beta software Software that is in the developmental stage, and not ready for commercial sale or release to the public. Software publishers often provide copies of beta software to independent testers and other software developers, who work with the program to find bugs and test for compatibility with other products.

binary field A database field that stores binary objects (such as clip art, photographs, screen images, formatted text, sound objects, and video clips) or OLE objects (such as graphs or worksheets created with a spreadsheet or word processor).

Glossary

binary large object (BLOB) (1) A graphic image file, such as clip art, a photograph, a screen image, formatted text, a sound object, or a video clip. (2) An OLE object, such as a graph or worksheet created with a spreadsheet or word processor; frequently used with object-oriented databases.

binary system A system for representing the two possible states of electrical switches, which are on and off (also known as *base 2*).

bit The smallest unit of data.

bitmap A binary representation of an image in which each part of the image, such as a pixel, is represented by one or more bits in a coordinate system.

bits per second (bps) A measure of modem transmission speed.

BLOB See *binary large object*.

block A contiguous series of characters, words, sentences, or paragraphs in a word processing document. This term is also sometimes used to describe a range of cells in a spreadsheet. Once a block of text or cells has been selected, the user can perform many different actions on it, such as moving, formatting, or deleting.

boot See *booting*.

booting The process of starting a computer. The term *bootstrapping* is also used. Both terms come from the expression "pulling oneself up by one's own bootstraps," which describes what computers must go through when being started.

boot record A small program that runs when the computer is started. This program determines whether the disk has the basic components of DOS or Windows necessary to run the operating system successfully. If it determines that the required files are present and the disk has a valid format, it transfers control to one of the operating system programs, which continues the process of starting up.

boot sector A part of the logical formatting process. The boot sector is a portion of a disk that contains a program that runs when the computer is first turned on and that determines whether the disk has the basic components necessary to run the operating system successfully.

border A paragraph format that displays a line on any side of a block. This type of formatting is often used to distinguish the block from regular text. Borders are generally applied to an entire paragraph or a group of paragraphs.

bottom-up design A design method in which system details are developed first, followed by major functions or processes.

bps See *bits per second*.

bridge A device that connects two LANs and controls data flow between them.

browser A software package that lets the user access the major components of the Internet, such as the World Wide Web, email, and so on.

bug An error in a computer program.

bulletin board service (BBS) An online information service tailored to the needs of a specific group of users.

Burst Extended Data Output (BEDO) RAM A very fast type of RAM, which is supported by only a limited number of CPUs—namely CPUs manufactured by VIA.

bus The path between components of a computer or nodes of a network. The bus's width determines the speed at which data is transmitted. When used alone, the term commonly refers to a computer's data bus.

bus network A network topology in which all network nodes and peripheral devices are attached to a single conduit.

button In graphical user interfaces, a symbol that simulates a push button. The user clicks a button to initiate an action.

byte The amount of memory required to store a single character. A byte is comprised of eight bits.

C

C A powerful third-generation programming language, widely used to develop commercial software. C is a portable language that can easily be transferred to different platforms.

C++ A third-generation programming language that is a superset of C and features object-oriented programming techniques.

cache memory High-speed memory that resides between the CPU and RAM in a computer. Cache memory stores data and instructions that the CPU is likely to need next. The CPU can retrieve data or instructions more quickly from cache than it can from RAM or a disk.

CAD See *computer-aided drafting or computer-aided design*.

CAE See *computer-aided engineering*.

CAM See *computer-aided manufacturing*.

card See *circuit board*.

carpal tunnel syndrome An injury of the wrist or hand commonly caused by repetitive motion, such as extended periods of keyboarding.

CASE tool See *computer-aided software engineering tool*.

cathode ray tube (CRT) A type of monitor or TV screen that uses a vacuum tube as a display screen. CRTs are most commonly used with desktop computers.

CBT See *computer-based training*.

CD See *compact disk*.

CD-recordable (CD-R) drive A peripheral device that enables the user to create customized CD-ROM discs that cannot be changed once created but can be read by any CD-ROM drive. CD-R drives are used to create beta versions and program masters and to archive data.

CD-ROM See *compact disk, read-only memory.*

CD-ROM drive A specialized type of disk drive, which enables a computer to read data from a compact disk. The term CD-ROM stands for Compact Disk Read-Only Memory. Using a standard CD-ROM drive and compact disk, the computer can only read data from the disk, and cannot write data to the disk.

Celeron An Intel processor designed for entry-level personal computers.

cell In a spreadsheet, the intersection of a row and column, forming a box into which the user enters numbers, formulas, or text.

cell address In a spreadsheet, an identifier that indicates the location of a cell in a worksheet. The address is composed of the cell's row and column locations. For example, if the cell is located at the intersection of column B and row 3, then its cell address is B3.

cell pointer A square covering one cell of a spreadsheet, and which identifies the active cell. The user positions the cell pointer in a worksheet by clicking the mouse on the cell or by using the cursor movement keys on the keyboard.

cell reference The address of a spreadsheet cell used in a formula.

central processing unit (CPU) The computer's primary processing hardware, which interprets and executes program instructions and communicates with input, output, and storage devices. In personal computers, the CPU is composed of a control unit and an ALU, which reside on a single chip on the computer's motherboard. In larger computers, the CPU may reside on several circuit boards.

Centronics interface The portion of a parallel printer cable that connects to the printer with a 36-pin plug. This interface is a standard developed by Centronics Corporation for the first dot-matrix printers.

channel A Web site that delivers information to your computer.

channel bar A bar that includes a series of icons that represent frequently used Web sites.

character animation The process of animating a character—such as a drawing of a person, animal, or some other organic or inorganic object—to create the illusion of movement. Once achieved only by manual techniques, character animation is now widely done using computers and special animation software.

character field See *alphanumeric field.*

character format In a word processor, settings that control the attributes of individual text characters, such as font, type size, type style, and color.

chart See *graph.*

chat Informal, real-time communication.

chat line An online service similar to a BBS, in which users can conduct live group discussions. Each keystroke is transmitted as it is entered.

choose See *activate.*

CIM See *computer-integrated manufacturing.*

circuit board A rigid rectangular card—consisting of chips and electronic circuitry—that ties the processor to other hardware; also called a card.

circuit-switched line A type of communications line in which access to the connection is constant until broken by either party. Circuit-switched lines are commonly used for telephone or modem transmissions.

CISC processors See *Complex Instruction Set Computing processors.*

class The attributes and functions that define an object in object-oriented program code.

class inheritance In object-oriented programming, the tendency for all subclasses to share the attributes and functions of the parent class.

click To select an object or command on the computer screen (for example, from a menu, toolbar, or dialog box) by pointing to the object and pressing and releasing the mouse button once.

client An application program on a user's computer that requests information from another computer through a network; also refers to the machine making the request.

client/server network A hierarchical network strategy in which the processing is shared by a server and numerous clients. In this type of network, clients provide the user interface, run applications, and request services from the server. The server contributes storage, processing, and printing services.

clip art Predrawn or photographed graphic images, which are available for use by anyone. Some clip art is available through licensing, some through purchase, and some for free.

Clipboard A holding area maintained by the operating system in memory. The Clipboard is used for storing text, graphics, sound, video or other data that has been copied or cut from a document. After data has been placed in the Clipboard, it can be inserted from the Clipboard into other documents, in the same application or a different application.

cluster On a magnetic disk, such as a hard disk, a group of sectors that are treated as a single data-storage unit. The number of sectors per disk can vary, depending on the type of disk and the manner in which it is formatted.

coaxial cable A cable composed of a single conductive wire wrapped in a conductive wire mesh shield, with an insulator in between.

COBOL See *Common Business Oriented Language.*

code The instructions or statements that are the basis of a computer program.

collaborative computing A system in which data and processing tasks are shared by several computers on a network.

Glossary

color monitor   A computer screen that displays computer data in color. A color monitor's range and intensity are related to video bandwidth, dot pitch, refresh rate, and convergence.

color separation   A computer process used to prepare full-color pages for printing. This process creates a separate page for each color found in the image.

column   (1) A vertically arranged series of cells in a spreadsheet, named with a letter or combination of letters. (2) In word processing, a document-formatting technique, in which the page is divided into vertical sections, like a newspaper's columns.

commands   Instructions that you issue to the computer, usually by choosing from a menu, clicking a button, or pressing a combination of keys.

command-line interface   A user interface in which the user interacts with the software by typing strings of characters at a prompt. MS-DOS is an example of a command-line interface.

commercial software   Software that is made available for sale to the public.

Common Business Oriented Language (COBOL)   A third-generation programming language used to create business applications. COBOL was developed by a government-appointed committee to solve the problem of hardware incompatibility.

common user access (CUA)   A system that makes use of similar graphical tools in several software products. The level of consistency in the interface makes software easier to learn and to use.

communications device   An input/output device used to connect one computer to another to share hardware and information. This family of devices includes modems and network interface cards.

communications program   Software used to transmit data between computers and terminals.

compact disk (CD)   A type of optical storage device, identical to audio CDs, which can store about 650 MB of data, or about 450 times as much as a diskette. The type of CD used in computers is called Compact Disk Read-Only Memory (CD-ROM). As the device's name implies, you cannot change the information on the disk, just as you cannot record over an audio CD.

compact disk read-only memory (CD-ROM)   The most common type of optical storage medium. In CD-ROM, data is written in a series of lands and pits on the surface of a compact disk (CD), which can be read by a laser in a CD-ROM drive. A standard CD stores approximately 650 MB, but data on a CD cannot be altered.

compiler   A program that translates a file of program source code into machine language.

Complex Instruction Set Computing (CISC) processors   Processors designed to handle large and comprehensive instruction sets. CISC processors are commonly used in the Motorola and Intel microprocessor lines.

compositing   The process of combining separate images to create a new image, as is done when the image of an actor is placed in front of a background image. Compositing is used in filmmaking, game design, and animation, and is increasingly being done with powerful computers and special software.

computer-aided drafting or computer-aided design (CAD)   The use of computers to create complex two- or three-dimensional models of buildings and products, including architectural, engineering, and mechanical designs.

computer-aided engineering (CAE)   The use of software that enables designers to perform analyses on designs, such as structural analysis or electronic circuit analysis, and determine the optimum materials and design components.

computer-aided manufacturing (CAM)   The use of software to create automated systems and to manufacture products, including the use of robotics.

computer-aided software engineering (CASE) tool   Software used to develop information systems. CASE automates the analysis, design, programming, and documentation tasks.

computer-based training (CBT)   The use of customized, interactive computer tools (such as multimedia presentations displayed from CD-ROM or online) to train employees in such areas as company policy, software, and personnel issues.

computer-generated imagery (CGI)   The process of using powerful computers and special graphics, animation, and compositing software to create digital special effects or unique images. CGI is frequently used in filmmaking, game design, animation, and multimedia design.

computer-integrated manufacturing (CIM)   The use of software to design products and integrate the production process with the accounting system to control inventory, ordering, billing, and scheduling.

computer program   A set of instructions or code executed by the CPU, designed to help users solve problems or perform tasks.

computer scientist   A person who studies computer theory and researches and develops new techniques in computer design and programming.

computer system   A four part system that consists of hardware, software, data, and a user.

condition statement   A feature of selection structure programming that directs program flow by branching to one part of the program or another depending on the results of a comparison.

configure   To adapt a computer to a specific need by selecting from a wide range of hardware and software options. Configuration may include installing new or replacement hardware or software, or changing settings in existing hardware or software.

context menu   In the Windows 95 and Windows 98 operating systems, a brief menu that appears when the user right-clicks on certain items. The menu—also called a shortcut menu—contains commands that apply specifically to the item that was right-clicked.

Control Panel   A dialog box that lets you change settings on your computer..

control flow   The order in which program statements are executed.

control unit   The component of the CPU that contains the instruction set. The control unit directs the flow of data throughout the computer system.

conversion   The process of replacing an existing system with an updated or improved version.

cooperative multitasking   A multitasking environment in which programs periodically check with the operating system to see whether other programs need the CPU and, if so, relinquish control of the CPU to the next program.

Copy   An application command that makes a duplicate of data selected from a document and stores it in the Clipboard without removing the data from the original document. The data then can be used in other documents and other applications.

copy protection   An antipiracy technique that prevents the illegal duplication of software.

counter field   A database field that stores a unique, incrementing numeric value (such as an invoice number) that the DBMS automatically assigns to each new record.

CPU   See *central processing unit.*

CRT monitor   See *cathode ray tube monitor.*

CUA   See *common user access.*

cursor   A graphic symbol on screen that indicates where the next keystroke or command will appear when entered. Representations include a blinking vertical line or underline, a box, an arrow, or an I-beam pointer. Also called the *insertion point.*

cursor-movement keys   The keys that direct the movement of the on-screen cursor or insertion point, including the up, down, left, and right arrows, and the Home, End, Page Up, and Page Down keys.

Cut   An application command that removes data selected from a document and stores it in the Clipboard. The data is no longer a part of the original document. While in the Clipboard, the data can be used in other documents or applications.

cyberspace   A term used to describe a vast electronic network in which everyday tasks, such as banking, research, and communication, are conducted via computer.

cylinder   All tracks bearing the same track number on both sides of a floppy disk or across all platters of a hard disk.

Cyrix   One of several manufacturers that make processors that mimic the functionality of Intel's chips.

D

DAT   See *digital audiotape.*

data   Raw facts, numbers, letters, or symbols that the computer processes into meaningful information.

data area   The part of the disk that remains free to store information after the logical formatting process has created the boot sector, FAT, and root folder (also called the *root directory*).

data bus   An electrical path composed of parallel wires that connect the CPU, memory, and other hardware on the motherboard. The number of wires determines the amount of data that can be transferred at one time.

data communication   The electronic transfer of data between computers.

data compression   The process of reducing data volume and increasing data-transfer rates by using a mathematical algorithm, which analyzes groups of bits and encodes repeating sequences of data.

data compression utility   A program that reduces the volume of data by manipulating the way the data is stored.

data-encoding scheme   The method that a disk drive uses to translate bits of data into a sequence of flux reversals, or changes in magnetic polarity, on the surface of a disk.

Data Encryption Standard (DES)   A common method of data encryption used for public transmissions that can encode data in 72 quadrillion ways.

data member   Class attributes in an object-oriented programming language.

data recovery utility   A program used to recover data files that have been mistakenly deleted or somehow rendered unusable; also called an *unerase program.*

data-transfer rate   The rate at which a data storage device can read or write data; expressed as bytes, KB, MB, or GB per second.

data warehouse   A massive collection of corporate information, often stored in gigabytes or terabytes of data. It can include any and all data that is relevant to the running of a company. All this data is stored in databases spread among many storage devices on computers running tens or even hundreds of central processing units.

database   A collection of related data organized with a specific structure.

database management system (DBMS)   A computer program used to manage the storage, organization, processing, and retrieval of data in a database; also called *database management software.*

date field   A database field that stores a date.

DBMS   See *database management system.*

debugger   Software that executes each program statement in sequence so that the programmer can track down and correct logic errors in the program.

Glossary

decimal system   The system that uses 10 digits to represent numbers; also called *base 10*.

decision support system   A software tool, often based on a spreadsheet or database, that generates reports from information in the system. These reports assist management in the decision-making process.

defragmentation utility   A program that reorganizes data on disk by rejoining parts of files split in the editing process and eliminating breaks between data units. By reorganizing data into contiguous sectors on the disk, this type of utility can improve disk access times.

density   A measure of the quality of a magnetic disk's surface; the higher the density, the more closely the iron oxide particles are packed and the more data the disk can store.

DES   See *Data Encryption Standard*.

descending sort order   Arranged in reverse alphabetic or numerical order, from Z to A or 9 to 0.

deselect   The opposite of select. In many applications, the user can select, or highlight, blocks of text or objects for editing. By clicking the mouse in a different location or pressing a cursor-movement key, the user removes the highlighting and the text or objects are no longer selected.

desktop   (1) In a computer operating system, the graphical representation of a desktop in which all files, utilities, and programs can be easily accessed by the user. (2) The most common PC model, sized to fit on a desk, with separate units for the CPU and the monitor.

desktop publishing (DTP) software   A program used to enhance standard word processing documents. DTP software creates professional-quality documents and publications using design, typesetting, and paste-up features.

development   Phase 3 of the systems development life cycle, in which programmers create or customize software to fit the needs of an organization, technical documentation is prepared, and software testing is begun.

device   Any electronic component attached to or part of a computer; hardware.

dialog box   A special-purpose window that appears when the user issues certain commands in a program or graphical operating system. A dialog box gets its name from the "dialog" it conducts with the user as it seeks the information it needs to perform a task.

digital   The use of numbers, or digits, to express units of data in a computer.

digital audiotape (DAT)   A magnetic storage medium that can store data at a very high density. Read by a DAT drive that has two write heads that write data with opposite magnetic polarities on overlapping areas of the tape, and two read heads that each read only one polarity or the other.

digital camera   A video camera that converts light intensities into digital data. Digital cameras are used to record images that can be viewed and edited on a computer.

digital convergence   The process of combining digital text, graphics, video, and sound into a single multimedia product.digital versatile disk.

digital versatile disk (DVD)   A high-density optical medium capable of storing a full-length movie on a single disk the size of a CD. Unlike a standard compact disk, which stores data on only one side, a DVD-format disk stores data on both sides.

digitize   The process of converting an image or a sound into a series of binary numbers (1s and 0s), which can be stored in a computer.

DIMM   See *Dual In-Line Memory Module*.

direct connection   One means of connecting multiple computers to one another, as in a network. In a direct connection, the computers are connected directly to one another by cables and network interface cards.

direct conversion   The complete transfer of all data and users from an existing system to a new system at one time.

directory   A tool for organizing a disk. A directory contains a list of files and other directories stored on the disk. A disk can hold many directories, which can in turn store many files and other directories; also called a *folder*.

discussion group   An electronic storage space where users can post messages to other users, carry on extended conversations, and trade information; also called a *bulletin board* or a *news group*.

disk drive   A storage device that holds, spins, reads data from, and writes data to removable floppy disks (diskettes) or nonremovable hard disks.

diskette   A removable magnetic disk made of a thin piece of flexible plastic, coated with iron oxide and encased in a plastic sleeve. Diskettes are used to load new programs or data onto a hard disk, transfer data between computers, or make a backup copy of data from a hard disk. Common diskette sizes include 3.5 inches and 5.25 inches; also alled a *floppy disk* or a *floppy*.

diskette drive   A device that holds a removable floppy disk when in use; read/write heads read and write data to the diskette.

distance learning (DL)   The process of using communications and computer technologies to provide instruction over a long distance.

distributed computing   A system configuration in which two or more computers in a network share applications, storage, and processing power; also called *distributed processing*.

DNS   See *Domain Name System*.

document   A computer file consisting of a compilation of one or more kinds of data. There are many different types of documents, including text documents, spreadsheets, graphics files, and so on. A document, which a user can open and use, is different from a program file, which is required by a software program to operate.

document area   In many software applications, the portion of the program's interface in which the active document appears. In this part of the interface, the user can work directly with the document and its contents.

document format   In productivity applications, settings that affect the appearance of the entire document, such as page size, page orientation, and the presence of headers or footers.

domain   A name given to a computer and its peripherals connected to the Internet.

Domain Name System (DNS)   A naming system used for computers on the Internet, consisting of an individual name representing the institution or person and the domain name, which classifies the type of organization, such as .com for commercial enterprises. DNS converts an e-mail address into the IP address for transmission.

dot pitch   The distance between phosphor dots on a monitor. The highest-resolution monitors have the smallest dot pitch.

double-click   To select an object or activate a command on the screen by pointing to an object (such as an icon) and pressing and releasing the mouse button twice in quick succession.

downloading   Retrieving a file from a remote computer; the opposite of uploading.

downward (backward) compatibility   The capability of a hardware device or a software product to interact successfully with the same software or hardware used by its predecessor.

drag-and-drop editing   See *dragging and dropping.*

dragging   To move an object on the screen by pointing to the object, depressing the mouse button, and holding down the button while dragging the object to a new location. Dragging also is used to activate commands, as when moving files in the Windows 95 Explorer.

dragging and dropping   Moving text or graphics from one part of the document to another by selecting the desired information, holding down the mouse button, dragging the selection to a new location, and releasing the mouse button.

DRAM   See *Dynamic RAM.*

draw program   A graphics program that uses vectors to create an image. Mathematical equations describe each line, shape, and pattern, allowing the user to manipulate all elements of the graphic.

driver   A small program that accepts requests for action from the operating system and causes a device, such as a video card or printer, to execute the requests.

drop shadow   In word processing and desktop publishing, a paragraph border style that is heavier on two contiguous sides, creating the illusion that the boxed paragraph is "floating" above the page.

DTP   See *desktop publishing software.*

Dual In-Line Memory Module (DIMM)   One type of circuit board containing RAM chips

dual-scan LCD   An improved passive matrix technology for flat-panel monitors in which pixels are scanned twice as often, reducing the effects of submarining and blurry graphics.

DVD   See *digital versatile disk.*

dye-sub (dye-sublimation) printer   A printer that produces photographic-quality images by using a heat source to evaporate colored inks from a ribbon, transferring the color to specially coated paper; also called *thermal dye transfer* and *thermal dye diffusion.*

dynamic RAM (DRAM)   The most common type of computer memory.

E

EBCDIC   See *Extended Binary Coded Decimal Interchange Code.*

e-commerce   The practice of conducting business transactions online, such as selling products from a World Wide Web site. The process often involves the customer's providing personal or credit card information online, presenting special security concerns.

editing   Making modifications to an existing document.

EFF   See *Electronic Frontier Foundation.*

EISA bus   See *Extended Industry Standard Architecture.*

electromagnet   A magnet made by wrapping a wire coil around an iron bar and sending an electric current through the coil. Reversing the direction of the current's flow reverses the polarity of the magnetic field. Electromagnets are part of the read/write heads used in magnetic storage devices.

electromagnetic field (EMF)   A field of magnetic and electrical forces created during the generation, transmission, and use of low-frequency electrical power. EMFs are produced by computers.

Electronic Frontier Foundation (EFF)   An organization created to provide research, policy development, and legal services for issues related to the expansion of electronic communications.

electronic mail (e-mail)   A system for exchanging written, voice, and video messages through a computer network.

electronic pen   An input device that allows the user to write directly on or point at a special pad or the screen of a pen-based computer, such as a PDA.

EMF   See *electromagnetic field.*

encapsulate   To include characteristics or other objects within an object in an object-oriented program.

Encapsulated PostScript (EPS)   A file format based on the PostScript printing language.

encryption   The process of encoding and decoding data.enhanced small device interface.

Glossary

enhanced small device interface (ESDI) An improvement on the ST-506 interface developed in 1983 by the Maxtor Corp.

(ESDI) A hard disk drive interface standard developed by Maxtor Corporation.

EPS See *Encapsulated PostScript.*

ergonomics The study of the physical relationship between people and their tools. In the world of computing, ergonomics seeks to help people use computers correctly to avoid physical problems such as fatigue, eyestrain, and repetitive stress injuries.

error-correction protocol A standard for correcting errors that occur when static interferes with data transmitted over telephone lines; examples include MNP2, MNP3, MNP4, and V42.

ESDI See *enhanced small device interface.*

Ethernet The most common network protocol, which usually is implemented using twisted-pair wires. Ethernet requires each computer on the network to take its turn to send data.

executable file The core program file responsible for launching software.

executing Loading and carrying out a program or a specific set of instructions; also called *running.*

expansion board A device that enables the user to configure or customize a computer to perform specific tasks or to enhance performance. An expansion board—also called a *card, adapter,* or *board*—contains a special set of chips and circuitry that add functionality to the computer. An expansion board may be installed to add fax/modem capabilities to the computer, for example, or to provide sound or video-editing capabilities. Also see *expansion slot.*

expansion slot The area of the motherboard into which circuit boards are inserted; connected to the bus in a PC.

expert system An information system in which decision-making processes are automated. A highly detailed database is accessed by an inference engine, which is capable of forming an intelligent response to a query.

Extended Binary Coded Decimal Interchange Code (EBCDIC) An 8-bit binary code developed by IBM to represent symbols and numeric and alphanumeric characters; commonly used today on IBM mainframe computers.

Extended Data Output (EDO) RAM A type of RAM, which is faster than FPM RAM and commonly found on the fastest computers.

Extended Industry Standard Architecture (EISA) A PC bus standard created by a consortium of hardware developers that extends the 16-bit bus to 32 bits. EISA buses are capable of accessing 16-bit and 32-bit devices.

Extensible Markup Language (XML) A proposed page-markup language that would replace HTML as the standard hypertext markup language for the World Wide Web. XML is built around the idea of letting anyone define a way to describe information presented in a Web page.

external modem A communications device used to modulate data signals. This type of device is described as "external" because it is housed outside the computer and connected to the computer through a serial port and to the telephone system with a standard telephone jack.

extranet A network connection that enables external users to access a portion of an organization's internal network, usually via an Internet connection. External users have access to specific parts of the internal network but are forbidden to access other areas, which are protected by firewalls.

F

FAQ See *Frequently Asked Questions.*

Fast Ethernet A networking technology, also known as *100Base-T,* that uses the same network cabling scheme as Ethernet but uses different network interface cards to achieve data transfer speeds of up to 100 Mbps.

Fast Page Mode (FPM) RAM The oldest and least sophisticated type of RAM, still used in many PCs.

FAT See *file allocation table.*

fax modem A modem that can emulate a fax machine.

fiber-optic cable A thin strand of glass wrapped in a protective coating. Fiber-optic cable transfers data by means of pulsating beams of light.

Fibre Channel Arbitrated Loop (FC-AL) A storage protocol that enables multiple computers to share storage media. FC-AL provides a large bandwidth to allow large amounts of data (up to 100Mbps) to be shared.

field The smallest unit of data in a database, used to group each piece or item of data into a specific category. Fields are arranged in a column and titled by the user.

fiery printer A color laser printer typically used to produce high-quality graphics; used by print shops and publishing firms.

file A set of related computer data (used by a human user) or program instructions (used by an application or operating system) that has been given a name.

file allocation table (FAT) In a diskette or hard disk, a table log created in the logical formatting process that records the location of each file and the status of each sector.

file compression See *data compression.*

file server The central computer of a network, used for shared storage. The server stores software applications and databases; also called a *network server, application server,* or simply *server.*

file server network A hierarchical network strategy in which the server is used to store and forward files to the nodes. Each node runs its own applications.

Glossary

file transfer   The process of sending a file from one computer to another by modem.

File Transfer Protocol (FTP)   A set of rules or guidelines that dictates the format in which data is sent from one computer to another.

filter   A DBMS tool that enables the user to establish conditions for selecting and displaying a subset of records meeting those criteria.

firewall   An antipiracy method for protecting networks. A network node acts as a gateway, permitting access to public sections while protecting proprietary areas.

flame   A jargon term used to describe negative, critical, or insulting messages posted in an Internet news group or chat room. Flaming can result in online retaliation in several forms, such as spamming, spoofing, expulsion from online groups, and so on.

flash memory   A type of nonvolatile memory, like ROM, which stores data even when the system's power is off. Flash memory is commonly used in digital cameras.

flatbed scanner   A scanner that can accommodate large pages and books. Scanning heads move under a glass cover to digitize data from the hard copy and transfer it to the computer.

flat-file database   A database file consisting of a single data table, which is not linked to any other tables.

flat-panel display   A thin, lightweight monitor used in laptop and notebook computers. Most flat-panel displays use LCD technology.

floating-point arithmetic   A method used to speed up the storage and calculation of numbers by reducing the number of decimal places through the use of scientific notation. It is the function of the computer's math coprocessor (also called a *floating-point unit*) to perform such calculations.

floating-point unit (FPU)   See *math coprocessor.*

floppy   See *diskette.*

floppy disk   See *diskette.*

floptical drive   A combination of two storage technologies, including floppy disk and optical disk technologies. Floptical drives include an ultra-high-density magnetic head that can write up to 20 tracks at a time, rather than just one track.

fly-by   A specially rendered animation, created in a CAD or 3-D graphics program, that creates the illusion that the viewer is moving past, around, or over an object such as a building. Designers often create fly-bys by using software cameras to constantly change the angle of view of the object.

folder   See *directory.*

font   The style of the letters, symbols, and punctuation marks in a document. Modern applications provide many types of fonts and enable users to use many different fonts in the same document.

footer   A recurring line or paragraph of text appearing at the bottom of each page in a document. Footers often include page numbers, the document's title, the name of the current chapter, or other information.

form   A custom screen created in a database for displaying and entering data related to a single database record.

format   In productivity applications, settings that affect the appearance of a document or parts of a document.

formatting   (1) The process of magnetically mapping a disk with a series of tracks and sectors where data will be stored. (2) The process of applying formatting options (such as character or paragraph formats) to a document.

formula   A mathematical equation within a cell of a spreadsheet. To identify it and distinguish it from other spreadsheet entries, a formula begins with a special symbol, such as a plus sign, an equal sign, or a parenthesis.

formula bar   A special toolbar above the spreadsheet window that displays the active cell address and the formula or data entered in that cell.

FORTRAN   A third-generation programming language designed to create mathematical and engineering applications.

fourth-generation language (4GL)   An advanced programming language used to create an application, such as a report writer.

FPU   See *math coprocessor.*

fragmented   Describes a file that has been broken into sections, which are stored on noncontiguous sectors of a disk.

frame   (1) In networking, a small block of data to be transmitted over a network. A frame includes an identifying header and the actual data to be sent; also called a packet. (2) In animation, a single still image that, when viewed with many other images in rapid succession, creates the illusion of motion. (3) In many software applications, a special tool that enables the user to place an object—such as a text box or an image from a separate file—in a document. The frame surrounds the object in the document, enabling the user to position and resize the object as needed.

freeware   Software that is made freely available to the public by the publisher. Freeware publishers usually allow users to distribute their software to others, as long as the software's source files are not modified, and as long as the distributor charges no fees or does not profit from the distribution.

Frequently Asked Questions (FAQ)   A document routinely developed by a news group, which lists the most commonly asked questions and their answers. FAQs help a news group's members avoid the repeated posting of the same information to the group.

Glossary

full duplex   The ability to send and receive data simultaneously over a common data path or communications link.

function   (1) In a spreadsheet, a part of a cell formula used to perform complex operations, such as adding the contents of a cell range or finding the absolute value of cell contents. (2) In programming, a block of statements designed to perform a specific routine or task.

function keys   The part of the keyboard that can be used to quickly activate commands, designated F1, F2, and so on.

G

G3   The current (as of this printing) line of Apple computers.

gateway   A computer system that can translate one network protocol into another so that data can be transmitted between two dissimilar networks.

GB   See *gigabyte*.

gigabyte (GB)   Equivalent to approximately one billion bytes; a typical measurement of data storage.

goal seeking   A data-analysis process that begins with a conclusion and calculates the values that will lead to the desired outcome, such as figuring a mortgage amount based on an affordable monthly payment.

Gopher   An Internet service that organizes resources into multilevel menus to make finding information easier; first created by the University of Minnesota to provide easy access to computers campus-wide.

goto statement   In programming, a statement that tells the program to move to a specific line of code, which may or may not be the next line in sequence.

graph   A graphic representation of numbers created from spreadsheet data; also called a chart.

graphical user interface (GUI)   A user interface in which actions are initiated when the user selects an icon or an option from a pull-down menu with the mouse or other pointing device. GUIs also represent documents, programs, and devices on screen as graphical elements, which the user can use by clicking or dragging; also called a *point-and-click interface*.

graphics program   Software used to create and manipulate original images or to edit images created in another application.

grayscale monitor   A monitor that displays colors ranging from white to black, including up to 256 shades of gray.

groupware   Application software that enables multiple users on a network to cooperate on projects. Groupware suites usually include scheduling and calendar software, e-mail, and document-management tools.

GUI   See *graphical user interface*.

H

hacker   An expert in computer technology who uses skill and innovative techniques to solve complex computing problems. Hackers are more notorious, however, for creating problems, such as invading private or governmental computer networks, accessing data from corporate databases, online extortion, and other activities.

half-duplex   The ability to send or receive data—but not do both simultaneously—over a common data path or communications link.

handheld computer   A personal computer that is small enough to be held in one hand. A handheld computer is much like a personal digital assistant (PDA) but usually features a tiny built-in keyboard.

handheld scanner   A scanner that can be held in the hand and used to scan narrow areas of data.

handle   A specialized portion of a frame, which enables the user to drag the frame to resize it. (See *frame*, definition 3.)

hard disk   A nonremovable magnetic storage device included in most PCs. A stack of aluminum or glass platters, each coated with iron oxide, enclosed in a hard disk drive.

hard disk drive   A device that consists of the hard disk platters, a spindle on which the platters spin, a read/write head for each side of each platter, and a sealed chamber that encloses the disks and spindle. Many hard disk drives also include the drive controller, although the controller is a separate unit on some hard disk drives.

hardware   The physical components of a computer, including processor and memory chips, input/output devices, tapes, disks, modems, and cables.

hardware maintenance technician   In an IS department, a worker responsible for maintaining and repairing hardware components used in the information system.

head crash   Describes the results when a read/write head makes contact with the surface of a spinning hard disk or diskette. The contact can damage the disk's surface or destroy the read/write head.

header   (1) The initial part of a data packet being transmitted across a network. The header contains information about the type of data in the payload, the source and destination of the data, and a sequence number so that data from multiple packets can be reassembled at the receiving computer in the proper order. (See *frame*, definition 1.) (2) A recurring line or paragraph of text appearing at the top of each page in a document. Headers often include page numbers, the document's title, the name of the current chapter, or other information.

Hertz (Hz)   The frequency of electrical vibrations, or cycles, per second.

hierarchical database   A database structure in which records are organized in parent-child relationships; each child type is related to only one parent type.

hierarchical file system A structured file organization system in which the root directory (also called a *folder*) may contain other directories, which in turn contain files.

higher-level language Languages designed to make programming easier through the use of familiar English words and symbols.

highlight To select a block of text or cells for editing. Selected text is highlighted—displayed in a different color from the remaining text in a document.

home page An organization's principal Web page, which provides pointers to other Web pages with additional information.

hot-swappable hard disk A magnetic storage device similar to a removable hard disk. A removable box encloses the disk, drive, and read/write heads in a sealed container. This type of hard disk can be added or removed from a server without shutting down the server.

HTML See *Hypertext Markup Language.*

HTTP See *Hypertext Transfer Protocol.*

hypermedia Text, graphics, video, and sound linked and accessible in a hypertext format.

hypertext A flexible software technology that provides fast and flexible access to information. The user can jump to a search topic by selecting it on screen; used to create Web pages and help screens.

Hypertext Markup Language (HTML) A page-description language used on the World Wide Web that defines the hypertext links between documents.

Hypertext Transfer Protocol (HTTP) A set of file transfer rules used on the World Wide Web that control the way information is shared.

Hz See *hertz.*

I

I-beam cursor An on-screen symbol shaped like a capital I that indicates the location of the mouse pointer.

icon Graphical screen elements that execute one or more commands when selected with a mouse or other pointing device.

IDE See *integrated drive electronics.*

image scanner An input device that converts printed images into electronic form. Sensors determine the intensity of light reflected from the page, and the light intensities are converted to digital data that can be viewed and manipulated by the computer; also called a *graphics scanner.*

implementation Phase 4 of the software development life cycle, in which new software and hardware are installed in the user environment, training is offered, and system testing is completed.

indent The distance between the beginning or end of a line of text and the left or right margin, whichever is closer.

Industry Standard Architecture (ISA) A PC bus standard developed by IBM, extending the bus to 16 bits. An ISA bus can access 8-bit and 16-bit devices.

inference engine Software used with an expert system to examine data with respect to the knowledge base and to select an appropriate response.

information superhighway The vast communications link that will allow access to government, industry, and educational data banks for all users. The information superhighway is similar to the Internet but will provide a single high-speed link in place of a network of systems.

information system A business computer application consisting of the rules and procedures established to deliver information to the users.

Information Systems (IS) department The people in an organization responsible for designing, developing, implementing, and maintaining the systems necessary to deliver information to all levels of the organization.

initializing See *formatting.*

ink jet printer A printer that produces images by spraying ink onto the page; prints at moderate speeds and is cost-effective.

input device Computer hardware that accepts data and instructions from the user. Input devices include the keyboard, mouse, joystick, pen, trackball, scanner, bar code reader, microphone, and touch screen, as well as other types of hardware.

input/output (I/O) Communications between the user and the computer or between hardware components that result in the transfer of data.

insertion mode In word processing, a text-entry mode. In this mode, when the user types characters, they are inserted into the document. If necessary, the computer forces existing characters apart to make room for the new text; existing text is not overwritten by new text.

insertion point See *cursor.*

install To transfer program components from a diskette CD-ROM to a hard disk and ready the program for operation.

instantiate In object-oriented programming, to create an object with all the attributes and methods associated with a specific class.

instruction set Machine language instructions that define all the operations that the CPU can perform.

integrated drive electronics (IDE) A common hard disk interface standard developed by Compaq Computer; places most of the disk controller circuitry on the drive itself.

Glossary

integrated pointing device A pointing device built into the computer's keyboard, consisting of a small joystick positioned near the middle of the keyboard, typically between the g and h keys. The joystick is controlled with either forefinger. Two buttons that perform the same function as mouse buttons are just beneath the spacebar and are pressed with the thumb.

Integrated Services Digital Network (ISDN) A digital telecommunications standard that replaces analog transmissions and transmits voice, video, and data.

Intel The world's leading manufacturer of microprocessors. Intel invented the first microprocessor, which was used in electronic calculators.

intellectual property Ideas, statements, processes, and other intangible items that a person can claim to own or have originated.

interactive The ability to react to and respond to external influences.

interactive media A software product that can react to and respond to input from the user.

interactive television A service that will allow viewers to select movies, shop, and participate in live broadcasts using phone lines, cable, and satellite communications.

interface See *user interface*.

internal modem A communications device used to modulate data signals. This type of modem is described as "internal" because it is a circuit board that is plugged into one of the computer's expansion slots.

Internet Relay Chat (IRC) A multiuser system made up of channels, which people join to exchange messages either publicly or privately. Messages are exchanged in real-time, meaning they are transmitted to other users on the channel as they are typed in.

Internet Service Provider (ISP) An intermediary service between the Internet backbone and the user, providing easy and relatively inexpensive access to shell accounts, direct TCP/IP connections, and high-speed access through dedicated data circuits.

interrupt request (IRQ) (1) A signal sent by the operating system to the CPU, requesting processing time for a specific task. (2) A signal sent by the keyboard controller to the CPU to indicate that a complete keystroke has been received.

intranet An internal network whose interface and accessibility are modeled after an Internet-based Web site. Only internal users are allowed to access information or resources on the intranet; if connected to an external network or the Internet, the intranet's resources are protected from outside access by firewalls.

IP address A unique four-part numeric address assigned to each computer on the Internet, containing routing information to identify its location. Each of the four parts is a number between 0 and 255.

IRIS printer A type of ink jet printer that sprays the ink on paper mounted on a spinning drum. Such printers can produce images with a resolution of 1,800 dots per inch.

ISA bus See *Industry Standard Architecture bus*.

ISDN See *Integrated Services Digital Network*.

ISP See *Internet Service Provider*.

J

Java A programming language, used for creating cross-platform programs. Java enables Web page designers to include movement and interactivity in Web pages.

Java applet A Java-based program included in a Web page.

joystick An input device used to control the movement of on-screen components; typically used in video games.

JPEG (Joint Photographic Experts Group) format A bitmap file format commonly used to display photographic images; compresses the bitmap, resulting in a loss of clarity while increasing the image refresh rate.

K

K5 A line of Pentium-class processors made by AMD. These chips are available in 100 MHz and 116.7 MHz versions, which are equivalent to the Pentium 133 MHz and 166 MHz processors, respectively.

K6 A line of Pentium-class processors made by AMD, which supports MMX technology and comes in speeds of 166 MHz, 200 MHz, 233 MHz, and higher—comparable to the Pentium Pro line of processors running at the same clock speed.

KB See *kilobyte*.

kerning A text-editing feature that adjusts the distance between individual letters in a word to make that word easier to read.

keyboard The most common input device, used to enter letters, numbers, symbols, punctuation, and commands into the computer. Computer keyboards typically include numeric, alphanumeric, cursor-movement, modifier, and function keys, as well as other special keys.

keyboard buffer A part of memory that receives and stores the scan codes from the keyboard controller until the program can accept them.

keyboard controller A chip within the keyboard or the computer that receives the keystroke and generates the scan code.

keyboarding Touch typing using a computer keyboard.

keyframe In animation, the primary frame in a motion sequence, such as the starting or stopping point in a walk cycle.

kilobyte (KB) Equivalent to 1,024 bytes; a common measure of data storage.

knowledge base A highly specialized database used with an expert system to intelligently produce solutions.

L

label Descriptive text used in a spreadsheet cell to describe the data in a column or row.

LAN See *local area network*.

land A flat area on the metal surface of a CD-ROM that reflects the laser light into the sensor of an optical disk drive; also see *pit*.

landscape orientation A document format in which the text is printed parallel to the widest page edge; the opposite of portrait orientation.

laptop computer A small, portable computer with an attached flat screen, typically battery or AC powered and weighing under 12 pounds; often called simply a laptop.

laser printer A quiet, fast printer that produces high-quality output. A laser beam focused on an electrostatic drum creates an image to which powdered toner adheres, and that image is transferred to paper.

LCD monitor See *liquid crystal display monitor*.

leading In desktop publishing, the amount of space between lines in a document. DTP software enables the user to precisely adjust this spacing, to make text easier to read.

library A collection of programs or functions that have been compiled and tested.

line spacing The distance between lines of text in a document. The most common examples include single-spaced and double-spaced. See also *kerning*.

liquid crystal display (LCD) monitor A flat-panel monitor on which an image is created when the liquid crystal becomes charged; used primarily in notebook and laptop computers.

listserv An e-mail server that contains a list name and enables users to communicate with others on the list in an ongoing discussion.

local area network (LAN) A system of PCs located relatively near to one another and connected by wire or a wireless link. A LAN permits simultaneous access to data and resources, enhances personal communication, and simplifies backup procedures.

logic error A bug in which the code directs the computer to perform a task incorrectly.

logical field A database field that stores only one of two values: yes or no, true or false, on or off, and so on.

logical format An operating system function in which tracks and sectors are mapped on the surface of a disk. Mapping creates the boot record, FAT, root folder (also called the *root directory*), and the data area.

logical operation One of the two types of operations a computer can perform. Logical operations usually involve making a comparison, such as determining whether two values are equal.

log on To access a computer system. The process of logging on often requires the user to provide a user identification code and/or a password before the computer system will allow access.

loop A program or routine that executes a set of instructions repeatedly until, or while, a condition is true.

M

machine language Strings of numbers defined by hardware design; directs the CPU to perform functions.

Macintosh operating system The operating system that runs on PCs built by Apple Computer. The Mac OS was the first operating system to use a graphical user interface, utilize plug-and-play hardware compatibility, feature built-in networking, and support common user access.

macro A tool that allows the user to store and then automatically issue a sequence of commands or keystrokes.

magnetic disk A round, flat disk covered with magnetic oxide, the most commonly used storage medium. Data is written magnetically on the disk and can be recorded over and over. The magnetic disk is the basic component of the diskette and hard disk.

magnetic storage A storage technology in which data is recorded when iron particles are polarized on a magnetic storage medium.

magneto-optical (MO) disk A storage medium that has the capacity of an optical disk but can be rewritten with the ease of a magnetic disk. Data is written to disk when a laser melts the plastic coating encasing the magnetically sensitive metallic crystals, allowing a magnet to change the orientation of the crystals.

mail merge The process of combining a text document, such as a letter, with the contents of a database, such as an address list; commonly used to produce form letters.

mail server In an e-mail system, the server on which messages received from the post office server are stored until the recipients access their mailbox and retrieve the messages.

mainframe computer A large, multiuser computer system designed to handle massive amounts of input, output, and storage. A mainframe is usually composed of one or more powerful CPUs connected to many terminals. Mainframe systems are typically used in businesses requiring the maintenance of huge databases or simultaneous processing of multiple complex tasks.

Glossary

maintenance Phase 5 of the software development life cycle, in which the new system is monitored, errors are corrected, and minor adjustments are made to improve system performance.

margin The space between the edge of a page and the main body of the document. Text cannot be entered within the margin.

massively parallel processing (MPP) A processing architecture that uses hundreds to thousands of microprocessors in one computer to perform complex processes quickly.

master page A special page created in desktop publishing software that contains elements common to all the pages in the document, such as page numbers, headers and footers, ruling lines, margin features, special graphics, and layout guides.

math coprocessor A computer chip that can be either separate from or part of the CPU and is especially designed to handle complex mathematical operations; also called the *floating-point unit* because it performs floating-point calculations.

mathematical algorithm A set of instructions, which a computer follows to carry out a given task. In the case of data compression software, mathematical algorithms are used to study the data to determine which portions—if any—can be removed to reduce file size.

maximum access time The maximum ammount of time it takes a drive to access data.

MB See *megabyte.*

MCA bus See *Micro Channel Architecture bus.*

media (1) The plural form of the term "medium." (2) In a network, the wire or cable used to connect the networked computers and peripherals.

MediaGX A microprocessor, made by Cyrix, which integrates audio and graphics functions and is available in 120 MHz and 133 MHz versions.

medium (1) In storage technology, a medium is material used to store data, such as the magnetic coating on a disk or tape, or the metallic platter in a compact disk. (2) In networking, a medium is a means of conveying a signal across the network, such as a cable. (3) In multimedia, a medium is a single means of conveying a message, such as text or video.

megabyte (MB) Equivalent to approximately one million bytes; a common measure of data storage.

megahertz (MHz) Equivalent to millions of cycles per second; a common measure of clock speed.

member function (method) A function of a class in object-oriented programming.

memo field A database field that stores text information of variable length.

memory A collection of chips on the motherboard or on a circuit board attached to the motherboard, where all computer processing and program instructions are stored while in use. The computer's memory enables the CPU to retrieve data quickly for processing.

memory address A number used by the CPU to locate each piece of data in memory.

menu A list of commands or functions displayed on screen for selection by the user.

menu bar A graphical screen element—located above the document area of an application window—displaying a list of the types of commands available to the user. When the user selects an option from the menu bar, a list appears, displaying the commands related to that menu option.

message A signal in an object-oriented program that is sent to an object, requesting it to perform a specific function.

Mhz See *megahertz.*

Micro Channel Architecture (MCA) bus A 32-bit PC bus standard developed by IBM; allows expansion boards to be configured by the software instead of manually.

microcode Code that details the individual tasks the computer must perform to complete each instruction in the instruction set; a necessary level of translation between program instructions and elementary circuit operations.

microcomputer See *personal computer (PC).*

microphone An input device used with multimedia applications to digitally record audio data, such as the human voice.

microprocessor An integrated circuit on a single chip that makes up the computer's CPU. Microprocessors are composed of silicon or other material etched with many tiny electronic circuits.

Microsoft Knowledge Base (KB) A searchable multimedia product that enables Microsoft customers and developers to find information and solutions about the Microsoft products they use.

millisecond (ms) Equivalent to one thousandth of a second; used to measure access time.

minicomputer A midsize, multiuser computer capable of handling more input and output than a PC but with less processing power and storage than a mainframe; often called a midrange computer.

MMX A microprocessor technology incorporated by Intel in the Pentium Pro, which increases the multimedia capabilities of a computer chip. MMX processors process audio, video, and graphical data more efficiently than non-MMX processors, enabling one instruction to perform the same function on multiple pieces of data, reducing the number of loops required to handle video, audio, animation, and graphical data.

model A three-dimensional image, which represents a real or imagined object or character; created using special computer software programs, including surface modelers, solid modelers, spline-based modelers, and others.

modem   An input/output device that allows computers to communicate through telephone lines. A modem converts outgoing digital data into analog signals that can be transmitted over phone lines and converts incoming audio signals into digital data that can be processed by the computer; short for modulator-demodulator.

modifier keys   The part of a keyboard used in conjunction with other keys to execute a command. The PC keyboard includes Shift, Ctrl, and Alt keys; the Macintosh keyboard also includes the Command key.

monitor   A display screen used to provide computer output to the user. Examples include the cathode ray tube (CRT) monitor, color monitor, monochrome monitor, flat-panel monitor, and liquid crystal display (LCD).

monochrome monitor   A monitor that displays only one color (such as green or amber) against a contrasting background.

monospace font   A font in which each character uses exactly the same amount of horizontal space.

Moore's Law   A commonly held (and so far accurate) axiom, which states that computing power doubles every 18 months. Named after Intel founder Gordon Moore, this "law" is expected to hold true well into the 21st century.

motherboard   The main circuit board of the computer, which contains the CPU, memory, expansion slots, bus, and video controller; also called the *system board*.

Motorola   A manufacturer of computer chips, most notably microprocessors and communications chips; the maker of processors used in Macintosh computers.

mouse   An input device operated by rolling across a flat surface. The mouse is used to control the on-screen pointer by pointing and clicking, double-clicking, or dragging objects on the screen.

MPC standard   See *Multimedia Personal Computer standard.*

MPEG (Moving Pictures Experts Group) format   A multimedia data compression standard used to compress full-motion video.

MS-DOS   The command-line interface operating system developed by Microsoft for PCs. IBM selected DOS as the standard for early IBM and IBM-compatible machines.

multimedia   Elements of text, graphics, animation, video, and sound combined for presentation to the consumer.

multimedia authoring   A process that combines text, graphics, animation, video, and sound documents developed with other software packages to create a composite product.

multimedia authoring software   An application that enables the user to incorporate images, text, sound, computer animation, and video to produce a multimedia product.

multimedia network   A specialized network that enables fast access to large multimedia files, such as audio, video, and animation files; often used in digital production and video studios.

multimedia PC   A PC capable of producing high-quality text, graphics, animation, video, and sound. A multimedia PC may include a CD-ROM or DVD drive, microphone, speakers, a high-quality video controller, and a sound card.

Multimedia Personal Computer (MPC) standard   The minimum hardware and software requirements for a multimedia PC, as defined by the Multimedia PC Marketing Council.

multitasking   The capability of an operating system to load multiple programs into memory at one time and to perform two or more processes concurrently, such as printing a document while editing another.

N

navigation   The process of moving through a software program.

needs analysis   Phase 1 of the software development life cycle, in which needs are defined, the current system is analyzed, alternative solutions are developed, and the best solution and its functions are selected.

network   A system of interconnected computers that communicate with one another and share applications, data, and hardware components.

network computer (NC)   A specialized, terminal-like computer that provides basic input/output capabilities to a user on a network. Usually comprising a keyboard, mouse, and monitor, NCs usually have no built-in storage device.

network database   A database structure in which any record type can relate to any number of other record types.

networking   The process of connecting computers, which permits the transfer of data and programs between users.

network interface card (NIC)   A circuit board that controls the exchange of data over a network.

network license   An agreement in which an organization purchases the right to use a program on a network accessible by several nodes. The total software cost is less than would be required to buy separate copies of the software for each machine.

network manager   See *system manager.*

network operating system (NOS)   A group of programs that manage the resources on a network.

network protocol   A set of standards used for network communications.

network server   See *file server.*

network version   An application program especially designed to work within a network environment. Users access the software from a shared storage device.

Glossary

new media See *multimedia*.

news A public bulletin board service on the Internet organized into groups representing specific topics of interest.

News group See *discussion group*.

NIC See *network interface card*.

nodes The individual computers that make up a network.

nonvolatile The tendency for memory to retain data even when the computer is turned off (as is the case with ROM); permanent and unchangeable.

NOS See *network operating system*.

notebook computer A smaller version of the laptop computer, weighing 5 to 7 pounds.

NSFnet A network developed by the National Science Foundation to accommodate the many users attempting to access the five academic research centers created by the NSF.

numeric field A database field that stores numeric characters.

numeric keypad The part of a keyboard that looks and works like a calculator keypad, with 10 digits and mathematical operators.

O

object A data item and its associated characteristics, attributes, and procedures. An object's characteristics define the type of object—for example, whether it is text, a sound, a graphic, or video. Attributes might be color, size, style, and so on. A procedure refers to the processing or handling associated with the object.

object embedding The process of integrating a copy of data from one application into another, as from a spreadsheet to a word processor. The data retains the formatting applied to it in the original application, but its relationship with the original file is destroyed.

object linking The process of integrating a copy of data from one application into another so that the data retains a link to the original document. Thereafter, a change in the original document also appears in the linked data in the second application.

Object Linking and Embedding (OLE) A Windows feature that combines object embedding and linking functions; allows the user to construct a document containing data from a single point in time or one in which the data is constantly updated.

object-oriented database A database structure in which data items, their characteristics, attributes, and procedures are grouped into units called objects.

object-oriented programming (OOP) A programming technology that makes use of reusable, modular components; includes the processes of encapsulation and inheritance and the ability to create an object before its exact character is known.

OCR See *optical character recognition*.

offline browsing The capability of a Web browser to enable users to read and navigate Web pages from a local hard drive when not connected to the Internet.

off-the-shelf application A software product that is packaged and available for sale; installed as-is in some system designs.

OLE See *Object Linking and Embedding*.

online Connected to, served by, or available through a networked computer system.

online service A telecommunications service that supplies e-mail and information search tools.

OOP See *object-oriented programming*.

operating environment An intuitive graphical user interface that overlays the operating system but does not replace it. Microsoft Windows 3.x is an example.

operating system (OS) The master control program that provides an interface for a user to communicate with the computer, manages hardware devices, manages and maintains disk file systems, and supports application programs.

operator The component of a formula that is used to specify the operation that you want to perform on the parts of a formula; includes arithmetic, comparison, and text operators.

optical character recognition (OCR) Technology that enables a computer to translate optically scanned data into character codes, which can then be edited.

optical drive A storage device that writes data to and reads data from an optical storage medium, such as a compact disk.

OS See *operating system*.

OS/2 A single-user, multitasking operating system with a point-and-click interface developed by IBM and Microsoft to take advantage of the multitasking capabilities of post-8086 computers.

output device A hardware component, such as a monitor or printer, that returns processed data to the user.

outsourcing The use of outside expertise to accomplish a task, such as hiring a freelance writer to produce user documentation.

overtype mode A text entry mode. In overtype mode, when the user types characters, they overwrite (and erase) existing text that appears to the right of the insertion point.

P

packet A small block of data to be transmitted over a network, which includes an identifying header and the actual data to be sent; also called a *frame*.

packet-switched A type of communications line in which data is broken into distinct, addressed packets that can be transferred separately. Access to the connection can be intermittent; commonly used for networks.

paint program A graphics program that creates images as a mosaic of pixels, or bitmaps.

palmtop computer See *personal digital assistant (PDA)*.

paragraph A series of letters, words, or sentences followed by a hard return.

paragraph format Settings that affect the appearance of one or more entire paragraphs, such as line spacing, paragraph spacing, indents, alignment, tab stops, borders, and shading.

paragraph spacing The amount of blank space between two paragraphs in a document. Typically, this spacing is equivalent to one line of text.

parallel conversion A conversion process that continues the use of an existing system while a new system is being implemented.

parallel interface A channel through which 8 or more data bits can flow simultaneously, such as a computer bus. A parallel interface is commonly used to connect printers to the computer; also called a parallel port.

Pascal A third-generation programming language that is highly structured and popular for its implementation of object-oriented extension; used for educational purposes.

passive matrix LCD Liquid crystal display technology, used for flat-panel monitors, that relies on a grid of transistors arranged by rows and columns. In a passive matrix LCD, the color displayed by each pixel is determined by the electricity coming from the transistors at the end of the row and the top of the column.

password A word or code used as a security checkpoint by an individual computer system or a network; verifies the user's identity.

Paste An application command that copies data from the Clipboard and places it in the document at the position of the insertion point. Data in the Clipboard can be pasted into multiple places in one document, multiple documents, and documents in different applications.

payload In a packet, the actual data being transmitted across a network or over telephone lines.

PC card A specialized expansion card the size of a credit card, which fits into a laptop or notebook computer and is used to connect new components.

PCD See *PhotoCD*.

PCI bus See *Peripheral Component Interconnect bus*.

PC video camera A small video camera, which connects to a special video card on a PC. When used with videoconferencing software, a PC video camera enables users to capture full-motion video images, save them to disk, edit them, and transmit them to other users across a network or the Internet.

PDA See *personal digital assistant*.

personal computer (PC) The most common type of computer found in an office, classroom, or home. The PC is designed to fit on a desk and be used by one person at a time; also called a *microcomputer*.

peer-to-peer network A network environment in which all nodes on the network have equal access to at least some of the resources on all other nodes.

Pentium An Intel processor utilizing a 32-bit microprocessor and superscalar architecture.

Pentium Pro An Intel processor utilizing a 32-bit microprocessor and capable of processing three program instructions in a single clock cycle. The Pentium Pro utilizes dynamic execution, which is the ability to execute program instructions in the most efficient order.

Pentium II An Intel processor based on a 32-bit microprocessor and holding 7.5 million transistors. The Pentium II supports MMX technology and dynamic execution, uses Slot One technology, and operates at speeds of 300 MHz and higher.

Peripheral Component Interconnect (PCI) A PC bus standard developed by Intel that supplies a high-speed data path between the CPU and peripheral devices.

personal digital assistant (PDA) A very small portable computer designed to be held in one hand; used to perform specific tasks, such as creating limited spreadsheets or storing phone numbers; also called a *palmtop*.

phase-change rewritable drive A type of optical storage device that enables the user to write to the disk more than once. A phase-change rewritable drive uses a laser beam to alter the molecular structure of the disk.

phased conversion A conversion process in which components of the replacement system are introduced gradually.

PhotoCD (PCD) An imaging system developed by Kodak to digitally record and store photographic images on CD-ROM.

photo-manipulation program A multimedia software tool used to modify scanned photographic images, including adjusting contrast and sharpness.

photorealistic Describes computer-generated images that are lifelike in appearance and not obviously models. Photorealism is becoming increasingly important as computer models are used more frequently in films, games, and multimedia products.

pilot conversion A conversion process in which a new system is tested and run by a selected group before it is fully installed throughout the organization.

pit A depressed area on the metal surface of a CD-ROM that scatters laser light; also see *land*.

pixel One or more dots that express a portion of an image; picture element.

plotter An output device used to create large-format hard copy; generally used with CAD and design systems.

Glossary

plug-and-play   An operating system feature that enables the user to add hardware devices to the computer without performing technically difficult connection procedures.

point   A standard unit used in measuring fonts. One point equals .02 inch in height.

pointer   An on-screen object, usually an arrow, used to select text, access menus, move files, or interact with other programs, files, or data represented graphically on the screen.

Point to Point Protocol (PPP)   A communications protocol used for linking a computer directly to the Internet. PPP features include the ability to establish or terminate a session, to hang up and redial, and to use password protection.

pointing device   A device that enables the user to freely move an on-screen pointer and to select text, menu options, icons, and other on-screen objects. Two popular types of pointing devices are mice and trackballs.

polarized   The condition of a magnetic bar with ends having opposite magnetic polarity.

polygonal modeler   A 3-D modeling program that builds images using an array of miniature polygons.

port   A socket on the back of the computer used to connect external devices to the computer.

portable   Describes software applications that are easily transferred from one platform to another, or hardware that can be easily moved.

portrait orientation   A document format in which the text is printed parallel to the narrowest page edge; the opposite of landscape orientation.

PostScript   A printing language created by Adobe Systems that produces high-quality images ready for the printing press.

PowerPC   Created through a joint venture by IBM and Motorola, a microprocessor designed to run both DOS and Macintosh-based software. Although the PowerPC never really gained market share, it set records for microprocessor performance.

PPP   See *Point to Point Protocol*.

preemptive multitasking   A multitasking environment in which the OS prioritizes system and application processes and performs them in the most efficient order. The OS can preempt a low-priority task with a more critical one.

presentation program   Software that enables the user to create professional-quality graphs and charts based on data imported from other programs, such as spreadsheets. Images are presented on paper, on transparencies, or as automated slide shows with incorporated sound.

printer   An output device that produces a hard copy on paper.

print job   A single request for printing services, made by a user on a network, to be printed on a networked printer. A print job can include one or multiple documents.

procedure   A name sometimes ascribed to blocks of reusable code. See also *subroutine* and *routine*.

processing   A complex procedure that transforms raw data into useful information.

processor   See *central processing unit (CPU)*.

productivity software   An application designed to help individuals complete tasks more efficiently. Examples include word processing programs, spreadsheets, graphics programs, and presentation software.

program   See *software*.

programmer   The person responsible for creating a computer program, including writing new code and analyzing and modifying existing code.

proportional font   A font in which the characters use varying amounts of horizontal space.

protocol   A set of rules and procedures that determine how a computer system receives and transmits data.

prototype   A working system model used to clarify and refine system requirements.

purchasing agent   In an IS department, the person responsible for purchasing hardware and software products.

push delivery   Technology that enables Web sites to automatically deliver preselected content to the user's browser.

Q

query   A search question that instructs the program to locate records that meet specific criteria.

Query by Example (QBE)   A database tool that accepts a query from a user and then creates the SQL code to locate data requested by the query.

QWERTY   A standard keyboard arrangement; refers to the first six letters on the top row of the alphanumeric keyboard.

R

random access memory (RAM)   A computer's volatile or temporary memory, which exists as chips on the motherboard near the CPU. RAM stores data and programs while they are being used and requires a power source to maintain its integrity.

range   In a spreadsheet, a rectangular group of contiguous cells.

read-only memory (ROM)   A permanent, or non-volatile, memory chip used to store instructions and data, including the computer's startup instructions. ROM's contents cannot be altered.

read/write head   The magnetic device within the disk drive that floats above the disk's surface and reads, records, and erases data on the disk. A read/write head contains an electromagnet that alters the polarity of magnetic particles on the storage medium. Most disk drives have one read/write head for each side of each disk in the drive.

real-time processing The ability to process information as it is received; provides immediate response to input.

record A database row composed of related fields; a collection of records makes up the database.

Reduced Instruction Set Computing (RISC) processor A microprocessor design that simplifies the instruction set, using fewer instructions of constant size, each of which can be executed in one machine cycle.

refresh rate The number of times per second that each pixel on the screen is scanned; measured in hertz (Hz).

register High-speed memory locations built directly into the ALU and used to hold instructions and data currently being processed.

relational database A database structure capable of linking tables; a collection of files that share at least one common field.

relative cell reference A spreadsheet cell reference that changes with respect to its relative position on the spreadsheet when copied to a new location.

remote administration The process of administering a network from a remote location, through a modem connection. The connection is established between the administrator's remote computer and a computer on the network—usually either the administrator's own node or a network server.

removable hard drive A magnetic storage device that combines the speed and capacity of a hard disk with the portability of a diskette. A removable box encloses the disk, drive, and read/write heads in a sealed container that can be moved from computer to computer.

render To create an image of an object as it actually appears.

repetitive stress injury (RSI) An injury to some part of the body caused by continuous movement. Computer-related injuries include wrist, neck, and back strain.

report A database product designed by the user that displays data satisfying a specific set of search criteria in a particular layout.

resolution The degree of sharpness of an image, determined by the number of pixels on a screen, expressed as a matrix.

resolution-dependent Describes an image whose appearance may change, depending on the resolution at which it is displayed.

resolution-independent Describes an image whose appearance will not change, regardless of the resolution at which it is displayed.

right-click When using a two-button mouse, to use the right mouse button to select an object or command on the screen.

ring topology A network topology in which network nodes are connected in a circular configuration. Each node examines the data sent through the ring and passes on data not addressed to it.

RISC processor See *Reduced Instruction Set Computing processor.*

ROM See *read-only memory.*

router A computer device that stores the addressing information of each computer on each LAN or WAN and uses this information to transfer data along the most efficient path between nodes of a LAN or WAN.

routine A name sometimes ascribed to reusable blocks of code. See also *procedure* and *subroutine.*

row A horizontally arranged series of cells in a spreadsheet, named with a number.

RS-232 The standard serial port configuration used for communications between the computer and peripherals.

ruler An on-screen tool in a word processor's document window. The ruler shows the position of lines, tab stops, margins, and other parts of the document.

running See *executing.*

S

sans serif A typeface without decorative finishing strokes on the tips of the characters; commonly used in headings.

scan code The code—generated by the keyboard controller—that tells the keyboard buffer which key has been pressed.

scanner An input device used to copy a printed page into the computer's memory and transform the image into digital data. Various scanners can read text, images, or bar codes.

screen saver A utility program that displays moving images on the screen if no input is received for several minutes; originally developed to prevent an image from being burned into the screen.

scripting language A list of commands within a program or an application that directs the program to perform specific tasks in a specific order.

scroll bar A vertical or horizontal bar displayed along the side and bottom of a window, which enables the user to scroll horizontally or vertically through a document by clicking an arrow or dragging a box within the scroll bar.

scrolling The movement of an entire document in relation to the window view to see parts of the document not currently visible on screen.

SCSI See *small computer system interface.*

SDLC See *systems development life cycle.*

section A user-defined portion of a document, which can have its own unique formatting.

sector A segment or division of a track on a disk.

seek time A measure of performance used for disk drives. A drive's seek time (also called its *access time*) is the maximum amount of time required to positions the drive's read/write heads over a given location on the disk.

Glossary

select (1) To highlight a block of text (in a word processor) or range (in a spreadsheet), so the user can perform one or more editing operations on it. (2) To click once on an icon and initiate its action.

serial interface A channel through which a single data bit can flow at one time. Serial interfaces are used primarily to connect a mouse or a communications device to the computer; also called a *serial port*.

Serial Line Interface Protocol (SLIP) A method for linking a computer directly to the Internet by using a phone line connected to a serial communications port.

Serial Storage Architecture (SSA) A networking protocol that enables multiple computers to share storage media. SSA provides large bandwidths, allowing large amounts of data (80 Mbps) to be shared.

serif A typeface with decorative finishing strokes on the tips of the characters; commonly used in the main body of text.

server See *file server*.

shading A paragraph format that displays a pattern or color as a background to the text; used to emphasize a block of text.

shareware Software that can be used for free for a specified time period. After that time, the user is obligated to purchase or register the product.

shell account A type of Internet access used by remote terminal connections; operates from a host computer running UNIX or a similar operating system.

SIMM See *Single In-Line Memory Module*.

Single Edge Connector A specialized motherboard slot, required by the Pentium II processor. Because the Pentium II requires this type of connector (also called a *Slot One connector*), new motherboard designs were required to accommodate the Pentium II chip.

Single In-Line Memory Module (SIMM) One type of circuit board containing memory chips.

Single Instruction Multiple Data (SIMD) process An architectural design enhancement on the Pentium Pro processor, the SIMD process enables one instruction to perform the same function on multiple pieces of data, reducing the number of loops required to handle video, audio, animation, and graphical data.

site license An agreement in which an organization purchases the right to use a program on a limited number of machines. The total cost is less than would be required if individual copies of the software were purchased for all users.

slide An individual graphic that is part of a presentation. Slides are created and edited in presentation programs.

SLIP See *Serial Line Interface Protocol*.

small computer system interface (SCSI) A device that extends the bus outside the computer, permitting the addition of more peripheral devices than normally could be connected using the available expansion slots.

soft format See *logical format*.

software A collection of electronic instructions that directs the CPU to carry out a specific task. Software usually resides in storage.

software piracy The illegal duplication of software for commercial or personal use.

solid model A 3-D model created in a solid modeling program, and which appears to be a solid object rather than a frame or polygon-based object.

solid modeler A 3-D modeling program that depicts an object as a solid block of material (such as steel or wood), which the user shapes by adding and subtracting material or joining with other objects. These programs incorporate the concepts of thickness and density.

sort To arrange database records in a particular order, according to the contents of one or more fields.

sorting The process of performing a sort operation on database records.

sort order The order in which database records are sorted, either ascending or descending.

sound card An expansion card that records and plays back sound by translating the analog signal from a microphone into a digitized form that the computer can store and process and then translating the modified data back into analog signals or sound.

source code Program statements created with a programming language.

source code analyzer A software development tool that examines a program and generates a report on many aspects of that program.

source file The file that stores instructions for the computer to execute.

spamming The act of distributing unrequested messages across the Internet or an online service. Spammers often flood news groups with messages and send e-mail messages to thousands of individuals. Spam messages often attempt to sell a product or service (like regular junk mail) but frequently carry negative, indecent, or obscene material.

spline-based modeler A 3-D modeling program that builds objects using mathematically defined curves.

spoofing The act of distributing unrequested messages that conceal the sender's identity. Spoofing is the same as spamming, but the spoofer's message identifies the sender as someone else or shows no sender's identity at all. This method protects the spoofer from retaliation from those who receive unwanted messages. See also *spamming*.

spooling The process of queuing multiple print jobs that have been sent to a networked printer. Print jobs are temporarily stored—usually on a hard drive in the network server, network print server, or a special print spooler—while they await their turn to be printed.

spreadsheet A grid of columns and rows used for recording and evaluating numbers. Spreadsheets are used primarily for financial analysis, record keeping, and management, and to create reports and presentations.

SQL See *Structured Query Language.*

star network A network topology in which network nodes connect to a central hub, through which all data is routed.

Start button A Windows 95/98 screen element, found on the desktop, which displays operating system options when selected. The Start button includes tools to locate documents, find help, change system settings, and run programs.

status bar An on-screen element in many applications; displays the current status of various parts of the current document or application, such as page number, text entry mode, and so on.

storage The portion of the computer that holds data or programs while they are not being used. Storage media include magnetic or optical disks, tape, and cartridges.

storage device The hardware components that write data to—and read data from—storage media. For example, a diskette is a type of storage media, whereas a diskette drive is a storage device.

storage media The physical components, or materials, on which data is stored. Diskettes and compact disks are examples of storage media.

storyboard A production tool that consists of sketches of scenes and actions that map a sequence of events; helps the author to edit and improve the presentation.

structured programming A programming process that uses a set of well-defined structures, such as condition statements and loops.

Structured Query Language (SQL) The standard query language used for searching and selecting records and fields in a relational database.

subclass A subset of a class in object-oriented programming.

subdomain A division of a domain address that specifies a particular level or area of an organization, such as a branch office.

subroutine The name most frequently ascribed to reusable blocks of code. See also *procedure* and *routine.*

supercomputer The largest, fastest, and most powerful type of computer. Supercomputers are often used for scientific and engineering applications and processing complex models using very large data sets.

superscalar A microprocessor architecture that allows more than one instruction to be processed in each clock cycle.

surface modeler A 3-D modeling program that depicts an object as an outer layer (a surface) stretched over a wire frame.

SVGA (Super VGA) An IBM video display standard capable of displaying resolutions up to 1280x1024 pixels, with 16 million colors.

swap in To load essential parts of a program into memory as required for use.

swap out To unload, or remove, nonessential parts of a program from memory to make room for needed functions.

Synchronous Dynamic RAM (SDRAM) A type of RAM that delivers bursts of data at very high speeds (up to 100 MHz), providing more data to the CPU at a given time than older RAM technologies.

syntax The precise sequence of characters required in a spreadsheet formula or in a programming language.

syntax error A bug in which the code is not entered correctly, so that the computer cannot understand its instructions.

system board See *motherboard.*

system call A feature built into an application program that requests service from the operating system, as when a word processing program requests the use of the printer to print a document.

system clock The computer's internal clock, used to time processing operations. The clock's time intervals are based on the constant, unchanging vibrations of molecules in a quartz crystal; measured in megahertz (MHz).

system manager The person responsible for ensuring that a system is secure, protecting data integrity, performing routine maintenance, and recovering lost data.

system operator (sysop) In an online discussion group, the person who monitors the discussion.

system software A computer program that controls the system hardware and interacts with application software; includes the operating system and the network operating system.

systems analyst The individual who analyzes and designs software systems and provides maintenance and support functions for the users.systems design Phase 2 of the software development life cycle, in which the project team researches and develops alternatives to meet an organization's computing needs.

systems design The second phase of the systems development life cycle.

systems development life cycle (SDLC) A formal methodology and process for the needs analysis, system design, development, implementation, and maintenance of a computer system.

Glossary

T

T1 A communications line that represents a higher level of the ISDN standard service and supplies a bandwidth of 1.544 Mbps; also called *PRI*.

T3 A communications line capable of transmitting a total of 44.736 Mbps.

tab stop A preset position in a document to which the cursor moves when the Tab key is pressed.

table A grid of data, set up in rows and columns.

tape drive A magnetic storage device that reads and writes data to the surface of a magnetic tape. Tape drives are generally used for backing up data or restoring the data of a hard disk.

taskbar A Windows 95/98 screen element, displayed on the desktop, which includes the Start button and lists the programs currently running on the computer.

TCP/IP See *Transmission Control Protocol/Internet Protocol*.

technical documentation Detailed documents that describe program or database structures, menu systems, screen layouts, data, and processing flow.

technical writer The person who documents the system, from the technical details needed by the systems managers to the procedural instructions designed for the end user.

telecommuter A person who works at home or on the road and requires access to a work computer via telecommunications equipment, such as modems and fax machines.

telecommuting To work at home or on the road and have access to a work computer via telecommunications equipment, such as modems and fax machines.

teleconferencing Live communications between two or more people using computers, telecommunications equipment, and e-mail software.

Telnet An Internet tool that provides a transparent window between the user's computer and a distant host system. Data is transmitted from the user's keyboard to the host, effectively taking control of the host computer to access data, transmit files, and so on.

template A preformatted document used to quickly create a standard document, such as a memo or report.

terminal An input/output device connected to a multiuser computer, such as a mainframe. A terminal consists of a monitor and keyboard but lacks its own CPU and storage.

text box In word processing and desktop publishing software, a special frame that enables the user to contain text in a rectangular area. The user can size and position the text box like a frame, by dragging the box or one of its handles. See also frame, definition 3.

text field See *alphanumeric field*.

text operator A component of a spreadsheet formula that combines two or more strings of text to create a single text string.

thermal-wax printer A printer that produces high-quality images by using a heat source to evaporate colored wax from a ribbon, which then adheres to plain paper.

thesaurus A text editing tool that lists alternative words with similar meanings.

thin client See *network computer*.

time field A database field that stores the time.

title bar An on-screen element displayed at the top of every window that identifies the window contents. Dragging the title bar changes the position of the window on the screen.

Token Ring IBM's network protocol based on a ring topology, in which linked computers pass an electronic token containing addressing information to facilitate data transfer.

toner A substance composed of tiny particles of charged ink, used in laser printers. The ink particles stick to charged areas of a drum and are transferred to paper with pressure and heat.

toolbar In application software, an on-screen element appearing just below the menu bar. The toolbar contains multiple tools, which are graphic icons representing specific actions the user can perform. To initiate an action, the user clicks the appropriate icon.

top-down design A systems design method in which the major functions or processes are developed first, followed by the details.

topology The physical layout of wires that connect the computers in a network; includes bus, star, and ring.

touch screen An input/output device that accepts input directly from the monitor. The user touches words, graphical icons, or symbols displayed on screen to activate commands.

track An area used for storing data on a formatted disk. During the disk-formatting process, the operating system creates a set of magnetic concentric circles on the disk: these are the tracks. These tracks are then divided into sectors, with each sector able to hold a given amount of data. By using this system to store data, the operating system can quickly determine where data is located on the disk. Different types of disks can hold different numbers of tracks.

trackball An input device that functions like an upside-down mouse, consisting of a stationary casing containing a movable ball that is operated by hand; used frequently with laptop computers and video games.

tracking Adjusting letter spacing within blocks of text to make the text easier to read.

trackpad A stationary pointing device that the user operates by moving a finger across a small, touch-sensitive surface; used with laptop and notebook computers.

TrackPoint   See *integrated pointing device.*

trainer   In an IS department, the person responsible for teaching users how to use a new system, whether hardware, software, procedures, or a combination thereof.

transaction   A business task, such as taking an order or preparing a time sheet.

transistor   Electronic switches within the CPU that exist in two states, conductive (on) or nonconductive (off). The resulting combinations are used to create the binary code that is the basis for machine language.

Transmission Control Protocol/Internet Protocol (TCP/IP)   The set of commands and timing specifications used by the Internet to connect dissimilar systems and control the flow of information.

tween   Abbreviation for "in-between." In animation, tweens are the frames that depict a character's or object's motion between keyframes.

twisted-pair wire   Cable used in network connections. Twisted-pair wire consists of four or eight copper strands, individually shrouded in plastic, twisted around each other in pairs and bound together in a layer of plastic insulation; also called *unshielded twisted-pair (UTP)* wire. Twisted-pair wire encased in a metal sheath is called shielded twisted-pair (STP) wire.

typeface   See *font.*

type style   An attribute applied to a text character, such as underlining, italic, and bold, among others. Most application programs provide a wide variety of type styles, which the user can freely apply to text anywhere in a document.

U

UART   See *Universal Asynchronous Receiver Transmitter.*

unerase program   See *data recovery utility.*

Unicode Worldwide Character Standard   A character set that provides 16 bits to represent each symbol, resulting in 65,536 different characters or symbols, enough for all the languages of the world; a superset of the ASCII character set.

Uniform Resource Locator (URL)   An Internet address used with HTTP in the format type://address/path. The URL specifies the type of server on which the file is located, the address of the server, and the path or location within the file structure of the server.

Universal Asynchronous Receiver Transmitter (UART)   A chip that converts parallel data from the bus into serial data that can flow through a serial cable, and vice versa.

UNIX   A 32-bit, fully multitasking, multithreading operating system developed by AT&T in the 1960s. A powerful, highly scalable operating system, UNIX (and variants of it) is used to operate supercomputers, mainframes, minicomputers, and powerful PCs and workstations. UNIX generally features a command-line interface, although some variants of UNIX feature a graphical operating environment, as well.

uploading   Sending a file to a remote computer; the opposite of downloading.

upward compatibility   The capability of a hardware device or a software product to interact successfully with all succeeding versions of software or hardware.

URL   See *Uniform Resource Locator.*

Usenet   A popular system of news groups accessible on the Internet and maintained by volunteers.

user   The person who inputs and analyzes data using a computer.

user assistance architect   The individual who develops the organization and structure of online documentation, such as Help systems or tutorials.

user documentation   Instructions or manuals that tell a user how to use a system.

user identification code   A code that identifies the user to the system; often the user's full name, a shortened version of the user's name, or the user's e-mail name.

user interface   The on-screen elements that enable the user to interact with the software.

V

value   A numerical entry in a spreadsheet, representing currency, a percentage, a date, a time, a fraction, and so on, which can be used in formulas.

variable   A part of computer memory that a program reserves as a placeholder for the data being processed.

vector   A mathematical equation that describes the position of a line.

Veronica   Acronym for Very Easy Rodent-Oriented Net-wide Index to Computer Archives; a keyword search tool that finds and displays items from Gopher menus.

vertical application   An application critical to the operation of an organization, such as accounting, order entry, or payroll.

VGA (Video Graphics Array)   An IBM video display standard capable of displaying resolutions of 640x480, with 16 colors.

video card   A specialized expansion board that enables the user to connect video devices—such as VCRs and camcorders—to the PC. This enables the user to transfer images from the video equipment to the PC, and vice versa. Many video cards enable the user to edit digitized video and record the edited images on videotape.

Glossary

videoconferencing Live video communication between two or more people using computers and videoconferencing software.

video controller A circuit board attached to the motherboard that contains the memory and other circuitry necessary to send information to the monitor for display on screen. This controller determines the refresh rate, resolution, and number of colors that can be displayed; also called the *display adapter*.

video RAM (VRAM) Memory on the video controller, called dual-ported memory, that can send a screen of data to the monitor while receiving the next data set.

virtual reality (VR) A computer navigation tool that projects the user into three-dimensional space using special devices designed to simulate movement and spatial dimension.

Virtual Reality Modeling Language (VRML) A special programming language that enables designers to create 3-D virtual environments (such as furnished rooms, shopping centers, and so on) for use in World Wide Web pages. Users with VRML-enabled browsers can navigate through these environments with a great deal of freedom, entering and exiting rooms, interacting with objects, looking through windows, and so on.

Virtual System Architecture (VSA) Processor technology created by Cyrix, which combines the memory, video card, and sound card in a single central processor.

virtual university Web sites that offer courses of college credit online.

virus A parasitic program developed as a prank that is buried within a legitimate program or stored in the boot sector of a disk. Viruses can be contracted when adding programs, copying data, or communicating online and will damage data, software, or the computer itself.

Visual Basic A fourth-generation programming language in which the programmer manipulates program components visually, and the code is generated automatically.

voice recognition An input technology that can translate human speech into text. Some voice recognition systems enable the user to navigate application programs and issue commands by voice control.

volatile The tendency for memory to lose data when the computer is turned off, as is the case with RAM; nonpermanent and alterable.

VRAM See *video RAM*.

W

walk-through A specially rendered animation, created in a CAD or 3-D graphics program, which creates the illusion that the viewer is moving through an object, such as a building. Designers often create walk-throughs by using software cameras to constantly change the angle of view of the object.

WAN See *wide area network*.

Warez news group An Internet news group where users share pirated copies of software.

Web page A document developed using HTTP and found on the World Wide Web. Web pages contain information about a particular subject with links to related Web pages and other resources.

Webview A feature of Microsoft Internet Explorer 4 and Windows 98, which enables the user to convert the Windows desktop into a Web browser called the Active Desktop. In this view, all documents, devices, Web pages, and so on, appear as hyperlinks rather than typical Windows icons.

what-if analysis A data analysis process used to test how alternative scenarios affect numeric results.

wide area network (WAN) A computer network in which two or more LANs are connected across a wide geographical area.

window An area on the computer screen in which an application or document is viewed and accessed.

Windows 3.0 An operating environment introduced by Microsoft in 1990 that could run 16-bit Windows and DOS applications, managed larger amounts of memory than its predecessors, and included the File Manager, Program Manager, and three-dimensional screen elements.

Windows 3.1 An operating environment introduced by Microsoft in 1992 as an upgrade to Windows 3.0; capable of running 16-bit Windows and DOS applications.

Windows 3.11 An upgrade to Windows 3.1; provides the basis for Windows for Workgroups, which includes built-in peer-to-peer networking and electronic mail capabilities.

Windows 95 A 32-bit operating system developed by Microsoft and released in 1995. Windows 95 features preemptive multitasking, plug-and-play capabilities, built-in networking, and the ability to access 16- and 32-bit applications.

Windows 98 An upgrade to Windows 95, Windows 98 includes a number of enhancements, including a built-in Web browser and Internet-related tools, online upgradability, and other features.

Windows CE A 32-bit operating system developed by Microsoft and released in 1997; designed for use on small handheld computing devices and to operate consumer devices and some industrial devices. The CE stands for "consumer electronics."

Windows NT A 32-bit operating system developed by Microsoft and released in 1993; designed for powerful workstations and restricted to running 32-bit applications; supports peer-to-peer networking, preemptive multitasking, and multiprocessing. The NT stands for "new technology."

Winsock Windows Sockets, a standard network interface that makes it possible to mix and match application programs from more than one developer to communicate across the Internet.

Glossary

wireframe model   A CAD tool that represents 3-D shapes by displaying their outlines and edges.

wireless communication   Communication via computers that relies on radio signals, including x-rays, ultraviolet light, the visible spectrum, infrared, microwaves, and radio waves, to transmit data.

word processing software   Software used to create and edit text documents such as letters, memos, reports, and publications.

word size   The size of the registers in the CPU, which determines the amount of data the computer can work with at any given time. Larger word sizes lead to faster processing; common word sizes include 16 bits, 32 bits, and 64 bits.

word wrap   A word processing feature that computes the length of each line of text as the text is entered.

workbook   A data file created with spreadsheet software, containing multiple worksheets.

workgroup application   A system in which two or more individuals share files and resources, working together to produce a product.

worksheet   The data file created with spreadsheet software.

workstation   A fast, powerful microcomputer used for scientific applications, graphics, CAD, CAE, and other complex applications. Workstations are usually based on RISC technology and operated by some version of UNIX, although an increasing number of Intel/Windows NT-based workstations are coming into popular use.

World Wide Web (the Web or WWW)   An Internet service developed to incorporate footnotes, figures, and cross-references into online hypertext documents.

write once, read many (WORM) drive   A permanent optical storage device that uses a laser to read data from the surface of a disk. After data has been written to the disk, it cannot be changed or rewritten.

WYSIWYG   A display mode that shows a document as it will appear when printed; stands for What You See Is What You Get.

X

Xeon   A newer version of Intel's Pentium II processor that features enhanced multiprocessing capabilities.

Index

Index

Index

Index

Index

media, 367
for backups, 118
for networks, 263
storage, 115
television, 368-369
See also multimedia; new media
MediaGX processors (Cyrix), 60
megabytes (MBs), 18
megahertz (MHz; unit), 53, 61
member functions, 425
memo fields, 227
memory, 18
cache memory, 55
in CPUs, 49
processing speed and, 52-53
in RAM (random access memory), 50-51
in ROM (read-only memory), 49-50
memory addresses, 50
address bus for, 54-55
menu bars, 160
menus, 160-161
Merced processors, 65
messages, 426-427
methods (member functions), 425
mice, 19, 77-80
trackballs and, 80-81
used with icons, 156
Micro Channel Architecture (MCA) bus, 54
microcode, 48
microcomputers, 27-30
processing speed of, 51-56
microphones, 19, 86-87
microprocessors, 16
invented by Intel, 56
parallel processing by, 61, 63-65
See also processors
Microsoft Corporation, 153
alliance between IBM and, 186-187
Internet utilities from, 169
MS-DOS operating systems by, 164, 177
multimedia hardware requirements of, 381-382
Open Software Definition (OSD) by, 304
Synchronized Accessible Media Interchange (SAMI) by, 90
Visual BASIC by, 430
Windows CE operating system by, 183-184
Windows NT operating systems by, 182-183
Windows operating systems by, 178-181
Microsoft Excel 97 (spreadsheet program), 212, 222
Microsoft Knowledge Base (KB), 376
Microsoft Network, 305, 309
Microsoft PowerPoint 97 (presentation program), 233
Microsoft Windows 3.x (operating environments), 178

graphics software on, 326
Microsoft Windows 95 (operating system), 153, 154, 178-179
forgeries of, 457
memory management by, 55
sound utilities in, 100
Microsoft Windows 95/98 (operating systems), 154
backup utility in, 175
command-line interface in, 164
data recovery and unerase utilities in, 175
drivers for, 172
DriveSpace utility in, 174
energy use controlled by, 451
file management in, 170
file name extensions in, 420
object embedding in, 167
preemptive multitasking in, 168
programs running in, 157-158
right-clicking mouse in, 156
Start button in, 157
taskbars in, 156-157
video displays under, 93
window control buttons in, 159-160
Windows Paint included in, 341
Winsock and, 309
Microsoft Windows 98 (operating system), 153, 154, 180-181, 189
memory needed for, 52-53
user interface in, 155-161
Web browser integrated into, 169
Microsoft Windows CE (operating system), 183-184
Microsoft Windows NT (operating system), 173, 182-183
data compression utility in, 174
parallel processing by, 61, 65
Start button in, 157
Microsoft Windows NT Server (network operating system), 183, 255, 268
Microsoft Windows NT Workstation (operating system), 182-183
Microsoft Word 97 (word processing software), 198, 222
Millennia Bug, 434
Millennium Problem (Y2K problem), 181, 428, 434
milliseconds (ms), 137
minicomputers, 27-28
MMX Single Instruction Multiple Data (SIMD) process, 58
MMX technology, 58, 60
models, 344
modems (modulators/demodulators), 20, 73, 247, 269-272
for Internet access, 308
modified frequency modulation (MFM), 140
modifier keys, 74-75

monitors, 19, 88-93
ergonomic issues involving, 448, 449
flat-panel, 94-95
screen savers for, 176
touch screens on, 20, 83-84
used simultaneously on Windows 98, 180
video controller cards for, 93-94
monochrome monitors, 88-89
monospace fonts, 201
Moore, Gordon, 51
Moore's Law, 51, 65
Mosaic (Web browser), 301, 302, 313
motherboards (system boards), 16, 46
expansion slots on, 103
Motorola Corporation, 56, 60-63
moving worlds, 356-357
MPC (PowerPC) family of Motorola processors, 62
MPEG (Motion Picture Experts Group), 382
MS-DOS (operating system). *See* DOS
multimedia, 367, 379-380
authoring of, 391
in business communications, 374-377
careers in, 392
creating, 388-391
in education, 371-373
future of, 393
hypermedia and, 383-386
networking, 382-383
testing of, 391
on World Wide Web, 372
See also new media
multimedia authoring, 389-390
multimedia computer-based training (CBT), 101
multimedia developers, 316
multimedia networks, 281-283
multimedia PCs, 100, 381-382, 384
Multimedia Personal Computer (MPC) standard, 381-382
multiprocessing (MP; parallel processing), 61, 65
multitasking, 57, 168, 179, 187

N

National Science Foundation (NSF), 292
navigation, in multimedia, 383-386
navigation systems, 10
needs analysis, 412-414, 433
Neidorf, Craig, 462
Nelson, Ted, 385
Netcaster (Netscape), 304
Netscape (firm), 169, 304
Netscape Communicator, 313
Netscape Navigator (Web browser), 169, 302, 313
Java applets supported by, 312

INDEX **535**

Index

Index

Index

Image Credits

Table of Contents

Chapter 1

6 (t)Aaron Haupt, (b)Doug Martin; **7** (t)NCR, (others)Tom Lippert Photography; **8** (tl)Smithsonian Institution, (tr) Chuck Savage/The Stock Market, (bl)JPL/NASA/Gamma Liaison, (br)NASA; **9** (b)SuperStock, (others)courtesy, with permission from, and under the copyright of Autodesk; **10** (t)Antonio Rosario/The Image Bank, (b)Sam Sargent/Gamma Liaison; **11** (t)LEXIS-NEXIS, (c)Intuit, used with permission, (b)The Image Works; **12** (t)US Department of Defense Camera Combat Center, (c)US Internal Revenue Service, (b)Dan Nelken/ Liaison International; **13** (t) Photofest, (b)Gamma Liaison; **14** AP/Wide World Photos; **17** Intel Corp.; **21** (t)Tom McCarthy/ SKA, (b)Geoff Butler; **24** screen shot reprinted with permission of Microsoft Corp.; **25** (t) Jose Lozano (others)screen shots reprinted with permission of Microsoft Corp.; **26** Cray Computer; **27-28** courtesy International Business Machines Corp. Unauthorized use not permitted; **29** Mark Romanelli/The Image Bank; **30** (t)courtesy International Business Machines Corp. Unauthorized use not permitted, (b)Toshiba **31** (t)courtesy International Business Machines Corp. Unauthorized use not permitted, (b)The Image Bank; **32 33** courtesy International Business Machines Corp. Unauthorized use not permitted; **34** (t)NCR, (b)Aaron Haupt; **35** (t)Toshiba, (b)courtesy Interna-tional Business Machines Corp. Unauthorized use not permitted; **38** USA TODAY; **39** (t)NASA, (b)Mouse Systems.

Chapter 2

46 Mark Burnett; **47** J. Raymont/ EIT; **50** (t)Intel Corp.,(b)Kingston Technology Corp.; **51** Hewlett Packard; **53** Newer Technology; **55** Mark Burnett; **56-58** Intel Corp.; **59** Mark Burnett; **60** (t) Intel Corp., (c)AMD, (b)Cyrix; **61** courtesy Sun Microsystems; **63** (tl tr) Motorola, (c)NEC, (b)courtesy Sun Microsystems; **64** Microsoft Corp.; **65** Al Fracekcvich /The Stock Market; **67** Intel Corp.; **70** (t)Cyberian Outpost,(b) Advanced Micro Devices; **71** Silicon Graphics.

Chapter 3

75 (t)screen shot reprinted with permission of Microsoft Corp., (b)Doug Martin; **77** (t)Toshiba, (b)screen shot reprinted with permission of Microsoft Corp.; **78** J. Arbogast/SuperStock; **80** Logitech; **81** (tl)Jay Silverman /The Image Bank, (tr c) courtesy International Business Machines Corp. Unauthorized use not permitted, (b)Gamma Liaison; **82** (t)screen shot reprinted with permission of Microsoft Corp., (b)FPG; **83** (t)Jon Feingersh/The Stock Market, (b)UPS; **84** (t)Bob Daemmrich/The Image Works, (c)courtesy International Business Machines Corp. Unauthorized use not permitted, (b)Federal Express; **85** AP/Wide World Photos; **86** Doug Martin; **87** Toshiba; **90** Starling Access; **91** Applied Optical Company; **94** courtesy International Business Machines Corp. Unauthorized use not permitted; **96 97** Hewlett Packard; **99** Hewlett Packard; **104** (tl c)Geoff Butler, (tr)courtesy International Business Machines Corp. Unauthorized use not permitted, (b)Mark Burnett; **106** Hewlett Packard; **107** AP/Wide World Photos; **108** courtesy International Business Machines Corp. Unauthorized use not permitted; **109** (b)Hewlett Packard; **112** (t)NetRadio Network, (b)PC Mechanic; **113** Advanced Recognition Technologies.

Chapter 4

116 (t)courtesy International Business Machines Corp. Unauthorized use not permitted, (c)courtesy Seagate Technology, (b)SyQuest; **117** Fujitsu; **118** screen shot reprinted with permission of Microsoft Corp.; **125** screen shot reprinted with permission of Microsoft Corp.; **126** Maxtor; **128** Syquest; **129** (t)Iomega, (b)courtesy Sun Microsystems; **130** (t)Hewlett Packard, (b)courtesy International Business Machines. Unauthorized use not permitted; **132** (t)Grolier, (c)courtesy Sun Microsystems, (b)Geoff Butler; **133** (t)Hewlett

Image Credits

Parkard, (b)courtesy International Business Machines Company. Unauthorized use not permitted; **134** (t)Micro Solutions, (b)Olympus America; **136** Interactive Media Corp.; **137** O.R. Technology; **139** Storage Computer; **141** Maxtor; **142** Hewlett Packard; **143** Mark Burnett; **145** (t)Olympus America, (b)Maxtor; **148** (t)Nico Mak Computing, (b)Strategia; **149** Iomega.

Chapter 5

154 Microsoft Corp.; **155** through **174** screen shots reprinted with permission of Microsoft Corp.; **175** (t)screen shot reprinted with permission of Microsoft Corp., (b)Symantec; **176** (t)Symantec, (b)Star Trek The Screen Saver by Berkeley Systems Inc.; **177** through **182** screen shots reprinted with permission of Microsoft Corp.; **183** Casio; **184 185** Apple Corp.; **186** courtesy International Business Machines Corp. Unauthorized use not permitted; **187** UNIX; **188** courtesy National Instruments, Austin, TX; **189** William Westheimer/The Stock Market; **190** screen shots reprinted with permission of Microsoft Corp.; **191** (t)Screen shot reprinted with permission of Microsoft Corp., (b)Apple Corp.; **194** (t)TUCOWS Interactive Limited, (b)Hewlett Packard; **195** Barnes and Noble.

Chapter 6

199 through **209** screen shots reprinted with permission from Microsoft Corp.; **210** Quark; **211** through **220**

screen shots reprinted with permission of Microsoft Corp.; **224 226** screen shots reprinted with permission of Microsoft Corp.; **228** through **237** screen shots reprinted with permission of Microsoft Corp.; **238** Hewlett Packard; **239** C.F.B. Mels/Westlight; **240 241** screen shots reprinted with permission of Microsoft Corp.

Chapter 7

248 Chuck Keeler/Tony Stone Images; **250** SuperStock; **251** Used with permission of Lotus Development Corp.; **252** screen shot reprinted with permission of Microsoft Corp.; **253** (t)Netopia, (b)White Pine Software; **254** screen shots reprinted with permission of Microsoft Corp.; **255** Doug Martin; **263** (t)Tom McCarthy/SKA, (b)Property of AT&T Archives. Reprinted with permission of AT&T; **264** (t)D. Sarraute/The Image Bank, (b)Farallon; **265** Doug Martin; **268** screen shot reprinted with permission of Microsoft Corp.; **269** reproduced by permission of Hayes Microcomputer Products; **271 272** Diamond Multimedia Systems; **273** Doug Martin; **275** Hewlett Packard; **280** Jeff Smith/The Image Bank; **281** William Taufic/The Stock Market; **282** courtesy International Business Machines Corp. Unauthorized use not permitted; **283** Lester Lefkowitz/The Stock Market; **284** (t)Tom McCarhty /SKA, (c)Property of AT&T Archives. Reprinted with permission of AT&T, (b)D. Sarraute/The Image Bank; **285** Diamond Multimedia Systems; **288** 3Com Corp.; **289** Novell.

Chapter 8

296 Qualcomm; **297** screen shot reprinted with permission of Microsoft Corp.; **300** Texas A&M; **303** AltaVista; **304** (t)YAHOO!, (b)America Online; **305** (t)Compuserve Interactive Services, (b)screen shot reprinted with permission of Microsoft Corp.; **306** Netcast Communications Corp.; **307** screen shot reprinted with permission of Microsoft Corp.; **312** permitted by author X.S. Zhou at StockSense; **313** Netscape; **315** Amazon.com; **316** Kodak; **317** Dale O'Dell/The Stock Market; **322** (t)Excite, (b)Deja News; **323** Hotmail.

Chapter 9

326 Doug Martin; **327** (tl)Rickabaugh Graphics, (tr)Wacom Technology Corp./Digital Metamorph, (bl)Michel Tcherevkoff (br)Intergraph Computer Systems; **328** Photofest; **329** Walt Disney/Kobel; **331** (t)Hewlett Packard, (b)Kodak; **332** Kodak; **334** Hewlett Packard; **336** Jasc Software; **337** (tl tr)Fractal, (b)Corel; **338** The Stock Market/Ryszard Horowitz; **341** Visio Corp.; **342** AutoCAD; **343** courtesy, with permission from, and under the copyright of Autodesk; **345** (t)Ryszard Horowitz/The Stock Market, (others) courtesy, with permission from, and under the copyright of Autodesk; **346** (t)Greg Phillips of Phillips Design Group LLC [www.pdgroup.com]; **347** (t)Photofest; **348** Greg Phillips of Phillips Design Group LLC [www.pdgroup.com]; **350 351** Adaptive Optics Associates; **352**

Index Stock; **353** (t)US Internal Revenue Service, (others)courtesy Triad Interactive; **355** screen shot reprinted with permission of Microsoft Corp.; **356** CBS SportsLine; **358** Graphsoft; **360** (t)Kodak, (cr)Jasc Software; **361** (t)courtesy, with permission from, and under the copyright of Autodesk, (c)Index Stock.

Chapter 10

368 FPG; **369** CNN Inc./Mark Hill; **370** Sega; **371** (t)The Food Network, (b)funschool.com; **373** Maxis; **374** (t)Jones Education Company, a unit of Jones International Ltd., (b)NASA; **375** (t)Netscape Communications Corp., (b)QVC; **376** screen shots reprinted with permission of Microsoft Corp.; **377** The Internet Movie Database Ltd.; **378** ADEC Distance Education Consortium; **379** Reproduced by permission of Pebble Beach Company, all rights reserved. Photo Brian Morgan; **380** Toshiba; **382** Packeteer; **383** Jose Lozano; **384** (l)LucasArts, (r)Activision; **385** screen shot reprinted with permission of Microsoft Corp.; **387** Caligari Corp., created with trueSpace; **392** courtesy International Business Machines. Unauthorized use not permitted; **393** Firefly Productions/The Stock Market; **394** (t)Sega, (c)funschool.com, (b)Maxis; **395** (t)Toshiba, (b)Caligari Corp., created with trueSpace; **398** (t)MSNBC, (b)Software Publishers Association; **399** CreateX Design.

Chapter 11

404 courtesy Sun Microsystems; **405** (t)Index Stock, (b)G.

Fritz/SuperStock; **406** (t)M. Smith/Blue Sky Software; **407** (tl b)SuperStock, (tr)Steve Niedorf/The Image Bank; **414** (tl)L.D. Gordon/The Image Bank, (tr)SuperStock, (b)B. Busco/The Image Bank; **415** (t)Alan Levenson/Tony Stone Images; **417** Used with permission of Lotus Development Corp.; **418** T. Rosenthal/SuperStock; **419** (c)Intuit, (b)Atari, **420** The Stock Market; **421** screen shots reprinted with permission of Microsoft Corp.; **431** (t)Jose Lozano, (b)screen shot reprinted with permission of Microsoft Corp.; **432** screen shots reprinted with permission of Microsoft Corp.; **434** courtesy International Business Machines Corp. Unauthorized use not permitted; **435** screen shots reprinted with permission of Microsoft Corp.; **436** Hewlett Packard; **437** Firefly Productions/The Stock Market; **439** (t)The Stock Market, (b)screen shot reprinted with permission from Microsoft Corp.; **442** (t)Digital Station, (b)courtesy Sun Microsystems; **443** Amazon.com.

Chapter 12

446 BodyBilt Seating; **447** (t)Fellowes, (b)Doug Martin; **448** Fellowes; **450** Fox Electronics; **451** (l)screen shot reprinted with permission of Microsoft Corp., (r)Environmental Protection Agency; **453** screen shot reprinted with permission of Microsoft Corp.; **454** Adobe; **455** (l)Claris, (r)courtesy the M.I.T. Media Laboratory/Richard Pasley; **457** Mark Burnett; **459** McAfree Antivirus; **460** Kensington Microware; **462 463** screen shot reprinted with permission of Microsoft Corp.; **466** (t)

MindSpring Enterprises, (b)courtesy Accepted Marketing; **467** Tom McCarthy/SKA; **470** Netscape Communications Corp. Used with permission. All Rights Reserved; **471** Corbis/Bettmann; **472** courtesy International Business Machines Corp. Unauthorized use not permitted; **473** Telegraph Colour Library/FPG; **474** (t)BodyBilt Seating, (c)Fellowes, (b)Fox Electronics; **475** (tl)Mark Burnett, (tr)courtesy the M.I.T Media Laboratory/Richard Pasley, (c)screen shot reprinted with permission of Microsoft Corp., (b)Tom McCarthy/SKA.

Appendices

482 (tl tr) Intel Corp., (cl)The Computer Museum, Boston, (cr)Property of AT&T Archives. Reprinted with permission of AT&T, (bl)Apple Corp., (br)Computerland; **483** (tl)Apple Corp., (c)Intel Corp., (br)VisiCalc; **484** (tl)Microsoft Corp., (tr)Bell Laboratories, (c)Used with permission of Lotus Development Corp., (bl)courtesy International Business Machines Corp. Unauthorized use not permitted, (br)Xerox Corp.; **485**(tl)Hewlett Packard, (tr)Intel Corp., (bl)Apple Corp., (br)Compaq; **486** (tl)Apple Corp., (tr)courtesy International Business Machines Corp. Unauthorized use not permitted, (cl)Intel Corp., (cr)Microsoft Corp., (bl)Adobe, (br)Hewlett Packard; **487** (tl)courtesy International Business Machines Corp. Unauthorized use not permitted, (tr)courtesy PhotoDisk, all rights reserved, (cl)courtesy International Business Machines Corp. Unauthorized use not permitted, (cr) Novell, (b)Apple Corp.; **488** (tl)Motorola, (tr)reprinted with permission courtesy NeXT Computer,

Image Credits

(bl)Intel Corp., (br)Donna Coveny/MIT News Office; **489** (tl)screen shot reprinted with permission of Microsoft Corp., (tr)The National Science Foundation Network, (c)courtesy International Business Machines Corp. Unauthorized use not permitted (bl) Apple Corp., (br)Symantec; **490** (tl)Microsoft Corp., (tc)Internet World, (tr)courtesy International Business Machines Corp. Unauthorized use not permitted, (bl)Intel Corp., (br)courtesy Motorola; **491** (tl) Apple Corp., (tr)America Online, (cl)Microsoft Corp., (cr)Intel Corp., (bl)Power Computing, (br)courtesy Motorola; **492** (t)Intel Corp., (b)courtesy Janet Reno.

ONE MAN'S JUSTICE

KT-416-643

ONE MAN'S JUSTICE

Akira Yoshimura

Translated from the Japanese by
Mark Ealey

CANONGATE

First published in the UK in 2003 by
Canongate Books Ltd, 14 High Street,
Edinburgh EH1 1TE

10 9 8 7 6 5 4 3 2 1

British Library Cataloguing-in-Publication Data
A catalogue record for this book is available on request
from the British Library

ISBN 1 84195 384 9

Typeset by Palimpsest Book Production Limited,
Polmont, Stirlingshire

Printed and bound in Italy by
LegoPrint S.p.A. (Lavis TN)

www.canongate.net

1

The boy's eyes were no longer on Takuya.

Each time the train lurched, the boy's head, covered in ring-worm, was buried in the gap between Takuya and the middle-aged woman standing in front of him. Takuya would lean back to create enough space for the boy to breathe. The boy looked up at Takuya repeatedly. There was a shadow of resignation in his eyes, a recognition of his powerlessness in the mass of adults, as well as a flicker of light, an entrusting of his well-being to this man who kept shifting back for him. Before long, however, the boy's head dropped. The strain of leaning to one side may have been too much for him, for now he hardly moved his head when he was pressed between the adults. The woman standing in front of them seemed to be the boy's mother, and Takuya could sense that he was holding on to the cloth of her work trousers.

The carriage was packed with people and baggage. Some had pushed their way in to stand between the seats, others perched on the seat backs, clinging for support to the luggage racks. No one spoke, and all that could be heard was a baby's intermittent hoarse crying.

The train slowed down. The sound of the wheels jolting over a joint in the tracks began at the front, rattled their carriage and clattered on to the rear of the train. There was a hum of voices as the passengers realised that they were approaching their destination, Hakata.

Takuya turned to look out the window. He wanted to be delivered from the suffocating atmosphere of the train, but at the same time he felt reluctant to step onto the platform in this city.

The train slowed more, shuddered slightly and came to a halt. The air filled with voices as people transformed the carriages into a bustle of activity. The boy winced as he twisted round to face

Takuya. Resisting the human tide, Takuya held the boy's gaze until he saw that a space had opened in front of him. Satisfied, he forced his way between the seats next to him to jump out the window and on to the platform.

Takuya looked around the concrete platform. The station was more or less as it had been when he left the city seven months ago, but scorched iron girders stood here and there, and the crossbeams of the roof's steel skeleton were exposed. He shuffled with the crowd across the platform towards the ticket gates.

Leaving the station, Takuya saw people milling around and peering into a cluster of makeshift wooden stalls. The hawkers' voices were animated, but the people on the street moved lethargically from one stall to the next.

The thought that someone in this crowd of survivors might recognise him made Takuya take the path that ran along the railway tracks for a short distance from the market to a stone bridge over a little stream.

A desolate expanse of charred buildings opened up in front of him. Once again he was astonished that so many homes could have been reduced to ashes in a single night.

Takuya set off along the road through the charred ruins. Though he had spent the last two years and four months of the war here, he had not expected ever to set foot in this city again. He knew deep down that it was unwise to go anywhere near the place.

The reason Takuya had left his home town to come here by train, ferry and then train again was a postcard he had received three days earlier. It was from Shirasaka Hajime, a former army lieutenant. Shirasaka had been born in the United States, but returned to Japan with his parents before the war, graduating from a private university before joining the Imperial Army. He had belonged to the same unit as Takuya, the Western Region Anti-Aircraft Defence Group, under the command of Western Regional Headquarters, and his knowledge of English had led him to stay on after the war as part of the staff winding up headquarters affairs in liaison with the Allied forces. The post-card, scrawled in his typescript-like handwriting, had mentioned that he was keen to see Takuya again, and suggested he come to visit soon.

Takuya was bewildered by the message. He had been in the same class as Shirasaka as a military cadet, but they hadn't been particularly close. In fact, at times Takuya had felt something akin to repulsion at the occasional manifestations of Shirasaka's foreign upbringing. In those days Shirasaka had seemed keenly aware of Takuya's feelings and made no attempt at friendship. Having been born and raised in America, a hostile country, Shirasaka was mocked and berated for his strange accent, and he was often on the receiving end of disciplinary action. Takuya didn't think this at all strange, in fact it mildly pleased him. Shirasaka was a tall, well-built man. These were certainly desirable attributes in an officer, but when Takuya thought of how this was the result of an ample American diet, he saw it as proof of an insidious disassociation from the Japanese people.

On orders from the commander of air defence operations at headquarters, Shirasaka had served as interpreter in the interrogation of captured American B-29 pilots who had bailed out when their bombers were shot down. Takuya had also been present, and had been surprised at Shirasaka's fluent English, which only aggravated his ill feelings towards the man. Shirasaka's English was completely different from what Takuya had learned as a student, and for the most part was unintelligible to him. Takuya could tell that the years he had spent in America had profoundly affected his character, and his natural way of conversing with the American fliers made Takuya doubt Shirasaka's trustworthiness. He would shrug his shoulders and shake his head without saying anything, and the Americans would look at him imploringly, appealing to him in muffled tones.

Takuya's feelings about Shirasaka had not changed since they had parted ways. And his impressions gained credence from the self-importance he had detected in ethnic Japanese American military interpreters on two other occasions. He imagined that Shirasaka would have used his English skills to ingratiate himself with the American military, and would doubtless be leading the same uninhibited life as those Japanese American interpreters.

Takuya tried to read between the few short lines on Shirasaka's postcard. Since the start of the Allied occupation, all mail had been censored by the Supreme Commander of Allied Powers in Japan (SCAP), and mail and documents from the staff handling the affairs of the now defunct headquarters would surely be strictly monitored. That Shirasaka had sent such a deliberate message to Takuya, to whom he had not been particularly close, must mean that he wished to see him urgently. As an interpreter, he would be in a position to assess developments on the Allied side, so it was possible he had come across information which concerned Takuya and was trying to pass it on.

After reading the card over and over again, Takuya had headed for Fukuoka, where Shirasaka was helping to wind up the affairs of the Western Command.

Walking along in the spring sunshine, he looked down at the road under his feet. He could see hairline cracks from the searing heat of the fires that had raged after the incendiary attacks. In places, holes in the asphalt exposed the soil beneath. Scorched roofing iron and rubble were piled on both sides of the road, and the occasional ruins of square concrete buildings and the tops of underground warehouses were all that was left standing.

In stark contrast to Takuya's parting impression seven months earlier, Fukuoka had acquired the settled desolation of a wasteland. Maybe it was because the burnt ruins were starting to return to the earth, or because all projecting objects had been removed, but this huge scorched plain seemed almost to shimmer in the heat. The sound of a piece of roofing iron that had come loose would approach on a gust of wind, then disappear into the expanse beyond the road. Here and there windblown piles of sand stood out in the arid lifelessness. Then, to the south, came the ominous sight of two gently sloping verdant hills. The hills were split to the east and west of a central ridge called Abura-yama, a vantage point from which the distant islands of Tsushima and Iki could be seen on a fine day. According to legend, during the reign of Emperor Shomu a monk named Sciga established a temple there and became known for the extract he made from the fruit of trees in the surrounding forest. The thicket where Takuya and his companions had executed the Americans, near the crematorium at Sanroku and not far from the hills in view, was linked inextricably to his memory of this city.

Shifting his gaze out to sea, he caught sight of a convoy of four US Army trucks moving along the coastal road, the beams from each set of headlights dancing in the clouds of dust thrown up by the vehicle in front. Some people said that the Americans drove with their headlights on during the day to flaunt the US military's affluence, and there was no denying the compelling nature of those shafts of light.

Ahead of him Takuya recognised a watchtower protruding from the burnt-out shell of a fire station. The building, or what was left of it, had a rough whitish look not dissimilar to that of unglazed pottery. Most of the outer walls had crumbled away, and rusty, glassless window frames hung loosely from the surviving structure.

Beyond the ruined fire station Takuya was stopped by the sight of a bank of pink cherry blossom. At the top of the road, up a gentle slope, was the former regional command headquarters building, encircled by a belt of cherry trees in full bloom. After the scorched desolation he had just walked through, Takuya found the vibrant pink of this hill strange to behold. Perhaps because it was surrounded by blossom, the old headquarters building radiated elegance rather than foreboding, as though it were a stately western manor. This gentle hill seemed somehow removed from the passage of time.

Takuya glanced to either side of the building. Sitting on the ferry and swaying inside the train, he had felt a faint distrust of Shirasaka's motives. It was easy to imagine Shirasaka, in the course of working with the occupation forces, developing a relationship which went beyond tending to the affairs of the former Western Command. Takuya thought that the postcard might even have been sent on the instructions of the Americans, to lure him into the open. He had decided to come here despite his apprehension because he assumed that, even if there were some basis for his fear, the situation would not have reached a critical stage.

Since the middle of the previous November, the newspapers had been full of reports of Japanese servicemen being tried and then executed by military tribunals for crimes committed overseas against prisoners of war. Even so, Takuya surmised that if the occupation authorities were suspicious of him they would have instructed the Japanese police to arrest him by now. And even if Shirasaka's card had been sent on the orders of the Americans, it was likely that they only wanted to carry out some routine preliminary questioning.

Moreover, Takuya felt sure that what they had done could not have been discovered by anyone on the outside. They had planned everything so carefully and so secretly that no civilian could have witnessed, or even been aware of, any part of the proceedings. There was no way, he thought, that this deed, carried out within a rigidly closed military system, could ever leak to the outside world. If the fact that executions had taken place was discovered, the headquarters staff would be culpable to varying degrees, and almost all of them would likely be implicated. That in itself, Takuya thought, would keep their lips sealed.

He concentrated his gaze on the low hill. It seemed deserted. There were no people or vehicles in sight anywhere around the building, nor on the road chiselled into the front face of the knoll. His eyes rivetted on the hill, he started walking forward. To one side a bent and broken water pipe protruded from the ground. Water flowed down the road, filling a hollow in an exposed patch of dirt and spreading out in a fan-shaped arc. Faint signs of moss could be seen just below the surface of the little pool, and at the bottom grains of sand glistened as though washed to perfection.

Takuya walked up the slope, stopping at the stone pavement in front of the building. The cherry blossom was just past its peak, and petals covered the ground.

The reception desk was unattended and the utter lack of sound suggested that the building was deserted, but a message on the wall, written on straw paper with an English translation typed beside it, invited visitors to make their way directly to the first floor.

Takuya stared ahead down the corridor. Hardly any of the windows had panes of glass and many had been boarded over completely, leaving the corridor dark and forbidding. The room Takuya had used was on the left, at the end of the corridor, but he felt no desire to go that way. He walked up the stairs to find the first floor bathed in sunlight. From there he followed an arrow drawn on a piece of paper stuck to the white wall. It pointed towards the section of the building where the offices of the regional commander and chief of staff had been located, and where the remaining affairs of the regional command were likely being attended to.

He paused before a door marked with a piece of paper bearing the word 'Entrance'. This room was connected directly to the chief of staff's office and had been used as the tactical operations centre. Worried that members of the Allied military might be inside, Takuya stood glued to the spot, trying to sense what was on the other side of the door. He could just make out voices, but couldn't tell whether Japanese or English was being spoken.

He reached for the knob and opened the door. Some old desks had been brought in and arranged in an L-shape on the right-hand side of the room. A man wearing a navy blue suit and an open-necked shirt was sitting with three men in uniform behind the desks. They hadn't noticed Takuya's presence and seemed to be poring over some documents. The man in the suit lifted his head and turned to look at Takuya. Immediately he stood up and walked round the desks toward the visitor.

He had longer hair now, so for a moment Takuya didn't recognise Shirasaka. Distracted, the three uniformed men turned as one to look toward Takuya, who recognised them immediately as non-commissioned officers from the old headquarters staff.

Gesturing as though to push him back, Shirasaka ushered Takuya out of the room and into the corridor, then guided him in the direction of the staircase before opening a door and beckoning him in. Shirasaka's hand movements and facial expression were new to Takuya. Evidently, in his association with the occupation authorities he had regained his American mannerisms.

Shirasaka sat down behind the single desk in the middle of the room. Takuya put down his rucksack, placed his service cap on the desktop and sat facing Shirasaka.

From Shirasaka's expression Takuya realised he had been right to assume that there was nothing frivolous about the decision to send him the postcard. But they had gone to great lengths to ensure that every scrap of evidence was destroyed, so surely there was no chance they had been found out. It could only have to do with the matériel or facilities previously under the jurisdiction of the now defunct headquarters organisation.

'Those American fliers . . . I'm afraid things have taken a bad turn.' Resting his elbows on the desk and knitting his fingers together, Shirasaka explained that the former army major-general who had been commander-in-chief, his chief of staff, and a colonel who had been an aide-de-camp to the commander-in-chief were being questioned by US Army intelligence officers attached to SCAP.

Taken aback, Takuya stared at him.

Shirasaka told him that the former senior officers from head-quarters had been detained for almost a month now. The questioning focused on what had happened to the crew members who had parachuted from the B-29 bombers shot down the previous year. American intelligence was carrying out its duties under article ten of the Potsdam Declaration, covering deten-tion and punishment of war criminals guilty of mistreatment of prisoners of war, and thus far not only had established the exact location of the crash sites of the B-29s downed by Japanese anti-aircraft units, but had also discovered that a total of fifty-eight crew members had survived the downing of their aircraft in the western headquarters administrative sector of Kyushu. On the basis of this knowledge, the investigators had gathered detailed information from civilian sources and learnt that of the fifty-eight, seventeen had been sent to prisoner-of war camps in the Tokyo area, and the remaining forty-one had been handed over to the military police – the *kempeitai* – by local police, and from there transferred to the custody of Western Regional Headquarters.

By all accounts, the investigation team had carried out a rigorous interrogation of western headquarters staff, and now knew that the crew members had, to a man, been either formally executed or disposed of to the same end. The 'bad turn' Shirasaka had referred to was that the headquarters staff had categorically denied issuing any orders to this effect, and insisted that the executions had been carried out arbitrarily by young officers.

'Incredible, isn't it?' said Shirasaka, shaking his head.

Takuya was dumbfounded. He was shocked not just that things could have been traced this far, but that senior officers in Western Regional Command, including the commander-in-chief himself, could have painted a picture so at odds with the truth.

During his days as the head of the Eleventh Army in China, the commander-in-chief had gathered a great deal of information about the movements of the US Army Air Force units flying out of China, and had done his utmost to use this knowledge after his posting to Western Regional Command. Surmising that the American build-up of airpower in China presaged air raids on Kyushu, he ordered the anti-aircraft intelligence network to focus their attention on the Korea Strait. His deduction had proved to be correct, allowing for early detection of the American bomber squadrons heading for Kyushu airspace, thereby giving local fighter units time to effect the optimum defence and inflict heavy losses on the incoming bombers.

This success had greatly enhanced his prestige within the army, where he was already widely renowned as a general of genuinely noble character. As composed and imperturbable as a man could be, he responded to each request for a sample of his calligraphy by writing the Chinese characters for 'Death, life, be as prepared for one as for the other.' That a man of his calibre should have brazenly divorced himself from his responsibilities was beyond belief.

Demobilised on the fifth of September of the previous year, Takuya had gone back to his home town. Soon after his return, he learnt that the occupation authorities had intensified their efforts to apprehend suspected war criminals.

On the eleventh of that month a warrant was issued for the arrest of those designated Class A war criminals, on charges of having participated in the 'formulation or execution of a common plan or conspiracy to wage wars of aggression'. Former prime minister General Tojo Hideki had shot himself in a suicide attempt when he realised that American military police had arrived at his home. The following day, it was reported that other high-ranking officials, including former army minister Field Marshal Sugiyama Hajime, former minister of health Major-General Koizumi Chikahiko, former minister of education Hashida Kunihiko, former commander of the North-east Region General Yoshimoto Sadakazu, former commander-in-chief of the Kwantung Army Honjo Shigeru, and former prime minister Konoe Fumimaro, had taken their own lives. The newspaper coverage included the full text of article ten of the Potsdam Declaration regarding Japan's surrender, stating: 'We do not intend that the Japanese shall be enslaved as a race or destroyed as a nation, but stern justice shall be meted out to all war criminals, including those who have visited cruelties upon prisoners.'

On the tenth of October Takuya read an article saying that warrants had been issued for the arrest of three hundred former staff of prisoner-of-war camps on charges of mistreatment of prisoners. The article, a release from the Associated Press office at General MacArthur's headquarters, stated that these suspects would be arrested by the Japanese authorities and handed over to Eleventh Army divisional headquarters in Yokohama, and that no stone would be left unturned until those guilty of mistreating prisoners of war were brought to justice.

Included in an article six days later, below the headline 'Bodies of Seven US Airmen Discovered – Parachuted to Ground during Tokyo Air Raids', was a statement from a spokesman for the Eighth Army Corps. It said that investigators had found the remains of two American fliers buried beside a Tokyo canal. Evidently the dead airmen had had their arms tied with thick rope and had suffered massive wounds to the neck and head. The clue that led to their discovery was provided by a young Japanese girl who, during the days of the air raids on Tokyo, had seen Japanese soldiers burying bodies wrapped in straw matting. The remains had been found in shallow graves full of muddy water, with the bodies clad only in flight jackets, sweaters and torn boots. The article also said that another five bodies had subsequently been exhumed from the grounds of a certain unnamed temple.

Not long afterwards, it was reported in the newspaper that trials of those suspected of crimes against prisoners of war had started, and that the first guilty verdict had already been delivered on the eighth of January. The man sentenced was a former army lieutenant who had been in charge of Ohmuta prisoner-of-war camp. An American prisoner of war by the name of Hurd had twice attempted to escape and in consequence had been thrown into the guardhouse. When he tried to escape a third time he was severely beaten. The military tribunal judged that the beating constituted serious mistreatment of a prisoner of war and sentenced the accused to death by hanging. Beatings were everyday occurrences in the Japanese army, so Takuya was shocked that merely beating an incorrigible escaper should warrant the death penalty.

Three days later, there were reports of assault charges filed against a junior officer at the Ohmuta camp, and charges of burning moxa on a prisoner's arm and slapping him across the face with an open hand against the commandant of another camp. Both officers were sentenced to death by hanging. Numerous similar cases were reported in succeeding days.

Amid all the press coverage, the articles covering the trial of the former commander-in-chief of Japanese forces in the Philippines, General Yamashita Tomoyuki, stood out to Takuya for their depiction of the stance that should be taken by a commander of an army corps. Yamashita's trial by military tribunal had been held in Manila and he was sentenced to death, but he did not hesitate to accept complete responsibility for the actions of his subordinates.

Takuya had assumed all along that the commander of the Western Region would take a position similar to Yamashita's. As the one who gave the orders in the Western Region, the commander would have been fully aware of what had happened under his command, and Takuya had firmly believed that if the facts of the matter were discovered the commander would take complete responsibility.

'American intelligence knows all your names and addresses. Things being the way they are at the moment, they will doubtless move to arrest you.' Shirasaka's speech was free of any trace of the rough language he had used to refer to fellow officers during his time as a lieutenant in the Imperial Army.

'What should I do?' asked Takuya dejectedly. He couldn't help but feel indignant at being told that those who had issued the orders in the first place were, only eight months after the dissolution of the Imperial Army, divorcing themselves from all responsibility for what had happened in that thicket near Abura-yama. Such things didn't happen in the army Takuya had known.

Shirasaka fixed his eyes on Takuya. 'Run for it. Hide somewhere,' he said in a soft yet compelling voice.

Takuya remained silent.

Shirasaka's eyes glistened as he spoke. 'Without a doubt, they'll hang you if you're caught. You'll die like a dog. Hide. Lieutenant Hirosaki came this morning. I sent him a postcard worded the same way as the one I sent you. I explained the situation and told him to lie low. He said he'd do his best, and now I'm giving you the same advice.'

When Takuya remained speechless, Shirasaka stood up and left the room.

Takuya remembered seeing a photograph in the newspaper which showed a former army lieutenant, sentenced to death for beating a prisoner of war, being led out of the courtroom by the American military police. If he were to end up that way, he would have no second chance to escape. There would be only the wait for the gallows. Takuya couldn't bear the thought that he, who had served his country so loyally, might be held captive by the occupation forces and forced to die such a humiliating death.

A wave of uneasiness came over him. The warrant for his arrest might already have been issued, and the occupation administration might have called upon those winding up the affairs of the former headquarters. Obviously, just being in this building was dangerous.

He stood and looked out the window. There were no people or vehicles moving towards the building, and a dusty haze shrouded almost half of the wasted terrain. A glint of bright light emanated from somewhere near the station.

The door opened and Shirasaka re-entered the room. Sitting down, he produced two pieces of paper from the inside pocket of his jacket and placed them on the desk.

'I gave Hirosaki these, too. They're papers for demobilised soldiers back from overseas. With one of these you can get food and other rations wherever you go, and they double as identification. I considered a few options and came to the conclusion that you should make out you're from Okinawa. It's occupied by the Americans, so a demobilised soldier wouldn't be in much of a hurry to get back there, which is a plausible reason for you to keep moving around the main islands. Write in a name that sounds Okinawan. Just in case, I'm giving you a second one to keep as a spare.'

Shirasaka pushed the papers toward Takuya. They already bore the official seal of the Western Command's Hakata office for demobilised military personnel, and the spaces for name and address were left blank. However he had obtained them, the documents looked very official.

Takuya put the papers in the inside pocket of his army jacket. 'I want you to give me my gun back,' he said.

Shirasaka stared hard at Takuya, a tinge of surprise spreading across his face. After the surrender, Takuya and the other officers had wrapped their twelve side-arms and a considerable quantity of ammunition in oiled paper and put them all into a waterproof bag, which had then been hidden in a secret compartment in the corridor of the headquarters building. In the bag was a collection of foreign- and Japanese-made pistols purchased with the officers' allowance for personal side-arms. Among them was Takuya's 1939 army pistol.

Takuya had forgotten about the pistol, but Shirasaka's explanation of developments and the words 'They'll hang you' had jogged his memory. He felt exposed and vulnerable without his gun, as though the wartime logic that an officer had to have a weapon on him at all times had returned to guide him.

Takuya realised that his war had yet to end. The enemy was close at hand, patrolling with sub-machine-guns slung from their shoulders, driving Jeeps and lorries through the streets of the cities and towns.

'Why do you need it?' said Shirasaka, a trace of trepidation in his voice.

'I just want to have it on me,' replied Takuya. Being armed was in itself more than reason enough. As long as his own war continued, a weapon would be indispensable.

Shirasaka's fists clenched within his folded arms. Takuya saw the tormented look on the man's face and realised that Shirasaka was afraid he might use the weapon to kill himself. On the twentieth of August, just days after the official document of surrender was signed, a navy lieutenant and a commander from the Kyushu munitions depot, distraught at the reality of defeat, had both committed hara-kiri in the woods near the Shoogaku temple, and since then there had been a rash of suicides by men named to stand trial for war crimes. Maybe it wasn't so strange of Shirasaka to interpret Takuya's wanting his gun back as a sign that he planned to kill himself.

'I want it back,' Takuya said in a calmer tone, hoping to allay Shirasaka's fears.

Shirasaka fidgeted. Propping his elbows on the desk, he rubbed his clenched fingers against his forehead, pushing his thumbs awkwardly into his cheeks.

'You used to have a Colt, didn't you? I like guns. I was attached to the one I had. I just want it back,' said Takuya softly.

His gaze still lowered, Shirasaka nodded several times, then grasped the edge of the desk and rose. Takuya turned to watch him leave the room. Any suspicion he might have harboured had vanished, nullified by the goodwill the man had shown in sending the postcard, providing him with papers and encouraging him to run. Shirasaka had probably felt unable to stand by and watch a former comrade-in-arms sent to the gallows, but maybe another part of the explanation was that, deep down, he felt an aversion to the 'trials' of those accused of war crimes. No doubt, thought Takuya, day-to-day contact with occupation forces staff had left Shirasaka nonplussed by their arrogance, and perhaps this had led him to obstruct their proceedings by encouraging his former comrades to flee. If the occupation authorities got wind of his actions, the severest of penalties would undoubtedly be meted out to him, too. Takuya felt a twinge of conscience, knowing that his request would commit Shirasaka to an even greater level of collusion, but it was overwhelmed by his desire to have the weapon back.

There was a faint sound of footsteps, then the door opened and Shirasaka reappeared, his expression strained as he returned to sit opposite Takuya. Glancing towards the door, he reached inside his jacket and offered Takuya the object he had been concealing. It was the pistol Takuya had carried during the war, but the months it had been out of his grasp made it somehow feel much heavier. The small box of ammunition that Shirasaka placed on the table sat there for several seconds before Takuya stuffed it into his rucksack.

Shirasaka pulled a pack of Lucky Strikes from his pocket and offered one to Takuya, who shook his head in refusal at the idea of smoking an American cigarette.

Takuya felt his composure return. Now that he was armed, he could at least resist his would-be captors and, if necessary, take his own life rather than submit to arrest.

'Well, then. I'd better go. Thanks for your help,' Takuya said, grasping his service cap and slinging the rucksack over his shoulder as he rose to his feet. Shirasaka stood up, stepped into the corridor and walked ahead of Takuya down the stairs.

Outside, Takuya thanked Shirasaka again and started down the cobbled road.

'Kiyohara!' he heard behind him. Takuya looked back and saw Shirasaka hurrying down the slope, eyes glistening. 'Don't go killing yourself,' he said imploringly, tears welling up.

Takuya didn't reply. He hadn't thought about how he would use the weapon, and he certainly hadn't made up his mind to end his own life. He would take everything as it came.

'Killing yourself would be meaningless,' said Shirasaka in an almost admonitory tone.

Takuya looked away from Shirasaka pensively, then started down the slope.

Maybe it was the reflection from all the burnt pieces of roofing iron, but the temperature down in the ruins of the city seemed higher than up on the hill. Takuya hurried towards the railway station, occasionally glancing back over his shoulder. Most of the knoll was hidden behind the remaining walls of the old fire station, and Shirasaka was not in sight. Beyond that, all he could really see was a glimpse of the pink cherry blossom at the top of the hill.

2

The he train left Hakata station.

His arms pinned to his sides in the crush, Takuya was jostled into the space beside the lavatory. There was so little room to stand that two men were crouched precariously on top of the wash-basins. The hair of the woman standing in front of him touched his face, a sour smell emanating from her scalp.

Takuya closed his eyes. Suddenly he found himself wondering how his American counterparts would be spending their days. Most of their officers would have been repatriated by now, and had no doubt been given a hero's welcome. Throngs of well-wishers would have welcomed them at the station and carried them home on their shoulders. Many would even receive medals for killing Japanese soldiers in battle. Takuya had killed one American. A tall, blond man who had taken part in incendiary attacks on Japanese cities, sending horrific numbers of non-combatants, old people, women and children to their deaths. If Japan had won, Takuya's act might even have earned him a medal, but now he had only his wits to keep him from the gallows.

There was no option but to get away. The impulse to flee was motivated not by fear of a noose around his neck but rather by indignation toward the victors. The Allies saw their own soldiers as heroes for killing Japanese and now sought to force a humiliating death upon Takuya and his defeated comrades-in-arms. The irony of it cut Takuya to the quick.

The train moved slowly down the track. By craning his neck, Takuya could just see over the mass of passengers to the outside world beyond the glassless windows. Before he knew it, it was early evening and the sun was setting.

There was a brief twilight, then dusk, before the darkness set in and the electric lights came on in the aisles. People got off each time the train stopped, but just as many seemed to get on, so there was no relief from the crush. The man pressed hard against Takuya's back seemed to be falling asleep on his feet. From time to time he gave way at the knees, forcing Takuya to do the same. Takuya could hear a light snoring just behind his head. His rucksack was slung over his shoulder, and through the cloth bag he felt the hard grip of the pistol against the small of his back. The gun was also probably pressing against the stomach of the man standing behind him, as now and then he seemed to pull back as if trying to avoid it.

The train pulled into Kokura station almost an hour behind schedule. Takuya pushed his way through the mass of bodies and alighted on the platform. There was a two-hour wait before his next train arrived on the Nippoo Line, but Takuya felt almost anchored to the spot. He made no move toward the next platform. He had instinctively boarded the train at Hakata, but now he was having second thoughts about actually going beyond here and returning home. Shirasaka had said that the Allied authorities already knew where Takuya was living, so it was entirely possible that the police would be waiting there to arrest him.

As he stood gazing at the black body of the train slowly receding from the end of the platform, he sensed that he wasn't completely ready to commit himself to fleeing. The occupation would continue virtually indefinitely, so he would have to be prepared to be on the run for the rest of his days. That would mean drawing a line in his current life, and before he could do that there were certain things he must do.

He was carrying very little cash, and to make good his escape he would need at least some money. He would also need to destroy anything at home that might be used to trace him. Besides, as he was unlikely to see his parents and younger brother and sister again, he wanted to say goodbye to them before setting off. He had to make one last visit home. Despite the risk, the pistol in his rucksack fortified the decision to return. If the authorities were waiting for him he could resist, and if escape proved impossible he could end it all on his own terms.

Takuya walked to the Nippoo Line platform. Under the pale station lights, another sea of people was crammed in from one end of the platform to the other, waiting for the incoming train. Spotting the scantest of spaces, Takuya sat down, placing his rucksack carefully between his knees. Beside him a young mother knelt changing her baby's nappy. As it lay face-up on the patchy concrete, the baby turned its eyes towards Takuya. Tiredness overcame him and he closed his eyes, letting his head drop forward. Perhaps because of the heat from the mass of bodies, the air on the platform was stifling, and in a moment Takuya had nodded off to sleep.

After a while he sensed people around him rising, and he opened his eyes and got to his feet. The whistle sounded and the train shot steam over the tracks as it pulled in beside the platform. Utter confusion followed, with people trying to get on before any passengers could leave the train. An angry exchange of voices ensued between those trying to climb in through the windows and those who blocked their entry from inside. Pushed from every direction, Takuya just managed to edge his way on board by stepping on the footplate at the end of one carriage.

The train jolted forward. Before long the bustle of voices and activity gave way to the monotonous beat of the wheels against the joints in the tracks.

A squadron of moths fluttered around the electric light outside the washroom, bashing themselves relentlessly against the misted glass cover protecting the bulb. Just when Takuya thought that at least one moth had decided to settle, wings trembling, on the metal top of the light fitting, it took off again to resume butting against the light, powder from its wings dropping visibly after each assault.

At station after station more passengers jostled their way on board, and by now it was decidedly uncomfortable. The crush was so oppressive that the rucksack on his back was being pushed downward, and he felt himself losing his balance.

The train pulled into Usuki station just before four in the morning. Takuya passed through the ticket gates and stepped out on to the road in the darkness. Usuki had not entirely escaped the ravages of war, but rows of antiquated wooden houses still stood on both sides of the street, as befitted the old castle town. The road wound through the town, with different buildings silhouetted round each bend. The moon was on the wane and the heavens teemed with stars. When he reached the outskirts he smelled salt in the air and heard the sound of waves breaking. Before long an expanse of sea opened up in front of him and he could make out a number of small boats moored to a little jetty.

Takuya made his way along the road beside the water. When he was near the ferry terminal he slipped under a canopy and sat down on the ground. Many people were sleeping there, lying or sitting under the eaves of the building. One man stirred and turned to look listlessly at Takuya, who had propped himself against the wooden wall, pulling his service cap down over his face and shutting his eyes. He was feverish and his joints felt tired and weak. The pistol felt hard yet reassuring through the cloth of the rucksack in his lap. His grip on consciousness loosened and he slipped into a deep sleep.

The sun beat down on his face more and more intensely. Takuya opened his eyes and, still seated, gazed out across the water. His lower back felt cold and his legs were numb. His sleeping companions were awake now, sitting or lying on the narrow pier.

Takuya pulled a paper bag from his rucksack and dropped a few dry roasted beans into his mouth. He hadn't had anything to eat since the afternoon of the previous day, but he wasn't really hungry.

As he chewed the beans his throat felt dry and he stood up, walked around to the rear of the building, drank some water from a tap and washed his face. He relieved himself on the dirt, and noticed that his urine was yellowish brown and frothy.

After a while a long queue formed on the pier, and he joined the end of it. Lice crawled over the scalp of the young girl standing in front of him. As soon as one hid itself in her hair another would appear immediately somewhere else, lift its rear end slightly, then burrow in among the roots of her hair.

After about an hour Takuya followed the others on to the boat bound for Yawatahama. Another forty-five minutes passed before the boat finally chugged laboriously away from the pier. Takuya found himself a corner of the deck near the bow and sat down.

The boat left the bay and passed close by Muku island on the starboard side before entering the Bungo Channel, where the smooth passage ended and a slight pitch and roll began.

Far off to the northwest he could make out the Kunisaki peninsula. The American B-29 bomber squadrons operating out of Saipan had often aimed to enter and leave Kyushu airspace at this landmark. Aircraft spotters were stationed all over the peninsula, as well as electronic listening devices to detect the approach of incoming aircraft. In the anti-aircraft strategic operations room of Western Regional Command they had processed the information, immediately alerted the air defence forces with an estimated point of incursion, and then provided them with a precise flight path to intercept the bombers.

As Takuya gazed at the peninsula, his mind returned to an incident involving the people of a fishing village at the tip of the landmass. Six months before the end of the war, a B-29 returning from a bombing mission was hit by fire from an anti-aircraft battery and brought down in the sea just off the fishing village. Three of its crew survived by parachuting into the water. The villagers put their boats out straight away, found the bomber crewmen and roughly pulled them into the boats before dumping them on shore. One of the three fliers was utterly terrified, running at the nose and convulsing uncontrollably. The villagers – men, women and children – beat the crewmen mercilessly until an old fisherman picked up a harpoon and ran it through one of the Americans. The official report on the incident described the old man's action as motivated by 'irrepressible feelings of indignation toward these outlaws who would violate the Imperial realm with the objective of slaughtering innocent old people, women and children'.

In all likelihood US military intelligence had already established that some fliers not only had survived their bomber going down, but had then been assaulted, and that one of their number had been killed. At the time, the actions of the villagers met with unquestioning approval, and they doubtless even felt something akin to pride about what had happened. But with the end of the war they, too, would be leaving for fear of pursuit by the American military.

Takuya stared toward the peninsula, now nothing more than a dim shadow in the distance. He realised that throughout the country countless people must be in the same predicament as he was.

The boat's pitch and roll remained slight, and all he really noticed was the monotonous beat of the engines. Before long Takuya fell asleep.

He was awakened by the sound of the boat's horn. The ferry pulled alongside a pier and a rope was thrown into the waiting arms of a man on shore. Takuya filed off the boat behind the other passengers.

Near the exit from the landing-stage there were two policemen in washed-out uniforms watching the passengers disembark nervously. Those carrying luggage tried to pass by the police, but almost all were ordered to enter a holding-pen set up to one side. They were confiscating any items, such as food, upon which the authorities had placed trading restrictions. The two policemen hardly glanced at Takuya and his battered rucksack as he walked past.

Takuya made his way to Yawatahama station, where he again joined a long line to buy a ticket. More than an hour later his turn finally came, and he headed toward the platform, ticket in hand. The train was waiting, a steam engine with four passenger carriages and two freight cars. As the passenger carriages were already packed, he squeezed into a space on one of the freight cars.

The whistle sounded and the train slowly headed southwards. Takuya sat back against the wall and stretched his legs out on the straw-covered floor. The train stopped at each station along the way, sometimes for quite a while at even the smallest of stations. Some of the floorboards in the carriage were missing, and he could see through to tufts of weeds growing among the sleepers and the stones on the tracks.

The sun was sliding down toward the west. Takuya felt the urge to relieve himself, so he grasped the sides of the opening through which he'd boarded, stood on tiptoe to clear the low outer wall, and urinated off the moving train. The sky was a brilliant red and the far-off ridges were tinged with purple.

The sun went down and the freight car was plunged into darkness. That night the stars were out in force, the moon one day further on the wane. Every so often, when the train rushed past electric signals, the freight car was bathed in a blaze of light, providing a split second's respite from the all-encompassing night.

The train pressed along the coast and, just as Takuya thought he glimpsed the black expanse of the sea, the engine and its carriages hurtled into a tunnel. From time to time he could make out lights from what must have been clusters of houses and fishing villages along the coast.

Takuya raised his head just enough to read the names on the passing station signs. He thought that the police might be keeping an eye on the station in the town next to his village, so he had made up his mind to leave the train one station short of his destination.

The train slowed and pulled to a halt beside the platform of a small station. He jumped down from the freight car, circled around it, crossed the tracks and walked through the ticket gates and out of the station. Avoiding the densely populated street, he made his way back along the railway line and started walking. The subtle bluish white of the steel tracks stretched before him into the distance, the clearly visible lights ahead reminding him that he had only a short distance to go.

When he was quite close to the town, he stepped down from the railway bed and walked along a path between two paddy fields. Perhaps because his eyes had become used to the dark, the waning moon seemed to illuminate everything around him. There was not a soul in sight.

Having skirted the town by following the paths through the paddy fields, he climbed up the white stone steps of the local shrine. Both the inner sanctuary and the shrine office were cloaked in darkness. He remembered coming here to pray with the villagers before joining the Imperial Army, standing among them in his university hat and uniform, the national flag slung over his shoulder. Pausing in the shrine gateway, Takuya took off his service cap and bowed toward the inner sanctuary.

Leaving the precincts of the shrine and its conspicuous smell of bark, Takuya followed a narrow, sinuous track cut into the hill behind the shrine. He had walked this path so many times when he was small that he knew it like the back of his hand, so he made steady progress over the protruding roots and potholes.

Takuya stopped under the boughs of a large pine. Below him, by the light of the moon, he could see the cluster of dwellings that made up the village where his family lived. There were about thirty houses, dotted along either side of the winding path, strung out between the hill where he was standing and the low knoll directly opposite. The sun rose from behind the hill overlooking the shrine and set behind the knoll on the other side of the village, so sunrise was late and sunset was early. The village was blessed with soil good enough to offset the shorter sunlight hours, which provided quality crops, especially mandarin oranges, for those working the land. The woods around the village were home to countless nightingales, whose pleasant warbling filled the air from early spring until autumn. This gave the village its name, Ohshuku.

Takuya's eyes traced the barely visible path through the village down to the area around his family's house at the foot of the hill. No sign of anyone on the path and no movement around the house.

Two dogs appeared on the path, trotting more or less side by side. They passed directly beside the house, then crossed the wooden bridge over the little stream. Takuya relaxed somewhat

– clearly the animals were not distracted by anything unusual around the house – but, just in case, he pulled the pistol out of his rucksack, loaded it and stuffed it in his belt before making his way down the slope.

Scanning the area, he cut through an open patch of weeds and jumped over the little brook. A light was on inside his house. When he was near the back door he could tell from the sound of running water that either his mother or his younger sister was washing something in the kitchen.

Takuya opened the door. His mother, standing in front of the sink, turned and welcomed him home. In the back room, his father sat hunched forward under an electric lamp, his reading glasses perched on the end of his nose as he read a newspaper. Making haste was Takuya's most pressing concern. Before long the peaceful world his family enjoyed would be shattered by the arrival of those seeking his capture. If they came while Takuya was still at home, the disruption would be all the greater for his family.

His mother asked if he had eaten but Takuya went straight into the living-room without answering. His father looked up. Takuya made sure his mother had gone back to her task at the sink before sitting down in front of his father.

In a quiet but deliberate voice, Takuya explained to his father how on the fifteenth of August the previous year, after the broadcast of the imperial rescript announcing Japan's surrender, he had taken part in the execution of American prisoners of war who had parachuted from disabled B-29 bombers. Now American military intelligence was on his trail and his capture was probably only a matter of time.

His father listened aghast.

'I have to go into hiding right away. I'm sorry . . . but can you give me some money please?' he said, fixing his eyes on the old man's face.

For a few seconds his father said nothing. Then, moving his gaze a fraction to the side, he whispered, 'So you've killed an American.'

'I cut his head off with my sword,' replied Takuya.

The old man stayed sitting where he was, not moving a muscle. A mournful look had come over his face.

Takuya stood up and walked over to his own room, switching the light on as he stepped through the doorway. He pulled out his photo album, stripped it of all the photographs taken since he had reached adulthood, and put them and his letters, diaries and address book in the wastepaper basket. This in hand, he stepped down on to the earth-floor section of the house and pushed the contents into the kitchen stove, lighting the paper with a match. His mother, not seeming to realise what Takuya was burning, dried her hands on her apron and walked into the living-room. He pushed the poker into the fire, checking that the papers were reduced to ashes before stepping back into the living-room.

There was a pile of notes on the low table in the middle of the room. To deal with the inflation that followed immediately after the war, the government had restricted the amount of money any householder could withdraw from a bank to three hundred yen per month, and one hundred yen per family member. Takuya knew that without the money on the table his family would inevitably struggle, yet he knelt down, took the notes, and stuffed them into the inside pocket of his jacket. His mother looked on apprehensively as she poured tea for the three of them. His father removed his glasses and sat motionless, staring vacantly into a corner.

Takuya rose to his feet and walked a couple of steps to the chest of drawers. He pulled out some socks and underwear and stuffed them into his rucksack along with a grey army blanket he took from the cupboard. His mother offered cups of green tea to the two men.

'Are you going somewhere?' asked his mother, looking inquisitively at her son.

'I have to go away. I'll be off in a few minutes,' he replied as he tied the cord on his rucksack.

'What? Tonight? It's late,' said his mother sharply.

'Where are Toshio and Chiyoko?' He thought he should see his brother and sister before he left.

'Chiyoko is in bed. She's coming down with a cold. Toshio is on the night shift. He won't be home for another hour or so,' replied his mother incredulously.

Takuya took a sip of the tea, picked up his rucksack, and got to his feet. He stepped into his shoes on the earth floor of the kitchen area.

'Why can't you go tomorrow?' asked his mother, her tone now slightly angry.

He swung his rucksack over his shoulder, opened the back door and stepped outside. His father slipped on his mother's clogs and followed him out. Takuya turned round to face his father, took off his service cap, and bowed his head.

'If they catch you they'll hang you, won't they?' the old man said hoarsely. Takuya nodded.

His father said, 'Go to the Sayama family in Osaka. They'll help you.' He handed his son a small parcel. Takuya nodded, then turned and walked away. He jumped over the little stream and headed straight across the grassy patch, on to the slope of the path up the hill. Like an animal trusting its natural instinct of self-preservation, Takuya decided that the safest way to return would be along the path he had used to come to the village.

He climbed the track at a brisk pace before pausing under the pine tree halfway up the hill. He looked down over the village, now half shrouded in a rising mist. The houses and the path were barely visible through the pale white murk, with only a few faint strips of light escaping from windows here and there.

Takuya opened the little package his father had handed him. Under two layers of paper were some two dozen cigarettes. To a father who would cut cigarettes in thirds with a razor and then smoke them stuffed parsimoniously into a pipe, these must have been even more valuable than money.

He sat down on one of the exposed roots of the pine tree, put a cigarette in his mouth and lit it. Having managed to get in and out of the family house safely, he felt somewhat relieved. He'd disposed of his remaining belongings, he had enough money to tide him over for a while, and he had a loaded pistol tucked in his belt. Even if a would-be captor spotted the light from his cigarette and rushed to catch him, Takuya was confident he could escape in the darkness over the track to the shrine and then beyond.

Only the faint gurgling of the little stream below broke the silence. He gazed at the area across the stream where his family house was. It was a small house for five people. Takuya had been born and raised in that house, and had commuted to middle school from there on the advice of his public servant father. He had gone on to high school and then to Kyushu Imperial University, paying what he could of the tuition by tutoring and delivering newspapers. Upon graduation he had gone straight into the Imperial Army. His younger brother, Toshio, had just graduated from a community college. Takuya's father had let him go on to university despite having to struggle on a meagre salary from the town civic office because he expected that Takuya would eventually take over the role of family breadwinner. Never in his wildest dreams could he have imagined his son stealing away from the family home in the middle of the night.

Takuya wondered how his family's position might be affected in the days and months to come. If it became public that his son was suspected of war crimes, Takuya's father might lose the job he'd held for so many years. The police would likely be pitiless in their pursuit, and would no doubt maintain the strictest surveillance over his family. Even the other people in the village might turn cold towards them. Takuya took comfort in the thought that, whatever happened, his family would understand that he had done nothing more than his duty as a military man, and that he was in no way a criminal. Surely that would give them the strength to endure the hardships that lay ahead, and he hoped that his brother and sister would look after his parents in his absence.

He stubbed out the remaining embers of the cigarette, took the pistol from his belt, unloaded it, and stuffed it between the folds in the blanket inside his rucksack. As he stood up and took one last look at his birthplace, the thought that he would likely never again set foot in the village, and just as likely never again see his brother and sister or his parents, saddened him.

Breathing in the cool night air, he set off again along the path. Around him in the darkness he could hear the chirps and cries of birds and the flutter of wings as they moved from branch to branch under the forest canopy.

He crossed through the precincts of the shrine and quickened his pace as he made his way along the paths between the paddy fields. The moon had progressed along its arc across the heavens, and by now was much higher in the sky. Takuya looked around as he hurried toward the station. Again, just to be safe, he wanted to board the train at least one stop down the line. A palpable feeling of satisfaction came over him. At last he was on the run and, at least for the moment, in control of his own destiny. It was similar to the feeling of suspense he had felt in the pit of his stomach when he was the officer in charge of the anti-aircraft defence operations room.

The lights of an incoming train came into view as it skirted round a hill and then straightened out alongside the river. Zigzagging through the paddy fields, Takuya drew steadily toward the tracks.

The train rumbled forward, spilling only a modicum of light on the outside world. Takuya stopped and watched as the train turned to the left in a long arc. The engineer was obviously working hard feeding coal into the boiler, as Takuya could clearly see the red-tinged silhouette of a man repeatedly bending and twisting in front of the firebox.

Staring at the tail-light of the last carriage as it moved into the distance, he started off again.

3

The first time Takuya set eyes on a crew member of a B-29 Superfortress it made an indelible impression on him.

On 16 June 1944, the bombing attack on Kokura and Yawata by B-29 Superfortresses operating from airfields in China was the first to target mainland Japan.

The first news that long-range heavy American bombers had been seen in China had arrived on the second of April that year, in a telegram from Imperial Army Headquarters in China, and from then on there were continual reports that the US Army Air Force was strengthening its presence around bases in China's Chengdu region. Recognising that this build-up very likely presaged attacks on targets in northern Kyushu, Imperial Headquarters followed the recommendation of Western Regional Command and ordered the Nineteenth Air Force Division, stationed in the northern Kyushu area, to begin preparations for a strategic defence under the direction of Western Regional Headquarters. Comprising two squadrons, the Nineteenth Air Force Division boasted seventy of the latest fighter planes, and could put thirty in the air at any one time, the pilots all veterans with over five hundred hours in the air. They had carried out hours of practice at night-time interception of heavy bombers, and had rehearsed their angles of attack again and again on a B-17 bomber that had been seized intact and airworthy in the early stages of the war in the Pacific. In conjunction with this preparation, anti-aircraft batteries were deployed in the northern Kyushu area, and joint exercises were carried out with the air force under the direction of Western Command to provide the optimum defensive screen.

At Western Command headquarters, an air defence intelligence unit was set up, and spotters posted to points all over the Korea Strait and Kyushu region, along with twenty-eight electronic detection stations. In addition, an intelligence network was established, involving further spotters, electronic devices and naval vessels outside the defensive perimeter proper.

At 11.31 p.m. on 15 June 1944, a report came in to Western headquarters from the electronic detection post on Cheju island that unidentified aircraft were moving eastwards. Forty-five minutes later, it was reported that the aircraft had crossed the line between Izuhara on Tsushima island and the island of Fukue in the Gotoh archipelago, and had then crossed the line between Izuhara and Hirado in western Kyushu, meaning that the aircraft were travelling at around four hundred kilometres an hour. At first it was thought that they might be Japanese spotter planes, but none was capable of flying at that speed and, as no friendly aircraft had been reported taking that flight path, it was judged that this intrusion must represent a force of enemy heavy bombers heading for the northern Kyushu area. The tactical operations centre reacted by immediately contacting the Nineteenth Air Force Division and the Western Region anti-aircraft batteries on special hotlines, and Takuya, as duty officer, issued a full air-raid alert for the northern Kyushu area in the commander's name.

Forty-seven aircraft attacked Kokura and Yawata that night, but they met with such determined resistance from fighters that the bombing they did manage before heading back to China was virtually ineffective. Seven American bombers were shot down during the attack.

At Western Command headquarters they had assumed that the intruders were B-17s, but inspections of the wreckage of aircraft shot down near the town of Orio in Fukuoka prefecture and Takasu in Wakamatsu city revealed that the planes were in fact the latest American bomber, the B-29 Superfortress. A crew member's own film of B-29s during flight, discovered amid the wreckage of one plane, confirmed the appearance of the new aircraft.

Subsequently, raids by US bombers based in China were made on Sasebo on the eighth of July; on Nagasaki on the eleventh of August, and on Yawata on the twentieth and twenty-first;

on Ohmura on the twenty-fifth of October, the eleventh and twenty-first of November, the nineteenth of December and the sixth of January the following year; but after that the B-29 bases were switched to Saipan, and attacks from mainland China stopped.

During those months, assisted by pinpoint detection of incoming aircraft by electronic detection stations and spotters, the fighters ensured that bombing damage was kept to a minimum, shooting down a total of fifty-one bombers while losing only nine of their own.

Of the American crew members who baled out of their disabled aircraft, seventeen survived to be taken prisoner. These men were escorted by the *kempeitai* to defence headquarters in Tokyo.

Then B-29s operating from bases in Saipan began a concerted bombing campaign on urban targets such as Tokyo, Osaka and Nagoya, and in March 1945 they again turned their attention to the Kyushu region. The Nineteenth Air Force Division defence was so effective that the numbers of American airmen parachuting into captivity increased dramatically. Previously such prisoners of war had been escorted to camps in Tokyo by the *kempeitai*, but in early April the Army Ministry issued a directive to Western Regional Command, delegating authority by stating that the crew members should be 'handled as you see fit'.

Six days after that order was received, a *kempeitai* lorry carrying twenty-four American airmen pulled up at the rear entrance of Western Regional Headquarters. The men were unloaded and shepherded in pairs into cells originally designed to hold local soldiers awaiting court martial.

That evening, together with a staff officer from the tactical operations centre, Takuya was assigned to guard the prisoners in the cells. The captive crewmen had just been given their evening meal trays, so when Takuya entered the holding cell area he saw tall, well-built men, some brown-haired and some blond, sitting in their cells eating rice balls flavoured with barley, or munching slices of pickled radish.

Takuya stood in the corridor and stared. The prisoners behind the bars were the first American airmen he had ever set eyes upon.

As the officer in charge of the air defence tactical operations centre, Takuya was among the most knowledgeable of the headquarters staff about the Superfortress bomber. Every time B-29 units intruded into the Kyushu region airspace, his staff painstakingly followed their incoming flight path and then tracked them as they headed off over the sea after completing their missions. Details such as the B-29's total wingspan of 43 metres, its wing surface area of 161.1 square metres, its fully laden weight of 47,000 kilograms, its top speed and altitude of 590 kilometres per hour at 9500 metres, its maximum range of 8159 kilometres with a 3-ton load of bombs, its ten 12.7-millimetre machine-guns and one 20-millimetre cannon and its maximum bomb load of 8 tons, were etched into Takuya's mind, and he had become very familiar with the appearance of the Superfortress by examining photographs of the aircraft – both in flight and as wreckage on the ground.

Hours of meticulous study of the B-29 enabled Takuya to deduce the likely target by determining the speed and course of the incoming bombers, and then, by calculating the intruders' time spent in Japanese airspace, how much fuel remained and, from that, the probable course and timing of their escape route.

To Takuya and his colleagues, who had followed the movements of these aircraft so faithfully since the previous year, the squadron of B-29s were a familiar, almost intimate presence. But now, seeing these American airmen standing and sitting on the other side of the bars, Takuya realised that all along his perception of the enemy had been limited to the aircraft itself, and that somehow he had forgotten there were human beings inside it.

He was surprised that most of them looked to be around twenty years of age, some as young as seventeen or eighteen. It shocked him to think of the Superfortresses he had tracked so meticulously, constructed with the latest equipment and instruments, being manned by young men scarcely past their teens.

Some of the men were the same height as the average Japanese, but most were around six feet tall, and all were endowed with sturdy frames and well-muscled buttocks. To men used to a diet of meat, the rice balls and pickled radish must have hardly even qualified as food. Nevertheless, they munched away at their portions, licking grains of rice off their fingers and biting noisily into the pickles.

Their facial expressions varied. Most avoided eye contact with their captors, but some, whose face muscles were more relaxed, gazed imploringly toward Takuya and his colleague. Others cast frightened glances at them.

In the end cell a fair-haired man lay on a straw-filled futon on the concrete floor, eating a rice ball. A dark bruise from a blow to the face covered the area from his nose to the point of his right cheekbone, and bandaging on his rib cage was visible through his unbuttoned jacket.

'This one's been shot with a hunting-rifle,' whispered the slightly built legal officer, appearing suddenly from behind. Takuya looked into the cell as the lieutenant read out the report prepared by the *kempeitai* on this particular American prisoner. The man had been a crew member of a B-29 involved in a night raid on Yawata and Kokura on the twenty-seventh of March. When his plane was hit, he had parachuted into the woods near Ono in the Oita area. People from a nearby village saw this and ran out to find the man, then clubbed him with sticks before shooting him through the shoulder and right lung with a hunting-rifle. Evidently the wounded airman had been handed over to the police by the villagers, and then on to the *kempeitai*, who had arranged for him to receive medical treatment before being transported to Western Regional Headquarters.

The man was obviously aware that people were watching him through the bars, but he ignored them, staring up at the ceiling as he ate. He seemed to Takuya to have long eyelashes and a remarkably pointed nose.

When he heard how the villagers had beaten and shot this American, Takuya realised that despite his being a military man, bound by duty to clash with the enemy, his own feelings of hostility toward the B-29 crews paled in comparison to the villagers'. Up to this point, his contact with the enemy had been limited to information about aircraft detected by electronic listening-devices or seen by spotters. In contrast, inhabitants of the mountain villages no doubt felt intense hatred when they saw B-29s flying over, as the objective of the bombers' mission was nothing less than the mass slaughter of civilians such as themselves. This hatred was the driving force behind their outbursts of violence toward the downed crew members.

It occurred to Takuya that these twenty-four American airmen in front of him were the embodiment of an enemy which had slaughtered untold numbers of his people. They had come back again and again to devastate Japanese towns and cities, leaving behind countless dead and wounded civilians. The idea that these men were receiving rice balls despite the virtual exhaustion of food supplies for the average Japanese citizen stirred anger in Takuya towards those in headquarters responsible for such decisions.

'Look at the awful shoes they've got on,' said the officer, with raw contempt in his eyes.

The prisoners' shoes were all made of cloth, reminiscent of those ordinarily worn when embarking on nothing more adventurous than a casual stroll. Some were torn at the seams. Considering the obvious inexperience of the young men manning the bombers, and their cheap footwear, Takuya wondered whether the much-vaunted American affluence was starting to wane.

After that day Takuya was never assigned to watch over the cells, but he took considerable interest in the decision about what to do with the men in them. No doubt the Army Ministry had delegated authority over the airmen because the intensified bombing attacks ruled out transporting prisoners to a central destination. This was evident from the concise wording of the order to 'handle as you see fit'. Even so, the precise meaning of 'as you see fit' was unclear.

Takuya thought back to the first raid by North American B-25 medium bombers just four short months after the start of the war. A force of sixteen enemy planes had taken off from an aircraft carrier and flown at low altitude into the Tokyo and Yokohama area to bomb and strafe targets before retreating toward China, where eight men from two planes that crash-landed near Nanchang and Ningpo had been captured by the Imperial Army. A university student at the time, Takuya remembered reading in the newspaper that the captured men had been tried by a military court on charges of carrying out bombing attacks designed to kill and wound non-combatants in urban areas, and strafing defenceless schoolchildren and fishermen. All had been found guilty as charged, and some were sentenced to death, others to terms of imprisonment. Takuya remembered seeing a photograph of the airmen wearing black hoods over their heads as they were led to their execution.

The fact that executions had been carried out after that raid surely left little room for debate over the fate of the twenty-four prisoners now in their custody. Once the B-29s moved their base of operations to Saipan, they began to concentrate their attacks on urban areas in general, as opposed to military installations and munitions factories. The Superfortresses gradually switched their targets, dropping huge quantities of incendiary bombs on medium-sized and even smaller towns outside the Kyushu and Shikoku areas. The extent of the devastation was immense; according to reports from central headquarters, more than a hundred thousand people had already been killed and over nine hundred thousand dwellings razed to the ground, affecting over two and a half million people. These fire raids were serious violations of the rules of war, so surely the handling of B-29 crew members would not be bound by provisions regarding the custody of normal prisoners of war.

Processing these prisoners began with interrogating them to acquire information which might help headquarters staff in their efforts against the bombing raids, and as the officer in charge of anti-aircraft intelligence, Takuya observed the interrogations. There were general questions about the number of aircraft at the bases in Saipan, as well as about the runways and hangars, followed by more specific questions about the scale of various kinds of facilities and whether or not there were plans for expansion, and then questions about the capabilities of the B-29, its weak points, and the flight paths used to enter and leave Japanese airspace. The interrogations were carried out both individually and in groups, and the captured crew members replied to the questions posed by the interpreter, Lieutenant Shirasaka, with surprising candour. The content of their answers was consistent, and there was no indication whatsoever that they had tried to co-ordinate their approach to the interrogation. All had some signs of fear in their eyes, but every so often one of them would shrug his shoulders, casually gesture with his hands, and even relax the muscles of his face slightly with the hint of a smile.

One nineteen-year-old crewman looked Shirasaka straight in the face and said he had taken part in twelve raids on cities such as Tokyo, Nagoya and Kobe. There was no mistaking the pride in his expression.

When asked to describe the scene inside the aircraft after dropping the bombs and turning back over the Pacific Ocean towards Saipan, one tall, blond twenty-two- or twenty-three-year-old smiled as he said something in quick reply. Shirasaka seemed momentarily taken aback, but then told the others the American had said that on the way back the B-29 crew members listened to jazz on the radio. Other airmen had replied to the same question by saying that crew members showed each other pornographic photos during the flight back.

When he heard Shirasaka's translations of these almost non-chalant remarks, Takuya felt an urge to lash out at the prisoner. While Takuya and his comrades had been doing their utmost to minimise the damage to their country, these men had been treating the bombing raids as sport. He had seen numerous photographs of wrecked B-29s with pictures of naked women painted on the fuselage beside flame-shaped marks indicating the number of bombing raids the aircraft had made, but now he knew that these men felt no remorse at all for having destroyed the lives and property of so many Japanese civilians.

Until that point, Takuya's image of the enemy had been

focused upon the aircraft itself, but now the people who flew it, dropped the bombs and manned its guns became his enemy. If there were twelve crew per plane and one hundred bombers taking part in a raid, this represented no fewer than one thousand two hundred of the enemy bent on raining havoc and destruction upon Japanese citizens. Each time he heard that Japanese fighters were engaging the intruders, in his mind's eye he pictured the American machine-gunners firing their weapons. When the bombers had reached their target, he imagined the bombardier looking through his sights and pressing the button to open the bomb-bay doors.

With the American landings on Okinawa starting on the twenty-sixth of March, air raids on the Kyushu region intensified dramatically. The following day and night, there were attacks by over two hundred B-29s on munitions factories in the Kokura and Yawata areas. On the thirty-first approximately a hundred and seventy Superfortresses attacked air force bases in Tachiarai, Kanoya and Ohmura. And on both the twenty-eighth and the twenty-ninth a force of approximately seven hundred and thirty enemy warplanes operating from aircraft carriers attacked air force and naval targets on the Kyushu eastern coastline and in the areas of Kanoya, Kagoshima, Miyazaki and Sasebo.

Repeated raids on the Tokyo and Nagoya areas lasted into April, and on the sixteenth locations in Kyushu were attacked by a combined force of about a hundred bombers and fighters. Raids targeting mainly air force installations in Kyushu were carried out on the seventeenth by approximately eighty B-29s, and then from the twenty-first to the twenty-ninth by a total of around eight hundred and forty Superfortresses. Takuya was kept frantically busy collecting information and issuing air-raid warnings.

During this time he came to think that these twenty-four prisoners would probably all be executed, but on the afternoon of the seventeenth of May, he heard that two of them had been removed from the holding-cells and transported by truck to the Faculty of Medicine at Kyushu Imperial University. The aide to the chief of staff who had told Takuya this said that one of the men was the crewman who had been shot through the lung with a hunting-rifle and that the other was an airman who had serious problems with his digestive organs. Both, he said, were going to the university hospital to receive treatment.

On hearing this, Takuya had thought that surely there was little need to take people to the hospital for medical treatment if they were to be executed soon, but he assumed there was a policy of having the prisoners as physically sound as possible at the time of the execution.

In May the air raids became even more relentless. In the eleven days between the third and the fourteenth, around two hundred and fifty B-29s and sixteen hundred and fifty carrier-borne aircraft attacked targets all over Kyushu.

Just after midnight on the twenty-third, a force of twenty B-29s dropped a large number of mines in the Kanmon Strait before heading east back over the ocean at around 1.40 a.m. In the air battle enacted under a canopy of stars the interceptors shot down four bombers and inflicted serious damage on four others. Takuya relieved one of his junior officers that night, taking off only his jacket before slipping into the bed in the rest area just off the operations room.

Awaking at eight the next morning, Takuya ate a simple meal of sorghum with barley rice before heading out to the tactical operations centre, a concrete structure half set into the ground behind the headquarters building. On the way he saw two prisoners being led along the corridor and out of the back door. Both wore black cloth blindfolds and their hands were manacled in front of them. They were accompanied by a doctor assigned to military duty and five soldiers carrying rifles with bayonets. The prisoners were pushed into an army lorry parked in the yard behind the building and the rear flap of the lorry's old tattered hood was pulled down and fastened. An army medical officer was with them, and Takuya guessed that these prisoners must also be going to the university hospital, although there were no obvious signs that they were wounded or ill in any way.

The lorry moved slowly out of the yard and down the slope, flicking up pieces of gravel with its rear tyres.

By late May, Western Regional Headquarters staff were working frantically to tighten defences in their region as part of Imperial Army Headquarters' decision to engage the enemy in a final decisive battle on the Japanese mainland.

In the Okinawa area, the American invasion force, comprising around fourteen hundred warships and almost two hundred thousand army and navy personnel, had already established a bridgehead on the island, but because of tenacious resistance the American advance was much slower than expected. In response to these landings, the Japanese mobilised a special attack force centred on the battleship *Yamato*, with kamikaze units smashing relentlessly into the oncoming American warships. The kamikaze attacks were a serious menace to the American force, but their only feasible approach to Okinawa was a course following the line of the Nansei islands, so they were easily detected by radar, allowing the Americans to intercept them with large numbers of fighter planes. As a result, losses were significant and most planes in these units were shot down before they could reach their destination.

The American ground troops, supported by bombardment from warships and strafing from fighters operating off aircraft carriers, gradually pushed forwards, and, though the Japanese provided determined opposition, they were eventually forced to retreat to the south-western corner of the main island of Okinawa, where they were now playing out the final act of their resistance.

With the fall of Okinawa just days away, the High Command predicted that the Americans would lose little time in turning their efforts toward a full-scale invasion of the Japanese mainland islands. Based on this assumption, plans were drawn up for the ultimate battle to defend the homeland, which centred on intense analysis of the enemy's situation. Essentially, the Americans' weak point was that they had to rely upon greatly extended supply lines stretching across the Pacific Ocean, and in contrast to previous battles, in which Japanese troops had had little choice but to make desperate banzai charges on far-flung Pacific islands, it was hoped that in a defence of the mainland itself the Japanese would have a decided advantage. Levels of available manpower were still high and, if the local populace was united in its support of the defensive effort, it was thought that there was a significant chance of victory. Public declarations were made that this decisive battle would by no means be a defensive struggle, and that it was indeed nothing less than an all-out offensive against the enemy.

There were numerous opinions as to the specific locations the Americans would target for their invasion, but in the end it was assumed that they would most likely select the southern Kyushu area, as that would allow them to use Okinawan airfields to provide fighter cover for the ground troops. In terms of specific landing-points, it was predicted that the invasion would primarily target the Miyazaki coastline, Ariake Bay and points on both the west and south coastlines of the Satsuma peninsula.

Imperial Headquarters relocated a number of units from Honshu to Kyushu and placed them under the command of Western Regional Headquarters. In accordance with orders from Tokyo, the extra troops were stationed around the locations judged most likely to bear the brunt of an invasion, and with the co-operation of local authorities and the general public work was begun on the construction of defensive positions. In addition, High Command dispatched a staff officer to Western headquarters, and other young officers who had completed a course of training at the Imperial Army's Nakano 'School' of subterfuge and intelligence activities were chosen to take command of, and begin tactical preparation for, units specifically designed to penetrate and disrupt the invading forces.

At the end of May, operating from repaired airfields in Okinawa, the Americans began a concentrated bombing offensive on the Kyushu area. On the twenty-eighth of May a combined force of about seventy bombers and fighters attacked targets all over southern Kyushu, and subsequently there were raids on both the second and third of June by a total of four hundred and twenty carrier-borne aircraft, followed by another combined force of some three hundred bombers and fighters attacking Air Force facilities.

By now the struggle in Okinawa had reached its finale, with the surviving defenders and large numbers of civilian refugees retreating to make a last stand at the southernmost tip of the island. An air of gloom hung over Western Regional Headquarters as staff listened in to the wireless communications of the defenders in Okinawa.

On the ninth of June, Takuya was told by the staff officer attached to the tactical operations centre that eight of the American prisoners were dead. Evidently they were the ones who had been taken in pairs from the holding-cells at headquarters to the Faculty of Medicine at Kyushu Imperial University.

He had been told that the first two captives transported to the university hospital were to receive treatment, but it now seemed that they had in fact been executed by medical staff. The prisoners had been sent to their deaths by a staff officer, Colonel Tahara, and Medical Officer Haruki, who had decided to use prisoners condemned to death as guinea pigs in experiments for medical research, and so requested that Professor Iwase of the First Department of Surgery use his good offices to facilitate it.

The two prisoners were anaesthetised with ether and carried to the anatomy laboratory, where they were laid on separate dissection tables. Professor Iwase operated to remove portions of the lobe of each of their lungs, but both men died from massive haemorrhaging when arteries were severed in the process. Subsequently, another six prisoners were brought to the anatomy laboratory, each undergoing surgery on his stomach, liver, or brain, the complete removal of the gall bladder, or injection of refined sea water into their arteries. All six died on the operating-table during this experimental surgery, and evidently both Colonel Tahara and Medical Officer Haruki were present on each occasion.

'They were all well anaesthetised and in a coma, so maybe it was a painless way to be executed,' whispered Colonel Tahara, adding that the bodies had been cremated on Abura-yama and the ashes buried.

The other staff in the tactical operations centre learnt about the eight prisoners in the course of that day. Colonel Tahara instructed them not to mention what had happened to anyone else, telling them that the official stance was to be that these prisoners had been sent to Imperial Headquarters in Tokyo.

While Takuya felt no particular emotion about their death, it struck him that executing them by means of experimental surgery was rather unusual. Still, regardless of the method used, he did not falter in his belief that it was only natural that they should die for their sins. In fact, more than anything, he felt increasingly indignant that the remaining prisoners were still alive and depleting precious food stocks in the headquarters compound.

That evening, in the headquarters judicial department, the remaining sixteen prisoners were arraigned before a formal military tribunal, and based on a re-examination of the transcripts of their interrogations it was confirmed that every one of the airmen had taken part in the bombing of urban targets. All were found guilty of the murder of non-combatants and, based on the tenets of international law, all were sentenced to death.

The following day, another seventeen airmen who had been captured after parachuting from B-29s shot down over Kyushu were delivered to the rear entrance of the headquarters building in a *kempeitai* lorry, then put into holding-cells together with the previous batch of prisoners. The cells were too small to handle the influx of prisoners, however, and with four men in each it was almost impossible for all of them to lie down. So the judicial department moved immediately to convert the litigants' waiting-room in their part of the building into an extra holding-cell for some of the newcomers.

Over the next few days, Takuya found himself virtually confined to the tactical operations centre. On the eighth of June, reconnaissance photographs taken by a plane flying over US Army Air Force facilities on Okinawa were delivered to headquarters. They showed clearly that the airfields in north and central Okinawa, along with those on Ie Island, were fully operational, and confirmed the existence of at least five hundred and twenty-three fighters and bombers. Takuya and his comrades all sensed that an intensification of the attacks on

Kyushu was imminent, and that the stage was set for a decisive battle for the homeland.

On the evening of the eighteenth of June, the mood at Western headquarters grew sombre. On the radio they had heard the farewell message from Lieutenant-General Ushijima Mitsuru, commander of the Thirty-second Army in Okinawa, to Imperial Headquarters in Tokyo, informing his superiors that he was about to give his life for the Emperor's cause. 'While our forces have fought with supreme heroism over the last two months, the enemy's overwhelming numerical superiority on land, sea and air means that this struggle has entered its closing stages. I most humbly report that the final preparations are in hand to lead those surviving soldiers to a glorious death.'

The final battle for Okinawa was a struggle of apocalyptic proportions. According to reports from pilots of reconnaissance planes, the pummelling of the southern tip of the island by concentrated bombardment from warships, ground-based artillery and the air was such that it looked as though there had been a huge volcanic eruption, with streams of tracer bullets, raging fires and plumes of grey and black smoke all adding a macabre effect to the hellish scene. Since the battle for Saipan and the struggles for the islands across the northern Pacific, non-combatants had been deeply embroiled in the conflict and had even lost their lives, together with the soldiers of each defending garrison. No doubt this tragedy had been repeated in Okinawa, with scores of old men, women and children losing their lives in the bombardment or choosing to die by their own hand.

That night, the news came that a force of fifty B-29s based in Saipan had attacked Hamamatsu and another thirty had raided the city of Yokkaichi, both attacks involving incendiaries and resulting in firestorms so destructive that the targets were virtually burnt to cinders. To date, the number of aircraft involved in bombing raids on targets in Japan had soared to over twenty thousand, claiming some four hundred thousand lives, destroying one million six hundred thousand homes and producing six million three hundred thousand refugees.

The next morning brought blue skies, with the meteorological office forecasting fine weather all over Kyushu. To those in the tactical operations centre, this meant a drastically increased likelihood of large-scale bombing raids, and orders were issued for spotters to be particularly vigilant.

The daylight hours passed uneventfully, and when the sun dipped low in the evening the bright red of the western sky signalled that another fine day would follow. Within minutes of the sunset the sky was a mass of twinkling stars.

That night, at 7.50 p.m., a report came in from an electronic listening-post set to cover the Hyuga coastline that a force of aircraft was heading north-west over that quadrant of the Kyushu defensive perimeter. As there was nothing to suggest that this was friendly aircraft on patrol, Takuya immediately assumed that it was a force of B-29s from Saipan and issued an air-raid warning to all areas of northern Kyushu.

Knowing that a lone Superfortress had flown a reconnaissance mission over Fukuoka the previous night, Takuya expected that before long Kyushu's largest city would bear the brunt of an attack. Thousands of tons of incendiaries had already reduced major urban centres such as Tokyo, Nagoya and Osaka to scorched wastelands, but so far the attacks on Kyushu had mostly been limited to military targets or munitions factories, and the island had been spared the saturation raids aimed at razing towns and cities to the ground. Okinawa was now completely in American hands, and it was likely that their next move would be to obliterate the cities of Kyushu before launching an invasion force on to its beaches.

Red lights lit up on the otherwise darkened map of Kyushu on the wall of the operations room as one report after another of aircraft intruding into the perimeter came in from electronic listening-points. The sequence of the lights indicated that the enemy bombers were proceeding on a course toward northern Kyushu.

Processing the incoming data, Takuya realised that this force, comprising around seventy aircraft, had split into two separate groups somewhere over Hita city in Oita prefecture. Around ten planes were continuing straight on their original course, while the other sixty had veered slightly to the north-west. It was presumed that the ten aircraft were on what would be the fifth mission to drop mines in the Kanmon Strait, adding to the total of eighty planes that had already done so, and that the other, larger group was heading for Fukuoka. When incoming reports confirmed beyond a doubt that Fukuoka was indeed the target, the tactical operations centre immediately issued an air-raid warning for the city and its environs.

The first word that intruders had entered Fukuoka airspace came from Dazaifu, just south-east of the metropolitan area, and was soon followed by reports of aircraft sighted above the city itself. Takuya knew from the data that the bombers were deploying at a low level over the city, and by now would have started their bombing runs. The intruders appeared to have followed the line of the Nakagawa river into the city and then dropped their load on Shin-Yanagi-Machi and the Higashi–Nakasu area, resulting in a rash of reports of fires raging in those areas.

Those in the tactical operations centre, a construction set partially into the ground and cased in reinforced concrete, were removed from the thunderous blasts of exploding bombs and the clamour of a city in the throes of incineration. Takuya and his fellow officers stood staring at the red lamps on the map of Kyushu stretched across one wall. The lights indicating the Fukuoka metropolitan area remained on, as did those representing the Kanmon Strait, confirming that the smaller force of ten aircraft had reached its predicted target.

Takuya sat motionless, staring at the map on the wall in front of his desk. Although the sky above the headquarters building was swarming with enemy planes, and the area around their safe haven was probably engulfed in flames, the atmosphere within the operations room was almost transquil. As the officer in charge of anti-aircraft intelligence, Takuya focused his attention solely on imparting information about the movements of enemy aircraft, and to him there was no difference between planes directly above and planes attacking a more distant region within the defensive perimeter.

Anti-aircraft batteries and searchlight units along the Kanmon Strait coastline had been reinforced in late May, and reports were now coming in that these units were engaging the Superfortresses dropping mines in shipping channels. Two hours after the initial sightings, these bombers seemed to have finished dropping their mines and had turned back south. Around the same time, reports began to come in that the force that had targeted Fukuoka had started to move in a southerly direction. The Superfortresses had clearly completed their mission and were heading back.

One by one, red lamps went out as the smaller force of intruders headed south from the Kanmon Strait, then joined up again over Hita city with the main force which had ravaged Fukuoka, and changed to a course directly south-east. A short time later the aircraft were detected crossing the line between Hosojima in Miyazaki prefecture and Sukumo in Kochi prefecture. Similar reports followed from the listening-points covering the line between Aojima farther down the Miyazaki coastline and Sukumo over in Shikoku, confirming that the bombers were about to disappear across the Hyuga Sea, heading back toward Saipan.

Orders were issued to give the 'all clear' for all areas of the Kyushu region, and only then was Takuya at last able to leave his desk. The enemy planes were officially recorded as having left Japanese airspace at 3.37 a.m., seven hours and forty minutes after the original intrusion.

Takuya wanted to see for himself what the situation was outside the confines of the operations room, and the lack of incoming reports meant in effect that he was finished for the night, so there was no reason not to slip away for a short time.

Delegating the remaining duties to his subordinates, Takuya hurried out of the room and down the dimly lit corridor. The moment he opened the double steel doors he was consumed by a deafening roar. Each breath of the superheated air seemed to scorch the inside of his lungs. Everything on the outside – the trees, the headquarters building, the ground – was bright red. Powerful gusts of wind lashed the branches of trees, and singed leaves danced across the ground.

Takuya stepped away from the doors and ran a few paces to the edge of the backyard, where he stopped, riveted by the terrifying scene before his eyes. Huge swirling towers of flames reached skyward from a seething conflagration covering an almost endless expanse below him. One thunderous roar followed another, resounding like waves crashing into a cliff, hurling sheets of fire and angry streams of sparks into the night sky. The barracks just to the west of where Takuya stood had been razed, and a frenzied swarm of soldiers were using hoses and buckets to throw water on to the headquarters building. The men were all tinged red, like everything else in this inferno.

Takuya had heard reports of cities being devastated by incendiaries, but the destruction he was witnessing far surpassed anything he had ever imagined. Like masses of towering whitecaps soaring up from a tempestuous sea, myriad flames pressed upward from the heart of the blaze. His face felt as if it was on fire, and billows of smoke stung his eyes.

The city contained no military installations or munitions factories, so the purpose of the fire raid could only have been to kill and maim civilians and reduce their dwellings to ashes. The thought flashed through his mind that the scene he was witnessing had been repeated time and again in other cities and towns all over Japan, with innumerable non-combatants sent to their deaths.

The strength of interceptor fighter units in Kyushu had been dramatically reduced by US bombing attacks on air force facilities in the area, and that night, too, there were no reports of Superfortresses being shot down by fighters, so the anti-aircraft batteries had more or less been left to defend the island's skies themselves.

Takuya blinked in pain as he gazed into the sea of flames.

Dawn came, and reports flooded into the tactical operations centre, outlining the damage in Fukuoka city. The fires had been extinguished by around 6 a.m., but apart from the Tenjin-machi and Hakozaki-machi areas, the entire city centre had been burnt to the ground, with an estimated ten thousand dwellings destroyed in the fires. Early accounts suggested that the death toll would be extremely high.

Subsequent reports described citizens who had fled during the night returning that morning to survey the smouldering embers of what had been their homes. Later several dozen people had gathered around the front gate of the headquarters complex, clamouring for the execution of the captive airmen. There were said to be a large number of women among the crowd, and some of them had been weeping as they screamed for the crewmen to be killed. No doubt they were infuriated at the thought that the Americans were still alive, safe from the blaze thanks to the fire-fighting efforts of the garrison. While the prisoners might have been afraid of being burnt alive, they also might have felt some kind of satisfaction in knowing that it was their compatriots who were raining death and destruction on the city below.

Takuya had little difficulty understanding the thinking of the people who had gathered in front of the main gate. The prisoners not only had burnt to death thousands of defenceless old men, women and children, but were now being kept alive with a steady supply of food that the average person in the street could only dream about. Surely there was no reason to let them live any longer.

'What the hell are they up to at headquarters? They should execute them as soon as possible,' muttered Takuya to himself.

Medical Officer Haruki's name was on the list of dead. In conjunction with his work as deputy head doctor at the military hospital adjacent to the headquarters building, he had been given the honorary rank of lieutenant, and he was attending a doctors' meeting when the air raid started the previous evening. Evidently he had been unable to make it to safety when their building caught fire. The casualty reports also listed the names of several non-commissioned officers and numerous enlisted men and civilian employees working at headquarters. Word also came in of family members of headquarters staff killed in the firestorms that had ravaged the city's residential areas.

Takuya could hear all this news being reported as he worked

at his tasks as anti-aircraft intelligence officer. A deterioration in the weather meant that raids were unlikely from Saipan-based aircraft, but all the same, as the possibility of more short-range attacks by bombers flying up the line of the Nansei Islands from bases in Okinawa could not be ruled out, Takuya paid particular attention to reports coming in from the southern Kyushu region.

He had just finished eating a late lunch of sorghum with barley rice and a piece of salted salmon when a staff officer from headquarters briskly entered his room, stepped up to Takuya's desk and announced in an impassioned voice, 'It's on.'

At Takuya's puzzled look, the lieutenant blurted out that eight of the prisoners in the holding-cells were to be executed, and that this was to be carried out immediately in the courtyard of what used to be a girls' high school, immediately behind the headquarters complex. Takuya was told that the prisoners were to be decapitated, and that headquarters staff with considerable experience in kendo had already been selected. Takuya was to arrange for two of his subordinates to be made available to participate in the executions.

Takuya nodded his understanding and beckoned the two sergeant-majors sitting on the other side of the room to come over to his desk. When he told them they would be taking part in the executions the colour drained from their faces and a look of trepidation came into their eyes.

'One good clean blow. Don't let us down,' growled Takuya.

The two men stood stiffly at attention as they barked their reply.

They were men with much longer service records than his, including combat experience at the front, and Takuya could not comprehend how they had the gall to show even a trace of apprehension at the mention of the executions. A rumour that one of the men had reputedly succeeded in beheading two Chinese prisoners with successive blows made their attitude all the more enraging. Possibly their stint at office work on the home front had dulled the mental hardness they would have honed on the battlefield.

Takuya watched as they put on their service caps, picked up their swords and left the room. By now a weather report that rain had started to fall in southern Kyushu had arrived. No sightings of any enemy aircraft were reported. Takuya's subordinates worked away collating the mountain of damage reports received from the city.

Around two o'clock the door opened and the two sergeant-majors walked in, one after the other. Takuya searched their faces for a hint of emotion. They were both pale but there was a strangely radiant look in their eyes. Their brows glistened with sweat as though they had come from vigorous exercise, and a tangible heat emanated from their bodies.

They stepped toward Takuya's desk and in an animated voice one reported, 'Duties completed, sir.'

'How was it? Did all go well?' asked Takuya.

'Yes, sir. We each executed one prisoner,' replied one of them, exhilaration lingering in his eyes.

'Well done,' said Takuya, nodding his approval. The two soldiers returned to their desks and wiped their brows with handkerchiefs.

Takuya heard that four regular officers and three non-commissioned officers had taken part in the executions that day, including Lieutenant Howa Kotaro of the accounts department, the only man who had volunteered. A graduate of Tokyo University, Howa was a mild-mannered man known for writing beautiful tanka poetry. That morning he had hurried down through the smouldering ruins of the Koojiya-machi area of Fukuoka to the house where his mother lived. It had burnt to the ground, so he waited for his mother to return from wherever she might have sheltered during the air raid. Casting his eyes over the sheets of roofing iron scattered across the ruins at the end of the little alleyway, he saw a black object resembling a scorched piece of timber. When he looked more closely and saw the gold-capped teeth showing from the gaping, burnt hole that had once been a mouth, he realised that this was the charred corpse of his mother. He wrapped her body in a piece of singed straw matting and asked a neighbour to look after it until he could come back to give her a proper funeral. Howa returned to headquarters and began working silently on his mother's coffin. Those attached to the tactical operations centre were in charge of organising the executions, but when Howa heard that the American airmen were to be killed, the request he made to the staff officer in charge of the operations room to be allowed to take part was so compelling that his name was added to the list. A member of the kendo club during his university days, Howa was the only man among the executioners to decapitate two of the prisoners.

While these executions temporarily relieved the frustration Takuya felt, each time he stepped outside the operations room and caught the horrific sight of a city razed to the ground, irrepressible anger and pain welled up inside him. According to reports issued by the municipal office, the death toll was over one thousand, with over fifty thousand families losing their homes and untold thousands of people injured in the firestorm. Everywhere there were dazed people sifting through the ashes of the scorched ruins. Here and there groups of men, women and children sat listlessly on the side of the road. Viewing such scenes, and contemplating the fact that these people were destitute because of the B-29 raids, he thought it an injustice that the remaining prisoners were still safe inside the headquarters building.

The day after the incendiary attack on Fukuoka city the key members of the headquarters staff moved to caves near Yamae village in the Tsukushi area, leaving behind only those who worked in anti-aircraft intelligence. After the attack on Fukuoka, the US Army Air Force started saturation bombing raids on other main cities and towns in Kyushu. First, on the twenty-ninth of June, a force of ten B-29s bombed Nobeoka in Miyazaki prefecture, and then Kanoya in Kagoshima prefecture. Beginning in July, attacks were made on cities and towns including Kurume, Yatsushiro, Nagasaki, Kumamoto, Oita, Omuta and Miyazaki.

Among those left to work on anti-aircraft intelligence, tension mounted as preparations were accelerated to meet the expected American landings on Kyushu. Defensive earthworks were being constructed everywhere, artillery pieces were placed in caves facing the sea, and special kamikaze attack aircraft were hidden in underground shelters.

Plans were also being made to strengthen the mobile reserve, the Thirty-sixth Army, by redeploying three infantry divisions from the Chugoku and Kinki areas, and by moving the pride of the mainland defensive forces – two elite armoured divisions and six reserve divisions – from the Kanto region to meet the enemy in Kyushu.

With such crucial forces being readied, Takuya began to sense that the last decisive moments of the war were close at hand. If the remaining armies played their part in the grand defensive strategy prepared by Imperial Headquarters, it would be possible for Japan to deal the American forces a body blow. There was no doubting Japan's advantage in terms of supply lines and the willingness of the ten million inhabitants of Kyushu to do their utmost to contribute to the success of the defensive effort. Though Takuya did not doubt that Japan would be victorious in the coming battles, he had a premonition that he himself would not live through the titanic struggle about to unfold. At least, he hoped, he would succumb knowing that he had inflicted the greatest damage possible on the enemy.

That summer was much hotter than average. The steel doors were usually pushed wide open, but because the tactical operations centre was encased in a thick layer of reinforced concrete it was oppressively hot inside the building, the lone fan sending a stream of hot air across the desks. Sweat dripping from their brows, Takuya and his colleagues went on processing incoming information and preparing the anti-aircraft defences for the next bombing raid.

Toward the end of July there was a dramatic increase in the number of enemy aircraft participating in each attack. On the twenty-eighth, a total of three thousand two hundred and ten planes attacked targets in the Kanto, Tokai and Kinki regions, while around six hundred and fifty carrier-borne planes made bombing and strafing sorties over Kyushu, some of the latter aircraft even going so far as to attack targets in the Korea Strait and the southern region of the Korean peninsula. The following day a force of three hundred and sixty-one carrier-borne bombers and fighters attacked targets in central and southern Kyushu. The same areas were attacked by three hundred and seventy-nine aircraft on the thirtieth, one hundred and forty-eight on the first of August, and another two hundred and twenty on the fifth of August. The fact that these attacks were concentrated on military and coastal installations was judged to be an indication that the American invasion of Kyushu was imminent, and Western Command headquarters was on constant alert for news that the invasion fleet had been sighted.

Near-windless days with clear blue skies continued, and the morning temperatures on the sixth of August presaged another sweltering day. Forecasting another large-scale attack that day, the tactical operations centre issued orders for no relaxation of the full-alert conditions in all areas of Kyushu.

Just after eight in the morning Takuya looked up from his desk, his attention caught by something distant, yet quite audible. It was a strange, almost rending sound, as if a huge piece of paper had been violently ripped in two. Seconds later a palpable shock wave jolted the air. His subordinates all sat stock-still, looking bewildered. No enemy planes had been reported in Kyushu airspace, and the sound they had just heard was clearly different from anything they had yet experienced. Takuya thought it might have been a distant peal of thunder.

Later that day, as expected, a combined force of a hundred and eighty bombers and fighters from bases in Okinawa attacked targets in southern Kyushu. Takuya was busy processing incoming reports and issuing orders to anti-aircraft defence units in that region.

That afternoon a communiqué from Imperial Headquarters in Tokyo notified them of the truth about the ominous sound and shock wave they had felt that morning. The message stated that at 8.15 a.m. two B-29s had intruded into Japanese airspace on a flight path over the Bungo Channel before sweeping north-east toward Hiroshima, where one of them had dropped a special new bomb which had caused extensive damage. It went on to advise that on no account was the extreme state of alert to be relaxed.

Western Command staff tried in vain to contact Central Regional Command headquarters in Hiroshima by telephone, but before long they received an updated report from Imperial Command in Tokyo to the effect that Hiroshima had been completely devastated, and tens of thousands of people killed or wounded. Considering that the sound and shock wave from the explosion had carried a full two hundred kilometres from Hiroshima to Fukuoka, Takuya and his colleagues realised that this bomb must possess a fearsome destructive power, far exceeding that of normal bomb technology.

Over the next several hours, a range of reports came in about the new bomb. Evidently, after being dropped it had descended attached to a parachute and had exploded several hundred metres above the ground, unleashing a blinding white flash of light, and punching a turbulent yellowish-white mushroom-shaped cloud up to ten or twenty thousand metres into the sky.

On the next day, the seventh, Imperial Command made a brief announcement on the radio regarding the bombing of Hiroshima. It stated that Hiroshima had been attacked by a small number of enemy B-29 aircraft and had suffered extensive damage, and that surveys were under way to establish the nature of the new weapon that had been used in this attack. Though reports from Imperial Command had mentioned nothing that specific, information had now been received to the effect that this new weapon was probably what was being called an 'atomic bomb'. The term itself was new to Takuya and his staff, but from the incoming reports it was clear that the weapon's destructive power was something completely unprecedented.

That evening Colonel Tahara, the staff officer assigned to the tactical operations centre, returned from a visit to Air Force Operational Command. The aircraft he had travelled in had stopped off in Hiroshima en route back to Fukuoka. He described how the city had been reduced to ruins, with corpses lying everywhere.

An air of oblivion hung over the staff in the headquarters

building, and no one uttered a word. Each struggled to understand how, in addition to devastating fire raids on towns and cities throughout the country, the American military could unleash a new weapon of such destructive power, expressly designed to kill and maim a city's civilian population. As fresh reports trickled in detailing the situation in Hiroshima, Takuya felt with increasing conviction that the American military had ceased to recognise the Japanese as members of the human race. Evidently, all the buildings had been destroyed and a large portion of the city's population annihilated in an instant. How, thought Takuya, did the thinking behind this differ from the mass incineration of a nest of vermin?

Two days later, on the ninth of August, news of grave concern was received at headquarters. The Soviet Union not only had unilaterally renounced the Soviet–Japanese Neutrality Pact, but had also declared war on Japan. Red Army forces were already advancing across the border with Manchuria to engage the Kwantung Army. It was clear that the timing of the Soviet offensive was linked to the dropping of the atomic bomb on Hiroshima, and now that the Russians had begun hostilities Japan was surrounded by enemies on all sides. Takuya sensed that the day he would be called upon to give his life for his country was near.

That morning at 7.40 a.m. a report came in from electronic detection posts that enemy aircraft had crossed the line between Aoshima in Miyazaki prefecture and Sukumo in Kochi prefecture on Shikoku island. Subsequently they were detected crossing the line between Hosojima in Miyazaki and Sukumo, so an alert was issued, followed by a full air-raid warning. But as spotters reported no sightings of intruders in that area of Kyushu, the order to sound the all clear was issued at 8.30 a.m. The high state of alert was maintained in the tactical operations centre, however, and when a report was received from spotters on Kunisaki peninsula that two Superfortresses had been seen heading westwards, the order to sound the air-raid sirens was reissued at 10.53 a.m.

The fact that only two B-29s were sighted, as in the attack three days earlier, pointed strongly to the likelihood that one of these intruders was carrying a bomb like the one that had devastated Hiroshima, and the course of the aircraft suggested that their target was a city in the northern Kyushu area.

The two aircraft continued westwards until they reached the city of Kokura, where they circled for a short time before the dense cloud cover evidently forced them to switch to a contingency target to the south-west. In view of the aircraft's flight path, the tactical operations centre staff speculated that the target had been switched to Nagasaki, so radio and telex messages were sent to that city straight away, to warn them of the approaching bombers and advise that everyone should be ordered to evacuate immediately. To avoid panic among the populace, however, no mention was made of the possibility that the bombers were carrying the same type of weapon that had destroyed Hiroshima.

Virtually incapacitated with anxiety, Takuya and his colleagues sat mesmerised by the red lamps on the wall map indicating the movement of the two B-29s. The lamps showed the planes moving inexorably over the Ariake Sea and then down across the northern section of the Shimabara peninsula, approaching Nagasaki from the north-east and seeming almost to stop for a moment over the city before heading east and then disappearing in the direction of Okinawa.

Queasy with foreboding, Takuya sat at his desk and waited for damage reports from Nagasaki. The only solace was the fact that they heard no sound and felt no shock wave like that experienced when the new bomb was dropped on Hiroshima.

Before long, however, his worst fears were realised. A report came in from Ohmura Air Force Base that a brilliant white light had been seen a split second before a thunderous explosion had rocked the ground where they stood, and a huge mushroom-shaped cloud had risen skywards above Nagasaki. There was no further communication until, after some time, reports began flooding in that the city had suffered extensive damage. Some information even suggested that the bomb had been dropped on a residential area in the northern part of Nagasaki. The bomb was obviously like the one that had destroyed Hiroshima. The thought that the tragedy visited upon Hiroshima had now been re-enacted in Nagasaki made it impossible for Takuya to remain sitting calmly at his desk.

Takuya heard that day that eight prisoners had been executed by headquarters staff who had been relocated to the caves near Yamae village. Apparently the executions had been carried out in the woods near the municipal crematorium at Higashi-Abura-Yama, to the south of Fukuoka. Among the staff were a number of officers from the Nakano 'School' of subterfuge, who were readying themselves to infiltrate enemy lines once the Americans landed. Evidently these men had used the blind-folded prisoners as targets to test the effectiveness of Taiwanese Takasago hunting-bows provided by a local archery club, but with such poor results that the idea of using them as weapons was abandoned. After the abortive experiment, the prisoners were taken one by one into a small clearing deeper in the forest, where they were beheaded. The bodies were then wrapped in straw mats and buried in shallow graves.

Distracted by the thought of the devastation inflicted upon Nagasaki, and frantically busy processing data and issuing air-raid warnings and all-clear signals following the attacks by a combined force of approximately three hundred bombers and fighters on targets all over Kyushu that day, Takuya registered what had happened to the American prisoners, but had no time to ponder their fate.

The following day, the tenth of August, another combined force of about two hundred and ten bombers and fighters darkened the skies of Kyushu, pummelling Kumamoto and Oita cities with incendiaries. In the course of two hours on the morning of the eleventh, over a hundred and fifty aircraft wreaked havoc on the city of Kurume, destroying four thousand five hundred homes. There was no respite from the raids; around two hundred planes attacked Kyushu on the twelfth, followed by another hundred and fifty B-29s on the fourteenth. Massive quantities of bombs were dropped on Kyushu, and there were even reports of large numbers of schoolchildren being killed in relentless strafing by American fighter planes.

By now, the urban centres in Kyushu had been reduced to ashes, the munitions factories all but destroyed, and food supplies diminished to such an extent that those living in the vicinity of the main cities and towns were on the verge of starvation. The destruction of most port facilities, the dropping of large numbers of mines into the sea and the lurking menace of enemy submarines made maritime transport virtually impossible, and since late July the frequent sorties by US fighters over southern Kyushu had virtually ruled out rail transport during daylight hours.

On the evening of the fourteenth of August Takuya heard from a colleague some news which he could hardly believe. Evidently the man had been told by an officer attached to the headquarters staff in the caves at Yamae that there were indications that some central government officials were prepared to accept the unconditional terms of the Potsdam Declaration, and that at noon of the following day, the fifteenth, the Emperor would be making a radio announcement of momentous importance. Apparently the broadcast would either ratify the acceptance of the Declaration or reject it, the likelihood of the former being very strong.

Surely this couldn't be true? The deployment of reinforcements, the preparation of weaponry and the strengthening of defences around anticipated landing-points in Kyushu had just been completed. Military installations and munitions factories might have been destroyed and cities razed, but there were still enough forces to repel the Americans. The decisive struggle was yet to come. Before its outcome was clear, it should be unthinkable even to consider surrendering.

This supposedly reliable information from government sources in Tokyo surely represented nothing more than the view of a small group of weak-kneed politicians, thought Takuya. Those people should be exterminated immediately for harbouring such treasonous thoughts on the eve of the decisive battle for the homeland.

He felt flustered as he attended to his duties. When he heard the seemingly interminable reports of American bombers and fighters attacking targets across the entire country, he couldn't help but think that this talk of surrender must be only a groundless rumour. Enemy aircraft were just as active that day as any other day, with some two hundred and fifty Superfortresses attacking targets in the Kanto, Fukushima and Niigata areas for several hours before midnight on the fourteenth. Within hours of those raids, a force of around two hundred and fifty carrier-borne aircraft made yet another wave of strikes on the Kanto area in the two hours after sunrise. Surely, thought Takuya, if the suggestion that the purpose of the Emperor's impending radio broadcast was to accept the Potsdam Declaration carried any credence, this would have already been conveyed to the Allies, who would in turn have ordered the American military to cease hostilities. The fact that as many as five hundred aircraft bombed and strafed targets all over the country from the night of the fourteenth into the early hours of the morning of the fifteenth was indeed proof that the war between the United States and Japan was continuing unabated.

After regaining his composure, Takuya slept for a few hours before returning to his post at 8 a.m. The weather forecast was for clear skies and high temperatures, so more large-scale air raids were expected in the course of the day.

As noon approached Takuya ordered his staff to assemble in the operations room. The men stood rigidly to attention in two neat rows. As he waited for the broadcast he thought that the Emperor could only be taking this unprecedented step to deliver words of inspiration to his people before the curtain went up on the final decisive battle for the homeland.

The hands of the clock reached noon, and after a recording of the national anthem the Emperor's announcement began. It was delivered in a strange, high-pitched voice, reminding Takuya of the prayers he'd heard recited by Shinto priests. Takuya and his comrades stood stiffly at attention, their heads bowed. The sound quality of the radio in the tactical operations centre was excellent, and the transmission of the Imperial rescript was heard clearly by all present.

Takuya listened intently to every word and lifted his head in disbelief on hearing the words 'We have ordered Our Government to communicate to the Governments of the United States, Great Britain, China and the Soviet Union that Our Empire accepts the provisions of their Joint Declaration.' The 'joint declaration' was obviously the Potsdam Declaration, acceptance of which meant nothing less than unconditional surrender.

Takuya felt suffocated. He couldn't believe this was happening. He had known that the war would some day come to an end, but he had always thought Japan would be the victor. Beyond a doubt, the current fortunes of war clearly favoured the enemy, and it might take months, even years, before the tide could be turned and victory claimed. By this stage, in his mind, the victory he had envisaged had been deferred to the distant future, which Takuya felt less and less confident he himself would see. In any case, it was unthinkable that the war should end in defeat. And to concede defeat in this fashion, before the decisive battle for the homeland, was even more inconceivable.

When the broadcast was finished Takuya felt faint, and he had to concentrate in order to prevent his knees buckling. The Emperor's words echoed in his head, leaving no room for other thoughts.

Takuya's men all stared at him, the bewilderment on their faces revealing that they had failed to comprehend the broadcast. Some even seemed buoyed by the Emperor's words, having interpreted the message as a veiled exhortation to redouble their efforts on the eve of the final struggle. Clearly the men were confused by the absence of the word 'defeat', and did not realise that Japan was about to surrender to the Allies.

Takuya turned toward the men, and in an emphatic tone said, 'It's all over. We've lost.' His strength draining from him, he shuffled back behind his desk and slumped into his chair.

The men remained as they were, staring at Takuya in disbelief. Moments later, muffled sobs could be heard from among the ranks. Propping his elbows on the desk, Takuya fixed his eyes firmly on the knots in its surface.

Eventually the men started to move silently back to their own desks.

Takuya wondered what would happen after the surrender. American warships would probably put US troops ashore all over Japan, and enemy aircraft would swarm on to surviving airfields, delivering loads of soldiers and weapons. No doubt the victors would waste little time in menacing the populace into submission as they went on to occupy all of Japan. Physically sound males would be forcibly relocated to work somewhere as labourers, and young women would most likely become the object of the victors' sexual desire. Those who resisted, he thought, would be thrown into prison or shot.

As if time had stopped, Takuya remained immobilised in his chair, a look of physical and mental exhaustion on his face.

The door opened and Colonel Tahara came in. When one of the men called the room to attention, Takuya stood up and bowed to his superior.

The colonel walked up to Takuya. 'You heard His Majesty's speech. We've had direct word from High Command that the Emperor has agreed to accept the Potsdam Declaration. Orders are to burn all documents at once,' he said hurriedly before disappearing out of the door.

Takuya turned to the men and barked out the order. 'Burn every document in the building. Now go to it!'

That defeat could become reality with such frightening ease dumbfounded Takuya. His notion of defeat had involved all branches of the Japanese Imperial forces choosing death before dishonour, and his own death had been a certainty in that scenario. Now he realised that there was nothing left for him to do. By this point, High Command would have already conveyed the news about the ceasefire to the air defence spotters and the electronic aircraft-detection posts, so there would be no more incoming reports to process, no more data to assess, no more air-raid alerts to issue. His duties had come to an end.

Unable to watch his men piling documents into boxes, Takuya left his desk and stepped out of the room. The corridor was busy with stern-faced men carrying armfuls of paper to and fro. Takuya walked down the hall and out through the steel doors at the rear of the building.

The sunlight was so brilliant that for a moment he felt dizzy. The trees, ground and stones all seemed to be parched white. He was overcome by a sense that the air was seething, engulfing him in myriad tiny air bubbles. He squinted as he fought the dizziness. In the rear courtyard, the soldiers had already started a bonfire and were burning piles of the documents that had been carried out through the back door. The fire was burning fiercely, the flames flickering like red cellophane in the midday sun.

From the rear entrance to the building, among the soldiers carrying bundles of paper, appeared the lieutenant from the legal affairs section, walking straight towards Takuya. His pursed lips were dry and his eyes glistened. Stopping in front of Takuya, he explained that the request he was about to make was an order from the major at High Command.

'The prisoners are to be executed. You are to provide two sergeant-majors to help. If we don't deal with the last of them before the enemy lands, they'll talk about what happened to the others. There are seventeen left. It's to be done straight away. People from headquarters staff up near Yamae village are waiting.'

Takuya understood that, to those at headquarters, the prisoners' execution was as important now as the burning of all the documents. They had already been sentenced to death, and the fact that hostilities had ceased had no bearing whatsoever on their execution.

Although his duties collecting data and issuing air-raid alerts had finished, Takuya once again sensed that his destiny was linked to that of the captured airmen. He had followed their actions for days and months on end, had busied himself to the very last collecting data about the aircraft that dropped the atomic bomb on Nagasaki, and had himself issued the air-raid alert and the order to evacuate the city. Takuya had been in a position to know the full extent of the damage caused by the bombing and strafing attacks carried out by these men. So far his duties had assigned him a passive role, but that was all over now, and the time had come, he thought, actively to show his mettle. Only then would his duties be finished.

At the time of the previous two executions, Takuya's responsibilities as officer in charge of the tactical operations centre
had kept him at his post, but the Emperor's broadcast released
him from all duties. I want to participate in the executions, he
thought. Taking the life of one of the prisoners with his own
hands would be his final duty. The lieutenant had said that the
executions would be carried out in order to dispose of remaining
evidence, but for Takuya it was something personal, something
he had to do as the officer in charge of air defence intelligence.

'Count me in, too,' said Takuya.

The lieutenant nodded. 'We'll be leaving soon,' he said, then
he hastened back into the building.

Takuya followed him through the steel doors and hurried
down the corridor to the air defence operations room, where he
called out to one of the two sergeant-majors. He was removing
documents from a filing-cabinet, but came quickly over to
Takuya when his name was called. His expression did not
change in the slightest when he was told that he was to take
part in the executions. A firm 'Yes, sir' was all he said.

Takuya ordered the second sergeant-major to continue burning the documents. Putting on his service cap, he walked out of
the room followed by the first one.

The prisoners, blindfolded with black cloth and their hands
tied together with twine, were being loaded into the backs of
two lorries outside. Takuya couldn't help being struck again by
the physical size of the men in front of him.

A sergeant and a couple of lance-corporals jumped up after
them and pulled down the canvas cover. The lorries moved off
slowly past the bonfire and down the gentle slope.

Takuya and the sergeant-major stood under a cherry tree
watching the hive of activity in the courtyard. Soldiers holding
bundles of documents hurried out to throw the papers on to the
fire, then scurried inside for more. The air was dead calm and
there was no sound except the snapping of the fire.

The major from High Command and the lieutenant from
the legal affairs section stepped out of the rear entrance,
accompanied by two enlisted men. They joined Takuya watching

the bonfire while the soldiers ran over to the garage. Moments later, there was an engine's roar as a lorry rounded the corner of the building and stopped in front of them. The major and the lieutenant jumped up into the cab while Takuya and his sergeant-major clambered into the back. A number of soldiers were already sitting in the back holding shovels, picks and coils of rope.

The lorry moved off. Takuya sat down on a coil of rope and looked at the charred ruins of the city from under the rolled-up canvas hood. Reports released in the days that followed would state that nine hundred and fifty-three people had been killed in raids on Fukuoka, and over fourteen thousand homes had been destroyed. Over two thousand people had been killed in both Kagoshima and Yawata and more than twenty thousand in Nagasaki, with the estimated death toll from air raids on all eighteen cities in Kyushu close to forty thousand. The execution of a mere seventeen prisoners, he thought, would hardly temper the outrage caused by the deaths of so many defenceless civilians in the fire raids.

The truck moved past piles of rubble and burnt roofing-iron which seemed almost to quiver in the hot haze. Takuya stared at the clouds of dust billowing behind the lorry as it rumbled forward. The engine raced as the vehicle began to climb the winding road up the hill. Before long the grassy slopes on either side of the road gave way to forest, with branches of trees brushing noisily against the sides of the canvas hood.

Moments after the lorry came out on to a flat stretch of road, it pulled over to one side, close against the face of the hill. Takuya jumped out of the back and saw that another two lorries and a smaller, khaki-painted vehicle had arrived before them. A sergeant standing on the road saluted Takuya and pointed to the left, in the direction of a bamboo grove.

Takuya and the others stepped off the road and down on to the raised walkway between two paddy fields. A battery of frogs launched themselves into the still water as the men thudded down onto the path. Within seconds Takuya and his comrades had left the track and were walking through the dense thicket of bamboo beyond the paddy fields. Mosquitoes buzzed everywhere, and Takuya waved his hand busily from side to side to keep them away from his face.

When they emerged into a small clearing he saw some officers and enlisted men from headquarters. The prisoners, blindfolded by strips of black cloth tied round their heads, were sitting huddled on the grass. Takuya went over to them.

To a man, the prisoners sat dejectedly with their heads hung forward. One was mumbling what might have been a prayer, and another, a very large man, was straining so hard against the rope round his wrists that he was almost toppling over.

Takuya noticed a group of officers from headquarters standing off to one side, a purplish-grey plume of cigarette smoke drifting straight up in the still air. When Takuya pulled out one of his cigarettes and lit it with a match, a few other officers stepped over to him and lit theirs from the flame. Puffing on his cigarette, Takuya stood gazing at the prisoners. The shrill chirring of what seemed like thousands of cicadas in the undergrowth around the small clearing had reached a crescendo, intense as a summer cloudburst. The sickly-sweet smell of wet grass hung in the air and the whirring of insect wings could be heard close by.

'Shall we get it over with?' said the major, throwing his cigarette into the grass and turning to Takuya.

Almost as if they had been waiting for him to issue the order, two enlisted men stepped forward and pulled a young blond prisoner to his feet. The American dwarfed the soldiers on each side of him.

They pulled him forward, but he moved uncertainly over the grass, his legs obviously weakened from his time in captivity. The major followed, and the four men soon disappeared into the forest.

Takuya stood smoking his cigarette, mesmerised by the noise of the cicadas. The glossy dark-green leaves of the trees glistened in the sunlight. As Takuya stared in the direction the four men had gone, he felt sweat trickling down the small of his back.

Before long he noticed movement among the trees. The major appeared, sword in hand, followed by the two enlisted men. The major's face was expressionless except for the faint hint of a smile at the corner of his mouth.

Another prisoner was dragged to his feet, a big, red-bearded man with a remarkably pointed nose. As soon as Takuya laid eyes on the muscular frame he instinctively stepped forward. He'd thought that this man had been executed long ago, but there was no mistaking it: this was one of the airmen who during the interrogations had casually replied that the bomber crews relaxed by listening to jazz on the way back to base. The man was held on either side by the two soldiers and led off down the path into the woods. Takuya followed close behind. He could almost feel the eyes of the other officers and men burning into his back. It doesn't have to be perfect, he told himself. As long as I end this man's days.

The prisoner was taken along a narrow track through the trees. Takuya gazed fixedly at the man's thick neck muscles as he walked into the forest.

4

Takuya dozed, slumped against the wooden wall of the freight car.

The previous night he'd walked along the coastal road as far as a town called Yoshida, but as the last train had left two hours earlier he had no choice but to sleep sitting on a bench in the cramped waiting-room. Once dawn arrived, he awoke and caught the first train out. It stopped at Yawatahama, where he would have to change trains, but the only thought in Takuya's mind at this stage was to put as much distance as possible between himself and his hometown.

Awakened by the shrill voice of the stationmaster, Takuya jumped down from the freight car on to the tracks. Afraid that there might be someone amid the throng in the station who would recognise him, he pulled the peak of his service cap down over his eyes and found himself a place to sit down at the end of the platform.

The train that pulled in two hours later was only going as far as Matsuyama, but thirty minutes later, after waiting over two and a half hours on the platform, Takuya boarded a train bound for the port of Takamatsu. On reaching his destination, he left the station, walked over to the dimly lit pier, and joined the long line of people waiting to board the ferry. Moments after he felt himself being pushed down into the crowded hold of the vessel, it started to move away from the pier, and in what seemed a very short time the boat reached the port of Uno, where Takuya then boarded a train bound for Okayama. It was already one in the morning by the time he disembarked. He was exhausted, but at the same time relieved that he had managed to distance himself safely from his hometown and make it to Honshu. Being just one more anonymous body in a sea of strangers must offer some degree of protection against arrest, he thought.

Following his father's advice, Takuya had decided to pay a visit to his mother's elder brother. At the end of the war his uncle had been an army colonel, responsible for overseeing military training in the country's schools. He was obviously a central figure in his mother's family, and Takuya's father had often expressed his respect for the man's integrity, giving pride of place on the wall to a framed piece of his calligraphy. There had seemed to be no doubt in his father's mind that the uncle would offer Takuya sanctuary.

Takuya, too, felt certain that his uncle would help. When he had joined the Imperial Army his uncle had written him a long letter, which, along with the usual congratulatory words and encouragement, seemed to Takuya to have been penned by someone who understood how it must feel to be joining the military without having had the chance to apply the knowledge he had gained at university. An uncle who could show such understanding, thought Takuya, would surely empathise with his participation in the execution and help him avoid capture.

After a little less than an hour, the Osaka-bound overnight train pulled into the station, so packed that there were even passengers standing on the couplings between the engine and the front carriage. There was no way Takuya could get on board, and before long the train slowly wrenched itself free from the throng on the platform. Shortly after daybreak another Osaka-bound train arrived, but again every imaginable space was taken. People were even sitting half out of the windows or perched precariously on the steps below the doors. The next two trains, one just before noon and the other in mid-afternoon, were just as crowded, and not until early evening did he manage to force himself into the window of a train from Okayama.

Stopping at every station, the train made its way down the line. After sunset, only scattered lights from houses and other buildings could be seen from the window. It was after ten o'clock when the train eventually reached Osaka.

Takuya followed the crowds through the turnstiles and out of the station. His eyes were met by a dark, overcast sky, without a glimmer of light from either the moon or the stars. Several rows of shacks had been thrown up as temporary housing immediately in front of the station, and he could make out the soft glow of an electric light here and there. Beyond that it was pitch dark.

Takuya knew that his uncle's house, which he had heard had miraculously survived the incendiary raids, was about thirty minutes away on foot, but as that would involve negotiating his way in the dark through the burnt-out ruins, he decided to spend the night in the relative safety of the station. He walked back in and found the waiting-area crammed with people. There were men, women and even children sitting and lying everywhere, waiting to board a train the next day or simply homeless and seeking shelter.

Finding a space beside a pillar in the concourse, he slipped his rucksack off his shoulder and sat down on the concrete floor. He was feverish, and he felt a creeping numbness in his legs. A warm, sickly smell, not unlike that of urine, hung in the air.

Feeling hungry, Takuya pulled the sweet potato he had bought at Okayama Station out of his bag and took a bite. At first it seemed to have no taste at all, but as he chewed a subtle hint of sweetness reached his tastebuds.

Suddenly, in the back of his mind, Takuya could hear a voice, a male voice, barely more audible than a whisper, muttering something like 'Lucia' or 'Luciana'. It was the word the red-bearded man had been saying to himself over and over again as he sat slumped in the bamboo grove.

Takuya's mind drifted back to that scene at Abura-yama the previous August. He remembered clearly how anxious he had been about whether he would be able to cut through the man's thick neck. He had concentrated on kendo for martial arts in high school, and had continued training during his days as an officer cadet, but all opportunity for further honing his skills with a sword had ended when he was posted to headquarters in Kyushu. Occasionally he had attended to his army sword, polishing it and then checking and sharpening the blade, but only to the extent necessary to keep it presentable in a ceremonial sense.

He remembered how flies had buzzed around the prisoner's head. There had been a light-brown birthmark on the man's neck, with a little tuft of soft red hair in the middle of it. Takuya remembered how he had stood there, seeing in his mind's eye the scene inside the bomber returning to base after a raid. When he pictured the red-haired man moving his head and shoulders to the rhythm of jazz, rage welled up inside him. This man must surrender his own life in return for those of the countless innocent civilians upon whom he had rained death and destruction.

Takuya remembered how the feeling of the sword striking something hard had jarred his palms. For some reason, the man's knees had jerked upwards with the first blow, a huge gash opening in the back of his neck as his head drooped forward. Takuya had swung his sword down another two times, but somehow recalled it now as three. He remembered his surprise at the relative ease with which he had severed the man's head, and how he had immediately felt a wave of pride and satisfaction.

Had it been 'Lucia' or 'Luciana'? Takuya wondered as he sat there against the pillar, rucksack between his knees. Could it have been the man's girlfriend, or was it his mother? Was it 'Lucia' or 'Luciana'? Takuya whispered to himself. Or then again, maybe it was part of a prayer.

If the major from High Command had given the order, Takuya would have been quite prepared to dispatch another one, maybe even two, of the prisoners. He had stayed there in the clearing and watched as each successive prisoner was led out of the woods, forced to sit down on the grass, and then beheaded. Takuya remembered how high his emotions had been running then. Watching, he had felt certain that he would do much better if he were asked to execute a second or even a third prisoner.

Suddenly, as Takuya sat there slowly munching the sweet potato, each bite tasting better than the last, a small hand was thrust in front of his face. He looked up to see a little boy, about ten years old, standing in front of him. The boy's shirt was open at the neck, revealing bones protruding from under tightly stretched skin so thickly caked with grime that it could almost have been burnt-on coal tar. A foul smell drifted from his body.

The boy's face showed no sign of emotion. His cheeks were sunken and his arms and legs astonishingly thin, his distended belly proof that he was suffering from malnutrition. The outstretched hand came nearer to Takuya's face. The boy clearly wanted some of the sweet potato. It was the first time Takuya had seen a homeless waif up close, standing there in filthy bare feet and wearing a shirt with one sleeve ripped open at the shoulder.

As Takuya stared at the child, guilt welled up inside him. His inability to protect this child and others like him had robbed the boy of his family and forced him to beg from adults to stay alive. Important as the remainder of the potato might be to stave off his own hunger, Takuya felt somehow obliged to share with the boy.

As he was about to break the sweet potato in half, the boy reached out and snatched it from his grip. Takuya looked up instantly, but the boy was already running as fast as his legs would carry him towards the exit. That he could find the reserves of energy to propel himself so nimbly and at such speed, around and over the human obstacle course covering the concrete floor and then out into the pitch darkness beyond the exit, was cause for amazement.

It never crossed Takuya's mind to pursue him. He sat motionless, staring out into the gloom of the night. He could still visualise the glint in the boy's eyes, a look of bold cockiness more fitting for someone twice his age. His eyes bespoke a reserve of worldly cunning and vitality behind his wretched appearance. Neither child nor adult, the boy seemed more like some kind of exotic creature. It disturbed Takuya to think that in just eight short months since the end of the war, the burnt shells of Japan's major towns and cities had become home to such waifs.

His own hunger pangs subsiding somewhat, he imagined the boy crouching down like a wild animal in the darkness of the ruins, casting furtive glances to each side as he wolfed down the remains of the sweet potato.

'Was it "Lucia" or "Luciana"?' Takuya whispered to himself.

Leaning back against the pillar, he closed his eyes. Putting his arms through the shoulder-straps of his rucksack, he secured the bag firmly on his knees. A deep sleep came over him.

There seemed to be no change in the outward appearance of his uncle's house, or at least what he could see of it over the high wooden fence around the property. A large wooden nameplate was attached to the gatepost, just as there had been the last time he visited. As he opened the gate he heard a bell ring just above his head. The garden was completely different from the way he remembered it. The only trees left standing were those hard up against the fence; the rest of the space had been dug up and turned into a vegetable patch. Buckets and straw mats lay here and there, and the ground was littered with pieces of fine straw. There was no sign of the shelves of bonsai trees that Takuya's uncle had been known to tend so lovingly.

Takuya slid open the front door. 'Is anyone home?' he called as he poked his head through into the entrance. A half-dozen slippered footsteps from down the hall brought his uncle out of the shadows. Takuya stiffened and bowed respectfully to the old man, but he couldn't help being taken aback at the physical change in his uncle. He had lost a great deal of weight and his skin was pale and pasty, as though he had aged years in a very short time. No doubt the want of proper food had taken its toll. There was no sign of the stalwart character he had once been known for. As Takuya followed the old man into the living-room, he couldn't help noticing how bare the inside of the house was.

His wife had gone out to buy some food, the old man said. The veins on the back of his wizened hands stood out as he made a pot of green tea.

There was no way, Takuya thought, that he could entrust his life to the feeble-looking old man sitting in front of him. His father's faith that his uncle would provide safe haven had obviously been based on an image of the man before the war was lost, which clearly no longer held true.

But then again, he might be reading too much into his uncle's physical appearance. Anyone who had spent so many years in the military would surely be stout of heart and mind, and not easily swayed by the vicissitudes of the last few years. Such a person would, he thought, be sympathetic to Takuya's role in the executions at Abura-yama, and therefore would help keep him safe from trial by the Allied authorities.

Takuya quickly came to the point in explaining the reason for his visit. His uncle sat silently, eyes half closed in concentration, as he listened to his nephew's story. Takuya's description of his own part in the executions immediately prompted an unmistakable expression of surprise on the old man's face.

Explaining that his father had recommended that he seek his uncle's assistance, he finished by saying, 'I need a place to hide.'

The old man looked at Takuya. A gap must have appeared in the clouds, for a beam of sunlight shone in through the glass door facing on to the garden, highlighting the light-brown spots running from his uncle's temple down the line of his cheekbone.

His uncle shifted his gaze from Takuya out to the garden. Takuya sat without moving and waited for his response.

Obviously unsettled, the older man adjusted his position before looking back at his nephew, and for a few seconds his mouth hung slightly open, as though he were at a loss for words. He moved his hands to his knees and straightened his back as he prepared to deliver his reply. Takuya sensed disappointment and a hint of contempt in his uncle's manner, and the reply he was given did nothing to dispel his unease.

'If you were acting on orders from higher-ranking officers, you've got nothing to fear from the Occupation authorities. You say that they deny giving the order, but a true military man wouldn't lose his nerve and run. Stand up in court and tell your story. Make them see the truth of the matter. That is your only option.'

His uncle was obviously putting on an act. His eyes betrayed a lack of conviction in the words he had chosen, and before he finished each sentence the momentum behind it faded away.

The newspapers were full of stories about former military men being condemned to death for little more than acts of assault on prisoners of war, so his uncle would have been well aware that 'standing up in court' would lead to nothing less than the death penalty. He was obviously afraid of having anything to do with someone on the run from the Allied authorities, and doubtless reluctant to stretch his limited food supply, even for a short time, by taking in another mouth to feed. Given his former position overseeing military education throughout the nation, he may even have feared the prospect of being investigated himself.

Takuya regretted having come all this way to visit his uncle. He had idled away the days since his demobilisation, but during that time he had come to resent what he saw as a growing tendency to denounce every aspect of the defunct Imperial Army. He felt something akin to pride for having been in the military, and was determined to live out the rest of his days without abandoning that feeling. The thought that his uncle could have served for so many years in uniform and then, with the war lost, become a completely different person made Takuya's blood boil.

He stared at his uncle, who was again gazing out at the garden. Most likely this man was barely justifying his place as the head of the family by working the meagre garden plot to help feed his wife and only daughter. The thought that his father had gone so far as to frame and display a piece of the uncle's calligraphy, the words 'great achievement' boldly proclaimed in resolute brushstrokes, now seemed rather comical.

Takuya stole a glance at the lintel behind his uncle, remembering that the last time he had visited it had featured a prized piece of calligraphy by an army general from the same village. It was gone, as was the photograph of his uncle resplendent in an army colonel's full-dress uniform. He had evidently chosen to purge himself of all vestiges of his military past, and in the process had been reduced to little more than a helpless old man, concerned solely with self-preservation.

'I'll give it some thought,' said Takuya, assuming a pensive expression to avoid injuring what was left of his uncle's dignity.

'That's what you must do. I really think you must go to court and make them understand the truth,' said the old man as he turned back to face his nephew.

There was no point in staying any longer, thought Takuya. He wished his uncle well and stood up to leave.

'Sorry I couldn't give you more than just a cup of tea, but with both my wife and daughter out . . .' said his uncle as he led Takuya back toward the entrance, a hint of relief in his voice.

Takuya bowed once again before stepping out through the gate, and regretted as he did so that coming all this way to Osaka by train and boat and then train again had been such a foolish waste of time. He sighed in annoyance at the thought that this futile exercise had depleted his precious funds.

Fences from the surviving houses defined the road on both sides. Takuya walked back the way he had come. Occasionally, broken sections of fence or low gates afforded him a view into people's gardens, which had all been transformed into vegetable plots. The pungent smell of human excrement reminded him of fields in the countryside.

He came out on to a main road. A tram swayed from side to side as it rattled noisily towards and then past him, men and women perched precariously on the steps at the front and rear of the carriage. The façades of the buildings on either side of the road suggested that they had once been shops, but now they were virtually deserted. Without exception, the people who had ventured out into the streets were gaunt and pallid. Some wore suit jackets and trousers, obviously bought in better times to fit fleshier frames; others, equally gaunt, sat beside the road dolefully clutching matchstick knees.

When Takuya turned right at the intersection, a simple bridge slung over a canal drew his attention. Two large lorries were parked one behind the other on the near side of the bridge, and he stopped and stared at what was going on in front of them. A noisy crowd of people, most of them children, stood stretching out their hands to those in the lorries. Two American soldiers sat in each lorry's cab, and there were more, with sub-machine-guns slung over their shoulders, seated in the back. The white star insignia of the American army was clearly visible on the doors of the lorries.

Takuya had never seen US Army vehicles or personnel up this close before. The soldier on the passenger side in the nearer lorry had his back to Takuya and was leaning half out of the window space in the door, apparently talking to those sitting under the furled hood in the back. The soldier in the driver's seat was staring in Takuya's direction.

Even though Takuya knew that these trucks certainly had nothing to do with his being in that street, the thought that they might very well be making random checks on passers-by made him want to turn back in the direction he had come from. Unnerved by the gaze of the soldier behind the wheel, Takuya shuffled to the side of the road as nonchalantly as he could and sat down on the dry ground, as though he were merely stopping to rest along his way. He wiped the sweat from his neck with a cloth from his pocket, then pulled out the bag of roasted beans he'd bought at a stall in front of the station and dropped a few into his mouth.

Takuya could hear the crowd of urchins still calling out to the soldiers, 'Haroo, Haroo!' He could not understand what on earth these children, and the adults standing behind them, could be doing milling around American military trucks.

As he sat contemplating the scene, he saw something quite astounding. The children had stopped calling out, and were now bent over, frantically scrambling to grab something off the ground. The adults who had been bystanders seconds earlier were also racing helter-skelter among the children, picking things up off the road. The soldiers in the trucks were throwing small objects out from under the furled canvas hoods. A black soldier in one lorry purposely threw them as far as he could, and one of his white comrades in the other one watched in fits of laughter as adults and children responded to his feigned throws. Takuya sat there aghast, transfixed by what he saw.

The slamming of cab doors was followed by the roaring of engines. The two vehicles edged slowly forward one after the other, and the crowd of people moved with them, adults and children breaking into a run as the lorries accelerated off down the road. The adults gave up after a few paces, but many of the children tore past Takuya in hot pursuit.

The lorries swung left round the first corner, leaving the young pursuers in a cloud of dust. The children stopped chasing and gathered at the corner of the intersection, and others who had not run after the lorries hurried past Takuya to join them and wait for the next truckload of Americans to appear. Some of them were holding their booty: pieces of chewing gum, chocolate bars and even cigarettes.

Takuya gazed at the crowd of children squatting and standing on the street corner and mused that, though the newspapers never mentioned this, it must occur every day, not just here but in all the towns and cities where the occupation forces were stationed.

Takuya got to his feet and started walking. Since the reduction of the cities of Japan to scorched wastelands was the work of the American military, he reasoned that the representatives of those who had committed such heinous acts should be the object of nothing less than revulsion. The sight of adults grasping at sweets in front of laughing Americans made Takuya feel sick to his stomach.

He crossed a bridge and faced an expanse of burnt ruins, a few makeshift shacks standing here and there to one side and a row of concrete buildings behind them. A cart pulled by an emaciated horse went past, soon to be overtaken by a man on a rickety old bicycle. There were potholes everywhere, and the cart and the bicycle bounced up and down as they moved along the road.

Takuya followed the road as far as the station. He couldn't shake off the image of adults and children milling around the American lorries. It was hard to believe that those people had lived through the same war he had.

Suddenly he was jolted by the unexpected sight of his younger brother, Toshio, walking toward him. Even though he was wearing his service cap pulled down low, there was no mistaking that tall, lean frame and distinctive gait. His brother had obviously seen Takuya, too, because he quickened his pace towards him. Takuya felt the energy draining from his body and a wave of foreboding struck him. His brother worked in their hometown post office and there was no chance that his work had brought him to Osaka, so he must have come to intercept Takuya at their uncle's house.

Takuya's brother stopped in front of him. His eyes were bloodshot from a sleepness night on the train and the pallor of his face betrayed weariness.

'The police came,' he blurted out. 'At five in the morning the day after you left. Two detectives and one constable.' Takuya felt himself flinch. Obviously his brother had followed him all the way to Osaka to alert him to the danger.

'What did they say?' Takuya asked timidly.

'They said that they had an order from the occupation authorities for you to report for questioning and that they'd come to take you in. They came inside and searched everywhere. Father told them you'd gone to visit a friend in Fukuoka and hadn't been back since. They told us to let them know if we heard from you or if you came home, but I think they'll have people watching the house,' said Toshio. His face was ashen grey.

'Did our father ask you to come and tell me?'

'Our mother and sister wanted me to as well. I got Mother to tell the people at work that I was ill and jumped on the train straight away. They all said you should make sure you stay away from home,' said his brother, in a voice barely more audible than a whisper.

'OK. Don't worry, I won't let them find me,' replied Takuya, thinking of his good fortune in deciding to leave his parents' house the night before the police turned up. His instinct had saved him then; if he stayed focused and alert, he should be able to keep one step ahead of the authorities.

'So you've been to Uncle's house, then?' said Toshio, a hint of doubt in his tone.

'That was a waste of time. He said a military man should come forward and straighten things out. It is ridiculous. He's just scared to get involved. He won't take me in because he's too worried about himself,' said Takuya, making a wry face.

'Really? Father told me to give him this sack of rice, since he was supposed to be looking after you and everything,' said Toshio disappointedly.

'He'll never let me stay there. All I got was a cup of tea. You can leave the rice with me,' said Takuya. The expression on his face was almost defiant.

Toshio put down his shoulder-bag, pulled a small cloth bag from inside it, and put it into his elder brother's rucksack.

'What will you do now?' he asked as he began walking beside Takuya.

'I've just remembered there's a fellow from Osaka University working in a steel company here. We were in the same officer training company. I may look him up while I'm here. He took part in executing the American airmen, too,' said Takuya without turning to look at his brother.

He felt an almost primordial instinct for self-preservation welling up inside him. Just as he had thought, the occupation authorities had instructed the police to arrest him on suspicion of involvement in war crimes. Unable to return home, he would have to stay one step ahead of those who wanted to put him behind bars.

'You'd better get straight back home, Toshio. If the police catch on to the fact that you're away, they'll realise you've gone to get in touch with me. You don't seem to have been followed, but you shouldn't be with me too long. Each of us should be on his way,' said Takuya, stopping to face his brother.

Toshio nodded reluctantly.

'Give the family my regards. I won't be in touch again. Just know that I'm lying low somewhere in Japan. Well, take care of yourself,' said Takuya, squeezing his brother's arm affectionately before turning away and crossed the road.

He strode along the path through the scorched ruins, not once pausing to look back. Since the end of the war, he had received just one postcard from this man Himuro, who worked at the steel company, and in it he had suggested that Takuya visit his company if he should ever be in Osaka. The company would be located among the buildings in front of him, which had somehow escaped the ravages of the bombing. He couldn't come this close without letting his friend know how serious his situation had become.

All the same, visiting Himuro's company might be as dangerous as returning home. No doubt Himuro had also been cited as a suspected war criminal, and so he might have already been taken into custody. Or maybe he had gone into hiding. The police might even have the company under surveillance, which would put Takuya at risk if he were to visit the premises.

He paused for a few seconds on the road leading to the steel company, then resumed walking, his gait more decisive than before. A moment's thought had brought him to the conclusion that, if his friend had not yet been arrested, he could not allow himself to get this close and then leave without alerting Himuro to the impending danger. Takuya had learnt from Shirasaka about the arrests of those directly below the commander-in-chief, and that the search had already begun for those who had carried out the executions of B-29 crew members, but it was highly unlikely that his friend, far away in Osaka, would be aware of these developments, and there was no doubt that for Himuro, too, capture would mean the gallows. Takuya remembered that Himuro had married while still at the university, and that his friend carried a photograph of his young wife in the inside pocket of his uniform. Himuro had always been the archetypal outgoing student, a gregarious man known for his raucous laugh. He had beheaded the oldest of the American airmen, a well-built thirty-two-year-old with deep-set, melancholy eyes.

Quite a number of people seemed to be moving in and out of the buildings here, considering the fact that virtually all factories had been destroyed and that the companies represented here would have long since lost all their production capacity. Maybe they were involved in buying and selling what was left of the factories and their contents.

Himuro's company office was housed in a relatively unscathed four-storey building. Takuya paused on the footpath and peered inside. On the wall just past the entrance he could see a piece of paper with the word 'Reception' written on it, and there was a wizened old man sitting at a desk on the other side of a little window.

Takuya steeled himself, took a couple of steps past the door, slid the glass window to one side at the reception desk and told the man he had come to see Himuro. When asked 'What's your name?' he thought for a second before blurting out the name of his form master at primary school, 'Masuoka Shigetaro.' The grizzled old receptionist looked over his shoulder and grunted a couple of words to a young woman sitting behind him. She rose and walked out into the hall and up the stairs. Himuro must still be around, thought Takuya.

People who were probably employees of Himuro's company came and went in the corridor. The range of the men's clothing was quite striking: from suits to army uniforms and overalls. One man even wore his spectacles held in place with black string looped round one ear to replace a missing sidepiece.

Before long Himuro appeared, looking sceptical as he walked down the stairs behind the young woman. He was wearing a baggy grey suit and had grown his hair quite long, parted neatly on the side.

When he recognised Takuya, his expression changed from suspicion to bewilderment.

'I've got to talk to you,' said Takuya, leading his friend out of the door and down the path. They turned past the bank at the corner and stopped on the other side of a telegraph pole. Himuro stood facing Takuya, waiting to be told the news.

'Things have taken a very serious turn,' said Takuya, and he went on to explain what Shirasaka had told him.

Himuro's jaw dropped. Maybe it was the weight he had lost, but he looked a mere shadow of the man Takuya remembered from their army days.

'I was sure it would be all right. We didn't leave anything that could be used against us,' said Himuro in a hollow voice.

'They worked out the number of prisoners who were handed over to headquarters from their investigations into the *kempeitai*. It seems the senior officers couldn't hold out against them and ended up telling them everything. No doubt the authorities will even know about the prisoners sent to the university medical school. By now they'll know everything,' said Takuya, and he saw Himuro's expression harden.

'I actually came here to Osaka hoping my uncle would give me a place to hide for the time being, but my brother came after me and told me that before dawn yesterday the police came to my parents' house looking for me. When I heard that, I thought they'd have already arrested you, being here in a big city like this. They won't be far away. For all you know they may be waiting for you at home right now. If we're caught we'll go straight to the gallows, I assure you,' said Takuya emphatically.

Himuro pressed his right hand hard against his forehead. 'They might come looking for me at work,' he said, glancing furtively over his shoulder.

'That's right. Who knows when they'll come? You know it's too risky to go back there. You've got to run for it now while you can,' said Takuya.

Himuro nodded in agreement, a look of utter consternation in his eyes. 'Where will you go?' he asked.

'I don't know. Even if I did, I wouldn't tell you. It's best if neither knows where the other's going. If one of us is caught and ends up being tortured, the other might be found. Neither of us needs that. I'm not trusting anyone from now on. There's no way I'll let them put a noose round my neck,' said Takuya in a clear, determined tone. Himuro nodded again, without replying.

'One thing, though: you'll need to get some money and food before you make your move away from here. This will help,' said Takuya, pulling the carefully folded identification papers out of the inside pocket of his jacket.

'If you show this you can get a ration book. Shirasaka gave me two, so you can have one of them. He told me to pretend to be from Okinawa and to say that going back there isn't an option. Just choose an Okinawan name and write it on the identification paper and you'll have a new identity.'

Takuya handed the form to Himuro. The square, red ink seal of the Western Region's Hakata administration office for demobilised servicemen validated it as identification for the bearer.

'Well, I'd best be on my way. Don't get caught,' said Takuya, squeezing Himuro's bony arm before he moved from behind the telegraph pole. He took half a dozen hurried steps across the road before stealing a glance back over his shoulder. Himuro had already gone.

Takuya headed back toward the scorched ruins. The area around the myriad makeshift huts in front of him was teeming with people. To get to the station Takuya would have to make his way through the crowd, so he pulled his cap down over his eyes to hide as much of his face as possible. He had last shaved when he left home to go to Fukuoka, so he now sported a considerable beard.

As he moved into the throng he heard a steady drone of hoarse male voices coming from huts on both sides of the path. Once he had worked himself comfortably into the flow of pedestrians, he craned his neck past the people walking alongside him to peer into the huts. He was taken aback by what he saw. There were people ladling curry from large pots into steaming bowls of rice and others selling steamed dumplings. People were handing over money in exchange for bowls of soup, vegetable porridge and noodles, and between these food stalls others hawked mud-brown cakes of soap or little open boxes of cigarettes. The pungent smells wafting from the stalls and the bustling air of the market left Takuya dazed as he arrived in front of the station.

There were men and women sitting everywhere on the cracked concrete floor inside the station, some curled up sound asleep.

Takuya found space to sit on the floor near the waiting-room and started to think about where he should go. Perhaps he should go north. If he went up to Hokkaido he should be able to find work in a mine without too much trouble, but the thought of heading in that direction and having to go through Tokyo, where SCAP headquarters were, weighed on him heavily.

Perhaps he should go south instead. One of his subordinates in the anti-aircraft tactical operations room had gone back to Tanegashima, and Takuya thought there was a good chance that this man would give him shelter. But getting there would involve passing through Kyushu, where the majority of those involved in the executions of the American airmen were living. Since investigations were likely to be centred in that region, it was difficult for Takuya to bring himself to head that way.

He tried to visualise the faces of comrades who hadn't taken part in the executions, searching his mind for someone who would treat him the same way as during the war, despite the collapse of the military and the scarcity of food and other essentials.

The face of one man came to mind, a corporal named Nemoto Kosaku. He had been attached to the tactical operations room and had always gone out of his way to help Takuya, ordering the soldiers on duty to change his bedding and make tea for him. Takuya remembered that Nemoto was from a little fishing village on Shoodo-shima in the eastern Inland Sea. An anti-aircraft observation post had been located there during the war, but there had been no other military facilities to speak of, so the occupation forces were unlikely to have stationed troops there. The fact that it was a fishing village also meant that they would probably not want for food.

Takuya also recalled that Nemoto had said he could get from his village to Kobe or Osaka by ferry, an option much more appealing to Takuya than another ride on a jam-packed train.

He stood up, walked over to the ticket window, and asked the way to the Osaka harbour ferry terminal.

'The pier?' muttered an old station worker sitting on a stool beside the entrance to the platforms, who then grudgingly told him the way.

Takuya started walking.

5

The ferry left Osaka that afternoon and arrived in Kobe in the early evening. For some reason it didn't depart that night, as it should have done, but stayed in port until early the next morning. The boat was jammed with passengers, but Takuya managed to find a spot on the deck to curl up and close his eyes. Shutting out the light focused his mind on himself.

An itchy sensation spread slowly down his back and he felt as if tiny creatures were crawling over his skin. In the crush on the train from his hometown to Fukuoka his clothes must have become infested with lice.

The ferry trip was long. The boat steadily threaded its way past islands of all sizes and shapes, but Takuya paid little heed to the view beyond the bulwarks, lying on his side munching a sweet potato.

He recalled the look of panic on Himuro's face and wondered whether his friend had taken his advice and fled straight away rather than risking going back to work. Maybe he had first tried to reach his wife to say goodbye. Either way, very soon the authorities would move to make an arrest, and whatever happened from now on, Takuya felt good knowing he had at least been able to warn his friend and give him the identification papers to help him on his way.

Takuya was as bewildered as Himuro that they had been found out despite their having left nothing that could be used against them. Colonel Tahara had called a meeting of all those involved in the executions to stress the importance of ensuring that not one scrap of evidence be left behind.

Although none of the POWs was alive to testify, there remained the problem of what would happen if the occupation authorities found out that forty-one American airmen had been transferred from the *kempeitai* to Western Command. Obviously, their first question would be about what had happened to those men. One suggestion was that they say they had all burnt to death when the camp in Fukuoka was destroyed in the incendiary raids. The problem with this, someone pointed out, was that they had no plausible explanation as to why the burnt bodies could not be exhumed for inspection.

After some debate, they had agreed that their story must involve the bodies disappearing altogether. Colonel Tahara had already sworn to silence all those who participated in the executions, and had told them that, if questioned, they were to say the POWs had been sent to Tokyo. It was decided that the story should be an extension of that, namely that the prisoners had all died in transit; that, given the already desperate situation in mid-July, and with no military aircraft available, two large fishing-boats had been requisitioned to transport the men. They were all told to say that both boats had sunk in the Kanmon Strait after striking American mines. If questioned further, they were to say that American aircraft and submarine activity had forced the two vessels to leave Hakata port under cover of darkness, and that no sooner had they entered the Kanmon Strait than both hit mines and sank without a trace. That area of water had been literally peppered with mines and such incidents had become an everyday occurrence, so this story had the ring of plausibility.

The only thing left was the actual disposal of the bodies. Almost half had already been cremated and the rest buried in a nearby graveyard, but it was decided that they should all be reduced to ashes and then disposed of at sea. The bodies were exhumed and hurriedly cremated and the ashes placed in urns before being loaded into a lorry, together with the ashes of those cremated earlier. Takuya rode in the front cab as the vehicle wound its way down to Hakata port. His charges sat on the wooden benches in the back of the truck, staring blankly anywhere but at the forty-one urns in front of them, now in bundles of threes and fours. A large fishing-boat moored to the pier was ready to take Takuya and his men far enough offshore to dispose of what the boat's crew had been told were boxes of military documents. About four kilometres east of Nokonoshima, Takuya ordered the forty-one urns dropped overboard.

By this time a wave of panic had struck northern Kyushu. Alarming rumours were circulating that, within hours of the Emperor's radio broadcast announcing defeat, US troops had begun landing in Hakata Bay, that black American soldiers had raped large numbers of local women, and that the Soviet Pacific fleet was steaming ominously toward Kyushu. The hysteria was fanned when many local government offices instructed their female staff to evacuate immediately. Crowds of frantic people carrying their belongings swarmed to the railway station in hopes of escaping to somewhere safe. The Moji Railway Company went so far as to bring in extra engineers and organise special train services to evacuate as many people as possible. Even on government-run lines, passengers were encouraged to board the trains without paying, to save time, and instead were given tickets requiring payment when they got off at their destination. These trains headed inland from northern Kyushu several times each day. Those who couldn't force their way inside the cars through doors or windows clambered on to the roofs, sat amid the coal in the engine tender, or even stood precariously on the cowcatcher at the very front of the engine.

This confusion had reigned for several days, but Takuya and his comrades felt secure in the knowledge that they had disposed of all evidence linking them to the executions. Even if the American military did come and occupy the burnt ruins of Fukuoka, he thought, how on earth could they ever discover that forty-one airmen had actually been taken prisoner?

Such confidence meant that Shirasaka's revelation that the Americans knew everything about what had gone on came as a tremendous shock, of course, and the realisation that they had seriously underestimated the Americans' investigation had filled Takuya with fear. At the same time, he felt ashamed that his lily-livered superiors had been so quick to break down under interrogation and tell all about the experimental surgery and the beheading of the surviving POWs.

The Americans were obviously not an enemy to be taken lightly, thought Takuya. They would certainly have ordered the Japanese police to move to arrest those suspected of war crimes, and would surely be carrying out independent investigations as well.

The boat sounded its steam horn and its progress through the water slowed as the engine was eased back. Takuya sat up and turned his gaze in the direction of the prow. The shore was not far away now, and he could make out a number of houses nestled below the low hills behind the village. Lines of small boats were moored at the shore on both sides of a short jetty sticking out at a right angle into the water.

Slowly edging forward, the ferry drew up alongside the little pier. Crewmen threw ropes to others waiting on the jetty, and in a moment the boat had stopped moving altogether. Takuya stood up and looked at the little village. Houses dotted both sides of the narrow, winding road that ran parallel to the shoreline. Almost all were of a single storey. The slopes behind the village were covered with terraced fields.

Takuya thought this looked an ideal place to hide. There was no chance of American lorries or jeeps appearing on the road, and a police station was highly improbable in a village this size. There would be very few people coming and going, so there was little chance of his being spotted by someone who might recognise him. Once familiar with the villagers, he thought, he should be able to get a job and stay here for quite some time.

Takuya followed the other passengers off the boat and on to the wooden pier. A group of old people were squatting on their haunches in one corner of the open area in front of the jetty, enjoying a chat with their friends in the sun. Takuya sauntered over to them and asked where he might find Nemoto Kosaku's house. Without moving to stand up, and almost in unison, two of the old men pointed down the road and explained how far to go and where to turn. Takuya followed their directions, walking up the road until he came to a small wooden bridge, which he crossed before turning right on to a narrow path up a slight slope. There were a number of houses along the path, but the old men had told Takuya that Nemoto's was the one on the left at the corner where this lane met the next. The house was quite small, but it had obviously originally been built to serve as a shop, too, as just inside the door, on the lower concrete floor section of the house, was an old counter. There were no goods for sale.

Takuya hesitated. The outward appearance of Nemoto's house suggested that the family was not likely to be able to put him up and feed him. Having been turned away by his own uncle, Takuya thought he should not expect too much from Nemoto. Defeat had swept away the obligations required of a subordinate to his superior.

But then again, he'd come not because he wanted to impose upon Nemoto's hospitality but to ask for assistance in finding a job. Reminding himself that all he wanted to do was start a new life here, and that there was no way he would allow himself to become a burden on Nemoto, Takuya stepped across to the entrance, slid the glass door to one side and called out to those inside.

A man's face appeared from behind the sliding door dividing the shop area from the rest of the house. It was Nemoto. His hair was cropped almost to his scalp, and he wore a vaguely suspicious look. The contrast between the bright sun outside and the shade inside seemed to make it difficult for him to identify who had arrived.

'It's Kiyohara,' said Takuya, removing his service cap.

'Lieutenant!' said Nemoto, jumping to his feet. He was clearly taken aback, but his face was the same picture of loyalty it had always been during his days as a corporal under Takuya's command.

Stepping down from the raised tatami mats on to the concrete floor of what had once been the shop, Nemoto apologised for the poor state of the place, but invited Takuya to come through into the living-area. When they were both inside, Nemoto knelt on the mats, placed his hands in front of him and bowed low to Takuya, thanking him for his kind guidance during their time together at headquarters. This polite reception embarrassed Takuya, but fond memories of Nemoto's devoted service during the war made him feel slightly more at ease.

As Nemoto moved to prepare a pot of green tea, his expression betrayed a growing suspicion as to the reason behind his guest's sudden appearance. When Nemoto knelt down again on the faded tatami mats, Takuya explained himself in a very calm, matter-of-fact manner. Nemoto, who knew about Takuya's involvement in the executions, quickly grasped the seriousness of this being found out by the occupation authorities.

Takuya went on to explain that he wanted to take refuge on the island and asked if Nemoto would help him find work.

Nemoto nodded and said, 'I understand. You're welcome to stay here with us in the meantime. As you can see, it's not the grandest place in the world, but what little we have is yours to use as your own.'

Takuya told him about the situation in Fukuoka and the other cities and towns he had seen from the trains in the last few days. As he described the bustle of the black market in Osaka, the village merchant in Nemoto seemed to rekindle and he keenly questioned Takuya about the things being sold in the market. During the war his family had opened a general store, but shortage of saleable goods had eventually put them out of business.

'Do you think it will be long before we can start buying things to sell again?' asked Nemoto earnestly.

'I have no idea,' replied Takuya. 'Everybody seems to be stretched just getting enough food to feed themselves these days.'

The rattle of the sliding glass door being pulled across was followed by the high-pitched voice of a small child. Nemoto got to his feet, stepped down on to the concrete floor and whispered something to those who had just come in. A little girl, five or six years old, peeped round the door at Takuya.

Nemoto stepped back into the room, followed first by a woman of about thirty and then by an elderly lady. He introduced the older woman as his mother and the younger as his wife. Both women bowed politely, the mother affording her guest a friendly smile as she thanked Takuya for the guidance and kindness he had shown her son during the war. It struck Takuya as somewhat unusual that, despite the fact that Nemoto was no more than twenty-four or twenty-five, he was already married with a daughter not too far from primary-school age.

As the two women led the little girl through the door into the next room, Takuya leant toward Nemoto and whispered that he did not want his part in the executions known to either of them. Nemoto nodded without saying a word.

That evening, Takuya sat with Nemoto's family at the low table in the living-room. The meal was rice gruel flavoured with pieces of potato, along with a little pile of tiny dried fish on a separate plate. In front of Takuya there was also one egg. Despite Nemoto's protestations, Takuya moved the egg across beside the little girl's chopsticks.

After the meal Takuya pulled the bag of rice out of his rucksack and gave it to the younger woman. Nemoto tried to refuse this contribution also, but Takuya, insisting, pushed the bag back into the woman's hands and pulled the cords closed on his rucksack. Seemingly resigned to accepting the gift, Nemoto guided Takuya to the third room, at the back of the house. Laying himself down on a futon for the first time in longer than he cared to remember, and soothed by the sound of the waves on the shore, Takuya soon fell into a deep sleep.

The next morning Takuya awoke just after nine. Nemoto's wife was nowhere to be seen, and the grandmother was looking after the little girl. After eating a late breakfast he shut himself away again in his room at the back of the house. It was one thing to give them a bag of rice, but he knew there was bound to be a limit to how long they would be prepared to share their food with him. While the older lady seemed quite happy with his presence, it was clear from the wife's expression that such feelings of generosity were not shared by all the family.

Occasionally Nemoto went out on an errand of one sort or another, but he seemed to spend most of his time sitting in the living-room next to the old shop part of the house. Whenever

Takuya came through to see him, he quickly placed an extra cushion on the tatami mat and poured him a cup of green tea. On one such occasion, ill at ease about having mistakenly assumed that Nemoto's being unmarried would make it easier to impose upon him, Takuya asked about the man's family.

'I didn't know you had a wife and child.'

Nemoto looked down at the floor. 'She's my elder brother's wife. He was killed during the war, so when I came back it fell to me to look after his wife and child. His daughter being so young . . . I felt sorry for her,' he said almost in a whisper.

The man's sincerity impressed Takuya, but more important, he now realised that the unusual situation the wife found herself in, losing her first husband and then being married to her brother-in-law, probably explained the hard, unfeeling look in her eyes.

'Any sort of work is fine, but can you help me get a job? I want to be able to look after myself, to rent my own place,' said Takuya. Nemoto didn't seem too concerned about putting Takuya up a little longer, but his wife gave the impression that their guest was quickly outstaying his welcome.

'Finding a place to live shouldn't be a problem, but work is another story. My wife has a job at a new salt refinery, built just a few months ago, but she's one of the lucky ones. There's just no work here. The fishermen have no fuel to take their boats out on to the water, and you can see how I spend my time, twiddling my thumbs because I have nothing to sell. Some people loaded themselves up with dried fish and kelp and went to Kobe to sell it, but most of them had it confiscated by the police when they arrived at the port, so no one goes any more,' explained Nemoto mournfully.

Takuya realised that he'd miscalculated the prospects of setting himself up in the village. There might be massive shoals of fish in the sea, but that counted for nothing if the fishermen lacked the means to get out on the water. It probably wasn't only a problem of fuel, either. They were just as likely to be short of the tools of their trade as everyone else around them.

'This is a fishing-village, so it's as good as dead if the fisher-men can't take their boats out. All that's keeping their hopes up is the rumour that special fuel rationing might be on the way. During the war hardly any fishing was done, so the fishing-grounds around here are full of fish waiting to be caught. If the fishermen can take their boats out, the number of jobs will start to increase. I doubt there'll be anything where you could use your university training, but something will come up to get you by. You've just got to wait a little while,' said Nemoto, trying to reassure his guest.

Nemoto was right; surely it wouldn't be too long before fuel got through to the fishermen. With agriculture obviously going to take more time to recover, stimulating the fishing industry was the quickest way to relieve the food shortages. So the government must be endeavouring to get fuel to the fishermen to help them feed the nation. Once fuel reached the village, Takuya thought, it would surely come back to life, and Nemoto's cash register would start to ring once again.

The request that he wait until then obviously implied an invitation to accept their hospitality for a little while longer, and this thought gave Takuya the fortitude he needed to endure the unwelcoming looks Nemoto's wife would doubtless cast in his direction. With gruel served at virtually every meal, the sack of rice he had given to Nemoto's wife should cover his food needs for at least a month. Takuya remembered that during their time in the army he had often shared his sake or rice crackers with Nemoto, so it was only natural that the man should help him now. As someone facing the prospect of death on the gallows, he must steel himself, he thought, and ignore the needs of others.

Takuya spent his days quietly in his room in the back of the house. Nemoto's wife was working on rotation with the other women of the village, two days on, then one day off. On her days off she either went down to the shore to look for kelp or shellfish, or went up into the woods behind the village to look for wild vegetables.

Soon Takuya noticed that Nemoto's family's attitude toward him seemed to be hardening from one day to the next. The wife avoided eye contact, and the grandmother's affable expression had disappeared altogether. Before he knew it, even Nemoto had less and less to say, and was clearly giving Takuya a wide berth by spending more time out of the house.

When eight days had passed since his arrival on the island, though he realised he was probably wasting his time, he asked Nemoto about his chances of finding a job. The family were finding it increasingly difficult to hide their annoyance at his presence, and this would obviously get worse the longer he stayed. He must find his own place to live, he thought.

'Well, there isn't . . .' said Nemoto, looking down to avoid Takuya's keen gaze.

'If there are no jobs at the moment, can you find me a place to live, then? I don't want to be a burden on your family,' said Takuya, hearing a hint of sarcasm in his own voice.

'A burden?' Nemoto's reply was barely audible, as though the thought had never entered his mind. But there was no doubt, thought Takuya, that Nemoto had been scolded by his wife for taking Takuya into their house, and was starting to regret making the decision.

'It's a very small village,' said Nemoto, still looking at the floor.

Takuya stared at the man's face, not quite understanding what he meant. Maybe this was a ploy to get the now unwelcome fugitive to leave his house.

'There are hardly ever any visitors in the village, so word spreads pretty quickly when someone does come. Everyone here knows that you're staying with us, and they're starting to ask me and my family a lot of questions. I've said that you're an officer from the same unit during the war, but . . .' Nemoto lifted his gaze. There was a glint in his eye as he plucked up the courage to speak his mind.

'I haven't said a word to my wife or my mother about you being on the run, but it's almost impossible to keep a secret on this island. I really don't think this is the best place for you to hide. I'm honoured that you thought to come here, but I'm starting to worry about the risk involved for you,' said Nemoto, his voice faltering at the end.

He clearly wanted Takuya to leave, but at the same time the genuine concern in his voice was unnerving. Takuya had not set foot outside Nemoto's house since the day he stepped off the ferry, but apparently the whole village was aware of his presence. He had thought a remote fishing-village would be an ideal place to hide, but now he realised that in fact the opposite was the case. Obviously he would be a fool not to take Nemoto's comments seriously.

Takuya pictured the heaving throng at the black market stalls in Osaka. He remembered shouldering his way through the crowd as hawkers on both sides of the narrow lane plied their wares in rough, husky voices. With each step he'd been jostled and pushed by those around him, but he recalled how losing himself in the crowd had produced a feeling of respite from the relentless tension of being on the run. Maybe he should seek refuge not in a quiet backwater but in a big city where he could more easily conceal himself.

'When's the next boat out? I want to leave,' said Takuya in an emphatic tone.

Nemoto looked taken aback, obviously worried that he had offended his guest. 'So soon? Please stay a little longer,' he said, a look of dismay in his eyes.

'No, you're right. It's not a good idea to stay here,' replied Takuya.

Nemoto implored him not to leave in such a hurry, but soon he gave in to Takuya's persistence about the ferry, and got to his feet and left the house to check the departure details.

A wave of apprehension came over Takuya at the thought of what might have been a fatal error of judgement in coming to this village. No doubt the police search would be both wide-ranging and focused on places where Takuya would be likely to seek refuge, so the addresses of his relatives, friends, and those close to him during the war would become targets of investigation. Nemoto's place would almost certainly come up eventually as a possible point of refuge for the police to check out. What on earth had made him come to such a dangerous place?

Now completely unnerved, Takuya looked furtively out of the window of the shop. A glum-looking old woman walked past with a young child clinging to her back. The sun beat down oppressively in the windless sky.

A few minutes later the glass door slid open and Nemoto stepped back into the house.

'There's a boat leaving for Kobe in thirty minutes. The next one after that is the day after tomorrow,' he said, kneeling down on the raised tatami mat.

'Good. I'll leave today,' said Takuya, and went through to the room at the back, where he grabbed his laundry off a piece of string drawn across the room and stuffed it into his rucksack. Nemoto looked anxious as Takuya stepped back into the living-room, ready to go.

'Why don't you go on the next boat, two days from now? This is a bit sudden, isn't it?' said Nemoto frantically.

'No, I'll go now. Thanks for putting me up. Give your family my regards,' said Takuya, sitting down to put on his shoes.

Nemoto went to the kitchen for a moment and returned with the bag of rice Takuya had brought. He placed it beside Takuya's rucksack, saying, 'Please take this with you. It's unopened.'

Takuya turned to look at Nemoto. 'I really am indebted to you. Keep it,' he said pushing the bag back into Nemoto's hands.

'No, I can't take it from you,' said Nemoto, looking embarrassed.

Takuya started lacing up his shoes. He knew he would need the rice to keep himself going on the run, so he did want to take it with him if he could. Nemoto was prepared to give it back, and there was no good reason not to go along with that. Takuya stood up, knowing Nemoto had just stuffed the bag of rice into his rucksack.

'You're too kind, you know,' he said, taking the rucksack from Nemoto and slinging it over his shoulder. He went outside and Nemoto followed, a couple of paces behind.

They walked down the road beside the river and crossed the bridge at the bottom of the slope. The water was running high so the tide must have come in. Half a dozen villagers standing on the jetty watched the two men approach. They smiled at Nemoto as he walked up to them. Takuya paid the fare to the man nearest the ferry and in return was given a piece of paper with the date and destination stamped on it in black ink. Holding the ticket, he turned and thanked Nemoto quietly for his kindness, and in response Nemoto stiffened to attention and bowed in military style.

The boat was brimming to the gunnels with passengers, many of them women and children. As Takuya threaded his way across the crowded deck to an empty spot near the prow, he wondered why so many of them were carrying such large loads of luggage.

The boat's engine rumbled to life and the rope was pulled free from the wooden bollard on the jetty. Takuya stood and looked to where Nemoto was standing with the other men. He waved briefly and Nemoto responded with a less exaggerated bow. The boat's horn sounded as the ferry moved away from the shore, and in moments Takuya had a clear view of the village and the hills behind it.

As he sat down again the reality of being a fugitive sank in once more. His uncle had wanted nothing to do with him, and his friend Nemoto had been able to offer safe haven for barely a week. Nemoto had been as honest and genuine as during their army days together, but an unemployed man with a family couldn't be expected to feed another mouth. The fact that he'd returned Takuya's rice unopened was a measure of his sincerity.

The thought of having taken back the bag of rice unopened made Takuya feel ashamed. They might only have served him rice gruel, but the knowledge that he had eaten their food for almost ten days and then come away with his own rice still untouched made him cringe with embarrassment. As he gazed out over the sea, his conscience troubling him, he caught sight of something glistening on the surface of the water. Almost instantly he realised that it was a school of flying fish, just like the ones he'd seen so often in the Uwa Sea offshore from his home in Shikoku. The noise of the boat's engine had probably sent the frightened fish jumping out of the water, skimming the surface before disappearing again with a tiny splash. Once the boat rounded the cape the shimmering fish were no longer in sight.

Takuya pondered his destination. He now felt sure that it would be dangerous to rely on any of his army friends, so obviously he should seek refuge with someone the police would never connect with him.

Recalling the names of those who had sent him New Year cards, he remembered Fujisaki Masahito, a friend living in Kobe. Fujisaki had been one year behind him at university, and the fact that his father was originally from Takuya's village had provided the two young men with something in common. The younger man had been exempted from military service on account of a bad limp, the result of a broken leg suffered in a fall down some stairs in his childhood. The New Year's message had said that their house had survived the bombing and that Fujisaki was helping to get the family business running again.

A police investigation would never trace him there, and as it was a big city he would have the advantage of being able to lose himself in the crowds. Takuya was inclined to pin his hopes of finding safe haven on Fujisaki, but having been turned away by his uncle and then having to leave Nemoto's house made him cautious. Wherever he went, it would be a struggle for people to ensure their own survival, let alone take on an outsider. And needless to say, being a fugitive was not going to help.

Gripped with anxiety, Takuya gazed out over the water until the glare off the sea made him squint and look away.

As his New Year card had suggested, Fujisaki's house was in a residential pocket of Kobe which had largely survived the ravages of the fire raids. Takuya had visited him twice during his university days, and the house looked just as it had then. He approached the house but went on past it, then stopped to lean on a lamp-post at the next street corner. After standing there nonchalantly for some time he turned back, but walked past once again without lifting a hand to open the latticed door.

He crossed the street and again paused under a lamp-post, this time turning casually to look towards the Fujisaki house. He could see strands of light leaking out from the edges of the blinds covering the windows. Because of his friendship with Fujisaki at university, Takuya felt sure that as long as he made the right approach and offered his bag of rice he could get them to put him up for at least a fortnight. But he wasn't so confident of Fujisaki's reaction if he told the full story about executing POWs and being on the run from the occupation authorities.

Memories of his time at Nemoto's house flooded back. Even with such a sincere former subordinate he had managed to last only eight days. Takuya tried hard to prepare himself first for astonishment and then for consternation at his unexpected appearance, feeling a foreboding he hadn't experienced when he'd left home for Osaka and then Shoodo-shima. At first the prospect of being tried by a victors' kangaroo court had made him determined to elude detection at any cost, but now, after a mere ten days, he was starting to flinch at the thought of relying on others. He felt preyed on by a mental weakness which would have been unthinkable in his army days.

Fighting back the anxiety, Takuya remembered the pride he had felt in being a lieutenant in the Imperial Army, and shuddered to think of the pathetic figure he cut standing there under the lamp-post. He stepped off the footpath and walked across the road to the house, stopping in front of the latticed door to the entrance before reaching to open it. Obviously it was locked from the inside, as it wouldn't budge.

He knocked lightly on the door frame. There was no reaction from within the house. When he knocked once more, a little louder, a light was switched on inside the glass door of the entrance.

'Who's there?' came a voice which Takuya recognised straight away as Fujisaki's.

'It's Kiyohara. Remember me from university?' said Takuya timidly.

He heard the scuffing of shoes over the concrete floor inside the entrance before the latticed door opened in front of him.

'Kiyohara san!' said Fujisaki, astonishment coming over his bespectacled face as he stood silhouetted by the electric light behind him. Takuya felt himself wavering as to what to do next. Obviously he would be invited inside, but he knew in his heart that he must explain himself before imposing any further.

'Can we talk out here? I want to tell you something,' said Takuya.

An incredulous look on his face, his friend stepped out beyond the latticed door and followed Takuya down the road. Takuya stopped and waited under the lamp-post for Fujisaki, who stared speechlessly at his unheralded guest. Takuya looked earnestly into Fujisaki's eyes and explained that he had fled from his own home after being cited as a war criminal, and that he had gone to Shoodo-shima but had to leave for Kobe to escape the little fishing-village's prying eyes.

'Can you put me up for four or five days, just until I find somewhere to hide? I've got some rice so I can feed myself,' said Takuya. But deep down he wanted to say a couple of weeks, or even a couple of months.

'You executed Americans? They'll hang you for that, won't they?' said Fujisaki with a hint of fear in his eyes.

Takuya nodded, thinking that Fujisaki must be unnerved at the idea of harbouring a fugitive.

'Anyway, come inside,' said Fujisaki, grasping Takuya by the arm.

'No, not yet,' he replied. 'Even if you say it's all right, what's your family going to say? Your father, in particular, must agree.'

Fujisaki stood thinking for a moment, then nodded, let go of his friend's arm, and turned to walk back to his house. Takuya watched him push open the door and disappear inside. Glancing furtively both ways down the dark street, Takuya hid himself in the shadows to one side of the lamp-post. The streets were deserted and dead quiet. The stars in the sky above were pale specks of light.

Takuya waited, staring at the latticed door. After a while he started to visualise Fujisaki sitting in front of his father, deep in conversation.

Suddenly the door opened and the two men seemed to step straight out of Takuya's dream on to the road. Fujisaki came out first, followed by his father, who was slightly balding on top but roughly the same height and physique as his son.

Takuya took off his army cap and bowed to the older man.

Fujisaki's father walked over to the illuminated area under the lamp-post. 'Come inside,' he said, grasping Takuya by the arm. He ushered him to the house and gestured for Takuya to step through the latticed door ahead of him. Inside the entrance, they took off their shoes and Takuya followed the other two down the narrow hall to a three-tatami-mat-sized room at the back of the house.

'It's not very big, but you're welcome to stay here until you decide on your next move,' said Fujisaki's father amicably before disappearing down the hall.

Takuya set his rucksack in a corner and sat down, after Fujisaki had swung out his bad leg to lower himself to the tatami floor. Takuya leant over and reached for his bag, from which he pulled out his sack of rice.

'I want you to take this,' he said, offering it to Fujisaki.

'You don't have to do that,' said his friend, fixing his eyes on the sack of rice.

'Take it, please. You can't put me up otherwise,' said Takuya.

Fujisaki nodded, got to his feet in the same awkward fashion, then carried the bag of rice out of the room and down the hall.

As Takuya pulled the cords tight on his rucksack he thought that he had done the right thing in taking the rice back from Nemoto. Without the rice he could never have brought himself to ask Fujisaki for shelter. Who knows, he thought, maybe the fact that he had his own supply of food had made the difference.

For the first time in days, he felt almost relaxed. He had given Fujisaki the equivalent of almost twenty-five days of government rice rations, which could always be blended with millet and other less nourishing grains.

*　　*　　*

The next morning Fujisaki asked Takuya to come through to the living-room and meet the rest of the family. He was married, and by the look of his wife – a frail-looking, pale young woman twenty-one or twenty-two years of age – she was not far away from giving birth. Fujisaki's mother was as friendly and welcoming as she had been when Takuya visited them as a student. She was now a little thinner, and the wrinkles on her face revealed how much she had aged over the past five or six years. Her questions about Takuya's hometown and her description of the night air raids on Kobe lacked none of the lively spirit Takuya remembered her for. As he answered her questions, it occurred to him that perhaps she had not been told the full story about his situation.

For breakfast they each had a bowl half full of rice gruel flavoured with a couple of thin slices of radish. Takuya joined the others round the table, the silence broken only by the occasional clicking of chopsticks. As he ate, Takuya looked across to Fujisaki and his young wife. There was certainly nothing out of the ordinary for a man of twenty-five, one year Takuya's junior, to be married and about to become a father, and as a couple they certainly gave the impression of being contented with their lot. Nevertheless, Takuya couldn't help being surprised that this delicate young woman, surviving on rations barely sufficient to keep herself going, was expecting a child. How much nourishment would rice gruel and radish provide for the baby? he thought. The fact that she was about to have a baby was testimony not only to her toughness but also to the strength of the family for not seeing this as anything out of the ordinary.

Takuya whiled away the hours in his room from morning till night from that day on. He borrowed a razor from Fujisaki and shaved each morning, washing himself in the cold tap water. The area behind the house was part of the workshop grounds, and he could hear the noise of the machines from his room. Power cuts were an everyday occurrence, and if he stood up, from the little window he could see the workers taking a rest, seated on wooden boxes.

Takuya felt quite uncomfortable at mealtimes. The usual fare was a combination of barley noodles, gruel and steamed bread flavoured with the odd piece of sweet potato, but occasionally they each had a whole sweet potato to themselves. Unlike at other times, the atmosphere round the dining-room table was decidedly gloomy, with no one saying a word. Though he had handed over his bag of rice, each time he sat down for a meal Takuya felt guilty that he was depriving them of part of their rations.

There's no way I'll be able to stay here long, he thought. In a fortnight Fujisaki's family will end up thinking the same way as Nemoto's. If it was just a matter of time, he mused, he must do everything in his power at least to delay the inevitable.

He took the demobilised soldier's certificate out of his inside pocket, recalling that Shirasaka had said that if he presented this to the local authorities he'd be able to get his share of rations. The false name he had written on it meant that it doubled as the papers he needed as a fugitive, and by using it to claim rations he could lessen the debt he owed the Fujisaki family.

Handing over the rice and giving them his ration allowance should at least help convince them of his goodwill on the food front, but spending every day in the little room at the back of the house doing nothing was undoubtedly a cause of annoyance to them. He was desperate to find a way to earn an income. But the country was overflowing with demobilised servicemen and residents returned from Japan's former empire, and with virtually all of the country's industrial and commercial sector destroyed there were very few potential employers. However much he might pound the pavements, there was little chance of finding work. Getting a job in Fujisaki's workshop would obviously be the best option by far.

That evening, Takuya asked Fujisaki if he could look at their university yearbook. Flipping through the pages, he found the name of a student from Okinawa, one year his senior, and began copying that man's name, Higa Seiichi, and Fujisaki's address, onto the demobilised soldier's card. When he had finished he called Fujisaki into his room and handed him the card, saying,

'If you show this to the people at the ward office they'll issue you a ration book. It's a false name, but you can claim the rations and use them for your family.'

Fujisaki looked down at the card and nodded.

'Then there's the matter of a job,' said Takuya. He explained to his friend that, if at all possible, he wanted to avoid being a freeloader, and so until he decided his next move, he wondered if there might be a job for him at Fujisaki's workshop.

Fujisaki seemed taken aback at the question, as his first reaction was to tilt his head to one side and knit his brow. But after a few moments he said, 'That isn't something I can decide by myself, but I'll speak to my father and see what he says.' With that he awkwardly got to his feet and left the room.

By now Takuya had come to realise that Fujisaki was a very different man from when he had been a student. At university he had been lively and extroverted, offsetting the fact that he had one bad leg. He'd been a broad-minded young man, not too carried away by issues, and not at all afraid to laugh out loud on occasion. There was little sign of those traits in Fujisaki any more. Working in the family business had obviously brought about some change in him, but his reaction to Takuya's request suggested that his heart wasn't in it and that he was just going through the motions. Even more worrisome was his increasingly brusque manner toward Takuya.

There was the sound of slippered footsteps in the hall, and the door to Takuya's room slid open.

'I've talked with my father, and he says orders are so low that we already have too many staff in the workshop. The only thing we might have for you to do would be making deliveries,' Fujisaki said, standing in the doorway.

'That's fine,' said Takuya, 'as long as I've got something to do.' He was a little uneasy, because it would of course take him out into the streets, but he could no longer bear the thought of doing nothing.

'I really feel bad letting you do that sort of work,' replied Fujisaki, with an embarrassed frown.

*   *   *

The next morning Takuya left the house with his demobilised soldier's card in his hand. Following Fujisaki's directions through the ruins, he soon came to the building being used as temporary municipal offices.

There was a hint of doubt in his mind as to whether the paper Shirasaka had given him would be safe to use, but the stamp of the Hakata office of the Western Region demobilisation office looked real, and the middle-aged man at the desk did not hesitate as he filled in the name 'Higa Seiichi' on the ration book.

Relieved at having passed the first hurdle, Takuya whispered his adopted name to himself. It sounded fine, almost suited him, he thought. From now on he would lead his life as Higa Seiichi. The name Kiyohara Takuya was a relic of his previous life and must play no part in his future.

When he got back to the house he handed the new ration book to Fujisaki, who was busy doing the company accounts in the living-room.

'I have a favour to ask of you,' Takuya said. 'Since I'll be walking around the streets making deliveries, I want to change the way I look. I'm a bit short-sighted, so I think perhaps I should start wearing glasses. Do you know of anywhere around here I can find them?' he asked.

Fujisaki tilted his head to one side for a few moments, looking thoughtful. 'The glasses I wore when I was in junior high school should still be in the drawer. In those days I didn't wear strong lenses, so they might actually be about right for you. I'll have a look,' he said, getting to his feet. He went up the narrow staircase across the hall.

When he handed the glasses to Takuya, he said, 'Well, they were there all right, but one sidepiece is missing.' They were basic black-rimmed glasses, just the sort junior high school children would wear. The left sidepiece was missing and the lenses were covered in a thin layer of whitish-grey dust.

Takuya blew on the glasses and wiped them with the cloth he had tucked into his belt. They were a bit strong, he thought, but probably wouldn't put any strain on his eyes. He attached some dark string to the left lens and hooked that over his ear.

Everything looked slightly blurred, almost as though he were looking at the outside world through a film of water.

Fujisaki led Takuya out of the back door to the factory area. In the corrugated-iron workshop a middle-aged man was pushing a foot pedal on the cutting-press, each movement of the machine producing a complete cardboard box ready to be folded into shape. A few metres away a man was brushing the company name in black ink through a thin metal stencil on to the cardboard, and beside him two women were working deftly to fold the boxes into shape and stack them to one side.

Takuya followed Fujisaki into the workshop, casually greeting each of the workers as they looked up from their tasks. Fujisaki introduced him to the man working the press as being from Okinawa, adding that he would be handling deliveries from now on. The cart he would be using was standing to one side. It had obviously seen better days, the wheels leaning inward and rust creeping along the handle frame, but it looked as though it could carry a decent load.

The next morning Takuya piled the cart high with boxes and pulled it out through the back gate. After passing several rows of houses which had survived the bombing, he walked down a road through the ruins, the sea now visible on his right, with a number of what looked like freighters anchored just offshore. The low range of hills straight ahead of him was covered in a thick blanket of green.

The cart creaked as it moved forwards. Takuya slowly wound his way downhill, straining against the handle with every step to keep it from getting away from him. The effort required him to stop more and more often. Sweat poured down his brow and clouded the lenses of his glasses.

At last he reached his destination, an improvised warehouse owned by a box wholesaler, hastily constructed down on the reclaimed land along the wharves. A surly-looking old man sitting in a shack marked 'Reception' took the delivery documents without saying a word. Then he got to his feet and waved his approval for the cart to be taken into the warehouse. After a quick check to see if the load matched the documents, the old man grunted that Takuya should unload his cargo and take it to the back of the big shed, where boxes and bags of all shapes and sizes were stacked neatly in rows.

After getting the man to stamp 'Received' on the job sheet, Takuya picked up the handle of his cart and started to retrace his steps to Fujisaki's factory. People had already begun building shelters here and there among the charred ruins. Men and women walked along the road, others rode past him on bicycles. Determined to avoid the gaze of passers-by, Takuya fixed his eyes on the ground ahead of him whenever someone approached.

No one around him could be trusted any more, he thought. Since the surrender, the newspapers had been full of articles espousing the tenets of democracy, renouncing in no uncertain terms anything to do with the politics or military of wartime Japan. The Imperial Army came in for the strongest criticism. Without fail, the thrust of the commentary was that Japanese militarists had started the war and that the Allied powers had had no choice but to respond in kind. Those charged with war crimes were cited as symbolising the outrages committed by the defunct Imperial Army, and without exception those writing the articles supported the measures being taken to rid the earth of such reprehensible criminals. On the radio, too, there were broadcasts exposing atrocities committed by the Imperial Army and denouncing those charged with war crimes. Ordinary Japanese citizens were nothing less than victims of the war, with the blame laid fairly and squarely on the military.

It seemed that, in keeping with such media coverage, the people in the streets would be falling into line with the intended message. Among the comments of prominent leaders of public opinion there had even been drastic statements to the effect that imposing the ultimate penalty upon war criminals was a requisite for establishing democracy in Japan.

Assuming this represented the new rationale for society, every passer-by was potentially as much an enemy for Takuya as the occupation authorities or the police. Any one of them who found out that he was charged with war crimes would be likely to go straight to the authorities. SCAP must know that he was on the run, so pictures of him would be on the walls of police stations all over the country. Each moment he spent in the public eye was fraught with danger. The only solace, he thought, was that confusion still reigned in Japan's cities. But that too might be false, for while the increase in crime involving vagrants and prostitutes must be keeping the police occupied, instructions from SCAP would surely give efforts to find and arrest war crimes suspects priority.

When he reached the factory Takuya sat down wearily on a straw mat inside the workshop door. He was exhausted from his labours, and the mental strain of cringing each time a passer-by cast more than a glance in his direction had taken its toll. Still, he was pleased that the day's work had at least slightly lessened the weight of his debt to the Fujisakis.

Looking through that day's newspaper, he saw that eleven Allied nations, headed by the United States, had charged twenty-eight military and political leaders, including former prime minister Tojo Hideki, as Class A war criminals. The acts in question were said to have been committed between 1928 and 1945, and fell into three major categories: conspiracy to commit aggression, aggression, and conventional war crimes, these last being further broken down into fifty-five separate counts. The article went on to state that the International Military Tribunal would first be considering charges against the Class A war criminals, and that the arrest and trial of the Class B and C suspects would soon follow. It closed with the comment that 'War criminals are the enemies of mankind, utterly repulsive beasts of violence.'

As he read the list of the twenty-eight men charged as Class A, he imagined that they would all end their days on the gallows. If this article was a reflection of current public opinion, the average Japanese citizen would agree with the Allied position, and therefore would no doubt call for the execution of all those implicated in such crimes. Who knows? he thought, maybe even Fujisaki and his family saw him as a 'beast of violence' for his part in killing the American airmen. He felt uneasy at the thought that he might not be safe where he was after all.

Power cuts were still happening every day, and production in the workshop languished far short of that required to generate any sort of profit. In one sense, the lack of electricity was a blessing in disguise, as without sufficient paper the workshop could not run to full capacity anyway. Takuya's delivery duties were limited to once every three days, and he spent the rest of his time picking up cardboard offcuts and bundling them for fuel, or sweeping the workshop and the open space behind the house.

Fujisaki's mother's attitude toward Takuya had changed discernibly. She often muttered, 'Getting rations is all very well, but stretching what we get to feed us all isn't so easy.' The amount and quality of the rations were now even worse than during the war. The designated staple, rice, was more often than not substituted with corn flour, potatoes or wheat bran, and the vegetable allocation was down to one giant radish per week, to be thinly sliced and divided up among several households. She often went out to the countryside with her son, hoping to barter a few articles of clothing for anything to help supplement the food rations.

The family's only entertainment was listening to the radio. Takuya sometimes joined them in the living-room to listen to the day's broadcast. There were programmes providing details about soldiers returning from overseas, and others for people seeking information on the whereabouts of family members in the armed forces. One interview with an economist made Takuya feel quite uncomfortable sitting in the living-room with Fujisaki and his family.

The economist forecast that Japan was on the verge of a food crisis of cataclysmic proportions, stating that the official current allocation of rice to each individual was barely enough to avoid starvation, and that when this absolute minimum requirement was calculated for the total population, the amount was almost twice the size of the previous year's total rice harvest. From this he deduced that at least ten million people would starve to death, and that most of them would be living in urban areas. He went on to say that no rice had reached Tokyo and other big cities for the last twenty days, and closed by saying that city residents must be prepared to eat grass to avoid starvation.

From around that time on, Fujisaki and his father both became increasingly taciturn. After dinner they either played games or sat silently reading the newspaper, neither one looking at Takuya. Takuya had no choice but to excuse himself as soon as the family had finished eating dinner.

More often than not, Takuya spent his evenings sitting in the little room at the back, squashing the fleas crawling over his clothes. Most of those he dispatched were a pinkish colour, gorged with blood which spilt out on to his fingernails as he crushed them. Occasionally he would hold a piece of underwear up to the electric light and find lines of delicately formed eggs, like tiny rosary beads, sitting neatly inside the stitching. He pierced each of them individually with a needle before going on to check the next piece of clothing. Other times, after he had got under the covers on his futon, he would take the pistol out of his rucksack and caress it in the semi-darkness. He wiped the barrel with a cloth and tested the tension of the trigger with his index finger. When he held it up to his nose, he could just detect the faint smell of gun oil.

In May, the opening of the International Military Tribunal for the Far East proceedings against Class A war criminals received daily coverage in the newspapers.

The attitude of the Fujisaki family to Takuya grew colder with each passing day. He had asked them to put him up for four or five days when he first arrived on their doorstep, but that was now more than three weeks ago. Though he was supposedly working to earn his keep, pulling the cart to the warehouse three times a week would hardly make the Fujisakis regard him as anything other than a freeloader. Almost certainly they would be reading the newspaper coverage of the war crimes trials, and by now could only see Takuya as an increasingly unwelcome guest.

On his way to the box wholesaler's warehouse one day in mid-May, as he guided his cart down a gentle slope in the middle of the ruins Takuya noticed two policemen walking up the road towards him. He regretted having pushed up the peak of his service cap so he could wipe the sweat off his brow, but he could hardly pull it down over his eyes now, so he simply trudged forward, looking at the ground as though he were tired out.

He edged the cart farther over to the other side of the road, away from the approaching policemen, his heart pounding furiously and cold sweat pouring down his neck.

The two policemen approached Takuya and his cart and then passed by, but just as he thought he was in the clear he heard one of the men say, 'You, there. Stop.'

Takuya felt the blood drain from his face, leaving him white and chilled. His first thought was to drop his cart and run for his life, but his feet were anchored to the spot. He turned half round sheepishly.

The closer of the two policemen stepped over to the cart and put one hand on the folded cardboard boxes. Bending over slightly, he lifted up each box in turn to look in the gaps between them.

'Where are these going?' he said, moving round in front of the cart. Takuya pulled the job slip from the inside pocket of his jacket, which was stuffed down in the load of cardboard boxes. He realised that the policeman was only checking to see if the load included any controlled goods, but all the same he was afraid that he might get a clear look at his face. The scar on his left cheek from where he'd cut himself on a branch as he fell from a tree as a child was still clearly visible, and the thought that this might give him away started a wave of panic which threatened to overcome him.

'Anything besides boxes on the cart?' asked the policeman, casting only a cursory glance at the paper before switching his gaze back to Takuya's face.

'No, nothing else,' said Takuya in a muffled voice.

The other policeman had by now moved round to the front of the cart. 'You're as white as a sheet, and the sweat's streaming off you. Something wrong with you?' he said, with a suspicious look in his eyes.

'Yeah . . . I came back from China with tuberculosis, but I have to work to buy food,' said Takuya, pursing his parched lips.

'Tuberculosis?'

'Yeah.'

'What's your name?'

'Higa Seiichi.'

'Higa?' said the policeman in a sceptical tone.

'Hi-ga,' said Takuya, tracing the characters out on top of the cardboard boxes. 'From Okinawa. It's a common name there.'

'Okinawa?' replied the policeman, apparently happy to leave it at that. The stern look had melted from his face as he ran his eyes once more over the cart and its load.

Satisfied that all was in order, he turned back to Takuya. 'You went white as a sheet when you saw us coming. So we thought something was amiss. If you're just ill, we won't hold you up any longer. On your way,' he said, and nodded to his colleague that they, too, should be off.

Takuya picked up the bar at the front of the cart and stepped off down the slope, feeling another deluge of sweat stream down his face. The policemen had probably mellowed at the mention of Okinawa, the only part of the Japanese homeland where combat had taken place. Shirasaka's advice had paid off in an unexpected way.

As Takuya manoeuvred the cart down the gentle incline, he chastised himself for the stupidity of his behaviour with the police. It was pathetic that losing his composure had obviously made them suspicious and led to their questioning him. Since being warned by Shirasaka in Fukuoka that he should flee, he had been back home and then on to Shoodo-shima after travelling through Osaka, and had caught sight of policemen on any number of occasions, but never had he been as intimidated as today. The incident with these two policemen brought home how much his nerve had weakened in this last month on the run. If he panicked every time he came across the police, it wouldn't be long before he gave himself away and was arrested. He longed somehow to instill in himself the backbone he had before the war ended.

Takuya recalled the policeman's intent gaze as he asked the questions. Although the glasses he'd borrowed from Fujisaki might have helped obscure it from view, the officer must have caught at least a fleeting glimpse of the scar on Takuya's cheek. Slipping the net this time didn't necessarily mean he'd be so lucky next time round, because the policemen could surely match what they had seen of his face today with the 'Wanted' posters they no doubt had on the wall back at the police station. If one of them did happen to see a resemblance, it wouldn't be difficult to go one step further and trace Takuya to Fujisaki's place through the box wholesalers. Suddenly the idea of Kobe as a safe haven was eclipsed by that of its being a trap ready to snap shut.

On the way back to the factory after dropping off his cartload of boxes at the warehouse, Takuya observed something that made him uncomfortable. To avoid the spot where he'd been questioned by the police, he took a detour through the busy streets near a bustling black market, where he saw a young American soldier with a Japanese girlfriend. The American was very tall, well over six feet, but the lithe young woman with him was also of impressive height for a Japanese.

She would have been twenty-one or twenty-two, had attractive, clearly defined features and a figure that suited the western clothes she was wearing. Her conservative make-up suggested that she was no streetwalker. On the contrary, she was probably from a good family. The two approached at a leisurely pace, her fingers entwined in his.

Forgetting his fear of American soldiers, Takuya watched the young woman, mesmerised. There was no mistaking the fact that she was delighted to be out walking with an American soldier. To Takuya, who had never seen Japanese couples holding hands like this in public, there was something lewd and inappropriate about the way the American and the young woman were behaving. But her relaxed smile made it clear that she paid no heed to the disapproving eyes turned their way.

Takuya could not understand how a young woman of her obvious breeding could have become familiar with an American soldier in the first place. It was inconceivable to him that someone who could surely manage an admirable match among her own should want to be seen walking hand in hand with a low-ranking American soldier. The couple walked past Takuya, the young woman leaning against her suitor.

Disheartened with the world, Takuya pulled his cart along the road between two lines of buildings that had been spared the ravages of the fire-bombing. There seemed to be an increasing number of people walking out on the streets.

Upon taking half a dozen more steps, he caught sight of another American soldier and his Japanese date. This couple were approaching on the footpath on the other side of the street, both laughing out loud at some private joke. Her showy clothes and garish make-up pointed clearly to her being a prostitute. The tall American had his arm round her shoulders, while his much shorter girlfriend had hers round his waist.

Takuya picked up his pace as he left the city centre and came back out onto the road between two broad expanses of burnt-out ruins.

That night he told Fujisaki that he wanted to move on to another city and asked if he would help him find a job. Fujisaki nodded, the relief on his face unmistakable.

Takuya took the following day off from work, saying he had a fever. He lay in his room, visualising over and over again the American soldier walking with his tall Japanese girlfriend. He tried to understand how this woman could walk hand in hand so jovially with someone who just nine short months ago had been the enemy. Had she forgotten that the Americans had destroyed Kobe and most other cities of any size in Japan? Had her anger with the American military for dropping atomic bombs on Japan and killing and maiming countless civilians already disappeared? It was to be expected that such bitterness would diminish with the passage of time, but surely the degree of fraternisation she displayed was unnaturally premature. But then again, the US military wanted for nothing, so associating with them would be beneficial in more ways than one. Maybe this explained her intimacy with the American, but somehow it had seemed more innocent than that, free of any ulterior motive. The faint, portentous rumble he had heard from the blast of the atomic bomb on Hiroshima. The horrific damage report from Ohmura air base after he had tracked the flight path of the two B-29s headed for Nagasaki. Obviously, the young woman had already stopped thinking about the tens of thousands who had died in those two attacks.

The thought of staying in Kobe and seeing many more scenes of such fraternisation was too much to bear. He wasn't just on the run, he thought, he was still at war. The feeling of the sword in his hand as its blade cut into the American airman's neck was still fresh in his mind, and the woman's name that the man had repeated over and over again as he sat there waiting in the bamboo grove still rang in his ears. That in the context of the same conflict there could be such a difference between himself and this woman baffled him. It was almost as though she had purged herself of all recollection of the war as she walked holding hands with the tall American.

Takuya had skipped breakfast and lunch that day, but his hunger pangs were so strong by late afternoon that he joined the family in the living-room for the evening meal of rice gruel.

Fujisaki's father asked if Takuya would be interested in going to Himeji. He explained that the owner of a company making matchboxes had set up a temporary office in Kobe to arrange the purchase of building materials needed to rebuild his burnt-out factory in Himeji. He went on to say that when he had telephoned this man about a job he had been told that, if Takuya was a good, reliable worker, he'd be prepared to take him on.

'What did you say about me?' asked Takuya.

'I told him that your name is Higa, and that you're a returned serviceman originally from Okinawa. I said that I'd given you some work as a favour to a friend.'

Takuya thanked Fujisaki's father and asked him to go ahead with the introduction. The chance to leave Kobe could not have come at a better time, he thought.

It was raining the next day.

Takuya left the house with the simple map that Fujisaki's

father had drawn for him. Rain dripped steadily off the peak of his cap, and he could feel the collar of his shirt becoming uncomfortably damp from the water trickling down his neck. His glasses kept clouding over, but he felt exposed without them, so there was no way he would take them off just for the sake of being able to see properly.

Fujisaki's father had mentioned a temporary office, but the factory chief was obviously just renting the premises of a vacant shop, whose old wooden sign above the door, paint flaking off at the edges, proclaimed it to be a fish shop. A desk was placed squarely in the middle of the concrete floor.

When Takuya stepped inside and announced himself, the glass door at the back of the room slid open and a diminutive man with close-cropped grey hair poked his head out to peer at Takuya. When he explained that he had come on the introduction of Fujisaki's father, the man, who was maybe fifty-five or fifty-six years old, stepped down on to the concrete floor and sat at the desk, pointing to a low stool for Takuya to sit on.

When asked about his background, Takuya said that he had been born in Okinawa and that after finishing high school he had joined the army, first being posted to Manchuria and then moving on to Kyushu as part of an air defence unit. He said he had finished the war as a lance-corporal and was twenty-six years old.

'Where are your parents?' the man asked.

Takuya replied that they were still living in northern Okinawa. The central and southern areas of Okinawa had been the scene of intense fighting, so he thought that saying his parents were alive, but in the north, seemed a more natural response.

The man explained that the preparations for rebuilding his factory in Himeji were all but complete. 'I'll give you a job. We're taking all the stuff I've collected here back to Himeji tonight by truck. Might be a bit rushed, but there's space for you on the truck. Can you go with us?' he asked.

'Yes, I can,' replied Takuya, without a second's hesitation.

'OK. Then be back here by late this afternoon. Regarding

your wage, we'll feed you, so how does six yen a day sound?'
he asked.

'That's fine,' said Takuya. It was more than enough, he
thought. His younger brother was getting almost four hundred
yen a month, but had said that he was doing pretty well if he
had more than one hundred and fifty yen left after food costs
were covered.

Takuya expressed his gratitude, bowed and left the 'office'.
The man seemed likeable. He might be running a factory, but he
seemed quite down-to-earth, much more humble than Takuya
had expected for a man in his position. The fact that Himeji
wasn't as big a city as Kobe meant that food would probably
be more readily available, and being able to leave that very day
was a stroke of luck. The rain began to ease off, with only an
odd drop disturbing the puddles here and there.

The promise of a steady income eased Takuya's mind, and
he thought that this might be an opportune time to do some
shopping with the money he'd been given by his father. If
possible he wanted to buy some new clothes and rid himself
of the army issue he'd been wearing since leaving his parents'
house in Shikoku.

Takuya trudged off toward the station. He knew clothes
weren't cheap, but he thought he could at least get a new hat.
Coming out on to a crowded street, he turned right and followed
the flow of pedestrians until he found himself in the middle of the
black market, a collection of shacks reinforced with old pieces of
corrugated iron. Most of the stalls were selling food, tobacco or
soap, and there was no sign of any clothing for sale.

After searching about ten minutes, he found a stall selling
shoes. There were leather boots of the kind worn by officers,
Air Force pilots' shoes and infantrymen's shoes lined up in
rows on sheets of newspaper, along with what looked like
virtually worn-out low-cut civilian shoes. In one corner of the
display there were several hats piled one on top of the other.
Takuya stepped over to that part of the table and began looking
through the hats. Most of them were military caps of one kind
or another, but there was one that was a bit different, the sort

of hat mountaineers would wear. He picked it up and tried it on. It was quite a good fit.

'How much is this?' he asked the young hawker who was sitting, legs splayed, on an apple box behind the display table. Takuya almost fell over when the young man replied, 'Eighty yen.' How could one hat be worth the equivalent of two weeks' wages at the job he was about to start? 'You can't make that a bit cheaper, can you?' he said to the hawker.

'It's almost new. This isn't cheap synthetic fibre, it's one hundred per cent cotton. OK, I'll do you a favour and knock the price down ten yen. That's the best I can do. Look how thick the material is. This is a quality product here,' he said, still perched self-assuredly on his apple box. The manner of this well-built young man reminded Takuya of the haughtiness of pilots just out of cadet training, who were known for carrying themselves as though they were a cut above everyone else.

Takuya stood and thought for a moment. He wouldn't have another chance to buy a hat, and if for seventy yen he could change his appearance and thereby make himself a little safer, maybe it wasn't so expensive after all.

He took seven ten-yen notes from the inside pocket of his jacket and handed them to the hawker in return for the hat. The young man counted the notes without saying a word, before stuffing them into his trouser pocket and looking past Takuya for the next customer.

As he walked away from the stall, Takuya took off his old service cap and put on the mountaineer's hat. A satisfied smile came to his face as he realised not only that the size was just right, but also that the brim of the hat would cover part of his face, just as his army cap had done.

The smell of food whetted his appetite. Sure that he had long overstayed his welcome at the Fujisakis', Takuya felt decidedly uncomfortable whenever he joined them for a meal. The idea of getting something to eat here in the market was appealing, and it would save him having to impose on them at mealtime again. Crowds were milling around in front of the men and women hawking plates of boiled *oden*, curry and rice, fried fish and bowls of rice gruel. He threaded his way across the flow to a little tin shack with a notice in front advertising bowl-size servings of tempura on rice. He placed his order and the middle-aged woman on the other side of the table scooped two helpings of rice into a bowl and passed it to the man standing next to her, her husband evidently, to put some pieces of vegetable tempura on top and pour on some broth before handing it to Takuya as he sat down at the table.

The deep-fried vegetables were more batter than anything else, but the rice and the broth poured on top were both piping hot and delicious. Takuya savoured each grain of rice and each sip of broth, reluctant to swallow them and cut short the ecstasy. Finishing every last scrap in the bowl, he pulled out two ten-yen notes from his pocket and handed them to the woman. It was somewhat ironic, he thought as he moved away from the tin shack, that there was so much food here in the black market when not far away the talk was of ten million people facing death by starvation.

When he got back to the Fujisakis' that day, the father told him that he had just spoken on the telephone to the factory owner who had offered Takuya the job earlier. Evidently the man from Himeji had been so impressed with Takuya's courteous and well-spoken manner that he was very keen to take him on.

'Everything he has now he has earned by the sweat of his brow, so if you work hard it won't go unnoticed,' said Fujisaki's father in an unusually cheerful tone.

Going to his room, Takuya took his clean loincloths and shirts down off the improvised washing-line and stuffed them into his rucksack before retracing his steps down the corridor to the living-room, where Fujisaki, in his mother's absence, handed over the ration book Takuya had lent them.

Kneeling on the tatami mats in front of Fujisaki and his father, Takuya expressed his gratitude for their hospitality, bowing so low that his forehead almost touched the floor. He repeated the performance for Fujisaki's wife when she came out of the kitchen. The slowness of her movements suggested that she was not too far from giving birth.

He went out to the factory and politely said goodbye to each of the workers before stepping out through the door at the back on to the road. The rain had stopped, and the sun was trying to force its way out from behind the clouds.

6

After dark the rain started falling again; it was light at first, but soon turned into a veritable downpour.

In the back of the truck there was a stack of corrugated iron, obviously salvaged from one or more bomb sites, a large box of nails and a collection of carpenter's tools. Terasawa, the man who had hired him, climbed up under the truck's hood with a pile of bedding in his arms and sat down behind the driver, a young man by the name of Kameya. Takuya sat down on the precariously small seat to the left of Kameya.

The engine roared to life and off they went into the rain. The hood stretched far enough forward to protect the driver from the elements, but the left side of Takuya's body was fully exposed to the rain. Soon his left trouser leg was so wet that spray came up from the saturated cloth, and in no time at all his left shoe felt as though it was filling up with the water running down his leg. His glasses were covered with drops of water, so he put them away in the inside pocket of his jacket.

Kameya did his best to avoid the potholes along the way, but once they came out on to the main road the ride was so bumpy that Takuya had to hold on tightly for fear of being bucked right out of the vehicle.

Occasionally a powerful beam of light would approach from behind. Each time Kameya pulled over to the left and slowed to a crawl as the light closed on them. There would be a tremendous blast from a horn and a US Army truck or Jeep would rumble past them.

'The Ame-chan scare me something wicked,' said Kameya, his eyes fixed on the road ahead. 'The other day I saw a truck driven by a Japanese overtake an American Jeep. The Jeep sped up and forced the truck off the road. They dragged the driver out of the cab and beat the living daylights out of him.'

After another hour of driving through the rain they pulled over and parked in an open space beside the road. The strain of trying to avoid the deeper-looking puddles and keeping a grip on the steering-wheel as the truck bounced in and out of big potholes had obviously taken its toll on Kameya.

When they came to a complete stop, Terasawa asked where they were. 'Just past Suma' was Kameya's reply.

After a short break they were back on the move. The going seemed a little easier once the rain eased off somewhat, but the truck's engine was straining so much that it sounded as though it might blow up any moment. After crossing a long bridge, they turned right and followed the road running along the embankment on one side of a river.

'This is Himeji,' said Kameya. Before long the neat row of houses came to an end, and wide, empty spaces opened up on both sides. The truck's headlights illuminated the area in front of them, and Takuya realised straight away that they were driving through another vast tract of bombed urban wasteland.

The truck turned into a narrow lane before stopping in front of some ramshackle houses.

Takuya stepped out of his side of the cab after Kameya had alighted from the right. His jacket and trousers were wet and heavy from the rain, and he felt chilled to the bone. Not far away he could see a train, the line of dim lights from its carriages chugging off to the right through the red-tinted smoke belching out from its smokestack. Takuya followed Terasawa and Kameya into the house.

Terasawa disappeared off to the other end of the house, while Kameya pulled a couple of futons from a pile of bedding in a corner of the room next to the entrance. After helping to set them out, Takuya stripped off his wet clothes, put on a dry shirt and loincloth he'd kept in his rucksack, and lay down on the futon.

As he closed his eyes, he could hear the train whistle in the distance.

He awoke to the sound of Terasawa's voice. Kameya pushed aside his bedcovers and sat up, rubbing his eyes. The rain had stopped and the morning sun shone brightly.

The clothes he had been wearing the previous day were still wet but, carrying his towel, Takuya followed Kameya outside dressed in his shirt and loincloth. Terasawa was standing with his hands cupped under the end of a broken water pipe sticking out of the ground, washing his face.

Takuya stood beside the lead pipe and surveyed the area around them. In every direction scorched ruins stretched endlessly toward the horizon.

His gaze settled on a point away to the north. Takuya had been on Sanyo line trains through this area before, but as it had always been at night he had never actually set eyes upon what was left of Himeji city. He knew that Himeji's White Egret Castle was one of the most famous of its kind in the country, but seeing it there in the distance, towering majestically above this desolate wasteland, rooted him to the spot in awe. The main donjon and a smaller one nestled into its side seemed to soar above the castle's steep white walls. Maybe it was because the air was so clear after the rain, but the whiteness of the donjon and turret walls seemed unusually bright in the morning sun, in vivid contrast to the green of the trees on the slopes surrounding the castle.

The sight of the castle, untouched in the middle of this scorched wilderness littered with rubble and burnt roofing iron, was bizarre. It must have been caught in the same firestorm that consumed the town, but as far as Takuya could tell, there was no trace of damage.

'The town was burnt beyond recognition. The Kawanishi Aircraft Works were just to the east of the castle, so they pounded that whole strip on the twenty-second of June, and then a really big fire raid on the night of the third of July burnt most of what was left. This area was hit on the same night,' said Terasawa, wiping his face and neck as he gazed out over the ruins.

'The castle did well to survive all that,' said Takuya, staring at its white walls in the distance.

'The night of the big fire raid, we fled up into the hills. When we came back the next day the castle was standing there, untouched. Everything around it had been burnt to ashes. Some of the pine trees just outside the castle walls caught fire and burnt, but the castle itself was unscathed. I can't tell you how happy I was when I saw it,' said Terasawa, keeping his eyes on the White Egret Castle as he went on to explain that most of the white plaster walls and the outlines of the moats had been camouflaged with netting because of concern that the castle would provide a perfect landmark for enemy bombers.

'The netting made her look really drab during the war, but when they took it off she was just as beautiful as she's ever been,' said Terasawa, obviously entranced by the sight of the castle and its towering white donjons.

Takuya's first job was to clear the burnt remnants of the previous set-up from the factory grounds. He and Kameya lived on site and two other men came in each day to work.

Terasawa's only son had been killed in the war in China, so he now lived alone with his wife.

The Himeji–Kobe area had boasted the highest number of factories manufacturing matches in Japan, and in contrast to the complete destruction of the factories within metropolitan Kobe, those concentrated along the coast near the town of Shirahama had somehow escaped the firestorms, and were continuing production with what poor materials were at hand. With matches already being produced, Terasawa was desperate to get his factory running again to make the boxes needed for them.

Terasawa's wife went out shopping virtually every day, coming back in the evenings with her rucksack full of food bought from acquaintances in farming-villages in the countryside or fishing-hamlets along the coast. She was a good-natured person who did her best to look after her husband's workers, sometimes even making shirts for them out of pieces of cloth she'd found along the way.

Trying to be as casual as he could, Takuya scrutinised the newspapers every day. He was most interested in anything concerning the investigations into Western Regional Command. Any information he could gather, he thought, must help him get a clearer picture of how safe, or indeed how dangerous, his situation was.

He found no coverage of matters concerning Western Regional Command, but there was a sudden spate of articles about the Class A war criminals, as well as details of those being tried overseas and in Japan for crimes in the B and C Classes. He couldn't help but notice that the words 'death by hanging' and 'death penalty' appeared frequently in all this writing. Both were used in an article about the verdict in a case against men found guilty of executing American airmen in Honshu. He read the article over and over again to himself.

One day towards the end of May, Takuya was poring over that morning's newspaper when he spotted an announcement made by a SCAP press secretary. It read: 'The Supreme Commander of Allied Powers in Japan has instructed the Japanese government to move immediately to freeze or confiscate any or all personal assets or property owned by people already arrested and incarcerated, or by criminals yet to be arrested and incarcerated. In particular, the possession of precious metals such as gold, platinum or coins, as well as stocks and bonds or bank deposit books will be subject to direct control.'

A harsh step indeed, thought Takuya. Not only would SCAP punish those found guilty of war crimes, but now it would go so far as to seize their property as well. If the individual had owned a house, the house and all its contents would be confiscated and the family turned out on to the street if the authorities saw fit. Surely this was no different from the laws of the feudal Edo period, which had punished a criminal's family for 'complicity by association'.

His mind drifted to his family back in Shikoku. His only property at his parents' house was his post office savings book and some government bonds, and his family wouldn't suffer in the least if those were confiscated. Even so, if the police decided to make a thorough search of the house, in the course of their investigation they would no doubt put considerable pressure on his parents and brother and sister to reveal what they might be hiding. Maybe they were even shunned by those around them for having spawned a war criminal.

Noticing that Takuya seemed preoccupied with one particular article, Terasawa's wife called out to him, her expression quite different than usual.

'Are you worried about your family back home? Is there something in there about Okinawa?' she asked sympathetically.

Takuya breathed a sigh of relief, reminded again that assuming an Okinawan identity had been a wise choice. If he could relegate Takuya Kiyohara to the past and become Higa Seiichi, maybe he would be able to lead a safe life from now on. In the short time since choosing it he had grown used to his new name. Maybe he was finally on the right track after all.

Despite long periods of heavy rain they made good progress clearing the factory grounds, and by the middle of June the task was complete. Terasawa had Kameya use the truck to bring in stacks of old boards, coils of wire and sheets of metal framing which he'd somehow acquired from merchants in town. Takuya and the other three men toiled away between downpours, following Terasawa's instructions as they laid the foundation for the new workshop.

The food situation in Himeji was just as bad as it had been in Kobe. Regulations governing the economy were still in place, and foodstuffs were subject to particularly strict control. The newspaper was full of articles about passengers at railway stations in the Himeji area being ordered off trains to have food they had bought or bartered at farms and fishing-villages confiscated. According to the newspaper, those caught transporting food more than once were charged under the economic control regulations, and all forms of black market activities were frowned on by the authorities.

In these circumstances, the food served in Terasawa's house became increasingly bland with each passing day. Most meals consisted of biscuits made from cornflower, salt and water, or bread baked with little pieces of sweet potato in it, and the only time rice appeared was in a thin soup or rice porridge. The Terasawas ate the same food as their live-in workers, and sometimes, as a special treat, Mrs Terasawa gave them some potato sweets or tobacco she had managed to buy on the black market.

The rainy season ended and summer came.

Prices continued to rise at a frightening pace. Postcards jumped from five sen to ten and then to fifteen in the space of a week. The monthly subscription rate for newspapers went from one yen and sixty sen to eight yen, and prices of goods on the black market virtually doubled overnight. Terasawa grumbled every day that he could barely keep up with the price rises on the building materials he needed to start up his factory again.

Takuya knew how fortunate he was to have found a job with Terasawa. In contrast to when he had had to sponge off Nemoto and Fujisaki, here he had a job, and the food on the table was part of the remuneration for his labour. Everyone, including the Terasawas, was friendly to him; all were quite happy calling him 'Higa' and obviously saw nothing suspicious about his claim to be from Okinawa. He was also completely used to wearing glasses, and by now was feeling a good deal more secure about his situation.

Occasionally, and quite unexpectedly, Takuya imagined that he heard something like the woman's name uttered over and over again by the American airman before he was killed. At other times, quite suddenly, he recalled the moment when his sword cut into the back of the airman's neck, and the strange sight of the man's knees jerking up violently came back to him. Each time this happened he felt unnerved, and more often than not he tried to calm himself down by furtively taking his pistol out of his rucksack and cleaning it behind the large pile of burnt iron and debris on the factory grounds.

If captured, he would be made to stand in the dock, told that he was to receive the death penalty, and then dragged to the gallows. When he imagined the agonising wait for that moment of truth, he thought it would be much better to take his own life. The American he had executed had managed to keep his composure to the end, but Takuya was not at all confident that he would be able to do the same.

There was still no word in the newspaper about the investigation of those in Western Regional Command. Shirasaka had already explained to him that high-ranking staff officers, including the commander himself, had been interrogated, and his younger brother had told him that the police had been to their house. But even so, it made him uneasy to think that there had been nothing in the newspaper about the executions, despite the fact that a good number of arrests must have been made by now.

When Takuya opened the newspaper after work on the twentieth of July, his eyes were drawn to a short article at the bottom of the front page. As he read it, his last vestiges of hope that the full truth about the executions would evade the investigators slipped away. Takuya could almost feel the colour drain from his face as he lifted his eyes from the newspaper. Under the headline 'Professor Iwase Commits Suicide', it read, 'War crime suspect Professor Kotaro Iwase of the Faculty of Medicine of Kyushu University hanged himself on the afternoon of the seventeenth in his cell at Fukuoka prison. He was fifty-four years old.'

Takuya remembered that he had observed an operation Iwase had performed on one of his subordinates who'd slipped and fallen from a truck, breaking his hip. The fact that the professor was being held at Fukuoka prison as a suspected war criminal was proof that the authorities had found out about the experiments carried out on the eight prisoners of war, making Takuya think that the others who had been involved must also have been caught. Army surgeon Haruki, who had suggested performing the dissections of live POWs, had been killed in the fire raids on Fukuoka, but Colonel Tahara, who had witnessed the operations as a representative of the tactical operations staff, would no doubt have been arrested with the others. Tahara had been involved in organising the executions of the other thirty-three airmen. Obviously he would have been grilled by his interrogators as to their whereabouts, so by now warrants for the arrest of all those who had taken part would have been issued, and it was highly likely that many were already in custody. The fact that Iwase had chosen to take his own life was probably an indication of the severity of the interrogations, and doubtless the prospect of dying on the gallows had been too much for him to bear.

Clearly, by now the occupation authorities must know all there was to know about the fate of the forty-one captured airmen.

Takuya looked up from the newspaper. A wave of apprehension came over him, as though suddenly he were cowering naked in the middle of a vast expanse with nowhere to hide. He felt as though he wanted to crawl into a cave deep in the mountains and hide there for the rest of his life.

That day Takuya had difficulty keeping his mind on the job, and two or three times Terasawa and his co-workers laughed at him for giving odd replies to their questions. He was suddenly on tenterhooks again, and these men seemed to represent nothing less than a threat to his life.

The summer heat intensified with each passing day.

When Terasawa had gathered all the building materials he needed, he got a man who had been a carpenter's apprentice before joining the army to come in and start the construction.

Kameya invited Takuya to accompany him on his trips to the black market, but the risk of being spotted in the crowd made him turn down every invitation.

Since the end of the war, the American forces had taken over the Suyari munitions works, and US Army Jeeps and lorries were everywhere on the streets of Himeji. New brothels, bars and shops catering to their needs sprung up virtually every week in the areas frequented by the Americans.

Kameya told him all sorts of stories about what he saw on his trips into town. He talked about the time he saw a young couple waiting for a train on the platform at Himeji station. An American soldier had swaggered over, grabbed the young woman by the arm and tried to drag her off, knocking her husband to the ground when he tried to intervene. He talked about the tawdry women he had seen brazenly consorting with

American soldiers in the streets, and how some of them had even set up a hut near the US military camp, where they solicited customers. Kameya said he had even seen these women shamelessly copulating with their American customers out in the open. He also told Takuya about the number of times he had witnessed innocent young women being accosted and dragged off to be raped by American troops. Evidently soldiers threw things from their vehicles for the locals to scramble after all the time, and he even described unscrupulous dealers who collected food scraps from outside the Americans' tents and boiled them up to sell as broth on the black market.

No way, thought Takuya, would he venture into the town centre if that was what he was going to find.

As he worked during the day, every few minutes Takuya stole a glance down each of the approach roads to the factory. The number of people throwing up shacks made from burnt roofing iron was gradually increasing, and there were even some out there living in what were to all intents and purposes crude mud huts. Whenever people approached the workshop grounds, Takuya scrutinised them to see if they posed a threat. He had decided that if someone did come with the intention of arresting him, he would first rush into the house to get his pistol and then dash down to the embankment by the river, where he'd fire some warning shots if followed. He had resolved to blow his brains out rather than be taken alive.

Deep inside, Takuya recognised that his feelings of outrage toward the American military for devastating his country were gradually mellowing, but that his fear was intensifying with each passing day. His reason for staying on the run was fear of the gallows.

On the thirteenth of August, Takuya found an article in the newspaper which raised his vigilance to yet another level. The headline read '*Kempeitai* Chief Flees. Female Companion Arrested'.

'When a warrant was issued for his arrest this April on charges of war crimes, former Imperial Army colonel and commander of the Tokyo *Kempeitai* Oishi Kojiro (forty years of age) of 1–16,

Kaga-Cho, Ushigome-Ku, Tokyo, mysteriously disappeared with his maid, Hirakawa Fumiko. However, Hirakawa was recently apprehended after being spotted by a policeman at Ueno Station while she was in the city to buy food supplies. She told police that Oishi was living in a village in the Nishi-Tama district, but when the agents moved to arrest him they discovered that he had already fled. According to Hirakawa, they had left suicide notes at their residence in Tokyo before absconding to Kawaji with what money and food they could lay their hands on. They had moved from one farmer's shed to another before eventually managing to rent a four-tatami-mat storeroom in a private house in Hikawa.'

Takuya tried to calm himself with a cigarette. It was strange to think there was another fugitive out there in exactly the same predicament as himself. He could almost sense the fear in Oishi, driving him to stay one step ahead of the police.

At the first opportunity, Takuya stepped behind a pile of building materials and scanned the article one more time. The arrest warrant for Oishi, chief of the Tokyo *kempeitai*, had been issued in April, about the same time the police had turned up at his parents' house in Shikoku. Obviously the SCAP authorities had issued a blanket order for the arrest of all suspects wanted on charges of war crimes. That Hirakawa's maid should have been apprehended on her way through Ueno station was proof that their photographs must be in circulation, and also that police agents were watching passers-by even in places as crowded as railway stations. This must be the case all over the country, so there would undoubtedly be police agents standing watch in and around Himeji station, holding photographs of war crimes suspects.

Obviously, when the maid confessed Oishi's whereabouts to the police, they would have rushed there, only to find that he had given them the slip once again. Oishi must have been constantly on the lookout, somehow sensing their approach and skilfully evading arrest.

This article taught Takuya a valuable lesson. Oishi had been lying low up in the mountains, but had kept sufficiently alert to recognise the impending danger and avoid capture by pursuers who no doubt had taken great care to approach as stealthily as possible. Takuya realised that no lesser degree of vigilance would be needed to keep himself safe from the gallows. His impulse was to cut the article out and save it as a reminder, but the risk of drawing attention to himself made him reject the idea.

After the corner supports of the warehouse had been erected the men started attaching the crossbeams. Perched precariously on lengths of wooden scaffolding, Takuya and the others toiled under the summer sun. The sweat from his brow had already stained the front of his mountaineering hat, and his face was so tanned that the skin was peeling from the bridge of his nose.

The clear view of the White Egret Castle gave Takuya the solace he needed to get through the day. Sitting majestically amid the desolation that once had been Himeji city, the castle seemed to project a feeling of stability, like a lead paperweight sitting on a sheet of rice paper. Its indomitable presence somehow buoyed and comforted him. It changed colour with the weather, light brown under an overcast sky, purplish in the evening sunlight.

The area around where the workshop was being constructed was known for its profusion of fireflies. They were so concentrated that at night the air above the river a short distance away glowed in the dark, and the luminescence seemed to spill over beyond the stream as thousands of the little insects flew out over the devastated land. Depending on the direction of the wind, there were also days when the house was enveloped by myriad tiny beads of light, while out in the desolate expanse pieces of twisted roofing iron and the rubble from white stone walls were illuminated, fading into and then out of sight.

Towards the end of August, three iron girders were stolen one night.

Incidents of theft were reaching epidemic proportions. Crops in the fields were plundered, and stories of cattle being stolen and butchered for their meat were not uncommon. A spinning-mill which had survived the fire raids had the glass taken from almost two hundred windows. Even lead water pipes were dug up and carried away. If people let their guard down for a moment, their bicycles, handcarts or even their shoes disappeared in a flash, and instances of luggage being stolen at the station were rife. Concerned about the materials he had to store outdoors, Terasawa made sure that at night everything was tied up with rope, but this had not deterred the thieves.

Judging from the number of girders taken, this seemed to be the handiwork of one person. If the thief had been a man of considerable physical strength, he certainly could have carried three of them at once.

Knowing how hard Terasawa had worked to obtain these girders, Takuya was incensed by the theft. The man was probably an incorrigible thief, whiling away his hours in the black market rather than working, and feeding himself with the proceeds of his criminal activities. The girders were to be used for building the warehouse, and without them construction was not possible.

Terasawa seemed disillusioned with everything, and spent his time walking mutely around the property.

That evening, he announced that the property would have to be guarded through the night. He seemed to think that, like a mouse that has found a source of food, the thief would definitely be back for more. The only way to stop him was to keep watch for the whole night, so it was decided that Kameya and Takuya would alternate shifts watching the yard. Terasawa said that he would do a shift as well, but Takuya insisted that it was the employees' duty and he should leave it to them. Beginning that night, Kameya kept watch from ten o'clock at night until one in the morning, when Takuya took over until daybreak.

While Kameya seemed to struggle on less than a full night's sleep, Takuya took it in his stride. Working through the night in the tactical operations centre had hardened him to the extent that, if he awoke some time before beginning his shift, he didn't hesitate to let Kameya go back to bed. Keeping watch until dawn with only an hour's catnap hardly affected him at all. Fatigue wasn't a problem, but the swarms of mosquitoes that appeared during the night certainly were. Together with Kameya he fashioned some bags out of cloth to cover their hands, and stitched together two hoods with small holes cut for their eyes. Their vantage point was the spot behind the metal drum used by the workers to bath in.

Just before dawn on the fifth day after they started their vigil, from his position crouched behind the drum, resting a piece of timber on his knees, Takuya noticed someone walking along the road in his direction.

Tiny bulbs of incandescence from the fireflies glimmered in the still night air as the person stopped in front of the yard, presumably to survey the scene before making his next move. Takuya remained motionless, only his eyes moving to follow the man as he walked off again toward the pile of building materials, just close enough now for Takuya to make out that this was no small individual. In the faint light from the stars in the clear night sky he was able to see that the man was manoeuvring a couple of steel girders on to his shoulder.

Takuya jumped to his feet and moved quickly from his spot behind the steel drum towards the thief. The man obviously heard Takuya, for no sooner had he taken a couple of steps towards the road than he swung round and dropped the girders to the ground with a clatter. Before the thief could make another move, Takuya swung his makeshift truncheon down on to the man's shoulder with all the force he could muster. After staggering three or four steps back towards the road, the man dropped to one knee, giving Takuya the chance to push him over, twist his arm up behind him and thrust a knee into the small of his back. The man was certainly well built. Takuya turned his head towards the house and yelled for those inside to come out and help. The man groaned slightly as he lay pressed to the ground, but showed no other sign of resistance.

A light flicked on inside the house, then the door burst open and Terasawa ran out into the yard. As Takuya held the man's legs, Terasawa shouted to his wife, who stood silhouetted in the doorway, to wake Kameya and get him to bring some rope. In no time the younger man was by their side, dressed in his underwear, holding a coil of rope.

As Takuya held the thief down, Terasawa and Kameya bound

the man's hands behind his back and tied his legs together with the same length of rope.

'Go get the police,' said Terasawa, panting from exertion. Kameya ran inside, put on his trousers and rushed back out again to the truck. He jumped into the cab, started up the engine and the vehicle rumbled out onto the road.

Takuya watched the truck move off down the road and a frown came over his face at the stupidity of what he had just done. Catching the thief meant, of course, that the police would become involved. They would come to ask questions, and as the person who had caught the thief in the act Takuya would be obliged to make a statement for their records. Giving a false name wasn't much of a concern, but the prospect of being recognised by someone at the police station terrified him. He was not at all confident that he could stay calm, and if he reacted the way he had when questioned on the road that time, he might very well arouse the suspicions of the police.

Maybe he should make a run for it now, he thought. The article about Colonel Oishi returned to his mind. Kameya had already been gone for a few minutes, but he still had plenty of time to escape before the police arrived. Maybe he should just stroll into the house, grab his rucksack and slip out of the back door. But then again, disappearing like that would alert the police to his real situation, and it wouldn't be difficult for them to trace his real name in their files on suspected war criminals. With the police stepping up surveillance at railway stations and street corners, it was obvious that they were doubling their efforts to close the net on the last fugitives. It wouldn't be wise to tempt fate by bolting at this stage.

Takuya considered his options. If he went to the police station, his chances of walking out again without attracting the police's suspicions were not good. Indeed, in the worst-case scenario he might very well be arrested and thrown behind bars.

He asked himself what Colonel Oishi would do in this situation, but the question merely reminded him of his own stupidity. The answer was simple: Oishi wouldn't have put himself at risk by catching the thief in the first place. During his training as an officer cadet, Takuya had done his best to memorise the sections of the field service code that covered engaging the enemy. He remembered that the instructions had stressed that, for a commander of men in the field, hesitation or inaction was even worse than choosing the wrong course of action. In the present situation, with the police being the enemy, perhaps boldly facing them was best after all.

'He's a big fellow, Higa. You certainly did well to catch him,' Terasawa said, looking down at the man lying trussed up in front of them. The thief had a prominent nose, set amid clear-cut features, and the service cap lying by his side suggested that he was a demobilised soldier.

Takuya brooded over his foolishness. If he had just moved out from behind the steel drum and yelled, the man would have dropped the girders and run away. Once the thief knew someone was guarding the building materials during the night, surely he wouldn't risk coming back. Takuya's task had simply been to prevent any further theft until the warehouse was built. That didn't necessarily mean catching the man to bring him to justice.

The stars faded and the sky took on a bluish tint.

Takuya vacillated between the two options open to him. Running seemed like a good idea, but he realised that if he fled now his pursuers would be much closer than ever before. Maybe trying to feign composure in front of the police was worth the risk.

The noise of an engine was soon followed by two faint beams of light rising and dipping as the truck approached along the bumpy road. Takuya pulled the brim of his mountaineering hat down lower and pushed his glasses further up the bridge of his nose.

There were two policemen sitting in the back behind Kameya. When the truck stopped they jumped down and rushed over to the thief lying face down on the ground. While the younger police officer placed his knee in the small of the man's back, the older one checked the thief's pockets, then untied the rope and snapped a set of handcuffs on him. They made the man kneel on the ground with his legs folded under him.

The older policeman appeared to know Terasawa, engaging him in what seemed to be friendly conversation. The part Takuya had played must have been mentioned, as the officer nodded and turned to walk over to him.

Takuya told himself to stay calm, but a slight grimace came over his face and he looked down at the ground while the policeman approached. A furtive glance towards the house allowed him to measure the distance between himself and his gun. If the officer's expression betrayed the slightest hint of suspicion, the moment they moved to arrest him he would dash into the house, grab his rucksack and flee out of the back door.

The sun was starting to rise, the earthen bank along the river coming faintly into view through the morning mist.

The policeman stopped in front of Takuya, pulled out a notebook and asked his name and age. Takuya replied that his name was Higa and that he was from Okinawa, which the officer quickly jotted down, his face the picture of concentration as he asked for details of the time and nature of the incident.

Each time Takuya sensed the policeman's eyes turning on him, fear surged up inside him. He was trying to avoid the gaze of his questioner without being too obvious, but he could see nothing but goodwill in the policeman's expression.

Terasawa sauntered over. 'Good job to have dropped this fellow with one blow. These army men are terrific, aren't they?' he said with a hint of triumph in his voice.

The policeman nodded and smiled at Takuya as he put away his notebook. Terasawa told Kameya to take the police back to the station, and the handcuffed thief was pushed up into the back of the truck. As the engine revved, the senior policeman saluted Terasawa and stepped up into the truck himself. The truck pulled out of the yard and off down the road.

Watching the vehicle move away, Takuya thought that he didn't seem to have attracted any undue suspicion during the questioning.

The scene was now bathed in morning sunlight and a plume of smoke rose into the air from the chimney above the kitchen.

Before long Kameya returned, and they all went inside to have the morning meal of rice gruel with thin slices of seaweed.

Obviously in fine spirits, Terasawa excitedly described how his heart had raced as he dashed outside to answer Takuya's call for assistance. Terasawa's wife and Kameya gave enthusiastic accounts of their own parts in the episode, Kameya explaining that the man hadn't said a word during the trip into town, and that he'd walked passively into the police station, his head hanging.

After finishing his meal, Terasawa got to his feet and went over to a cabinet in the corner of the room, where he opened the lid of a small wooden box and took out two packs of Lucky Strike cigarettes. 'Well done,' he said, handing each of the men a packet.

Kameya looked curiously at the packaging before breaking the seal.

'Try one,' said Terasawa. Takuya opened his packet and pulled out a cigarette. The paper was of good quality and the pleasant smell of tobacco wafted out of the box. Holding it between his fingers, Takuya noticed how much thicker it was than the Japanese ration cigarettes, and that the tobacco was packed much more evenly. To Takuya, these cigarettes symbolised all he had heard about the material wealth and affluence of America.

He lit it and inhaled. It certainly smelt nice, and tasted as though it had been made from good-quality tobacco, but it was far too pungent for his uninitiated palate and he coughed as soon as he inhaled the smoke. Terasawa laughed happily at the scene in front of him.

They completed the 'workshop' that evening. At least, it was called a workshop, but in actual fact it was only a square structure with sheets of roofing-iron nailed on to the top and sides. Most of the floor was just bare ground, with only a small section covered with recycled wooden boards.

The next morning, the carpenter turned his attention to the construction of the warehouse. Terasawa and Kameya went out in the morning in the truck and returned in the afternoon loaded with a jumble of machines, motors, belts and shafts, which the men hauled straight away into the workshop. Takuya played his part in assembling the machinery, but as he worked he stood in such a way as to keep a clear line of sight down the road in the direction of the police station. He still couldn't shake his lingering uneasy feeling that the police might have recognised his face from wanted posters and at that very moment might be on their way back to arrest him.

In the evening of the fifth day after the thief's capture, Terasawa returned from town saying he had stopped at the police station and found out some details about the man. Evidently he was a known criminal, a specialist in the theft of metal goods, which he then sold through a broker. When the broker was arrested, he in turn had spilled the beans about the full extent of his betrayer's activities. The man was a demobilised soldier, as Takuya had guessed, and had moved to Himeji by himself to start his life of crime after losing his family in the fire raids on Osaka.

'The police were really pleased about this one. They think he'll probably admit to still more crimes,' said Terasawa, cutting a cigarette in half and stuffing the tobacco into a clay pipe he held in his hand. Putting the pipe in the corner of his mouth, he turned to Takuya and said, 'I didn't think of this till after I left the police station, but I think I'll get them to give you some sort of award for this. I know all the top brass down there, so if I say something they'll take notice. That was quite a criminal you nabbed here, and you should get something for it.'

Takuya was flabbergasted. Getting an award would require him to go to the police station and give more details of his personal history. He would have to meet all sorts of police officials, and in the process they would more than likely work out his real identity.

'I can't have you doing that,' said Takuya in a strained, high-pitched voice.

The faintest of smiles appeared on Terasawa's face before he replied. 'I won't have to stand up and shout about it. You really caught a big one here. The police will be more than happy to give

144

you an award for your efforts,' he said as he picked out the last
bits of tobacco from his pipe.

Takuya's mind raced as he tried to think of a way to get out
of this predicament.

'He's a demobilised soldier just like me. I couldn't accept an
award for putting a fellow soldier behind bars. And remember,
he lost his whole family in the war, so he must have been beside
himself. I couldn't accept an award for capturing someone like
that,' he said, raising his voice.

'I see,' said Terasawa, obviously recognising that there was
no point in pressing the matter further. His wife smiled warmly
across the table at Takuya.

After that there was no more mention of awards, and no
policemen turned up to discuss Takuya's capture of the thief.

The machinery had all been installed in the workshop and
test runs had gone without a hitch. Terasawa obviously still had
considerable funds left, because he purchased a large handcart
and had a telephone put into his house.

One day the owner of the match factory turned up on his
bicycle and had a long talk with Terasawa. By all accounts the
quantity of matches being produced was steadily increasing and
with it the demand for matchboxes.

Even into September, the late summer heat showed no signs
of abating.

Takuya spent his days pulling the cart to fetch materials from
a timber-processing yard at a little town down near the coast.
There was a press there which cut out the shapes for large and
small matchboxes from pine boards.

He was uneasy about walking around on the streets, but with
the construction of the warehouse complete the only job left
for him was pulling the handcart. Using a splitter machine, the
men in Terasawa's workshop cut the boxes out. Two recently
hired middle-aged women then stuck the striking-paper on to
the outside of the boxes. They were obviously experienced, and
kept up a steady pace with no problem at all.

With Kameya now also working on the striking-paper, Takuya
found himself in charge of carrying all goods and materials in and

out of the factory. He wrapped a hand towel round his head and wore his mountaineering hat on top of that to avoid being burnt by the late summer sun as he traipsed through the ruins to pick up materials at the timber-processing yard or the paper wholesalers. He always made a point of choosing the less crowded paths.

On the morning of the twenty-fifth of September, Takuya opened the newspaper and found the article he had been fearing all along. The name of the commander at the regional headquarters was printed boldly under the headline 'Jailed in Sugamo Prison'.

'The Judiciary Division of SCAP has announced that the following seven high-ranking officers of the Japanese Imperial Army have been arrested and are being held in Sugamo prison in relation to the unlawful killing in Fukuoka of thirty-three crew members from B-29 bombers,' it read. Those arrested were the lieutenant-generals in command of the Western Regional Forces and the Sixteenth Army, and of the southern Kyushu-based Fifty-seventh Army; the chief of staff of the Sixteenth Army; a major-general who had been second in command in the Western Region; a colonel in charge of the Western Region Air Defence Tactical Operations Centre; a major; and finally Lieutenant Howa Kotaro, listed as a company officer attached to headquarters.

Although this was the first article about the POWs since the coverage of Professor Iwase's suicide, Takuya knew instantly that this meant the SCAP authorities now knew every last detail about what happened to the airmen. Like Professor Iwase, these officers would have undergone relentless interrogation in Fukuoka prison, and only after they had told all they knew would they have been transported to Sugamo prison in Tokyo, where Class A war criminals were incarcerated.

Most of those listed were elite, high-ranking officers bearing ultimate responsibility for what happened under their command, but seeing Howa Kotaro's name unnerved Takuya. Distraught and incensed by his mother's death in the fire raids on Fukuoka the previous night, Howa had volunteered to take part in that day's execution and had decapitated two of the airmen. Of the seven men imprisoned at Sugamo, only Howa had actually been involved in carrying out the executions rather than giving the orders to do so. His arrest must mean that by now Takuya had also been designated a war criminal. He stared fixedly at the name Howa Kotaro in the last line of the article.

In a column further down the page, in fine print, he read that ninety-three war criminals had been put to death in Rabaul, and another hundred and twenty-three in Australia. Many more were probably meeting the same fate all over the Pacific, thought Takuya.

The mornings and nights grew cooler as autumn approached. The trial of the Class A war criminals was approaching a climax, and articles covering each day's developments in court filled the newspapers.

One afternoon, on a day one of the regular power cuts occurred, a local government officer came and sprayed DDT round Terasawa's house, sprinkling some of the white powder in the hair of all the workers, and even shoving the funnel down into their jacket sleeves and trousers. The officer explained that lice had been identified as the cause of the spread of typhus through the country, and that three thousand people had died. He went on to say that there had already been outbreaks of the disease in the Himeji area.

'This spraying is ordered by the occupation forces, who have supplied us with the DDT and the spraying equipment,' the man reported in an official tone before climbing back into the truck and driving away.

Takuya and the other men followed the orders and left the white powder on their bodies for the rest of the day. The effect of the pesticide was startling. The itchiness and the sensation of tiny creatures crawling over his skin disappeared in no time, and the number of flies and mosquitoes in the house dropped dramatically.

'The Americans certainly don't do anything by halves,' muttered Terasawa as he ran his fingers through his powder-covered hair.

Takuya hauled ever-increasing loads of materials into the

workshop, and matchbox production was soon in full swing. The men and the machines seemed to be in almost perpetual motion, and on the wooden floor of the workshop the women, sitting on old, worn-out cushions, toiled away tirelessly, sticking paper covers on to the completed boxes. Terasawa racked his brain thinking of ways to keep a supply of glue ready for his workers, and when flour, a key ingredient, wasn't available he bought scraps of cheap wheat-gluten bread, which was boiled to produce a substitute. It worked just as well as flour and water, so from that point on Terasawa's wife got up early every morning and boiled up the day's supply of glue.

Before long, the system changed so that Kameya used the lorry to bring in the materials while Takuya devoted his energies solely to delivering the completed boxes to the match factory.

He loaded the handcart as high as he could and trudged out along the street to the match factory. It was a real struggle to get the cart up the slope to the bridge, and when he made it up on to the long wooden structure he always paused to get his breath. The bridge was showing signs of age and disrepair, with long sections of the handrail rotted away and gaping holes visible in the upright supports, where ornamental iron fittings had been removed to be melted down during the war.

There was a magnificent view of Himeji castle from up on top of the bridge. The whiteness of the walls of the donjons and turrets was truly spectacular. One of the workers at Terasawa's factory said that many people believed the castle had survived the inferno only because the Americans had recognised its historical value, and had therefore ordered the B-29s to leave it standing. But Takuya gave this theory little credence. He thought the suggestion that an air force which had incinerated cities and towns all over Japan, and then dropped two atomic bombs, would be concerned with sparing historic buildings was nothing but propaganda.

After crossing the bridge he came out in front of a row of old houses which had somehow escaped the conflagration. There was a gradual incline off to the left, and a line of hills on the right. The road threaded its way through the little valley in a way that reminded him of his own village back in Shikoku.

At this point Takuya always stopped to rest and cast his eyes over the gentle slopes on both sides. Every time he paused there, the line of the road and the low hills to the east and west caused memories of home to come flooding back. Often he stood there gazing at the hills and thinking of his father. With SCAP ordering all assets of war crimes suspects frozen or confiscated, there was a very real chance that his father would have lost his job in the public service. Each time Takuya stopped, he visualised his father standing by the back door to the family house, ready to hand over the packet of cigarettes.

The match factory was in a place called Shirahama, amid a cluster of several dozen factories. It was a good five-kilometre haul from Terasawa's workshop. A large operation, it bustled with more than a hundred workers.

Takuya announced his arrival to a young man in the office, who led him round to the warehouse beside the rear entrance of the factory, where he unloaded his cargo. In the warehouse there were stacks of small and large matchboxes and men were busy loading them on to horse-drawn carts.

While he waited for his receipt to be stamped, he peered into the factory. It was the first time he had seen how matches were actually made, and he watched the workers and machines with interest. The young office worker explained the names of the machines, the manufacturing process and the materials used.

Sometimes while he was waiting, horse-drawn carts delivered bales of matchsticks. The workers arranged them on trays, where they were painted with paraffin before the head was dipped in potassium chlorate mixed with fish glue. The matches were then dried and taken out to the area where the women workers packed them into boxes. They sat on both sides of a long table grabbing the matches and putting them neatly into boxes at a dizzying pace. From years of experience, each one of these women could virtually guarantee that any box would contain the required eighty-five matchsticks. Red phosphorus striking-paper was attached and stamped with the company's trademark, and finally the boxes were wrapped, ready to be dispatched.

Restrictions of everyday commodities had been lifted when the war came to an end, but the unregulated sale of daily essentials such as matches and food was prohibited. The 'Match Supply Regulations' of 1940 were still in place, so the government bought up all the matches produced and distributed them to organisations running the disbursement of rations. Every match manufacturer was plagued with a shortage of materials, and as matchbox supply could not keep up with demand, matches were often shipped loose in bags rather than in boxes.

No wonder the match manufacturer was happy that Terasawa had started making boxes for them. Every time Takuya arrived with a load of boxes they brought him out a steamed potato or a little bowl of potato starch soup.

The best wood for making matches was white willow from Hokkaido, but as this was almost entirely unavailable they had to make do with local pine. The problem with pine was its lack of strength when cut to match size, which led to waste during the manufacturing process. Apart from this, the paraffin, red phosphorus and fish glue were all of inferior quality, and the supply was inadequate, forcing manufacturers to thin their materials to get by, resulting in a much less effective product.

Takuya delivered matchboxes to the factory day after day. The leaves of the trees on the surrounding hills took on autumn colours, and before long Takuya was hauling his load through swirling eddies of yellow and brown leaves.

Terasawa, Kameya and the others went to a barber's in an enclave of town which had more or less survived the bombing, but because he was wary of being recognised, Takuya got Kameya to cut his hair with some electric shears.

Occasionally Takuya would look into the long, narrow mirror hanging on a post in the house and see a completely different face from that of his days as an army officer. The outline of his face had completely changed. He was gaunt, and his skin was deeply tanned from hours of labour under the sun. The change in his eyes was particularly striking. The piercing look had disappeared, replaced by an unsettled look of apprehension. When he tried to force an angry glare, he could produce no more than a weak and unconvincing grimace.

But that was all right, he thought. The transformation was certainly dramatic, considering that only six months had passed since he had begun his life as a fugitive, but for someone in his position the change was hardly undesirable. If the photographs being used now by the authorities were from his days in the army, there was a good chance, he thought, that even if he was stopped no one would be able to make the connection. The glasses were now part of his normal appearance, and it was almost as though the months of hard work had sculpted the features of his face anew.

The temperature dropped, and there was frost in the morning. The food shortages worsened. Although the government had announced that staple rations of rice were to be increased, more often than not only potatoes and the like were available, and even they were increasingly slow coming through. The newspapers reported an increase in the number of unemployed every day, and there were often stories about people dying of starvation in the big cities.

Takuya reminded himself once again how fortunate he had been to find a job with Terasawa. Having a ration book didn't guarantee enough food to survive, and the only place anyone could get proper sustenance was still the black market. To be blessed with a job where his employer provided food and shelter must be extremely unusual. Takuya counted his lucky stars that he had come across someone as decent as Terasawa.

Nineteen forty-six came to a close and a new year began. On New Year's Day they had rice cakes delivered, and ate them in traditional *zooni* soup. The rice cakes weren't as sticky as they should have been, and felt rough on the tongue. The first snow fell, and when Takuya awoke the next morning the mountains in the distance were covered in a white blanket.

When work started again after New Year, a twenty-seven-year-old man called Kimijima was taken on to manage the procurement of materials in the match factory. Takuya often conversed with him in the course of his work. Kimijima was a thin man with penetrating eyes, and the way he wore his naval service cap suggested that he had actually served in the Imperial Navy. He told Takuya he had been a petty officer on a destroyer which had been sunk in the Pacific. He had drifted in the sea for five hours before being picked up. He explained that the scar on his neck was a burn mark from when the ship burst into flames when she was hit.

When Kimijima asked Takuya about his background, he told him that he had been a lance-corporal in the army. The younger man still had the air of someone whose character had been forged in an atmosphere of harsh discipline. Takuya couldn't help but think that there was little left in his own nature to remind him that he, too, had once been a military man.

Occasionally he passed a policeman approaching from the opposite direction. Other times American soldiers in Jeeps would thread their way through the pedestrians, leaving clouds of dust in their wake. Each time Takuya lowered his already well-concealed face toward the ground as he pulled the cart down the road.

One day when the snow was disappearing from the surrounding hills, Takuya was on the way back from delivering a load of boxes to the match factory when he heard someone call to him from behind. When he looked round he saw two men approaching, one about thirty-five or thirty-six and the other not much over twenty. For a second he felt the colour drain from his face at the thought that they might be plain-clothes policemen, but a closer look put his mind at ease. The older man was wearing a jacket and leather boots, and the younger an Air Force flight suit. Both looked unusually healthy and strong.

Still wary, Takuya turned slowly to face them.

The younger man sidled up to him and offered him an American military cigarette. Takuya declined, saying he didn't smoke.

The older man started talking, at first beating round the bush but eventually explaining that they had seen Takuya delivering boxes to the match factory and followed him on his way back.

'Anyway, can you help us get some matches? We'd really appreciate it,' he said, familiarly placing his hand on the cart.

Takuya replied that his job was to deliver boxes and that he wasn't in a position to get matches for them. He did not let on that he knew very well they were suggesting he steal from the match factory.

'So you can't get some for us? We'll pay whatever price you say,' said the man irritably.

Takuya shook his head. 'I can't do that. Not my line, I'm afraid,' he said, shaking his head as he pushed the cart forward down the road.

'Not your line, eh?' said the man with a chuckle as he walked alongside Takuya. After a few paces, looking intently at Takuya's face from the side as though to try to decide whether or not he should give up, he grabbed the handle and stopped the cart. He pulled out a pencil and scribbled a name and address on a piece of paper.

'You can find me here. Remember, I'll pay good money whenever you have matches to sell,' he said, stuffing the piece of paper in Takuya's jacket pocket as he let go of the handle.

Takuya trudged along the road back to the workshop.

Eager to demonstrate his honesty, that night he showed Terasawa the paper and told him what the man had said.

'It's a dangerous world we live in, isn't it?' muttered Terasawa as he stared at the piece of paper in his hand. He told Takuya that controlled goods such as matches were sold on the black market, and that, while some of them were probably stolen, a sizeable number of match manufacturers were illicitly selling their products to dealers in black-market goods. Evidently these matches were made of better-quality materials than those supplied for rationing, so they hardly ever broke and were far easier to light.

The blossom came and went on the cherry trees. Takuya recalled the belt of cherry trees in full bloom around the headquarters building. Shirasaka had undoubtedly finished winding up the affairs of Western Regional Command and returned to his hometown. Takuya had been on the run for twelve months now, although it felt much longer.

The two men who wanted him to steal matches did not approach him again. The trees and bushes on both sides of the road were flush with the green of spring, and the air around the road through the hills was alive with birdsong.

Prices ran wild on the black market. The same large bottle of sake that had cost thirteen yen in February was now, two months later, selling for one hundred and nine yen. In the same time, a monthly newspaper subscription went from eight yen to twelve yen fifty sen, and a postcard costing fifteen sen had shot up to fifty sen.

By this stage, it was a struggle to keep up the production of matchboxes with the gradually increasing output of the match factories. Materials were scarce, wood more and more difficult to come by. Often only half the amount of timber ordered was available.

Terasawa made the rounds of the timber dealers, but soon concluded that the supply situation would get worse before it got better, and struck upon the idea of producing his own wooden sheeting. He instructed his workers to erect a makeshift work area beside the warehouse and bought a second-hand sawing-machine. No one knew how he managed to get it but, before long, loads of rough-sawn pine started to come in by rail.

Near the end of the rainy season, production started on the timber sheeting. The saws whirred and rumbled and pine boards were stacked up one after another, wet and pressed thin to make the material, which would then be dried out in the sun. Soon this new source of materials increased production in the workshop dramatically.

7

Not a day went by when the trials of Class A war criminals didn't dominate the newspapers. There were also excerpts from Tojo Hideki's response to the prosecutor's questions about the execution of some of Major Doolittle's airmen who had taken part in the first air raid on Tokyo in 1942. Tojo maintained that this raid had been a clear violation of international law because its specific objective had been to slaughter defenceless civilians, including women and children. For this reason, he stated, he had not hesitated to grant his chief of staff, former Field Marshal Sugimoto, permission to execute the captured crewmen. At the same time he insisted that full responsibility for this action lay with himself and no one else. Tojo went on to say that executions of POWs by subordinates on the instructions of their commanding officers had been accepted practice in the Imperial Army, and that holding these men to account was unjust. However, the reality of the situation was that many officers and lower-ranking soldiers had already been hanged. Tojo's testimony would undoubtedly have no bearing whatsoever on the fate of someone, such as Takuya himself, who had beheaded an American POW.

The articles about the war crimes trials left Takuya depressed, but those about food were equally disheartening. By now food shortages far exceeded what could be safely endured; supplies of rations were an average of twenty days late across the country, and nothing had reached Hokkaido for three months. The economist's prediction of ten million people dying was obviously no exaggeration, and dramatic increases in deaths from starvation were reported in big cities such as Tokyo and Osaka, with truckloads of bodies collected every day.

There were no stories of people starving to death in Himeji, but increasing numbers of women and children were going out to the rural areas to barter for food. They took articles of clothing and the like to farming-villages and exchanged them for pitiful amounts of produce.

Amid all this hardship and privation, Terasawa's timber sheet operation led to some unforeseen good fortune for Takuya and the other workers. The scraps and sawdust produced in the process of making the wooden sheets were highly sought-after by salt manufacturers, to use as fuel when boiling sea water to distill salt. After dark, in exchange for the timber scraps, they would secretly deliver bags of salt, a controlled item, to the workshop. Merchants would in turn come offering foodstuffs in exchange for salt, and occasionally farmers living nearby brought in vegetables or beans to barter. Small though the quantities were, Terasawa would then pass on to his workers some of the food or salt he had acquired.

There were times, as Takuya worked away hauling matchboxes, when he thought that maybe he could live the rest of his life like this, without anyone ever discovering his true identity. During the eight months he had pushed the handcart between Terasawa's workshop and the match factory in Shirahama, never venturing beyond that five-kilometre stretch of road, the only people who had ever called out to him had been black-market dealers, and he had never once felt in danger.

As summer came, the sun's rays became more intense. Day by day Takuya plodded along the road in front of the handcart, breathing heavily as beads of sweat formed on his brow and trickled down his neck. On rainy days he covered his cargo with a canvas tarpaulin, put on a raincoat and trudged off toward Shirahama. By now the precise location of every pothole and exposed stone in the road was so clear in his mind that he unconsciously avoided the obstacles on his way to and from the match factory.

One drizzly, hot day, just after Takuya had finished making his delivery of boxes, the young worker in charge of the stores led Takuya to a desk at the back of the warehouse. Something about the man's expression was out of the ordinary. When they reached the desk the man went out through a side door, returning a moment later with the factory manager and Kimijima, the former naval petty officer in charge of materials procurement.

When he saw the looks on their faces, Takuya felt himself flinch. The normally affable factory manager wore a particularly stern expression, his eyes betraying pent-up anger. A feeling of foreboding came over Takuya. His first thought was that somehow the men in the match factory had discovered his real identity, and now the manager was going to question him about his past. The blackness of his hairline stood out in stark relief against his deeply furrowed brow.

The manager sat down and began to explain the situation. On Sunday, two days earlier, Takuya had made a delivery of matchboxes to the factory, and on Monday, when stock was taken, it was discovered that ten packs, each holding ten boxes, were missing. He said that the old caretaker had opened the warehouse door to let Takuya in to unload his boxes on Sunday, but other than that no one had access to the storage area, which naturally made Takuya the prime suspect.

Relieved to know that his identity was not at issue, Takuya protested vehemently against the unfairness of the manager's allegations. Obviously, it was because he was just another shabbily dressed labourer that he was the object of this ridiculous accusation.

The manager ignored Takuya's protestations of innocence, repeating that if he owned up to the crime nothing would be done. The young clerk glared at Takuya as if he were a criminal.

Continuing to shake his head in denial, Takuya had a sinking feeling that this would end up in the hands of the police. If he were to be questioned as a suspected thief, there would be an investigation into whether he had any prior convictions, and the police would no doubt go through their wanted posters as part of that process. The next step would inevitably be identification and arrest. To have the police involved was obviously the last thing he wanted, but Takuya couldn't bear the thought of being suspected of stealing from anyone.

The factory manager was unshaken in his insistence that

Takuya must have done it. Takuya shook his head vigorously in denial.

An uncomfortable silence followed, then the factory manager glared at Takuya and walked out of the warehouse.

Takuya too went outside. He didn't want to leave knowing that they still thought that he was the culprit. Thinking of the look in the eyes of the manager and the clerk made him so humiliated and incensed that he trembled with emotion.

'Don't worry about it,' said Kimijima from behind.

Takuya turned to face him. He felt a sudden desire to tell this man everything about his past. Of all people, Kimijima would surely understand his situation; he would know that he wasn't the sort of man who would commit such a stupid crime.

'I may be pushing a handcart these days, but . . .' was as far as Takuya went before clamming up.

'I know what you're saying. I know you're no labourer. You've got a family and a proper job back in Okinawa. Not that those things count for much these days. At least pulling a cart is a job, and brings in money to buy food,' said Kimijima, trying his best to be comforting.

If only he could open up to Kimijima and at least have this man understand both his innocence and the desperate nature of his situation, thought Takuya.

He took a couple of steps toward Kimijima and tried to bring himself to say something to him, but his lips wouldn't move. Kimijima certainly wasn't the sort to blab to the police, but he might tell people close to him, who might in turn tell others, and before long the police would be bound to pick up on the story.

Deep down he still wanted to confide in Kimijima, but he was relieved that he had held his tongue, at least on this occasion. Looking to Kimijima for support made him feel pathetic.

'Suspecting you this way without a shred of evidence . . . it's just ridiculous,' said Kimijima with a trace of anger in his voice.

Takuya stopped in front of the office and bowed his head to Kimijima, then wrapped the hand towel round his face and put on his mountaineering hat.

He stepped behind the handle of the cart and started to push it out of the yard. Before he had gone half a dozen steps he felt tears rolling down his cheeks. He asked himself why he was crying. He hadn't done anything to justify being suspected of this theft and had done his best to deny it, so there was nothing for him to regret. What was he so sad about? Was it the fact that he was someone who had graduated from university and gone on to reach the rank of lieutenant in the Imperial Army, only to become a suspected criminal, a labourer with a hand towel wrapped around his face, pushing a cart?

Recently he had realised that since coming to Himeji he had gradually changed into someone quite different from his previous self. One day, as he was hauling his cart along the road, he had noticed a woman, probably out shopping, walking a few paces in front of him. She was carrying a makeshift bag, made from what had once been the Japanese national flag. It appeared that she was using it to carry potatoes, but when Takuya saw this, rather than feeling anger, he had just looked away. Maybe he was starting to change with the times, too, like the young woman walking hand in hand with the US serviceman. Smoking American military-issue cigarettes no longer felt the least bit strange. All that remained was the fear of being caught by the American military. Maybe the tears were a sign of how delicate his nerves had become after all this time on the run.

When he got back to the workshop he said nothing to Terasawa about the accusations. He had explained about the two black-market dealers approaching him on the road and trying to get him to steal from the match factory, so if he told Terasawa about the stolen matches there was a chance his boss would think that he had given in to temptation and actually committed the crime. Furthermore, the lack of evidence meant it was highly unlikely that the match-factory manager would ever mention the incident to Terasawa.

The next day, Takuya hauled a load of boxes to the match factory as usual. Requesting a change to another task would only increase the match-factory manager's suspicions of him, and if he told Terasawa about what had happened, in order to be relieved of his delivery duties, the odds were good that his boss would take steps to protest Takuya's innocence. Terasawa's connections with the police being what they were, it was possible that he might even ask them to lend a hand in clearing Takuya's name.

Definitely, the right way to proceed was to continue doing deliveries, he told himself. To guard against further accusations, every time he arrived at the match factory he now stopped in front of the office and waited until one of the workers came out to escort him. When he went into the warehouse to unload his boxes, he always asked the stores clerk to accompany him, and if for one reason or another the clerk had to go back inside Takuya waited outside, leaning on the empty handcart, until the man came back and verified that everything was in order. Nonplussed by this approach, the clerk was sometimes sarcastically servile, but Takuya kept his replies short and impassive and remained unperturbed. Sometimes he bumped into the factory manager, and when their eyes met the manager just kept walking, a decidedly uncomfortable look on his face.

The power cuts were as frequent as ever, so to maintain production levels they started operating the machines before dawn. Takuya got up earlier, too, to lend a hand carrying the pressed timber sheets and the striking-paper. This summer there were many more fireflies than the previous year, and little specks of light flickered everywhere around the workshop.

The heat abated and the first signs of autumn appeared.

One day in mid-September, coming back from his deliveries and wanting to take a short rest, Takuya pulled his empty cart up the embankment between the road and the river. The breeze felt refreshing against his skin, which was moist with sweat from his toil, and a panoramic view of the countryside opened up in front of him.

As he sat down against the cart and wiped his face and neck with his hand towel, he spotted something blue down in the expanse of reeds between the river and the embankment. It looked like a pair of trousers. Straining to see through the rustling reeds, he made out a pair of feet protruding from the trouser legs. Maybe a young couple was there, trying to enjoy themselves away from prying eyes. As the reeds swayed and hummed in the next strong gust of wind Takuya got a clearer view of the blue cloth of the trousers, then he caught sight of the man's shirt and the back of his head. He was obviously alone.

Takuya lit a cigarette. The reeds bent over again with the next gust of wind and the man lying in the reeds was exposed to view once more.

Each time the wind blew strongly enough to move the reeds, Takuya found his eyes drawn to the man. The sweat on his face was almost dry by now. In the distance he could see a train slowly pulling out of the station just this side of Himeji castle. There was no one to be seen anywhere near him. The only person visible was some distance away along the embankment, a woman dressed in a dark work kimono, bent over picking wild vegetables.

Maybe this man had been doing the same and was taking a rest before starting again. Takuya remembered how he used to pick bamboo shoots and parsley in the woods and fields around his village, and thought that if there were something edible down among those reeds, perhaps he should go and pick some for himself.

Hat in hand, Takuya got to his feet and walked down the embankment and on to a little path through the sea of reeds. They were so high that each time the wind blew, the fluffy tops brushed against his face.

Before he had taken many steps along the winding path a faint sickly-sweet smell brought him instinctively to a halt. The black, swollen feet of a dead body were poking out of the blue trousers. From a distance it might have seemed as though the man was taking an afternoon nap, but the terrible smell of decaying flesh wafting in Takuya's direction was unmistakable.

Waving his hand in front of his nose at the stench, Takuya watched as the wind flailed the reeds against the man's body. The man lay face down, his shirt pushed up to reveal the reddish-black skin on his back.

Takuya edged backward two or three steps before turning

round and scurrying a few more paces back down the path. The sickly-sweet smell of death still clung to his clothes, and as he scrambled up the embankment he was hit by a wave of nausea.

Back beside his handcart, Takuya retched as he stared at the blue cloth down among the reeds. Had the man been murdered, or had he starved to death? Takuya had seen only the man's feet and part of his back, but he guessed that the man had probably been at least middle-aged. He knew he should report it to the police, but of course that was the last thing he intended to do. Being questioned by the police was just too risky.

The dead man has nothing to do with me, he thought. Eventually that woman picking wild vegetables, or maybe some children playing in the reeds, would find the body. If the man had simply collapsed and died on his way somewhere, his body would be carried away and disposed of.

Takuya lifted the handle of the cart and started walking. The revolting smell persisted, clinging to him. He retched again and again as he walked down the road. This smell was different from the one that had wafted up from the shallow graves when they had exhumed the decapitated bodies to destroy the last evidence of the fate of the American airmen. That smell had been something akin to wet, rotting cardboard, but it was equally pungent. Maybe there was a difference when a corpse decomposed in the sun.

Despite having no proof, Takuya somehow sensed that the man had died a natural death. But if that was so, why had he wandered off the road and down into the reeds? Had he been so hungry that he'd remembered his childhood days and gone searching for birds' nests? Or had he ventured down the embankment to look for wild vegetables? The thought of that poor man lying there dead, face down among the reeds, deeply affected Takuya.

He tried to picture the families of the men who had been executed in that clearing in the bamboo grove. They would have had parents, perhaps brothers and sisters. Their families would have mourned their deaths and no doubt despaired at the fact that there were no remains on which to focus their grief.

As a crewman on a B-29, the man whom Takuya had beheaded had been party to the slaughter of countless Japanese, but the clear memory of the man in his mind included nothing of what Takuya imagined a murderer might look like, no suggestion of anything criminal. He had just been playing his part as a cog in the wheel of the American war machine in its attacks on the Japanese mainland and, even if that had resulted in the slaughter of civilians, it was unlikely that he felt any guilt about his part in the process. To him, there may have been only a tenuous connection between the bombs that tumbled out of his plane's bomb bay and the carnage down on the ground.

Takuya mused that his involvement in the executions was essentially the same in nature as the actions of the man he had killed, in that both were merely carrying out their duties as military men. The difference was that whereas the killing committed by the American had been by bombing, which precluded witnessing the bloodshed, Takuya's act had involved wielding the sword with his own hands as he beheaded the airman. The fact that the American had killed countless people as opposed to Takuya's one victim brought him some comfort.

Takuya shook his head and frowned. He wished he had never seen that blue cloth. As recollections of that afternoon in the bamboo grove swirled inside his head, he felt ashamed of his loss of nerve. These days he hardly ever checked his pistol to make sure it would be ready for that moment of truth if he was cornered, and he even doubted he'd have the courage to pull the trigger if the worst came to the worst.

The reeds waved this way and that before bending right in unison as a gust of wind blew from downstream. Takuya fixed his eyes on the ground and pulled the cart off down the road.

Temperatures dropped with each passing day. There were no articles in the newspaper about a murder, and, as the body in the reeds must have been found by now, the authorities must have decided that the man had died a natural death.

Takuya delivered his cartloads of matchboxes, his routine unchanging from one day to the next. He had attached a long canvas strap to two points on the deck of the cart so he could move it more easily, and, once a hard knot of muscle formed under the skin on his shoulders, pulling the cart was no problem at all.

The first colours of autumn could be seen on the low hills near Himeji. Fine weather continued, with pleasant days followed by glowing red sunsets.

One day towards the end of autumn, when the reds and golds of the surrounding hills had begun to mute to softer yellows and browns, Takuya saw something that made him stop in his tracks and stare down the road. A convoy of four US Army trucks, their canvas canopies rolled up, was moving towards him, kicking up clouds of dust.

He had often seen American lorries and Jeeps trundling along the main road and over the reinforced concrete bridge just downstream from the rickety old wooden bridge he pulled his cart across, but never once had he seen them using this old road. It was barely wider than the wheelspan of a big lorry, making it impossible for two vehicles to pass. Maybe they were lost, or maybe they had decided to take a shortcut. There were no side paths to push the cart off into, and all that separated the road from the paddy fields on both sides was a narrow ditch.

The lorries were coming towards him at considerable speed, but for the life of him he couldn't think what he should do. His load of matchboxes stuck out on both sides of the cart, so if he didn't move it off the road there was no way a lorry would be able to pass.

For a second he thought of turning round and heading for the last crossroad, but that was almost a kilometre back down the road, so there was no way he could make it in time. There was nothing to do but push the cart to one side of the road and hope that the lorries would be able to squeeze past. He summoned all his strength and hurriedly pushed the cart back a few metres to a spot on the side of the road where it was slightly wider than where he had been standing.

The sound of the trucks' engines and tyres grew louder as the front vehicle closed rapidly on him. The sunlight reflected off the windscreen so he couldn't see inside, but he could see an elbow sticking out of each of the windows.

The lorry's horn blasted the air for what seemed an age, leaving his ears ringing. The full width of the road was taken up as the convoy bore down on Takuya and his cart. Fear seized him at the thought that the driver might not slow down at all, and would instead choose to smash both the cart and Takuya out of the way. The tyres looked enormous, and the chassis with its white star on the side was far higher than that of any Japanese vehicle he had ever seen.

The sound of the horn was followed by the screeching of brakes, as the lorry halted ten metres short of the handcart. Takuya clasped the bar tightly as he stood his ground. Shouts of surprise came from the soldiers sitting in the back of the lorry, and heads poked out to check why they had stopped so suddenly. Seconds later the vehicle was engulfed in the cloud of dust floating up from behind.

A fresh-faced young soldier leant out of the window on the passenger side, yelling something and gesticulating excitedly at Takuya to get out of the way. Evidently enraged, he shouted the same thing again and again with increasing urgency.

Takuya moved the cart. His vision seemed to blur for a moment as sweat poured down his forehead. He manoeuvred the cart forward and backward to get it as far off the road as he could.

The horn rent the air once again before the vehicle started to roll forward. Edging the cart back, he looked up to see a husky, red-faced man sitting behind the steering-wheel. The man leaning out of the window on the passenger side was still furiously shouting something at Takuya. The lorry closed on him, and the wheels kicked up little stones as they turned.

Realising that it was impossible to keep the cart up on the road, Takuya stepped down into the ditch, pulling the handcart with him. One of the wheels slipped down off the road and Takuya leant over sideways trying to keep the cart from toppling over. He threw all his weight against the cart's metal bar and just managed to stop the weight of the load from tipping the cart into the rice paddy.

The truck rolled forward on a course which would take it within inches of Takuya's cart. The soldiers in the back, both black and white men, seemed to be laughing as they looked down at Takuya. They all had sub-machine-guns slung over their shoulders or resting against their knees as they stood peering down over the side.

As Takuya concentrated all his might on keeping the cart from slipping into the paddy field, he pitched his gaze diagonally up at the Americans. Maybe this looked comical to the soldiers, for a gale of laughter erupted from them. This was the first time he had seen foreign military up close since the afternoon of the day the war ended. Every one of them seemed to be smiling.

As the leading lorry passed him and moved off down the road, the second one approached slowly. Once again the back was full of soldiers looking down at Takuya and his cart perched precariously at the side of the road. A round-faced man with mousy hair leant out of the passenger window, smiling widely at Takuya. He couldn't have been much more than seventeen or eighteen years old. The cab went past and the back came level with Takuya. Again the soldiers smiled down at him, their eyes seemingly genial. Takuya could sense a fawning, obsequious expression coming across his own contorted face.

Suddenly one of the soldiers thrust his upper body forward and swung the steel helmet he had been hiding behind him down onto Takuya's head. The lack of anywhere to retreat, and the speed with which the helmet was wielded, made the blow impossible to avoid. The other soldiers must have been waiting for that moment, because a loud cheer went up from them. Takuya caught sight of a black soldier giving the culprit a few congratulatory slaps on the shoulder as he felt himself and the cart slowly tipping over sideways into the rice paddy. The load of matchboxes spilt into the water and Takuya felt his face slap hard into the mud.

The soldiers' jubilant faces quickly moved out of view, and

the remaining lorries accelerated down the road now that the obstacle had been ejected from their path. The clouds of dust settled and the noise of the engines faded into the distance.

Barely conscious, his eyes almost shut, Takuya's first thought was to see this as an officer of the Japanese army being insulted by a lowly American soldier, but for some reason this didn't anger him in the slightest. He just couldn't understand the grinning looks on the young soldiers' faces, their joyful animation as they celebrated Takuya's difficulty. He felt that the soldier's smashing him over the head with a steel helmet was part of some frivolous game, like the bomber crews whiling away their time inside the B-29s by flipping through pornographic magazines and listening to jazz.

Some time passed before he slowly opened his eyes again. There was no pain, but his ears were ringing as though a hundred cicadas had got inside his head. He tried to get up, but the side of his face was stuck to the mud and wouldn't move. His vision seemed to be all right, for he could see the bar of the cart directly above his head, as well as the canvas strap hanging down on top of him. Beyond these he could see the clear blue sky, with only a few delicate clouds.

A man dressed in peasant clothes appeared. Takuya felt himself being lifted and dragged out of the paddy field and up the slope, where he was helped into a sitting position on the side of the road. Some more men, probably ten in all, appeared around him. Some tried to push the cart up out of the mud, and others carried his spilt cargo back up on to the road. A man wearing shorts asked him something, and while Takuya could sense himself replying, the sound of his own voice was drowned out by the ringing in his ears.

He looked up at the blue sky and the clouds moving across it. There were women in work clothes among the crowd. Takuya could feel someone holding him in an upright sitting position.

People were milling around the handcart, stacking the load back into place. The cicada-like ringing seemed to echo from one side of his head to the other.

Terasawa appeared in front of him, talking frantically. Again he felt himself answering but was unable to hear his own reply. Kameya's face came into view, and Takuya felt himself being lifted into the lorry. The glare of the sun made him squint.

He closed his eyes.

8

Takuya spent three days recuperating in bed.

'You poor thing,' said Terasawa's wife every time she put some food down beside his pillow. The ringing in his ears was gone, but he still had a splitting headache.

Evidently a farmer working in a nearby field had seen Takuya toppling into the rice paddy with his handcart. The people who came to his assistance after the trucks left had seen the company name painted on the cart and sent someone to report the incident to Terasawa, who had rushed to the scene with Kameya in the lorry.

'We told the police, but they just nodded and said that when it comes to the occupation forces there's nothing they can do,' explained Terasawa in a despondent tone.

Takuya couldn't imagine pulling the cart again. If US Army trucks had chosen that road once, they might choose it again, and if he got in their way a second time the same thing might happen again. He sensed a strange malevolence in those cheerful Americans. Their physical size equally overwhelmed him. Thinking of how intimidated he felt now, he couldn't believe that just two years ago he had the nerve actually to stand up and behead one of their countrymen.

When Takuya asked timidly if he could be switched from deliveries to a job in the workshop, Terasawa agreed without a moment's hesitation. He said that he understood Takuya's reluctance to get back out on the road, and that another man had been asking for a job doing deliveries.

For four days Terasawa's wife nursed the swollen wound on Takuya's head with antiseptic. Five days after the incident, Takuya came back to work again on light duties, and two weeks after that, when he was fully recovered, he started on heavier duties, carrying pieces of timber around the workshop.

By now the hills in the distance were covered with a white blanket of snow.

Orders for matchboxes went up with the increase in the black-market production of matches. Production capacity was pushed to the limit, and to compensate for the time lost during the day because of the power cuts.

At the end of December, Terasawa's wife's niece, a well-built twenty-five-year-old by the name of Teruko, came to live with them to help with the housework. She got up early in the morning to help Terasawa's wife boil the sticky concoction they used as glue each day. In addition she helped with the cooking, washing and cleaning, and went out to collect the week's rations.

A bathroom was added on to the house and hot water was generated by burning the scraps and sawdust from the workshop. Terasawa let the staff who lived away from the workshop take turns soaking in the new bathtub after work. He also followed rises in the wage market, and increased his workers' wages as often as he could. At the end of that year, Takuya's live-in wage was raised to one thousand three hundred yen a month.

Kameya sometimes spent his spare cash down in the brothels near the station, returning late at night.

'Do you want to come down sometime?' he asked Takuya, holding up three fingers to indicate that three hundred yen would buy the services of a young lady for an hour.

Takuya smiled and said nothing.

Lugging timber around in the workshop was hard work, but not having to venture outside lifted a weight from his mind. As when he'd been pushing the handcart, most days he kept a small towel wrapped round his face, more for function than disguise now.

In his free time Takuya gazed at the white walls of Himeji castle or tried to imagine what was happening in his village back in Shikoku. Almost two years had passed since he left home. He wondered what his parents and brother and sister had done during that time, and whether his father and mother were still in good health. They must be wondering what had happened to him, too. The police would be checking their mail, so sending them a letter was too risky. All the same, he wished he could put their minds at ease with the knowledge that, for the time being, he was still alive and safe.

As New Year approached, Terasawa bought a stack of greeting-cards and, after stamping each of them with the company seal, got Teruko to address them, which she did in immaculate, precise handwriting.

Takuya toyed with the idea of sending a New Year's card to his parents. He could write Terasawa's company address, he thought, but of course he would have to use a false name, something new, neither Kiyohara Takuya nor Higa Seiichi. At first glance his family would think it strange to be receiving greetings from a stranger, but they'd soon recognise his handwriting and realise that he was safe and well, living in Himeji.

After thinking it through this far, Takuya suddenly changed his mind. Maybe he was slowly starting to cave, he thought. When he left his parents' home, Takuya had told himself that there would be no return, and that he would never see his family again. He had known that evading the authorities hinged on cutting the bonds with his home, and that was as true now as it had been two years earlier.

But, as time passed, Takuya's resolve started to waver. Sending New Year's greeting-cards was so ritualised that receiving one from someone with whom you normally had very little contact was nothing out of the ordinary. Surely the police wouldn't notice his one card among the dozens of others? He pondered a little longer, convincing himself that there was no risk involved. Letting his family know that he was still alive was something he just had to do.

After getting one of the company-stamped cards from Terasawa, Takuya thought hard about what to write. Something as bland as possible would be best, and addressing it to his younger brother rather than his father would make it safer still. He wrote 'New Year's Greetings' at the top, followed by 'Wishing you and your family all the best for the year to come.' They were very nondescript words, but he was sure that his family would read between the lines and recognise his message.

That night, Takuya went to the mailbox in front of the makeshift ration distribution centre. There was a chance that a member of his family might try to visit him at the address on the card, but surely they would realise that this could be fatal for him.

He headed back home with an extra spring in his step at the thought that even a tenuous connection was about to be made with his family.

At dinnertime on New Year's Day, 1948, Terasawa brought in five bottles of beer and a large bottle of sake for them to drink with their meal of rice cakes and vegetables boiled in soup. He had even obtained some dried fish to supplement the meal. By all accounts match production in the area was increasing by leaps and bounds, and Terasawa's production of boxes, and therefore profits, was also rising. By this stage he had increased the number of staff to almost twenty workers.

Terasawa often spoke of hearing rumours that the match market was about to be deregulated later that year, with the old wartime rationing and control regulations possibly being abolished. He told them that, while the overall quality of the matches was still inferior, production levels were basically meeting demand, so the regulations were becoming pointless. Terasawa said public discontent was running high over matches which frequently snapped or failed to light properly, and that government offices in Tokyo and Osaka were starting to handle appeals from citizens' groups for something to be done about the situation.

'There's certainly something farcical about making matchboxes when more than half of what goes in them is going to break anyway,' Terasawa lamented.

The front page of the morning newspaper on New Year's Day contained a long message to the Japanese people from General Douglas MacArthur, supreme commander of the Allied Powers, in which he laid out a plan for Japan's future as a nation. Takuya scoured it for mention of war criminals, but found nothing.

After the New Year's holiday came to a close, however, the newspapers featured lengthy articles almost daily, recounting the proceedings in the Tokyo trials of Class A war criminals. Takuya read every one of them, but since that article the previous September about the imprisonment in Sugamo of the high-ranking officers, there had been no further mention of the POWs held by Western Regional Command, something which worried him intensely.

Although he had long since recovered from the physical damage caused by the encounter with the American soldiers, emotionally he was far from healed. The pitiful feeling of helplessness he had experienced as the helmet smashed down on his head was still rooted in his mind. It was a feeling less of humiliation than of having been absolutely crushed in defeat. Everything they did seemed lighthearted, he thought. If they caught him they would probably make a comedy out of leading him to the gallows and placing the noose round his neck. He remembered that the Americans had adorned the B-29s with caricatures of naked women and pictures of flames painted on the fuselages to show how many raids they had taken part in.

On his job carrying timber around the workshop Takuya kept a lookout for anyone approaching from outside. Houses were being built in the vicinity of the railway station, and the boundaries of this new residential area were gradually pushing farther out.

With the price of materials increasing at a frightening pace, Terasawa decided that the best thing would be to stock up on timber and striking-paper and, as the existing warehouse was already full to capacity, to build another one next to it.

It appeared more and more likely that the sale of matches would be deregulated soon, and an article in the newspaper on the twentieth of January reported that a special ration of matches was to be given to each household. Families with three members could buy two small boxes, those with six people four boxes, ten people eight boxes, and ten boxes could be purchased by households comprising ten or more people. The price was set at one yen twenty-three sen, and normal ration coupons for household goods would suffice. This was proof that production levels were at last starting to meet demand.

Maybe the news that matches were going to be removed from the list of regulated goods was encouraging more operators to start manufacturing, for the number of stranges coming in to buy large quantities of matchboxes had increased considerably. Thick wads of notes were handed over in exchange for cartloads of matchboxes. The buyers, dressed in all sorts of clothes, were obviously black marketeers, and none of them knew much at all about the product they were looking to buy. Every time these strangers approached, Takuya worried that they might be plainclothes policemen.

With the drop in temperature came occasional light flurries of snow. The icy winds that blew across Himeji stole the feeling from Takuya's hands, and that winter he again developed painful chilblains on his ears, fingers and toes.

The new houses built near the station hid the lower part of Himeji castle from view, but the white towers and donjons stood out in stark relief against the clear blue of the winter sky.

Towards the end of January the newspapers were dominated by articles about the poisoning of twelve workers at the Shiina-machi branch of the Imperial Bank, but in early February Takuya found one that mentioned Western Regional Command. On the second of February the legal department of the US Eighth Army had announced the names of twenty-eight people, comprising sixteen military personnel, including the commander-in-chief of Western Regional Command, and twelve staff of the Faculty of Medicine at Kyushu Imperial University, who had been charged and would be tried together publicly by the Yokohama military tribunal. The charges were divided into the three broad categories of vivisection, cannibalism, and the unlawful execution of B-29 crew members, with a note at the end of the article to the effect that Professor Iwase of Kyushu Imperial University had already taken his own life.

Takuya had secretly hoped that the trial of the seven officers from Western Regional Command, including the commander-in-chief, who had been held in Sugamo prison since September

1945, had already ended. Now he knew that in fact it was just about to start, and that the number of people charged had increased to sixteen. The article he had read almost a year and a half ago had mentioned seven suspects incarcerated in Sugamo prison, six of them high-ranking officers, and the other, Lieutenant Howa Kotaro, the only one who had actually taken part in the executions. That the number of suspects had increased to sixteen meant that another nine of the soldiers who had participated in the executions must have been arrested and charged.

Takuya had taken part in only one of the three executions, so he didn't know for certain how many people had been involved altogether, but he surmised that it must have been around fourteen or fifteen, meaning that including himself there were still four or five men at large. Shirasaka had mentioned giving Lieutenant Hirosaki demobilisation papers and telling him to run, and Takuya had done the same for his friend Himuro in Osaka. If those two men were still at large, another two or three more must be on the run.

SCAP would have wanted to start the trials, and would have instructed the Japanese government to arrest the remaining suspects. The government in turn would have entrusted the police with the task, which they were no doubt doing their utmost to carry out. Again Takuya felt as though the net was somehow closing in around him.

He started to feel uneasy about having sent the New Year's card to his family in Shikoku. Using a false name was one thing, but maybe he shouldn't have used a card with his real address in Himeji printed on it. But then again, if the police had been suspicious about the card they surely would have sent someone to Terasawa's workshop by now. He assumed that the fact they hadn't was proof that the card had slipped past the censors unnoticed.

Takuya tried to imagine the lives his comrades were leading as fugitives. Like him, they would have assumed false names and tried to change their appearance, and would probably be leading secret lives somewhere as labourers. They would no doubt pay just as much attention as he did to the newspapers, and would have seen this article. How wonderful it would be, thought Takuya, if they could all evade capture.

The Class A war criminals' trials entered their closing stages, and towards the end of February there was further mention in the newspaper of those in Western Regional Command. The article first covered the charges against those involved in the experiments on eight captured airmen in the Faculty of Medicine at Kyushu Imperial University, then went on to describe how, after the experiments, the livers of the dead airmen had evidently been extracted, marinated in soy sauce, and served at the officers' club of Western Regional Command. Takuya hadn't heard anything about livers being eaten, and thought that it must be a mistake.

Accompanying the indictment was an explanation of the background to the charges, which further increased Takuya's anxiety. The names of those charged were preceded by the statement that although Western Regional Command had tried to conceal the truth by stating that the eight airmen who died on the operating tables in Fukuoka had been killed in the atomic bombing of Hiroshima, 'the full story had finally been revealed after hundreds of interrogations had been carried out all over the country'. Takuya thought this testified to the rigour of the investigations undertaken by the occupation authorities.

After reading this article Takuya decided it was almost a miracle that he hadn't been caught.

The police had probably already traced his movements as far as his uncle's house in Osaka, then on to Corporal Nemoto's on Shoodo-shima, and from there to his friend Fujisaki in Kobe. They would have been unrelenting in their questioning, and while each of his friends would no doubt have admitted to giving him shelter for a short time, the fact that he was still a free man was obviously due to the fact that Fujisaki and his family had not let on that they introduced him to the Terasawas.

The temperature started to rise as spring approached.

'Do you want to try your hand at keeping the accounts? You seem to write pretty well, and I think my wife and niece are right when they say that lugging wood around the workshop doesn't really suit you. They're always on at me about it,' said Terasawa to Takuya as he sat taking a break on a pile of wood.

Takuya didn't know what to say.

'I remember you saying that you finished high school in Okinawa. The warehouse is in full operation and stock is streaming in, so we need to keep a proper inventory of things. Want to give it a try?' said Terasawa, offering Takuya a cigarette.

Takuya could sense the goodwill behind the offer.

His boss might only have finished primary school, but he treated his workers with an innate generosity which formal education could not teach. He had led a hard life and was extremely demanding when it came to work, but his kindness ensured that a proper balance was maintained. He implied that the idea behind the offer wasn't his, but Takuya had no doubt that Terasawa had thought it all up himself.

The thought of changing jobs made Takuya uneasy. Moving wood around the workshop allowed him to stay in an isolated environment, while if he were to look after the company accounts he would be obliged to go out into the public eye to arrange deliveries and collect payment from clients. He wanted to turn down the offer, but could think of no good excuse.

The prospect of not having to toil away in the workshop was certainly appealing. Although he had been a sportsman during his university days, labouring required a different sort of physical and mental hardness which was starting to take its toll. Deciding that it might seem peculiar if he turned down Terasawa's kind offer, Takuya consented to change jobs.

Beginning the next day he sat behind a desk in the large concrete-floored space in the front part of the house. Obviously there could be no more wrapping a hand towel round his face while he worked, nor could he wear his mountaineering hat all the time. He felt exposed and unnerved without what he now realised had been, at least in his mind, crucial elements of disguise.

Terasawa came in and handed over some money, telling

Takuya to go and buy a new pair of glasses to replace the ones he had repaired with a piece of string.

Glasses were the only means he had left to make his face less recognisable in a crowd, so he willingly took the money from Terasawa and went to an optician in an area of town which had largely survived the fire raids. There wasn't much to choose from, but he picked out some with dark-brown horn rims and asked the shopkeeper to fit them with quite strong lenses. He tried them on and looked in the mirror on the counter. The rims of the glasses Fujisaki had given him had been relatively thin, so they hadn't made much difference to the way he looked, but these new ones altered his appearance considerably. On the way back to the workshop he tossed his old glasses on to a pile of rubbish by the side of the road.

The two women made quite a show of their surprise upon seeing Takuya, and Terasawa commented jokingly that he looked like a completely different person, which of course eased his fears somewhat.

Takuya set himself conscientiously to his new job. The accounts book Terasawa gave him was nothing more than a large exercise book with the word 'Accounts' written on the cover. While he thought he should hide the fact that he had a degree in economics by keeping the books as simple as possible, he knew that he would have to use some basic bookkeeping practices in order to maintain the accounts properly. He ruled some blue and red lines on the pages and organised them into workable columns.

Terasawa was impressed when he saw what Takuya had prepared.

'When I say high school, it was a business school, actually,' said Takuya, looking a little embarrassed at the praise.

Terasawa's niece brought cups of green tea to Takuya's desk mid-morning and mid-afternoon. She also told him that amid the desolation a charred plum tree had actually started blooming. Two little clumps of blossom had appeared on one branch sticking out from the blackened trunk, and quite a few people had come to see this. She added that she had noticed couples standing under the tree looking up at the pink flowers.

Teruko often whispered to him that she would be glad to mend his clothes, or do other little jobs for him.

On the eleventh of March, Takuya read in the newspaper that the trial of those involved in the experiments at Kyushu Imperial University had begun at the Yokohama military court. The article described how three hundred people, including foreigners, the families of the accused, and reporters from Japan and overseas, had packed into the public gallery, and how the accused, the public prosecutors and other lawyers had filed into the court, followed by members of the military tribunal. After one of the public prosecutors read out the charges, each of the accused, including the commander-in-chief of Western Region, had pleaded not guilty, and the day's proceedings were closed after the chief prosecutor made his opening address to the court.

Six days later Takuya came across an article which, in its own way, indicated the probable fate of the accused from Western Regional Command. It reported on the sentencing of naval garrison personnel on Ishigaki island who had been involved in the execution by decapitation, and subsequent bayoneting of the corpses, of three American fighter crewmen. The chief of the military tribunal had sentenced two of the forty-five accused to imprisonment with hard labour, and found another two not guilty, but had sentenced the remaining forty-one men to death by hanging.

Logically speaking, no more than three garrison soldiers had actually beheaded the American airmen, so the others must be the officers who had ordered the execution and those who had bayoneted the corpses. That the list included many soldiers of the rank of corporal or below served to confirm this, the officers undoubtedly having ordered the bayoneting to prepare the soldiers for the battles to come. Such practices were almost routine in front-line units, and there was no place for the will of the individual soldier to intervene in the process. Nevertheless, it was SCAP's position that several dozen soldiers should receive the death penalty regardless of whether they had been acting on orders from their commanding officer to mutilate the dead bodies. By this reasoning, Takuya and those of his comrades who had actually beheaded B-29 crew members could expect nothing less than the gallows.

He often woke up in the middle of the night and found it hard to get back to sleep, worrying about how someone he had passed in the street had looked at him, or how a man standing on the street corner had seemed to be peering curiously into the factory area. Since taking on his office duties, he had to make regular trips to the bank and to clients in order to receive payments for boxes. Occasionally, he had gone as far as the railway station to arrange for the shipment of an order of matchboxes by freight train. Every time he left the confines of the company premises, the thought that he was stepping into public view unnerved him. At times he thought that for his peace of mind he should take his pistol with him, but he knew that the nerve he would need actually to use it had long since vanished, so it stayed in his rucksack.

Takuya started to think that being attached to Western Regional Command Headquarters had been a stroke of very bad luck. The other graduating cadets had been scattered to postings throughout Japan and overseas. Within the anti-aircraft defence corps, some had taken up positions with ack-ack units and others had gone to command electronic aircraft detection groups. If only he hadn't been assigned to headquarters, he thought, he wouldn't be on the run, but would probably be sitting in an office somewhere, content with his lot.

He thought back to the time when the lieutenant from the legal affairs section had told him to pick out two sergeant-majors to take part in the executions, and regretted having offered to do his part, too. He had volunteered from a feeling of outrage toward those who had carried out countless incendiary raids, as well as not one but two atomic bombings on Japanese cities, seeing the execution of the B-29 crewmen as a natural and indisputable response to such acts of barbarism. But after the war there had been no adverse media comment about the bombings, the primary objective of which had been to slaughter defenceless civilians. SCAP censorship had probably played a part in this but, even so, the average person in the street was just as reluctant to say anything. Women offered their bodies to American soldiers for money, children grovelled in the streets for sweets, and men bought what the Americans didn't need to sell for their own profit. They must have erased from their minds all memory of the houses being burnt to cinders and the lives lost in the firestorms. Not an iota of hatred about what had happened seemed to remain among the populace.

Takuya, too, came to the realisation that his anger with the American military had all but evaporated. Did the time after a war act as some sort of filtration process, whereby all memories and experiences were expunged from the present and relegated to the past? All that remained in Takuya's mind was the undeniable fact that he had beheaded a POW and the relentless anxiety of being on the run.

He started to rethink the meaning of the badges he had worn as an officer in the army. Wearing an officer's badge was an article of faith, a sign that one was not afraid of dying, and Takuya had held true to it during his days in uniform. However, since leaving the army, the fear of death dominated his every moment, and the fact that such a change should occur in the two short years since he left his parents' house seemed incredible. Whenever he went out on business he took the less-used roads and walked with his eyes cast slightly downward. If he had to go to the Sanyo line freight station, he furtively slipped the duty station worker a box of matches from Terasawa, smiling obsequiously and acting as ingratiatingly as he could in order to avoid giving the impression that he'd been an officer in the army.

Down on the embankment the cherry trees were blossoming, and crowds of people were said to be flocking in for a festival which was being held at the Ryuumon temple near the sea. Slowly society seemed to be moving back towards normality.

On a day when they knew that the power was to be off, Takuya went with Terasawa and the others to the beach to collect shellfish. The women got up early and cooked some rice with soybeans to use for making rice balls. One of the day workers and his family joined them, and Kameya drove them all to the sea in the lorry.

They crossed the bridge over the Ishikawa river and drove through the residential area of Shirahama, where many of the match factories were located. The beach was on the edge of town, not far from the little fishing-port of Mega, so they could see fishing-boats heading back in after a day out at sea. Men and women in sedge hats were working in the belt of salt fields stretching out on one side.

At this first view of the sea in two years Takuya relaxed immediately. It was a beautiful calm day, and in the distance he could see several small islands, each covered in a lush blanket of green. A shoal of fish must be just off to the west, as the water was agitated by fish breaking the surface. Seabirds took turns plunging out of the sky into the mass of fish, or sat bobbing up and down on the water's surface.

There were crowds of people there that day, all bent over scraping away at the sand. Here and there, the sun's rays reflected brightly off puddles of sparkling clear water.

Takuya and the others dug away at the sand with metal clamps they had brought from the workshop. They found small clams everywhere, but occasionally, to everyone's delight, they uncovered a really big one. Every so often, Takuya straightened up and stretched his back, surveying the area around them. At the water's edge, he could see little waves curling white at the top before dropping on to the shore. The sea was slightly greener than how he remembered it near his home. Off in the distance a black freighter slowly threaded her way between the islands.

Terasawa sauntered over to him, metal clamp in hand and an old straw hat on his head.

'Higa,' he said, as he bent over to scrape at the sand. Takuya turned to face him.

'My wife asked me to speak to you about this. Um . . . What do you think of her niece, Teruko? To marry, I mean? You know what our situation is. Losing our son in the war means that we have no one to take over the business after us. My wife likes you, you know,' said Terasawa, as he dug some little clams up and placed them neatly on the sand.

'Teruko seems to have a soft spot for you too, so why don't you think about it?' said Terasawa. Then he stood up straight, picked up the clams and walked off toward the bucket.

Takuya wasn't surprised. In fact, he had almost expected such an approach. On more than one occasion Teruko had flashed her platinum-capped teeth at him in a way that betrayed the feelings Terasawa had alluded to, and the gleam in her eye when she looked Takuya's way had not escaped him, either.

Teruko was a straightforward, pleasant young woman. Her sturdy, buxom presence had certainly served to remind Takuya of the opposite sex. No doubt she would make an admirable wife. Terasawa had implied that they wanted Takuya to consider taking over the company, and he did not doubt that the Terasawas would make ideal in-laws. Maybe marrying their niece, having a family and living out the rest of his days in Himeji wouldn't be such a bad idea.

But after a few moments he shook his head. If he were to marry Teruko and become Terasawa's adopted son, he could not keep his past a secret. A commitment to marry the niece would have to be predicated on his telling them the truth about himself. Getting them to understand his situation must come first, he thought. But Takuya knew that he couldn't bring himself to make such a confession, and that therefore his only choice was to turn down Terasawa's offer.

At lunchtime, they all retired up onto the grassy dune beyond the beach to sit on straw mats and unwrap rice balls. Teruko sat on the edge of the bank and placed a hand towel neatly on her lap before starting to eat her own lunch with chopsticks. Terasawa kept them entertained with funny stories and Teruko covered her mouth with her hand as she laughed happily at his jokes.

In the afternoon, the line of waves breaking on the beach crept closer as the tide started to come in, shepherding the people with their buckets full of clams back towards the grassy dunes. When the sea had reclaimed all but the last few yards of sand, Takuya and the others retreated up the slope and loaded the day's haul of shellfish into the lorry.

Off they went. Teruko sat holding on to the side of the lorry with one hand as she pushed the hair off her face with the other.

That night, after he had crawled into his futon, Takuya told himself that the time had come for him to leave the Terasawas. He'd been with them for two years now. Staying in one place was never wise for someone on the run, and the fact that he had been with the Terasawas for this long was obviously the main reason behind the suggestion that he marry their niece. If Takuya were arrested now, the authorities would suspect that Terasawa had given him shelter despite knowing what he had done. He decided to leave Himeji before he burdened Terasawa with repercussions from his past.

The next day, on his way back from a visit to the bank to deposit the week's receipts, he dropped in at the local employment agency. If he were to look for a different job, it would be best to avoid the cities and instead hide somewhere like a coal mine up in the mountains. Spending time in the bowels of a mine, away from prying eyes, would surely bring him peace of mind, he thought. Men and women were going in and out of the agency, and inside a throng of people lined up in front of the workers standing behind a counter on the other side of the room. Waiting his turn would require more time than Takuya had that day, so he decided to come again the next morning.

As he turned to leave, he saw a poster beside the door advertising for labourers in the Ikuno mine. Almost certainly they needed to advertise like this because many people were unwilling to work there.

That night he casually asked Kameya about the location of the Ikuno mine and learnt that it was a silver mine, further inland, to the north of Himeji.

Looking at the map on the wall above his desk, Takuya thought it seemed an ideal place to hide. It was right in the middle of Hyogo prefecture, about halfway between the Harima Sea and the Sea of Japan. The symbol on the map indicating the exact location of the mine showed that it was in a gorge between two lines of mountains. A quick look at the railway timetable told him it was just under an hour and a half from Himeji on the Bantan line. Being up in a heavily wooded area meant that, if the police did come to arrest him, it would not be too difficult to evade them by slipping away into the forest. Working underground, he would never need to be seen by anyone apart from his co-workers.

Suddenly Takuya felt extremely uneasy about being in Himeji. If he continued to parade around town in broad daylight, before long the police would recognise him. Also, with the bombed-out areas gradually filling up with new houses, more people who knew him might move back into the city, which obviously increased the likelihood of his being identified by the authorities. At the same time, he couldn't help but be worried about Fujisaki's family. They knew that he was working at Terasawa's workshop, and if the police tracked him as far as the Fujisakis they might well crack under interrogation and divulge his whereabouts. That the Fujisakis knew his whereabouts was a danger he was only now beginning to appreciate fully. The only way to circumvent this potentially disastrous situation was to distance himself from the Terasawas and to keep his move to the Ikuno mine a secret.

Takuya felt himself losing his composure. At times he was completely immobilised by the premonition that the police were about to appear and arrest him.

Three days later, when the power supply was off, Takuya went to the employment agency to get the forms to apply for work in the Ikuno silver mine. When he returned to Terasawa's house, he slipped the forms between the pages of his accounts book and, checking that no one was likely to disturb him, furtively started filling them in. The figure for mine workers' wages on the forms was several times higher than the average wage in Himeji.

When Takuya went into the living-room that evening, the sound of running water told him that Terasawa's wife and their niece, Teruko, were in the kitchen doing some washing.

Terasawa was smoking a cigarette as he read the newspaper spread out on the low table in the middle of the room. Takuya sat down on the other side of the table, his legs folded under him in formal style, and without beating about the bush said that he wanted to quit his job. Terasawa lifted his eyes from the newspaper and stared in bewilderment at him.

Takuya saw straight away that Terasawa was hurt. Two years had passed since the Terasawas had taken him on. Their warm support was the only thing that had saved him from starvation.

'Is this because I asked you about Teruko? If that's the case, don't worry about it. Forget I ever mentioned it,' said Terasawa remorsefully.

'That isn't the reason,' Takuya replied instinctively.

'Well, what is it then?' said Terasawa, looking him squarely in the face.

Takuya was at a loss for words. He regretted that he hadn't at least concocted an appropriate excuse for quitting his job. If he allowed Terasawa to think that the talk of marriage was the reason, Teruko would be needlessly offended. Of course he bore no ill will toward the Terasawas, and he did not want to see them hurt.

'You know I don't have anyone to take over from me, so I just thought that it might be good if you and Teruko got together. But if you're not keen on the idea it doesn't matter. Are you worried about your parents? If so, why don't you get them to come to Himeji? I know it may not be so easy to leave Okinawa these days, but . . .' Terasawa pushed his glasses back up the bridge of his nose, the women's laughter from the kitchen seeming to finish his sentence.

Takuya looked away and hung his head. He could not bear betraying Terasawa's kindness.

He flushed with a sudden urge to confide in Terasawa. He could feel himself starting to panic, and fidgeted uncontrollably as he looked up at the ceiling. He took a deep breath to try to calm himself down, but felt his face turn red, as though all the blood in his body were rushing to his head. In his mind he could hear two opposing choruses of voices, one telling him that it was wrong to hide the truth from Terasawa any longer, the other that he shouldn't do anything on impulse which could not be rectified afterward.

Terasawa sat looking dejected, saying nothing.

'To tell you the truth . . .' Takuya began. As he spoke, the voice of caution seemed to repeat itself over and over again in the back of his mind. He felt himself break out in a cold sweat. Nevertheless, once he had uttered the first short sentence, the words flowed as though they had been a script waiting to be articulated. It was almost as if his mouth were moving independently of his mind. He could feel a faint nervous spasm in his knees start to spread through the rest of his body.

Terasawa's gaze was fixed on Takuya's face, his expression one of utter astonishment. Though his fear of the possible consequences of his decision was undiminished, Takuya continued with his confession, a powerful surge of emotion driving him on.

Takuya felt his eyes moisten as he finished his story.

Terasawa sighed, and his hands shook slightly as he filled his pipe with tobacco and struck a match to light it.

'So that was it. From the day I met you I thought you weren't just some ordinary man off the street,' he said. He sighed again, more deeply this time, but then turned his gaze back to Takuya as though he had just decided something, and said in a hushed but forceful tone, 'You did well to own up to that. Leave it to me. I won't say a word, not even to my wife or niece. Wherever you go it would be dangerous. Best to stay here, I'd say. I'll make sure you're safe.'

Takuya bowed deeply, said nothing as he stood up, and returned to his own room. A wave of fatigue came over him as he sat down on his futon. While he had been happy to hear Terasawa's kind words of support, he agonised that the punishment might not stop at him if his true identity were discovered. Speaking about his past against his better judgement was proof that he had come to rely too heavily on Terasawa's goodwill. Takuya resolved to stick to his plan to go up to Ikuno and hide away in the depths of the mine.

He had decided to return the forms for the job at the Ikuno mine the next time the workshop was closed due to power cuts, but when that day came he could not bring himself to walk out of the gate and go to the employment agency. In part, he did not feel determined enough to shake himself free of his dependence on the Terasawas, but the main reason was his apprehension at being unable to imagine what life would be like underground in the mine. He could no longer find the mental fortitude necessary to push himself to move again.

The rainy season started.

Dressed in a long raincoat, Takuya trudged around the streets collecting payments and taking them to the bank. Terasawa's attitude toward him had become slightly more respectful of late, and whenever he saw Takuya helping to unload incoming materials he called over one of the other workers to do it instead.

A few days of thunderstorms brought the rainy season to an end. With the government having announced that the regulations covering the sale of matches would be lifted in autumn, a large number of would-be manufacturers started up businesses, which led to a dramatic increase in the demand for matchboxes. As orders began coming in from factories in the Kobe area, Takuya found himself increasingly busy organising large consignments to be shipped there by freight train.

One day Takuya plucked up the courage to go to the black market and buy himself a pair of blue trousers, a shirt, some second-hand black shoes and a felt hat. A change of clothes was one thing, but he couldn't bring himself to go further and visit the barber. The thought of sitting in the barber's chair, his face exposed for all to see, made him continue letting Kameya cut his hair with the electric clippers.

Whenever he left a piece of clothing out in his room, Teruko would take it away and return it later that day nicely washed and ironed. Terasawa's wife was obviously behind this, but Takuya chose to say little more than a casual thank you each time he found the clothing back in his room.

Fine weather continued and the temperature steadily rose.

The number of power lines in the area around the workshop increased, and they could often hear cicadas clinging to the pole beside the gate to the company grounds.

At the end of July match manufacturers had managed to obtain a small quantity of white willow from Hokkaido, so good-quality matches were being produced again. As more goods circulated in the market, the skyrocketing prices that had continued since the end of the war started to ease, and the freeze on access to savings was removed. On top of this, reports appeared in the newspapers that the price of vegetables and seafood was starting to fall below the prices regulated by the government. The meals at Terasawa's gradually improved, and the dining-table was occasionally graced by large bowls of rice mixed with real barley.

Takuya noticed that articles about the war crimes trials had all but disappeared from the newspapers. Once in a while there was mention of the trial of a Class A war criminal, but it was never more than the briefest of coverage. Terasawa had obviously kept his word about not telling his wife or niece about Takuya's past, for there was no noticeable change in their attitude to him.

The summer that year was unusually hot.

On the twenty-eighth of August, Takuya found an article in the newspaper reporting that a verdict had been delivered in the case against the men involved in the experiments carried out at Kyushu Imperial University. Three medical staff from the university, the commander of Western Region, and a total of five staff officers from the tactical operations centre had been condemned to death by hanging, while two other university staff and two headquarters staff had been sentenced to life imprisonment. The article closed by stating that the trials of those involved in the execution of B-29 crewmen would commence very soon.

Takuya sensed that the Allied administration was moving into the final stages of dealing with Japan's part in the war. The military tribunal's adjudications would close with the trials in Tokyo of the Class A war criminals and those staff of Western Regional Command involved in the execution of POWs. Takuya mused that, after these trials were finished, the danger of capture might abate as his pursuers became less zealous.

Early the next morning, Takuya was overseeing the shipment of a consignment of boxes. A very large order for various sizes had come in from a match manufacturer in Kobe, and Takuya had to organise its transport by horse-drawn cart to the freight station, and then its loading on to the train.

He stood on the platform at the Sanyo line freight station, checking that everything was in order as the cargo was loaded into the freight car. The workers were stripped to the waist, their back muscles glistening in the sun and their arms and chests speckled with pieces of straw packing stuck to the sweat from their toil.

The man in the guardroom stuck his head out of the window and called to Takuya that there was a telephone call for him from Terasawa. He told the men to stop loading until he got back, walked over to the office and put his hand in through the window to take the receiver.

Terasawa's hollow-sounding voice came over the telephone line, telling Takuya to drop everything and run for it. 'Go to Okayama. I've got a friend who makes matchboxes there who will help,' he said. He blurted out the address of the place before telling Takuya that two detectives from a city near his home had turned up at the workshop together with one from Himeji Central Police Station, and had left hurriedly when Kameya said that Takuya was at the freight station. 'Run for it! They must almost be there! Go to Okayama!' said Terasawa, now almost shouting into the telephone.

'OK,' Takuya replied, and he leant in through the window to replace the receiver. He turned and looked down the road leading to the workshop. All he could see was a horse-drawn cart moving slowly along the parched dirt track, and an old woman dressed in dishevelled clothes with a baby on her back.

Terasawa's words imploring him to run rang in his ears, the name and address of the man in Okayama echoing in his head. If I go now everything will be all right, he told himself, amazed at how calm and collected he was. As he stood beside the guardroom, it occurred to him that he wanted to check with his own eyes that someone had actually come to arrest him. For a moment he couldn't believe that he could be so deliberate at a time like this, but he told himself that there was still time to wait and see them before making his escape.

A man wearing an open-necked shirt appeared a short distance down the road. Two other men soon followed, one of whom crossed to the other side, picking up his pace as he neared the platform. The second man had close-cropped grey hair, suggesting that he was much older than the other two.

Takuya couldn't understand why he hadn't turned and run already. It was almost as though his joints had locked and his feet were set in concrete. He knew that all he had to do to escape was to jump down on to the tracks and thread his way to safety through the lines of freight cars. Nevertheless, he stood glued to the spot, watching the three detectives hastening toward their goal. The tallest of the three looked quite young, not much more than twenty or twenty-one years old.

Takuya was at a loss. A feeling of inertia seemed to have come over him, as though the mental strain of two years on the run had disappeared, leaving nothing but lassitude. Even if he evaded capture, he would doubtless end up being caught somewhere else, he thought. Maybe he wasn't as good at being a fugitive as he had thought. He had done all he could to stay at large, and he had no strength left to push himself any further.

Enough, he told himself. The three men walked into the station, casting studied glances at everyone, until almost at the same moment all three recognised Takuya.

One of the younger men clambered up on to the platform. The other made to seal off the path to escape by walking farther down the footpath and stopping in front of the freight car. The grey-haired man walked over towards the guardroom and up the stone path to the platform to stand in front of Takuya.

'Takuya Kiyohara?' he said. Takuya nodded, watching dolefully as the detective pulled out a set of handcuffs. He told himself over and over again that this was all right, this was the way it was always going to end.

His father was there waiting at Himeji police station. As soon as he saw Takuya walk into the room he hung his head and started sobbing uncontrollably. He was still weeping as he began to explain himself in beseeching tones. He told his son that the police investigations had been relentless from the day after Takuya had made his escape, with all his family, relatives, friends, and even his teachers from primary and high school, being interrogated one by one. Within weeks of Takuya's disappearance, the atmosphere at the municipal office had soured so much that he had quit his job. A month ago he had been taken into custody for another round of interrogation, the police insisting that he must know where Takuya was hiding. He described how the police had told him that the three other men from headquarters had been arrested after their parents had confessed their whereabouts, and that they were all trying to put the blame for everything on Takuya. His interrogator had kept telling him that, because of this, Takuya must receive the heaviest sentence, and the only way to prevent it was to bring him before the court as quickly as possible.

As they had decided that Takuya's father was not going to try to escape, they had let him sit outside and sun himself in a spot where they could see him. Not wanting to be a public burden, he spent much of his time outside, weeding the police grounds as payment for the meals they provided. His father had realised that the false name on the New Year's card had really been Takuya, but, fearing that writing a reply would lead to disaster, he had gone no further than to copy the address in Himeji on to the reverse side of the paper attached to the straw festoon adorning the family's Shinto altar in the living-room, burning the greeting-card after he had done so. After being held for about a month, and increasingly worried about what his interrogator had said about Takuya's remaining at large leading to a heavier sentence, he had told the police about the address written on the festoon.

'What have I done? I wish I were dead,' Takuya's father sobbed, burying his face in his hands.

Early that evening, some sushi rolls were delivered to the

holding-cells by one of Terasawa's workers. Two other men were being held in the same cell as Takuya, so he shared the food with them.

Later that same night, he was handcuffed and taken to Himeji station by two detectives. When he walked in he saw his father and Terasawa standing beside the ticket window. Terasawa handed the detectives some cigarettes and matches before fixing his forlorn gaze on Takuya.

The police must have contacted the station beforehand, because there were seats reserved for them on the train. Takuya sat between the two detectives and looked out of the window as the train slowly moved away from the platform. The moon was out and the sky was clear, so he could make out the silhouette of Himeji's White Egret Castle, but before long it faded into the distance and disappeared.

The next day, just after eleven o'clock in the morning, the train pulled into Tokyo station, and from there Takuya was taken directly to the Tokyo metropolitan police station. After a brief round of questioning he was put into a cell. When asked how he had acquired the pistol and ammunition, he said nothing about Shirasaka, instead saying that he had brought them home to Shikoku after the war ended and had buried them in the forest behind his parents' house.

After breakfast the next morning he was taken on foot to SCAP headquarters. His interrogator, a twenty-seven- or twenty-eight-year-old American officer who spoke good Japanese, asked him about his rank and posting during his years in the army. He pulled out the wanted poster they had used in their search, smiling as he said, 'You're just a little boy here.' It was a photograph of Takuya's face, enlarged from the class photograph taken when he graduated from high school. They must have got the original from one of his classmates, he thought.

Later that day Takuya was driven through the main gate at Sugamo prison in a US Army truck. A burly military policeman escorted him into a room off the courtyard, where he was made to strip to his underwear before being photographed and fingerprinted.

From there he was led down a long corridor into a cell. The American military prison guard pushed the steel door shut with his foot and locked it. The prison clothes Takuya had been given had the letter 'P' stencilled in black on the back of the shirt, both arms, the back of the trousers and the front of each trouser leg.

On the second of September, with a second-generation Japanese-American army sergeant acting as interpreter, the questioning by the public prosecutors and lawyers began. It didn't take Takuya long to understand that what Shirasaka had said about the commander of Western Region and other high-ranking officers trying to evade responsibility was obviously true. They were all insisting that the executions had been carried out arbitrarily by junior officers and their men, rather than because of any orders from above. This, of course, flew in the face of what Takuya knew to be true. The deputy chief of staff, the colonel in charge of the tactical operations centre, the headquarters legal officer and a number of headquarters medical officers had all been present at the executions, which should surely remove any doubt as to whether consent had been granted by those at the very top echelons of command.

Apart from one small window at the back, Takuya's cell was defined by concrete walls and a heavy steel door. He spent most of his time sitting there quietly by himself, but at bath time, twice a week, he had a chance to see the other prisoners, among them some of those who had served in Western Regional Command.

When Takuya bowed to higher-ranking officers, they did little more than casually acknowledge his presence before looking away. He wasn't sure whether this was because they were indignant at what they viewed as his cowardice in fleeing in the face of arrest, or because they felt pangs of conscience at the thought that their statements about ordering the executions had compromised Takuya and the other more junior men. Their long confinement seemed to have weakened them physically, for their faces looked gaunt and pale.

Lieutenant Hirosaki, who had been given blank identification papers by Shirosaka, and Lieutenant Himuro, whom Takuya had advised to escape from Osaka, were there, too. Both men described in hushed tones how they had let their parents know where they were hiding and how this had ultimately led to their arrest. As with Takuya's arrest, the parents of these two men had broken under the pressure of interrogation, divulging their sons' whereabouts on the assumption that they were thereby helping to avert the worst of punishments. Apparently, this had been a calculated scheme to round up the last fugitives.

Himuro told Takuya that a former colonel from the tactical operations centre of High Command had insisted in court that the indiscriminate bombing of Japanese cities and towns by the US Army Air Force was a violation of international law, and that the people responsible for such attacks were the ones who should be brought to justice. Takuya was impressed by the man's courage, but at the same time, knowing that criticism of the American military in front of a military tribunal could only lead to the heaviest possible penalty, he realised that he could never bring himself to say anything so provocative when his turn came to speak in court.

About a month after Takuya entered Sugamo prison, he happened to pass the former commander-in-chief of Western Regional Command in the corridor as the old man carried his meal on a tray back to his cell. Maybe it was because he had lost so much weight, but in his baggy prison clothes the commander looked frail and ordinary, a completely different person from the one Takuya remembered. The intimidating presence he had had in his lieutenant-general's uniform was gone, leaving behind only a haggard old man.

On the eleventh of October, in the military court in Yokohama, the first public hearing was held in the trial of those from Western Regional Command. Takuya was one of thirty-five accused, including the commander-in-chief. They all pleaded not-guilty to the charges against them.

The public hearings were a long process. Takuya and his fellow accused travelled each day by bus through the black-market area in front of Shinjuku station, down Shibuya Doogenzaka, through Oosaki and Shinagawa to the military court of the

American Eighth Army in Yokohama. Upon arriving at the courtroom they ate a simple midday meal from a mess tin while sitting on the floor in the makeshift holding-room, made their appearance in the courtroom and then returned by bus to Sugamo prison. As a precaution against suicide, before they were returned to their cells when they got back to the prison, they were made to strip naked to allow an MP to check their ears, noses, mouths and anuses to make sure they were not bringing back any poisons.

Every time Takuya attended the court sessions he was astounded that every one of the high-ranking officers from headquarters persisted in completely denying giving orders to carry out the executions of the American airmen. In the face of determined questioning by the public prosecutor, even the deputy chief of staff and the colonel in charge of the tactical operations centre, both of whom had actually witnessed executions, were adamant that no orders had been issued from above to dispose of the POWs. The only thing that now concerned these shadows of men in prison clothes was saving their own lives. That this would mean compromising the lives of others meant nothing to them. They were different people now. The poise and assurance they had demonstrated when they were in uniform was gone.

From all appearances, they seemed terrified by the prospect of death. Their faces were ashen and their replies to questions were halting, as though they were afraid that choosing the wrong word might be fatal. There were some among them whose voices trembled with fear as they spoke. The expression 'strung up' was being used in Sugamo to mean death by hanging, and it was clear that these men were choosing their words very carefully in a desperate attempt to avoid being 'strung up' themselves. Takuya couldn't help but notice that when one of the American military prosecutors directed his gaze at one of these men, he literally stiffened with fear, his every word of reply filled with apprehension.

From time to time thoughts of regret entered Takuya's mind for not having escaped at the freight station, but he always returned to the conclusion that doing so would only have served to postpone the inevitable. The more contact Takuya had with the prison MPs, the American military prison guards, and the judges, prosecutors and lawyers sitting in court, the more he came to the realisation that America's omnipresent military had total control of the country. Even if he had managed to evade his pursuers at the freight station, the Americans' control of society was so comprehensive that his capture would have been only a matter of time.

From other inmates, he learnt that about a month earlier the commander of the Tokyo *kempeitai*, Oishi Kojiro, had been incarcerated in Sugamo prison. He had managed to stay one step ahead of the authorities until they discovered that he was working in a coal mine and moved swiftly to arrest him. Many of Takuya's fellow inmates said that Oishi's staying at large so long was proof that his *kempeitai* background had equipped him well for stealth and deception, but the fact that even someone as careful as that could be captured brought home the inevitability of his own arrest.

Takuya, struggling against the fear of death as he spoke, testified in court that his own subordinates, the two sergeant-majors, had taken part in the executions only because of his orders. Shortly after this, a major posted to Fukuoka from Imperial Headquarters gave evidence to the effect that Takuya's participation in the executions was in compliance with orders he himself had given, and that these orders had of course originated at the very top of the chain of command in the Western Region, a statement which directly contradicted the testimony given by the highest-ranking officers. It seemed as if any suggestion that the US Army Air Force's indiscriminate incendiary raids on Japanese cities might have been a violation of international law had been ruled out from the start, for the defence lawyers made no mention of this in any of their statements.

On the twelfth of November, Takuya heard that verdicts had been reached in the trials of the Class A war criminals, and that seven of the defendants, including former prime minister Tojo Hideki, had been condemned to death by hanging. Another sixteen, including former navy minister Shimada Shigetaro, had been sentenced to life imprisonment. Two men were given fixed terms of imprisonment. Only seven received the death sentence, which was fewer than Takuya had expected, giving him a faint glimmer of hope that he might escape the noose.

Day after day, he and the other defendants rode in the bus from Sugamo prison to the military court in Yokohama. No one spoke along the way, so there was nothing for him to do but cast his mournful gaze out of the little windows at the outside world, or hang his head and close his eyes, thinking of the past. Occasionally he visualised himself stepping out of the command centre and seeing Fukuoka consumed by flames, or remembered the sight of the two B-29s heading towards Nagasaki, then that shrill voice over the radio from Ohmura air base minutes later, reporting the devastation of the city. But these images were now no more than vague memories from days long gone by. There wasn't a hint of emotion involved in their recollection. The anger he had once felt at the American bombers who had obliterated Japan's cities with incendiaries was all but gone.

By the time the American soldier wielding the steel helmet knocked him unconscious as he clutched his handcart on the edge of the paddy field, he had probably already joined the rest of his countrymen living in a new, postwar world, he thought. Even then he had felt no hatred of them, only an obsequious terror. And now, in his hazy memory of it all, his strongest feeling was relief that he'd been lucky enough to get away as lightly as he had. He remembered the fawning look he had directed toward the American soldiers in the lorry just before being struck with the helmet, and knew that that expression had become a virtual fixture on his face since he had entered prison.

They were allowed to wash themselves in the bath twice a week, but most of the time the MP guarding them screamed for them to get out of the bathtub after what seemed like only a few moments. Takuya and his fellow inmates would strip while they waited in the corridor, ready to rush into the bathroom when the MP gave the word, and shave and wash themselves frantically in the short time available. Some sat there leisurely washing themselves, but more often than not Takuya was flustered by the guard's shouts, and left before he could soak in the bath. In the morning, too, he leapt out of bed the moment he heard the guard yelling and the crash of a boot against the steel cell door. Not a day went by when Takuya did not feel intimidated by his captors' overpowering physical presence.

He often thought about his father, reduced to a sobbing wreck in the police station. He had aged dramatically, the skin of his face loose around the jowls. Takuya sent two postcards to his family. Outgoing messages were limited to one hundred and fifty characters, but nothing that required more space to write about came to mind, so this posed no problem. His father had spoken of wanting to be dead, but Takuya was reassured knowing that his strong-willed mother and loyal brother and sister were there to provide support.

Most inmates had family problems. Anyone accused of being a war criminal sullied the family name, so the relatives of those in Sugamo were not received kindly by those around them. Takuya had heard of marriage arrangements for sons and daughters being called off, job offers rescinded and children being refused entry into schools and universities because their father was in Sugamo. The wife of Takuya's friend Himuro had returned to her parents' house while her husband was on the run, and filed for divorce as soon as she heard he was in Sugamo. Like so many other inmates who had been married, Himuro put his seal on the papers and sent them back as requested.

There were even cases in which the parents or wife of an inmate had been so distressed that they had committed suicide. In the early weeks, because many inmates succeeded in taking their own lives, the Americans had instituted considerably more rigorous body searches and left the corridor and cell lights on through the night. As a precaution against the transfer of poison or razors, those who were yet to be sentenced were refused visits from people outside the prison.

On two occasions, from inside his cell Takuya sensed fellow inmates being taken out to be executed. Apparently, notification that the sentence was to be carried out always occurred on Thursdays, when the prisoner was moved to a special cell for his last night before being executed the next day. That summer, five new sets of gallows were constructed in the execution compound.

One Thursday Takuya overheard a prison guard calling out the name of an inmate in a cell a few doors down from his. He heard the door being unlocked and the man stepping out into the corridor, saying his last farewells to the men in adjacent cells. The footsteps soon faded out of earshot and silence was restored after the steel door in the corridor leading to the adjoining wing was shut behind them. Takuya later heard that the man had been executed the next day.

About two weeks after that, Takuya again heard someone quietly bidding the other inmates farewell, then breaking out into an old Imperial Army song as he disappeared down the corridor. That man was one of four hanged the next day.

News travelled quickly around Sugamo on the twenty-fourth of December that seven people, including former prime minister Tojo Hideki, had been executed the previous night. There were showers that day, and through his cell window Takuya could see raindrops against an otherwise clear sky.

The trial of those from Western Regional Command was entering its final stages.

Takuya felt as if he were playing a part in a bizarre stage play. It was as though each of the accused was frantically trying to climb on top of the others to keep from drowning. As each day passed the atmosphere among the men became more tense, their expressions betraying a growing desperation. Takuya was no different from the others, aware that he was tied into a life-and-death struggle with the rest of the accused. When he heard another defendant's answers to the prosecutor's questions being framed to compromise his own position, and therefore edge him closer to the gallows, Takuya felt himself stiffen and his mouth go dry. When he in turn made a statement, he could almost feel the other defendants' gazes burning into the back of his neck. By this stage, like all the other accused, Takuya was focused on nothing but his own chances of survival. Any difference in status that had previously existed between superiors and subordinates had long since disappeared. It was every man for himself.

When he was alone in his cell he sometimes imagined the moments before his death – the noose being slipped round his neck, the trapdoor falling open and his body dropping half through the hole with a jolt. If only he could avoid the pain that must come the moment before death, he thought, hoping that it would all end the very instant the trapdoor swung open. When Takuya thought of the minutes before stepping up to the gallows, he was filled with trepidation. He wondered if he would be able to hold himself together long enough to walk up the steps unassisted. Those who kept their composure to the very end would be eulogised, he told himself. He, too, must keep his dignity and stay calm until the moment he died.

He recalled the scene in the bamboo grove before the American airmen were executed. They must have been terrified by the prospect of death, but they all did exactly as they were told, walking off through the undergrowth and kneeling down to await their fate. Was it pride, or perhaps even vanity, he wondered, that stopped them from causing a commotion? The instant the sword touched the man's neck, his body had jerked upward, as though his legs had unleashed the last action of his mortal coil. Would something similar happen when a man was hanged, Takuya wondered, and were the stories true about faeces and urine being released at the moment of death?

That night Takuya got no sleep, tossing and turning for hours on his straw mattress. It was rumoured that suicides among inmates yet to be sentenced were on the rise, and as Takuya's sentencing approached he felt that, if the opportunity arose, he would like to end it all himself.

The deliberations in court drew to a close, and it was announced that the sentences of those from Western Regional Command would be passed on December the twenty-ninth.

That day Takuya was taken from his cell, handcuffed and led out into the rear courtyard. Some inmates were already standing in neat lines, others were being led out by MPs to join the assembly. Many had bloodshot eyes and puffy faces, so it was obvious that Takuya was not the only one going without sleep.

They were ushered on to a waiting bus, and escorted by Jeeps at the front and rear carrying armed MPs. When everyone was seated the bus moved off, picking up speed once they left the Sugamo compound and drove through the streets of Tokyo and then down the main road toward Yokohama. Takuya gazed out of the window along the way, but nothing caught his eye.

Eventually the bus came to a halt in front of the court building, from where they were all led into an anteroom. Takuya avoided looking at the others, instead staring down at the polished wooden floor.

After a short wait an MP told them to move out of the room. When Takuya got up from his chair his knees and ankles felt strangely weak, as though all the strength in his legs had drained away. They were made to form a line and file down the corridor, the commander-in-chief's diminutive figure walking in front of Takuya. The former lieutenant-general's close-cropped hair was now completely white, as thin and soft as baby's down, and the skin on his neck hung loose, deep wrinkles moving ever so slightly with each step.

As always, their handcuffs were removed in the corridor before they filed into the courtroom. A large United States flag took pride of place high on the wall behind the judge's seat. Below it was a framed photograph of President Truman, flanked by photographs of General MacArthur, Supreme Commander of Allied Powers in Japan, and General Walker, commander of the United States Eighth Army. Takuya and his fellow accused remained standing as the lawyers, public prosecutors and judge entered the court. Out of the corner of his eye he could see an MP in a white helmet standing beside the door behind the seats for the defendants. The US Army colonel in charge of the proceedings started to speak, at first addressing the court, but soon looking down at the documents in front of him as he read out the verdicts in a monotone. Takuya sat motionless and stared at the deadpan expression on the man's face.

The colonel looked up again and, turning his head slightly

toward the defendants' seats, began to speak. The interpreter repeated the verdict in Japanese.

Takuya recognised the commander-in-chief's name despite the colonel's peculiar American pronunciation. His heart pounded as he stared at the colonel's lips reading the charges, the verdict and the sentences. Takuya understood very little English, but knew that it was a guilty verdict and recognised the words 'death by hanging' at the very end. The translation that followed confirmed that he was not mistaken.

Suddenly Takuya was overwhelmed by a feeling of suffocation, as though a trapdoor had swung open underneath him and a noose were closing on his neck. The deputy chief of staff's name was read out in a perfunctory tone amid a familiar-sounding stream of English, and again the words 'death by hanging' rang in the court. In quick succession, the names of the other high-ranking officers were read out, including that of the former colonel in charge of the tactical operations centre. All of them were sentenced to death by hanging.

His knees started to tremble. He shuddered, and staying on his feet became a painful struggle. The sentences of the soldiers from Ishigaki Island who had beheaded and then bayoneted the bodies of three American pilots came to his mind. Forty-one of the forty-five accused had been sentenced to death. Takuya and his comrades from Western Command had killed a total of thirty-three men, so it went without saying that their crime was much worse than that of the coastguards, and therefore the words 'death by hanging' would surely be read out after each of their names.

As they moved down through the ranks, next came the lieutenants. Both legal affairs officers were condemned to death, and after their names and sentences had been read out Takuya recognised the name of Lieutenant Howa Kotaro. He had thought the fact that Howa's mother had been killed in the fire raids on Fukuoka might have been seen as an extenuating circumstance, but again the words 'death by hanging' rang out.

By now Takuya had lost all hope. His own action had been no less extreme than those of the two legal affairs officers or

Lieutenant Howa. His name would be next, he thought, but instead the name of the young officer cadet was read out in the same American pronunciation, again followed by the death sentence. Takuya's head started to spin. His legs went numb and his knees felt as though they would buckle any second.

Next came the name of the staff officer who had ordered Takuya to take part in the executions. The set English expressions describing the charges were read out in the same sombre tone, but the words at the end were different. Takuya was sure that rather than an expression mentioning 'death', he heard the word 'life'. As he tried to understand the difference, the interpreter translated it as a 'life sentence'.

Himuro's name was read out next. Takuya concentrated as hard as he could on each individual word, and again he picked out the expression 'imprisonment for life'.

'Ta-ku-ya Ki-yo-ha-ra,' said the chief of the military tribunal. Takuya gazed intently at the colonel's lips. His sense of time seemed to have deserted him, because the space between one moment and the next seemed like an aeon. The charges were read in full and again Takuya thought he heard the word 'life' among the words explaining the sentence.

Another wave of shaking came over him and he felt a chill run down his spine, then barely controllable nausea. The culmination of years and months of unrelenting suspense had passed in an instant. He was not going to be strung up after all. A wave of emotion pushed the physical sensations into the background, but for a fleeting moment, until the interpreter confirmed it, he thought that maybe he had misheard his sentence.

The remaining defendants' sentences continued to be announced in the same monotone English followed by the interpreter's Japanese, but by now the words no longer registered with Takuya. He stared at the American flag, at the same time repeating to himself the words 'life sentence'.

After a short while the tenor of the announcements seemed to change, and the words 'not guilty' could be heard following the charges.

Realising that the English announcements had come to an end,

Takuya returned his gaze to the chief of the military tribunal. The American colonel shuffled his papers into order on his desk and rubbed his cheeks slowly with both hands.

Suddenly a voice could be heard from down in front of Takuya. Incredulous, the chief of the tribunal turned to see what was happening.

Takuya could just make out a muffled sobbing two rows down, as well as the sound of someone breathing hard and trying to keep back tears. Looking toward the front, Takuya saw a little old man moving forward from the line of seats, his head quivering slightly.

The old man was pleading tearfully that he hadn't given any orders to kill POWs. His voice trembled as he spoke. Obviously the strain had got the better of him, for he stood ramrod straight, almost as though someone had inserted a board down the back of his shirt.

Takuya felt ashamed to see this old man grovelling before the court, insisting to the members of the tribunal that, though he might have been sentenced to death in the earlier trial of those involved in the vivisection of POWs at Kyushu Imperial University, and had now received the same sentence in this trial, he had never given anyone orders to do such things, and that this decision was regrettable in the extreme.

Takuya felt he had witnessed something he would have preferred not to see, and looked away. He shut his eyes, but could still hear sniffling from the former commander-in-chief. The old man Takuya had respected as a famous general was now openly weeping.

A different American voice said something in English, which the interpreter quickly translated as the announcement of the end of the proceedings.

Takuya and the others turned to the right and, after being handcuffed once again by the MPs, filed out of the courtroom.

In the makeshift holding-room down the corridor, they were given their evening meal in army-issue mess tins. Takuya had no appetite, but he knew that he must eat. He dug his spoon into the white rice mixed with barley and chewed away at the pieces of tasteless dried fish.

Three hours after leaving Tokyo they were back on the bus to Sugamo. The sun was starting to set and the western sky was tinged with red.

Out of the left side of the bus Mount Fuji was visible in the distance as they crossed the Rokugo Bridge over the Tama river. With the sun sinking behind it, the snow on the mountain took on a light shade of purple.

9

Takuya was moved into a different cell to begin serving his sentence.

Soon after New Year 1949 his father and brother came to visit him. Through the three layers of heavy wire mesh separating them Takuya had only a blurred view of their faces, but he could see his father blinking uncomfortably, wiping his eyes repeatedly with a handkerchief. Seeing them stare at the handcuffs and the leather band wrapped round them made Takuya feel decidedly uncomfortable.

When their time was up an MP came over and led Takuya's two visitors out of the interview room.

In the end nine people, including the commander-in-chief, had been sentenced to death, five to life imprisonment, one to forty years of hard labour, four to thirty years, three to twenty-five years, four to twenty years, one to ten years, and one to five years. Seven were found not guilty. Evidently, four of the men who had taken part in the executions, Howa being one of them, were sentenced to death because their involvement was judged to be voluntary, whereas Takuya and the others who received various prison terms were deemed to have been acting in response to orders passed down the chain of command. That night, the nine men sentenced to death were moved to another wing of the prison.

Takuya spent his days uneventfully, going along with prison routine. Having avoided the gallows, he started paying greater attention to prison life. The food was dreadful. The staple component of most meals was a rice sludge made from what the other inmates said could only be chicken feed, and the soup that sometimes accompanied it was little more than miso-flavoured water with a few tiny pieces of vegetables in it. On the rare occasions they were served bread it came lightly buttered, the fat already starting to separate. Eating, getting up and going to bed took place at set times. When Takuya thought of how he'd managed to avoid the gallows, his face relaxed. He might be destined to spend the rest of his days in prison, but he was happy to be alive.

Just after the rainy season started Takuya's younger brother came to visit again. He said their parents and sister were well, and that with the sale of sake having been liberalised a month earlier their father was now enjoying a drink every night before going to bed. He went on to announce cheerfully that he'd received a pay rise at work.

Takuya listened patiently before telling his brother not to come any more. With their father having left his job, it couldn't be easy for his brother and sister, so the money needed to get from Shikoku to Tokyo and back was better spent on keeping the family fed, he said. His brother nodded from the other side of the steel-mesh dividing-screen.

Newspapers were not allowed in Sugamo. Instead there was a simple mimeographed tabloid put together by the inmates, but it featured nothing more than wood-block prints depicting prison life, some satirical verse, the occasional cartoon and a column of letters to the editor. There were effectively no sources of information about life in the outside world.

Several days of hot, humid weather set in.

One evening, through his cell window Takuya caught sight of fireworks bursting one after another in the night sky. A voice from the next cell told him that it must be from the river festival at Ryogoku. There was no sound with them, but the brightly coloured strands of light seemed to trace flower petals in the darkness before trailing away to nothing. When two or three went off at once the night sky was illuminated with splashes of brilliant colour, soon followed by an audible sigh from those watching from the cells. As Takuya stood staring out of his window at the fireworks, he thought that at last the confusion that had followed defeat in the war was starting to dissipate.

Autumn came and went and the temperature dropped.

Takuya hadn't smoked since entering Sugamo. There was an

allocation of five cigarettes a day for those who wanted them, and the guards walking up and down the corridor would light them if asked. But Takuya felt so nervous about calling the guards over that before long he had lost all desire to smoke.

One day in the third week of November, when Takuya was on his way back to his cell with a tray of food, the old man walking beside him started talking.

'You men were really lucky, you know,' he said calmly. The man was a former colonel in the Imperial Navy who had been sent to Sugamo on a life sentence just after the prison was opened.

Noticing Takuya's puzzled expression, the man began to explain what he meant.

In the early trials, he said, many people had been condemned to death for little more than slapping prisoners of war, and only after two years had the punishments started to get lighter. He said things had changed markedly after the forty-one navy coastguard troops from Ishigaki island were sentenced to death in mid-March 1948, almost three years after the surrender. The judgement of those from Western Command in the last of the war crimes trials, with most of the accused escaping the hangman's noose, was proof that the American position on war crimes had changed dramatically. United States policy toward Japan was at a turning-point, he explained, with the Americans moving away from treating Japan as a former enemy, and instead trying to entice her into their camp as a friendly player in the increasingly complicated political situation in Asia. This new stance, he said, was manifesting itself in all sorts of areas, one of them being the handling of war criminals.

Before the war, this man, now well on in years, had been a naval attaché at the Japanese Embassy in Washington, and at the time of the surrender he had been an intelligence officer at Imperial Headquarters.

'Do you follow what I'm saying?' he asked, smiling faintly.

He told Takuya that after graduating from the Imperial Naval Academy he had studied at a university in the United States, and that since he spoke fluent English he was acting as a liaison for the American military authorities with former Imperial Navy personnel in Sugamo. Obviously, it was through his continuous contact with the Americans that he had detected this subtle change in direction, and as he had some knowledge of world affairs in general he was able to make the connection between American policy toward Japan and the effect this had on the issue of war crimes.

Takuya thought the man's observations were probably very accurate. There was certainly no doubting the fact that punishments had become much less severe with the passage of time, as his own case illustrated. As the man said, luck had indeed been on Takuya's side.

On reflection, he realised that there had even been a change in the attitude of the American prison guards. The ones who had treated the inmates with spiteful severity had suddenly disappeared, replaced by more pleasant, cool-headed characters. The MPs were much more lenient about the inmates' time in the bath, and occasionally even winked affably at the men. The food situation throughout the country must have been gradually improving, because the quality of the prison food seemed better; and the time inmates were allowed to spend outside was extended.

On the twenty-fourth of December, Takuya was reminded of just how perceptive the former navy colonel's conclusions had been. That night, the Christmas message from the US Army colonel in charge of Sugamo was pasted to the wall in each wing of the prison. It detailed a number of improvements for the inmates, as well as specific reductions in the sentences of those serving shorter terms. These were to go into effect immediately. Two days later forty-six men were released on parole, followed by another sixteen on the thirty-first of December.

The atmosphere in Sugamo became even more hopeful in early 1950. In the first week of March, the prison superintendent announced parole for all inmates serving short sentences, and rumours immediately started circulating that sentences might even be reduced for those in for life or still awaiting execution. This proved to be the case, with reductions of sentence announced for all those remaining on death row. Word spread around the prison that all nine men from Western Regional Command who had been condemned to death, including the former commander-in-chief, were to have their sentences commuted to life imprisonment.

Thirty-four of those involved in the executions on Ishigaki island had their death sentences reduced to prison terms, so, including the Ishigaki garrison commander, former navy colonel Inoue Otsuhiko, only seven people remained on Sugamo's death row.

Everyone expected that they, too, would be reprieved, but early in the evening on the fifth of April, these seven men were notified that they were to be moved to cells in a different wing of the prison, in preparation for the carrying out of their sentences. Two days later, at thirty-two minutes after midnight, Colonel Inoue and three others were hanged, followed to the gallows twenty-five minutes later by former navy lieutenant Enomoto and two others. The Japanese prison chaplain told the other inmates that after they had eaten a meal with the men they had made their way through the rain to the execution yard singing the 'Battleship March'.

When the Korean war broke out that June, the American approach to the occupation of Japan was further relaxed, and one after another the remaining inmates had their sentences commuted. Takuya was no exception, and his term was reduced from life to fifteen years.

Around this time, Takuya found himself considering the war crimes trials in a new light. By rights, a trial should represent the precise application of the law, with the verdict being the strictly impartial result of due process. But the war crimes trials seemed to be heavily influenced by world affairs, with the severity of the sentencing varying greatly from one trial to the next and the original sentences often commuted within a short time of being delivered, which surely threw into question their legal foundation, and suggested that judgements were made by the victors however they saw fit. Although it pleased Takuya to know that many condemned men had escaped the gallows, and to have had his own sentence reduced, he couldn't help but think that these trials had been nothing more than an arbitrary set of judgements, distant in the extreme from what he imagined a trial should be.

With the escalation of the conflict on the Korean peninsula, the pace of changes in Sugamo accelerated. American prison guards dispatched to the front were replaced by Japanese staff, which brought more dramatic improvements in the conditions for the inmates. In September of the following year, 1951, the San Francisco peace treaty was signed, and once it came into force the administrative responsibility for running Sugamo was transferred to the Japanese government, which soon allowed stage shows and even sumo wrestling troupes to entertain the inmates.

Takuya closely followed the bewildering changes happening around him. People were being released one after another, and five-day paroles offered to anyone who chose to apply. Inmates were even allowed to leave Sugamo during the day to work in the city, and before long the prison gate was witnessing a veritable commuter rush in the morning and early evening. By this stage Sugamo was no longer a prison in the true sense of the word.

About this time Takuya heard that the former commander-in-chief was receiving treatment in the prison hospital for a neurological disorder. A short time later word went round that the old man had died in the middle of the night, filling the air with bloodcurdling screams of agony before he succumbed. The news aroused no emotion in Takuya. It was as though he were hearing of the death of an old man with whom he had no connection.

Takuya chose neither to seek work in companies during the week nor to go on work parties outside the prison, and he did not apply for five-day parole. Those who worked in companies during the week brought back newspapers as well as stories of the changes in the outside world, but Takuya scarcely ran his eyes over the headlines, and paid little attention to the other men's gossip. The regular stage shows held little appeal for him, so he spent his days quietly in his cell. Such entertainment was supposedly organised as a special favour to the inmates, but this 'benevolence' only served to annoy Takuya.

In early November 1954, he noticed an article in the newspaper forecasting a rice harvest of around four hundred million bushels, the largest in history. The food in the prison was now all Japanese, and in both quality and quantity it had tangibly improved.

Early in January 1955, Takuya's father died of tuberculosis. The prison officials encouraged Takuya to go and visit his family, saying they would grant him special parole, but he stubbornly refused their offers, finding their displays of sympathy nothing more than an unwelcome intrusion.

In a letter from his younger brother, Takuya read that the attitude of the people at home to war criminals had completely changed, the general opinion now being that these men were in fact victims of the war, and that, though it might have been an unofficial offering, the town officials had sent the family a condolence gift after the death of Takuya's father.

Takuya ripped the letter up and threw it away. He knew that the expression 'victims of the war' was in common usage, but still felt that these words were of no relevance to himself. He wrote a reply to his brother, saying that having beheaded an American POW he in no way fell into the category of victim. When he remembered once having read an article describing war criminals as 'enemies of mankind, utterly repulsive beasts of violence', he felt an overpowering bitterness towards those who, in the space of seven or eight short years, could simply change their minds on such a crucial issue. It annoyed him that his brother could be foolish enough to pass this on as though it were good news.

The release of the Class A war criminals who had avoided the death sentence continued, and the fewer than two hundred inmates remaining in Sugamo were all moved into the same wing.

In February 1957, nine years after he had entered Sugamo Prison, Takuya was released on what was termed 'parole'.

He felt no elation as he stepped out through the prison gate.

The first thing that struck him was how many well-dressed men and women were out walking in the streets. From the window of the tram he could see rows of houses and newly constructed buildings, neon signs everywhere and all kinds of cars on the neatly paved roads.

Everything he saw made him feel uncomfortable, as did the thought that he was now thirty-seven years old, with the prime of his life behind him. Merely looking at the streets and the people in them made him angry.

Just after nine o'clock that night he boarded the express train bound for Uno, from where he would take the ferry across the Inland Sea to Takamatsu in Shikoku, and change again to the train for Uwajima. In his pocket was an envelope holding the money he had been given by the Demobilised Soldiers' Bureau to cover the cost of returning home.

All the seats in the train were clean, and with few people on board he had no problem finding a place to sit. In the row in front of Takuya, a young woman sat slumped against the shoulder of the man sitting next to her, and diagonally across from him on the other side of the carriage a middle-aged man poured himself a glass of sake. Outside, neon lights lit up the streets beside the tracks.

Takuya wiped the lenses of his glasses, clouded by the steamy air inside the carriage. His short-sightedness seemed to have worsened in the last few years.

Leaning against the metal window frame, Takuya closed his eyes. His younger sister had missed her chance to find a husband when she was still in her twenties and had married a widower the previous spring, while his brother had married three years earlier and now had one young child. In her last letter, Takuya's mother had recommended that he get married as soon as he left prison, even going as far as to enclose a young woman's photograph for him to consider, but he had sent it straight back without comment. Marriage held no appeal for him. All he really felt like doing at the moment was lying down and resting on a tatami-matted floor.

From time to time he opened his eyes and gazed drowsily out of the window.

Eventually the first signs of dawn came and the sun started to rise.

Takuya left his seat to wash his face and clean his teeth in the washroom at the end of the carriage. When the train reached Osaka station he stepped down on to the platform and bought a boxed lunch at the nearest kiosk. Trains came in and departed from the other platforms, with waves of people rushing up and down the stairs.

As the train approached the outer suburbs of Kobe, for a brief moment Fujisaki's face flashed in front of his eyes. The train rumbled on through Akashi and Kakogawa.

Thoughts of Terasawa and his wife came to his mind. Takuya had sent them two or three postcards in his early years in Sugamo and had received letters of reply with gifts of rice crackers, but their correspondence had dried up several years ago.

He turned his head to look out of the window again. Fields had been replaced by rows of houses, and Himeji castle had come into view in the distance. It almost seemed to rotate slowly as the train drew nearer on the last curve of track into the city. Heavy grey snow clouds hung low in the sky.

The idea of returning home was less and less attractive. If he went back to his parents' house, his mother would probably weep at the sight of him and his brother and sister would probably be just as tearful. He would have to go and pay his respects at his father's grave and talk to the relatives and friends who would gather to welcome him back. The prospect of all this was still annoying, something he preferred to put off as long as possible.

The train slowed as it approached the station. Takuya took his bag down from the luggage rack above his head, put on his overcoat and went to the door.

As he stepped down on to the platform he saw that the station had been completely refurbished, with new benches and kiosks on each platform. He walked out on to the street. The area in front of the station was packed with shops and large buildings.

All the roads looked in good condition, and a wide tar-sealed boulevard stretched from the station to the castle's soaring walls. The green of the pine trees surrounding the castle stood out in stark contrast to the gleaming-white plaster walls of the donjons and towers, and the light brown of the stone buttresses provided a distinctive outline against the surrounding scenery.

Gazing at the White Egret Castle as he walked, Takuya headed along the road beside the railway tracks, and crossed over them at the first intersection. Before long he passed the employment agency he had visited years ago. Still on the same spot, it was now a larger, permanent structure, surrounded by rows of houses probably built as part of a municipal housing project. There were new houses and shops on both sides of all the streets he passed, so Terasawa's factory would have been enlarged and the old house knocked down and replaced.

Takuya walked down the tarred road until he got as far as the pachinko parlour, where he stopped. Almost ten years had gone by since he had left Himeji. Terasawa and his wife would be old by now, or they might even have died while Takuya was in prison. Their niece would have been adopted as a daughter, then would have married and taken over the business.

Takuya tried to imagine what meeting Terasawa would be like after all these years. All they would have to talk about would be how things were in the past, and once that was over conversation would quickly dry up. He had sent Terasawa a postcard expressing his gratitude and had received a reply, so maybe that was where he should leave it. Indeed, if they had adopted Teruko and she had married and started a family, she would probably feel obliged to offer little more than a perfunctory welcome. The prospect of having to make conversation with Teruko's husband hardly inspired enthusiasm.

He took a deep breath before turning round and walking back down the road toward the station. The idea of getting off the train and visiting Terasawa seemed ludicrous now. That part of his life was too long ago, over and done with. As he stood at the railway crossing a Tokyo-bound train gradually accelerated away from the platform and past him to the right.

As the last carriage passed, the barrier at the crossing lifted and Takuya walked back across the tracks and down the road to the station.

Inside the station, he went over to a kiosk and bought a box of matches. An *ukiyoe*-style picture adorned the label on the top of the box. When he turned the box over he found the name of a match factory in Shirahama, Himeji, printed in small characters. The matchsticks had a healthy lustre, and their vermilion heads were all the same shape and size.

He struck one. The match didn't break and the head ignited cleanly at the first attempt. Enticed by the paraffin soaked into the wood, the flame slowly moved along the stick. It was a small, brilliant light.

He blew out the match and tossed it into a trash can, then looked up at the big timetable above the ticket window to find the next train heading west.